Indigenous Recall

The Return to Sanity

Volume 2 of the Lipstick and War Crimes Series

by Ray Songtree

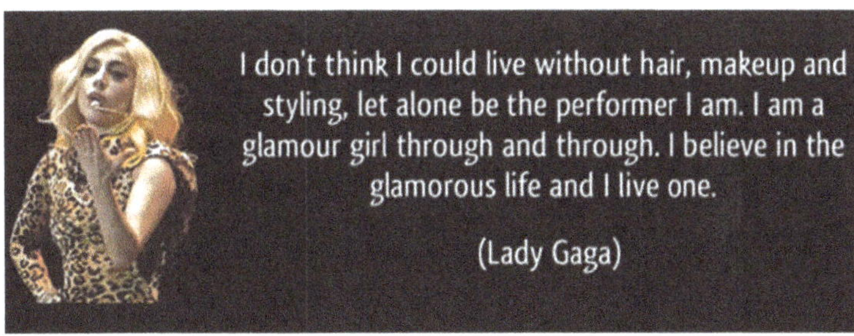

She believes in over consumption. She believes in vanity.
She spreads it to the populace and is supported in doing so.
Over consumption is based on taking
from others, who are left without enough.
This is enforced by the military. Vanity leads to violence.
Lipstick and War Crimes

Kauai Transparency Initiative International

Since we are all psychic, there is no such thing as intellectual property. Intellectual property is an oxymoron. The two words do not combine to make a rational statement because the intellect has no form, and property allegedly does. What intellectual property could mean is we don't want others to take advantage of our work. It can also mean that a for-profit corporation registers whatever it wants and claims it has the legal right to restrict access. In this way nature and even creativity is being commodified. The law is based on an oxymoron.

The author makes no claim to own any concepts in this writing, nor any of the images. The intent of this writing is educational and all revenues will go back into the promotion of education through non-profit Kauai Transparency Initiative International. The use of possibly copyrighted material for critique or eduction comes under "Fair Use" in accordance with, Title 17 U.S.C. Section 107 of the US Copyright Law. For more information go to: http://www.law.cornell.edu/uscode/17/107.shtml. If you wish to use copyrighted material from this book for purposes of your own, that go beyond 'fair use,' you must obtain permission from the copyright owner. Otherwise, portions of this book may be used for non-profit distribution as per Creative Commons License.

I urge the reader to purchase books from which excerpts were taken. See endnotes.

Mission Statement: Kauai Transparency Initiative International believes that human nature is loving. "Right to know" leads to informed choice which leads to local stewardship. When government and industry are honest and open with citizens and consumers, people will naturally choose health for themselves and future generations. A mother protects her child. KTII exists to help causes that work for transparency and disclosure. The goal is an informed loving society on Kauai and afar, brought about by tipping society toward responsible awareness through honest education.

KTII was founded by Ray Songtree in 2011.

To make tax-deductible donations, to inquire about affiliate programs or for speaking/workshop/concert inquiries, see KTII.org

Indigenous Recall, Vol. 2 ISBN 978-1-941293-23-2 *Paperback*

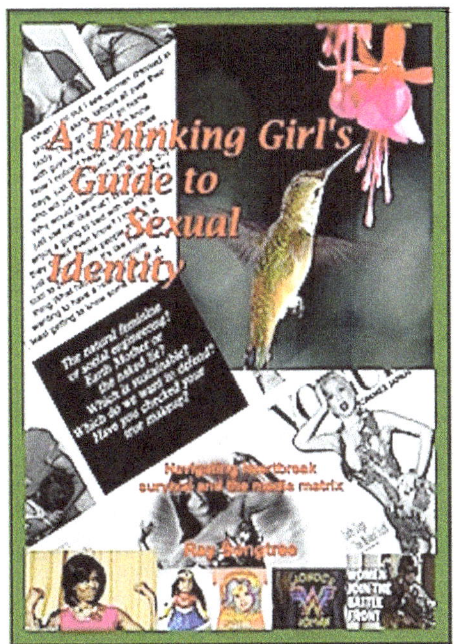

Volume 1 of the *Lipstick and War Crimes Series* by Ray Songtree has been published with different covers and different introductions for different demographic groups. This is not about money, it is about tipping diverse groups towards balance with their ecologies, by abandoning an artificial heartless globalist technocracy. *Zen and the Art of De-programming* has Buddhist, Christian, and Indigenous introductions included. *Begging Faith* has Christian introduction. *Indigenous Re-call* has indigenous intro. *A Thinking Girl's Guide to Sexual Identity* (students), *Feminism Revisited*, *She Promised Me Paradise* (Hawaiian souvenir edition) and *Lipstick and War Crimes* editions are available also as Vol. 1 (they have no introduction.) The Zen edition is the most comprehensive. Bulk or wholesale rates are available on bookstore page at Lipstick-and-War-Crimes.org. Translation or affiliate ideas welcomed. Contact www.KTII.org

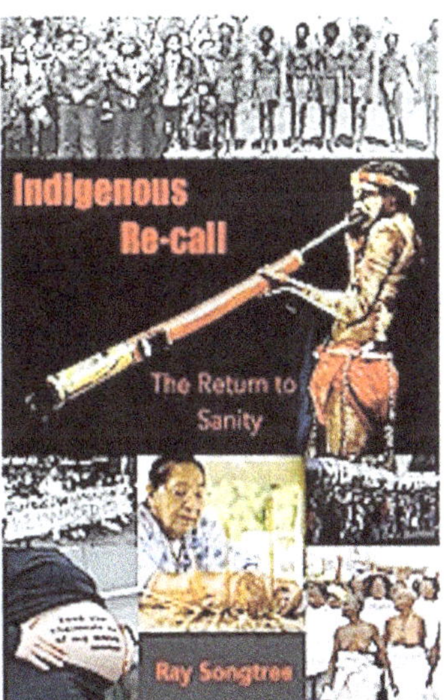

Caste of Characters in Vol. 1: "Mother of Feminism" CIA agent Gloria Steinem, Miley Cyrus, Jane Fonda, Albert Einstein, Madonna, Obama and his true father, Shirley McClain, lesbian Katherine Hepburn, Henry Kissinger, secret elitist Oprah Winfrey, Alice Walker, CIA Hugh Hefner, Kate Upton, Warren Beatty, Katy Perry, Soviet defector Yuri Bezmenov, Hillary Clinton, Beyoncé Knowles, Papua New Guinea, Jay-Z, Marilyn Monroe, Gaga, Warren Buffet, Shakira, Kristina Aguilera, Hero Cathy O'Brien, Fukashima, Pharrell Williams, Angelina Jolie, Bill Gates, Elizabeth Taylor, Nelson Mandela, and your mind…

Vol. 2 Editions. Student, Christian, Zen, Jewish, India, and Jennifer Lopez editions. All volumes in series are stand alone, however, Vol 2 is the most historical and encompassing. Find E-books online. Search "Ray Songtree." All these editions are the same book with different introductions.
The Spanish edition is called *Lápiz Labial & Crímenes de Guerra*.

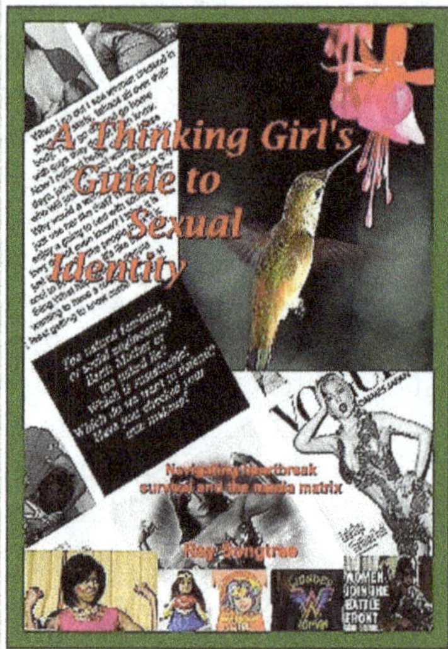

Christian, Zen and Indigenous Introductions

Christian Introduction

Christian, Zen and Indigenous Introductions

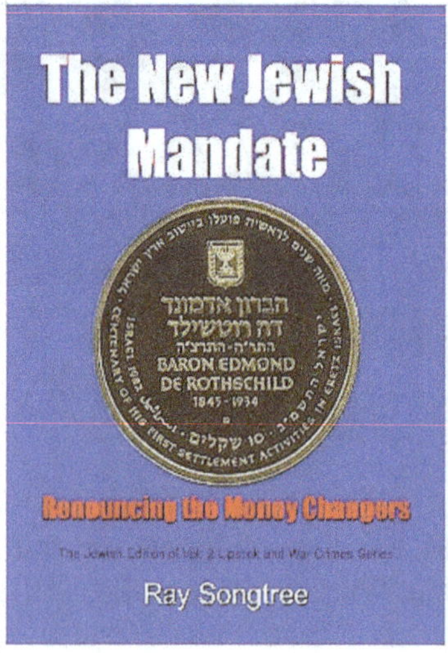

Jewish Introduction for friends and critics of Israel

Introduction for India Black and White interior

Christian and Indigenous Introductions

Vol. 3 is called *Henry and Beyoncé* He an exalted mk-ultra handler and she an exalted victim. (Vol. 1) Both are cogs of same machine to entrance and trick us. Vol. 3 deprograms the origins of followship. "Progress" has no realistic goal. Beyoncé's "Billionaire Girl's Club" dumbs us down.

Superbowl Halftime Show - Beyonce,

"Ignoring the future and looking fabulous"

Above foreground, severely wounded Richard Larry Weaver. Below, author Ray Songtree and *USS Liberty* survivor, Richard Larry Weaver, who discovered that the submarine *USS Amberjack* fired a torpedo and hit his ship in the infamous false flag attack of June 8, 1967 off the Gaza coast that was blamed solely on Israel. (Israel and U.S. receive orders from the exact same globalists.) Larry has had 36 surgeries. The Great Mystery arranged our meeting. Larry's Mother-in-Law and my Mom were friends at an elderly accommodations on Maui.

I include these photos of Richard Larry Weaver to honor and thank him for his investigation and to acknowledge the mysterious spirit that brought us together for our common work of seeking truth and justice. Larry does not endorse all views in the series. The reader can hear his radio interview at link below.

https://lipstick-and-war-crimes.org/1967-uss-liberty-attacked-by-submarine-uss-amberjack-crew-member-blows-whistle/

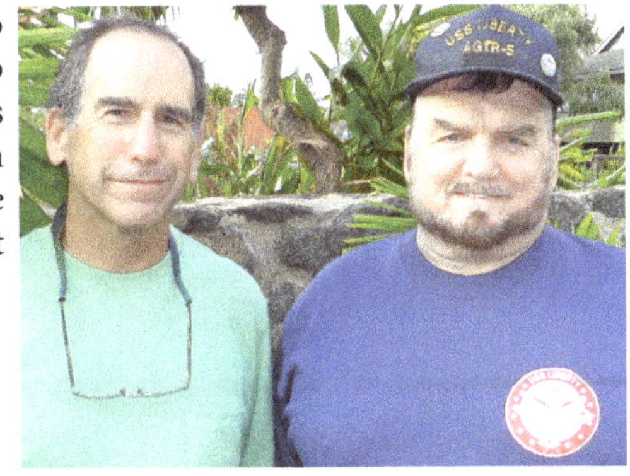

Introduction to the Indigenous Edition of Vol. 1, Lipstick and War Crimes

This edition is specifically for indigenous descendants, mostly Native Americans, but also Pacific Islanders, Australians, South Americans, Africans, and Asians.

"Indigenous Recall" has two meanings. Indigenous people are asking that the broken defective dominant culture be recalled as a defective product. The other meaning is they have to recall, recollect who they really want to be. "Indigenous Recall" places First Nation people as central, which I believe they are. Technological, disassociated people will be dinosaurs soon.

"The Return to Sanity" will have meaning when the criminals at the top are exposed for all to see. "Return to Sanity" also refers to rolling back the insane for-profit industrial lifestyle, which has no future because of resource depletion. People who are worried about over population don't understand what Monsanto or Bill Gates or Apple Inc. are about. Without doubt, population will decline due to all the poisons and wireless frequencies that have already been deployed. Steve Jobs was murdered to get his conscience out of way of Apple's push for dangerous wireless technology. (See www.bioinitiative.org) Apple Inc. no longer offers a wired keyboard for example, and Cloud technology makes us dependent on dangerous wireless technology.

My Japanese sensei, Kobun Chino Roshi, who was also Steve Job's sensei, was drown to eliminate his influence on Jobs' conscience. Doctors who have cures for cancer are getting murdered to insure cancer kill rate (See http://whale.to/a/persecuted_doc_h.html and BurzynskiMovie.com) Of course, murder and genocide is well known to indigenous peoples. However, and this is important, we are *all* at risk now.

Stolen generations, Australia and Pennsylvania, images from Vol. 2 of Lipstick and War Crimes. Now children are being stolen by schools and media because parents are asleep.

On the upper right of front cover of this book is a photo of Australian Aboriginal men. Please notice they have on chains. What was their crime? Their crime was that empire arrived and defined their ancient lifestyle as criminal. A century later, we now behold the new chains... The center photo on cover shows a concert performance with a didgeridoo ...

What do you see in this picture? Do you see a woman looking up at a didgeridoo?

This series will wake you up so you learn to see how we are tricked and socially engineered. The photo is of a young woman being trained to be a sex slave. She has on lipstick and makeup, so she is looking for attention. She is Asian so the target of photo shoot is Asian girls. She is holding a phallus between her legs and her mouth is open for oral sex. This is the subliminal message. And this message is effective. This is what our young people are exposed to.

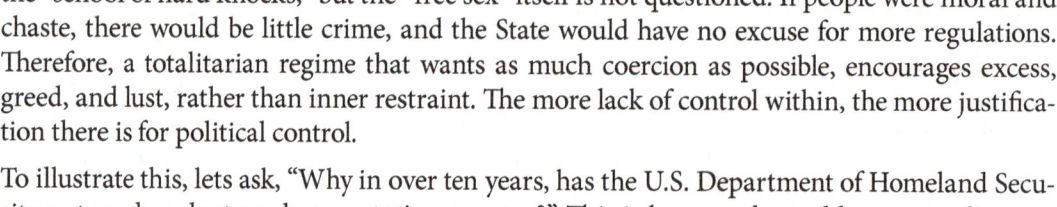

When our attention remains below the waist, we might not question who controls the direction of society. This is intentional.

It is up to we who are awake, as their community, to shield young people and give them the smarts to avoid this kind of psychological manipulation.

Since many people have lost inner guidelines, promiscuity brings the "school of hard knocks," but the "free sex" itself is not questioned. If people were moral and chaste, there would be little crime, and the State would have no excuse for more regulations. Therefore, a totalitarian regime that wants as much coercion as possible, encourages excess, greed, and lust, rather than inner restraint. The more lack of control within, the more justification there is for political control.

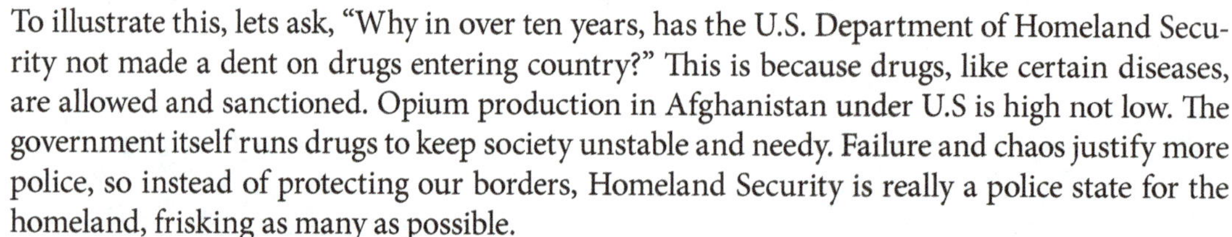

To illustrate this, lets ask, "Why in over ten years, has the U.S. Department of Homeland Security not made a dent on drugs entering country?" This is because drugs, like certain diseases, are allowed and sanctioned. Opium production in Afghanistan under U.S is high not low. The government itself runs drugs to keep society unstable and needy. Failure and chaos justify more police, so instead of protecting our borders, Homeland Security is really a police state for the homeland, frisking as many as possible.

Allowing crime enables enforcement.

For our entire lives, the entertainment industry has run "free sex" values to create more immorality and less inner integrity. The goal is a society where people depend on outer government laws to govern them. This reinforces need for "more security." So, promiscuity is a sophisticated road to enslavement under a government that will "take care of you." Promoted contraception and promiscuity has intentionally created a population of children without committed fathers and without a strong family. In their minds, Big Brother will provide.

Authentic indigenous cultures don't train their girls to be sex toys. Sex means motherhood. Ancient cultures know what is sacred. The road to healing our communities will require a rejuvenated ancient culture that is connected, not disconnected. As stated in mission statement, human nature is loving. "Original sin" was invented by Emperor Augustine. Our nature is loving because our natural state is connected...

Now, let's explore the disconnection...

A friend invited me to the Big Island of Hawaii for a dawn ceremony at top of Mauna Kea volcano. We flew over from Kauai and met some men who said they were descendants of Ali'i, the old royalty. They were drinking alcohol near some tide pools. The dawn ceremony had perhaps 35 people attend. No Hawaiians were there except family members of the hosts. The rest, perhaps 50%, were White, like we two from Kauai. After the ceremony, listening to people talking, I learned it was all about getting grant money from the NASA observatory.

Most readers here are non-indigenous. We are disconnected. We have no homeland or ecology. We move to where we can find a job, and see the Earth as scenery, not a place where we grow, hunt, or gather sustenance. Nature is for recreation, not living and dying. The 'aina (the land-spirit-environment in Hawaiian) is a place to take photos. Our actual home is in a place called Sidewalk-Anywhere.

There are also people of native blood reading this who think of themselves as indigenous, but live exactly like non-indigenous people. Let's get very real. We are our lifestyles, not how we fantasize. Everyone needs to stop dreaming of entitlements, which only take us further from our roots. To survive in a century with depleted resources and coming shortages we will need to recall how to produce with our own hands. A natural authentic indigenous person doesn't take handouts because they are not part of the something-for-nothing system. They are producers. We need to become indigenous if we want a sustainable future for the next generation. Too many people are pretending to be natives.

The present global technological civilization, with 3.5 million people in cities, is unsustainable and will fail. We all know this but live in denial like some miracle will save the day. The elite, who are planning ahead, are ignoring environmental diseases like Alzheimer's and Autism. Slow kill wireless frequency is being pushed globally, as are dangerous unneeded vaccines.

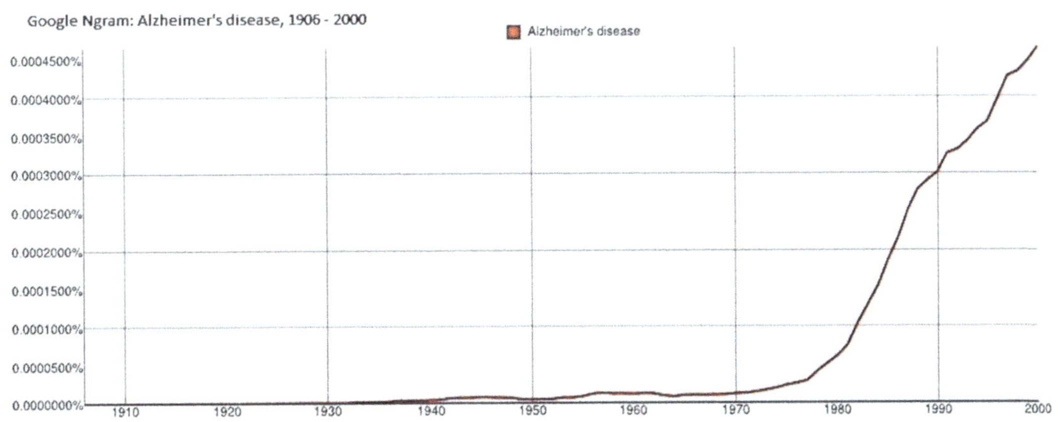

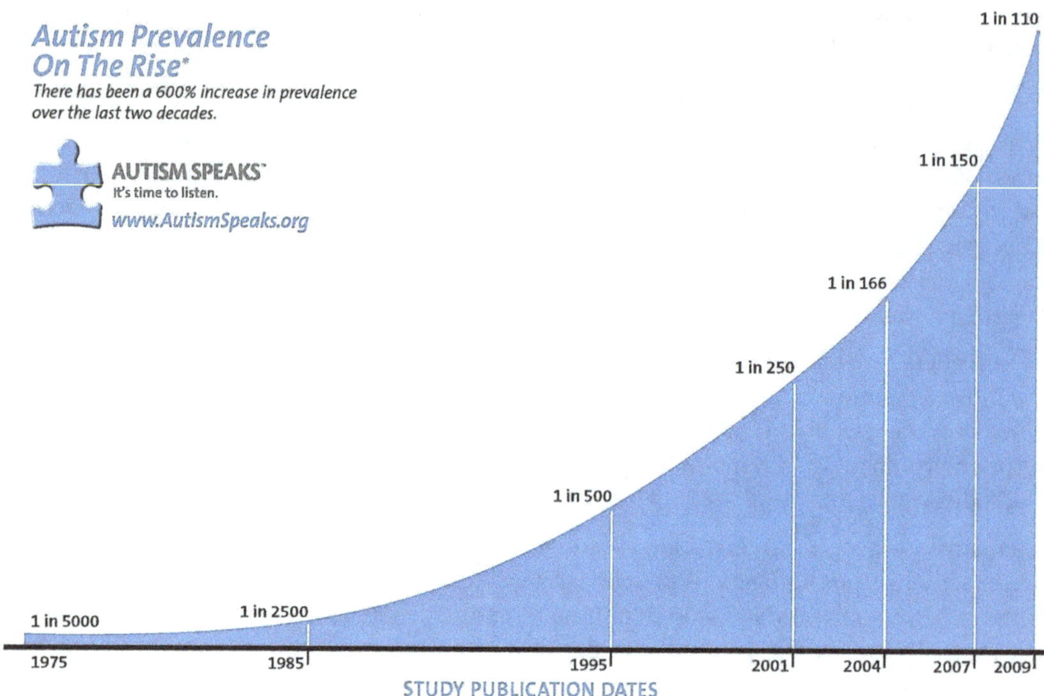

In the elite timeline, there will be nothing natural or indigenous left. *Their* high tech civilization with far fewer people, who are under their complete control, is *their* sustainable plan. They will bring down the population intentionally. Slow kill operations are already taking their toll. The rate of cancer and genetic diseases will sky rocket as the graphs show. Please see what is written on the pregnant woman's tummy on front cover of this book.

There are still authentic indigenous people who get food and water from the land. They are being eliminated as quickly as possible by the "market" and school curriculums (World Bank 'Early Childhood Initiative' promoted by singer sex-object Shakira, Vol. 3). Native natural people are considered to be an obstacle to "progress" by World Bank. Here the non-indigenous reader probably agrees with the elite. You probably discount indigenous people who "don't matter." This is because you live in Sidewalk-Anywhere. Be careful. I am going to show how we have been socially engineered to support destruction. In doublespeak, "progress" means destruction.

Yet, a part of us feels something deeper than tolerating destruction. Nature is natural and is our Mother. We want connection. In contrast, the artificial is unnatural and is our enemy. Inside we know this. The way out of destruction is to go back to innocence, not to try to fix insane "progress" with something new that is also unnatural. A drug won't cure a drug.

In nature there are no "clean freaks" who use toxic chemicals to sterilize their homes. There is no stigma against dirty fingernails or crooked teeth. Walking barefoot is okay. Most of us hate nature. We hate the Earth and don't want to get close to her. We were steered this way.

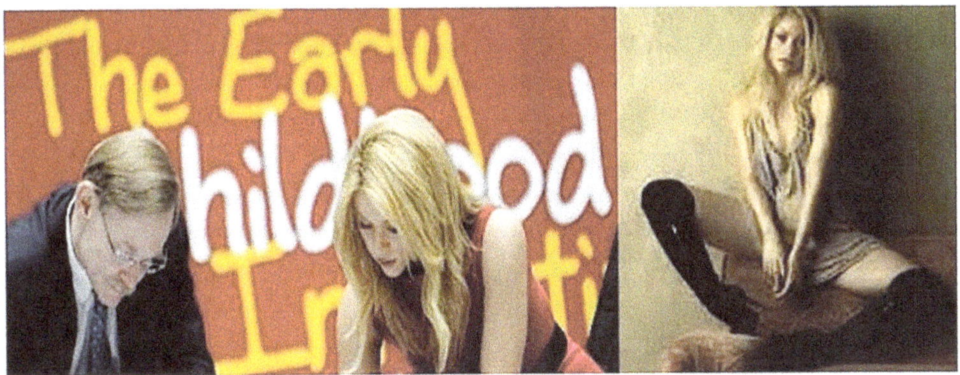

Shakira, a Colombian singer with dyed blond hair, covered extensively in Vol. 3 of series, was invited by World Bank to promote "Early Childhood Initiative" education in order to globalize all children and bring all cultures into the "formal economy" of debt.
The Common Core U.S. School Curriculum by Bill Gates Sr., a former Planned Parenthood head, will be merged with a global education system to create global mono-culture and destroy regional and indigenous diversity. This is already happening.
Shakira claimed on The Voice *talent contest to have 70 million Facebook followers.*
Here we see the values being promoted worldwide by Obama and World Bank.

If we stay below the waist, we might not notice who is governing us.

The attack on indigenous people is mirrored by the attack on *the natural within us all.* This is a big realization that all of us, whatever our race, can share. This attack is organized. Just as the British Empire was the business model of the banksters who controlled Britain (Vol. 2), the world wide assault on the natural is a plan, a program. Why is the World Bank involved with global education? It is to further colonize the entire world's minds. We are being steered.

Pop culture, though foreign to some readers, infects all children through images, like the one above of the young Asian woman. We need an alternative to "entertainment." We need to create this alternative for the next generation. The globe is now controlled by pop culture.

* * *

My visit to the far north of Australia a few years ago, to be with native people on their 40,000 year old homeland, went well. All doors opened. I found myself led mysteriously to meet some of the few activists I had seen on videos online. However, I was a stranger. I did not know their language. (Actually their town of 700 people spoke 9 languages.) Why should they trust me, when their grandparents were massacred and a cell tower was built over the grave?

To my surprise, there was nothing I could help them with because they were on welfare and had no motivation to do anything. They owned almost nothing because if they owned, say a knife, they would have to lend it when asked, and so they didn't have a knife. They had welfare.

No one could afford a vehicle, so they would have gambling nights, and the winner might win $20,000 with which they would buy a Toyota in Darwin that they would share with their extended family until the washboard roads destroyed the rig a year later. They looked forward to factory built vehicles, not to a sustainable future. Natural life is tough. Mosquitoes are waiting. The easy way is welfare. In nature extra energy is not wasted. Because of the outside input from industrialization, we all take a short cut. Native American plains people adopted canvas tipis. It was easier than bison hides. Energy must be conserved. But what about the future?

In Arnhemland, I met "traditional land owners" who were given this title by the Australian government. Divide and conquer begins with private property. The "traditional land owners" were approached and persuaded to sell some land, so the government could build a police compound and a prison in their own town. This was the next step of empire. Australia, hardly a sovereign country, was going to bring civilization to the heart of Arnhemland, and that meant the dominant culture's laws and police. I was adopted by this family, but my respect drifted away when I saw how they had betrayed their own people.

I saw first hand how a people can be demoralized. The Yolngu of the far North had met their first white man only 85 years ago. This is how they were assimilated … young men were flown around the world as musicians in the 70's. They returned globalized, non-indigenous.

The grocery stores now sell blue soda pop. There was no alcohol in this part of Australia, but they had kava. It is a prison camp. The people have no representation. There is no officially recognized self-rule. In angry reaction, there is an underground force. This force is disconnected from the female elders. There was spirit possession and murder. There was also a Christian community, which didn't confront anything as it was led by disconnected Whites. (See introduction to Christian Edition at Lipstick-and-war-crimes.org, free.) There was also real faith. One man I loved, had it. He, by the way, became a grandfather when he was 28.

Girls become women as soon as their nipples come out. My daughter was only 7 so she was underage. Arranged marriage based on a complex totem system is the tradition, but with pop music and movies (which we will review in this series) another new norm is now unmitigated sexual attraction. (Sound familiar? This is globalism.) My lovely friends met at a K-Mart in Darwin. But they took the relationship very seriously and were very loyal. They had found real love and integrity. Their young teen son was flown to Melbourne for a field trip by school system to help assimilate him and make him globalized, non-indigenous.

The one elder who recognized me, asked me to stay and help the elders who had been crushed by "The Intervention." This 2007 government intervention, (now officially called "Stronger Futures," which is doublespeak for weaker futures) lied in media about extent of child molestation, and invaded reserves with armed troops "to save the children." It was a cultural assault, hidden as a "humanitarian intervention," a common ploy of Western hegemony. (Our soft side is invoked to justify bombs. Thus, U.S. has been in scores of wars in last 50 years. Saving others means obliterating them, as in Libya.) In Arnhemland, Empire wants the minerals. I told this elder that all the white people here were also slaves. This was new idea for him. So he asked me to help out, but I had a child with me and needed to go, and I was disheartened by what I saw. My mission there, to connect with something ancient, would take a new form of being an advocate for a goal that is the opposite of global. I am now an advocate for what is most worthwhile, something local.

I did learn remarkable things. The people there never speak the name of someone who has died. Imagine how free of history and it's prejudices they are! The dead are left to re-birth and are not disturbed. We hunted crabs in the mangroves, and when I told my friends that I don't normally eat the guts, they asked "Why not?" No need for plates or silverware; the kangaroo or goose is thrown directly on the fire and is eaten with hands. No furniture, what for? To be far from the Earth? The invasive out of control Asian water buffalo are slaughtered by government with helicopters. I see in future that the bulldozed garbage pits will be used to trap buffalo. Water buffalo meat is so tough it can hardly be eaten, but a new aboriginal lifestyle will evolve around this meat source. The buffalo wipe out the billabongs (ponds and lakes). Invasive cane toads are poisonous, and have killed off other sources of food. The ecology is changing and so will the aboriginal lifestyle. And the mosquitoes are waiting.

I learned there are spirits who are territorial. When I entered the reserve I did my own ceremony. I didn't realize that the reserve was so big that I would have had to do a ceremony for each location. I was attacked by spirit for my error. This was new for me. I had not encountered entities like this before. My local friends encountered them daily and were afraid to go out at night. The spiritual leaders have lost power. The people are prey.

On the reserve there are continual meetings with mining representatives who want to strip mine the land for aluminium (Australian spelling). The place was overrun by White people who were there for all kinds of "humanitarian" reasons. Most are there to make as much money as possible as contractors, just like Iraq. They act polite. They respect nothing but their own wallet. So again, the example for the natives is that White people can't be trusted.

When I returned to Hawaii, someone I know, who was adopted into the Lakota Tribe, told me his best friend was murdered with a knife by his son, who was having sex with his own mom. When the father confronted the son, he was killed. Utter madness. When I told someone I had been in Australia with Aboriginals, he told me about the incest discussed openly at Pueblo meetings in New Mexico. He wanted to know if things were as dysfunctional where I had visited.

I told him that all this dysfunction was planned. Of course bringing casinos into Native American reserves would bring prostitution and graft. Of course drugs are furnished, just like in African American communities. Of course outside jobs created a disparity in lifestyles and jealousy and the community loses cohesion. Or course home rule and real power have been stripped from the people so they could fit into the puppet countries that we call "nations," most created by the British for the UN. And so, of course, there is little social order. In nature the community self regulates with a diversity of wisdom and perspective. In broken communities, disfunction runs rampant until the police state steps in. As stated, illicit sexuality is a tool to bring about political dominance. Internal regulation and conscience needs support. Break the community and the individual is adrift. Then we experiment, and now we have half our kids without a committed father. Take a deep breath. So what do we do? Who will be society's elders?

Each of us, no matter what our ethnic background may be, need to realize that factory items will become unaffordable. Already, a bankrupt financial system holds itself up with lies. In U.S., 47 million people are on food stamps while jobs are out-sourced. Over 100 million Americans receive some kind of government support. The Social Security system goes into more debt each year. It must fail. I knew this when I was a teenager, that by the time I could receive social security, the system would be broken. We all know this.

Those that are living closer to nature and to the side of the doomed dominant culture, offer the viable alternative. This fact must stay in our minds and plans. Indigenous people need to teach their children as much of the old ways as possible; not just ceremonies, but skills. They also need to be open to teachers of skills from other races and tribes. Non-indigenous people need to connect with the farmers and ranchers and indigenous of your area because they know the land. You probably don't. Your world will fail, but nature will still be here.

The Maori of New Zealand knew over 400 plants. They knew every plant in their area. Of course they did. They had no sidewalks.

When I visited Hotevilla in Hopi-land Arizona, in the early 70s, I fetched water for Grandpa David from a spring. When I went back later there was a tall water tower. I couldn't remember if it had been there the first time or not. The water tower is run on electric pumps with parts that will become unavailable. It is just a matter of time. The pumped water allowed the town to grow beyond its natural size. Even in Hopi-land, there needs to be people who know the old ways and live to the side of the dominant convenient culture.

All this is daunting, of course. However, you the reader can wake up. We have been colonized. Our minds and values and hopes and dreams have been colonized. We think the Earth is dirty, but it is not, it is the Earth. We can peel back the colonization and get back to the root of our human experience. There is still wilderness and we must visit it soon, alone, and with patience. When we touch the Earth, we need to touch her as a family member, not a tourist. We can plant something. We can harvest it. We can learn to store food. Humans are omnivores. We can learn what to do if there is no toilet paper or matches in the store.

This first volume of the *Lipstick and War Crimes Series*, starts to connect how *the attack on our inner virtue parallels the attack on the environment and anyone who lives naturally.* Purification in a time of imperialistic mono-culture means *diversification and autonomy.*

Something disconnected can be re-connected. The solution is old and simple.

Indigenous Recall: The Return to Sanity

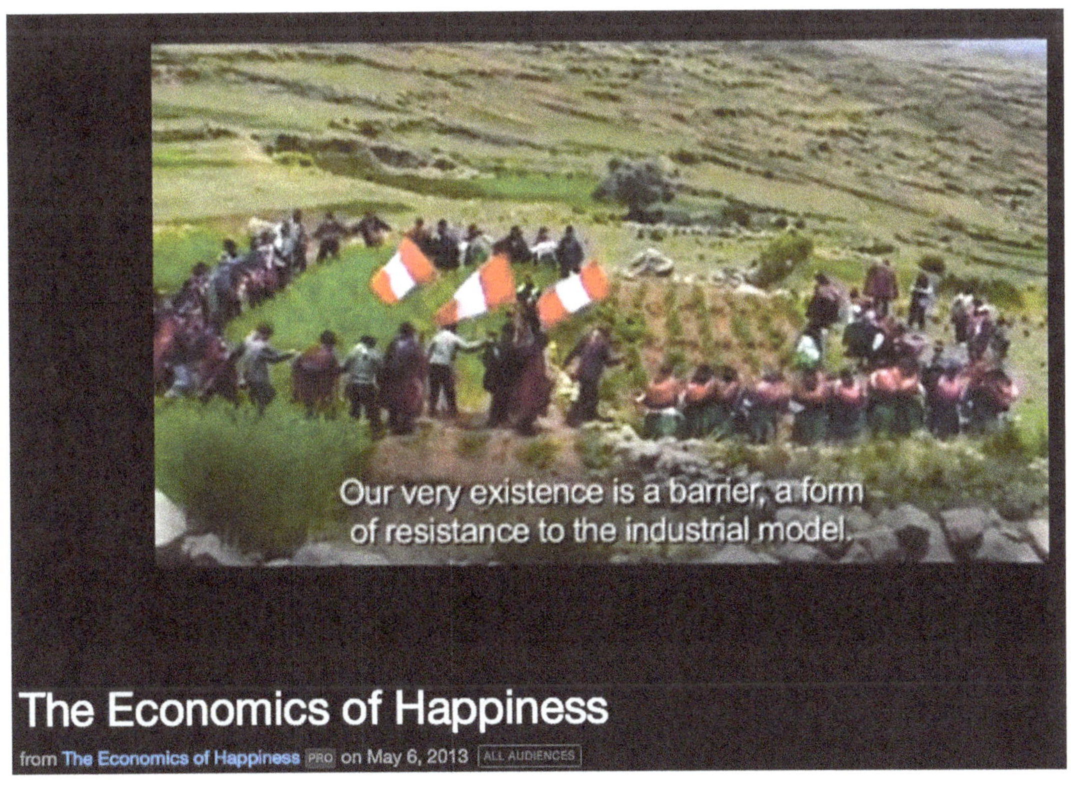

The Thanksgiving Myth: Reflecting on Land Theft, Betrayal, and Genocide

By Sarah Sunshine Manning, The Hampton Institute, November 24, 2015

As Thanksgiving approaches, many schools throughout the U.S. are making preparations for the standard, and all too cliché, Thanksgiving Day lessons, and fairy tale-esque Thanksgiving plays.

And more often than not, the school Thanksgiving activities are largely based on what ultimately amounts to myth, created to serve the imaginations of the dominant society, and simultaneously functioning to erase the tragedies of Indigenous nations.

The myth usually goes a little something like this:

> Pilgrims came to America, in order to escape religious persecution in England. Living conditions proved difficult in the New World, but thanks to the friendly Indian, Squanto, the pilgrims learned to grow corn, and survive in unfamiliar lands. It wasn't long before the Indians and the pilgrims became good friends. To celebrate their friendship and abundant harvest, Indians in feathered headbands joined together with the pilgrims and shared in a friendly feast of turkey and togetherness. Happy Thanksgiving. The End.

From this account, the unsuspecting child might assume a number of things. Firstly, they may assume that pilgrims merely settled the New World, innocently, and as a persecuted people, they arrived to America with pure and altruistic intentions. Secondly, children might assume, and rightfully so, that Indians and pilgrims were friends, and that this friendship must have laid the framework for this "great American nation."

So, what exactly is the harm in this school-sanctioned account of history? Understandably, the untrained eye may not notice the harm in such a myth, as most Americans are victim to the same whitewashed lie as the rest, and dismantling a centuries-old myth certainly does prove challenging.

But the first lesson for educators and adults to digest is the fact that this narrative is egregiously whitewashed and Eurocentric on many levels. Moreover, it is a lie, which serves to rob American children of valuable historical lessons.

Truth be told, this beloved lie was packaged solely for nationalistic consumption when, following the bloody Civil War, President Abraham Lincoln declared Thanksgiving a national holiday in 1863. Back then, Americans were desperately in need of unity and inspiration. Hence, the myth of the first Thanksgiving was born to inspire and unite.

Beyond the myth, and the seemingly good intentions of Abraham Lincoln (who actually despised Indians) the actual story of pilgrims and indigenous people went down much differently.

As a social science educator, I strongly advocate for the unabridged study of human history; for the many valuable lessons imbedded in the stories of our past. Changing any story, essentially, means short-changing American society from some extremely valuable lessons – lessons that function to plant the seeds of social consciousness and humanitarian evolution.

So let's take a look at a different version of history; a fuller version, and hopefully, extract some meaningful lessons from our shared past:

> One day, the Wampanoag people of the Eastern coast of the Americas noticed unfamiliar people in their homelands. These unfamiliar people were English pilgrims, coming to a new land which they dubbed "America," in order to settle and create a new life.
>
> The Wampanoag were initially uneasy with the settlers, but they eventually engaged in a shaky relationship of commerce and exchange. Also, in observing that the pilgrims nearly died from a harsh winter, the Wampanoag stepped in to help.
>
> The Wampanoag chief, Massasoit, eventually entered into agreements with the pilgrims, and, on behalf of the Wampanoag Nation, decided to be allies while each nation coexisted in the same space together. At one time, the Wampanoag and pilgrims shared in a meal of wildfowl, deer, and shellfish.
>
> After Massasoit's death, the Wampanoag nation became weakened as a result of disease contracted from the English. It wasn't long before the pilgrims began tormenting surrounding tribes, burning entire villages to the ground, while indigenous men, women, and children lie sleeping.
>
> Uneasy with the growing cruelty, greed, and arrogance of the new people in their homelands, the Wampanoag began to distrust the pilgrims. The pilgrims soon demanded that the Wampanoag submit to them, and give up all their weapons.
>
> Shortly after, the pilgrims and Wampanoag were at war, and in the end, the pilgrims rose victorious. At the close of the war, the Wampanoag were nearly decimated, and the son of Chief Massasoit, Metacom, was killed by the pilgrims, dismembered, beheaded, and his head impaled on a spear outside of Plymouth. Metacom's young son was sent to the West Indies as a slave, along with numerous other Wampanoag and surrounding tribes.
>
> A day of Thanksgiving was declared, and to celebrate, the pilgrims kicked the heads of dead Indigenous peoples around like soccer balls. (This was not the end …)
>
> As indigenous nations throughout America were continually betrayed by European settlers, killed by disease, germ warfare, hunted for bounties, sent overseas as slaves, and ultimately pushed out of their homelands and onto prison camps (now commonly known as reservations), few survived the depressing conditions. As a result of centuries of historical trauma, indigenous nations today have staggering rates of depression, mental health disparities, suicide, and deaths due to alcohol and drugs. Indigenous people continue to struggle to cope with historical trauma, and heal deeply embedded wounds which stem directly from colonialism. This, still, is not the end.

The lessons to be gained from the truths of history are many, and conversely, those lessons are lost in whitewashed myths.

While glossing over the very real consequences of colonialism, the mythical version of Thanksgiving creates a fairy tale of land theft, betrayal, brutality, and genocide, virtually functioning to erase the very real and traumatic experiences of entire indigenous nations. This phenomena of whitewashing and outright erasure of indigenous history, in many instances, is not only inhumane and oppressive to the indigenous people, but it is also unfair to all Americans who stand to learn from rich and equally tragic history. [The program of slavery is to deny any expression of truth, and to indoctrinate everyone with myths.]

Without question, colonialism is great for the colonizer, and disastrous for the colonized. [The British call their slave states "Protectorates."] Colonization reduces entire populations, and leaves generational wounds that linger stubbornly for centuries. This is a lesson that all Americans must heed.

As a result of propagating the mythical version of Thanksgiving, American children and adults alike, become confused about history, and moreover the Thanksgiving lie outright prevents a collective American understanding of the contemporary struggles of Native American people today.

Without understanding the 500 years of colonial impact on indigenous people, scores of bigoted attitudes have emerged, as Americans cannot seem to wrap their heads around the many struggles of tribal communities today that stem directly from [continuing] colonization.

To be sure, the Thanksgiving myth has many consequences, and aside from breeding ignorance and reinforcing bigotry, the myth silences the already marginalized indigenous people, who desperately need to hear, share, and tell our [true] story as a part of the healing process.

It is time to let go of the myth and embrace truth, and we must start in schools, where young children look to their teachers with inquisitive eyes as the all-knowing authorities. [However the Federal Common Core Curriculum is dedicated to programed lies.]

As educational institutions, schools must be progressive in bravely moving toward truth, while moving away from any semblance of ongoing myth-sanctioning.

This change is long overdue, and all of our children deserve truth, meaningful lessons, and a robust dose of humanitarian development. And the great news is: our entire world stands to benefit from it.

Depending on the age of students, different degrees of the story can and should be told. Educators can find ideas here.

And conversely, the myth, the school plays, and the story of happy Indians and friendly pilgrims needs to be abandoned, wholesale. This leveling out of myth creates space for new conversations and lessons of unity, and deeper understandings of what it truly means to be a good human being, and that is something to be thankful for.

Sarah Sunshine Manning (Shoshone-Paiute, Chippewa-Cree) is a mother, educator, activist, and an advocate for youth.

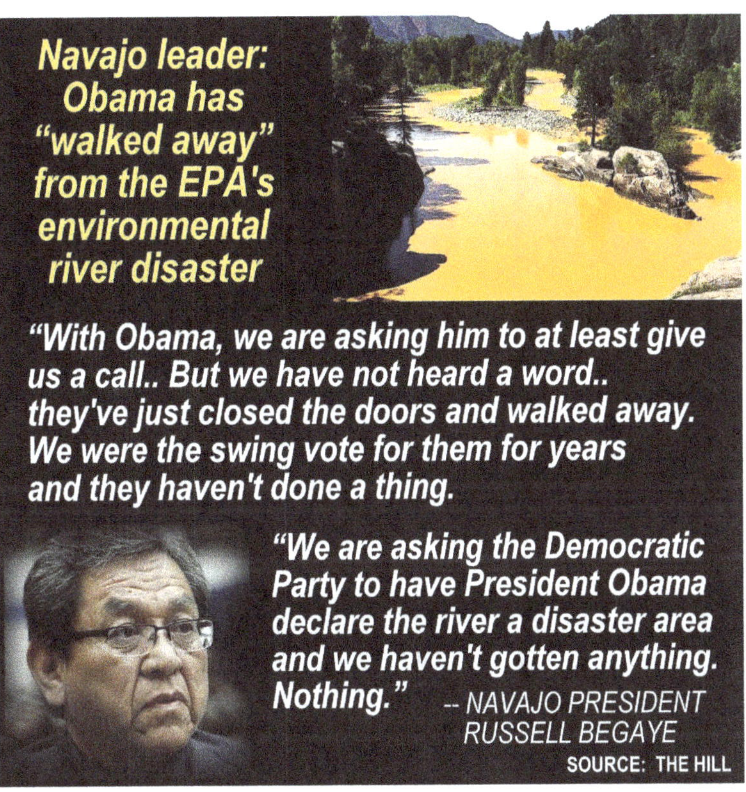
Navajo leader:
Obama has
"walked away"
from the EPA's
environmental
river disaster
"With Obama, we are asking him to at least give us a call.. But we have not heard a word.. they've just closed the doors and walked away. We were the swing vote for them for years and they haven't done a thing.
"We are asking the Democratic Party to have President Obama declare the river a disaster area and we haven't gotten anything. Nothing."
-- NAVAJO PRESIDENT RUSSELL BEGAYE
SOURCE: THE HILL

Speech - "For The World to Live, Europe Must Die"

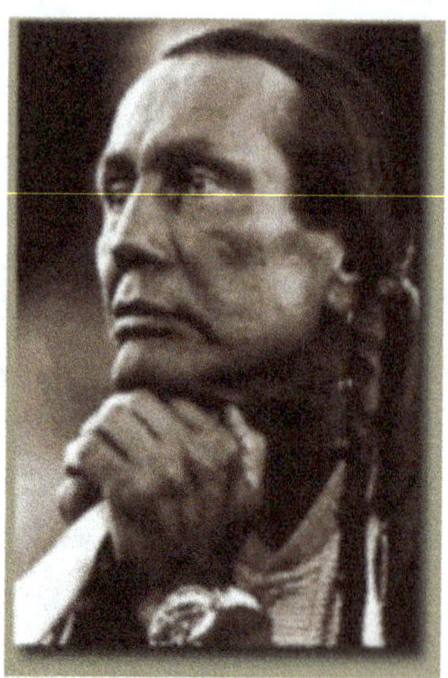

The following speech was given by Russell Means of the Oglala Lakota in July 1980 before several thousand people who had assembled from all over the world for the Black Hills International Survival Gathering, in the Black Hills of South Dakota. Only 80 years before he was born, his people were living their ancient and sustainable lifestyle and hunting buffalo. Russell Means did not have the internet to uncover what we know now. We now know that the British Empire and colonialism was a Rothschild business model. Here, Russell Means ties in the arrogance of monotheism [I know THE truth], which is manifesting today as total control through technocracy.

Technocracyinc.org "–founded in 1933. Developing a new system for government; a social structure that will prevent poverty, corruption and an imbalance in the distribution of wealth and resources."

Total control, total rationing, to bring "Peace on Earth." In my opinion this is the most profound speech I have ever come across – Author. [Brackets are mine.]

Russell Means ... Black Hills International Survival Gathering, July 1980

"The only possible opening for a statement of this kind is that I detest writing. The process itself epitomizes the European concept of "legitimate" thinking; what is written has an importance that is denied the spoken. My culture, the Lakota culture, has an oral tradition, so I ordinarily reject writing. It is one of the white world's ways of destroying the cultures of non-European peoples, the imposing of an abstraction over the spoken relationship of a people.

"So what you read here is not what I have written. It is what I have said and someone else has written down. I will allow this because it seems that the only way to communicate with the white world is through the dead, dry leaves of a book. I don't really care whether my words reach whites or not. They have already demonstrated through their history that they cannot hear, cannot see; they can only read (of course, there are exceptions, but the exceptions only prove the rule). I'm more concerned with the American Indian people, students and others, who have begun to be absorbed into the white world through universities and other institutions. But even then it's a marginal sort of concern. It's very possible to grow into a red face with a white mind; and if that's a person's individual choice, so be it, but I have no use for them. This is part of the process of cultural genocide being waged by Europeans against American Indian peoples' today. My concern is with those American Indians who choose to resist this genocide, but may be confused as to how to proceed.

"(You notice I use the term American Indian rather than Native American or Native indigenous people or Amerindian when referring to my people.) There has been some controversy about such terms, and frankly, at this point, I find it absurd. Primarily it seems that American Indian is being rejected as European in origin—which is true. But all the above terms are European in origin; the only non-European way is to speak of Lakota—or, more precisely, of Oglala, Brule, et.—and of the Dineh, the Miccousukee, and all the rest of the several hundred correct tribal names. There is also some confusion about the word Indian, a mistaken belief that it refers somehow to the country, India. When Columbus washed up on the beach in the Caribbean, he was not looking for a country called India. Europeans were calling that country Hindustan in 1492. Look it up on the old maps. Columbus called the tribal people he met "Indio," from the Italian in dio, meaning "in God.")

"It takes a strong effort on the part of each American Indian not to become Europeanized. The strength for this effort can only come from the traditional ways, the traditional values that our elders retain. It must come from the hoop, the four directions, the relations: it cannot come from the pages of a book or a thousand books. No European can ever teach a Lakota to be Lakota, a Hopi to be Hopi. A master's degree in "Indian Studies" or in "education" or in anything else cannot make a person into a human being or provide knowledge into the traditional ways. It can only make you into a mental European, an outsider.

"I should be clear about something here, because there seems to be some confusion about it. When I speak of Europeans or mental Europeans, I'm **not** allowing for false distinctions. I'm not saying that on the one hand there are the by-products of a few thousand years of genocidal, reactionary European intellectual development which is bad; and on the other hand there is some new revolutionary intellectual development which is good. I'm referring here to the so-called theories of Marxism and anarchism and "leftism" in general. I don't believe these theories can be separated from the rest of the European intellectual tradition. It's really just the same old song.

"The process began much earlier. Newton, for example, "revolutionized" physics and the so-called natural science by reducing the physical universe to a linear mathematical equation. Descartes did the same thing with culture. John Locke did it with politics, and Adam Smith did it with economics. Each one of these "thinkers" took a piece of the spirituality of human existence and converted it into a code, an abstraction. They picked up where Christianity ended: they "secularized" Christian religion, as the "scholars" like to say—and in doing so they made Europe more able and ready to act as an expansionist culture. Each of these intellectual revolutions served to abstract the European mentality even further, to remove the wonderful complexity and spirituality from the universe and replace it with a logical sequence: one, two, three. Answer!

"This is what has come to be termed "efficiency" in the European mind. Whatever is mechanical is perfect; whatever seems to work at the moment—that is, proves the mechanical model to be the right one—is considered correct, even when it is clearly untrue. This is why "truth" changes so fast in the European mind; the answers which result from such a process are only stopgaps, only temporary, and must be continuously discarded in favor of new stopgaps which support the mechanical models and keep them (the models) alive.

"Hegel and Marx [A paid Rothschild frontman] were heirs to the thinking of Newton, Descartes, Locke and Smith. Hegel finished the process of secularizing theology—and that is put in his own terms—he secularized the religious thinking through which Europe understood the universe. Then Marx put Hegel's philosophy in terms of "materialism," which is to say that Marx de-spiritualized Hegel's work altogether. Again, this is in Marx' own terms. And this is now seen as the future revolutionary potential of Europe. Europeans may see this as revolutionary,

But American Indians see it simply as still more of that same old European conflict between being and gaining. The intellectual roots of a new Marxist form of European imperialism lie in Marx'—and his followers'—links to the tradition of Newton, Hegel, and the others.

"Being is a spiritual proposition. Gaining is a material act. Traditionally, American Indians have always attempted to be the best people they could. Part of that spiritual process was and is to give away wealth, to discard wealth in order not to gain. Material gain is an indicator of false status among traditional people, while it is "proof that the system works" to Europeans. Clearly, there are two completely opposing views at issue here, and Marxism is very far over to the other side from the American Indian view. But let's look at a major implication of this; it is not merely an intellectual debate.

"The European [Rothschild] materialist tradition of de-spiritualizing the universe is very similar to the mental process which goes into dehumanizing another person. And who seems most expert at dehumanizing other people? And why? Soldiers who have seen a lot of combat learn to do this to the enemy before going back into combat. Murderers do it before going out to commit murder. Nazi SS guards [created by Rothschilds, funded by Wall Street] did it to concentration camp inmates. Cops do it. Corporation leaders do it to the workers they send into uranium mines and steel mills. Politicians do it to everyone in sight. And what the process has in common for each group doing the dehumanizing is that it makes it all right to kill and otherwise destroy other people. One of the Christian commandments says, "Thou shalt not kill," at least not humans, so the trick is to mentally convert the victims into nonhumans. Then you can proclaim violation of your own commandment as a virtue.

"In terms of the de-spiritualization of the universe, the mental process works so that it become virtuous to destroy the planet. Terms like "progress" and "development" are used as *cover words* [doublespeak] here, the way victory and freedom are used to justify butchery in the dehumanization process. For example, a real-estate speculator may refer to "developing" a parcel of ground by opening a gravel quarry; development here means total, permanent destruction, with the earth itself removed. But European logic has gained a few tons of gravel with which more land can be "developed" through the construction of road beds. Ultimately, the whole universe is open—in the European view—to this sort of insanity.

"Most important here, perhaps, is the fact that Europeans feel no sense of loss in this. After all, their philosophers have de-spiritualized reality, so there is no satisfaction (for them) to be gained in simply observing the wonder of a mountain or a lake or a people in being. No, satisfaction is measured in terms of gaining material. So the mountain becomes gravel, and the lake becomes coolant for a factory, and the people are rounded up for processing through the indoctrination mills Europeans like to call schools.

"But each new piece of that "progress" ups the ante out in the real world. Take fuel for the industrial machine as an example. Little more than two centuries ago, nearly everyone used wood—a replenishable, natural item—as fuel for the very human needs of cooking and staying warm. Along came the Industrial Revolution and coal became the dominant fuel, as production became the social imperative for Europe. Pollution began to become a problem in the cities, and the earth was ripped open to provide coal whereas wood had simply been gathered or harvested at no great expense to the environment. Later, oil became the major fuel, as the technology of production was perfected through a series of scientific "revolutions." Pollution increased dramatically, and nobody yet knows what the environmental costs of pumping all that oil out of the ground will really be in the long run. Now there's an "energy crisis," and uranium is becoming the dominant fuel.

"Capitalists, at least, can be relied upon to develop uranium as fuel only at the rate at which they can show a good profit. That's their ethic, and maybe that will buy some time. Marxists, on the other hand, can be relied upon to develop uranium fuel as rapidly as possible simply because it's the most "efficient" production fuel available. That's their ethic, and I fail to see where it's preferable. Like I said, Marxism is right smack in the middle of the European tradition. It's the same old song.

[Capitalists and Communists were both created by the Rothschilds to work their plan of divide and conquer and total destabilization, thesis-antithesis>synthesis, to create their high tech New World Order, built on the destruction of everything organic-spiritual.]

"There's a rule of thumb that can be applied here. You cannot judge the real nature of a revolutionary doctrine on the basis of the changes it proposed to make within the European power structure and society. You can only judge it *by the effect it will have on non-European peoples.*

[Whenever entitled rich nations people talk about their god "progress," they willfully deny the collateral damage.]

"This is because every revolution in European history has served to reinforce Europe's [Rothschild] tendencies and abilities to export destruction to other peoples, other cultures and the environment itself. I defy anyone to point out an example where this is not true.

"So now we, as American Indian people, are asked to believe that a "new" European revolutionary doctrine such as Marxism will reverse the negative effect of European history on us. European power relations are to be adjusted once again, and that's supposed to make things better for all of us. But what does this really mean?

"Right now, today, we who live on the Pine Ridge Reservation are living in what white society has designated a "National Sacrifice Area." What this means is that we have a lot of uranium deposits here, and white culture (not us) needs this uranium as energy production material. The cheapest, most efficient way for industry to extract and deal with the processing of this uranium is to dump the waste by-products right here at the digging sites. Right here where we live. This waste is radioactive and will make the entire region uninhabitable forever. This is considered by industry, and by the white society that created this industry, to be an "acceptable" price to pay for energy resource development.

"Along the way they also plan to drain the water table under this part of South Dakota as part of the industrial process, so the region becomes doubly uninhabitable. The same sort of thing is happening. The same sort of thing is happening down in the land of the Navajo and Hopi, up in the land of the Northern Cheyenne and Crow, and elsewhere. Thirty percent of the coal in the West and half of the uranium deposits in the United States have been found to lie under reservation land, so there is no way this can be called a minor issue.

"We are resisting being turned into a National Sacrifice Area. We are resisting being turned into a national sacrifice people. The costs of this industrial process are not acceptable to us. It is genocide to dig uranium here and draw the water table—no more, no less.

Now let's suppose that in our resistance to extermination we begin to seek allies (we have).

"Let's suppose further that we were to take revolutionary Marxism at its word: that it intends nothing less than the complete overthrow of the European capitalist order which has presented this threat to our very existence. This would seem to be a natural alliance for American Indian people to enter into. After all, as the Marxists say, it is the capitalists who set us up to be a national sacrifice. This is true as far as it goes.

"But, as I've tried to point out, this very "truth" is deceptive. Revolutionary Marxism is committed to even further perpetuation and perfection of the very industrial process which is destroying us all. It offers only to "redistribute" the results—the money, maybe—of this industrialization to a wider section of the population. It offers to take wealth from the capitalists and pass it around; but in order to do so, Marxism must maintain the industrial system. Once again, the power relations with European society will have to be altered, but once again the effects upon American Indian peoples here and non-Europeans elsewhere will remain the same. This much the same as when power was redistributed from the church to private business during the so-called bourgeois revolution. European society changed a bit, at least superficially, but its conduct toward non-Europeans continued as before. You can see what the American Revolution of 1776 did for American Indians! It's the same old song.

"Revolutionary Marxism, like industrial society in other forms, seeks to "rationalize" all people in relation to industry —maximum industry, maximum production. It is a materialist doctrine that despises the American Indian spiritual tradition, out cultures, our lifeways. Marx himself called us "pre-capitalists" and "primitive." Pre-capitalist simply means that, in his view, we would eventually discover capitalism and become capitalists; we have always been economically retarded in Marxist terms. The only manner in which American Indian people could participate in a Marxist revolution would be to join the industrial system, to become factory workers, or "proletarians," as Marx called them. The man was very clear about the fact that his revolution could occur only through *the struggle of the proletariat, that the existence of a* massive industrial system is a precondition of a successful Marxist society.

[The same banksters funded both the industrial revolution and Marx]

"I think there is a problem with language here. Christians, capitalists, Marxists... All of them have been revolutionary in their own minds, but none of them really means revolution. What they really mean is a continuation. They do what they do in order that European [Rothschild] culture can continue to exist and develop [globalize and monopolize] according to its needs.

"So, in order for us to really join forces with Marxism, we American Indians would have to accept the national sacrifice of our homeland; *we would have to commit cultural suicide and become industrialized and Europeanized.*

"At this point, I've got to stop and ask myself whether I'm being too harsh. Marxism [created by Rothschilds] has something of a history. Does this history bear out my observations? I look to the process of industrialization in the Soviet Union since 1920 and I see that these Marxists have done what it took the English Industrial Revolution 300 years to do; and the Marxists did it in 60 years!

"I see that the territory of the USSR used to contain a number of tribal peoples and they have been crushed to make way for the factories. The Soviets refer to this as "the National Question," the question of whether the tribal peoples had a right to exist as people; and they decided the tribal peoples were an acceptable sacrifice to industrial needs. I look to China and I see the same thing. I look to Vietnam and I see Marxists imposing an industrial order and rooting out the indigenous tribal mountain people.

"I hear a leading Soviet scientist saying that when the uranium is exhausted, then alternatives will be found. I see the Vietnamese taking over a nuclear power plant abandoned by the U.S. military. Have they dismantled and destroyed it? No, they are using it. I see China exploding nuclear bombs, developing nuclear reactors, and preparing a space program in order to colonize and exploit the planets the same as the Europeans colonized and exploited this hemisphere. It's the same old song, but maybe with a faster tempo this time.

"The statement of the Soviet scientist's is very interesting. Does he know what this alternative energy source will be? No, he simply has faith. Science will find a way. I hear revolutionary Marxists saying that the destruction of the environment, pollution, and radiation will be controlled. And I see them act on their words. Do they know how these things will be controlled? No, they simply have faith. "Science will find a way."

"Industrialization is fine and necessary." How do they know this? Faith. "Science will find a way."

"Faith of this sort has always been known in Europe *as religion. Science has become the new European religion [technological "dominion"]* for both capitalists and Marxists; they are truly inseparable; they are part and parcel *of the same culture.* So, in both theory and practice, Marxism demands that non-European peoples give up their values, their traditions, their cultural experience altogether. We will all be industrialized science addicts [glued to a smart phone] in a Marxist society.

"I do not believe that capitalism itself is really responsible for the situation in which American Indians have been declared a national sacrifice. No, it is the European tradition; European culture itself is responsible. Marxism is just the latest continuation of this tradition, not a solution to it. To ally with Marxism is to ally with the very same forces that declare us an acceptable cost.

"There is another way. There is the traditional Lakota way and the ways of the other American Indian peoples. It is the way that knows that humans do not have the right to degrade Mother Earth, that there are forces beyond anything the European mind has conceived, that humans must be in harmony with All Relations or the Relations will eventually eliminate the disharmony.

"A lopsided emphasis on humans by humans—the European's arrogance of acting as though they were beyond the nature of All Related things [Because they believe in a concept, not a connection]—can only result in a total disharmony and a readjustment which cuts arrogant humans down to size, gives them a taste of that reality beyond their grasp or control and restores the harmony. There is no need for a revolutionary theory to bring this about; it's beyond human control. The natural peoples of this planet know this and so they do not theorize about it. Theory is an abstract; our knowledge is real.

"Distilled to it's basic terms, European faith —including the new faith in science—equals a belief that man is God. [Manmade "progress" is supposedly divine.]

> [*"And God said, Let us* make man in our image, *after our likeness: and let them have* dominion *over the fish of the sea, and over the fowl of the air, and over the cattle, and over all the earth, and over every creeping thing that creepeth upon the earth."* – Genesis 1:26]

"Europe has always sought a Messiah, whether that be the man Jesus Christ or the man Karl Marx or the man Albert Einstein. *American Indians know this to be truly absurd.* Humans are the weakest of all creatures, so weak that other creatures are willing to give up their flesh that we may live. Humans are able to survive only though the exercise of rationality since they lack the abilities of other creatures to gain food through the use of fang and claw.

"But rationality is a curse since it can cause human beings to forget the natural order of things in ways other creatures do not. A wolf never forgets his or her place in the natural order. American Indians can. Europeans almost always do. We pray our thanks to the deer, our relations, for allowing us their flesh to eat; Europeans simply take the flesh for granted and consider the deer inferior. After all, Europeans consider themselves godlike in their rationalism and science. [They think that their] *God is the Supreme Being; all else must be inferior.*

[This is the mono-theism. One god is true, MY god only!]

"All European tradition, Marxism included, has *conspired to defy the natural order of things.* Mother Earth has been abused, the powers have been abused, and this cannot go on forever. No theory can alter that simple fact. Mother Earth will retaliate, the whole environment will retaliate, and the abusers will be eliminated. Things will come full circle, back to where they started. That's revolution. And that's a prophecy of my people, of the Hopi people and of other correct peoples.

"American Indians have been trying to explain this to Europeans for centuries. But, as I said earlier, Europeans have proven themselves unable to hear. The natural order will win out, and the offenders will die out, the way deer die when they offend the harmony by over-populating a given region. It's only a matter of time until what Europeans call "a major catastrophe of global proportions" will occur. It is the role of American Indian peoples, the role of all natural beings, to survive. A part of our survival is to resist. We resist not to overthrow a government or to take political power, but because it is natural to resist extermination, to survive. We don't want power over white institutions; we want white institutions to disappear. That's revolution.

"American Indians are still in touch with these realities—the prophecies, the traditions of our ancestors. We learn from the elders, from nature, from the powers. And when the catastrophe is over, we American Indian people will survive; harmony will be reestablished. That's revolution.

"At this point, perhaps I should be very clear about another matter, one which should already be clear as a result of what I've said. But confusion breeds easily these days, so I want to hammer home this point. When I use the term "European," I'm not referring to a skin color or a particular genetic structure. What I'm referring to is a mind-set, a worldview that is a product of the development of European culture. Peoples are not genetically encoded to hold this outlook, they are acculturated to hold it. The same is true for American Indians or for the members of any other culture.

"It is possible for an American Indian to share European values, a European worldview. We have a term for these people; we call them "apples"—red on the outside (genetics) and white on the inside (their values). Other groups have similar terms: Blacks have their "oreos;" Hispanics have "coconuts" and so on. And, as I said before, there are exceptions to the white norm: people who are white on the outside, but not white inside. I'm not sure what term should be applied to them other than "human beings."

[Exactly. A spiritual person is color blind and sees the soul.]

"What I'm putting out here is not a racial proposition but a cultural proposition. Those who ultimately advocate and defend the realities of European culture and its industrialism are my enemies. Those who resist it, who struggle against it, are my allies, the allies of American Indian people. And I don't give a damn what their skin color happens to be. Caucasian is the white term for the white race: European [Rothschild hegemony coming out of monotheism] is an outlook I oppose.

"The Vietnamese Communists are not exactly what you might consider genetic Caucasians, but they are now functioning as mental Europeans. The same holds true for the Chinese Communists, for Japanese capitalists or Bantu Catholics or Peter "MacDollar" down at the Navajo reservation or Dickie Wilson up here at Pine Ridge. There is no racism involved in this, just an acknowledgment of the mind and spirit that make up culture.

"In Marxist terms I suppose I'm a "cultural nationalist." [Which the New World Order hates, and which all of us must become. We must preserve our families.] I work first with my people, the traditional Lakota people, because we hold a common worldview and share an immediate struggle. Beyond this, I work with other traditional American Indian peoples, again because of a certain commonality in worldview and form of struggle. Beyond that, I work with anyone who has experience the colonial oppression of Europe and who resists its cultural and industrial totality. Obviously, this includes genetic Caucasians who struggle to resist the dominant norms of European culture. The Irish and the Basques come immediately to mind, but there are many others.

"I work primarily with my own people, with my own community. Other people who hold non-European perspectives should do the same. I believe in the slogan, "Trust your brother's vision," although I'd like to add sisters in the bargain. I trust the community and the culturally based vision of all the races that naturally resist industrialization and human extinction. Clearly, individual whites can share in this, given only that they have reached the awareness that continuation of the industrial imperatives of Europe is not a vision, but species suicide. White is one of the sacred colors of the Lakota people—red, yellow, white and black. The four directions. The four seasons. The four period of life and aging. The four races of humanity. Mix red, yellow, white and black together and you get brown, the color of the fifth race. This is the natural order of things. It therefore seems natural to me to work with all races, each with it's own special meaning, identity and message.

"But there is a peculiar behavior among most Caucasians. As soon as I become critical of Europe and its impact on other cultures, they become defensive. They begin to defend themselves. But I am not attacking them personally; I'm attacking Europe. In personalizing my observations on Europe they are personalizing European culture, identifying themselves with it. By defending themselves in this context, they are ultimately defending the death culture. This is a confusion which must be overcome, and it must be overcome in a hurry. None of us has energy to waste in such false struggles.

"Caucasians have a more positive vision to offer humanity than European culture. I believe this. But in order to attain this vision *it is necessary for Caucasians to step outside European [Rothschild] culture—alongside the rest of humanity—to see Europe for what it is and what it does.*

"To cling to capitalism and Marxism and all the other "isms" is simply to remain within European culture. [The world of mind programming.] There is no avoiding this basic fact. As a fact, this constitutes a choice. Understand that the choice is based on culture, not race! Understand that to choose European culture and industrialism is to choose to be my enemy. And understand that the choice is yours, not mine.

This leads me back to address those American Indians who are drifting through the universities, the city slums, and other European institutions. If you are there to learn to resist the oppressor in accordance with your traditional ways, so be it. I don't know how you manage to combine the two, but perhaps you will succeed. But retain your sense of reality.

"Beware of coming to believe the white world now offers solutions to the problems it confronts us with. Beware, too, of allowing the words of native people to be twisted to the advantage of our enemies. Europe invented the practice of turning words around on themselves. You need only look to the treaties between American Indian peoples and various European governments to know that this is true. Draw your strength from who you are.

"A culture which regularly confuses revolution with continuation, which confuses science and religion, which confuses revolt with resistance, has nothing helpful to teach you and nothing to offer you as a way of life. Europeans have long since lost all touch with reality, if they ever were in touch with it. Feel sorry for them if you need to, but be comfortable with who you are as American Indians.

"So, I suppose to conclude this, I would state clearly that leading anyone toward Marxism is the last thing on my mind. Marxism is as alien to my culture as capitalism and Christianity are. In fact, I can say *I don't think I'm trying to lead anyone toward anything.*

[Exactly. A sovereign person does not make others into followers. Buddha and Jesus were not channelers, they were sovereign beings. Jesus doesn't wants me to follow, he wants me to stand up! Buddha's dying advice after 40 years of teaching was "Be a light onto yourselves."]

"To some extent I tried to be a "leader," in the sense that white media like to use that term, when the American Indian Movement was a young organization. This was a result of a confusion that I no longer have. You cannot be everything to everyone. [We can not lead others, we only end up leading dumbed down followers. The leader then becomes an icon, no longer human.] I do not propose to be used in such a fashion by my enemies. I am not a leader. I am an Oglala Lakota patriot. This is all I want and all I need to be.

"And I am very comfortable with who I am."

Russell Means (1939-2012)

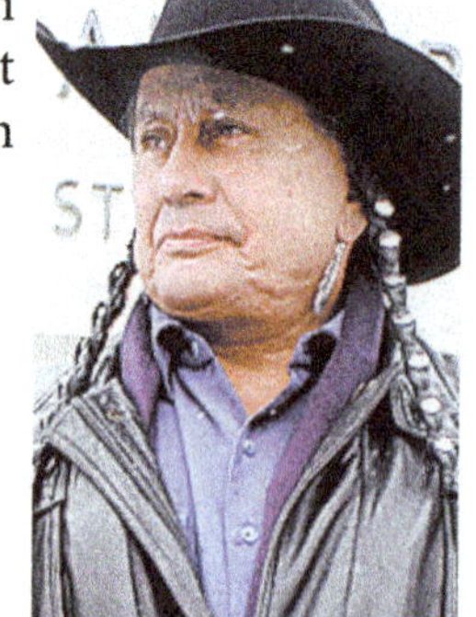

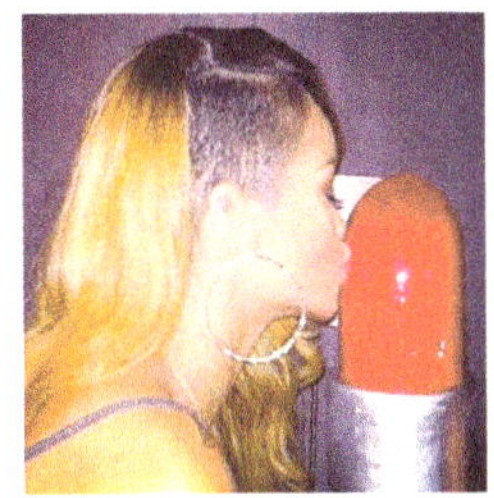

Rihanna, "Diva" of seductive materialism

Table of Contents

(Cast of Characters)

War Criminal Henry Kissinger

Meet the Author 1

David Menongye – Hopi | Kobun Chino Roshi – Zen Master | Steve Jobs | John and Mina Lansa – Hopi | Thomas Banyacya – Hopi | David Holmgren – Permaculture | *YouTube – The Disclosure Project Press Conference, May 2001* | *YouTube – 9/11 Loose Change* | David Icke | Yolngu People – Arnhemland, Northern Territories, Australia | Song – "This Land is Your Land" by Woodie Guthrie | *Youtube – Operation Deep Forest* –NSA attack on Maori in New Zealand | David Wilcock | Movie – *Elisyium* (2013) – Matt Damon | song "I'm Yours" by Jason Mraz | Glossary terms summary

Chapter 1 Organized Consumerism 15

Movie – *Finding Nemo (2003)* | Song – "I Get Out" – Lauryn Hill | Movie – *Captain America (2014)* – Robert Redford | Ralph Nader | "Logo" Barack Hussein Obama | Movie – *Brave* (2012) – Disney/Pixar in Mandarin | The Peace Corp | Graeme Wearden – *Guardian* | George Soros | Albert Einstein | Normon Dodd – 1954 Congressional Committee | Rockefeller, Guggenheim, and Carnegie Foundations | George Bernays, Father of Public Relations | Using crisis | George Bush Sr. (George Herbert Walker Bush) – Pedophile (U.S. spelling) and War Criminal | Iranian Prime Minster Mosaddeq killed – 1953 CIA Operation Ajax – overthrow of Iran's democratically elected government | Shah of Iran | Ayatollah Khomeini | Osama bin Laden | Alice Bailey – "New World Order" – 1918 | UN Lucis Trust – (formally Lucifer Publishing) | Erica Carle – *The Intelligent Student's Guide to the New World Order* | Education 2000 | Naomi Klein – Author *Shock Doctrine* | J.P. Morgan – *Rothschild* Bankster | *Cutout* Winston Churchill | Jon Christian Ryter – Researcher | *Cutout* FDR – Franklin Delano Roosevelt | Senator Claremont Pell – Earthquake Weapons 1976 | HAARP (High Frequency Active Auroral Research Program) | Goldman Sachs Inc. | C. Edward Griffin – FED *Hero* Whistleblower | AMA – American Medical Association | FBI Chief Ted Gunderson – exposes rampant child sacrifice for satanic rituals – Gunderson was murdered with arsenic | Henry Kissinger – Pedophile and War Criminal | Robert McNamara – Viet Nam era war criminal becomes President World Bank | Zbigniew Brzezinski – author of *Between Two Ages: America's Role in the*

Technetronic Era | *Cutout* Bill Gates – On trial in India, 2014, for vaccine crimes | Prince Philip | Donald Rumsfeld | Leuren Moret – *Hero* Whistleblower | FEMA – Federal Emergency Management Agency (Creates and manages emergencies) | Johann Adam Weishaupt – Founder of Illuminati 1776 | *Virtue* by author

Chapter 2 All the Man's Kings 41

Amschel Rothschild – Father of Modern Banking | Andrew Hitchcock – Rothschild *Hero* Whistleblower The *Rothschild* Timeline | George Washington | Henry Jackson | Benjamin Franklin | Nathan Mayer Rothschild – England | Jacob (James) Mayer Rothschild – France | Prince William IX of Hesse-Hanau | East India Company | Napoleon Bonaparte | Wellington – Battle of Waterloo | Thomas Jefferson | Kalmann (Carl) Mayer Rothschild pals with Pope Gregory XVI | Karen Hudes – World Bank Whistleblower | Guiseppe Mazzini – Illuminati agent | Jack Ruby – Paid assassin of Oswald | Lee Harvey Oswald – Framed | John C. Calhoun – Vice President under Andrew Jackson | Jacob Schiff – Foremost Rothschild agent in U.S. Founded FED, ADL, NAACP, and | Bolshevik Revolution | British Prime Minister Benjamin Disraeli | Cherokee and Creek Native Americans – Trail of Tears | Karl Marx – Rothschild Employee | Karl Ritter – Anti-thesis of Communist Manifesto | Friedrich Wilhelm Nietzsche | Abraham Lincoln | Tsar Alexander II – Rothschild enemy | John D. Rockefeller – Standard Oil funded by Rothschilds | Frederick Engels | David Allen Rivera – Author | Warren Buffet | *Cutout* Arnold Schwarzenegger | The FED – Federal Reserve a private Rothschild bank that refuses to be audited | ADL – Anti Defamation League | James Earl Ray – Exonerated in (censored by Media) 1999 trial, Shelby Tennessee. Did not kill Martin Luther King. | NAACP – National Association for the Advancement of Colored People | Collin Powell – War Criminal | Condoleezza Rice – War Criminal | *Cutout* Oprah Winfrey | *Sellout* Jessie Jackson | Eddie Murphy – Owned | Cynthia McKinney – *Hero* Whistleblower | Movie – *The Monuments Men (2014)* directed by George Clooney | Jesus | Buddhism

Chapter 3 The Mask Comes Off 61

Paul A. Volker – *Roth-efeller* minion | The Bilderberg Group for real | Edmond de Rothschild | Sharon Percy Rockefeller | Andrew Gavin Marshall – Researcher | Pawns in a Game | *Cutout* Vladimir Lenin | *Cutout* Adolf Hitler | *Compromised* Mahatma Gandhi | *Compromised* Woodrow Wilson | *Cutout* Chairman Mao | *Cutout* Stalin | *Cutout* Bill Clinton | *Cutout* George Bush Jr. | Color Revolutions and Arab Spring | Salvador Allende – Chile – Murdered by Kissinger | Operation Condor – South America – Kissinger | Bill Van Auken – Researcher | John Kennedy Jr. – murdered 1999 | Yom Kipper War – 1973 – a la Bilderberg Group | UN Agenda 21 – You are to live in a Smart City where you will be happy. | *Compromised* Dalai Lama | Song "If I Ain't Got You" by Alicia Keys | Vandana Shiva – *Hero* GMO, Seed, Women's activist India | Chinese environmental activists | Walmart | WTO World Trade Organizations | IMF – International Monetary Fund (Noose) | Nelson Mandela | Ryan Shapiro – Researcher | Hermann Kallenbach – Gandhi's handler | Gopal Krishna

Gokhale – Gandhi's mentor | Joseph Lelyveld – New World Order minion | Bob Marley – Artist, song writer, truther

Chapter 4 Entitlement, The Bad Boy 75

Cutout Australian Prime Minister Paul Keating | *Cutout* Australian Prime Minister John Howard | Martyr Senator Paul Wellstone – another airplane crash | Fake Swine Flu – practice for false flag Ebola | Sharyl Attkinson – *Hero* Journalist | CDC – Center of Disease Control (Controlling the Dissemination of Cancer and other diseases) | RFID chips | More Lipstick Please: George Orwell | Urban Blight | Noam Chomsky | Song "Ramona" by Bob Dylan | Sir Baldwin Spencer – Snob explorer aboriginal communities | Palestinian Children Killed | Emperor Nero | Geo-engineering – Weather modification plus ionizing atmosphere for other programs

Chapter 5 Freedom for the Rich 93

Chapter 6 The Ocean Is Broken 95

Greg Ray – Sailor | Plankton Decline – Not discussed | Geo-engineering | Global Dimming | Elana Freeland – author of *Chemtrails, HAARP, and the Full Spectrum Dominance of Planet Earth* | Dead Fish | Dane Wigington – *Hero* Whistleblower GeoEngineeringWatch.org | Vincent Freeman – Nanotechnology Whistleblower | Transhumanist Agenda | *"If it's covered up, it's true."* – Chuck Cannon | Autism graph | Alzheimer's graph | Prostate Cancer UK graph | Hepatitis C, UK graph | NAS Graph Tennessee | Food Stamp – Ration Graph | Soil Erosion Graph – We inherit reality, we don't create our own reality. | Water per Capita Graph | Cell Tower/ Electro Sensitive Graph | Sanctioned Diseases | Bertrand Russel | Fluoride | USAF Major George R. Jordon – Fluoride | Mike Adams – *Hero* Whistleblower – NaturalNews.com | Mercury | EMF Pollution – Electro Smog | "Smart" Meters | Dirty Electricity – Switching Mode Power Supply | Josh del Sol – *Hero* Whistleblower – Producer of film *Take Back Your Power* | Breast Cancer | FCC – Intentionally obsolete safety standards | Bioinitiative.org – Thousands of studies show long term danger of wifi | Five Danish Ninth Grade School Girls – *Hero* Whistleblowers | Another Fake Pandemic | Gary Null and Richard Gale – *Hero* CDC Whistleblowers | No Ebola epidemic, case numbers disappearing in Liberia | Dave Hodges – CDC and Bill Gates own patents on Ebola | Monsanto Inc. | Ebola Vaccine impossibly produced in a few months | Bioweapons Lab at epicenter of Ebola in Sierra Leone | Jane Burgermeister – Vaccine Agenda *Hero* Whistleblower | The Bill Gates You Should Really Know | Email by Author | Bill and Melinda Gates – The rich will manage us for our own good and make sure we want it. | Gates – Global Food Supply | Gates – Geo-engineering | Gates – Vaccine Deaths | Gates – Trial in India names Gates | Kenya WHO sterilization campaign | "Depopulation Vaccine" in Kenya and Beyond by *Hero* journalist Jon Rappoport

Chapter 7 Just Look In the Mirror. 159

Song "Man in the Mirror," sung by Michael Jackson | Concept *Disconnecting vanity* | Movie *Brave* (2012) in Spanish | song "A Thousand Years" by Christina Perri | Patrick Henry | Furor David Rockefeller | Richard Henry Pratt – Carlisle Indian School | General Philip Sheridan | Denise Oliver Velez – American *Indigenous Hero* Whistleblower | The Disney Weapon | Gloria Steinem – CIA agent | song "Can't Hold Us Down," by Disney brat Christina Aguilera | song "Stand By Your Man" by Tammy Wynette and Billy Sherrill | The 1970s Illuminati ISIS | Madonna | Cher | song "Stronger Than Me" by Amy Winehouse | Katherine Hepburn – promoted by Howard Hughes | Lady Gaga | Unregulated cosmetics | song "Once in a Lifetime" by Talking Heads | Prostituting Ourselves | Selling Disconnection | song "From This Moment" by Shania Twain | song "Danny's Song" by Kenny Loggins | song "Take a Look at My Face," Smokey Robinson | Gay – origins of word | King Louis XIV – "L'etat cc'est moi" (I am the state) (and King of Fashion) | Breast feeding or fetish? | Michelle Obama | Women join the battle front

Chapter 8 Shamelessness and the All-Seeing-Eye 195

"Ella" – 17 year old talent show contestant | *American Idol, X-Factor, The Voice* | Simon Cowell – Freemason | Reinhard Mohn – Nazi heir, controls X-Factor | Demi Lovato – Disney brat | Selena Gomez – Disney brat | MK-ULTRA mind programming | Tim Olstad – talent show contestant | King Frederick William I – Prussian compulsory schools | The Disney Machine | Miley Cyrus / Hannah Montana | Ted Schwarz – Author *Secret Weapon* | Katy Perry – Another music industry *cutout* | Britney Spears | Christina Aguilera | Someone is Watching | George Washington | Warren Buffet | Madonna and Spears/Aguilera | Madonna and Cyrus | Charlie Chaplin | Trans-humanism | Hillary Clinton – Lesbian/Bi-sexual | Posers as Teachers | Jennifer Lopez | The Zionist music industry | E. Michael Jones culturewars.com | Larsha Moon on Mass Enslavement through Sex | song "Live It Up" by Jennifer Lopez, Britain's Got Talent 2013 | Gag Order | Lady Gaga | Elton John | Disney Inc. | Walt Disney – another *cutout* | Fritz Springmeier – Author of *The 13 Illuminati Bloodlines* | Robert Kennedy Jr. on families | song "Born This Way" by Gaga | song "Alive" sung by Dami Im | Maltese Cross | Queen Elizabeth | song "God Save the Queen" by The Sex Pistols | Knights of Malta and Sovereign *Military* Order of Malta | Rothschilds | Shakira – another "diva" Illuminati *cutout* | Adolf Hitler | Benjamin Disraeli | "Sir" Norman Schwarzkopf | "Sir" Collin Powell | Madeleine Albright | "Sir" Henry Pedophile Kissinger | "Sir" Brent Scowcroft | "Sir" Alan Greenspan | "Sir" George Pedophile Herbert Walker Bush | "Sir" Ronald Reagan | "Sir" J. Edgar Hoover | "Sir" Tom Jones | "Sir" Mick Jagger | Freemasons | Rihanna | Celine Dion | New Age Movement | Deepak Chopra | Image – The California drought | Movie – *Why Are They Spraying* (2012)

Meet the Author

My first memory was tremendous clashing banging sounds. My mom was holding me and we had just left the apartment on Octavia Street in San Francisco. Existence was an electric blue stick figure. The pulsing of that moving blue current of light and melody with the shape of a little stick man was me, my awareness, my being. I opened my eyes to the street and sidewalk and saw and heard the tall buildings and cars and smashing sounds. It was very, very loud and frightening. You might say it was a rude awakening.

I came into this world. I was a little baby—I don't know how old, but too young to walk.

When I was three years old, my Dad took me fishing at Coyote Point on San Francisco Bay. I caught a little bright silver perch and had it up on the pier and I was flinging it around on the end of the line. He started screaming to stop.

You remember things like that.

That was the first spiritual lesson ... Respect and kindness. Another was my mom cringing because her finger nail accidentally had gouged my skin ... Kindness and guilt. My younger brother crying because I had bullied him, and my later shame ... Remorse and shame.

When I was four in nursery school the teacher asked me, "Do you believe in God?" I had no idea. She took another boy on her lap and said, "Johnny believes in God and I love Johnny." Prejudice.

You remember things like that.

My aunts and uncles. My cousins. The pets, the desert, the mountains, the kelp beds ... these were my roots. I grew up in a beach town in southern California. I was lucky because my parents were avid campers and loved the wilderness. I saw endangered California Condor flying as a youth in the backlands behind Santa Barbara. They don't fly there now. Most of the world's 7 billion people have never spent a night in the wilderness, let alone months, as I have. Most of the world has never seen virgin forests, and thus, they have no baseline with which to contemplate our relationship with the ancient natural world.

For most people, nature is not ancient. For most people, nature is not *the Great Mystery* because they've never spent days and weeks in the silence that exposes every speck of *vanity* and strips us of the ability to name.

I remember hiking in the wilderness in the Sierras under deep blue skies. I remember looking up. There were con-trails of water vapor that disappeared behind the jets. But now the sky is covered with sprayed trails?

The sprayed trails now fan out and cover the sky. They are not con-trails.

As a teenager in the Los Angeles basin, I learned that our water was pumped from over the mountains. I remember thinking, "That won't last," and I looked up from my school desk and said to myself, "I'm outta here."

I wasn't inspired by college and when a friend offered me a free ticket to London, I took it, and then traveled overland through Europe, Turkey, Iran and Afghanistan to Pakistan and India. That was before the wars. More foundation for kindness was my 1973 stay with Lama Yeshi and Zopa Rinpoche near Kathmandu, Nepal. They introduced me to the Vow of Service. [1]

The writings of Peruvian Carlos Castaneda was pivotal for me, particularly *Journey to Ixtlan* which is one of the few books I would recommend to someone interested in the spiritual path. One sentence in an earlier book of his led me to stop drinking alcohol for the rest of my life.

In India I had an experience where the universe turned inside out. I talk about it in my only youtube you can find on line. This took many years to integrate. It was disorienting and I had no support.

I returned to college and checked out all the different spiritual lineages and teachers I could find. In my first private interview with Kobun Chino Roshi (we called him Kobun), he approached me as I was sitting and staring down at a patio table. He said, "It's like looking at the moon." He knew, as I did, that when the universe turns inside out, here and there don't mean anything anymore. There really is no space between anything. It is all the mind, and the picnic table was no further away than the moon. He told me I was very young to have this experience.

In my whole life I've only met a few people who know about what I just spoke of. As Kobun could see me, I can see this in others. It's the difference between a window that is open and one that is not. When it is open, there is no otherness. It is mind to mind.

But I've also learned there is more than one kind of awakening, and what I can see is different than the kind of sight that others have available to them. This means there is no one direction for soul evolution; there are countless directions. This realization undercuts the kind of universal understanding that our ego often tries to seek. I just can't go there any more. Evolution is multi-directional and no map can map it.

(Kobun happened to conduct the marriage ceremony for famous Apple CEO, Steve Jobs, which I will discuss later. Kobun died mysteriously.)

* * *

Another important experience was my 1975 stay with blind David Menongye, in Hopiland, Arizona. He sat next to me and told me where to drive to a boulder on which the Hopi Prophecy is drawn. He was blind but he could see.

Grandpa David took me down into the kiva where I listened to John and Mina Lansa in their ancient tongue. These people were legends for me.

In the words of Hopi elder John Lansa, as translated by Thomas Banyacya …

> *"There is a spiritual seeing of things* **that can't be explained.** *There are shrines in the spiritual center, which are markers for spiritual routes which extend in all four directions to the edge of the continent. Through our ceremonials, it is possible to keep the natural forces together. From here at the spiritual center, our prayers go to all parts of the Earth. Our prayers maintain the balance that keeps all things well and healthy. This is the sacred place. It must not have anything wrong in it. It must never be defiled. We want it organic the way it has always been. Leave the land in the hands of the Hopi to take care of everything for all the people. We know how to farm. Only people who know how to grow things will survive. Through prayer, people can develop* **in their own way** *as the Hopi have."*

I would like to add here that, until we each see the entire world as sacred, we will abuse her.

When I was in India I saw a Tibetan woman who could make things disappear. The crowd around her was both captivated and gobsmacked terrified. As she walked, she would hit a stick on the ground, throw it up and it would disappear. I didn't observe her long enough to see where the sticks were coming from. I've thought about that later. But I saw her strike one against the ground and heard it also. The crowd was like a ring around her moving down the road. They were afraid to get too close to her. I saw the ring of people approach where I was sitting on a stone wall with two boys. I didn't budge so they stuck with me. Then we were in the ring of spectators and I saw what everyone else was seeing. Then the ring moved past us and all I could see were peoples' backs. I saw this with my own eyes. The horror on one women's face was confirmation for me. We all saw it. The boys joked with me that I wasn't afraid.

When I came back to college, I hung around Swami Muktananda, a siddhi. Siddhis have siddhi powers. It is a phase beyond what is available in Zen Buddhism. I saw him materialize water. It wasn't a trick and few who were present even noticed. It was done for a practical purpose, because a pitcher of water had run out, and only the guy holding the pitcher and perhaps myself knew what happened. These were good experiences that let me know that the world is not what I was told it is. It is also rather humbling, because I don't know what these people were doing.

In 2005 at the age of 52, I went on a trip with my grown son and he brought a book by Australian author David Holmgren, *Permaculture: Principles and Pathways Beyond Sustainability.* The book began with a Peak Oil Production graph. The graph showed that since discovery in 1847, oil production skyrocketed and then leveled off around the year 2000. And then the graph showed the depletion we can expect. There will be less oil every year as we slide down the back side of the peak. This is true because the easy oil has already been extracted. On the downside of the graph, it said "period of social unrest." And I saw that, and I turned to my son and said, "This book is true."

More demand for oil has caused prices to increase. In the coming ten years available oil will go down while demand continues to go up. The price will strain us all. Oil will be sought in deeper and deeper places, until it eventually becomes unaffordable. Oil is the cheapest and easiest fuel to use with the most uses, and civilization as we know it is based on oil. Fertilizer and plastic and synthetic clothing is made from oil. The *Globalists* know all about this, but have not warned the public.

When my son and I returned home from this trip, we spent a month doing research on the internet. One subject led to another. We saw lots of documentary videos. Every few days we would discover something new which blew us away. Some of the knowledge was shocking to my psyche. It would take a couple of days to recover. If you want to be really shocked, watch this one on YouTube, *The Disclosure Project Press Conference, May 2001.*

For some reason Peak Oil websites were mentioning 9/11. I couldn't understand that and so I did a YouTube search for 9/11. A watershed moment occurred when I watched the video, *9/11 Loose Change* and saw the 47 story tall building, called World Trade Center 7, fall in a perfect symmetric controlled demolition at 5:30 in the evening of September 11, 2001.

We were never shown this on television.

It fell perfectly into its own footprint. It was not hit by an airplane. It was a steel building over 740 feet tall. That is like over two football fields. It is impossible that it could turn to dust in 10 seconds due to burning office furniture on a few floors. It was very obviously a controlled demolition, as anyone can see if they watch this video. [2] To bring down a building perfectly like this would require weeks of professionally placed explosives. It was planned in advance. All this became apparent to me in an instant.

Perfect controlled demolition on 9/11 at 5:30 PM. 47-story tall World Trade Center 7 is the black rectangle in center of photos

More shocking is that the demolition was announced on the ground in advance so that the area was cleared of personnel. BBC even reported the "collapse" 20 minutes before it happened. Since the actual collapse of WTC 7 was never shown by the Media, it had to mean the Media was in on a cover up of whatever really happened that day.

I was sneering at the "conspiracy theory" in *9/11 Loose Change* up to that point. I watched the perfect symmetric dustification of this huge building and my jaw dropped. I said, "Oh sh*t."

The elephant was in the room. I had been lied to. Everyone had. Conspiracy wasn't theory. Conspiracy was fact. I was living in a mad world of lies, and wars were being waged based on these lies. Blood for what? For whom? I ordered every book written on 9/11. I was enraged.

I have spent the last 9 years going back to "university" in the form of self-guided study, trying to get a grasp on what is going on in this world. Other friends on my mailing list constantly updated and deepened my study. Conspiracy is indeed a fact, not a theory, which millions are investigating for the first time in history. This large body of researchers make up, in my opinion, the prophets of our times.

* * *

To clear ourselves of deception, all the methods of deception need to be understood, otherwise we will think we now know "the truth," without correcting the mind that receives information.

I've learned never to believe anything, but to see everything as messages that might be useful. I no longer assume data is reliable. The facts I share in this book are actually descriptions. This is what I'd like the reader to learn. Words are just words. The "facts" in this book will get more factual as more truth is exposed over time. The facts here are much more true than what the Media has fed you. Therefore, whatever you thought was "true" will be challenged. I'm going to connect a lot of dots for you and I have to be repetitive as the circle of understanding grows and includes more history and more evidence. At the same time I am weaving in an analysis of the moral basis for an alternative to the present dysfunctional society, which we are hurting ourselves with. I present an overview in the first few chapters and then the evidence comes on hot and heavy. This widening circle of connected dots is what can change your life by changing how you digest information. As you come across new information you can use concepts like *doublespeak* and *cutout* (See Glossary) to see the face behind the mask.

Through my study, I've learned that most of the intelligent people I meet are not informed. They believe and feel what they do, based on controlled dis-information. The fact that peoples' feelings and passions, including my own, can be manipulated, is difficult to witness. Everyone in the world is programmed by their cultures, but our roots were hijacked in the last century and what we call "our values" are being steered by people who do not respect virtue. Our values are being manipulated so that we might become the first culture ever without virtue.

It's amazing how many billions of people believe the same lies. For example the three laws of thermodynamics are only theoretically true in a "closed system," but there are no closed systems. Yet intelligent people trained in science and teaching science, believe the "laws of physics," forgetting that they are make believe. And billions of people are just as trapped. We end up seeing many people as intelligent, but ignorant. And then we look at ourselves even more closely.

And the real kicker, as I said, is that our values have been programmed. Our ethical coordinates were placed with *social engineering* programs. We are told since we were children to be proud of our flag. Years pass and we find ourselves working for banksters protecting their corporations as security guards in a *military* occupation, murdering freedom fighters in other countries. (The word bankster is combination of words banker and gangster, and is growing in usage as it accurately describes the creation of credit from nothing, in which no value backs up the bank paper "loan," and the world is put in debt with the police backing up the alleged "loans." Charging interest rates was called usury in the past.) Should we come home from a war of occupation and teach our children to be proud of our flag?

I'll say that again.

It is not just the history and science that have been lies, it is also the designed values that were pushed on us when we were kids, that were false.

What is marriage? What is sex? What is freedom? What is progress? What is valuable? Believe it or not, your answers are very different than how people answered these same questions for thousands of years. There is very little that is normal about modern values. Our values were designed in some back room and made tasty enough that we swallowed them. I know that's hard to believe but this book will show how our children are being distorted right in our own homes.

* * *

On the horizon of everyone's understanding is the unknown. I'm still learning.

The only other person I know of who is trying to submit a synthesis of spiritual and political awakening is David Icke of the UK. (I'm not discounting Christian or Patriot efforts, but these often don't ask adherents to let go of the *dominant culture* (See Glossary) religion. For example, Jehovah Witnesses don't take part in commercial holidays but are still mainstream consumers. They still believe humans are supposed to have "dominion" over their Earth Mother. I feel that *hero* whistleblower Icke is also *dominant culture* because he doesn't discuss *consumerism* as a central problem.)

Icke is worthy of respect, even if you don't agree with every thread he talks about. I don't always agree with him, but I respect him very much. I don't agree with his understanding of past prophets. Their stories may be embellished to the point of being just fables, but they existed, and some are still alive in realms that are still important to our faith now. I have had experiences with people who supposedly died. They still exist. Jesus still exists, and I know this, and I value him, even though I'm not a Christian. There are many other great beings who we can't see, but they are active here and valuable.

Those who ridicule Icke usually take a few statements out of volumes of his research, and judge him. David Icke is an altruistic spokesperson of history that is hidden from us by false "news." That makes him a *hero.* He connects the dots to show the corruption and crime behind all the fictions. Icke will expose rampant pedophilia in government. Your network news will not! But his view is not the perfect view, nor is mine or yours. The critic has to decide, are you with Icke against pedophilia or not? You'd better take sides! There is nothing grand about heckling a whistleblower. We have some real crimes that need to be busted.

Anyway, we don't want to all agree. That would be *monoculture* . We are individuals with unique sight so why would we criticize someone for seeing differently than ourselves?

The reason we are so critical of others is that we are still infected with the *dominant culture,* which is one of the main themes of this *End of Technocracy Series.* Instead of being independent sovereign beings, we tend to think like competitors, each striving for our king-of-the-mountain position in the eyes of others. "I'm the man! I know what's going on!"

This is why we pick pick pick at anyone who tries to make a difference. We are like chickens forever fighting in a pecking order. How foolish! If I am unique, you are unique. If we don't disagree, how can I learn something from you?

Picking on others and smearing them is what our oppressors do. (Those would be the people who didn't tell us what really happened on 9/11.) If we are to emancipate ourselves from their dominance, we need to emancipate others from our ridicule.

* * *

I hadn't been to Australia for many lifetimes. I returned in 2012 to see how my ancient family was doing. They weren't doing well at all. I found that most of my brothers and sisters were dead, and I, at age 59 was an elder. My stay with a small group of Yolngu families in Arnhem Nation, in the far hot north of Australia, was depressing and heart rending. What was most depressing is that integrity and honesty had been destroyed by welfare. Deeper than laziness was no motivation. When there was any motivation, it was to get substances to get stoned.

The government is actively disenfranchising the Aboriginal communities of Australia with a disgusting new law with the hypocritical *doublespeak* (See Glossary) name "Stronger Futures." The attempt by community elders there to organize anything has been sabotaged by this new imperial attack from the government of Australia. The police on the ancient homelands, act like they are in Sydney. It was as bad as what I saw in Tibet with the Chinese government. Mining for "*progress*" comes first, people come second.

I stayed with families who had met their first *dominant culture* White Man less than 80 years ago. I learned that every part of an animal is edible, all the guts. I learned that whether you are white or black, mosquitoes are waiting for you. I learned that paranormal experiences were daily fare for these people and that they were afraid of the spirit world and afraid to go out alone at night. This is not how their grandparents lived, and, interestingly, the same fear is now present far away in the Amazon. My spiritual bedrock and my new political literacy came to bear on understanding their social and cultural plight, which is not unique, but a classic example of *dominant culture* abuse of *indigenous people* (See Glossary).

Unless the reader knows someone from an *indigenous* culture, it is difficult to understand how we look in their eyes. We look like greedy invaders because, in fact, we are. It's good to try to understand this.

I will take an example from a song which many Americans know, written by Woodie Guthrie ...

This land is your land, this land is my land
From California, to the New York skyline,
From the redwood forests, to the gulf stream waters
This land was made for you and me.

Well I roamed and I rambled, and I followed my footsteps
Through the sparkling sands of her diamond deserts,
And all around me, a voice was calling
This land was made for you and me.

The lyrics sound pleasant enough, "We can share this continent." But the lyrics only sound nice if one pretends that Native Americans hadn't been here already for thousands of years. Native Americans know North America as a living place, not an empty canvas upon which a factory culture should be stamped. They know this land in a way most Americans are not even interested in learning about. Most Americans don't know the soil and water and plants and animals, so how is Guthrie saying "This is your land, this is my land?" He is singing this as a *dominant culture* Globalist who wants to replace corporations (*dominant culture)* with collectivism (*dominant culture),* and use the land as abusively as the corporations, but in the name of "the people." Who will organize "the people"? The *Globalists.*

As I went walking, I saw a sign there
And on the sign it said "No Trespassing."
But on the other side it didn't say nothing,
That side was made for you and me.

Woodie's idea of community property sounds nice. Then, if that is how he feels, the land actually already has a community owning it. The ancient locals. But being a member of the *dominant culture,* he couldn't see that. "You and me" was white people, who magically will all agree about everything.

If there isn't someone guarding the ecology, it can be abused. In ancient Hawaii, the fish harvest was strictly regulated, so that it could be sustainable! There is not freedom from responsibility in Nature. So the back side of the sign needs to say something, like Aloha Aina. Love this Land.

The song "Waltzing Matilda" in Australia is similar. It sounds nice, except this song is for a ruthless raping invader who drew straight lines on ancient homeland, claimed territories for the "Crown" and feels patriotic now singing it.

Australia is a symbol of what the whole world has experienced at the hands of the monster banksters from Europe, who were the ones who funded the British Empire. In only two hundred years, the entire continent of Australia was raped. Even today, the crime is not healed, nor has it been arrested. Every *indigenous culture* world wide is under the same pressure. Please see video *Operation 8, Deep in the Forest* on YouTube.

A government attorney in Bolivia told me, "There are no *indigenous people.* They were overrun 50 years ago." Could this be true?

Our present "modern" idea of progress, which we all bow to like it is God, is creating a toxic dump for our children to clean up. What is so magnificent about this? What are we so proud of? Also in our landfills are cultures that were clean and slow and sane, which were destroyed by our infection, our desire to dominate. Like drunks with our zippers down, we call this "progress."

* * *

I hope to help young people return to a *Purification Path.* I feel I am qualified to do that. To help. The un-sustainability of both our rate of consumption and the amount of bull s**t we are asked to believe, convinces me that we will return to a *Purification Path.*

Suppressed "free energy" systems need to remain suppressed until we jettison the *dominant culture* from our consciousness and replace it with a nourishing culture. The Earth and the other two million species don't need free energy chain saws and free energy bulldozers and free energy water pumps. Free energy on a limited planet will destroy resources even faster. It will have to be licensed and regulated, which will give the ultimate excuse for Big Brother and the *Globalists* to have a one world government. I'm warning all the good people jumping on the free energy tech band wagon, that until *consumerism* is replaced by Purification, free energy will guarantee a global lock down. We each need to slow down, not speed up. It is time for quality, not more quantity. It is time to slow down and connect.

Some people call this transition away from abuse, "ascension." I feel that's backwards. I honestly don't think we are going forward to some new consciousness. I feel we need to return to something. Back to normal. There are people who have predicted dates for some big moment, some big shift. There were people like David Wilcock who promoted 2012 as the year he would ascend. He didn't want to be here any more. He is older and wiser now.

The shift is much like the light before dawn. For us to wait for the sun to peak over the horizon is fine, but we can see plenty in the dawn light and we need to start shifting right now.

A transition back to sanity won't happen overnight and wishful thinking won't get anyone to "heaven" or to some "fourth or fifth dimension of consciousness." The idea that some galactic level of energy will change people's karmic habits is, to my mind, a denial of our responsibility to reform ourselves.

I find it odd that people who live a decadent lifestyle think they are evolved.

The coming exposure of the shocking crimes of our wanton leaders will be our rite of passage into a rejuvenation ethic. Our role models will not be the filthy rich elite, but the salt of the Earth. Our heroes will be the slow people, who are still incarnating among slow *indigenous cultures.*

Because of *resource depletion* (See Glossary), my sight on this is accurate. Slowing down is our future. Either that or we will be enslaved on a *technocratic* (See Glossary) prison planet run by elite *Globalists*, as in the recent movie *Elysium* (2013) with Matt Damon.

Yuppie high tech "utopia" is based on denial of our impact upon others. I expose these deceptions in the pages you are about to read. The truth is going to win and we are going to slow down. There is no sane way to drive a hot rod. We are going to walk. It is just matter of time. And this old walk is a positive future, representing true progress from the insane "Russian roulette game" we are now playing with nature herself.

* * *

My writing is meant to help catalyze awareness and *move us toward a tipping point* where *transparency* will overwhelm secrecy. There are thousands of others doing this work and the reader can be one of them.

I sincerely feel it is time to turn off the TV. It is time to take stock of our situation. True women, it is your time to rise up. True men, it is your time to rise up.

As we get off our sleepy sofas and stand up, we need to ask, "What am I buying each day that is killing off so many species? Why do we women paint our faces? Why are there birth defects in Fallujah and who will clean this up? Who is spraying our atmosphere, under what authority? Why are schools still offering poisonous tuna fish to students? [3]

For many reading this book, the truth will be painful. It is a book for seekers, not a book for entertainment. But I love music and I love the human spirit, so I think you well feel that also. I include the music of our times, which is both an oracle for our feelings and the medium of our decadence. For those who have a hard time with hard information, I fully share your grief. Yes, I cry. But kindness is never ending, I can promise that. Your heart needs enlightenment, which is only available now through alternative sources like this.

To love with appropriate care requires truthful coordinates. These truthful coordinates are not "facts." Truthful coordinates come from studying the consequence of choice.

What we want are ethical coordinates for making wise choices.

My mentors are many. I acknowledge each of you with references. My information cannot be completely accurate, nor can the information from any of my sources. We are all learning together, and we don't want to ever stop learning. I tried to verify all references, but verification is never perfect. So please, read this book as a researcher, not as a believer or non-believer. Words are stories. Words are descriptions.

I apologize in advance if my writing style is pedantic or blunt. It is just a way of expression. Many people want things very soft and sugar coated, because any other way is not politically correct for them. I'm not good at being politically correct! For me, there is not even time to be polite now. Those yelling "fire" loudly are heroes to me. Paul Revere didn't ride around whispering.

The book is written as a flow of consciousness. The subject is holistic so I could not organize a perfectly linear presentation. I mix psychology with ethics with history because without the inner understanding we won't know how to see our place in the revealed history. So when an economic graph follows a Diva's shameful photo, please see the connection. Lipstick hides the dark side. I hope the reader can connect the dots that I have tried to make a circle with. You are in the center of this circle.

The choir of truthers is growing, and I ask you to please join us. Keep studying and share what you learn. Let us tip this world toward *informed choice* and let us choose connection and responsibility …

– Ray Songtree June 2014

I've been spendin' way to long
checking my tongue in the mirror
and bending over backwards just to try to see it clearer
but my breath fogged up the glass, so I drew
a new face and laughed

I guess what I'm singin' is there is no better reason
to rid yourself of vanities and just go with the seasons
Its what we aim to do, our name is our virtue

– from song "I'm Yours" by Jason Mraz

Glossary of Terms with Central Concepts

Each of us is a series of choices. There is no difference between our choices and their consequences (karma) which, combined, makes up who we are. We are not a mind or a body that makes choices. We are choice.

We exist as choice within context. We think in our heads that we are bodies separated from context, but when we quiet down, we realize we are not separate, we are more or less connected. This is not an intellectual conclusion. It is a quiet and dynamic experience, an actual return towards what is our true nature. Awakening is not a destination, but a simplification that becomes too quiet to name and grows ever deeper.

In the inescapable context that surrounds us, are other beings. In respecting and appreciating their inalienable right to be here, we choose morality. Thus we live in a moral "universe." ***We can never be free of responsibility.*** *This is an absolute truth that even atheists can embrace. So our choice is to be stuck in our heads and separated and abusive, or to quiet down and connect from the heart and claim our personal sovereignty and do something positive.*

By simplifying and awakening, we help others awaken. By dropping Consumerism, we help others drop Consumerism. By strengthening our own community, we undercut the Globalist plan to centralize and control everything. Re-localization will reverse monoculture and de-throne the parasitic structures of corruption that are threatening to kill the planet.

Since no two of us make the same choices, there is friction within the multi-verse. There is no "universe" or one-verse. There is no universal message or solution. There is no one "humanity." There is no utopia or heaven. Wherever beings choose, there is multi-verse and multi-choice and friction. A spiritual "believer" forgets this and masks this reality with a dogma such as "peace" or "spiritual evolution" or the one and only God, or the one and only Truth. There is no one peace, there is no one direction of evolution, there is no up, there is no Godhead that has infinite sight or keeps tabs on infinite choices, there is no way to express a truth that encompasses infinite choices. Structured belief is a blindness.

Rather than live in dogma, a sovereign individual lives in action that is increasingly informed by connection. That connection includes other dimensions that cannot be explained, but in English we use the words luck, synchronicity, grace, tao, God, spirit, providence to refer to this connection and the beings we connect with. I cannot explain this, nor can anyone.

We used to live naturally within an ecological community. This is our indigenous roots. Until we return to living naturally within an ecological community, we will kill bioregions with indoor living that blindly rips off the outdoor world. We must both dethrone the Globalist parasites, and touch the Earth again. Thereby we will touch Spirit again and take responsibility for that, each as sovereign individuals. Simplification will survive the disease we call "progress." Overconsumption and monoculture are doomed, but we are not. Young people will adapt!

It is suggested that the reader see the Glossary of Central Concepts at the end of the book before reading further, as it is illustrated with long explanations for the terms that shape the plot presented. Here is the list of terms which will appear in italics throughout text.

1. *Cage theme*
2. *Compassion*
3. *Consumerism*
4. *Controlled media*
5. *Co-opt*
6. *Cutout*
7. *"Democracy"*
8. *"Developed" countries*
9. *"Developing" countries*
10. *Disconnecting vanity*
11. *Dominant culture*
12. *Doublespeak*
13. *Entitled*
14. *Evil*
15. *"Freedom"*
16. *Globalists*
17. *Globalization*
18. *Grasping desire*
19. *The Great Mystery*
20. *Hero*
21. *His-story*
22. *Indigenous people*
23. *Informed choice*
24. *Inverse relationships*
25. *Military*
26. *Monoculture or monopolization*
27. *Personal sovereignty*
28. *Predictive programming*
29. *"Progress"*
30. *Purification path*
31. *Recovering from "development" countries*
32. *Re-localization*
33. *Resource depletion*
34. *Roth-efellers*
35. *Rothschild*
36. *Sanctioned disease*
37. *Social engineering*
38. *Technocracy*
39. *Transparency*
40. *Unsustainable*
41. *Urban people*
42. *Vanity*

Chapter 1

Organized Consumerism

The purpose of life is many purposes, thank goodness.

Developing kindness, however, seems to be a very different purpose than hoarding power. Cooperation is different than scheming to take advantage of others. Nourishing is different than abuse. Growing food is different than stealing it.

It is not just an appearance that our society is out of control and sick. It truly is out of control and sick! It is also not just appearance that things are getting worse. Things are definitely getting worse! For those who think this is negative or absurd, or that we don't have problems, you may not have noticed that the U.S. is printing 30 billion dollars per month to stay afloat! You may not know that 100 million Americans receive some kind of welfare. You might not know what is going on with the seas or the rivers or the skies because the Media is not mentioning this.

Many have outlined these issues. This book goes deeper, however. This book is about empowerment and responsibility and turning the tide. It is my faith that people are good and when truth exposes deception, people will call for goodness.

In this book series we will be asking if we might be deceiving ourselves and not even knowing it. We will be asking where we got our values. We will be asking whether we have time or mind anymore for lipstick.

Environmental problems, or problems with *resource depletion*, or trade disagreements, or covert war crimes, are all symptoms. Someone made these things happen. Someone didn't care. There is a deeper sickness that is manifesting as whatever dysfunctions we see around us.

Some people say the big problem is just too many mouths to feed or cars on the road. I say that is just half of it. They are overlooking what we all have in our heads, our desires, what we think we are here for, and how we listen or not listen to conscience. Interestingly our thinking has changed as a mass phenomenon, because our thinking was *socially engineered*. (See Glossary) Trends were pushed and this has affected our choices in mass.

Society's choices have changed because each of us has a new narrative in our heads that was placed there step by step. Each of us have become a home for a new culture that didn't exist one hundred years ago. From how we see ourselves in the *vanity* mirror, to the kinds of food we expect each meal, to the wars we support with our taxes, our values have changed.

It is our values that have caused the dysfunctions we see manifest around us. I know it's more comfortable to blame the bad guys, but that isn't going to work, because even after we throw this corrupt leader or that bankster in jail, or arrest 100,000 of them, we still have what they planted in our heads for a century. We still have our habits, our dysfunctional goals, which were engineered and advertised into us … So now what? What do we replace them with?

After escaping from the apartment aquarium, the fish are still trapped in plastic bags. They are not free. They hadn't planned for what comes after the revolution. From movie Finding Nemo (2003), *by pre-Disney Pixar.*

It is true that there are corrupt institutions, which for centuries have been living like parasites off of us. We will study them. And yes, they have used every psychological trick to push corporate values. And their push has been to take advantage of us, no doubt. The crime of intentional disparity is obvious. But are these institutions acting alone or did we help them?

In examining the roots of dysfunction, there are visionaries who say an outside force is distorting our dimension. Some people think we are being used by other civilizations. Maybe that explains where electricity came from or advanced mathematics. I say, maybe, but so what? Maybe we are all slaves to mine minerals to build space craft for aliens. Maybe. But so what? And maybe these unearthly beings are evil, because for them, the end justifies the means. Maybe for all that.

But who cares what someone else thinks? Who cares what visionaries think? There is something more essential that is more powerful than an "outside force."

* * *

The reader is conscious. We are alone together, you and I. You are not a victim. You are not a result.

You are consciousness. I respect you and I wrote this for you. We are capable of conscious choice. We each are still central to our own experience of existence. The I is still the I. The I is still choosing. We care. We are moral. We have a say in the matter.

Your spiritual destiny is based on the momentum of your character. Mine too. We are not victims, we are choosers.

Our power is in choice, and our choices have changed. Whatever manipulations have occurred, someone decided to go along with it. And we can decide to not go along with it any more. We are not stuck. We don't have totally free will, but we have choice. We can simply decide that we won't cooperate with or enable abuse anymore.

It is something we decide within, and then we watch, almost as a witness, how that decision changes what we give our energy to. We take a stand. It is a decision you can choose to make within.

I get out, I get out of all your boxes
I get out, you can't hold me in these chains
I'll get out
Father free me from this bondage
Knowin' my condition
Is the reason I must change
I won't support your lie no more
I won't even try no more
If I have to die, oh Lord
That's how I choose to live
... Cause now I'm choosin' life, yo
I take the sacrifice, yo
If everything must go, then go
That's how I choose to live.

– from song "I Get Out" by *Hero* Lauryn Hill

How and why our choices changed needs to be examined, but the central crucial source of the problems in the world is that *we allowed ourselves to adopt a materialistic value system.*

Some would say we didn't have a choice, as it was forced on us at gunpoint just as a "free market system" and "free trade" is being forced at gunpoint all over the world today. This is true and I appreciate that. We have seen local farmers everywhere run out of business by IMF (International Monetary Fund) policies and currency manipulation and new "food safety" laws. I do appreciate that, however the fulcrum of power as sovereign beings is not how we react, but in how we make the next choice, with whatever latitude we have. Even in concentration camps, people have shown that they can choose hatred or not choose hatred, choose faith or not choose faith.

(I want to say right here, that there is a time to stop the Red Coats and that is a choice also. I'm referring to the Continental Army of 1775 who stopped the British. It is not hatred to defend your family. (Vol. 5) All security personnel reading this need to understand, you must be on the right side of history in the struggle between corruption and virtue. *Military* and law enforcement officers might want to think deeply about the questions that surface in the movie *Captain America, The Winter Soldier* (2014), starring Robert Redford.)

In seeking solutions we cannot keep endlessly dissecting problems. There are millions of people who have read about societal problems for decades and done nothing about it. We can study scandals forever, but we aren't exercising our power of choice.

The top planners and corporations have steered our choices, but they are *our* choices. *Personal sovereignty* (See Glossary) means we take responsibility for our decisions. We are accountable.

You have a say in the matter. You have power.

* * *

> "Most Americans have given up on themselves. They have rationalized their futility. That's easy to do, and they make excuses for themselves as to why they can't show up at a town meeting, or even show up to vote locally, or collar their member of Congress, or start a new citizens' group. And it is easy to rationalize futility because, let's face it, there is a 1% that does have a huge amount of wealth and power. And the 1% has blurred the difference between local, state, and federal government and corporate power, (which is called corporatism).
>
> "It [The 1%] also has a hundred ways to tell young people and children, "Don't bother." They often do it with distraction and entertainment [Lipstick]. They do it with pharmaceuticals. They do it with reprimands in the third grade or fifth grade. [And by molding standards and fashions.]
>
> "They commercialize education. The students do not grow up learning about civic history, the way they learn about *military* history and electro history by a two party tyranny, and [they learn] about the building of the railroads and so on and so forth, but they don't learn about civic history and *the struggle for justice* which, in his better moments, Senator Daniel Webster called the great work of human beings on Earth."
>
> – *Hero* Ralph Nader June 2013 [4]

The base of the economic pyramid, we billions, are becoming aware that there is no economic recovery in sight because of population/*resource depletion* (Glossary). (Right here some readers might say there is no such thing as overpopulation, but I must ask you, have you ever raised mice or fish or weeded a garden?) College students get it. There are very few jobs waiting for them. The idea of "success" is morphing and that's good, because "endless growth" is an *unsustainable* ponzi scheme.

We as a civilization are facing an imminent shock and then slow or fast collapse depending on how far one lives from agricultural areas. Those of us, like myself, who live where 90% of food is imported, with a one week supply on hand, are very vulnerable. Lucky for Hawaii, if we change our choices we can grow enough food for ourselves. But how about Phoenix or Toronto or Tokyo or Leningrad or Addis Ababa or Sao Paulo? Because of "overshoot" (See Glossary – *Resource Depletion),* an emergency is upon all of us, really, no matter where we live. Since endless growth is impossible, there is going to be a contraction. The supply lines are going to falter with more children on Earth than ever before.

If you remember nothing else from this book please remember what I just wrote.

The need for service and *compassion* for the next generation has never been more compelling, nor the sacrifice required, more dear. But we must direct this service from our own hearts and homes, and not be followers of those now in control of society. We must not replace one world government with another one world government. So when the state offers help in organizing community groups in your area, be suspicious. They are already feeding almost all children breakfast and lunch every day in elementary school. The state is feeding the kids, not the parents.

We are being conditioned. The best help is for the govenment not to interfere with community organization so that we neighbors can come together as responsible individuals and parents, without Big Brother's *doublespeak* kindness. There is a need to serve each other, not a need to be served a ration or to be served some "community restoration" under a global hierarchy, which is what the UN is all about these days.

We are reminded constantly of the fact of imminent collapse in movies. (This is called *predictive programming* – Glossary). Few of these messages lead us to prepare. The obstacle to preparing is that our entire value system must adapt and this isn't easy when we are busy applying lipstick. The only people who really understand what we are facing are the "preppers" and they are misrepresented on network TV as extremists, when they actually have common sense. We all know a collapse is becoming ever more probable, but we live in denial. We need to change that denial today.

If so-called *"progress"* is not sustainable, then it isn't progress is it?

* * *

A new corrupt set of values is now within us and is blinding us to reality. We think we are superior and modern but we are heading for a cliff. For real.

We are each now hosts for a culture that is parasitic upon the Earth and upon our own selves. This is the interesting point. All my life I have heard environmentalists who deny spirit, and I've also heard spiritual people who are ecologically illiterate.

Please, everyone, we need to eat *and also*, "man does not live on bread alone."

Our culture needs to be grounded with reality which is ecology, *and also* grounded in faith which is our spiritual paths.

So now the reader knows, when I say we need to wake up, I am suggesting we need to wake up to *both* ecology and spirit. Not one or the other. Both.

Today our lifestyle and even our government budgets are borrowing from our children's future. This is resource and tax cannibalism. We have become disconnected. Our preoccupation with our own selfish "pursuit of happiness" has become dangerous.

We used to touch and know the Earth. This connected our hearts. We knew our families. We knew our traditions. We knew our water sources and our plants. We knew what worked and what did not. We were wise.

Our true spiritual natures have a parasitic infection. Until we clean up ourselves, we are all marching toward suicide. Until we regain our connection and our wisdom, we are walking a road of destructive ignorance. Only an idiot eats himself to death. Only a monster steals his child's next meal.

* * *

I feel that eliminating confusion leads towards clarity. This is a constructive approach. Utopia is a day dream. It's better to clean ourselves of beliefs than hold onto unrealistic beliefs like "world peace" or "progress." I'm sorry if that hurts some readers' feelings, but reality had never included utopia. So rather than wish, I think it is better to do. It's better to just keep cleaning our minds and establishing our gardens.

The goal of a lot of inventions is the idea that they will fix things. They won't. A new carburetor won't fix the desire for a joy ride. Hydrogen cars won't fix the problem that people think happiness is somewhere else.

It is difficult to imagine that less is more, but the truth is that we don't need some new invention, we need to change why we think we are here.

When purification replaces "more and faster" as a life ethic, things that seemed impossible will happen. If we can keep the boat lightweight it will float and we will live to see the sun rise over the sea.

Purification might be a new concept for some. If we are cleaner today than yesterday, will be more able to deal with whatever life presents? Yes.

And what is NOT helping us? What is not helping is ignoring the problems because we are too busy putting on lipstick and caught up in our "look" or consuming data in front of a monitor or hand held device. Cheaper sensual or intellectual entertainment is not going to help. Faster broadband is not going to help. You can't eat the next generation of toys. I feel hand held phones and devices are now the new opiate of the masses.

Unfortunately, we often can't imagine that what captivates us is exactly what is preventing us from finding "solutions."

In 1992 President Bush Sr., declared "The American lifestyle is non-negotiable." In February 2006 his son, Bush Jr. said, "America is addicted to oil," without any hint of changing the addiction. His statement was misleading. We are not addicted to oil but to stuff and speed. A new fuel won't correct our addiction to more speed and more stuff. Seeking alternatives to fossil fuels won't help the addict. A new fix is not the answer.

If the American lifestyle of over-consumption is non-negotiable, the rest of the world can just stay poor, right Mr. Bush? And guns will be used to enforce this, correct?

Lipstick and war crimes.

The people who wrote those Bush speeches come from the same think tanks that dictated FDR's speeches in the 30s and what comes out of Barack Hussein Obama's mouth now. (I call him "Logo" Obama. His true father and CIA past and is introduced in Vol. 1.) The obsession with more stuff and more speed goes way beyond this administration or that.

* * *

Our preferences and obsessions were sold to us and today are being sold faster and more blatantly then ever before. This affects what we think we need to consume, how we think we need to behave, and yep, how we think we need to think.

The corrupt values of corporate *Globalists* are now inserted into Hollywood themes and children's DVD's all over the planet. The destruction of old cultures seems to be America's new culture.

One subliminal message in this poster is the "smart city" in background. Where are the farmers? There are none. Where is the feminine? Gone.

The Peace Corp, for example, has the "altruistic goal" of teaching the rest of the world about "America." The goal is assimilation and *monoculture.* The Peace Corp is at war with all other cultures by inserting American values everywhere it goes.

So let's introduce the use of the expression *doublespeak* here, which I cover in the Glossary. The Peace Corp really means the Cultural War Corp.

When a President of the United States says Americans won't change our addiction, or that the American lifestyle of over consumption is non-negotiable, this is threatening to other nations, because *Los Estados Unidos* uses more resources per capita than most other countries *and* has over 1000 *military* bases worldwide. *Consumerism* has the largest and most advanced *military* regime behind it. The *military* (See Glossary) exists to "protect American interests." That means American thievery. So when Bush Sr. told a Rio Summit audience that America wouldn't tighten its belt, everyone understood that the imperial heel of American might was here to stay. And of course, all were too terrified to boo.

* * *

Consumerism is never really challenged within our culture because *consumerism* is the milk from which the rich banksters skim the cream to make the butter of their concentrated wealth and power. And since the elite control the conversation, the truth about this is never revealed. Yes, there really is a financial elite who concentrate wealth and power.

Eighty-five people alive today, who we can be sure know each other, control as much wealth as half the human race, 3.5 billion people.

> "*The Oxfam report* found that over the past few decades, the rich have successfully wielded *political influence* to skew policies in their favor on issues ranging from financial deregulation, tax havens, anti-competitive business practices to lower tax rates on high incomes and cuts in public services for the majority. Since the late 1970s, tax rates for the richest have fallen in 29 out of 30 countries for which data are available, said the report.
>
> "This 'capture of opportunities' by the rich at the expense of the poor and middle classes has led to a situation where 70% of the world's population live in countries where inequality has increased since the 1980s and 1% of families own 46% of global wealth."
>
> – Graeme Wearden, *Guardian*, January 20, 2014

Without our addiction to "more stuff," the rich could not feed off of us or lead us. We would be non-participants. If every community worked for self-sufficiency the elite wouldn't matter. The top of the pyramid would have no base.

But at this point, the financial elite are in control and are pushing for more control as fast as possible. Most disconcerting is that they are attempting to convert all children to the mind programming that they have prescribed. The bait that they lure us with is more stuff and more speed, which we could call *consumerism.* Once we bite at the bait and get hooked, the mind programming is in us.

The mind programming is that the more we eat, the more we are. Not so. We need to consume very little to be magnificent beings.

We have become like asses with a carrot dangling in front of our faces, and that carrot is the promise of more more more.

We have been paid off with goodies so we think this is going to work. But it won't keep working. And the elite know this, so they are now leading us for something more than their own monetary gain. They want something else. They are using their influence for something else.

Who is leading us? Who are they?

> *"South Africa is in the hands of international capital."*
>
> – George Soros, *Davos Economic Forum,* 2001

For now, when I say "they," I am referring to the richest people in the Western world who exercise the most power. "They" are internationally established and have no loyalty to any nation or religion or ethnicity. They are only loyal to their "grand chess game" of monopoly, which means seeking ever more power *over* others. And "they" have been organized for centuries, as you will see.

Many of the controlling cabal are not on that list of 85 people. They are hidden and control more than wealth. They control most of the *military* of the world and can make decisions that, say, the Joint Chiefs of Staff at the Pentagon are not aware of. They are a hidden shadow force and we know they exist because whistleblowers have revealed them, and the Media doesn't cover the whistleblowers because it is "too controversial." This means that whoever is controlling the Media has a vested interest in stopping the whistleblower leaks. This means the whistleblowers were telling the truth.

The Globalist Illuminati are an association. They own the 85 richest people because they are more dangerous. They are the top gangsters, complete with hit men and safe houses.

Their base of operations seems to be the financial "City of London," Wall Street, and Basel, Switzerland (which coordinates the worlds's central banks under one leadership). Some say these people are descendents of ruling classes that go back thousands of years, but I won't trace them that far here. Two and a half centuries is enough for these books. I will prove "they" are organized, and are dedicated to politics, policy, war and *social engineering*. But remember what I said, that "they," as an outside force, are not as important as the reader reading this.

* * *

> *The ruling class has the schools and press under its thumb. This enables it to sway the emotions of the masses.*
>
> – Albert Einstein

How many readers feel that Albert Einstein was a "conspiracy theorist?"

> "In 1954, a special Congressional Committee investigated the *interlocking web* of tax-exempt foundations to see what impact their grants were having on the American psyche. The Committee stumbled onto the fact that some of these groups had embarked upon a gigantic project to rewrite American history and incorporate it into new school text books.
>
> "Norman Dodd, the committee's research director, found, in the archives of the Carnegie Endowment for International Peace [benign name, right?], the following remarkable statement of purpose:
>
> > "The only way to maintain control of the population was to obtain control of education in the U.S. They realized this was a prodigious task so they approached the Rockefeller Foundation with the suggestion that they go in tandem and that portion of education which could be considered as domestically oriented be

taken over by the Rockefeller Foundation, and that portion which was oriented to International matters be taken over by the Carnegie Endowment.

"The Rockefeller Foundation agreed to take on the domestic portion of the task. The purpose of all this interest in history, was of course to rewrite it. Dodd explained:

"They decided that the success of this program lay in the manner in which American history was to be presented. They then approached four of the then most-prominent historians—such as Mary and Charles Beard—with the suggestion that they alter the manner in which they were accustomed to presenting the subject. They [were] turned down flat, so ... they decided they [had] to build a coterie of historians of their own selection.

"The Guggenheim Foundation agreed to award fellowships to historians recommended by the Carnegie Endowment. Gradually, through the 1920s, they assembled a group of twenty promising young academics, and *took them to London*. [The *Rothschild* bankster family's British outpost, as we will soon see. The non-fiction thriller begins.] There they briefed them on what was expected of them when they became professors of American history. That twenty were the nucleus of what was eventually to become the American Historical Association.

"In 1928, the American Historical Association was granted $400,000 by the Carnegie Endowment to write a seven volume study on the direction the nation was to take. The thrust of these books, according to Dodd was that "the future of this country belongs to collectivism and humanism." [These are *doublespeak* words for giving up one's unique community ties to become a faceless cog directed by Big Brother.]

"Dodd concluded from his study that these tax-exempt foundations—by virtue of the fact that they pay for these studies—lay at the heart *of a group* determined to destroy the United States. [Convert the U.S. into a member of the New World Order.]

These educational changes were applied very gradually, so as not to alarm the general American populace, but they have been documented." [5]

Well, Albert was not a conspiracy theorist. He knew what he was talking about, but people like you and I don't know about this, because the schools controlled by the "ruling class" that he mentions, never told us about all the elements of the conspiracy. (Globalization you didn't get in school.) The fact that what Norman Dodd discovered was never told to us in Media or in schools, lets us know the stories were true. So please open your mind, because most of the evidence I will present, you have never heard before.

I will use many examples, but because pop music culture is affecting hundreds of millions of young people, and this is being broadcast from presidential ceremonies to Super Bowl half times, and appears to be the cutting edge of Globalist culture-scaping, I will cover the music industry example of "lipstick" in some detail. But let's continue with opening up our ethical situation.

* * *

The *Globalists* don't want to only control elections and laws. They also want to dictate attitudes and values about our sense of identity. Just as education was taken over, so has every other venue of public discourse including the entertainment industries. This insures that public sentiment/standards won't get in their way. Whether it be corporate goals like convincing women to smoke cigarettes "because it is fashionable," or political/resource goals like smearing some Middle Eastern leader as a "dictator" and then murdering him, *our sense of identity and ethics* is being manipulated. We are being steered.

> In 1928 George Hill, president of the American Tobacco Company, hired Edward Bernays to expand the sales of his Lucky Strike cigarettes. Recognizing that women were still riding high on the suffrage movement, Bernays used this as the basis for his new campaign. He *co-opted* it. Feminism was *co-opted.* He consulted Dr. A.A. Brill, a psychoanalyst, to find the psychological basis for women smoking. Dr. Brill determined that cigarettes, which were usually equated with men, represented equality if women could smoke also, so a "torches of freedom" Media event was organized where hired girls smoked in a parade on camera. The "emerging market" of women smokers was opened up. It is estimated 100 million people died from tobacco related diseases in the 20th century.

* * *

Since "they" are secretive manipulators and thieves, one of the values they need to have vanish is virtue itself.

They don't want people to make a fuss about their crimes. And, as I will show, they are succeeding in destroying virtue as an ideal in young people, which will hurt many young people for life. In the short run, by keeping us jaded, they are free to do whatever they want. In the long run, there is less resistance to our civil liberties simply disappearing.

The fact is that what was legally or ethically outrageous just five years ago is now acceptable.

Am I exaggerating? Listen to this short speech at Harvard Law School. Link video. [6]

It is not enough now to be "in the know" and be cynical. It is time to shout that an illegal government as described at Harvard is not acceptable. The parasitic Illuminati are afraid of moral courage because they don't have any. Your commitment to a new ethic will turn the tide. So we'll see what you do when you finish this series and realize your mind is blown, as mine was.

Using crisis

> *The world can therefore seize the opportunity [the culmination of Operation Desert Storm] to fulfill the long-held promise of a New World Order where diverse nations are drawn together in common cause to achieve the universal aspirations of mankind.*
>
> – George Herbert Walker Bush, March 6, 1991

President George Bush Sr. helped plan the "opportunity" of Operation Desert Storm, 1990-1991, where 400,000 Iraqis were killed or wounded in 100 hours, one of the worst war crimes in history. Here is a little background, so we can understand where Bush was coming from with *his handlers'* grand aspirations.

1953: Iran's democratically elected Prime Minster Mosaddeq is overthrown in CIA Operation Ajax. The U.S. helps place the Shah who rules with iron fist for 26 years and returns generous oil contracts to the UK and others.

1979: Ayatollah Khomeini returns to Iran after being protected overseas for 15 years to foment Muslim anger for coming planned wars with Muslim nations. He was transported to Iran from France with a plane full of European journalists, so it couldn't be shot down. He was placed.

1980-1988: War between Iran and Iraq with both sides using U.S. *military* weapons. The U.S. gives Iraq strategic intelligence, knowing Iraq would use it for chemical weapon attacks that would kill thousands, a war crime. [7]

The mustard gas factories in Iraq were funded through Chilean intermediary corporations that were funded by Chase Manhattan Bank. "DEA informant John Pastis said Chalmers assured him that the US government had approved the deals. In 1988 Chalmers floated plans to construct a $3 billion PC-2 mustard gas complex in Iraq, later built by Bechtel." [8]

In this period 1978-1992, the U.S. creates Mujahideen to fight against Russians in Afghanistan and places CIA operative Osama bin Laden.

1990: The U.S. sets up Iraq to invade Kuwait to initiate Operation Desert Storm, covered in last chapters of this series.

Was Operation Desert Storm some new "opportunity" or a move in a long running chess game?

Please let me de-construct Bush's criminal *doublespeak* statement ...

"The world can therefore seize the opportunity ..."

Who is the world? There is no such thing. So he means the *Globalists.* And here we see a common theme in Globalist thinking, that a tragic catastrophe is an "opportunity."

"to fulfill the long-held promise"

What long held promise? There is no such thing. Again he is talking to insiders in their common plot to control the planet and he is projecting that thinking into the masses to *socially engineer* our expectations and values. He is referring to the plotting of ancient occult societies.

"of a New World Order"

The Globalist banksters started this wording as evidenced by this scan of a book below, which identifies the League of Nations as the New World Order. The League of Nations, precursor to the UN, was created by the Rothschilds, the most influential banking family for three hundred years.

> The New World Order, by Frederick Charles Hicks. (Garden City & New York: Doubleday, Page & Co., 1920, pp. viii, 496.)
>
> This work is in reality a treatise on the new international law of today as it has been affected by the League of Nations and the recent treaties. Most of those who have studied international law up to the present time have felt that numerous changes have taken place during

We also see the term "New World Order" in the writing of Alice Bailey (1880-1949) [9] who developed the Lucis Trust (David Rockefeller and War Criminal Henry Kissinger were on the Board of Directors) that today has great influence at the United Nations. Lucis Trust was a permutation of Lucis Publishing, formally known as Lucifer Publishing, founded by Bailey and her Free Masonry husband in 1922. The Freemasons are major characters in this book.

From watered down Wikipedia ... "The objectives of the Lucis Trust as stated in its charter are: 'To encourage the study of comparative religion, philosophy, science and art; to encourage every line ["full spectrum dominance"] of thought tending to the broadening [homogenizing] of human sympathies and interests, and the expansion [*monopolization*] of ethical religious and educational literature; to assist or to engage in activities for the relief of suffering and for human betterment [as defined by the puppet masters]; and, in general, to further worthy efforts for humanitarian and educational ends. [*Social engineering*]'

"The Lucis Trust's publishing company was founded in the early 1920s as the Lucifer Publishing Company. The Lucis Trust says that the name was probably chosen *to honor Lucifer.* The name was changed in 1925 to the **Lucis Publishing Company.** In Latin *lucem ferre* means "to bear light" and *lucis* means *of light.* [The *evil co-opt* of light that claims to be THE light, Vol. 4] The company has headquarters in New York City, London, and Geneva. [The three centers of Illuminati ... Wall Street, the financial "City of London" within London, and Switzerland, where the The International Bank of Settlements in Basel presides, as mentioned, ruling over all the world's central banks.]

"The Trust is established in Great Britain under the title 'Lucis Trust Ltd.,' in Switzerland as 'Lucis Trust Association,' and in the Netherlands as the 'Lucis Trust Stichting.'

"As part of the "World Goodwill at the UN" project, they are developing a process of defining new Sustainable Development Goals for humanity [as a *monoculture*] after 2015 when the Millennium Development Goals expire." [Luciferian satanists are planning your slave New World Order future.] – Wikipedia

> "In the preparatory period for the **new world order there** will be a steady and regulated disarmament. It will not be optional. [It will be forced at gunpoint by the 'humanitarian *Globalists*,' who will monopolize 'security.'] No nation will be permitted to produce and organize any equipment for destructive purposes or to infringe the security of any other nation." [Nations will exist only in name, under the gun of the *Globalists*.]
>
> – Alice Bailey

Now that we have traced the bankster and satanic origins of The New World Order, we return back to the 1991 Bush Sr. speech, as he gloated over the slaughter in Operation Desert Storm …

"where diverse nations are drawn together in common cause to achieve the universal aspirations of mankind."

Diverse nations have no common aspiration! The people in the rice paddies don't know anything about the people harvesting corn or potatoes somewhere else. So here Globalist Bush is claiming to speak for the hearts of billions of people. This isn't just pompous. This is predatory. Let's now remove the *doublespeak* and hear what Bush actually said …

> *We Globalists can therefore seize the opportunity to fulfill our long-held goal of our World Order where we will bring together the worlds nations and end their sovereignty, including the U.S., so there will be just one government in the world, ours.*
>
> *And we will use the ideal of ending war to seduce the populace, while buying off the leaders who will convince their people to wear chains for peace.*
>
> *To allegedly end war, we will wage continual war and have the largest military in the world.*
>
> *To have the support and complicity of the American public we will trick people with patriotism, lie in the Media about evil regimes and claim we are defending democracy, while installing puppets, and looting resources.*
>
> *To keep everyone dumbed down we will provide a fat standard of living and the more obesity, the better.*
>
> *To keep young people immobilized, we will provide drugs and sexuality to make them incoherent and unable to have a political stance.*
>
> *With more single moms, the population will gradually become more fragmented and loyalty to family will incrementally become loyalty to Big Brother, who will provide the essentials for life.*
>
> *Therefore, listen up, humanity with universal aspirations! The American lifestyle is non-negotiable!*

* * *

"The Final Act of the Uruguay Round, marking the conclusion of the most ambitious trade negotiation of our century, will give birth - in Morocco - to the World Trade Organization, the third pillar of the **New World Order,** along with the United Nations and the International Monetary Fund."

– from full-page advertisement by Morocco [puppet] government
in *The New York Times* April 1994

Thus, the Bush Sr. statement about New World Order was not poetry. The *Roth-efellers* (Glossary) created UN, IMF, WTO and much much more. We therefore see that the President of the United States is just a puppet, a *cutout* (Glossary) who reads a script to seed our minds.

The Intelligent Student's Guide to the New World Order

www.conspiracyarchive.com/NWO/Intelligent_Students_NWO.htm – By Erica Carle

What is the New World Order?

The essence of the New World Order (NWO) or world management system is that it is management by social engineers, rather than government based on a written constitution. How you are affected by this management system depends on what the social engineers decide the system should do for you and require of you. The social engineers and system managers think of themselves as scientists applying the scientific method to the control of group behavior. Your behavior and your relationships are regarded as the subject of investigation and control by those who call themselves social scientists. You are among their test animals, and you have no say in, and often no knowledge of, experiments that involve you. If the NWO is totally implemented, your independence, individuality, and freedom will be gone.

There is nothing new about the idea of managing others, or even of controlling the whole world. That has been the goal of social philosophers for thousands of years. However, we need not go back over ancient history. We are concerned primarily with what has been going on in our own generations. This we can understand quite well if we confine ourselves to the Nineteenth and Twentieth Centuries.

Goals of the New World Order

To begin to understand the New World Order (NWO) you need to forget what you have been told about philosophical differences between Republicans and Democrats; left and right; Socialists and Libertarians; business and labor; liberal and conservative; black and white, etc.. The planners of the New World Order know they must use, influence, and cater to all of these groups to accomplish the goals they are seeking, which are:

1. Consolidate everything.
2. Commercialize everything.
3. Classify everything.
4. Claim everything.
5. Control everything.

From EDUCATION 2000, A Holistic Perspective, II. Plan for Implementation

"What does *transforming* education look like? [Emphasis mine, remember word transform!] Where are the people who can mobilize change? [de-stabilization/consolidation] What constituencies should participate in this process? We believe that to generate the momentum necessary to take teaching and learning to its *next stage* will require a vast network of participating *transformers.* These individuals and organizations represent a *broad spectrum* of society. They include young people, local communities, families, teachers, teacher educators and academics, educational associations, United Nations organizations, business, government & local/national education leaders, model holistic schools, citizen groups for social change, media." [10]

Boxed screen shot below from same url as above. www.ties-edu.org/GATE/Education2000.html

United Nations Organizations

We believe that the United Nations and its allied organizations advocate an educational vision and a mission commensurate with our own. GATE seeks to work in partnership with groups in the sphere of the United Nations, including NGOs (non-govermental organizations). Our intent is to create reciprocal working relationships.

Example #1. Several members of the GATE Steering Committee serve on the Seed Advisory Committee for the Global Education Program for Peace and Universal Responsibility at the United Nations' University for Peace in Costa Rica. The project's mission is: *To design and implement a global education program which can foster a consciousness of universal responsibility within each member of the human family, in order to assure a more peaceful and sustainable world for future generations.*

Example #2. GATE has been networking with various branches of UNESCO to develop a series of World Conferences on Education. The purpose of these conferences would be to: explore today's critical issues in education, investigate innovative techniques and models, and create a global reform movement with a ten year action plan. The conferences would model the non-hierarchical process of new leadership and would be organized according to the following tracks:

1. Critical issues in education
2. Global citizenship and ecological education
3. Education for all
4. Innovative strategies and techniques
5. Spiritual education
6. Peace and education
7. The media and education

The beautiful cool sounding language above is a great example of total *doublespeak.* What is being described is Full Spectrum Dominance, in which "education," meaning indoctrination, will even include "spiritual education." "Universal Responsibility" means no one has any personal responsibility or territory or sovereignty or stewardship. "Peace" was just described in the Alice Bailey quote. The "human family" means no diversity. "Consciousness" means everyone under the same mind control. A "sustainable world" (without local stewardship) means everyone gets factory rations. "Sustainable world" does not mean a sustainable ecosphere or unpolluted ground water or unpolluted skies. Think of the geo-engineering jet trails (Pages 92, 97-98, 143 261). Use of the word "non-hierarchical" is just insincere *co-opt* of criticism of the hierarchal pyramid of power.

Only a hierarchal pyramid of power can enforce the goals of Education 2000 and the New World Order. The "vast" number of organizations that have bought into this *doublespeak* is daunting. That is why I wrote this book for you. *Globalization* you didn't get in school.

* * *

The *Globalists* can't move ahead in the game of monopoly if there are no players. If nations were friendly and living at peace and the citizens were just going along living their ancient lifestyles, the parasites would be completely blocked from any influence. A virus can't do much with a strong immune system. So the society must be injured to create an opening.

Destabilization/consolidation is how to get the players moving. To do this, crisis is injected. As you will see later in book, the U.S. terrorized, lied to, and then dumped 1.1 million North Vietnamese into South Vietnam's ancient agrarian society in 1954. These abducted people were dropped off without provisions or supplies and had to become bandits to survive. Thus, ancient stable Vietnam was introduced to the process of destabilization/consolidation. Now the *Globalists* would have players who need "help."

Destabilization/consolidation isn't just used in foreign policy, but in everything the *Globalists* touch, including your mortgage, your debts, your job, your children, what is on your TV, what is in your newspapers, and what is on your computer screen. Peace and harmony doesn't sell. Fidelity doesn't make a soap opera interesting. Crisis is their opportunity and spreading dysfunction is their joy ride.

Virtually every war in the last two hundred years was a Globalist power play. The bankster *Globalists* ran the drugs out of India and Burma (and now out of Afghanistan), and paid the African slavers for centuries. Even as I write this, the enormity of these centuries of horror stabs my heart. For traditional people around the world, the past five hundred years has been hell on Earth.

But before I blame this monster or that, I have to remember that *the culture* has supported domination, at least since Genesis was written. Let's blame the willingness to be part of a *dominant culture* for what really happened and is still happening. (Kudos to writers of the recent film *Noah* (2014), for putting the words of the *dominant culture* in the mouth of the bad guy, the enemy of Noah.)

* * *

The *Globalists* use crisis to reshuffle the deck of society's cards *their* way. Naomi Klein's book *Shock Doctrine* is worth understanding. When the banksters cause booms or depressions or housing bubbles or recessions by increasing and then decreasing money supply, the crisis brings an opportunity for buying property and factories cheap and using a desperate work force. That's good business for those who planned the crisis. Also, "selling short" on the stock market allows insiders to profit from a downside turn. This is how J. P. Morgan made even more fortunes in 1929. Here is proof that the Great Depression was orchestrated.

> "On Tuesday, October 29, 1929, the short sellers would begin shorting the market. [Betting the price of stocks would go down.] Calls would go out from JP Morgan & Company. The messages contained only one word. "Sell." As the roller coaster ride began that day, American financier Bernard Baruch brought an illustrious visitor with him to the New York Stock Exchange. Baruch's guest, England's former Chancellor of the Exchequer, Winston Churchill, was brought to the center of American commerce at 11 Wall Street for a reason.

> "... Most conspiracy chroniclers were convinced that Churchill, who did not hold public office again for a decade, was singled out by the money barons to witness the power possessed by the international bankers who could, at will, collapse the monetary systems of any, or all, of the nation states of the world, bring about a major recession, or inflate or deflate any nation's currency—or worse, pit one nation against another in war.
>
> "... And, it appears they wanted a witness. Churchill was to be that witness ..."
>
> – by Jon Christian Ryter, August 2, 2011 [11]

There is other evidence that Churchill was an insider already, and was placed using his trumped up fake heroism in the South African Boer Wars. Churchill knew he was no *hero*. He was a placed *cutout* and a liar. Therefore, in my opinion, Churchill was brought to the New York Stock Exchange to witness the market crash that would devastate the world, not to witness it with surprise, but to witness the crash as part of his apprenticeship. Four million men in the U.S. were homeless during the Great Depression that followed. The depression set the U.S. up for socialist programs by FDR whose grandfather was a drug runner for the *Rothschild* banksters. I'm not making this up. All these "leaders" were placed.

Most economists are taught that the "70 year business cycle" is caused by market forces, as if bankster manipulation doesn't exist. The banksters are the ones funding university education to control curriculum as shown above, thus economists are not taught about the financial pyramid that controls us, and most would deny, with snobbish academic certainty, that a financial conspiracy could possibly exist. I just proved that the stock market crash of 1929 was orchestrated. Snobbishness aside, this non-fiction thriller has no legs unless the reader opens her or his mind.

* * *

Catastrophe can be due to financial crisis, war, medical, geological, or weather causes. There are weapons to create many kinds of crisis and they have been used for decades, but this is a big secret. Most readers have not heard of tectonic (earthquake) weapons or gene specific viruses that are created to attack certain ethnic groups. Most people have never heard of the tens of thousands of studies by the *military* to determine the ways electro-magnetic and radio and microwave frequencies can be used to create diseases, or affect hormone levels, or almost anything. It is difficult for most people to imagine that the U.S. has a way to create tsunamis.

Let me start with tectonic weaponry. Like climate engineering, Earthquake (tectonic) weaponry is a science, at least 50 years old. This science was discussed by Senator Claremont Pell in Congress in 1976. [12] It is possible to bounce low frequency electro-magnetic waves through the atmosphere with a system called HAARP and focus them below the ground at a specified place, and over many hours or days, an earthquake can be triggered. Ionized atmosphere from geo-engineering jet trails which were mentioned with an image in the Introduction, helps this weaponry. Many of the devastating earthquakes in the past 50 years were man made, particularly in Jungua (Mandarin for China), but more recently in Chile, Haiti and New Zealand. [13] The December 2004 tsunami in Indonesia/Thailand was also man made, with Collin Powell and Jeb Bush doing reconnaissance work. Fukushima was another New World Order manmade tsunami, but is too detailed for me to address here. See evidence here. [14]

Hurricane Katrina in 2005, was geo-engineered, as was the Cyclone Nargis of Myanmar in 2008, and much more. The recent floods in Pakistan and the Midwest were not natural. [15]With a bit of study you will be on board. Study "HAARP" online. Another recent intentional crisis was the 2010 Gulf Oil Spill, which is easily seen by the intense *military*/media coverup and bathtub death of *Hero* Whistleblower Mathew Simmons who was about to testify in court. [16].

(When doing historical or scientific research on the internet, I suggest ignoring Wikipedia or anything that does not ask hard questions. I use Wikipedia references in this book to show the mainstream Wikipedia *"his-story"* (Glossary) which is watered down, but sometimes damning enough. Usually the top five links on a search are the official story, not the whistleblower story. Always find the whistleblower story in a web search by adding words like exposed, revealed, questioned, danger, conspiracy. As an exercise, do a search for "Vaccine health," and then compare with a search for "Vaccine dangers." Or do a search for "Oklahoma bombing," and then do a search for "Oklahoma bombing conspiracy." Then weed through those for the ones that give references. Official sounding academies are sources of funded data. Find out who is on the Board of Directors and this will become clear. If you see Goldman Sachs or Rockefeller, run!)

On a less dangerous level, shock doctrine or crisis creation is used routinely when products are intentionally designed so they will wear out and need to be replaced to fit a projected future revenue stream. A car that drove for 500,000 miles would destroy the "market" for more cars. This isn't shock doctrine, but is similar. Planned obsolescence is a pre-conceived business strategy of insuring future market demand, and so is shock doctrine which insures need for re-build. Halliburton and KBR made billions rebuilding Iraq as one example. In Iraq, money was made selling the arms, then rebuilding, and of course obtaining the contracts for the oil, which controls price.

Destabilization/consolidation programs such as planned obsolescence include seeding the population with live virus to make sure the "flu season" arrives, even in tropical Hawaii, [17], so the pharmaceutical companies can have a predictable market and revenue stream. For this reason, too, your American Medical Association doctor is never trained in prevention or nutrition and can only prescribe Big Pharma drugs.

> "As mentioned previously, the Rockefeller and Carnegie foundations traditionally worked together almost as one in the furtherance of their mutual goals, and this certainly was no exception. The Flexner brothers represented the lens that brought both the Rockefeller and the Carnegie fortunes into sharp focus on the unsuspecting and thoroughly vulnerable medical profession."
>
> – *He Who Pays The Piper—Creation of the Modern Medical Establishment;*
> G. Edward Griffin

> "The American Medical Association was founded in 1847 and incorporated in 1897. In the early 1900s, the AMA realized that there needed to be some changes in medical education. Medical practice and education in some areas left a lot to be desired (poor training and understaffed medical schools). It created the Council on Medical Education, with the purpose of evaluating countrywide medical training and making [centralized] improvements where needed. However, they didn't have enough money to do this. Enter Rockefeller and Carnegie and their funding and [self-funded] popularity.

> The president of the Carnegie Foundation, Henry Pritchett, met with the AMA and offered to take over the entire Council on Medical Education project.
>
> "Here was the classical "philanthropic formula" at work again. Have others pay a major portion of the bill (the AMA had already done most of the work. The total Carnegie investment was only $10,000.), reap a large bonus from public opinion (isn't it wonderful that these men are taking an interest in upgrading medical education!), and gain an opportunity to control a large and vital sphere of American life." – G. Edward Griffin
>
> "—In the 1800s, the American Medical Association (AMA) resented their competitors who drove down the cost of medical care and drew away customers;
>
> "—The AMA called upon the strong arm of government force to vanquish the competition, it did so through regulating medical schools;
>
> "—A report was commissioned calling for the standardization [*monopolization*] of medical education; this was the Flexner Commission;
>
> "—The report of the Commission concluded that there were too many doctors and medical schools in America and recommended reducing the number of schools. The public outcry generated by [in favor of] the [well publicized] report convinced Congress to declare the AMA the only body with the right to grant medical school licenses in the United States." [18]

Pharmaceutical companies don't exist to keep the population healthy. They exist to live off the population, and by controlling medical schools (so that your doctor never studied prevention or nutrition), Big Pharma insures its monopoly. Dear reader, if you want to avoid flus then eat chemical free food, get exercise, spend time outdoors, develop a strong immune system and avoid vaccinations and those who take them. The live virus in the vaccines is contagious. When vaccination week for school children occurs, kids who didn't get the vaccination, as well as those that do, suddenly get sick. It is a business model for profit, having nothing to do with health. Health is based on strong legs, not crutches, and strong immune systems, not pills or needles.

* * *

If the reader applies this way of analyzing how failure or crisis is used to bring about new opportunities, to everything in modern life, then you can start to understand how *Globalists* plan for the future. They plan failure and destruction and crisis and disease in advance.

> I need to go a bit deeper here, to how we each process decisions. It is difficult to imagine that there are people without ethics or conscience. However, this is a harsh inaccurate judgement. Every reader here, and I also, have secrets that we will never tell anyone ever. You have secrets that you deny to yourself … things that are so private that you (and I) intentionally forget them …mistakes we would rather not remember.
>
> Mind control, which I can't cover deeply (see Vol. 1), involves creating a place of denial, or even multiple personalities, where secrets or even behavior can be stored. Soldiers are mind controlled to deny their own humanity. The music industry artists, who we will meet in the coming chapters, have been mind controlled to deny the impact of their

stage presence. When we do something behind someone's back, we deny we did it, so each of us knows what denial is—don't deny it!

Involvement in crimes, like the Nazi experience which involved millions of Germans, (my entire extended family in Europe died under the Nazis), or the Israeli crimes against humanity with Palestinians, or the Iraq Holocaust which has not ended and has involved millions of American soldiers, requires putting large arenas of activity into that inner place of denial/secrecy. Crime requires lying.

The *Globalists* know they are involved in crimes against humanity, but this is put into a place of denial (lies) so that it is disappeared (verb). "You saw nothing, you were never here." This makes the *Globalists* disconnected from reality or truth.

They develop a criminal mind that step by step is devoted to the big secret, which gets bigger and deeper as they work themselves up the ladder of power. To go up the ladder they have to prove they can be trusted with heinous secrets. They have to be willing to compromise themselves. They have to "make bones" as in the movie *The Godfather*. "Making bones" literally includes satanic rituals as revealed by FBI Chief Ted Gunderson. (Search Ted Gunderson on YouTube) These rituals are used by secret societies like the Freemasons and Skull and Bones societies, both which are filled with high government officials.

The Vatican tolerates pedophilia because pedophilia is a rung on the ladder to child sacrifice by which they control the dark fear of *transparency* in the hierarchy of their corrupt "church." This may be unbelievable to some, but keep reading. The way the pyramid of power remains extremely secretive is that the top players in business, in government, and even in the Church, have been inducted gradually into sexual perversion, blackmail, and then satanic rituals. Power is not earned—it is dispensed. The most powerful people in our world are owned and live in a prison of heinous secrecy that re-frames their psychology and disconnects them. This plays out as the *vanity* of their lives.

Of course, these people are terrified of exposure, and this makes them absolutely loyal to the conspiracy they are a part of. This is why I will focus on the sexual programming of the music industry in coming chapters. We are all being inducted into lust and perversion and split personalities in order to uphold a pyramid of denial, which upholds the pyramid of abuse. Lipstick and war crimes.

Behind the cosmetic mask is fear of exposure. The dark is threatened by the light of *transparency*. (Hence the name of the non-profit that produced this book, Kauai Transparency Initiative International.) Conspiracy is threatened by the clear *compassion*ate mind and heart which is our birthright, and, so, we are being *socially engineered* to lack virtue and paid off by *consumerism* to forget our spiritual bedrock, our natural clear mind. *Grasping desire* (see Glossary) has replaced serenity and penetrating insight.

Hero Ralph Nader's quote above was taken from a short talk at Harvard Law School, and there he asked the students what level they were, and most were freshman. And in the youtube, he nods his head and explains that the older students get roped into careers working for the very law firms who exist to circumvent the law. The older students had entered the step by step process of denying truth and had lost the moral courage which the younger students still have. They compromised themselves and live in denial and have too much shame to come to listen to a *Hero* like Nader.

> The middle and top Globalist players are different than you and I who have not taken the dangerous road. But the difference is only in degree. No one is perfect, but their imperfection is demonic. For most of us, success is building something beautiful that others can also experience. We share, we don't hoard. But as parasites, these *Globalists* don't build or share, they steal.
>
> This is difficult to comprehend for we who believe in beauty and love. Well, we say we believe this, but our lifestyle is hedonistic, which is hurtful to those on the other end of *consumerism.* But this is hidden from us. If we knew what our products really cost in terms of suffering in other nations, we would pause. Most of us don't harbor intentional cruelty, which I call "evil."
>
> Trickle-down *evil* is alive and well in the U.S. since World War II when the U.S. had impunity to explore raw political power. As we will learn, the Illuminati banksters funded all sides of World War II so that THEY won the war, and America's political power since 1945 is really THEIR political power. This took an entire citizenry down the road of crime, much as the citizens of ancient Rome were inducted into a culture as entitled grotesque slave masters. Remember, America was built on slave labor and the Native American Holocaust. Those who are proud of America need to keep remembering we stole this land and are still crushing the locals who remain. We have learned to deny the shadow of power. The shadow of power is abuse.
>
> I believe the *Globalists* even go further. They deny love. I am using this next word only as a metaphor, not as an actual ego, but it is hard to understand the syndrome of Lucifer, because Lucifer is a shadow, not a light like the love in our hearts. The criminal mind lives as a shadow, and has no source. The criminal mind is the abandonment of source.
>
> It is difficult to put this in words. The resolution will come one day when the top *Globalists* sit face to face with people who have good hearts and the abusers confess before the world, until the abusers finally break down in tears. (I'll return to this in last chapter.)
>
> Until we re-connect these people with their own hearts, we will be spreading toxic souls through the multi-verse.

Returning to our discussion of shock doctrine and planned destruction as a business model for "progress," the *Globalists,* of course, have analyzed their client base. They have analyzed overpopulation and really don't want some random collapse due to over extended supply lines and material breakdowns. *That is just poor planning.*

So as businessmen, they ask, "What would be the best number of people in a perfectly controlled world? What is the plan? Let's use some computer models to come up with our ideal number … hmmm …. How will we arrive at that number? Hmmm, we can eliminate those extra people in famines, or in a big war, or maybe slowly, using different kinds of diseases … hmmm … Maybe a combination of programs would be best. If it's a slow gradual kill, no one will notice, and we won't have to see as much gore, either, which is messy. If we have multiple cancer causing agents, no one will be able to determine the cause. Hmmm. "

Now we are back to danger because these *Globalists* have forgotten what love is and can't imagine a cooperative solution that includes empowering the masses. Quite the contrary …

What I just outlined about population targets is not theory. There is plenty of evidence for the above programs. Just so the reader knows, coming from a Zen background, I really have little tolerance for speculation. What I write here was informed by evidence. I can't cover all the evidence; that is what the internet is for, but the evidence is piling up now every day as more and more *hero* whistleblowers come forward.

> "Dr. Henry Kissinger proposed, in his memorandum dated April 24, 1974, titled 'Implications of world wide population growth for U.S. security & overseas interests), to the National Security Council (NSC) that 'depopulation should be the highest priority of U.S. foreign policy towards the Third World.'
>
> "He quoted [cited] reasons of national security, and that the U.S. economy will require large and increasing amounts of minerals from abroad, [to indulge], especially from less-developed countries ... Wherever a lessening of population can increase the prospects for such stability, population policy becomes relevant to resources, supplies, and to the economic interests of the U.S. [U.S. is puppet spear point of the New World Order.]
>
> "Depopulation policy became the top priority under the NSC agenda, Club of Rome and U.S. policy makers like Gen. Alexander Haig, Cyrus Vance, Ed Muskie and Kissinger. According to a NSC spokesman at the time, the United States shared the view of former World Bank President Robert McNamara [who was given his bankster position in the New World Order for murdering millions of Vietnamese as Secretary of State] that the "population crisis" is a greater threat to U.S. national security interests than nuclear annihilation. In 1975, Henry Kissinger established a policy-planning group in the U.S. State Department's Office of Population Affairs. The depopulation "GLOBAL 2000" document for President Jimmy Carter was prepared.
>
> "It is no surprise that this policy was established under President Carter with help from Kissinger [right photo and front cover] and Brzezinski—*all with ties to David Rockefeller* [emphasis mine]. The Bush family, the Harriman family—the Wall Street business partners of Bush in financing Hitler [to be discussed soon]—and the Rockefeller family are the elite of the American eugenics movement. [... Including the father of Bill Gates. Gates was placed so that Microsoft was Illuminati controlled from the beginning, while Apple Inc. was hijacked later.] Even Prince Philip of Britain, a member of the Bilderberg Group, is in favor of depopulation:

> "'If I were reincarnated I would wish to be returned to earth as a killer virus to lower human population levels' (Prince Philip Duke of Edinburgh, leader of the [phony front] World Wildlife Fund, quoted in 'Are You Ready for Our New Age Future?' Insiders Report, American Policy Center, December 1995).
>
> "Secretary of Defense Donald Rumsfeld has been proposing, funding and building Bio-Weapons Level 3 and Level 4 labs at many places around the U.S., even on university campuses and in densely populated urban locations. In a Bio-Weapons Level 4 facility, a

single bacteria or virus is lethal. Bio-Weapons Level 4 is the highest level legally allowed in the continental U.S.

"For what purpose are these labs being developed, and who will make the decisions on where bio-weapons created in these facilities will be used and on whom? More than 20 world-class microbiologists have been murdered [silenced] since 2002 [this news is widely corroborated], mostly in the U.S. and the UK. Nearly all were working on the development of ethnic-specific bio-weapons (search Smart Dust, Roboflies &) …"

– from article "Kissinger, Eugenics, and Depopulation"
by *Hero* Whistleblower Leuren Moret, November 20, 2004

FEMA ***is amassing a staggering supply of unexplained burial vaults that would hold millions of bodies. Through history, criminal governments plan genocidal depopulation by design. U.S. government labs create race specific bio-weapons, W.H.O. forces vaccines containing mercury and cancer viruses? Fluoride toxic water? Aluminum in chemtrails? Doing the math?***

Coming soon to your neighborhood? FEMA will not explain this. These coffins are not being stock piled for a slow kill, but for something much quicker and more catastrophic. If you are frightened you should be. And it is pre-meditated. Still comfortable?

People with almost unlimited funds do, in fact, plan obsolescence and crisis, so they can replace the old system with their new system, and with each rebuild, a more *technocratic* society can be deployed. (See Glossary *Technocracy*).

A recent example of *technocracy* is the simultaneous *world wide* roll-out of electric utility "smart meters," with the "green" excuse that "smart grid" would save energy. This was a lie. The excuse has allowed cancer causing RF emission devices to be placed on every house, which are more dangerous than cell phones, and repeater stations, similar to small cell towers, in every neighborhood. [19] The "smart meters" are also a surveillance tool. (More on electro-magnetic frequencies in Chapter 6.) This is *technocracy* to the letter. And of course, in the rebuild, billions were made, and whole industries created to tow the Globalist line.

The *Globalists* don't want stability and peace. Not at all. The Freemasons are a secret society, (Page 246-257) that is part of the Illuminati complex, and their motto is "Order Through Chaos." It means *their* order through our chaos. One of the Freemason symbols is the bee hive for a "well ordered" society, ruled by secret meetings! Freemasonry is the opposite of community or democracy. It is based on secrecy and manipulation. It is freedom to control others in secret.

The Illuminati founder Johann Adam Weishaupt (6 Feb 1748 – 18 Nov 1830) was big on the "Hegelian Dialectic," which views change as a linear progression in which opposing forces of thesis and antithesis bring about a synthesis. This has been translated as problem-reaction-solution (See this 4 minute explanatory youtube [20]), in which the planner creates a problem usually with violence, steers the reaction with media, and delivers the pre-planned solution, as a new law or institution or culture. We will cover this more in later chapters.

The *Globalists* want change and upheaval so they can keep turning over the sod of society and place bets and investments with their insider information. As stated, for over two hundred years, war and depression has been created to profit the instigators. From the French Revolution in 1789 [21] to the Ukraine protests in 2014 [22], and ISIS in the Middle East (last chapter), the same program of destabilization/consolidation, replacement, cover up and yellow press (See *controlled media* in Glossary) has been practiced *by the same group.* (I know some readers are thinking "conspiracy theory" right now, but that is your conditioning. Albert is looking over your shoulder and saying, keep reading!)

Their goal is to run the agenda of the whole world step by step by step. This centuries old commitment to power/crime always has new recruits who want to "succeed." Most of the top players are family of trusted insiders, but new recruits by the hundreds of thousands are needed, who will sublimate their ethics, so that the system keeps moving forward based on the payoff. Remember the Harvard law students example above. Here also is recent exposé recording conversations at the FED. [23]

One could say that the *dominant culture* (Glossary) consists of hit men, and now women, who are recruited and paid off by their crime bosses. Crime pays in a materialistic culture. This parasitic culture does not create, it steals from nature and natural people. Because of this embedded will to ripoff, crime is normalized. Nature is not rejuvenated, nature is exhausted and that thievery is what is controlling our values and our impact on all living things.

I call "them" the *Globalists*, but others use words like "The Cabal," or the "New World Order." I also use the word "Illuminati," because the roots are real and satanic values are now being propagated through symbols all around us. The term "bankster" is good, as it combines words "banker plus gangster." These threads are all connected by … debt.

Virtue

In the dominant culture, we are encouraged to be weaklings. The individual is dependent on the industrial gang, and is not sovereign. He or she is not a strong link but an obedient link. We might have muscle or brains, but not sovereign integrity.

As a member of the dominant culture, the reader is probably too ignorant and dependent and physically weak to grow food. As a woman, you are probably too dependent and fearful to lay down in the bush and birth a child on your own. If you are a man, you are probably too weak and uneducated to know how to make anything. All you know is to play with a keyboard or touch pad. You are removed from nature and dependent on modern industrial dominance. We used to each be strong.

To offer an alternative, Gandhi advocated spinning your own cotton, to break the grip of monopolistic industrial dependence.

In the vain culture, pride is a function of approval. Worth comes from social recognition. If we appear worthwhile, we think we are worthwhile. In the dominant culture, there is little personal sovereignty and much elbowing for rank. Dependence and rank is valued and exalted, codified and called worthwhile.

It is conforming to rank, and being proud of rank, that makes gang violence possible. War criminals are actually violent sheeple conforming to their criminal gang/herd. They are not strong people, they are weak sheep. The dominant culture wants us to be weak so we will be silent and tolerate abusiveness.

The opposite of false pride based on approval would be the self-esteem of taking the time to meet one's maker, The Great Mystery, one on one. To do this, a seeker must be very strong and drop pride.

This kind of self-esteem is actually humble, so the man or woman with real self esteem looks for humbleness in his/her own eyes. "Am I humble?," he or she asks. "Am I humble?" "Am I humble?" "Am I humble?"

Morality is maintaining a lack of vain selfish pride. "Treat others as you would like to be treated" becomes our norm, not a proud position in a pecking order. We just can no longer acquiesce to abuse!

With our own commitment to our own sense of purification and humility, we are no longer weak and dependent. What we care about is our own honesty, openness and impeccable lack of false pride. In our own eyes. This can be our inner spiritual commitment. This has been called 'faith.'

We cannot be corrupted anymore by seeking approval.

From there, we can find our strength. From there, virtue springs. Our self-importance has stepped out of the way. The water of virtue can flow …

Chapter 2

All the Man's Kings

"... Monarchs and Ministers of all countries courted his advice and were guided by his suggestions."

The name *Rothschild* comes up for good reason. Being the chief banking swindler family in Europe for centuries, they heard about everything and in mafia manner, eventually controlled their turf ... Europe. And through *their* British Empire, they gained control of most of the world and went to war against other colonial (thievery) nations for even more territory. They used surplus money and gold looted from India to help in other international projects. *Their* East India Company kicked the Dutch East India Company out of South Africa. The Rothschilds created Zionism and control Israel, which henceforth, I will always call "*Rothschild* Israel," to distinguish it from the victim citizens of that so-called country. When I was in Bolivia I saw the name *Rothschild* in a museum. They created and control the U.S. Federal Reserve (FED) and are peas in a pod with the Rockefellers. (Important ... Please see Glossary *Roth-efellers* Page 344)

> "The *Rothschild* dynasty is, without a doubt, the pioneer of international finance. Mayer Amschel Rothschild, the first of the family to open a bank, was honored by *Forbes* magazine as the seventh most influential businessman of all time and the inventor of modern banking."
>
> – *Business Insider* December 23, 2012

Forbes sucks. We will see some *Forbes Magazine* covers that showcase slavery and satanism, later in this book.

Below are just a few highlights from the *Rothschild* history. One version of the full history can be found on line, *History of the House of Rothschild* by Andrew Hitchcock, which I have amended below because I found more, or different, or contrary history. The great bulk of the following chronology is from Hitchcock. It is good to read more than one account. [24] (I said I wouldn't go back over 250 years.)

> "Please do not automatically assume someone you meet with the name *Rothschild* is part of the *Rothschild* criminal network. Furthermore, and most importantly, the majority of Ashkenazi Jews are innocent and not part of this network. Check the facts out for yourself first. This article is designed to inform people who the enemy is [The *Rothschild* New World Order], not single out people of a particular race or people with a particular surname, who may have nothing to do with this *Rothschild* criminal network."
>
> – *Hero* Whistle Blower Andrew Hitchcock

1743: Mayer Amschel Bauer, an Ashkenazi Jew, is born in Frankfurt, Germany, He is son of Moses Amschel Bauer, a money lender and the proprietor of a counting house.

Moses Amschel Bauer places a red sign above the entrance door to his counting house. This sign is a red hexagram (which geometrically and numerically translates into the number 666) which under *Rothschild* instruction will end up on the Israeli flag some two centuries later. [*Rothschilds* created, funded, managed Zionists from day one, so this is easily possible.]

1760: During this decade Mayer Amschel Bauer works for a bank owned by the Oppenheimers' in Hanover, Germany. He is highly successful and becomes a junior partner.

Following his father's death, Bauer returns to Frankfurt to take over his father's business. Bauer recognizes the significance of the red hexagram on his father's door and changes his name from Bauer to *Rothschild* ("Rot," is German for "Red," "Schild," is German for "Sign," pronounced Row-t Shildt in German, not Roth-child).

Now, as Mayer Amschel *Rothschild*, he discovers that General von Estorff is attached to the court of Prince William IX of Hesse-Hanau, one of the richest royal houses in Europe, which gained its wealth by the hiring out of Hessian soldiers to foreign countries for vast profits (a practice that continues today in the form of exporting "peacekeeping" troops throughout the world [and "contractors" in Iraq and other nations. That is … mercenaries]).

He therefore makes the General's re-acquaintance on the pretext of selling him valuable coins and trinkets at discounted prices. As he plans, *Rothschild* is subsequently introduced to Prince William himself, who is more than pleased with discounted prices he charges for his rare coins and trinkets, and *Rothschild* offers him a bonus for any other business the Prince can direct his way.

Rothschild subsequently becomes a close associate with Prince William, and ends up doing business with him and members of the court. *He soon discovers that loaning money to governments and royalty is more profitable than loaning to individuals, as the loans are bigger and are secured by the nation's taxes.* [Loans secured by enforced taxation which benefits the parasitic aristocracy or elite.]

1769: Mayer Amschel Rothschild is given permission by Prince William to hang a sign on the front of his business premises declaring that he is "M. A. Rothschild, by appointment court factor to his serene highness, Prince William of Hanau."

1770: Mayer Amschel Rothschild draws up plans for the creation of the Illuminati and entrusts Ashkenazi Jew, Adam Weishaupt, a Crypto-Jew who was outwardly Roman Catholic, with its organization and development. [Rothschild funds Illuminati]

1773: Amschel Mayer Rothschild is born, the first of Mayer Amschel Rothschild's sons. He, like all his brothers who follow him, will enter the family business at the age of 12. [They are mind programmed.]

1776: Adam Weishaupt officially completes his organization of the Illuminati on May 1 of this year. The purpose of the Illuminati [according to Hitchcock] is to divide the goyim (all non-Jews) through political, economic, social, and religious means. The opposing sides were to be armed and incidents were to be provided in order for them to: fight amongst themselves; destroy national governments; destroy religious institutions; and eventually destroy each other.

[On a deeper level, the purpose of the Illuminati is domination of the connected intuitive side of ourselves by the ego, "the *vanity* that disconnects," which finds self-importance, or false pride, through divide and conquer manipulation. "Good" connection "goes bad" and the parasites reap profit by consuming what once was connected. This *vanity* is an insatiable shadow that can never be appeased and moves forward seeking ever more control and influence, as it is out of touch with connection, also called "source."]

Weishaupt soon infiltrates the Continental Order of Freemasons with this Illuminati doctrine and establishes lodges of the Grand Orient to be their secret headquarters. This was all under the orders and finance of Mayer Amschel Rothschild and the concept has spread and is followed within Masonic Lodges worldwide to the present day.

Weishaupt also recruits 2,000 paid followers [He didn't have this kind of money, he was funded by Rothschild] including the most intelligent men in the field of arts and letters, education, science, finance, and industry. They were instructed to use the following methods in order to control people.

1. Use monetary and sex bribery [definitely still happening today] to obtain control of men already in high places, in the various levels of all governments and other fields of endeavor. Once influential persons had fallen for the lies, deceits, and temptations of the Illuminati they were to be held in bondage by application of political and other forms of blackmail, threats of financial ruin, public exposure, and fiscal harm, even death to themselves and loved members of their families. [In our times everything is secretly photographed or recorded, and the target is then owned by fear of exposure. This now includes almost everyone, as Edward Snowden has revealed.]
2. The faculties of colleges and universities were to cultivate students possessing exceptional mental ability belonging to well-bred families with international leanings, and recommend them for special *training in internationalism, or rather the notion that only a one-world government can put an end to recurring wars and strife.* [In this paradigm, spiritual discipline doesn't exist and won't bring peace; only a top-down world government with total enforcement power will save us "from ourselves," according to the Illuminati. The Church does the same by saying our nature is evil. It is not. Our nature is clear with karma on top of it. Instead of a spiritual bottom-up solution through education, a top-down solution that entails dumbing everyone down was the prescription for society's ills.] Such training was to be provided by granting scholarships to those selected by the Illuminati. [In the U.S., the "Ivy League" schools provided the *cutouts* for new generations of Globalist minions.]
3. All influential people trapped into coming under the control of the Illuminati, plus the students who had been specially educated and trained, were to be used as agents and placed behind the scenes of all governments as experts and specialists. This was so they would advise the top executives to adopt policies which would in the long-run serve the secret plans of the Illuminati one-world conspiracy and

bring about the destruction of the governments and religions they were elected or appointed to serve.

4. To obtain absolute-control of the press [at that time the press was the only mass-communications media which distributed information to the public] so that all news and information could be slanted in order to make the masses believe that a one-world government is the only solution to our many and varied problems.

[This accurately describes what has evolved out of this group.]

1777: Nathan Mayer Rothschild is born.

1784: Illuminati founder [Rothschild employee] Adam Weishaupt issues his order for the French Revolution to be started by Maximilien Robespierre in book form. This book was written by one of Weishaupt's associates, Xavier Zwack, and sent by courier from Frankfurt to Paris. However, in route there, the courier is struck by lightning. [For those who don't think there are invisible realms that intervene, you are mistaken. The visible spectrum we can see is only a sliver of reality. This lightening strike seems too "coincidental" to be discarded as random, in my opinion.] The book detailing this plan is discovered by the police and handed over to the Bavarian authorities.

As a consequence, the Bavarian government orders the police to raid Weishaupt's Masonic lodges of the Grand Orient, and the homes of his most influential associates. *Clearly, the Bavarian authorities were convinced that the book that was discovered was a very real threat by a private group of influential people, to use wars and revolutions to achieve their political ends.*

1785: The Bavarian government outlaws the Illuminati and close all the Bavarian Masonic lodges of the Grand Orient. Mayer Amschel Rothschild moves his family home to a five story house in Frankfurt which *he shares with the Schiff family.* [Remember the name Jacob Schiff.]

1798: John Robison, who in 1783 was elected General Secretary of the Royal Society of Edinburgh, publishes a book entitled, *"Proofs of a Conspiracy Against All the Religions and Governments of Europe Carried on in the Secret Meetings of Freemasons, Illuminati and Reading Societies,"* and gives details of the whole *Rothschild* Illuminati plot.

He advised how he had been a high degree Mason in the Scottish Rite of Freemasonry, and had been invited by Adam Weishaupt to [continental] Europe, where he had been given a revised copy of Weishaupt's conspiracy. However, although he pretended to go along with it, Professor Robison did not agree with it and therefore published his book. The book included details of the Bavarian government's investigation into the Illuminati and the French Revolution.

That same year, on July 19, David Pappen, President of Harvard University, lectured the graduating class on the influence Illuminism was having on American politics and religion. [The Illuminati are real, not make believe, as we will see in the music industry.]

At the age of 21, Nathan Mayer Rothschild leaves Frankfurt for England, where, with a large sum of money given to him by his father, he sets up a banking house in London.

1798: *It was not my intention to doubt that the* ***Doctrines of the Illuminati****, and principles of Jacobinism, had not spread in the United States. [Demonic Jacob Frank in Chapter 21] On the contrary, no one is more truly satisfied of this fact than I am. [They are here]. The idea that I meant to convey, was, that I did not believe that the Lodges of Freemasons in this country had [yet], as Societies, endeavoured to propagate the diabolical tenets of the first [the Illuminati], or pernicious principles of the latter [Jacobinism] (if they are susceptible of separation). That Individuals of them [Illuminati] may … actually had* ***a separation of the People from their Government in view, is too evident to be questioned.***"

– George Washington, 1st President of the United States (1789–1797),
from a letter written on October 24, 1798,
which can be found in the Library of Congress. [25]

[President Henry Jackson was a Freemason and was a major enemy of the Illuminati banksters, so George Washington's view seems supported. There is controversy about Ben Franklin as a Mason or Washington's true agenda. [26] I won't touch that here.]

1806: Napoleon Bonaparte states that it is his "object to remove the house of Hess-Cassel from rulership and to strike it out of the list of powers." [Assassinate] On hearing this, Prince William IX of Hesse-Hanau flees Germany, goes to Denmark and entrusts his fortune valued at $3,000,000 at that time to Mayer Amschel Rothschild for safekeeping.

1808: Moses Montefiore and Nathan Mayer Rothschild loan the British Treasury £3,200,000 (used to service the debt owed the privately operated Bank of England operated by Nathan Mayer Rothschild), in return are given an exclusive grant of trading privileges with all countries of the Indian and Pacific Oceans, between Cape Horn and Cape Good Hope for the newly chartered joint stock corporation which *Rothschild* controlled: the British East India Company.

1810: Sir Francis Baring and Abraham Goldsmid die. This leaves Nathan Mayer Rothschild as the remaining major banker in England.

Nathan's brother, Salomon Mayer Rothschild goes to Vienna, Austria and sets up the bank, M. von Rothschild und Söhne.

1811: The charter for the Rothschilds Bank of the United States runs out and Congress votes against its renewal. Nathan Mayer Rothschild states, "Either the application for renewal of the charter is granted, or the United States will find itself involved in a most disastrous war." Congress stands firm and the Charter is not renewed, which causes Nathan Mayer Rothschild to issue another threat, "Teach those impudent Americans a lesson. Bring them back to colonial status."

1812: Mayer Amschel Rothschild dies. In his will he lays out specific laws that the House of Rothschild were to follow:

- all key positions in the family business were only to be held by family members;
- only male members of the family were allowed to participate in the family business; this included a reported sixth secret bastard son. (It is important to note that Mayer

Amschel Rothschild also had five daughters, so today the spread of the Rothschild Zionist dynasty without the *Rothschild* name is far and wide);

- the family was to intermarry with it's first and second cousins to preserve the family fortune (of the 18 marriages by Mayer Amschel Rothschild's grandchildren, 16 were between first cousins, a practice known today as inbreeding);
- no public inventory of his estate was to be published; [He was a living lie.]
- no legal action was to be taken with regard to the value of the inheritance;
- the eldest son of the eldest son was to become the head of the family (this condition could only be overturned when the majority of the family agreed otherwise).

Straightaway Nathan Mayer Rothschild was elected head of the family following his father, Mayer Amschel Rothschild's death.

Jacob (James) Mayer Rothschild goes to Paris, France to set up the bank, de Rothschild Frères.

1814: With regard to the $3,000,000 Prince William IX of Hesse-Hanau had entrusted to Mayer Amschel Rothschild for safekeeping, what happened next is from the *Jewish Encyclopaedia,* 1905 edition, Volume 10, page 494, which states,

> "According to legend this money was hidden away in wine casks, and, escaping the search of Napoleon's soldiers when they entered Frankfurt, was restored intact in the same casks in 1814, when the elector (Prince William IX of Hesse-Hanau) returned to the electorate (Germany). The facts are somewhat less romantic, and more businesslike."

This last line indicates the money was never returned by Rothschild to Prince William IX of Hesse-Hanau. The *Encyclopaedia* goes on to state, "Nathan Mayer Rothschild invested this $3,000,000 in gold from the East India Company knowing that it would be needed for Wellington's peninsula campaign."

On the stolen money Nathan made, "no less than four profits: On the sale of Wellington's paper which he bought at 50 cents on the dollar and collected at par; on the sale of gold to Wellington; on its repurchase; and on forwarding it to Portugal."

1815: The five *Rothschild* brothers work to supply gold to both Wellington's army (through Nathan in England) and Napoleon's army (through Jacob in France), and begin their policy of *funding both sides in wars.* Banksters love wars because they are massive generators of risk free debt. This is because they are guaranteed by the government of a country, and therefore the efforts of the population of that country, and it doesn't matter if that country loses the war because the loans are given on the guarantee that the victor will honor the debts of the vanquished.

While the Rothschilds are funding both sides in this war, they use the banks they have spread out across Europe to give them the opportunity to set up an unrivaled postal service network of secret routes and fast couriers. The posts these couriers carried were opened by these couriers and their details given to the Rothschilds, so they always were one step ahead of current events. [The original NSA, Google and Facebook, for real. Under the same management!]

Furthermore, these *Rothschild* couriers were the only merchants allowed to pass through the English and French blockades. It was these couriers who also kept Nathan Mayer Rothschild up to date with how the war was going, so he could use that intelligence to buy and sell on the stock exchange.

One of Rothschild's couriers was a man named Rothworth. When the outcome of the Battle of Waterloo was won by the British, Rothworth took off for the Channel and was able to deliver this news to Nathan Mayer Rothschild, a full 24 hours before Wellington's own courier.

At that time British bonds were called *consuls* and they were traded on the floor of the stock exchange. Nathan Mayer Rothschild instructed all his workers on the floor to start selling *consuls.* This made all the other traders believe that the British had lost the war so they started selling frantically. [Similar ploy was used in New York in 1929.] Therefore the *consuls* plummeted in value, which was when Nathan Mayer Rothschild discreetly instructed his workers to purchase all the *consuls* they could lay their hands on.

When news came through that the British had actually won the war, the *consuls* went up to a level even higher than before, leaving Nathan Mayer Rothschild with a return of approximately 20 to 1 on his investment.

This gave the *Rothschild* family complete control of the British economy, now the financial centre of the world following Napoleon's defeat, England set up a new Bank of England, which Nathan Mayer Rothschild controlled.

Interestingly, 100 years later the *New York Times* would run a story stating that Nathan Mayer Rothschild's grandson had attempted to secure a court order to suppress publication of a book which had this insider trading story in it. The *Rothschild* family claimed the story was untrue and libelous, but the court denied the Rothschilds request and ordered the family to pay all court costs.

Back to 1815—this is the year Nathan Mayer Rothschild makes his famous statement,

> *"I care not what puppet is placed upon the throne of England to rule the Empire on which the sun never sets. The man who controls Britain's money supply controls the British Empire, and I control the British money supply."*

He would go onto brag that in the 17 years he had been in England he had increased the £20,000 stake given to him by his father, 2500 times to £50 million.

The Rothschilds also used their control of the Bank of England to replace the method of shipping gold from country to country and instead used their five banks spread across Europe *to set up a system of paper debits and credits, the banking system of today.*

By the end of this century, a period of time that was known as the "Age of the Rothschilds," it is estimated that the *Rothschild* family controlled half the wealth of the world.

However something that did not go well for the Rothschilds this year, was the Congress of Vienna, which started in September, 1814 and concluded in June of 1815. The purpose for this Congress of Vienna was for the Rothschilds to create a form of world government, to give them political control over much of the civilized world.

Many of the European governments were in debt to the Rothschilds, so they figured they could use that as a bargaining tool. However, Russia's Tsar Alexander I, who had not succumbed to a *Rothschild* central bank, would not go along with the plan, so the *Rothschild* world government plan failed.

Enraged by this, Nathan Mayer Rothschild swore that some day he or his descendants would destroy the Tsar Alexander I's entire family and descendants. Unfortunately he was true to his word and 102 years later [Rothschild funded Bolsheviks, organized by Jacob Schiff in New York] would act upon that promise [murdering everyone in the Czar's family, including the children.]

Interestingly, world government fanatic and Ashkenazi Jew, **Henry Kissinger** [war criminal on cover of this book], did his doctoral dissertation on the Congress of Vienna. [Kissinger is a Bilderberg Group chief, Obama consultant, See Vol. 1]

1816: The American Congress passes a bill permitting yet another *Rothschild* dominated central bank, which gives the Rothschilds control of the American money supply again. [Alexander Hamilton, who married into the New York elite, was pro-central bank.] This is called the Second Bank of the United States and is given a twenty year charter. The British war [of 1812] against America therefore ends with the deaths of thousands of British and American soldiers, but the Rothschilds get their bank. [The war wasn't specifically about the bank.]

1816: *"I sincerely believe, with you, that* ***banking establishments are more dangerous than standing armies.****"*

– Thomas Jefferson, 3rd President of the United States (1801–1809) and principal author of the United States Declaration of Independence (1776), in a letter written to John Taylor on May 28, 1816

"The central bank is an institution of the most deadly hostility existing against the Principles and form of our Constitution. I am an Enemy to all banks discounting bills or notes for anything but Coin. If the American People allow private banks to control the issuance of their currency, first by inflation and then by deflation, the banks and corporations that will grow up around them, will deprive the People of all their Property, until their Children will wake up homeless on the continent their Fathers conquered."

– Thomas Jefferson

[The continent stolen from *indigenous people!* Jefferson authorized the 1803 Louisiana Purchase, where scores of ancient cultures were "bought" from France for $15 million. Some feel there was no reason to pay France, because they no longer exerted *military* will in North America, thus Jefferson's integrity is questioned. What the U.S. bought from France was looting rights. This was backed up by the idea of "manifest destiny" where the *dominant culture* felt that dominance justifies itself, and there is no higher purpose. The Mormons later used the same rationale for destroying ancient cultures in Utah. The same for New Zealand, Australia, Africa, etc. The alleged Christians used genocide of the Canaanites in the Bible as precedent. Jefferson didn't believe the Bible and had fossils in his foyer, but didn't question the privileged, self-entitled *dominant culture,* which is what the Old Testament is all about and what our current environmental crisis is all about.

If Jefferson is going to invoke the legacy of successful conquest in quote above, then conquest is the world he lives in and can only expect more of. What was before conquest? He didn't know. He was a slave owner who was deeply in debt to carry on his self-entitled lifestyle. He could not afford to free his friends and lovers who were "his" slaves. He did not interact with the *indigenous ancient people* who never cut down the forests in tens of thousands of years. Jefferson did not serve a vision of Nature, based on balance. He wrote of the "pursuit of happiness" without defining it, which makes the Declaration of Independence deeply flawed. The *indigenous* were independent .... What about *their* declaration of independence? I would like to see Patriots wrap their minds around this. We need to step beyond conquest. Culturally we are cannibals eating up other cultures and now ourselves.]

1818: The French secured massive loans in 1817 in order to *help rebuild* after their disastrous defeat at Waterloo. [They took loans for the war also.] *Rothschild* agents bought vast amounts of French government bonds causing their value to increase. On November 5 they dumped the lot on the open market causing their value to plummet and France to go into a financial panic. The Rothschilds then stepped in to take control of the French money supply.

[So we've seen three examples, the Waterloo battle scam, this 1818 scam, and the 1929 stock market crash as *Rothschild* destabilization/consolidations manipulations. However, the devaluation of a nation's currency does the same, and has crushed people in Argentina, Mexico, Thailand, and many more. *Globalization* opens nations to manipulation, where their disaster is an "opportunity" for the parasites. So expect it, everyone, no matter where you live. If things are going smooth, watch out. If you have equity, it will be broken down and stolen. Your economy will be an "opportunity." Because the U.S. is now bankrupt, any fund is raided, like the Superfund for toxic cleanup, or pension funds. To have any savings in stocks or paper now is very blind. Corporation or government debts are erased in same manner, so if AIG Insurance owes millions of people a plan based on years of premiums, they just erase it and say they can't pay. Then AIG was bailed out, but did they re-instate the cancelled policies? No. Disaster is their "opportunity." And because the parasites run your government, your government cannot be trusted to take care of you. Wake up everyone. I made italics the words "help rebuild" above, because the "opportunity" of rebuilding and "helping" requires disaster.]

This was the same year the Rothschilds were able to loan £5,000,000 to the Prussian government.

1821: Kalmann (Carl) Mayer Rothschild is sent to Naples, Italy. He would end up doing a lot of business with the Vatican, and Pope Gregory XVI subsequently conferred upon him the Order of St. George. Also, whenever the Pope received Kalmann, he would give him his hand rather than the customary toe to kiss, which showed the extent of Kalmann's power over the Vatican.

[This version is disputed by Karen Hudes who says Vatican controls the Rothschilds. This needs more research. We do know the Jesuits were a *military* force and Illuminati founder Adam Weishaupt, through Rothschild, initiated a competing system with Jesuits. [27]]

1822: The emperor of Austria made the five Rothschild brothers Barons. Nathan Mayer Rothschild chose not to take up the title.

1823: The Rothschilds take over the financial operations of the Catholic Church, worldwide. (Hitchcock does not reference this, so this needs to be researched. We know that the Rothschilds and the Vatican are in bed together, but we don't know who is "on top.")

1827: Sir Walter Scott publishes his nine volume set, *The Life of Napoleon* and in volume two he states that the French Revolution was planned by the Illuminati (Adam Weishaupt) and was financed by the money changers of Europe (The Rothschilds).

1832: President Andrew Jackson (the 7th President of the United States from 1829 to 1837), runs the campaign for his second term in office under the slogan, "Jackson And No Bank!" This is in reference to his plan to take the control of the American money system to benefit the American people, in order to stop profiteering by the Rothschilds.

1833: President Andrew Jackson starts removing the government's deposits from the Rothschild-controlled Second Bank of the United States and instead deposits them into banks directed by democratic bankers.

This causes the Rothschilds to panic, and so they do what they do best, contract the money supply causing a depression. President Jackson knows what they are up to and later states, "You are a den of thieves vipers, and I intend to rout you out, and by the Eternal God, I will rout you out!"

1834: The Italian revolutionary leader, Guiseppe Mazzini, is selected by the Illuminati to direct their revolutionary program throughout the world, and would serve in that capacity until he died in 1872.

1835: On January 30, an assassin tries to shoot President Jackson, but miraculously both of the assassin's pistols misfired. [Others say there was only one pistol.] President Jackson would later claim that he knew the Rothschilds were responsible for that attempted assassination. [The assailant] Richard Lawrence, who was found not guilty by reason of insanity, later bragged that powerful people in Europe had hired him and promised to protect him if he were caught.

[Jack Ruby, who killed Lee Harvey Oswald, the innocent government covert agent framed for death of JFK, makes similar claim on this youtube. [28] The same group has been doing this for centuries.]

The Rothschilds acquire the rights in the Almadén quicksilver (Mercury) mines in Spain. This was at the time the biggest concession in the world. Mercury was a vital component in the refining of gold or silver and this gave the Rothschilds a virtual world monopoly.

1836: *"A power has risen up in the government, greater than the people themselves, consisting of many and various powerful interests, combined in one mass, and held together by the cohesive power of the vast surplus in banks."*

– John C. Calhoun, Vice President of President Henry Jackson (1825 – 1832) and U.S. Senator, from a speech given on May 27, 1836 [This is a great quote and even more true today.]

Following his years of fighting against the Rothschilds and their central bank in America, President Andrew Jackson finally succeeds in throwing the Rothschilds out of America, when the bank's charter is not renewed. It would not be until 1913 that the Rothschilds would be able to set up their third central bank in America, the Federal Reserve, and to ensure no mistakes are made, this time they will put one of their own bloodline, **Jacob Schiff,** in charge of the project.

Nathan Mayer *Rothschild* dies and the control of his bank, N. M. Rothschild & Sons is passed on to his younger brother, James Mayer Rothschild.

1840: The Rothschilds become the Bank of England's bullion brokers. They set up agencies in California and Australia. [For the gold rushes]

1841: President John Tyler (the 10th President of the United States from 1841 to 1845) vetoes the act to renew the charter for the Bank of the United States. He goes on to receive hundreds of letters threatening him with assassination.

1844: Salomon Mayer Rothschild purchases the United Coal Mines of Vítkovice and Austro-Hungarian Blast Furnace Company that would go on to be one of the top ten global industrial concerns.

Benjamin Disraeli, an Ashkenazi Jew (who would go on to become British Prime Minister twice—the only admitted Ashkenazi Jew to do so) publishes *Coningsby*, in which he characterizes Nathan Mayer Rothschild as "the Lord and Master of the money markets of the world, and of course virtually Lord and Master of everything else. He literally held the revenues of Southern Italy in pawn, and Monarchs and Ministers of all countries courted his advice and were guided by his suggestions." [Kissed his a**.]

[According to Disraeli's biographer, Robert Blake, the character of Sidonia in the book *Coningsby* is a composite between Lionel de Rothschild and Disraeli himself.]

> *"The world is governed by very different personages from what is imagined by those who are not behind the scenes."*
>
> – from *Coningsby*, or *The New Generation*

1845: Andrew Jackson (7th President of the United States) dies. Before his death he was asked what he regarded as his greatest achievement. He replied without hesitation, "I Killed The Bank." [He has this placed on his tombstone.]

[Jackson resisted the *Rothschild* banks but was responsible for the *dominant culture* removal of 125,000 Native Americans, including the Creeks and Cherokee, from the southeast states. Families with elders and children were forced at gunpoint to march thousands of miles to desolate Oklahoma, an ecology they knew not, in the Trail of Tears. This march was worse than the Death marches in Philippines that victimized American soldiers captured by Japanese in World War II. Patriots might think Andrew Jackson a *hero*, while Native Americans want the truth told and this monster's face removed from the U.S. twenty dollar bill. The reader should weigh your response to this carefully. Did Jackson represent sectarian bravery or virtue? How would you feel if you were Native American? This book will repeatedly point out that our relationship with *indigenous people* and the Earth Mother must be healed, or we are guilty of the same abuse the banksters have been guilty of. Stealing. More than that, until we live like *indigenous people*, we will be trying to outsmart, trick, deceive Nature and continue destroying Her. Yes that is radical opinion, but time and *resource depletion* are on my side. And for you heading for the stars, that will grow old, and how will you treat the next Mother Earth you find? The fix is inside us, not new technology.]

Jacob (James) Mayer Rothschild (who by now had married his niece, Betty, Salomon Mayer Rothschild's daughter), now known as Baron James de Rothschild, wins the contract to build the first major railway line across the country. [France]

This was called the Chemin De Fer Du Nord and ran initially from Paris to Valenciennes and then joined with the Austrian rail network built by his brother (and wife's father—all sounds a bit sordid, doesn't it) Salomon Mayer Rothschild.

[Transportation would speed up resource exploitation and homogenization of cultures. The goal was as much extraction and influence as possible to prove "power" by the individuals involved, who were disconnected from the consequences on the ground. I call this *disconnecting vanity.* Our vanity calls unsustainable extraction "progress."]

1847: Lionel De Rothschild, now married to the daughter of his uncle, Kalmann (Carl) Mayer Rothschild, is elected to the parliamentary seat for the City of London. A requirement for entering Parliament was to take an oath in the true faith of a Christian. Lionel De Rothschild refused to do this as he was Jewish and his seat in Parliament remained empty for 11 years until new oaths were allowed.

1848: Karl Marx, an Ashkenazi Jew, publishes, under commission from the Illuminati League of Just Men "The Communist, "The Communist Manifesto." Interestingly at the same time as he is working on this, Karl Ritter of Frankfurt University was writing the antithesis which would form the basis for Freidrich Wilhelm Nietzsche's "Nietzscheanism." This Nietzecheanism was later developed into Fascism and then into Nazism and was used to foment the first and second world wars.

[Nie·tzsche·ism: the philosophy of Nietzsche 1844-1900, emphasizing the will to power *(grasping desire* and *vanity* – Glossary terms) as the chief motivating force of both the individual and society. Neitzsche was a German philosopher noted for his *concept of the superman* [oh brother!] and his rejection of traditional Christian values. Since the satanist Illuminati Rothschilds financed both Communism and Fascism, it is not surprising that both rejected Jesus Christ and both persecuted Christians. Stalin killed millions and Hitler killed Jehovahs Witnesses. Christians are now being undermined and harassed in the U.S., and called "hate groups" for supporting traditional biological family.]

Marx, Ritter, and Nietzsche were all funded and under the instruction of the Rothschilds. The idea was that those who direct the overall conspiracy could *use the differences* in ideologies to enable them to divide larger and larger factions of the human race into opposing camps so that they could be armed and then brainwashed into fighting and destroying each other, and particularly, to destroy all political and religious institution—the same plan put forward by Illuminati founder Weishaupt in 1776.

1849: Gutle Schnaper, Mayer Amschel Rothschild's wife dies. Before her death she would nonchalantly state, "If my sons did not want wars, there would be none."

1852: N.M. Rothschild & Sons begins refining gold and silver for the Royal Mint and the Bank of England and other international customers.

1856: *"There is ... a power which we seldom mention in this House ... I mean the secret societies ... a great part of Europe—the whole of Italy and France and a great portion of Germany, to say nothing of other countries—is covered with a network of these secret societies [Masons] ... They do not want constitutional government; they do not want ameliorated institutions ... they want to change the tenure of land, to drive out the present owners of the soil and put an end to ecclesiastical establishments ..."*

– Benjamin Disraeli, British Prime Minister, July 14, 1856 speech in the House of Commons. [This isn't in his novel, this is out front.]

1861: President Abraham Lincoln (16th President of the United States from 1860 until his assassination in 1865) approaches the big banks in New York to try to obtain loans to support the ongoing American Civil War. As these large banks were heavily under the influence of the Rothschilds, they offer him a deal they know he cannot accept, 24% to 36% interest on all monies loaned. Lincoln is very angry about this high level of interest and so he prints his own debt free money [the Greenbacks] and informs the public that this is now legal tender for both public and private debts.

1862: By April $449,338,902 worth of Lincoln's debt free Greenbacks have been printed and distributed. He states,

> *"We gave the people of this republic the greatest blessing they ever had, their own paper money to pay their own debts." [Money without interest payments]*

Also

> *"The government should create, issue, and circulate all the currency and credit [interest free] needed to satisfy the spending power of the government and the buying power of consumers.*
>
> *The privilege of creating and issuing money is not only the supreme prerogative of government, but it is the government's greatest creative opportunity. The financing of all public enterprise, and the conduct of the treasury will become matters of practical administration.*
>
> *Money will cease to be master and will then become servant of humanity."*
>
> – Abraham Lincoln

That same year *The Times* of London publishes a story containing the following statement,

> "If that mischievous financial policy, which had its origin in the North American Republic, should become indurated down to a fixture, then that government **will furnish its own money without cost.** It will pay off debts and be without a debt. It will have all the money necessary to carry on its commerce. It will become prosperous beyond precedent in the history of civilized governments of the world. The brains and the wealth of all countries will go to North America. That government must be destroyed or it will destroy every monarchy on the globe."

[This is why I, the author, call all royalty by a more accurate name ... parasites.]

1863: President Abraham Lincoln discovers that the Tsar of Russia, Alexander II (1855-1881), is having problems with the Rothschilds as well, as he is refusing their continual attempts to set up a central bank in Russia. The Tsar then gives President Lincoln some unexpected help. The Tsar issued orders that if either England or France actively intervenes in the American Civil War, and help the South, Russia would consider such action a declaration of war, and take the side of President Lincoln. To show that he meant business, he sends part of his Pacific Fleet to port in San Francisco and other ships to New York.

The *Rothschild* banking house in Naples, Italy, C. M. de Rothschild e figli, closes following the unification of Italy. The Rothschilds use one of their own in America, John D. Rockefeller, to form an oil business called Standard Oil which eventually takes over all of its competition.

[This statement by Hitchcock is not quite what I found in my research. John D Rockefeller made friends with James Stillman, President of Rothschild First National City Bank. It can be understood they had business ties. Stillman's two daughters married John D. Rockefeller's nephews. From here on it is obvious that the Rockefellers and the Rothschilds were in bed with each other, no pun intended. The *Roth-efellers.*]

1864: *Rothschild* man, August Belmont, who by now is the Democratic Party's National Chairman, supports General George McClellan as the Democratic nominee to run against President Abraham Lincoln in election. Much to the anger of Belmont, President Lincoln wins.

[Did the reader get that ... U.S. party politics were and are controlled by Rothschilds.]

1864: Europe –This entree is from *Final Warning: A History of the New World Order, Illuminism and The Master Plan for World Domination* by David Allen Rivera, 1994.

> "On September 28, 1864, Marx and Engels founded the International Workingmen's Association at St. Martin's Hall in London, which consisted of English, French, German, Italian, Swiss, and Polish Socialists, who were dedicated to destroying the "prevailing economic system." It later became known as the First Socialist International, which eight years later spread to New York and merged with the Socialist Party.

"Marx wrote to Engels: 'I was present, only as a dumb personage on the platform.'"

"James Guillaume, a Swiss member, wrote: 'It is not true that the Internationale was the creation of Karl Marx. He remained completely outside the preparatory work that took place from 1862 to 1864 ….'"

[Again, we find evidence that the Illuminati did in fact control the growing Communist movement, but not to deal with the problems of workers and industry; rather it was to instigate riot and revolution, just as in Bolshevik Revolution, Iran 1953, Libya, Ukraine, Venezuela and scores of other destabilization/consolidation programs.]

"The Marxist doctrine produced by the Association was accepted and advocated by the emerging labor movement, and soon the organization grew to 800,000 dues-paying members.

"Even though Marx publicly urged the working class to overthrow the capitalists, in June, 1864, in a letter to his uncle, Leon Phillips, Marx announced that he had made 400 pounds on the Stock Exchange. It is obvious that Marx didn't practice what he preached, and therefore didn't really believe in the movement he was giving birth to. He was an employee, doing a job for his Illuminati bosses.

"Nathan Rothschild had given Marx two checks for several thousand pounds to finance the cause of Socialism. The checks were put on display in the British Museum, after Lord Lionel Walter Rothschild, a trustee, had willed his museum and library to them."

– David Allen Rivera

[Marx was placed by the Rothschilds. May all socialists and communists please wake up. You are being fooled and used. May all who hate communists also wake up. Capitalism is run by the bankster Illuminati also.]

Back to Hitchcock timeline …

1865: In a statement to Congress, President Abraham Lincoln states, "I have two great enemies, the Southern Army in front of me, and the financial institutions in the rear. Of the two, the one in my rear is my greatest foe."

Later that year, on April 14, President Lincoln is assassinated, less than two months before the end of the American Civil War.

Following a brief training period in the Rothschild's London Bank, **Jacob Schiff,** a Rothschild, born in their house in Frankfurt, arrives in America at the age of 18 with instructions and the finance necessary to buy into a banking house there. The purpose of this was to carry out the following tasks. [Hitchcock lists four tasks, but gives no source for this information so I do not include it here.]

Nathaniel de Rothschild becomes Member of Parliament for Aylesbury in Buckinghamshire.

1875: On January 1, **Jacob Schiff,** now Solomon Loeb's son-in-law, takes control of the banking house, Kuhn, Loeb & Co. [Members of this same firm managed the Rockefeller Family businesses through the 20th century]. He goes on to finance John D. Rockefeller's Standard Oil Company, Edward R. Harriman's Railroad Empire, and Andrew Carnegie's Steel Empire with *Rothschild* money.

[From the late 1800s to present, the Rothschilds basically went underground, and the Rockefellers were more visible. The Rothschilds controlled Treaty of Versailles, and creation of Israel, which throughout the book I will refer to as "*Rothschild* Israel," which is accurate—more details to come. Also, from 1875 forward, I call this family the *Rothefellers,* see Glossary.]

2002: "The power of the *Rothschild* family was evidenced on 24 Sept 2002 when a helicopter touched down on the lawn of Waddedson Manor, their ancestral home in Buckinghamshire, England. Out of the helicopter strode **Warren Buffet**—touted as the second richest man in the World, but really a lower ranking player—and Arnold Schwarzenegger, at that time a candidate for the Governorship of California. Also in attendance at this two day meeting of the World's most powerful businessmen and financiers, hosted by Jacob Rothschild, were James Wolfensohn, president of the World Bank and Nicky Oppenheimer, chairman of De Beers. Arnold went on to secure the governorship of one of the biggest economies on the planet a year later. That he was initiated into the ruling class in the Rothschilds' English country manor suggests that the centre of gravity of the three hundred trillion dollar *Rothschild* cartel is in the U.K. and Europe, not the U.S." [29]

(Please see online, this breathtaking analysis of the Rothschild's support in creating the Secessionist movement for U.S. Civil War, the Freemasonry ties, the assassination of Lincoln, drug running to replace lucrative slave trade, creation of KKK, support of the Bolshevik Revolution, links to Mafia, and activities of the racist Rothschild Anti-Defamation League. [30])

* * *

The *Rothschild* family had a bit of influence on modern history and society's relationship with Nature—does the reader not agree? Rockefeller, Harriman, and Carnegie companies would create "foundations" spoken of in Dodd quote above (Page 23-24), which acted together under one Illuminati direction to successfully *socially engineer* American culture.

Please now recall what Einstein and Nader said. This is real folks.

I will refer the reader to the internet now to read the rest of Andrew Hitchcock's version of *Rothschild* history and to compare it with other versions, particularly, *The Great American Adventure,* a history of law, which will be very surprising, by retired Judge Dale. [31] As I've said, if an article does not ask hard questions, but just "explains," then don't trust it, because it is mind programming, not research. Also see "Secret History of America's Beginnings Series" on Youtube.

Jacob Schiff (see year 1865 above) would go on to create the Federal Reserve (FED) in 1913, after blackmailing President Woodrow Wilson. 1913 would also see creation of Internal Revenue Service, FBI, and zionist Anti-Defamation League. Schiff would also create the NAACP (National Association for the Advancement of Colored People) in 1909, which would be controlled by *Rothschild* Jews for its first 13 years. The Rothschilds are not altruistic, and were involved in slave trading the previous three centuries. The purpose of NAACP was to use racial issues to take down existing institutions in the process of attaining "synthesis" or "singularity."

Now that the reader is becoming familiar with Globalist *doublespeak*, let's translate this NAACP mission statement …

> *"to ensure the political, educational, social, and economic equality of rights of all persons and to eliminate racial hatred and racial discrimination."*

When we understand the character of the *Roth-efellers*, we see that this, like other platitudes, cannot be sincere. So what does it really mean? It can be translated easily as "Homogenization under New World Order." When we consider that the *Rothschild* League of Nations at that time had same "universal aspirations" as NAACP, and that war criminal Bush Sr. promoted these "universal aspirations" in 1991 (Page 25-28), we realize that the NAACP is not about bringing Blacks to equality with Whites, but bringing all people, world wide, to equal control under a *monoculture* .

> *Monoculture* is built on hatred, while love is based on tolerance, which tolerates diversity. *Monoculture* is intolerant of diversity and tries to destroy diversity. Love accepts diversity. Hatred enforces *monoculture.* Thus, "equality," which creates *monoculture* , really means intolerant hatred, masked as "being fair."
>
> A *dominant culture* is hateful to other cultures and tries to homogenize, incorporate, and absorb them.
>
> Real fairness would lovingly uphold tolerance for diverse standards.
>
> I know this will be hard for the reader to accept at first. Dear reader, you don't want to become a robot. You want to be unique and unequal to anyone who has ever lived, and if you have your own standards, those need some way of expression, otherwise you don't have your own standards, and you are just a software program responding to the keyboard played by someone else. In fact, you are unique, not equal. I learn from you because you are not a clone. We are not equal, we are diverse.

The NAACP is another of hundreds of fronts. It is run by the Illuminati, and that is why the NAACP and Jessie Jackson and "Logo" Obama have never mentioned the 1999 Shelby Tennessee Trial that exonerated James Earl Ray and implicated the government in the death of *Hero* Martin Luther King. [32]

Oh, you didn't hear about this trial! Were you confused by PBS specials that continue to name James Earl Ray as killer, when he was exonerated in a U.S. court? Do you think PBS tells the truth? Do you think third generation CIA agent Obama is sincere every year on Martin Luther King Day? Why hasn't "Logo," or Collin Powell, or Condoleezza Rice, or Oprah Winfrey, or Jessie Jackson, or Eddie Murphy blown the whistle about this 1999 trial?

Why is the exonerated James Earl Ray still vilified in all official *his-stories?* Well, it is to hide the true murderers, obviously. All these "Black" people just mentioned are owned. They are Black on the outside and Illuminati on the inside. Unlike *Hero* Cynthia McKinney!

"Ever since I came to Congress in 1992, there are those who have been trying to silence my voice. I've been told to sit down and shut up over and over again. Well, I won't sit down and I won't shut up until the full and unvarnished truth is placed before the American people."

– *Hero* Cynthia McKinney

The NAACP is also very quiet about protesting the racism we see in the proportion of Black prisoners in U.S. jails or in protesting the CIA drug running in Black communities.

Sincere people at NAACP are like the sincere people in many NGO's (Non-Government Organization) and even in government who simply do not understand that the game is rigged. Those at the top of these organization surely know something is up, but haven't read a book like this. The NAACP and Martin Luther King Center have not produced whistleblowers. I'm sorry to hurt peoples feelings, but the only popularly well-known Black heroes to my limited knowledge, in recent times, were Bob Marley, rap artist Tupac, Michael Jackson, U.S. Representative Cynthia McKinney, and Lauryn Hill. (Page 17) The first three were assassinated, McKinney was given another Black woman as opposing funded candidate to run her out of office, and Hill was jailed and then smeared as "crazy," which she says has given her more freedom, because the press leaves her alone now. (Do not read Wikipedia biographies of any whistleblower, as Wikipedia smears them and tells lies. Wikipedia will never explain who is harassing a whistleblower, because Wikipedia is a tentacle of that harassment. Never give money to Wikipedia)

The Rothschilds' overwhelming mafia influence continues today. In the recent movie *The Monuments Men* (2014) directed by George Clooney, the script goes out of its way to mention Rothschild as an "art collector" to dis-inform the public as to what this bankster family really is. Clooney, then, is controlled. Period.

* * *

The New World Order is an old plan. Jesus warned us very clearly about it. The Roman Empire was a harbinger of what was to come ... slavery ... in which nature was captured and displayed in coliseums for slaughter. I'm emphasizing the *dominant culture's* outlook toward nature here.

"They" exist in their own eyes to control our world by controlling interest rates, which controls debt, which controls capital, which controls "development," which controls jobs, which controls your power to consume your little piece of the pie. Mother Nature is the pie being cut up and distributed. Your income, whatever it is, is your ration for taking part in *their* system. Cutting up the pie for so many billions of people to have more speed and more stuff causes overgrazing and pollution, both environmentally and morally.

What runs the whole machine is the mantra that "more is better." This makes us insatiable, insuring that we keep pushing *their* wheel.

The Earth is "collateral damage" in the Globalist effort to control all people, because they respect nothing. Until we understand that banks control all industry, this doesn't make sense. It is not some independent "industrialization" that is hurting the Earth, it is those who control the release of new technology and new factories. And it is not "capitalists" that are hurting the planet, it is those who control the capital, which means, controlling the loans. At the top are not corporations. At the top are interest rates controlled by a very small group. Remember the example of the Great Depression and the stock market crash and the crashes just listed in Hitchcock's *History of the Rothschilds.* A very small group brought these about. In most cases, one person. With that power of life and death over corporations, the New World Order can and does place their own people on the boards of most companies and in the administrations of most governments. *With control over policy and taxes, we the slaves pay the wages for the entire structure.*

"They" hope to be the financial bosses of the world and in many ways are already. There isn't a place that is not affected, as evidenced by Microsoft and Apple in every city on globe, or plastic items in the most remote villages. Bill Gates was placed, as his father was a head of *Roth-efeller* sponsored Planned Parenthood. [33] Steve Jobs was assassinated with a cancer weapon to get him out of the way before knowledge of wireless dangers (See Bioinitiative.org) would reach his Buddhist heart. (I believe my friend and elder, Kobun Chino Roshi (Page 3) was also killed, along with his young daughter, in an "accident" in Switzerland, to eliminate any influence he might have had on Steve Jobs.)

Apple Inc. is now entirely a Globalist operation and the reason your Macintosh computer has a wireless keyboard or your iPad has no ethernet port is to increase EMF (electro-magnetic frequency) smog and accelerate the EMF "slow kill" rate. As Michael Jackson sang, "They don't care about us." Phones have a warning in the settings to keep the phone 15 mm from your body. Why haven't you heard about this? An avalanche of cancer is coming. "Apple has issued a safety warning in every iPhone user manual—but, they deceptively printed it in tiny print and located it in a section where no one will see it." [34]

A Buddhist wouldn't do that. Steve Jobs was "removed."

* * *

Another example of successful *Globalization* is Coca Cola or Disney Inc. As I hope the reader knows, coke causes tooth decay, and as we are going to see in this non-fiction thriller in which the reader plays a major part, Disney causes moral decay. Both coke and cartoons make people weaker and more malleable.

Yes, various countries still have some sovereignty, but as *Globalization* crushes forward, especially through trade agreements and children's movies and games, pop music, fashion and tourism, the world's diverse ethnic and cultural differences are blurring, making us all a common "market" for more *social engineering* and ever more control.

On August 29, 2014, The *Wall Street Journal* published an article by war criminal, pedophile [35], Bilderberger (next chapter), *Roth-efeller* minion, Henry Kissinger (introduced in Vol. 1), who appears on the front cover of this book …

> *"The international order thus faces a paradox: its prosperity is dependent on the success of globalization, but the process produces a political reaction that often works counter to its aspirations."*
>
> – War Criminal Henry Kissinger, August 29, 2014

The prosperity of the "international order," (meaning New World Order—there is no other one) is at odds with morality and diversity. Thus, of course, there is a "political" reaction to the "aspirations," meaning machinations, of the elite banksters.

1) "Prosperity" is *unsustainable consumerism* that will increasingly only be available to the few, while the buying power of the masses, disappears. We are seeing the constricting of "prosperity" everywhere, except places like China, which is destroying its own environment in heedless, globalist, *dominant culture,* Earth hating frenzy. (See environmental reality in China, Vol. 5)
2) The "international order" is based on state terrorism.
3) "The political reaction" is the response by anyone with *personal sovereignty* and a sense of dignity, to abuse and *monopolization.*
4) There are no aspirations of *globalization* except total control.
5) Why is the *Wall Street Journa*l giving this decrepit monster any coverage? Oh, oops, it is the *Wall Street Journal!*

"The international order [*Roth-efeller* New World Order] thus faces a paradox: its prosperity [of the top elite] is dependent on the success of *globalization* [controlling all markets, controlling everything], but the process [of destroying nations, destroying communities, destroying local cultures, destroying local control and destroying the oceans, waters and skies] produces a political reaction [cries of the victims growing to rage] that often works counter to its [the elite's] aspirations [secret scheming]."

* * *

How is the reader doing? These first five chapters lay our foundation for questioning. The sixth chapter is an in your face reality check. And then I start to get personal with your *socially engineered* sexuality. But let's get through these first few which outline our state of cultural confusion.

I'm aiming at your world view. I want to shake it from inside out. What is Ray trying to say here? There is an urgency. Who is looking at these words?

Chapter 3

The Mask Comes Off

The reader might wonder, "If there really is a global conspiracy to control everything, how could it possibly be hidden?" From the above history of the *Rothschild* family that we just read, a global conspiracy wasn't hidden to anyone high in government. But the *controlled media* and school curriculums fed you lies about free press, democracy, and human rights when in reality, what history has been about is consolidation of power, right up to today.

It is very hard to believe that such a big secret could be kept secret, but our knowledge of the world is limited to what we see and hear and read. There has been no free press for a hundred years. (see *controlled media* – Glossary) If a whistleblower is not publicized, then you never would hear about her or him. And whistleblowers are almost never publicized. More often they are smeared, fired, or killed.

To put a face on this, let's take just one example of the many influential individuals in our world now, who demonstrate the reality of a banking *social engineering* conspiracy.

1991: Former Federal Reserve Board Chairman 1979–1987, **Paul A. Volcker** becomes Chairman of the European Banking firm J. Rothschild, Wolfensohn and Co.

Wikipedia leaves out the *Rothschild* name, and just calls the banking firm "Wolfensohn and Co." This is because Wikipedia, which almost always appears at top of globalist Google searches, is globalist censored information and cannot be trusted.

I find it pleasing that the Rothschilds want their name hidden, forcing them into a cage of their own secrecy. I am pleased they are on the run. The more they hide, the greater the chance that they will someday figure out the aberration of their lives. They might realize they are making a big mistake with their choices. They might realize they are hiding from truth and are quite mad.

Here is some history that controlled Wikipedia does share about **Paul Volcker** ...

> "As of October 2006, Paul Volcker is the current chairman of the board of trustees of the influential Washington based financial advisory body, the **Group of Thirty.** [Has reader never heard of this group? Why not? Who censored it from your world view?] He has had a long association with the **Rockefeller family,** not only with his positions at **Chase Bank** and the **Trilateral Commission,** but also through membership in the **Trust Committee of Rockefeller Group, Inc.,** which he joined in 1987.
>
> "That entity managed, at one time, the **Rockefeller Center** on behalf of the numerous members of the Rockefeller family. He is former chairman and an honorary trustee of **International House,** the cultural exchange residence and program center in New York City. He is a founding member of the **Trilateral Commission** and is a long-time member of the **Bilderberg Group.**"

Every *Roth-efellers* group named above has secret meetings to plan economic cycles, wars, technocratic roll-out (Smart Grid), domestic and foreign policy, and other little details like that about your future.

2009: *Roth-efeller* minion Paul Volcker becomes "Logo" Obama's Chairman for the Economic Recovery Advisory Board. In other words, Volcker is a *Roth-efeller* agent, inside and out, and is *still* in power, and actually helps control puppet "Logo" Obama. Is this "change you can believe in?" (Logo's campaign slogan.)

> "Leaked documents from the 1955 Bilderberg Group conference discuss the agenda to create a European Union and a single EU currency, decades before they were introduced, disproving once again the debunkers, who claim that Bilderberg has no influence over world events. Leaked papers from the meeting which took place from September 23-25 1955 at the Grand Hotel Sonnenbichl in Garmisch-Partenkirchen, West Germany, were released by the Wikileaks website yesterday ..."
>
> – Infowars.com, May 8, 2009

The Bilderberg Group (Volcker is "long term member") is composed of elite royalty, rich corporate heads, and *military* security chiefs. They meet secretly each year to discuss your future without telling you what they are discussing. The reason they meet in person, believe it or not, is to be mind programmed into more *disconnecting vanity* (See Glossary) and to give up another piece of their conscience and *personal sovereignty.* One could call this group commitment to *disconnecting vanity* and *entitlement,* some kind of "bonding." The Bilderberg Group could be called the Cockroach Group because, like cockroaches, they like to hide in the dark. Queen Elizabeth is a member.

"The European founders of the **Bilderberg Group** included Joseph Retinger and Prince Bernhard of the Netherlands. Prince Bernhard had, incidentally, been a member of the Nazi Party until 1934, three years prior to his marrying the Dutch Queen Juliana, and had also worked for the German industrial giant, I.G. Farben, the maker of Zyklon B, the gas used in concentration camps.

"On the American side, those who were most prominent in the formation of the **Bilderberg Group** were **David Rockefeller,** Dean Rusk (a top official with the **Council on Foreign Relations (CFR)** who was also then the head of the **Rockefeller Foundation),** Joseph Johnson (another CFR leader who was head of the **Carnegie Endowment** [controls U.S. education]), and John J. McCloy (a top CFR leader who became Chairman of **Chase Manhattan Bank** in 1953 and was also Chairman of the Board of the **Ford Foundation.**

"The fact that the major American foundations, **Rockefeller, Carnegie, and Ford,** were so pivotal in the origins of the **Bilderberg Group** is not a mere coincidence. The foundations have, since their founding at the beginning of the 20th century, been the central institutions in constructing consensus among elites, and creating consent to power. They are, in short, the engines of *social engineering,* both for elite circles specifically, and society as a whole. As Professor of Education Robert F. Arnove wrote in his book *Philanthropy and Cultural Imperialism:*

> "Foundations like **Carnegie, Rockefeller, and Ford** have a corrosive influence on a democratic society; they represent relatively unregulated and unaccountable concentrations of power and wealth which buy talent, promote causes, and, in effect, establish an agenda of what merits society's attention. They serve as "cooling-out" agencies, delaying and preventing more radical, structural change. They help maintain an economic and political order, international in scope, which benefits the ruling-class interests of [alleged] philanthropists and philanthropoids—a system which ... has worked against the interests of minorities, the working class, and Third World peoples."

The names above were founders of the Bilderberg Group, while below is an outline of the *Rothefeller* control of Bilderberg Group ...

> "Certainly, while *Rothschild* interests have remained in the Bilderberg Group, as evidenced by Edmond de Rothschild having been a member of the Steering Committee, and Franco Bernabe, Vice Chairman of Rothschild Europe, being a current Steering Committee member, the Rockefeller interests seem to be most dominant."
>
> "Not only is **David Rockefeller** sitting as the single individual of the Member Advisory Group of the Steering Committee, but close Rockefeller confidantes have long served on the Steering Committee and been affiliated with the Bilderberg organization, such as:
>
> - Sharon Percy Rockefeller;
> - George Ball, a long-time leader in the **Council on Foreign Relations,** who was Undersecretary of State for Economic Affairs in the Kennedy and Johnson administrations;
> - Henry Kissinger [Front cover], long-time Rockefeller aide [worked for **Nelson Rockefeller** for ten years] and American imperial strategist;
> - Zbigniew Brzezinski, who co-founded the **Trilateral Commission** with **David Rockefeller** [and trained Obama, when Obama was supposedly going to Columbia];
> - Joseph E. Johnson, former U.S. State Department official and President of the **Carnegie Endowment for International Peace;**
> - John J. McCloy, former Chairman of the **Council on Foreign Relations** (superseded by **David Rockefeller**), former Assistant Secretary of War, Chairman of **Chase Manhattan Bank** (where he was superseded by **David Rockefeller**), former Trustee of the **Rockefeller Foundation,** Chairman of the **Ford Foundation,** and President of the **World Bank;**
> - James Wolfensohn, former President of the **World Bank** and Trustee of the **Rockefeller Foundation.**

- Jessica T. Matthews, a current Bilderberg Steering Committee member, who is representative of not only a continuation of Rockefeller interests, but also of the continuing influence and role of the major foundations. She is President of the **Carnegie Endowment for International Peace,** served on the National Security Council under Zbigniew Brzezinski, was a senior fellow at the **Council on Foreign Relations** (at which David Rockefeller remains as Honorary Chairman), is a member of the **Trilateral Commission**, is a trustee of the **Rockefeller Foundation,** and has served on the boards of the Brookings Institution, the **Rockefeller Brothers Fund** and the Joyce Foundation.

– Andrew Gavin Marshall, June 16, 2011 [36]

The reader is asked to remember these deep and wide Rockefeller influences when we review David Rockefeller's incredible schizophrenic memoirs in another book of the series. Already mentioned, Queen Elizabeth, the richest woman in the world, is a Bilderberger. We will explore her cult and pedophile background shortly. (See video *The Zion King* online)

The CEOs of Facebook, Google, and Amazon Books now attend Bilderberg meetings, but considering all three were placed and made famous, exactly like the music industry divas and the presidents and prime ministers we will meet soon, this is no surprise. Facebook 2010 slogan was "Making the world more open and connected." Forcing "openness" to destroy boundaries and sovereignty, and "connecting" everyone through centralized *monoculture* (See Glossary) is exactly what the New World Order wants. And this is planned … in secret meetings!

Pawns in a Game

The bankster *Globalists*, who now use Google, Facebook, Amazon, Bill Gates, the CIA, PBS, Oprah and anyone influential (that was allowed to become influential), placed Vladimir Lenin, a funded change agent. They placed Hitler. They placed Churchill. They placed Gandhi. They placed Woodrow Wilson and Franklin Roosevelt and Mao. They placed Stalin and Bush Sr. and Clinton and Bush Jr. and Logo Obama. They probably placed your politicians in your country also. And if your citizens pushed through a real democratic initiative, the CIA came in and created a *coup d'état* to install bought-off politicians. If your country had a revolution in the last century, it was probably paid for by the banksters. This definitely includes the "color" revolutions and the "Arab Spring" in year 2011. [37] (Vol. 5)

I assure you, the reader, that the leaders of your country are either bought off, or know they are under threat. In Central America, the grisly death squads and attacks on Liberation Theology Priests and Nuns were CIA funded. Salvador Allende of Chile fell in 1973 under the planning of one of our main characters in this book, once again, Monster Henry Kissinger. [38]

Under CIA and Henry Kissinger, Operation Condor was a campaign of assassination and intelligence-gathering dubbed as counter-terrorism (See School of Americas, Vol. 5) conducted jointly by the security services of Argentina, Bolivia, Brazil, Chile, Paraguay, and Uruguay in the mid-1970s. They also exchanged cruel torture techniques (genital mutilation, Vol. 1), like near drowning and playing the sound recordings of victims who were being tortured to their family.

At least 80,000 people disappeared and were systematically murdered without trial. Targets were alleged "terrorists," but in reality victims were political opponents and their families. The U.S. organized Operation Condor was a Globalist destabilization/consolidation program.

> **March 2013:** "A trial that opened Tuesday in Buenos Aires is the first to consider the totality of crimes carried out under Operation Condor, a coordinated [by U.S.] campaign by various U.S. backed Latin American dictatorships in the 1970s and 1980s to hunt down, torture and murder tens of thousands of opponents of those regimes.
>
> "Operation Condor was prosecuted in the name of a crusade against "terrorism." Its methods in many ways prefigured the systematic and continuing crimes carried out by the [Obama] U.S. government decades later with its use of "extraordinary rendition," torture and "targeted killings."
>
> "The case will take up the disappearance and murder of 106 people, the greatest number of them Uruguayans, but also Chileans, Paraguayans, Bolivians, Argentines and one Peruvian.
>
> "While other cases in both Spain and Italy have touched on the crimes carried out under Operation Condor, the Argentine trial is of far greater historic weight. This is the country in which an estimated 30,000 workers, students, left-wing activists, intellectuals and others targeted by the regime are believed to have been abducted and executed, and where the greatest number of killings of foreigners was carried out.
>
> "Those who organized Operation Condor included the *military* regimes in Argentina, Chile, Uruguay, Brazil, Bolivia, and Paraguay. Peru and Ecuador also participated in some of the operation's crimes. The U.S. government, and in particular, former Secretary of State **Henry Kissinger** (Gloria Steinem's boyfriend, Vol.1), provided crucial support for the bloody repression carried out under the mantle of Condor."
>
> – Bill Van Auken, Global Research, March 07, 2013 [39]

(Interestingly, I've seen no updates posted on the internet in English about this trial in the past two years.)

Only a few leaders world wide are somewhat independent, and they can be targeted with very sophisticated weaponry. Cancer, Alzheimer's and other diseases can be created with directed energy weapons. Directed energy weapons are used to bring down airplanes. Many leaders, including scores of American congressmen and celebrities like young John Kennedy Jr. (Page 80), have been killed this way. [40] These directed energy weapons can dissolve buildings, as we will see when we study 9/11 in Vol. 5.

* * *

As just one perfect proof that an international criminal conspiracy actually impacts our daily lives, the Yom Kippur War between Israel and Arab countries in 1973, was planned at a Bilderberg Meeting in order to create an international oil crisis. The war would be an excuse for New World Order controlled OPEC to raise prices. Duped Americans would blame "Arabs."

> "The May 1973 meeting of the Bilderberg Group occurred five months prior to the extensive oil price rises brought about by the Yom Kippur War. However, according to leaked minutes from the meeting, a 400% increase in the price of oil was discussed, and meeting participants were creating a plan [on] how to manage the about-to-be-created flood of oil dollars." [41]

The planned Arab-Israeli war and planned OPEC backlash would cause the entire world to suffer an oil shortage and a price increase. The money made by the OPEC nations with inflated prices would be "recycled" as investments in U.S. banks. Placed by Nelson Rockefeller, **Henry Kissinger** was key to instrumenting this plan, and this is why he gained so much power. When someone knows what chips are about to fall, they can place their bets. In the graph below note how the 25 year stable price of oil (red) then shot up after the Yom Kippur War.

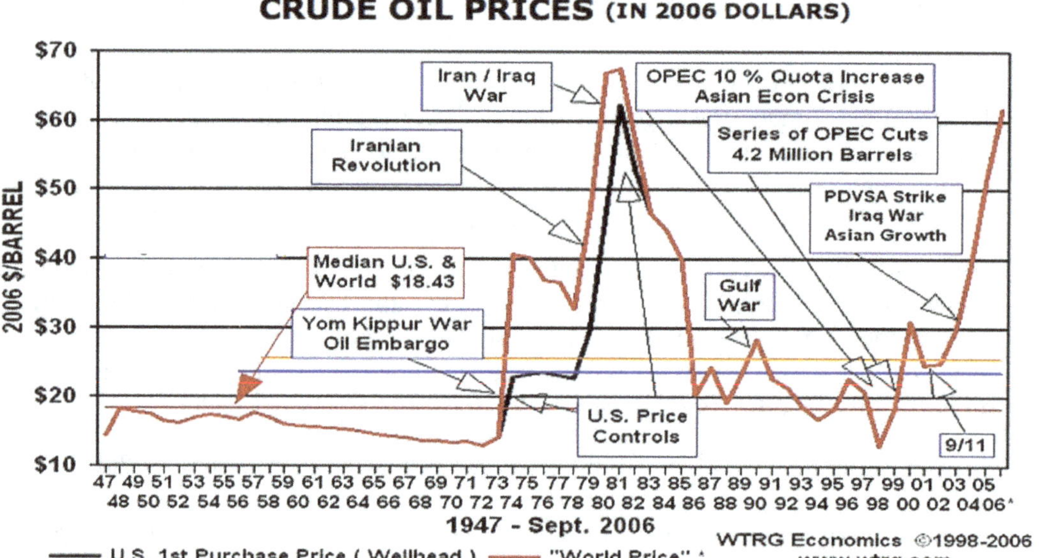

> "In 1979, the Iranian Revolution spurred another massive increase in the price of oil. The Western nations, particularly the United States, had put a freeze on Iranian assets, effectively restricting the access of Iran to the global oil market. The Iranian assets freeze became a major factor in the huge oil price increases of 1979 and 1981." Added to this, in 1979, British Petroleum cancelled major oil contracts for oil supply, which, along with cancellations taken by Royal Dutch Shell, drove the price of oil up higher.
>
> "... However, in 1979, the Federal Reserve, now the lynch-pin of the international monetary system, which was awash in petro-dollars (oil profits invested in U.S. dollars) as a result of the 1973 oil crisis, decided to take a different action from the one it had taken earlier." ...

Paul Volcker [who we just met] became the new Chairman of the Federal Reserve System, and immediately took drastic action to fight inflation by radically increasing interest rates. The world was taken by shock. This was a policy that would not only be felt in the U.S. with a recession, but was to send shock waves around the world, devastating the Third World debtor nations.

"This was likely the ultimate aim of the 1970s oil shocks and the 1979 Federal Reserve shock therapy. With the raising of interest rates, the cost of international money also rose. Thus, the interest rates on international loans made throughout the 1970s rose from 2% in the 1970s to 18% in the 1980s …" [Mistakenly blamed on President Carter by some.]

"The IMF "negotiated standby loans with debtors offering temporary assistance to states [nations] in need. In return for the loans, [nations] agreed to undertake structural adjustment programs (SAPs) …

"The nature of SAPs is such that the conditions imposed upon countries that sign onto these agreements include: lowering budget deficits, devaluing the currency, limiting government borrowing from the central bank, liberalizing foreign trade, reducing public sector wages, price liberalization, deregulation and altering interest rates. For reducing budget deficits, precise "ceilings" are placed on all categories of expenditure; the state [the nation that is no longer sovereign] is no longer permitted to mobilize its own resources for the building of public infrastructure, roads, or hospitals, etc.

"Joseph Stiglitz wrote that, "… In some cases the agreements stipulated what laws the country's Parliament would have to pass to meet IMF requirements or 'targets'—and by when." Further, "The conditions went beyond economics into areas that properly belong in the realm of politics," and that "the way conditionality was imposed made the conditions politically *unsustainable*; when a new government came into power, they would be abandoned. Such conditions were seen as the intrusion by the new colonial power [the *Globalists*, or New World Order] on the country's own sovereignty."

– Andrew Gavin Marshall [42]

By manipulating prices, the entire structure of most governments, their economies, their people's living conditions *and their culture* came under the dictates of the *Globalists*. Colonization has never ended.

Financial destabilization leads to consolidation of control. Total world control is the goal, not making money per se, but gaining more power, by undermining local strength.

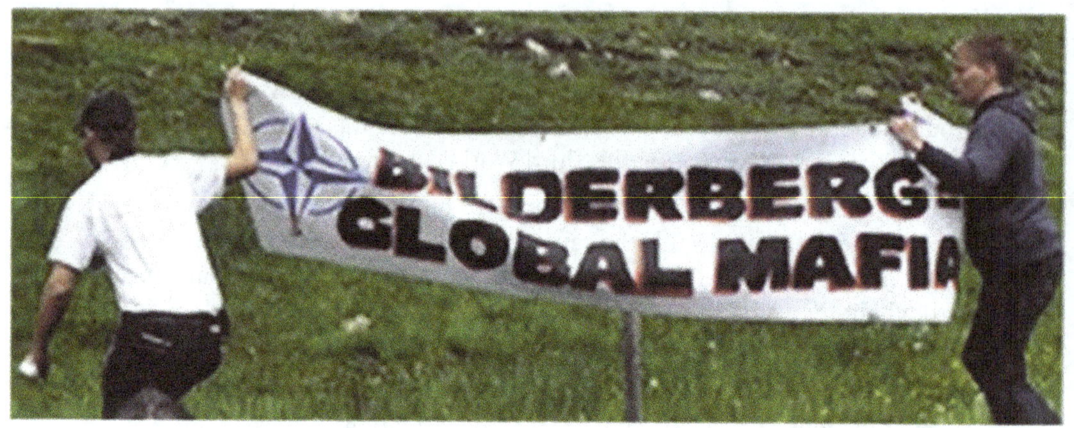

* * *

In the past, the *Globalists* did not control us because we all used to live as *indigenous* free people in direct relationship with the Earth Mother, with no landlord or banks. For example, before 1954, there was not really a South Vietnam, there were just people living in ancient tribal territories growing food. Same for much of Libya and Afghanistan. Actually, this is true for most rural areas in the "undeveloped" countries 50 years ago. Even today there are places too "poor" = self-sufficient to be involved in *globalization*, but these people are now targeted. They are the "BOP," the bottom of the pyramid.

Of course, the ancient way of being free of government was not paradise. The "good old days" were more free of bureaucracy and toxins, but not free of adversity. There will never be freedom from adversity because the multi-verse (formally called universe) is always changing, and the attempt to get beyond adversity, and not go along with nature, destroys nature. Spiritual people don't fight nature, they live in balance with her.

This way of talking about nature was also *co-opted* (See Glossary) by the insincere UN in their Agenda 21 "green sustainability" language of 1992. (This is the subject of another book series, on *co-opt* of environmental movement.) They invited lots of *indigenous* people to the UN as poster boys and girls, and then ignored everything they had to say. The UN is still doing this. The policy of taking American Indian chiefs to meet the Great White Father continues today, with *indigenous* leaders invited to the UN to be given prostitutes, drugs, and any and all temptations, and then given large sums of money from NGO foundations. The poster elders, taken right out of the bush, are paid off and completely corrupted in the process. I saw this in Bolivia. They are not given a thousand dollars, they are given $200,000 dollars to keep them quiet. Instead of protecting their ancient culture, they pollute their community with disparity, materialism, envy, and *grasping desire* that will induct them into the "emerging market and the formal economy."

Earth Mother is what our bodies are made of. Everything we can see except the sun, moon, and stars is the Earth Mother. This kind of talk in UN Agenda 21 is used to trick people to think the new laws respect nature. They do not at all. In trying to "protect" nature, a *monoculture* order is to be stamped on to every continent. Diversity is to be smashed, and that is not nature.

(One person used extensively by the *Globalists* as a poster boy is Tibet's seemingly naïve Dalai Lama, who I met in 1974.)

Both the web of ecology and the economic pyramid are moving toward collapse. *And the Globalists know this.* This is why they have a big seed vault on a remote island in Norway. This is why they produce TV shows like *The Day After,* viewed by 100 million people in 1983 to subliminally *(predictive programming)* prepare us for doom and fear and dependence on Big Brother, rather than prepare you, as I am doing, for *rejuvenation of the culture itself.*

Globalist *"progress"* is *doublespeak* for disaster, which is what the future is looking like under their leadership. When we get hip to this, we can sabotage their plans and try something sane like working with our neighbors instead of only for our own retirement. A comfortable retirement is not in the cards for most people, no matter how much you think is in your IRA account. I promise it will be raided and be reduced to nothing. The future is lean, not fat.

Some people live for the fortune
Some people live just for the fame
Some people live for the power, yeah
Some people live just to play the game

Some people think that the physical things
Define what's within
And I've been there before
But that life's a bore

So full of the superficial
Some people want it all
But I don't want nothing at all
If it ain't you baby

Some people want diamond rings
Some just want everything
But everything means nothing
If I ain't got you

– from song "If I Ain't Got You" by Alicia Keys

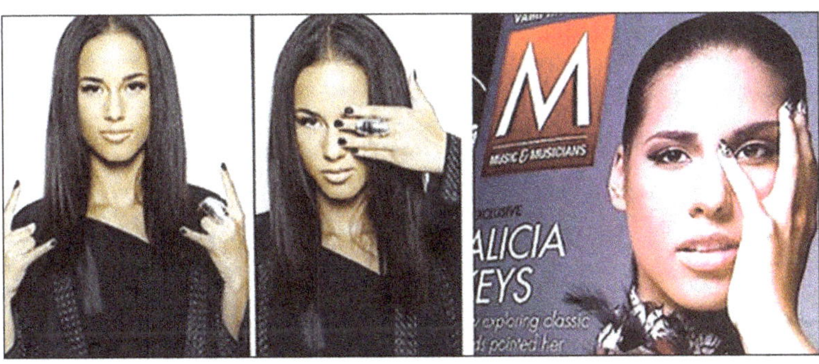

Alicia Keys is a brilliant musical artist, but to become famous, she had to play the Illuminati game, which we will explore in coming chapters.

* * *

The terms "One World Government" or "New World Order" means monopoly or *monoculture*, in which no culture is to have its own independent unique identity. Everything will be concentrated under one authority, one law, one code, if the *Globalists* get their way.

Globalization is about control, not about "economics." Some people who have not studied *doublespeak* are confused by terms like "free trade." Free trade has penalties for not participating. It is hardly free. Countries are forced into "free" trade agreements by fear of being left out, which amounts to economic sanctions. That force is what is called control. Just like *indigenous* poster boys, all leaders and diplomats and generals are wined and dined and given prostitutes and boys (sorry, it's true) and bribed into being part of "progress." "Free trade" means "controlled trade" with strict severe regulations.

Globalization is a continuation of colonization. In Africa some call it "re-colonization." In South America it is called "land concentration." In Australia it is called mining. In Europe and North America it is called "outsourcing." In India or China, each with over a billion people, there are very rural people and ultra *urban people*. I understand *globalization* the way GMO activist Vandana Shiva of Delhi sees it. *Globalization* is a crime.

"Nature shrinks as capital grows."

– Vandana Shiva

- **Chinese environmental activist faces prison sentence for …**
  www.washingtonpost.com/world/chinese-environmental-activist-faces …
  BEIJING — A retired Chinese forestry official who became an environmental activist campaigning against deforestation and overdevelopment on China's southern …
- **Chinese Activist Accuses Apple Supplier Foxconn of …**
  online.wsj.com/article/SB10001424127887323681904578643790739425074 …
  August 02, 2013 A prominent Chinese activist is taking aim at Apple Inc. supplier Foxconn and a lesser-known manufacturer in a recent report that accuses the …
- **China's environmental activists — FT.com** www.ft.com
  Environmental activists often point to the emergence of social media such as Weibo as a turning point for their cause. "people were like shattered glass …" [Remember this quote when we look at words to song "Skyscraper" (Chapter 15)]
- **China's Environmental Activists — Organic Consumers …**
  www.organicconsumers.org/articles/article_28353.cfm
- **China's repression of activists continues unabated — The …**
  www.washingtonpost.com/opinions/chinas-repression-of-activists …
  January 23, 2014 · CHINA'S COMMUNIST leaders ought to regard activists like Xu Zhiyong as allies in their effort to reform the country's … environmental and social ills.

The *Washington Post,* which ran some of these articles, is a Globalist rag. I include these above, because it is the West that exported industry to China in the 1990s with tremendous investments. Clinton's "free trade" resulted in most countries losing their industrial base, which is now run by wage slaves in China with the Mother Earth there being severely polluted. All this to keep us dumbed down with Walmart cheap crap which Walmart founder claimed was "raising our standard of living." Walmart is a study in itself.

What is progress? What is a high standard of living?

* * *

The corporate aspect of *Globalization* is organized using trade agreements through the World Trade Organization (WTO), World Bank and IMF, which are all *Roth-efeller* creations. Trade agreements override the sovereignty of nations by making various governments conform to an outside model. The governments change the laws for their citizens to tow the line of the model. The biggest impact is that nations cannot protect themselves from cheaper overseas products, which destroys local markets and thus local communities. Mission accomplished for the *Globalists* who want their convenient-to-manage *monoculture*.

The government aspect of *Globalization* is organized by the United Nations, which was a second attempt after the League of Nations failed. The 1919 Treaty of Versailles and the League of Nations were headed by the *Rothschild* banksters. As chronicled above, the control freak Rothschilds owned half the world's wealth in the 18th century and funded a wide and deep intelligence network. They intermarried with British royalty. The British Empire was their project. They never left India or South Africa, so if you adulate Gandhi or Mandela, that's because you were fooled by *controlled media* and false biographical movies. The *same money system* that created the governments these men overthrew are still in place and *creating the laws of these countries now.*

I went to Pretoria to take part in a vigil at the hospital for Mandela's recovery. I meditated on the sidewalk and made friends with international news crews. I found out later he had already died, and we were all tricked. It is impossible that Mandela was not under mind control protocols while he was in prison. He entered as a communist and came out in favor of "privatization." South Africa is a land of barbed wire … to keep out the natives. If hearing that the myth you put on a pedestal was a puppet, I don't mean to hurt your feelings, but this book is about waking up. Our values, the people we hate or love, are sold to us.

Was Mandela a complete sell out? In my opinion, no. In 1990 he stood up to Puppet Clinton who did not want him to visit Gaddafi, who had financed Mandela in the struggle against apartheid. Without Gaddafi's support there would still be apartheid in South Africa. In recent news, 24 years later, Mandela was under surveillance by the FBI when he came to the U.S. in 1990 because they didn't trust him. That means the *Globalists* were afraid of a *hero* with a mind of his own.

"The FBI documents, which were partially redacted, were released to Massachusetts of Technology doctoral candidate Ryan Shapiro, who had filed a Freedom of Information Act. "What's missing from these documents is often as illuminative as what's disclosed," Shapiro said." [43]

> "No country can claim to be the policeman of the world and no state can dictate to another what it should do. Those that yesterday were friends of our enemies have the gall today to tell me not to visit my brother Gaddafi. They are advising us to be ungrateful and forget our friends of the past."
>
> – Nelson Mandela, Tripoli, May 18, 1990

> "As we are liberated from our own fear, our presence automatically liberates others."
>
> – Nelson Mandela

Here are some more quotes showing that Mandela was not owned by the *Globalists* ...

> "I have also invited Brother Leader Gaddafi to this country. And I do that because our moral authority [the *personal sovereignty* of conscience] dictates that we should not abandon those who helped us in the darkest hour, in the history of this country. Not only did the Libyans support us, they gave us the resources for us to conduct our struggle, and to win. And those South Africans who have berated me for being loyal to our friends, can literally go and jump into a pool."
>
> In a 1999 speech: "Israel should withdraw from all the areas which it won from the Arabs in 1967, and in particular Israel should withdraw completely from the Golan Heights, from south Lebanon and from the West Bank."
>
> "The UN took a strong stand against apartheid; and over the years, an international consensus was built, which helped to bring an end to this iniquitous system. **But we know too well that our freedom is incomplete without the freedom of the Palestinians."**
>
> On the U.S. preparing its war against Iraq in 2002: "If you look at these matters, you will come to the conclusion that the attitude of the United States of America is a threat to world peace. **If there is a country that has committed unspeakable atrocities in the world, it is the U.S. They don't care for human beings."** [He was right. U.S. has killed 1.5 million people so far in Iraq and poisoned the land with uranium ammunition, causing birth defects.]

As far as Gandhi, I know the inside story of that incarnation intimately and that is the energy behind this writing. Gandhi was used. He was given land by *Rothschild* handler Hermann Kallenbach for his Tolstoy Farm in South Africa and then brought to India by East India Company moderate Gopal Krishna Gokhale. His Jewish handler was Herman Kallenbach. He was placed in every sense of the word and the movie about him lies about this. He wasn't discovered in India; he was *co-opted* in South Africa. Gandhi's greatness was steered and used. The part of him that was great was trivialized in a recent biography by a Globalist minion named Joseph Lelyveld, a former executive editor of the *New York Times*. The biography doesn't quote Gandhi, just describes his toenails. Gandhi's legacy is a thorn in the little remaining conscience of the *Globalists* because he was coming from a place of *personal sovereignty*, though was confused. The facts about Gokhale aren't quite forthcoming in Gandhi's autobiography. Memoirs are always streamlined it seems. Gandhi had an appendicitis without anesthetics. [44] He was more than a nice guy or an idealist or a politician, and has served numerous and diverse lifetimes on Earth, but he was used. India never got independence, as proven by how GMO company Monsanto Inc. (eugenist Bill Gates is big investor) is protected in India, while destabilizing/consolidating huge sections of the agrarian base.

Any new influence, talent, personality, invention is quickly incorporated or *co-opted* by the all seeing *Globalists*. When you have unlimited funds and live for control, this is what you do. You cover all bases so you can win EVERYTHING.

As noted, the *Globalists* create wars so they can loan to both sides of conflict, whose governments will then pay off the loans using our taxes. Their war machine keeps on truckin'. War is the greatest business of the banksters with guaranteed pay back. With a small investment in buying off or blackmailing government leaders (*cutouts*) (See Glossary), they reap access to the tax base of the world. Another small investment is creating protests, movements, covert cells, supplying arms, supplying anything needed. This is actually the true history we are never told.

Until all the covert operations are exposed, we simply don't know the history of the world.

The process of *Globalization* or New World Order had gone even further then infiltration. The *Globalists* actually create movements from scratch, and create opposition to those same movements from scratch to force issues. A few examples are the Tories (Loyalist Colonists), the Secessionists, the Confederates, the KKK, Communism, Fascism, Zionism, Islamic Fundamentalism, New Age Movement, Feminism, Gay Movement, Zeitgeist Movement, Occupy Movement and the destabilizing groups in Ukraine and Venezuela.

These were all funded from the first day, and are spun by the *controlled Media* in the way the *Globalists* want it spun. Let's admit, please, that corporate media is where we obtain our world view.

The most famous examples of opposing players in the fixed game are the Republican and Democratic parties. If you study who funds them, contributions are given to both sides from the same sources! Each of these contributions helps buy a plank in a candidates platform, and the politician is roped in for life.

"Movements" are funded through proxy "non-profit foundations," which are actually just promotional organs used to save taxes, by groups like Ford, Carnegie, Rockefeller and Gates. Billionaire George Soros, quoted above, personally funds 1500 activist groups. This is not philanthropy, it is hegemony.

When the 1919 League of Nations failed because Americans had independent thoughts and really didn't want a treaty that overrode Congress, the Rothschilds initiated several programs to change American culture and politics. **The Council of Foreign Relations (CFR)** was later set up by the *Roth-efellers* to change American public sense of national identity and to place candidates. *Rothschild* bankster J.P. Morgan had bought up the 25 leading newspapers in 1915. (See Glossary *controlled media*) The education conspiracy which Dodd discovered (Page 23-24), and Einstein and Nader spoke of, was another thread of this plan.

Globalization is the most well funded and organized *social engineering* conspiracy that this planet has ever seen.

* * *

Globalist thinking is now a part of our vocabulary. Every time any of us speak in terms of global justice or global fairness or global anything, we are speaking as *Globalists.* Whenever we ask, "what should be the direction of society?," we are saying there is only one society. Every time we use the word "humanity" the way Bush Sr. said "the world," as if there is only one culture, we are minions of the Illuminati. We aren't the super rich, but we talk like them.

Unless you live in Leningrad or Sao Paulo, these are not your neighborhoods to plan for. But we are all so concerned with "the world." This is distraction. If the *Globalists* weren't so busy intervening everywhere, international news would be in the travel section. Local issues, as Nader warned us, are ignored. This disconnects us from our real responsibility close to home and we fail to be watchdogs and caretakers in our own neighborhoods.

Is your neighborhood 100% free of pollution, crime, or corruption?

This is where we should be focused. But the *controlled media* distracts us in mass. One news story can be shoved before millions of people and distract from what is happening in a million backyards. We only have so many minutes in the day. How many minutes do you spend paying attention to things you have no influence over? We should clean ourselves first, then our homes, then our neighborhoods, then our communities. This strength is the only reality we can really experience. The rest is mostly sensationalist gossip if you think about it.

My work is to convince you to cut off the *Globalists* and their values, and make yourselves and your communities strong.

Globalism is a head trip, not a way of life. In giving our power to the head trip, we have less power to make decisions that will really matter to us. Retaining power for our own decisions for our own way of life is what is called *personal sovereignty.*

To practice *personal sovereignty,* conserve your own energy. You will see that lipstick is a drain. Maybe I should clarify what I mean by lipstick here. *Lipstick is indulgent vanity which distracts us from what is really important.* When you stop supporting lipstick, you will stop giving away attention. You will choose quality over quantity. You will have more mind for that part of us that "does not live by bread alone."

> *Emancipate yourself from mental slavery,*
> *nobody else gonna free your mind ...*
>
> – from "Redemption Song" by Bob Marley

Chapter 4

Entitlement, The Bad Boy

Globalism and *personal sovereignty* are in conflict, not only in policies of the International Monetary Fund (IMF), but in our very own psychological loyalties.

Both the IMF and your psychological attitude has been organized for you, by the same people. Unbelievable? Conspiracy theory? We will examine "lipstick" and you will see that this is no theory.

Personal sovereignty is integrity and integrity depends on inner character which stands on its own feet. *Personal sovereignty* is where you can always win.

The *Globalists* don't have *personal sovereignty* because they feel they are the *entitled* elite and can *depend* on everyone else and use everyone else because they are royalty. This sounds criminal ... however ... we emulate them! We want to be royalty too!

Entitlement (See Glossary), like *consumerism*, is being exported and injected into all social venues. "I deserve high consumption." This is what we tell ourselves is "success" or "progress." "The American lifestyle is non-negotiable."

"Infinite growth is our future," is the Globalist mythology. We worship "prosperity" without question. The herd that never questions this crock are called *sheeple,* combining words sheep and people.

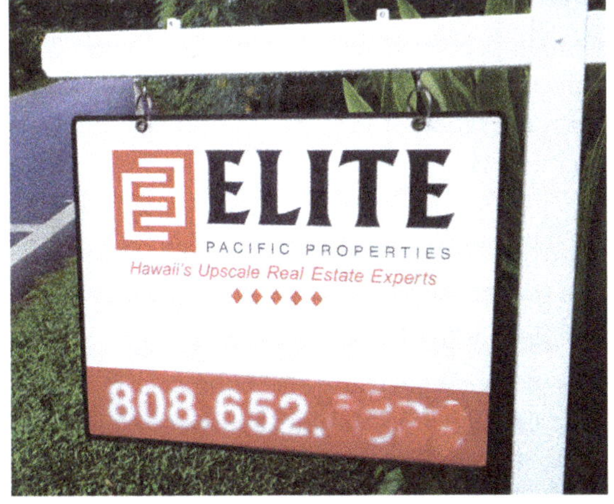

So, besides *consumerism* (I want I want I want), the attitude of being vain and *entitled* (I deserve, I deserve, I deserve) is also being propagated in our values and beliefs. The sheeple are supposed *to expect* more more more. We compare ourselves to the rich and judge ourselves as poor. Our children are taught to say they are "bored" if they don't have more more more. We wish we could walk on the red carpet too. Our civilization's values are based on envy. Be a King for a day! Then we will have arrived at fame *(vanity)* and fortune (excess). Then we too can be *entitled* at the highest level ... drool.

We will get into sassiness soon enough, but I want to emphasize that *when we examine the link between lipstick and war crimes, self-entitlement is the bad boy.*

Self-entitlement kills our virtue, our sense of decency, and our sense of responsibility to others besides ourselves. It makes us greedy creeps. This is why the elite, who are in fact serial killers, are described as psychopaths by many analysts. Self-entitlement is another way, perhaps, to say "*disconnecting vanity.*" (Glossary)

Self-entitlement is the expectation of high-consumption and to hell with anything else. Me me me. A psychopath is not connected with a greater whole. She or he is all about number one, my life, my needs, my "success."

Self-entitlement works with *consumerism* to extract as much as possible, sucking everything else dry.

* * *

The word "royalty" is *doublespeak* for parasites. Yes, in my opinion, all royalty everywhere are elitist parasites leeching off others, usually with the aid of terrorism. "Bow or your head will be cut off!" I'm talking about the Emperor of China and the Ali'i of Hawaii and King Henry VIII and Shogun so-and-so and Pharaoh what's-his-name and the Maori chiefs and the Incan warlords and every other royalty anywhere. All were bully parasite gangsters who indulged in self-entitlement at the expense of others.

(If there is one good thing about technology it might be the internet, because "succeeding" at the expense of others will get revealed publicly more and more, and *our hearts and our compassion will stop justifying disparity.*)

People with *personal sovereignty* don't terrorize others and rip them off.

But we are complicit. We "small people" also lack *personal sovereignty* when we comply with Globalist planning. It is a big mistake when we let "them" make choices for us. We are not practicing *personal sovereignty* when we act like sheeple. Accepting any "free" benefit from the government is an example.

("Small people" is how British Petroleum Chairman Carl-Henric Svanberg described the general population in 2010, who were getting sick and dying from his Gulf Spill, chemical Corexit spray operations and worse. The real people, not small, are still getting sick. Search "Blue Plague" on internet.)

The elite *Globalists* want more power. They can never have enough. They are insatiable and controlled by *grasping desire.* (See Glossary) Because they aren't using their influence for balance and reciprocal give and take with others, whatever they have in their hearts falls into a black hole and they need more, more, more.

It is in giving back and recycling care that we are rejuvenated, but they don't know about this because they are stuck in this make believe place of "owning." The ego doesn't exist but they *think* it does. No one owns anything, but *disconnecting vanity* thinks it does. The navigating intellect (within all we human types), has become bloated and has blocked the flow from their hearts. This navigating intellect is oh so proud of "getting ahead." And the elite try to feed this *vanity,* but *vanity* can't give back, it can only suck everything to hold itself up. So there they are, in the purgatory of one way grasping.

Having more money than they could possibly spend, the super rich turn to manipulation of society as their game. So now they are not only grasping stuff, they are grasping power *over* others.

So lets stop here for a second …

They *need others* to prove their power.
So then, power over others is not their own power.
It is dependent power (oxymoron).
This is not *personal sovereignty*
or connection with spirit within.
This is a power trip that takes
the opposite direction,
away from openness and communion
and toward relative position,
me over you.
This is duality
and being lost,
not unity and true knowing
that needs nothing
and loves others.

In their game they like to display their proof of winning so they can gloat in an imagined legacy. If they are super rich, they build things like the Taj Mahal or the Rockefeller Tower or the Clinton Library or this monument or that. These monuments do not stand for virtue, they are monuments to *vanity*. Every ancient man-made "wonder" is the same.

If a person who is controlled by *grasping desire* is not rich enough to build a monument, maybe he or she will go shopping and buy a new car or a new dress! It is the same *vanity*. Most of us are part of this *grasping desire* mind set. If you want to show something off, it is *vanity*, period!

This is why poor people are often more soulful than the wealthy. A miser has money, but will find some way to show it off *rather than share*. To get super rich you have to know how to hoard.

Do *indigenous people* have *vanity* and *grasping desire*? Absolutely yes! But our modern *vanity* is a fashion sold to us. It is now *cultural* to feel *self-entitled*. This is new. We all think we are kings and queens. In fact our girls are taught to be "princesses." There are simply no other role models for young girls except princesses, female warriors, or deranged proud sluts who are "awesome." The goal for most girls now is to always be on stage. It is not enough to sing, one has to have a microphone and strut your stuff and have swagger and attitude.

The elite compete with each other and have award ceremonies and big parties. When "Logo" Obama visited the UK in May 2011, he brought 500 people as his entourage. We paid for that. This is how royalty try to impress each other. If you notice how his wife (her/his gender is in question) dresses, there is nothing humble about her. She likes being royal. She is different than any other first lady before her. She is royal.

Those ruled by *vanity*, then love to give each other medals and titles. "Lord" this and "Lord" that, "Emperor of the Sun," "So and so the Great," "The Sun King." This is somehow meaningful to them. Their "love" is pointed toward the self, and is self-absorbed, is self-centered, is self-indulgent. Their "love" is lipstick.

People ruled by *disconnecting vanity* live for the appearance of importance which, as I've said, *depends* on underlings to prop up this image. Even if they might have to pay an audience to applaud, they exalt in the pride of "success." Me me me, I am so grand grand grand. *Even if they have to lie in their memoirs, they will do so.* When I think about this, it seems quite insane. How can they take pride in a lie? Don't they realize history will reveal the lie and they will be remembered as a liar? Bill Clinton is incredible. I wonder if he lies to himself in his sleep?

They need the adulation of others for self-esteem. This means they really don't have self-esteem, doesn't it? Exactly.

Vanity creates this puffed up "self" while true self-esteem is selfless. Why do I say that? You see, *personal sovereignty* melts into altruistic service as we grow spiritually. The more of a truthful listening heart we have, the less me-me-me remains. It is as if the quiet has power. But it is not power to mess with others, it is the power to be responsible. This inner quiet manifests as *compassion.* So we could say it is selfless.

People ruled by *vanity* live to put their thumb on others, while they themselves live under the thumb of their own *vanity.* We've all seen megalomaniacs. The reader has met puffed up bullies and knows about wife beaters, so we all know how negative it can be. And every one of us has to guard against this in our own selves. This syndrome certainly isn't new. It is an ancient character fault, outlined in most myths and epic stories that formed the moral coordinates for past civilizations.

However, this *vanity* is now *organized* like never before, to convert all of us to vain values and chasing. All advertising is based on making us feel lacking and we are supposed to answer this by being vain and wanting status.

The traditional epic stories taught about virtue. In the modern world, we strive for "success" and our heroes lack virtue. Our "heroes" and "idols" are women painted up to look like sex objects and war criminals who bomb civilians. We idolize lipstick and war crimes.

The fact that we have pride in this is some kind of testimony about our vulnerability to darkness.

I call this disease "*disconnecting vanity*" because it disconnects us from virtue, which is what we wisely seek by living a life of *inner personal sovereignty.* Virtue nurtures health. Lack of virtue decays to sickness.

* * *

The very same leaders who call for peace and "green" international laws are the ones funding wars and building polluting factories. What comes out of Globalist mouths in terms of platitudes is opposite to what they invest in. The *Globalists* are con men and actors. They are *nice guys* in public and *sneaks* behind closed doors.

Having almost unlimited funds, they can, as mentioned, manipulate any opposition to get their way. When I say unlimited funds, consider that the 10 *Rothschild* affiliated banks who *are* the FED have collected interest on every dollar they printed for one hundred years.

To control both sides of an issue, the mega rich *Globalists* buy off and place mouth pieces, called *"cutouts."* A *cutout* is like a paper cartoon with clever message that the banksters cut out of a newspaper and pin on a bulletin board. Then the next day they cut out another cartoon character and replace the first. Most politicians are funded replaceable *cutouts* or place holders. New face, same bulletin board. In other words, the bankster Globalist Illuminati fix the game so that one administration after another has the same policies. This allows them to frame the entire debate and the outcome.

A *controlled media*, (formally called the yellow press) steers the public reaction to the policies read out loud by the *cutouts* from the Globalist script. Obama, Bush Jr., Clinton, Bush Sr., Reagan, Carter, Ford, Nixon, Johnson. None of these *cutouts* wrote their own speeches or came up with policy.

Do you think Democrat Carter was much different than Republican Nixon? Henry Kissinger, who handled Republican Nixon's foreign policy, worked for Nelson **Rockefeller** for ten years. Zbigniew Brzezinski, who handled Democrat Jimmy Carter's foreign policy, also created the Trilateral Commission with David **Rockefeller.** The Rockefellers are the American branch of the *Rothschild* global bankster network.

So the *Roth-efellers* controlled the foreign policy of a "Republican" and then a "Democratic" administration. Nixon or Carter, Republican or Democrat, twiddle dee or twiddle dumb.

More *cutouts?* David Cameron, Gordon Brown, Tony Blair, John Major, Margaret Thatcher, James Callaghan, Harold Wilson, Edward Heath.

Down under? Anthony Abbott, Kevin Rudd, Julia Gillard, John Howard, Paul Keating, Robert Lee …

These people have no say in policy. They are mouthpieces. Electing them is just a big game to trick the masses into thinking we have some say. We don't. All these presidents and prime ministers were and are owned and controlled by the *Globalists.*

Australian Prime Minister Paul Keating apologized for the horrific treatment of Aboriginal peoples in 1992, same year as the Rio Summit and Agenda 21. No coincidence there. Both the Keating speech and Rio were insincere tricks. The grotesque "Intervention" against native communities in Northern Territories for trumped up reasons by the Howard administration in 2007 [45] is proof that Keating was just a *cutout* and did not set policy. Australia wants to destroy the last traditional people in Northern Territories to get the minerals. The 1992 Keating speech was just a fluffy feel-good event which changed nothing. His speech just mollified people. That is the job of politicians.

None of these *cutouts* can be trusted. We didn't really elect them. If you web search "voting machine fraud," you will find unanswered questions. My theory, and this is just my pondering, is that campaigns are funded to bring about as much of a split 50/50 vote as possible, and then the voting machine can just tweak a tiny percentage of votes to bring about the desired winner. The winner will be the one who most embraces Globalist thinking. The opponent is just there to give voice to what looks like a fair debate. I share this possibility for others to weigh. Maybe it has some merit.

Our "elected" officials were advertised into our lives, funded to win, and must tow the line once in office or they will be run out by a funded opponent, the way *Hero* Cynthia McKinney was defeated. Or if too popular, they will be "terminated with extreme prejudice." Executed. Seriously, no joke. Four American Presidents have been assassinated, and all by the banksters.

Hero Senator Paul Wellstone from Minnesota died in a plane crash in 2002, as did John Kennedy Jr. in 1999 (mentioned above). These were assassinations. Wellstone was one of the only Senators standing up to the Bush administration's repeated lies, and his voter support surged when he voted against war in Iraq. [46] John Kennedy Jr. had printed an exposé about Israel in his magazine *George*.

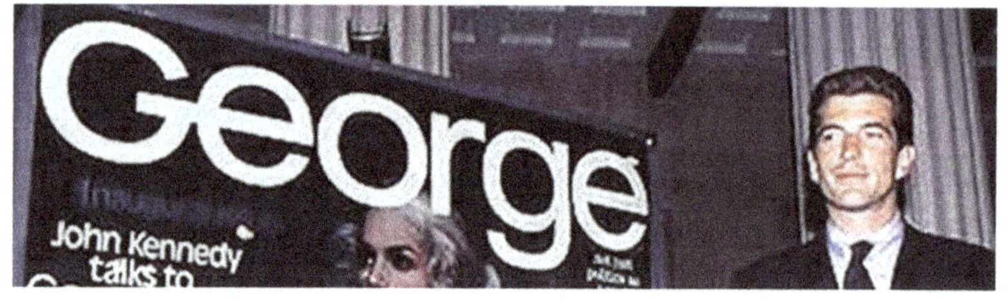

For those who think it impossible that a U.S. Senator would be assassinated by the *Globalists*, just keep reading. The pattern is outrageous and I hope you are outraged. This book isn't only about lipstick and I hope you become angry. (But if you've been programmed by the New Age Operation, you won't, because you've been castrated. (Pages 259-260)

As alluded to, if control through bribes doesn't work, the banksters have thugs on salary and *always have.* The thugs include the FBI, CIA, MI6 (UK), Mossad (Israel), TSA, NSA, etc. etc. Government covert ops are not independent from the banksters. Please understand there is only one pyramid of power in the world and it is based on debt.

Russia, China, India and many other countries are starting to break away from the "Anglosphere," as the oil thuggery and bankruptcy of the U.S. becomes ever more obvious. This is making the *Globalists* desperate, by the way.

They had hoped for a real pandemic in 2009, but it fizzled, and now the WHO is disgraced for calling a nothing flu a "pandemic," as they and the CDC had organized that fake swine flu scare. I had tracked the Center of Disease Control count each day, and it went up a power of 10 every eight days, 40, 400, 4000, 40,000 and then they suddenly stopped counting. Those numbers proved to be a lie, as exposed by *Hero* CBS reporter Sharon Attkisson who was stone walled when asking for information from CDC. And it ends up there were never 800 deaths in Mexico city from the swine flu. It was all a media fabrication in real time. [47]

The CDC is a front, and every health department in the world should break from them. The *Roth-efeller* World Health Organization cannot be trusted. WHO actually changed the definition of a pandemic *during* the swine flu crisis so that any flu, any year, could now be declared a "pandemic." [48]

The swine flu was not as deadly as they had planned. It did not produce a worldwide emergency in which the economy of world could have been shut down, rebooted, and consolidated under martial law. The *Globalists* are no longer on schedule and in control and are running now on contingency plans. They are out of step as disclosure is breathing down their necks, as the world wakes up.

By SHARYL ATTKISSON CBS NEWS *October 27, 2009, 6:05 PM*

Freedom of Information: Stalled at CDC and D.C. Government

Shares / Tweets / Stumble / Email More +

(CBS)

In August 2009, CBS News made a simple request of the Centers for Disease Control and Prevention for public documents, e-mails and other materials CDC used to communicate to states the decision to stop testing individual cases of Novel H1N1, or "swine flu." When the public affairs folks at CDC refused to produce the documents and quit responding to my queries altogether, I filed a formal Freedom of Information (FOI) request for the materials. Members of the news media are entitled to expedited access, which I requested, since this was for a pending news report and on an issue of public health and interest.

The Obama administration made a commitment to a "new era of open government," as stated in a presidential memorandum on the Freedom of Information Act (FOIA). On March 19, 2009, Attorney General Eric Holder issued new FOIA guidelines to "restore the public's ability to access information in a timely manner."

Two months after my FOI request, the CDC has yet to produce any of these easily retrievable materials. Sadly, this is of little surprise. This has become standard operating procedure in Washington.

* * *

The Illuminati prey on peoples' highest wishes. They use the soft part of us, the part that cares and hopes, and they work it to their advantage. That is the art of a con artist, to win trust and take advantage of it.

Platitudes like "peace" and "green" and "human rights" and "*democracy*" and "*freedom*" are just used to make the *cutouts* sound popular. They will really say anything. Peoples' sincere hopes are used as excuses for more and more regulations to give *Globalists* even more control. We have to stay "safe" after all. Has the reader noticed that the standards of safety keep getting more and more invasive?

> "The recommended childhood vaccination schedule has changed dramatically over the years, with children now receiving upwards of 30 vaccines, including multiple combi-

> nation vaccines, before the age of six. And in many cases, doctors and nurses administer half a dozen or more vaccines all at once during a single visit to make sure children get all these shots and to save time. But according to data compiled from the government's *Vaccine Adverse Events Reporting System* (VAERS), as many as 145,000 children or more have died throughout the past 20 years as a result of this multiple vaccine dose approach, and few parents are aware of this shocking fact."
>
> – Naturalnews.com [49]

The U.S. *military* has a long tradition of using its soldiers as medical guinea pigs.

> "In recent years, with the involvement of pharmaceutical executives like Donald Rumsfeld with the Department of Defense, the trend has accelerated. Now hundreds of thousands of U.S. servicemen and women receive vaccines that are untested and experimental in nature.
>
> "On October 16, 2006, the Department of Defense announced that it will resume its previously court-halted anthrax vaccination program and that troops who do not agree to receive the six-injection series voluntarily will be faced with disciplinary action."
>
> – The Roots of Gulf War Illness … Video [50]

The need for ever more "health" now requires new laws which makes the state health program mandatory. These laws will give more profits to the related industries. The laws establish a penalty for not participating. The public becomes a captive market. We are caged.

Hold on! This is my body isn't it? You see, this gets very personal, very quickly.

Now, by law in the U.S., citizens do not have rights over their own bodies. "Obama-Care" legislation passed in October 2013 mandates implanted "Radio Frequency Identification" (RFID) chips in all Americans [51], though, this is not mentioned in mainstream news.

Obama-Care allows chipping of the entire population … "The HR 3962 Bill is an exact copy of the HR 3200 Bill except for just a few words removed concerning the RFID Microchip, but the ability to chip every citizen of the United States is still in the bill. Read Pages 1501 thru 1510 housedocs.house.gov. Then read Class II Special Controls Guidance For FDA Staff www.fda.gov." [52] Children in the state of Wyoming have received implanted RFID chips without their parents' consent. [53]

One company that makes breast implants for women includes RFID chips in the implant …

"Breast augmentation is one of the most popular cosmetic surgery procedures, with a staggering 300,000 women in America alone receiving breast implants every year.

"*Establishment Labs*, a major breast, body and facial aesthetic company which has offices in both Europe and America, recently announced that it has teamed up with *VeriTeQ* to produce breast implants, 'with a radio frequency identification (RFID) tag built in, with the goal of providing information about the implant to a patient long after the device has been inserted into her body … The CEO previously tried to market the implantable microchip as a replacement for the credit card.'" [54]

In January 2014 Motorola Mobility, owned by Globalist controlled Google, announced it had patented its "e-tatoo" that can read sub-audible impulses or "thoughts," so that the user can control devices remotely with his/her thoughts.

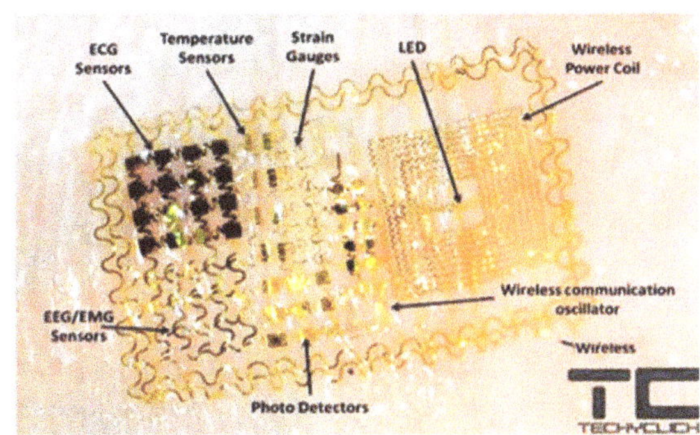

Techies are excited by *any* new technology and many young people who don't have *personal sovereignty* yet, will jump to be wired and "cool." Society will then move another step toward "trans-humanism," the melding of technology and biology, all with proprietary software which most people don't question.

"Progress" has secrets. *"Progress"* includes more control *over you.*

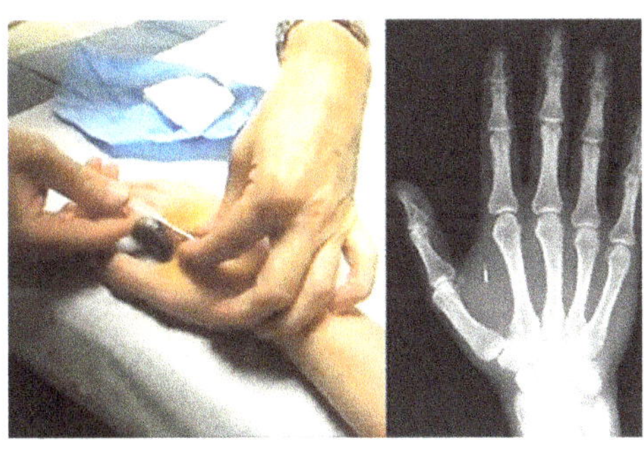

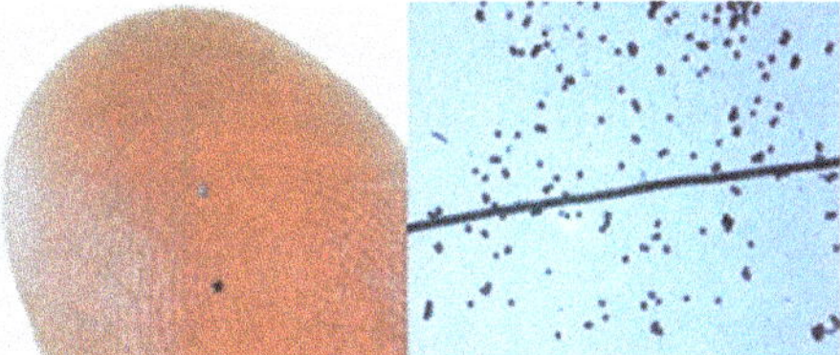

Hitachi 2012 RFID chips can be injected.

Something is being pushed on us. If Big Brother is taking care of me, do I get to be an adult or will I always be a subordinate? Will the choices concerning my own body be taken away from me? It appears this is happening already. What about the body of my child, or the body of my grandchild? Must I lose *personal sovereignty* and become an irresponsible parent in order to be a good citizen in the eyes of the state? (The *Globalists* won't say it out loud but their answer is, "Exactly!")

Like frogs slowly getting boiled, we see there is something wrong but accept it with resignation. "You can't stop progress." "I gotta work." "Yea, its terrible."

What do we get out of being in this system? This is where *consumerism* steps up to feed us candy, toys, and lipstick to dumb down the question.

"The world is messed up, but at least I am content." Admit it, this is how you and almost everyone you know thinks. *Entitlement is the bad boy.*

According to our corporate values, the purpose of life is to consume as much as possible. As long as we get "food and games," (bread and circus), we will predictably go along with the Emperor. That is why it is called food and games.

But why should we? Unlike the Emperor, we can be aligned with spirit. We aren't trapped in disconnection like our elite. The trick for us now is to surprise the *Globalists* and stop being addicted to their food and games and do something on our own. It's easy. We will choose virtue and service to the next generation over more stuff and more speed.

MORE LIPSTICK PLEASE

Consumerism is the glue that binds we peons within the "One World" system. *Consumerism* is God for most people. That is, any spiritual values that we had when we lived more naturally and close to the Earth and knew what simplicity was, have been replaced by *grasping desire* for more stuff.

While the American dream remains in place to tempt everyone to chase the carrot and create more carbon emissions, the same *Globalists* who hold the carrot in front of us, want nations to tax themselves for carbon emissions! (Global military geo-engineering creates extreme climate and droughts to fake CO2 crisis.)

This makes no sense until one understands that the *Globalists* have virtually no altruistic or sincere fiber in their character. They could care less about anyone's welfare except their own. They are serial killers, don't forget. To think they want to do anything for the environment while living posh lives and keeping armies of thugs, is not very perceptive. These people are poisonous snakes and that is how they got where they are.

Doublespeak is the language of the forked tongue. The hope to *live off of other people's labor* is the dominant value of our times and it trickles down from the top who are doing just that. And we accept this as normal because we can't remember how we lived when we had an *indigenous* lifestyle.

Indigenous peoples can't even take part in nine-to-five forty-hour-a-week slavery. For most of the world it is 60-70 hours of work. In China (Jungua), laborers have no day off. They work 7 days a week. No sabbath.

Indigenous people don't make good "workers" or good soldiers because living by a time clock goes against their *personal sovereignty.* Martial existence denies the heart. We are made of wind earth fire rain, not gears and wires. *Indigenous peoples* are not inured to regimentation. They aren't mind controlled and phony. They aren't part of the machine cutting up everything. Living for the weekend means dying for the week, and they don't buy it. Saving money to get ahead of the rest of their cousins has no thrill. There is no future to waste time thinking about, when time doesn't exist because one lives in the now.

I doubt any *indigenous people* will ever read this book, as they don't need to.

Most of us have to answer to a foreman who works for an administrator who answers to a CEO who meets in a back room with a Board of Directors who trick and lie to faceless stockholders who are ripped off by the banksters. The average person's goal is to be rich like our master banksters.

This is the "something for nothing" ambition. "I too can be a baron! I won't have to work anymore. Somehow I will live off of other peoples' work. I will sit on the porch of the plantation mansion and sip lemonade!"

This is the general goal in the pyramid-pecking-order-culture that we live in. Winning the lottery means we don't have to work anymore and we can consume as much as we want. The goal of athletes and entertainers is to get rich and "live like a king."

The fact that every king was a greedy miser who subjugated others is something we don't talk about. So this deceit is really in us. We imitate and laud people who really have done little to be proud of. When it is taught in schools how they got so powerful, and the crimes they committed are heaped up in a giant pyramid shaped pile of sorrow, who will want to emulate them? That day is coming.

Just as "Logo" Obama lied about ending wiretapping in his 2008 campaign speech, the woman on the street closes one eye about the problems that our lifestyle brings to other countries and to environment. The way trickle-down deceit works is we have to lie about the crimes of our bosses in order to live with the fact that we work for them.

"In a time of universal deceit, telling the truth is a revolutionary act."

– George Orwell

This American dream of something for nothing luxury, is spreading worldwide. But it is a bankrupt dream. While the world thinks America is rich, 47 million Americans are on food stamps.

If we stopped chasing the American Dream and demanded some long term solutions, we couldn't be farmed any more. Our masters want compliant domesticated farm animals, not people who are centered in their own power and object to corruption.

This is why *personal sovereignty* is being undercut.

Welfare is a way of paying off people to be quiet. And this money isn't coming from anyone's taxes, so no sense in complaining about that. That whole anger is a nice divide-and-conquer myth we should drop. Funds for welfare are just being typed into accounts by the FED. If you don't believe it, research "quantitative easing." A giant slush fund without any accountability (the *Rothschild* FED refuses to be audited) sloshes back and forth, as the *Globalists*, in their elitist boat, try to stay afloat on top of it.

Meanwhile the Earth is about to tell us, loud and clear, that she is running out of everything our civilization claims it needs. I mentioned Peak Oil in the Introduction, but it's really Peak Everything. Many rich nation citizens are squealing in surprise. The middle class is shrinking and nothing on Earth will change this. "The American Dream is now a farce but, shhhhh, don't say anything!"

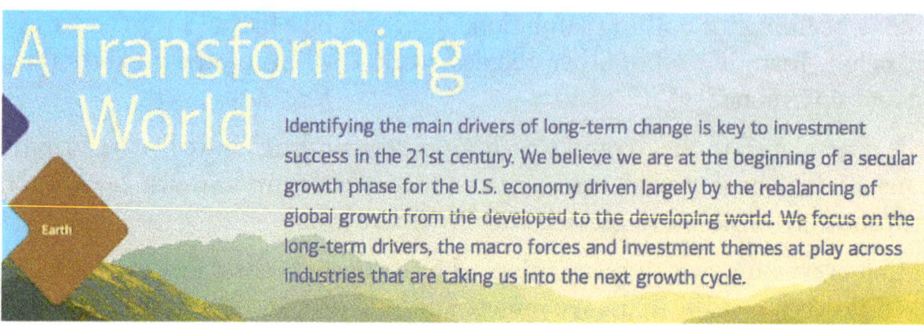

A Transforming World
Identifying the main drivers of long-term change is key to investment success in the 21st century. We believe we are at the beginning of a secular growth phase for the U.S. economy driven largely by the rebalancing of global growth from the developed to the developing world. We focus on the long-term drivers, the macro forces and investment themes at play across industries that are taking us into the next growth cycle.
Earth

The companies that try to organize investment in "long term change" want to attract people who are chasing the carrot of something-for-nothing profit. They hope investors will invest with them as people go homeless outside their doors. One eye closed. It is just con-artist foolery. Transformation to what? Something healthy for the whole world, or something profitable for the few? Something more or less polluted? "Growth" doesn't mean anything good for someone on the ground, it means relative position of a corporation on a stock exchange.

"Four billion low-income consumers, a majority of the world's population, constitute the base of the economic pyramid (BOP). New empirical measures of their aggregate purchasing power and *behavior as consumers* suggest significant opportunities for *market-based approaches* to better meet [create through advertising] their needs, increase their productivity [making things for the cities] and incomes, *and empower their entry into the formal economy.*" [... and disempower their independence from the Globalist economy.] [55]

For the analysts who wrote this, human beings and cultures that are thousands of years old are just market opportunities. Imagine that 4 billion people are now just "BOP."

The word psychopath might be appropriate here.

The market no longer simply supplies the demand of the public; the market leaders now create the demand. To control the market one must control desires and "behavior as consumers." To control desires, one must control values.

For me, these analysts are insane and I would write them off and forget them, except that their bosses control programs from the Peace Corp to the U.S. *military.* (See Glossary)

So ... our economic language now includes the "Bottom of the Pyramid." Then, for these analysts, who exactly is at the top of the pyramid?

Please remember the quote above as we explore the character of the *Globalists.*

URBAN BLIGHT

It almost appears that indoor people of the city are at war with the outdoor people in rural areas, and want to transform the countryside into a factory to supply their indoor needs.

But despite their antipathy for country living, it is the city dwellers who are the endangered species. Their indoor lifestyle constitutes a structural reason for over-consumption which cannot be sustained.

Consumerism isn't found where people live close to nature and are self-sufficient. The 70% of Africans who live as subsistent farmers are not the source of *consumerism* and it's trickle down deceit, and yet their self-sufficient world is judged as "undeveloped." They are targeted as the "BOP." Whoa! They don't need "development!" They are already self-sufficient!

> "Canadian mining operations are just destroying large parts of the world."
>
> Noam Chomsky said that "Canada is trying to take the lead in destroying the possibility of decent survival: that's what it means to exploit the tar sands, and the gold mining in Colombia, and coal mining, and so on .... That means destroying the world in which your grandchildren might be able to survive: that's the Canadian idea now."
>
> Chomsky added that "There is resistance: in Canada it's coming from First Nations. But it's worth remembering that that's a world-wide phenomenon. Throughout the world, the *indigenous* populations are in the lead. They are actually taking the lead in trying to protect the Earth. That's extremely significant."
>
> – tworowtimes.com November 9, 2013

We might ask, what value system would name something that is already working as "undeveloped?" Remember, many *"developed" countries* (See Glossary) are not at all self-sufficient. *They are the dependent countries.* The "developed nations" go and "colonize" independent countries, *destroy their independence,* dictate cash crops, and then gloat on their porches sipping lemonade.

England produces very little. England cannot feed itself. While it is claimed 78% of the UK economy is "services," the bulk of this is "financial services and real estate services." The proud claim that London is one of the worlds's largest financial centers is a *doublespeak* way to say that London controls the debt, and therefore the economies, of much of the world.

What do the banksters get out of this? Well, they produce nothing, yet as transaction gatekeepers, they live a high consumption lifestyle. The world is supposed to look up to London or New York as great cities, but these are dependent economies based on usury. They produce nothing. The banksters just organize extraction from everyone else. So what do they get? They get a free ride and an aura of glory to hide the rip-off.

* * *

So then, the goal of "development" in the "developed world" means sustaining a "something for nothing" lifestyle, where we "developed" people live off of desperate workers overseas, and then judge them as being "undeveloped."

We also import migrant workers to do the labor which our teenagers disdain. But they should disdain manual work because we are superior, right? "Manual work is too low for we *entitled* ones. We are *developed* after all." This is where the words *vanity* and *entitlement* start having relevance. Please understand that this attitude is what supports abuse everywhere.

Should the nations that depend on everyone else, be considered superior? In what way? More devious? More decadent? More indulgent? More disconnected?

There is a population problem in *every* country, not a development problem. Young people are leaving the countryside to look for non-existent jobs in the cities. They will soon have to return to the countryside as the cities are *unsustainable*. What value system would want to change everyone's relationship with the Earth and lead them to the pointless cities? Well, it doesn't take much searching to see where the mixed up guidance is coming from ...

Ramona, come closer, shed softly your watery eyes,
The pangs of your sadness will pass as your senses rise
For the flowers of the city,
Though breath like are death like some times.
And there's no use in trying, to deal with the dying,
Though I cannot explain that in rhymes...

– from song "Ramona" by Bob Dylan

Our *consumer values* are based on the *vanity* and drunkenness of "developed world" city life. These drunk cities import "stuff" from everywhere else to keep themselves drunk. The reader might ask, "What is he talking about, who is drunk?"

When we don't know where our food comes from, when we don't know where our waste goes, when we don't know why our family is getting cancer, when we realize we are lied to constantly by government, but keep watching the news anyway, we do this because we are ingesting something to keep ourselves in a pleasant stupor.

We even stay in a stupor as to what impacts our children. How do we explain that people are not worried about their children's future? We inebriate ourselves with distractions. We want to always be busy and distracted.

Maybe we are not drunk, maybe we are ostriches with our heads in the sand, but look at every grocery store now. Look how large the wine section is. While everyone knows the future looks grim, we are not hiding our heads in the sand, we are partying as much as possible. We "live for the weekend." There are hundreds of millions of people who drink beer most nights. There is a beer factory in Lhasa! This partying value system commands the advertising that negatively impacts the entire world.

It is the inebriated attitude that *"We are here on Earth to party!"* that enables irresponsibility.

* * *

When I was visiting the ancient locals of Arnhemland, Northwest Territory (NT), I read a book by Sir Baldwin Spencer who visited that area when the aboriginal communities were still living their 40,000-year-old lifestyle. That was only 90 years ago. He commented, with what seemed to me some snobbery, that the peoples' lives were devoted to eating as much as possible, day after day after day. He seemed to be saying that "developed civilized people" like himself were not devoted to the same thing.

We are devoted to not only eating as much food as possible (35% of Australians are obese) but *consuming everything else as well.* Baldwin Spencer's lifestyle consumed more metals and fossil fuels and chemicals than the people he had the wealth to visit. Incredibly, he didn't notice this. His sense of superiority and self-entitlement and blindness was the end result of his superior "modern" lifestyle. He was a "Sir" after all!

Wealth blinds us.

That sense of superiority, which kept him blind, is like a drunkenness, because it is based on indulgence and over-consumption. To get to his alleged superiority, nature was crushed. But that was okay, because "that's progress" and the proof of progress is we get to feel superior. Does the reader understand this circle of craziness?

I'm drunk, so I buy a big car I can't really afford that allows me to drive to the liquor store and buy more liquor which I share with my friends when I show off my big car. It is a circle of irresponsibility. However, in our times it is very dangerous ...

Now, I buy a warship and bring in cavalry, and I kill and crush the *indigenous people* and bring in cattle, which destroys their ecology, to feed my cities. I then tell my children that because I killed, raped and stole from them, they must be inferior! Since they are supposedly inferior, I will continue crushing them by "developing" them and forcefully bring them into the "formal" economy. This will benefit corporations from my country, whose *military* I pay for with my taxes. My country produces almost nothing.

"But that's progress." Is it?

If another nation is not contributing to overconsumption then we have to go "save them."

Believe it or not, thousands of international NGO's (Non-Government Organizations), which have at their disposal greater budgets than many countries, are busy trying to "help" other countries by changing them forever. In reality they are serving as the agents of transitional companies and Western interests. They are "helping" bring self-sufficient cultures into the "emerging market" as if they hadn't been getting along just fine for thousands of years. Some NGOs have promoted 'liberation movements' or civil wars such as in Albania, Afghanistan, Northern Iraq and Sudan. Amnesty International is example of an NGO that justifies foreign wars by the U.S. by falsely claiming overseas abuse. See video. [56] Behind the NGO's is the U.S. *military* (Glossary) with 55,000 special ops overseas. With friends like that, who needs enemies?

* * *

It used to be resources that the colonists sent back to the head thieves in Europe. Now resources are called "commodities," and the banksters skim the cream off of every trade electronically.

To "capture markets," as in the NATO takeover of Iraq and Libya, the war criminals (troops) are sent in for lame lying reasons, like "weapons of mass destruction" which, oops, didn't exist. I will say this many times, if we were told the truth, there would be no more war. Wars are based on lies.

In *doublespeak*, war criminals are called "warriors" or "heroes." To join the *military* is to volunteer to become a war criminal. Why do I say that? Ninety percent of the casualties in modern warfare are civilian. I'll go further ... to salute the flag of the United States now is to nod to war crimes.

A UN report documents 1,319 civilian deaths and 2,533 injuries in Afghanistan in the first six months of 2013, a 23 percent increase over the same period in 2012. The study finds "a 14 percent increase in deaths, 28 percent increase in injuries and 23 percent increase in total civilian casualties."

The outer conquest reaps the spoils of war, but there is an inner sacrifice that reaps spiritual poverty. A disconnected psyche is one of the downsides of winning a war. This is a point we do not examine enough.

The penalty of winning is deferred shame. The guilt of what one has done is deferred to a later date when conscience percolates up to the surface. *Vanity* and lying patriotism builds a firewall around the heart so this won't occur.

This is why I use the words *disconnecting vanity,* because we have to deny our crimes, and we become schizophrenic. The soldiers we will be meeting in this series became like Jekyl and Hyde characters, trying, but never succeeding in forgetting what they saw and did to innocent men, women, and children.

"Winning" in a world of conquest is losing spiritually.

However, because the *dominant culture* is ruled by *disconnecting vanity,* it is too vain to see the disconnect and realize the spiritual sacrifice that comes from making someone else a loser.

Indigenous people worldwide experienced the same thing. An onslaught of mineral prospectors overran their lands, backed up by soldiers on horseback. These prospectors were hoping to strike it rich so they could have their "something for nothing" lifestyle and sip lemonade. This onslaught continues today. When I was in Arnhemland, Australia, in 2012, mining companies were trying to lobby the community to allow strip mining for aluminum. The onslaught has not stopped. We are still trying to eat as much as possible. After all, we need aluminum for all those beer and soda cans.

Almost everyone wants to be like our rich bosses and have luxury and free time to "eat as much as possible day after day." The aboriginal lifestyle consisted of gathering food and relaxing and having time for art and dance and story telling. We only have time to sit in front of a television and be *socially engineered.*

So how, in any way, is our lifestyle superior?

It is this superior attitude, the *vanity* side of the "*disconnecting vanity*" that helps us be so disconnected.

Proud to be dysfunctional

* * *

It is the cities (where 50% of the world's 7 billion people now live) that are sucking nature dry and trying to "develop" every other place. *Urban people* don't see the Nature they are impacting. They don't understand they are draining resources and leaving toxins for future generations. The physical disconnection from the natural world that supplies our daily needs makes urban abuse of Nature not only possible, but certain.

Natural rural people eat food that comes from the hand of someone they probably know. A neighbor caught the fish and traded with them for something else. But city people have no idea what it takes to put sushi on a plate. City people eat food packaged with plastic and impregnated with chemicals and transported with fossil fuels and grown by machines in ways that destroy the soil. Fast food, for example, uses heaps of packaging. We aren't seeing progress, we are seeing destruction. Big Ag isn't "feeding the world." Big Ag is feeding city people at the expense of everything else.

The traditional rural lifestyle is not the problem. It is the cities. The cities are parasitic on the countryside, and, as it turns out, the *self-entitled consumer habits of the cities are parasitic on our inner spiritual selves also.*

However, it gets even more unbelievable.

Beyond the impact of too many people wanting too much, there is something worse for Nature that is hidden in plain sight. This is one of the biggest control scandals ever … the geo-engineering projects … the control of weather and the dimming of sunlight …

Atlanta at I-75 &
N. Marietta Parkway
Atlanta GA

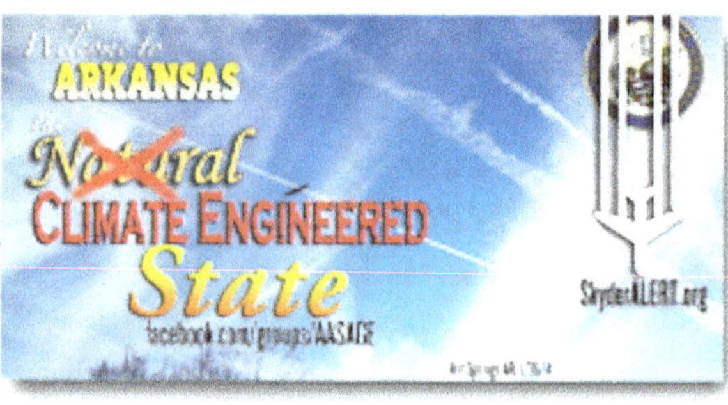

1852 Higdon Ferry Rd.
Hot Springs, AR

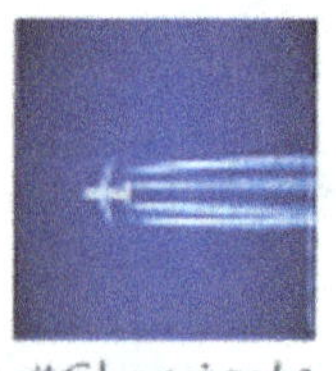

Various locations
Lansing, Michigan

CHAPTER 5

Freedom for the Rich

I'd like the reader to think about this.

Chapter 6

The Ocean Is Broken

"What was missing was the cries of the seabirds which, on all previous similar voyages, had surrounded the boat. The birds were missing because the fish were missing."

Exactly 10 years before, when Newcastle yachtsman Ivan Macfadyen had sailed exactly the same course from Melbourne to Osaka, all he'd had to do to catch a fish from the ocean between Brisbane and Japan was throw out a baited line.

"There was not one of the 28 days on that portion of the trip when we didn't catch a good-sized fish to cook up and eat with some rice," Macfadyen recalled.

"But this time, on that whole long leg of sea journey, the total catch was two. No fish. No birds. Hardly a sign of life at all.

"In years gone by I'd gotten used to all the birds and their noises," he said.

"They'd be following the boat, sometimes resting on the mast before taking off again. You'd see flocks of them wheeling over the surface of the sea in the distance, feeding on pilchards."

But in March and April this year (2013), only silence and desolation surrounded his boat, as it sped across the surface of a haunted ocean. North of the equator, up above New Guinea, the ocean-racers saw a big fishing boat working a reef in the distance.

"All day it was there, trawling back and forth. It was a big ship, like a mother-ship," he said. And all night it worked too, under bright floodlights. And in the morning Macfadyen was awoken by his crewman calling out, urgently, that the ship had launched a speedboat.

"Obviously I was worried. We were unarmed and pirates are a real worry in those waters. I thought, if these guys had weapons, then we were in deep trouble." But they weren't

pirates, not in the conventional sense, at least. The speedboat came alongside and the Melanesian men aboard offered gifts of fruit and jars of jam and preserves.

"And they gave us five big sugar-bags full of fish," he said. "They were good, big fish, of all kinds. Some were fresh, but others had obviously been in the sun for a while.

"We told them there was no way we could possibly use all those fish. There were just two of us, with no real place to store or keep them. They just shrugged and told us to tip them overboard. That's what they would have done with them anyway," they said.

"They told us that his was just a small fraction of one day's by-catch. That they were only interested in tuna and, to them, everything else was rubbish. It was all killed, all dumped. They just trawled that reef day and night and stripped it of every living thing."

Macfadyen felt sick to his heart. That was one fishing boat among countless more working unseen beyond the horizon, many of them doing exactly the same thing. No wonder the sea was dead. No wonder his baited lines caught nothing. There was nothing to catch ...

"I've done a lot of miles on the ocean in my life and I'm used to seeing turtles, dolphins, sharks and big flurries of feeding birds. But this time, for 3000 nautical miles there was nothing alive to be seen ..."

Back in Newcastle, Ivan Macfadyen is still coming to terms with the shock and horror of the voyage.

"The ocean is broken," he said, shaking his head in stunned disbelief.

– *Greg Ray* [57]

Why don't we hear about this as the biggest story of our lives? Why is this, in fact, being hidden from us? With a quick internet search for "plankton decline," we see that scientists are trying to warn us of even worse ocean problems. Yet, this news too, is buried beneath celebrity gossip and sectarian squabbles and the general party lifestyle we look forward to each weekend.

- **Plankton In Big Decline, Foundation of ...**
  www.huffingtonpost.com/2010/07/29/climate-change-plankton ...
  July 28, 2010: WASHINGTON — Despite their tiny size, plant plankton found in the world's oceans are crucial to much of life on Earth. They are the foundation of the ...
- **Short Sharp Science: Phytoplankton in decline: bye bye ...**
  www.newscientist.com/ ... /2010/07/phytoplankton-in-decline-bye-b.html
  Jul 29, 2010: Ocean life is being wiped out from the bottom up. The global population of microscopic plants that float in ocean water and support most marine life has ...
- **Zooplankton decline reported in North Atlantic**
  news.msn.com/science-technology/zooplankton-decline-reported-in ...
  Microscopic creatures that make up a critical link in the ocean food chain declined dramatically the first half of this year in the North.
- **Phytoplankton in decline across world's oceans**
  www.naturalnews.com/031925_phytoplankton_oceans.html

We dream of something that we ourselves are destroying. Is that sane? But the Globalists have an answer for us ... "Smart Cities" (Doublespeak for eventual work labor camps where everyone will be happy.)

The reader might search the words "climate engineering." Below you will see the little that has been disclosed about this science. Also please check "geo-engineering." You will also find disinformation in the form of professional looking articles that are 80% or 90% true, but the 10% steers you to wrong conclusions and entirely omit any controversy. (Unless a report includes downside risks, don't trust it.)

"**Geo-engineering** is the deliberate modification of the planet's environment by the addition or subtraction of a resource or energy input on a massive scale.

"[Revealed] Geo-engineering projects on Earth, often introduced [felicitously] as a means of combating climate change, have included space mirrors, sulfur-spraying in the stratosphere, cloud seeding and proposed oceanic carbon sequestration."

A more accurate term for geo-engineering is "weather warfare." The alibi for spraying the atmosphere is to reflect the sun to stop global warming, which might explain some of the plankton die-off.

"Since measurements began in the 1950s, scientists have discovered that there has been a decline of sunlight reaching the Earth; they called it global dimming." (Search Global Dimming on YouTube)

The real reasons for the massive spraying of the atmosphere, including from space shuttles, are not altruistic, or we would have heard about it. It is being done secretively. That tells us quite a lot. Many readers have never heard about this. The *Globalists* never do anything for "the small people." This is something to remember. They are never altruistic. Goodness is such a wee bit of their character that we can ignore it for now. Maybe reading books like this will up the percolation of conscience for them.

The result of 70 years of geo-engineering is devastating the bio-sphere. The rainfall of entire continents is now programmed. Most extreme climate is now intentional, bringing about more destabilization/consolidation. The reader might be confused by this. Why would the *Globalists* want to bring about that much havoc?

The *Globalists* have their hands on more data than anyone else. They own NASA for goodness sakes! They know exactly what is going on with *resource depletion*. They know about overpopulation. They plan ahead.

Remember the bankster *Globalists* funded all sides in World War II, including Hitler and Imperial Japan. 50 to 80 million people died in that bankster funded war. Havoc, or even depopulation, is simply not a concern for psychopaths.

While our skies are being sprayed, the Globalist controlled entertainment industry is conditioning people to think there is something normal about it.

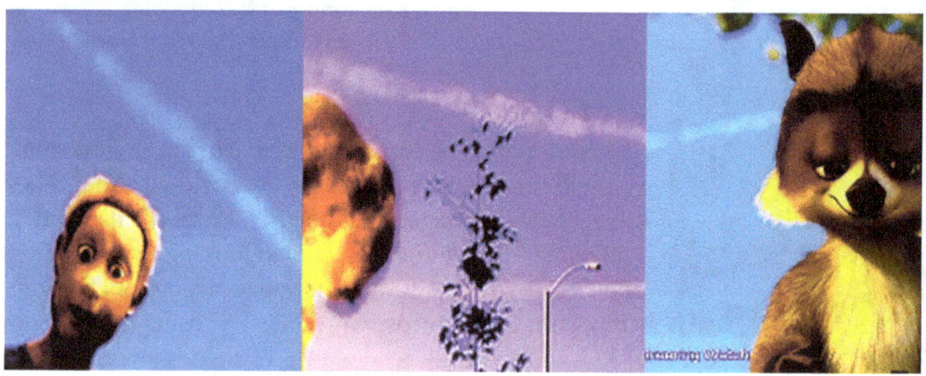

Cartoons and movies are conditioning another generation to think of trails of chemicals loaded with nano sized conductive metal particulates, as normal and not unusual. We are breathing and ingesting nano particles of aluminum, barium, strontium, polymers, and fibers. (See new Book *Chemtrails, HAARP, and the Full Spectrum Dominance of Planet Earth* by Elana Freeland) Not only do such particles deprive the atmosphere and soil of moisture, but they are undermining our immune system. Another reason for ionizing the atmosphere is the propagation of electro-magnetic waves for many undiscussed purposes … If these programs were positive we would have heard about them.

Below we see what the inside of a chemtrail plane looks like. The right plane has windows like a passenger jet; in the left one, the *Globalists* didn't even remove the luggage compartments. From the ground, they look like passenger jets. Tricky, eh? These are covert operations to trick us.

Just as plankton death is *not* being robustly discussed, neither is the die-off of other animals …

Mysterious Animal die-off around the world …
beforeitsnews.com › Mass Animal Death. In July 2013, Bees, Whales, Fish … mammal and fish die-offs around the world … Fraser Island off the …

Reports of dead birds and fish still coming in from around …
www.newsnet5.com/ … news/ … fish-still-coming-in-from-around-the-world

Samples from the cows have been shipped off to a local … Hundreds of fish have died on the …

Tens of thousands of dead fish wash ashore on South Carolina …
usnews.nbcnews.com/_news/2013/ … stretch of beach in South Carolina Tuesday, officials said, at least the second such occurrence in the region in …

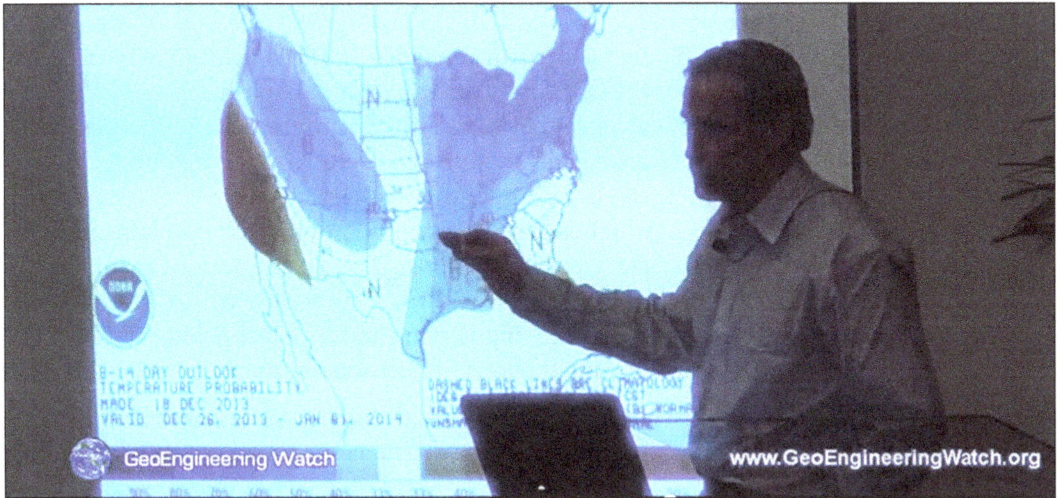

> *"Those people, our brothers and sisters in the military, who are doing things they don't understand the ramifications of, if we could reach them, I believe they would refuse to participate. I believe that is our chance of stopping this issue. Because we need them on our side. We need them to understand what they are doing to their fellow civilians. So we all have to work together to bring this issue to light."*
>
> – *Hero* Whistleblower, Dane Wigington

I recommend this excellent YouTube video that gives analysis of the California drought. By the time you read this there will be more investigation available. Wigington shows how the cold summer of 2014 in eastern U.S. with hot in west was geo-engineered. Unless we see significant rain in California, much more than California will be effected. [58] When you see news about mass forest fires, you are looking at the intentional result of geo-engineering which guaranteed will be blamed on "Global Warming" for ever more restrictions.

Some more highly recommended videos which the reader can find online …

Look Up

What in the World Are They Spraying?

Why in the World Are They Spraying?

Vincent Freeman – Hour 1 – Chemtrails Pathogen, Xenobiology & Engineered Bacteria, April 4, 2014

> "Vincent Freeman is a molecular biologist and artificial intelligence scientist who has worked on classified programs at some of the top-50 defense contractors. He has also conducted genetic and biological analysis for the National Institutes of Health (NIH). Vincent is currently volunteering his time as a senior consultant to the Carnicom Institute, a non-profit research organization whose goal is to identify and **expose covert geo-engineering and bio-engineering.** Vincent will discuss his current project that involves 'reverse-engineering' the fundamental structural biology involved in the 'chemtrails' pathogen. He is working closely with Clifford Carnicom to accomplish this task. Vincent will explain the biological evidence they have and explain the eerie properties of cross domain bacteria, a type of **genetically engineered** bacteria/nanomachine. In the second hour, we'll discuss Morgellons disease and how the population is already exposed and infected regardless of whether they have symptoms or not. He explains how infection can be proven via multiple scientific methods and what can be done to inhibit Morgellons growth. Also, Vincent discusses where CI is going in terms of research. Later, we discuss the evidence of covert bio-engineering and nanotechnology and how it works, as well as how these factors might play into the **trans-humanist agenda**. [59]

There is no longer natural weather on planet earth. What?! This, like many other hidden realities, seems far fetched until the evidence is examined. The natural ancient life of the whole planet is now at risk.

The general mining of the planet to feed a few generations of urban consumers is devastating; however, the ongoing geo-engineering experiments for 70 years for political reasons is catastrophic. I suggest that the reader start looking up at the sky whenever possible. That is your sky, your air, your children's air.

When something is covered up and not discussed in our "news," this tells us the *Globalists* don't want us to know something. The cover up is part of the evidence. As Chuck Cannon, a peer of my father told me, "If it is covered up, it's true," … one of the wisest things ever said to me.

I would like to share some hard facts before we get into the music industry part of this book. We need a reality check sometimes.

Not even the rise of disease in our times of *"progress"* is alarming enough to be on the front page of our awareness.

Autism has increased 600% in the last twenty years. What?! As you can see on the graph, it is not genetic. Something in our "superior," "developed" lifestyle is very wrong. Autism shows no sign of leveling off at all. This is another undiscussed catastrophe. By the time you read this, 1% of children in some "developed countries" will be mentally challenged [retarded] for life and the mainstream is not blowing the whistle about it. *And as the graph shows it will become much worse.*

It is being covered up. This tells me that this might be an intentional "destabilization/consolidation" operation. To restate it, autism may be a Globalist attack *because it is being kept secret*. The cover up needs to be exposed and explained. We need accountability right now.

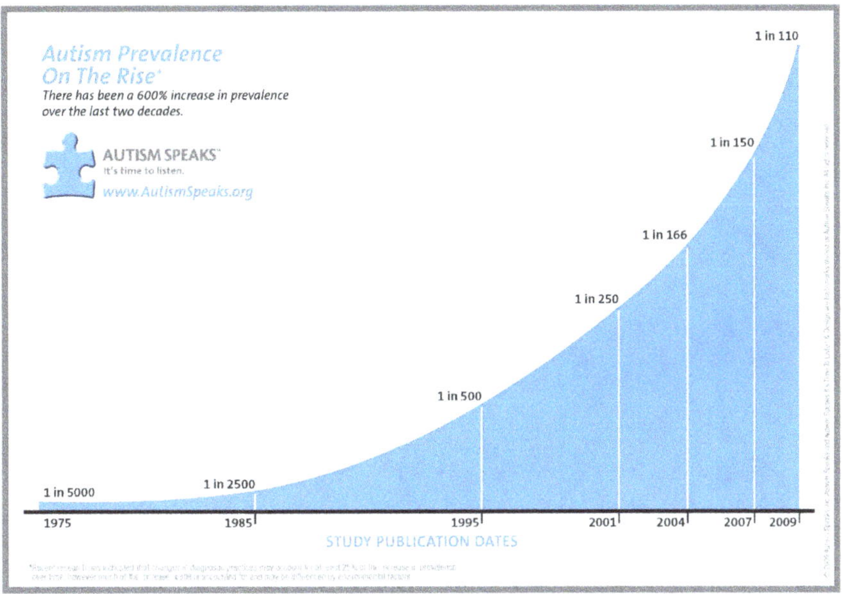

What has caused Alzheimer's disease to increase in graph below? Your government is not concerned.

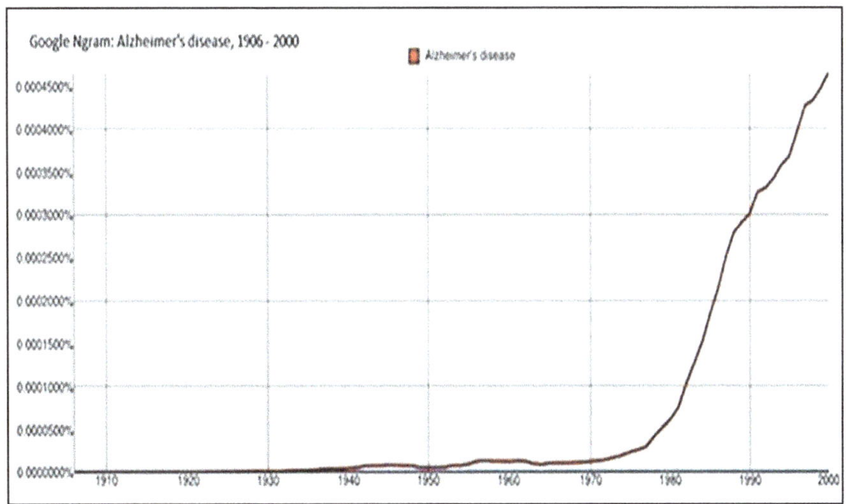

Prostate cancer incidence in the UK in ten years.

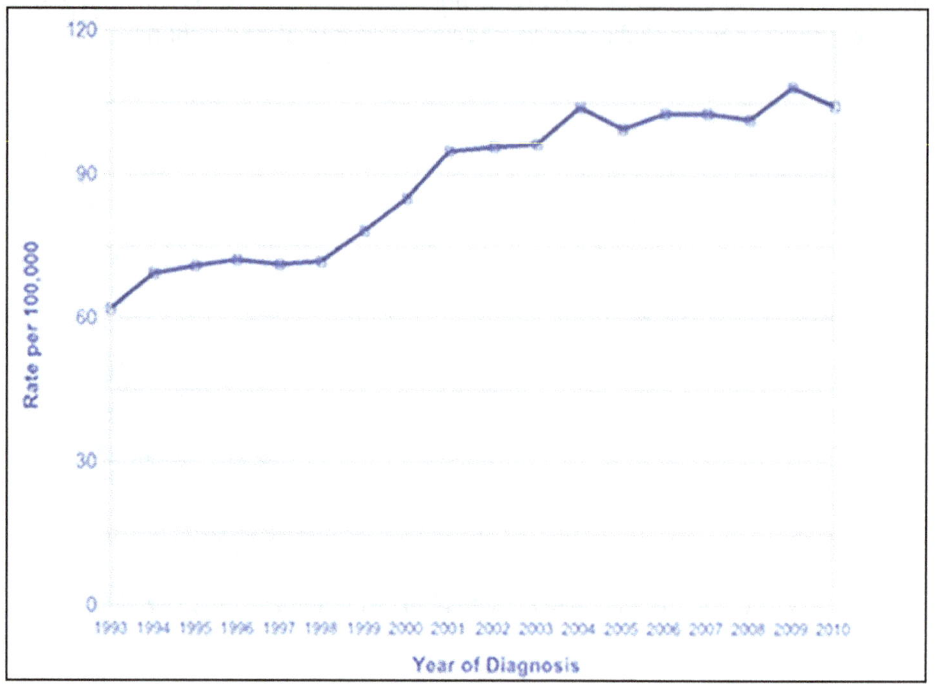

Figure 1: Cumulative laboratory reports of hepatitis C infection from England: 1992–2010

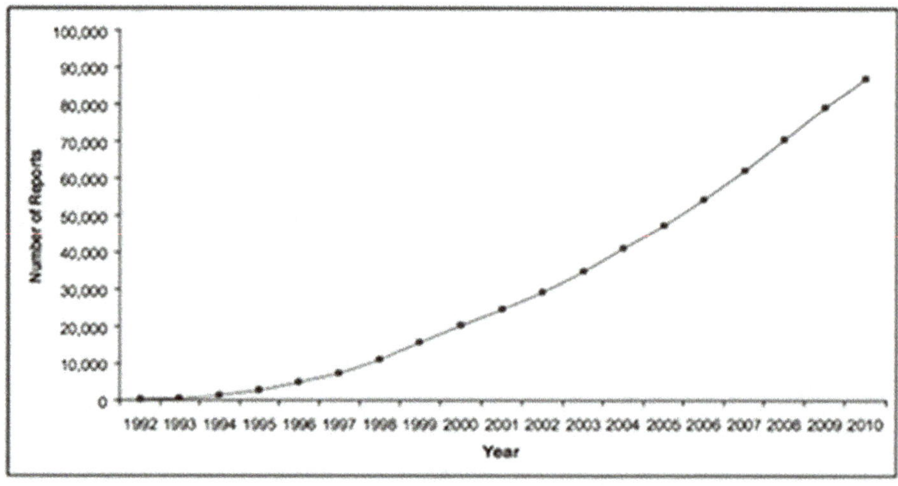

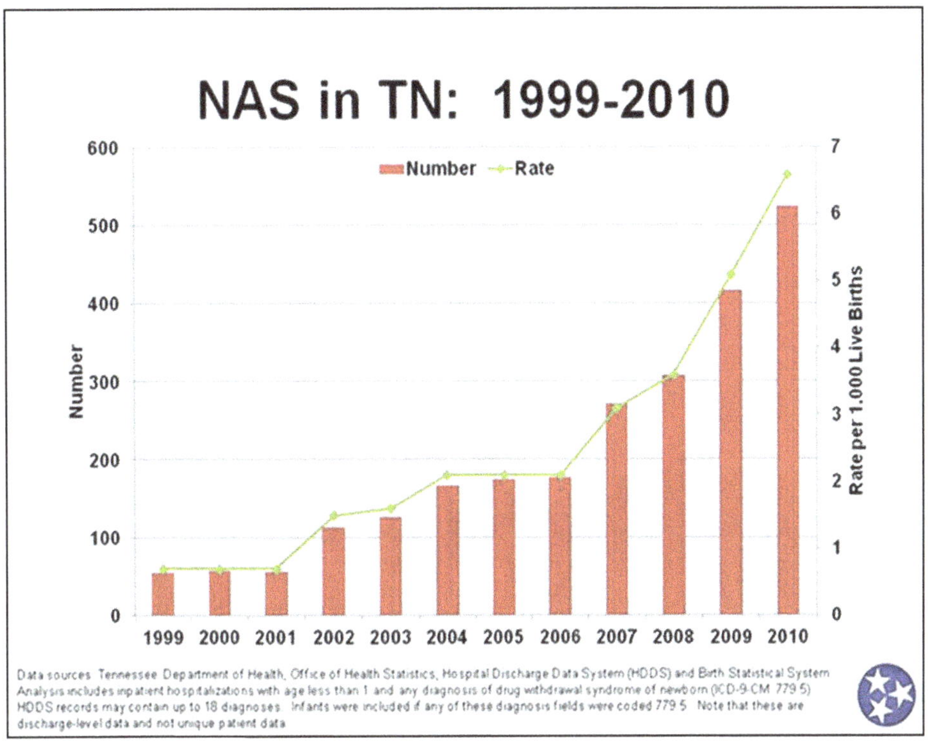

NAS refers to infants after birth, who experience symptoms of withdrawal when they no longer receive drugs from addict mother's umbilical cord. The rate of drug use in Tennessee among child-bearing women has increased 1000% in 15 years. "Progress?" America is "the greatest country in world," right? Is "America" worth going overseas and killing for, "to serve your country?" How about fighting for health in our own communities?

Now after seeing those graphs, please ask … "Is my government taking care of me and my neighbors?" How great is America or UK with statistics like this? Should we be proud of our flags, or should we demand some honest reporting in the media and some action by our representatives to find out how we are poisoning ourselves?

Or maybe we should be asking, "Who is poisoning us?" I have already explained the why part … Just good planning on the part of our masters to reduce the population.

Behind the logic of too many people and resource decline are the planners who make decisions in secret and covet their own power and influence above all else. These people just happen to be criminally insane. As stated previously, informing the masses with truthful information is anathema to their program.

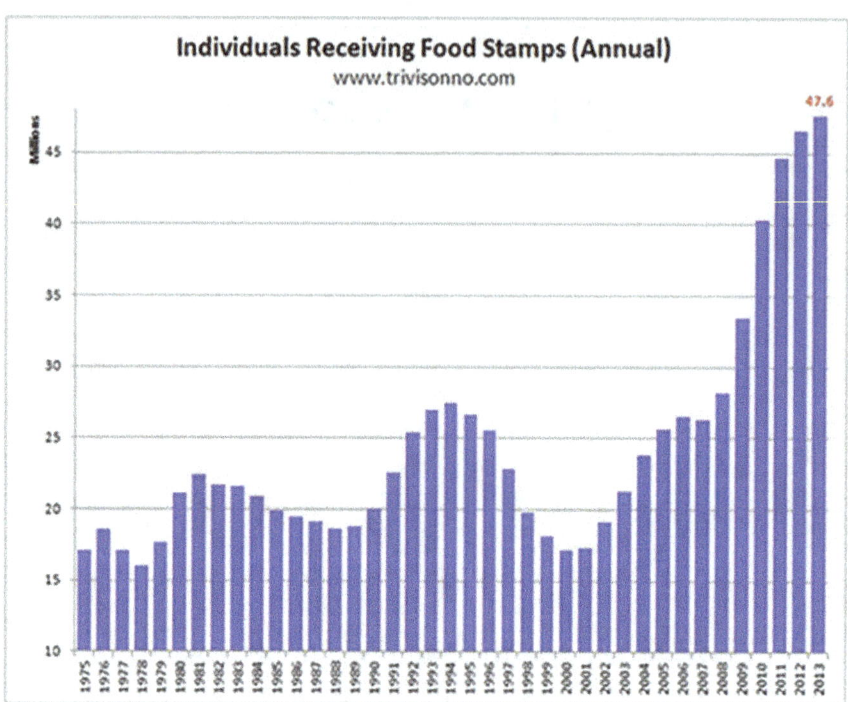

The rise in food stamp usage is intended to be permanent, as the population is conditioned to receive rations. I am serious. The noose is tightening. The population will be choked.

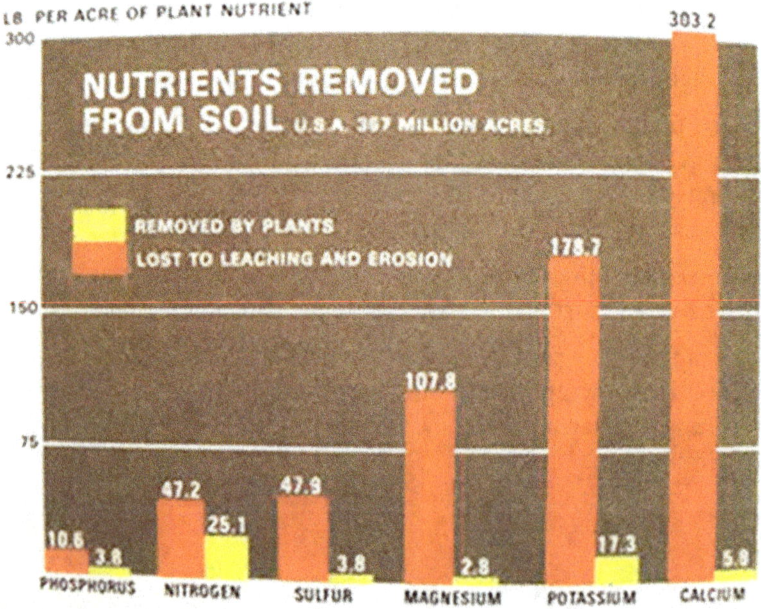

Unlimited usage on a limited planet is not sustainable, whether you think this or that. The reality is beyond philosophy. It is reality, and no, we do not create our own reality. Wake up!

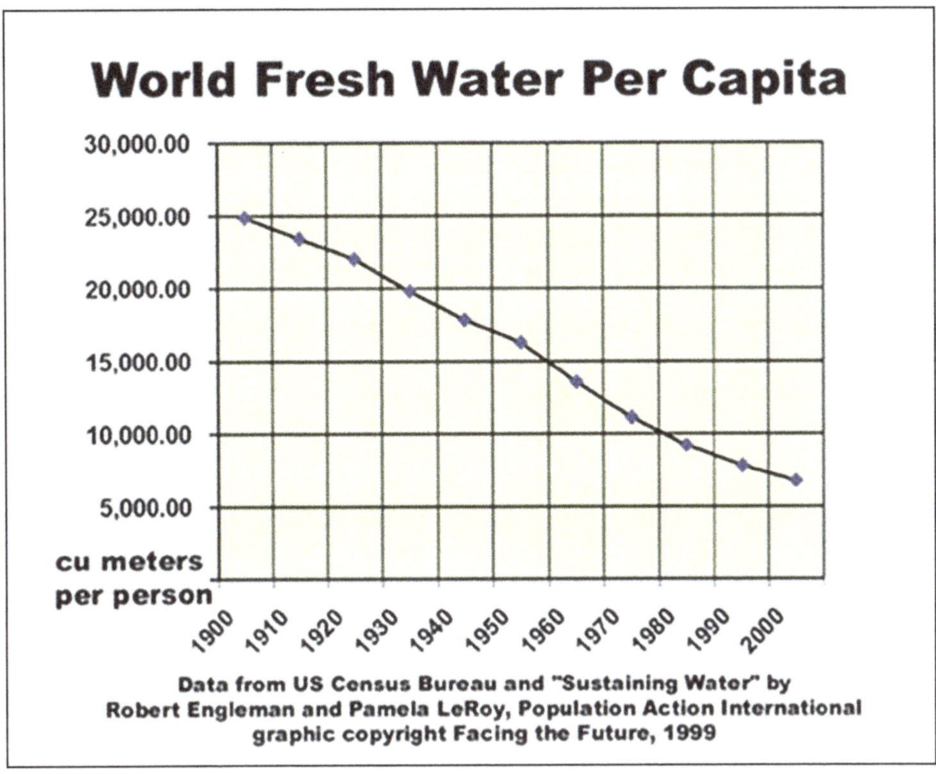

Frequency of Electro-Hypersensitivity Symptoms Based On Distance to Cell Phone Base Station

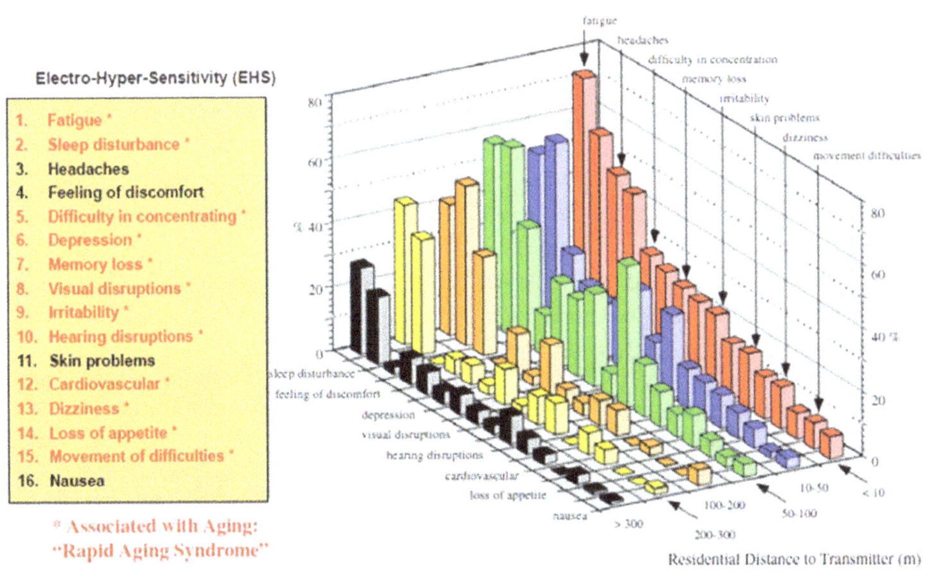

SANCTIONED DISEASES

The topic of ignored, or as I call them, *sanctioned diseases* (See Glossary) is too broad for the general overview I am offering and could be a book in itself, but I would like to mention three poisons as examples … Fluoride, mercury, and electromagnetic frequencies, (EMF). A more complete list of 20 topics in a well researched condensed article can be found here. [60] I believe the callous sanctioning of these environmental contaminates is part of the insane eugenics agenda coming out of the *Roth-efeller* UN. *"Sanctioned diseases"* drifts into "intentional diseases," and then into bio-weapons, which is too technical for anyone but microbiologists.

> "Perhaps by means of injections and drugs and chemicals, the population could be induced to bear whatever its scientific masters may decide to be, for its good." [In the technocrat's eyes, meaning their benefit, not society's.]
>
> – Bertrand Russell, *The Scientific Outlook* 1931

FLUORIDE

> "The first [actually second after Stalin Russia] occurrence of fluoridated drinking water on Earth was found in Germany's Nazi prison camps. The Gestapo had little concern about fluoride's supposed effect on children's teeth; their alleged reason for mass-medicating water with sodium fluoride was to sterilize humans and force the people in their concentration camps into calm submission."
>
> – Joseph Borkin, *The Crime and Punishment of I. G. Farben* [Corp.]

> "USAF Major George R. Jordan testified before Un-American Activity committees of Congress in the 1950s that in his post as U.S.- Soviet liaison officer, the Soviets openly admitted to … "Using the fluoride in the water supplies in their gulags (concentration camps), to make the prisoners stupid, docile, and subservient. " Fluoride, or Hydrofluorosilic acid (H 2 SiF 6), is not naturally occurring but is a waste by-product derived from the industrial manufacture of aluminum, zinc, uranium, aerosols, insecticides, fertilizers, plastics, lubricants and pharmaceuticals. It is also a Part II Poison under the UK Poisons Act 1972 ranking in toxicity above lead and just below arsenic. Fluoride is one of the basic ingredients in both PROZAC (FLUoxetene Hydrochloride) and Sarin nerve gas (Isopropyl-Methyl-Phosphoryl FLUoride). American toothpastes containing fluoride are by law obliged to state, '"WARNING: Keep out of reach of children under 6 years of age. If you accidentally swallow more than used for brushing, seek professional help or contact a poison control center immediately." [61]

The following were links I found by searching on NaturalNews.com, which I recommend. Kudos to Natural News "Health Ranger," *Hero* Whistleblower Mike Adams. Natural News has free subscriptions for news updates sent to your email.

September 7 - Mike Adams, NaturalNews Editor

37 lies Americans tell themselves to avoid confronting reality

Have you noticed the incredible detachment from reality exhibited by the masses these days? The continued operation of modern society, it seems, depends on people making sure they don't acknowledge reality (or try to deal with it). "Denial" is what keeps every sector...

 8,688

Harvard research links fluoridated water to ADHD, mental disorders …
February 25, 2014 … Building upon earlier research published in 2006 that dubbed fluoride as a "developmental neurotoxicant," the new review included a …
www.naturalnews.com/044057_fluoridated_water_adhd_mental_disorders. html

Water fluoridation news, articles and information:
6/24/2012 - The year before water fluoridation began in the United States, the entire dental profession recognized that fluoride was detrimental to dental health …
www.naturalnews.com/water_fluoridation.html

Bombshell: Syria's 'chemical weapons' turn out to be sodium fluoride
Sep 3, 2013 … If these chemical names sound familiar, that's because sodium fluoride is the same toxic chemical that's routinely dumped into municipal water …
naturalnews.com/041883_syria_chemical_weapons_sodium_fluoride. Html

PROOF: Chinese industrial fluoride suppliers openly list sodium floride
August 31, 2012 Fluoride-pushing doctors and dentists who try to contaminate your water supply with fluoride are promoting their deadly agenda …
naturalnews.com/037024_sodium_fluoride_insecticide_proof.html

Sodium fluoride news, articles and information:
9/18/2012 We've just released a new, hard-hitting mini-documentary on sodium fluoride. This is a must-see video for anyone who wants to know …
naturalnews.com/sodium_fluoride.html

Israel commits to ending water fluoridation by 2014, citing major …
Sep 16, 2013 Israel's Ministry of Health has made a bold ruling against artificial water fluoridation, reversing more than 15 years of forced …
naturalnews.com/042079_water_fluoridation_israel_health_concerns. html

Eight reasons why water fluoridation has failed modern civilization
February 4, 2013 As it turns out, so-called "optimal" fluoride levels in water do not protect the health of children or adults, and regular exposure to fluoride in water …
naturalnews.com/038949_water_fluoridation_failure_toxic_chemicals. Html

Seven ways to naturally protect yourself against fluoride toxicity …
February 23, 2013 More than 200 million Americans today are forcibly exposed to toxic fluoride through their public water supplies, and many more …
www.naturalnews.com/039221_fluoride_toxicity_protection.html

MERCURY

Saving the environment and saving our children is the same story. There is no separation. Environmental dangers from intentionally allowed pollution may be the issue that forces you to become an active civil participant as Ralph Nader spoke of in first chapter.

I have a neighbor who lives very close to me who went to hospital for nerve problems. He had poisoned himself and became permanently disabled from eating tuna (ahi) daily. Tuna is a predator fish that is near the top of the ocean food chain and collects higher concentrations of heavy metals such as mercury, which poisoned my neighbor, who as an industrial human, is at the very top of the food chain. Yet in 2005, NOAA produced a pdf *entitled Keeping Hawaii Seafood Safe to Eat* which states ... "No cases of poisoning reported from open ocean fish." So was my neighbor the first person ever? The deceit in the following report tells me that the reporters were dodging hard evidence of danger.

What about
ahi, is it safe?

Yes. There are no reported cases of mercury poisoning associated with Hawaii's open ocean fish, including tuna, marlin and swordfish.

No adverse health effects were found in children born to mothers that ate 12 meals of fish (like Hawaii's fish) in the Seychelle Islands.

The known health benefits of fish in the diet appear to outweigh any potential adverse health effects of low-level mercury exposure from a diet of open ocean fish.

Is mercury poisoning a problem in Hawaii?

No single case of mercury poisoning from the consumption of Hawaii fish has been reported. Also, no cases have ever been reported that specifically implicated open ocean fish like swordfish, tuna or marlin anywhere in the world.

What fish cause mercury poisoning in Hawaii?

No Hawaii fish species are known to have caused mercury poisoning.

It is very fine print, but at top right of above image, it says in blue print on its side, "State of Hawaii, Hawaii Seafood Promotions Committee." Now, does the reader think this NOAA sponsored report contains a bias? The statement above says two things. There is a NO problem, and there is a "potential" problem but is outweighed by "known health benefits." If there is no problem, what is being outweighed?

This NOAA piece of government/industry propaganda is a good example of why we can't trust government studies. The report states "A more appropriate study of health effects from fish consumption involved a population of mothers in the Seychelle Islands that ate an average of 12 meals of fish per week ... The Seychelle Island diet of fish includes yellowfin tuna, skipjack, bonito, wahoo, jacks and other fish similar to those found in Hawaii."

Hold on! *Indigenous people* eat fish caught from small boats in shallow water, catching almost exclusively smaller fish that are not high on food chain. The Seychelle diet *may sometimes* include larger fish, but these people are not eating the top predators 12 times a week. The wording is misleading, and this is typical of the lying, twisting, greed oriented *social engineering* that is called education. The purpose of this study was not education, it was to promote consumption. If the study listed all the species eaten in Seychelle Islands, most were not the top predators where heavy metals accumulate.

NOAA includes this image of "guidance" below which makes one believe that the Seychelle diet consists of twelve 6 ounce steaks of yellow fin tuna per week! See wording on left. All the agencies named are *Roth-efeller* fronts, particularly EPA and FDA. Do search online, "revolving door FDA, EPA, USDA, or FCC" and find out which corporations, such as Monsanto, control so called regulatory agencies.

Guidance for pregnant women for safe fish (ex. yellowfin tuna steaks) **consumption aimed at reducing prenatal mercury exposure of their children.**

AGENCY OR SOURCE	GUIDANCE*
EPA-FDA Joint Advisory 2004	1 meal/week
World Health Organization (WHO)	2.3 meals/week
Agency for Toxic Substance and Disease Registry (ATSDR)	3 meals/week
Seychelle Island Child Development Study (Univ. Rochester)	12 meals/week*

* *A "meal" is a 6 oz. portion of fish.* ***Average fish consumption without any adverse health effects.*

In Hawaii, many people eat ahi (tuna) several times a week, beyond the EPA guidance, and remember, mercury is cumulative, so this report above is criminally negligent. I exposed the *Roth-efeller* Big Pharma World Health Organization on Page 81. The authors of this NOAA/ Dept. of Commerce pdf, *Keeping Hawaii Seafood Safe to Eat,* J. John Kaneko, Brooks Takenaka and Paul Bartram are guilty of misleading the public. Someone else arranged the graphics who worked for PacMar, Inc., but with a disclaimer at end of pdf, the government leaves the authors to hang alone. Shame shame shame.

The Seychelle Island people eat a lot of fish, and *sometimes* they eat the top of food chain fish. This NOAA/industry "report" (advertisement) is misleading and therefore lying to the public to promote the big fish industry and tourist industry, as stated explicitly in beginning of pdf. They did this to tie in all the commercial interests to think of their wallet first, not the health of their descendants. The *unsustainable* fishing industry is decimating big fish populations, and sea life in general, as we saw with "The Ocean is Broken" story that began this chapter. *Globalization* depends on making people selfish. Then no one will stand up for self-sacrifice, balance, truth or health. These human qualities will be ignored to enable the consumerist disconnection with nature. God has become profit by wastefully cutting corners around conscience.

"Undocumented health affects" in text from same NOAA pdf to right, simply means "true symptoms that industry funded universities and New World Order governments refuse to investigate." Remember, universities are controlled by big business donations. Science, which I will cover in another book of series, is for sale to the highest bidder, and honest scientists are terrorized (Page 38). Who will suffer from this? Everyone and everything.

> Necessary to reduce mercury exposure from the diet. But the known health benefits of eating fish should be carefully weighed against the undocumented health affects of low-levels of mercury in open ocean fish. Women of child bearing age and young children should follow their doctors' advice.

NOAA dodges responsibility with disclaimers in text, such as, "While further studies are being completed, women should follow their doctor's advice." See, they warned us that presently, right now, mercury poisoning in fetuses is a health issue, but after misleading you with their propaganda, the danger is your doctor's problem. After reading there is "NO PROBLEM," how many people will make an expensive appointment with a doctor to get a recommendation about how much tuna they should eat? How many doctors have researched the corrupt EPA?

Does your doctor know that EPA's response to Fukashima airborne radiation was to stop monitoring radiation! Does your doctor use EPA recommendations? Yes, because she or he is then off the hook. The EPA will say "consult your doctor" and your doctor in court will cite EPA. So, no one is accountable.

Personal sovereignty (Glossary) means we take responsibility for each of our decisions. You are not a sheep under some celestial Shepard or a sheeple under the Illuminati (to be covered shortly: the all-seeing-eye). To make good decisions we need honest information and we must insist on *personal sovereignty* (integrity) from all spokesman. They in turn must demand accountability from all agencies. When this happens, a lot of people will go to jail and health will become the new "pursuit of happiness."

SYMPTOMS OF AUTISM IN CHILDREN	SYMPTOMS OF MERCURY POISONING IN CHILDREN
Loss of Speech	Loss of Speech
Social Withdrawal	Social Withdrawal
Reduced Eye Contact	Reduced Eye Contact
Repetitive Behaviors	Repetitive Behaviors
Hand-flapping, Toe-walking	Hand-flapping, Toe-walking
Temper Tantrums	Temper Tantrums
Sleep Disturbances	Sleep Disturbances
Seizures	Seizures

From the Spanish Edition of *Lipstick and War Crimes*

Evaluación de la concentración de mercurio en diversas marcas de atún enlatado comercializadas en la ciudad de Cartagena de Indias

"Evaluation of The Mercury Concentration in Various Brands of Canned Tuna Sold in the City of Cartagena De Indias, Colombia"

Juan Manuel Sánchez Londoño

Código: 598924

Universidad Nacional de Colombia, Facultad de Medicina, Departamento de Toxicología, Convenio Universidad de Cartagena, Colombia

2011

A study conducted by a Master's Degree student from the Department of Toxicology, Faculty of Medicine at the National University of Colombia, concluded that consumption of different brands of tuna sold in city of Cartagena de Indias posed a risk to consumers. The danger is implied in tuna consumption.

The study compared 41 samples of tuna sold in Cartagena and analyzes the total percentage of mercury (T-Hg) to conclude that the general population, and especially children, pregnant women, and people with heart problems, is at a high risk.

Despite the denial from the government, and the companies involved in the production of tuna, the study is conclusive by showing statistical analysis of levels of mercury. Many of these brands are not only sold in Cartagena, although this was location of study, but are distributed throughout Colombia and neighboring countries.

Brands were classified as A, B, C, and D ... "The average concentration of T-HG in samples of canned tuna of four brands available in the market of the city of Cartagena de Indias was (0.86 ± 0.09). Brand C can be considered as low risk with values (0.31 ± 0.13ppm). Brand B can be considered as moderate to high risk, while brands A and D have a very high risk *(even more than warned by WHO)* and are considered unacceptable."

The results show that in ALL cases there is a present risk. The author also accompanied the document with recommendations in which he says this information needs to be available to consumers, in order to prevent any tragedy associated with mercury contamination.

However, as can be seen in press clippings at that time and since, "Invima" (The National Institute of Food and Drug Monitoring) demerit this serious study, which was carried out at the largest University of Colombia, one of the most important universities in Latin America, and they argue that the levels of mercury in tuna are safe. [The exact same thing happened in Hawaii. This then, is allowed risk, or allowed incidence = *sanctioned disease.* Also, not mentioned is that mercury accumulates in body, and like EMF, which we are about to look at, the chronic long term exposure *is not regulated ANYWHERE.]*

100 Percent of Fish in U.S. Streams Found Contaminated with Mercury
Mar 3, 2010 "This study shows just how widespread mercury pollution has become in our air, watersheds and many of our fish in freshwater streams."
www.naturalnews.com/028284_fish_mercury.html

Mercury exposure and children's health Sept. 2010.
serious health hazard for children. This article provides an extensive review of mercury exposure and children's health.
ncbi.nlm.nih.gov/pubmed/20816346

Too Much Tuna Means Too Much Mercury for Kids
Sept. 19, 2012 A coalition of consumer groups says kids should eat much less canned tuna to avoid mercury poisoning. In a new report issued today … www.webmd.com

Too Much Tuna Can Cause Mercury Poisoning In Children
Children should be consuming considerably less canned tuna, otherwise their risk of serious mercury poisoning could become a public health issue in years to come …
medicalnewstoday.com/articles/250554

Mercury alert: Is canned tuna safe to eat?
Tuna can contain mercury, so parents must choose wisely when serving it to their kids, and *be aware that school lunches may have unsafe levels.* [Depopulation agenda is alive and well in our public schools.] edf.org/oceans/mercury-alert-canned-tuna-safe-eat

NRDC: Mercury Contamination in Fish - Protect Yourself and …
Eating fish contaminated with mercury, a poison that interferes with the brain and nervous system, can cause serious health problems, especially for children …
www.nrdc.org/health/effects/mercury/protect.asp

Consumer Reports – Mercury in canned tuna still a concern
Jan 2011, Canned tuna, Americans' favorite fish, is the most common source of mercury in our diet. New tests of 42 samples from cans and pouches of …
consumerreports.org/cro/magazine-archive/2011/january/food/mercury-in-tuna/overview …

Meanwhile industry/government lies continue unabated …

FDA Stuns Scientists, Declares Mercury in Fish to be Safe for Infants …
December 17, 2008 … This FDA decision on mercury in fish has alarmed EPA scientists who called it "scientifically flawed and inadequate."
www.naturalnews.com/news_000622_mercury_fda_fish.html

Fish and Mercury Truths
Eating fish is safe. Commercial fish poses no concern. www.aboutseafood.com/

EMF Pollution – Electro Smog

"No concern." Did you see the last words from Aboutseafood.com above? This is the dumbing down mantra for the masses. "Don't ask questions."

This is exactly how the bought-off electric utilities everywhere were instructed to talk about Smart Meters, which are the new (in some places government mandated) electrical meters on your home or business. Smart Meters measure how much electricity your home uses. The same talking points in Hawaii were used in South Africa and South Korea to lie to the masses. Not one utility anywhere has shown that Smart Grid and Smart Meters are cost effective. It was a *Roth-efeller* New World Order *Globalization* program. The lie is that Smart Meters conserve electricity. They do not. They require electricity to function and are for rationing, not conservation. Selective rationing. And they record much more than we are told with their proprietary software. The "all-seeing-eye" is planned to be in every home with a depopulation component.

"The Technocratic Age is slowly designing an every day, more controlled society. The society will be dominated by an elite of persons free from traditional values, who will have no doubt in fulfilling their objectives by means of purged techniques, with which they will influence the behavior of people and will control and watch the society in all details. ***It will become possible to exert a practically permanent watch [all -seeing-eye] on each citizen of the world."***

– Obama Columbia University mentor Zbigniew Brzezinski

Wireless, so called "Smart" Meters are also used for water and natural gas usage. The older analog meters had a spinning dial and produced no EMF (Electromagnetic Frequency). The new digital "Smart Meters," (a name chosen to sell the technocrat, surveillance, depopulation wet dream to the masses by dumbing us down with *doublespeak* semantics. The name also incites our *vanity*. Oh, how "smart" progress is! And how "smart" I am to be part of it! How "smart" I am to become dependent on a machine!) produce both wireless and EMF pollution due to "dirty electricity from "switching mode power supply."

New Critical Problem with 'Smart' Meters: The Switching Mode Power Supply
www.takebackyourpower.net/news/2012/10/06/new-critical-problem ...

Warning – New Sources of Harmful Dirty Electricity – Sam Milham, August 16, 2013

"In the last month, I have been contacted by two women, driven out of their homes by illness caused by neighborhood installation of water pumps with variable frequency drives (VFD) or variable speed drives (VSD) or controllers. These are solid state devices which replace mechanical motor switches to control motor speed and torque by *varying motor input frequency and voltage.*

"One was a solar powered water pump using a maximum power point tracking (MPPT) controller to maximize charging of batteries which powered a water pump motor. The other was a VFD on a replacement deep well pump motor. When this pump was running, dirty electricity levels in the house spiked as did the primary neutral to earth voltage dumped into the earth at a transformer near the house. These devices all interrupt current flow and generate high levels of high frequency voltage transients or "dirty electricity." – See: belden.com/docs/upload/Building_a_Reliable_VFD_System_WP.pdf

Relationship of electric power quality to milk production of dairy herds.

"2013 March 1: Dairy farmers were the first to recognize the problem, since installation of Variable Frequency Drives on milk pump motors caused an immediate drop in milk production. [A biological response] A 10 millivolt change in dirty electricity in the milking parlor floor equals a change of about a pound of milk per day in each cow.

"VFDs are also being put on the motors of many new air conditioners and furnace fans. The inverters and controllers on residential and commercial photovoltaic solar systems and wind turbines all generate "dirty electricity." – ncbi.nlm.nih.gov/pubmed/23416176

[Human beings will also have a biological response. Duh!]

Health and privacy controversies concerning the globalist, world wide, 2011 roll out of Smart Meters have been sidelined by the globalist controlled mainstream news … Lawsuits are tied up in court.

Updated Report on How Smart Meters Invade Privacy
The report has now been updated …
smartgridawareness.org/2014/08/ … on-how-smart-meters-invade-privacy

No More Privacy: Smart Meters Are Surveillance Devices
Have you heard about the new "smart meters" that are being installed in homes all across America? Under the guise of "reducing greenhouse gas emissions" and …
endoftheamericandream.com/archives/no-more-privacy-smart-meters-are …

Comparing Cell Phone and Smart Meter Radiation
Can you trust your utility to look after your health and safety? PG&E's smart meter emits RF radiation levels far higher than a cell phone.
Stopsmartmeters.org/ … /comparing-cell-phone-and-smart-meter-radiation

Comparing "Smart" Meter RF Emissions to Cell Phones
www.youtube.com/watch?v=aOabFJlenz4

Smart Meters Radiation Exposure Up to 160 Times More Than Cell Phone
Daniel Hirsch, … by comparing to a cell phone for one moment in time.
www.electrosmogprevention.org/public-health-alert/smart-meters …

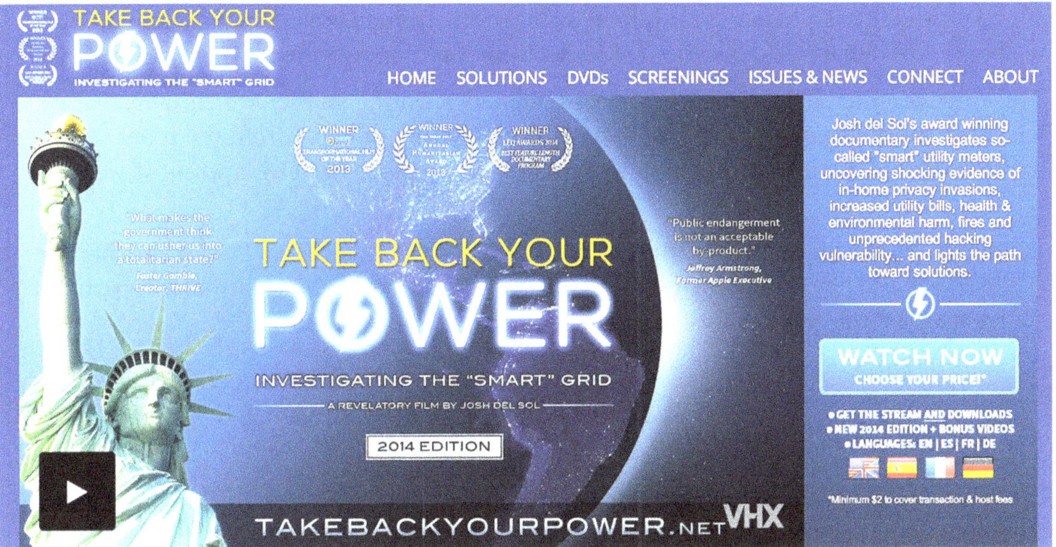

Power packed documentary video at Takebackyourpower.net

Letter by Josh del Sol, September 9, 2014

http://pubcit.typepad.com/clpblog/2014/09/legal-and-public-health-problems-of-the-wireless-age.html

> "I have great concern that a former senior lobbyist for the cellular telecom industry (Tom Wheeler) has been planted to run the FCC, an organization whose "safety" guidelines [Using SAR, specific absorption rate] for microwave radiation have been identified as "inapplicable" by the U.S. Dept of Interior, NIOSH, EPA, Amateur Radio Relay League Bio-Effects Committee, and even FDA (back in 1993).
>
> "These FCC guidelines actually permit 100x more radiation than countries such as China, Poland and Russia.
>
> "And in June 2014, CDC (Center of Disease Control) broke ground and publicly posted a cell-phone use precaution on their website, only to redact it in August amidst apparent pressure from the wireless industry, following the information going somewhat viral amongst groups aware of what appears to be a greater cover-up.
>
> "For the past 3 years, I have been researching the issue of health harm from wireless technology, as part of making the investigative documentary "Take Back Your Power" (www.TakeBackYourPower.net), which exposes a panoply of issues brought about with the deployment of "smart" meters.
>
> "The smart meter deployment has been incentivized through $11B of stimulus funds, by what appears to be a corporately-run government also keen to illegally snoop on in-

home activities and move in the direction of sweeping austerity measures throughout the utility industry. [Author would say that the corporations are just greedy minions who are easily bought off by the *Roth-efellers*. In this case, the taxpayers went trillions of dollars into debt because of the *Roth-efeller* orchestrated 2008 housing bubble/economic crisis, and this is where the $11 billion dollars came from to buy off industry to come on board with Smart Grid and Smart Meters. Stimulus money came from our tax dollars!]

"There are literally thousands of peer-reviewed scientific studies which demonstrate either the biological harm (directly) or the plausibility of harm from the types of microwave radiation which are being deployed throughout the U.S. and most western countries.

"On an increasing basis, I feel agreement with a growing number of PhD whistleblower scientists and physicians, including Dr. Dietrich Klinghardt who identifies this particular story as "the great issue of our time."

Sincerely, Josh del Sol, Producer and Director,
Take Back Your Power: Investigating The "Smart" Grid

The following is a list of links generated at
newsmedicalworld.blogspot.com

Transmitting Smart Meters ... are a public health threat. ... the exposure to microwave and radio wave radiation from these meters is involuntary and continuous ...
www.electricalpollution.com/smartmeters.html

Smart Meter Comments - EMF Safety Network
Oct 18, 2011 - If we had the choice, would we choose a car with a cancer-causing smart meter radiation device attached to it that radiates our children while ...
www.emfsafetynetwork.org/?page_id=1223

"Smart" Meters: More Radiation Than a Cell Tower
Aug 22, 2011 – PG&E and other utilities claim that wireless 'smart' meters emit a fraction of radiation compared to other common wireless devices.
stopsmartmeters.org/ ... /smart-meters-more-radiation-than-a-cell-towe ...

'Smart' Meters Violate FCC Radiation Exposure Limits Says New
Jan 7, 2011 – "The reality is that 'smart' meters emit radiation of a power and frequency that has been linked with DNA disruption, pathological leakage of ...
stopsmartmeters.org/ ... /smart-meters-violate-fcc-radiation-exposure-li ...

Comparing Cell Phone and Smart Meter Radiation
Sep 4, 2011 – From our friends at Burbank Action: The utilities are telling us that smart meters emit less radiation than cell phones ...
stopsmartmeters.org/ ... /comparing-cell-phone-and-smart-meter-radiat ...

Smart Meter Radiation - 3 Things You Must Know
Oct 19, 2011 – Don't be fooled, smart meter radiation is dangerous. There is a growing body of scientific studies to support this …
electricsense.com/ … /smart-meter-radiation-3-things-you-must-know/

Smart Meter Dangers
the inauguration of smart meters with grudging and involuntary exposure of millions to billions of human beings to pulsed microwave radiation should …
smartmeterdangers.org/

Smart Meter Radiation Risks
Jun 8, 2011 – Are Smart Meters health hazards? Smart Meter radiation emissions are far more serious than admitted, claim independent EMF studies.
www.earthcalm.com/5582/emf-dangers … /smart-meter-radiation-risks …

But of course, industry lies again …

Smart Grid: Meters safer than cell phones and microwaves
Radio frequency emissions from smart meters fall within FCC safety standards and are much lower … www.smartgridnews.com/artman/publish/Technologies_Metering_News/ …

Here is an attack piece worded to offset validity of Biointitiative.org

wifiinschools.ca/the-bioinitiative-report/

"The results of the analysis showed that, of the 33 expert groups, only one – the BioInitiative Report – reached the conclusion that RF posed a health risk."

The reader might ask, who funded the other 32 groups? Why is American Academy of Pediatrics not listed? Or HeartMD Institute? Simple, the lying industry who cares only about their own wallets stacked the deck and found 32 "groups" to ignore all warnings.

The U.S. Federal Communications Commission (FCC) safety standards are based on literally the degree to which Electromagnetic Frequencies (EMF) or Radio Frequencies (RF) can heat body tissues.

So "Safe EMF" just means not hot EMF. If a Smart Meter doesn't make your body hot, then it is "safe." If a wireless modem doesn't heat your skin, it is "safe." If a wireless baby monitor doesn't heat your child's brain, it is "safe." If a cell phone in your bra doesn't heat your breast, it is "safe."

The reader can find statements by the American Cancer Society, CDC, FDA, FCC, and many others that say there are NO health risks from Radio Frequencies. These statements are written up exactly, almost word for word, like the mercury propaganda piece I shared above. They are lying. See www.bioinitiative.org for the studies they deny and ignore.

Doctors warn of breast-cancer link to keeping cell phone in bra

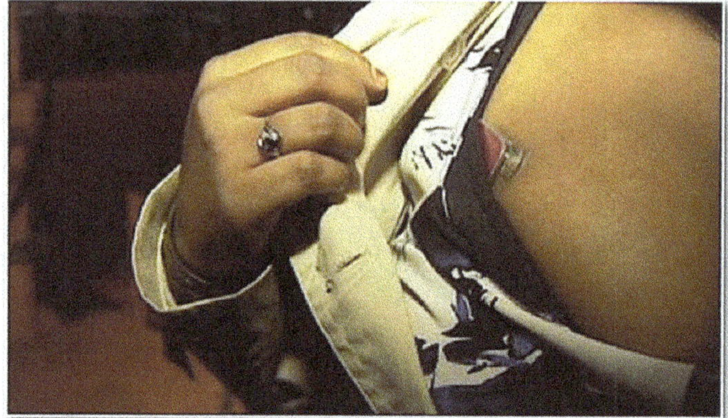

Cell phone bra breast cancer link special report

KTVU.com

OAKLAND, Calif. — Could where you carry your cell phone make you sick? Some doctors say they're seeing evidence of breast cancer that could be linked to where some women keep their mobile phones.

Tiffany Frantz and other young women tell KTVU it's convenient way to hold on to their cell phone. "I put my cellphone right in my bra," said Frantz.

Related

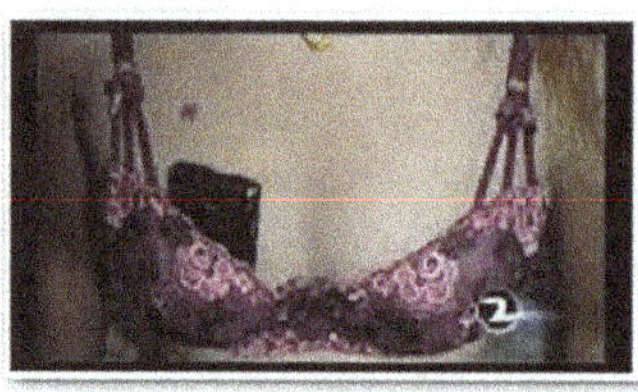

SPECIAL REPORT: Keeping cell phone in bra may lead to breast cancer

However, her mother Traci Frantz expressed misgivings. "We never took it seriously until after she was diagnosed," said Traci Frantz.

At the age of 21 years old, Tiffany got breast cancer.

"Her tumors were exactly where her cellphone had been against her skin her bare skin for about six years," said Traci Frantz. Their family has no genetic or other risk factors. Surgeons ended up removing Tiffany's left breast.

"It's kinda coincidental that it's right where I kept my cellphone," said Tiffany.

Coincidence? Donna Jaynes got breast cancer at 39. Her family also no had risk factors for cancer. Her doctor showed KTVU the dots where her tumors developed just a half an inch beneath her skin.

"All in this area right here, which is where I tucked my cellphone," said Jaynes. She said she did just that for ten years. She had a mastectomy.

"I thought cellphones were safe. I was under the impression that they were," said Jaynes.

I recently wrote this guest editorial for a local newspaper …

Is Wireless Tech Dangerous in Schools?

Wireless tech is new, and just as second hand smoke was proven to be hazardous, wireless frequencies are also hazardous.

- **Blackberry Torch:** "Use hands-free operation if it is available and keep at least 0.98in (25mm) from your body when turned on and connected to the wireless network. Reduce call time."
- **Apple iPhone:** "When using near your body for voice calls or for wireless network data, keep iPhone at least 15mm (5/8in) away from the body and only use accessories that do not have metal parts. Again maintain at least 15mm separation from the body."
- **Nokia C6:** "Maintain a normal use position at the ear at least 15mm (5/8in) away from the body. Any accessory should not contain metal and should position the device the above-stated distance from the body."

These guidelines protect the companies in case of a lawsuit, but in fact, wireless devices are dangerous much further away from body, as the very weak signals mimic the very faint electrical signals which govern our metabolism and in a chronic electro-smog environment, biological disruption occurs.

Home Smart Meters are at least 160 times more powerful than cell phones (Search internet "Hirsch Smart Meters")

The most important thing to know about wireless tech is that exposure standards by FCC (Federal Communications Commission) are obsolete. FCC uses Specific Absorption Rate (SAR) to measure whether a frequency heats your body. In 1993 the following comments were made about SAR (heat) standards …

- National Institute for Occupational Safety and Health (NIOSH): The FCC's standard is inadequate because it is based solely on one dominant mechanism—that adverse health effects are caused by **body heating.**
- Food and Drug Administration (FDA) "FCC rules do not address the issue of long-term, chronic exposure to RF fields."
- Environmental Protection Agency (EPA): The FCC's exposure guidelines are "seriously flawed.."

Over the past 10 years medical researchers collected almost 2000 studies showing that long term exposure to wireless frequencies cause cancer, genetic disruptions in the body cellular metabolism, and other diseases and reactions. (See Bioinitiative.org) Their research shows that FCC should be focusing on biological response to electromagnetic frequencies, and not worrying whether the new tech heats tissue.

But FCC has ignored criticism, because the FCC is actually controlled by the very industries that it is supposed to regulate. Just do search for "FCC revolving door" on internet to see how FCC and industry are in bed together.

On August 29, 2013, the American Association of Pediatrics submitted a letter to the FCC (http://bit.ly/17tQclg) …

> "As radiation standards are reassessed, the AAP urges the FCC to adopt radiation standards that: **Protect children's health and well-being.** Children are not little adults and are disproportionately impacted by all environmental exposures, including cell phone radiation.
>
> "Current FCC standards do not account for the unique vulnerability and use patterns specific to pregnant women and children. It is essential that any new standard for cell phones or other wireless devices be based on protecting the youngest and most vulnerable populations **to ensure they are safeguarded throughout their lifetimes."**

There are serious questions about wireless safety. Therefore, it is irresponsible for our schools to spend money on expensive routers, modems, iPads and other wireless tech. It is also prudent for Kauai Island Utility Cooperative to issue a warning about the Smart Meters and not penalize people for opting out.

Kauai residents are urged to become informed consumers. Kauai parents are urged to help educate our teachers and principals and superintendent. The state will resist bottom up reform, however we must convince authorities that caution is justified with new technology.

Many people are getting dizzy, losing sleep, and worse from, not just their own house meter, but from the dozens of "Smart Meters" on homes of neighbors. Still Smart Grid News, above, pushes the lie that RF emissions from Smart Meters are safe, using the obsolete corrupt FCC bulls**t standards. Please pardon me, dear reader, but the New World Order is "killing us softly."

Again, one of the best websites for medical research about wireless dangers is Bioinitiative.org

Or you can be sheeple …

> *"Diet, injections, and injunctions will combine, from a very early age, to produce the sort of character and the sort of beliefs that the authorities consider desirable, and any serious criticism of the powers that be, will become psychologically impossible."*
>
> – Bertrand Russell, *The Impact of Science on Society, 1952*

Student Science Experiment Finds Plants won't Grow near Wi-Fi Router

By Global Research News
Global Research, June 08, 2014
mnn.com and Global Research 30 May 2013

Region: Europe
Theme: Science and Medicine

 86.4K  62K  664  487  174  100K

Ninth-graders design science experiment to test the effect of cellphone radiation on plants. The results may surprise you.

Five ninth-grade young women from Denmark recently created a science experiment that is causing a stir in the scientific community.

It started with an observation and a question. The girls noticed that if they slept with their mobile phones near their heads at night, they often had difficulty concentrating at school the next day. They wanted to test the effect of a cellphone's radiation on humans, but their school, Hjallerup School in Denmark, did not have the equipment to handle such an experiment. So the girls designed an experiment that would test the effect of cellphone radiation on a plant instead.

Photo courtesy of Kim Horsevad, teacher at Hjallerup Skole in Denmark.

The students placed six trays filled with *Lepidium sativum*, a type of garden cress into a room without radiation, and six trays of the seeds into another room next to two routers that according to the girls calculations, emitted about the same type of radiation as an ordinary cellphone.

Over the next 12 days, the girls observed, measured, weighed and photographed their results. Although by the end of the experiment the results were blatantly obvious — the cress seeds placed near the router had not grown. Many of them were completely dead. While the cress seeds planted in the other room, away from the routers, thrived.
The experiment earned the girls (pictured below) top honors in a regional science competition and the interest of scientists around the world.

Thousands of suppressed scientific papers revealing wi-fi dangers are available at www.Bioinitiative.org. Wi-fi is being used to lower life expectancy and is part of de-population agenda. Cancers from wi-fi are sanctioned diseases.

It is fairly certain that industry funded scientists will debunk this experiment and the idea will be publicized widely that there is nothing to be concerned about. However, I have found no follow up news about this experiment in English, so, it appears it is being ignored. Ignored??? Meanwhile, I suggest that the reader do as I have ... hard wire everything in your home and talk to your neighbors about EMF pollution.

These girls deserve our respect. They noticed that sleeping near a wireless device had a biological effect and they investigated. This is true girl power! Protecting health!

ANOTHER FAKE PANDEMIC

One automatically thinks that Disease Control means trying to stop disease, but the CDC is a New World Order organization that studies diseases so it can manage them, not stop them. Just as FEMA (Federal Emergency Management Agency) helps produce emergencies it can manage (more in last chapters), so does the Center of Disease Control, which controls where and when diseases will appear. Managing includes creating new strains of disease and disseminating these strains to harm the public world wide in targeted campaigns. The reader can quickly research the fake SARS, Bird Flu and Swine flu scares, all manufactured by the CDC.

CDC Votes in Favor of a Flu Vaccination Assault on Americans' Health

– by Richard Gale and Gary Null, the Progressive Radio Network, July 2, 2010

A central principle of democracy is freedom of choice. We can choose our political party, our religion, and the food we eat, but this does not seem to be the case when it comes to our medical choices and our freedoms to make them.

The recent unanimous 11-0 vote by the members of the Centers for Disease Control's Advisory Committee on Immunization Practices (ACIP) favoring every American over the age of six months receive the flu influenza vaccine is one more attempt by our federal health officials to open up our bodies to the free market capitalism of pharmaceutical coffers. It is another step to mandate a vaccine across the nation, a policy that has many supporters in the pro-vaccine science community. [Since this article, California now has mandatory vaccines]

[There are many doctors and scientists who are publicizing strong doubts about vaccine safety, yet the CDC, which was already shown on Page 81 to be untrustworthy, has an "advisory committee" where not one of eleven members considered a precautionary principle. Unanimous, in this case, means all these people are *cutouts* who voted as instructed.]

The vote raises an alarm about our federal government's scientific integrity, and calls into question its true allegiance and purpose: to protect the health of American citizens or increase Big Pharma profits. If the recommendation were ever enforced, the U.S. would be the only nation in the world with mandatory flu vaccination. However, what our investigations show and what differentiates the U.S. health agencies from the health ministries in other nations, is that in the U.S. federal health system Big Pharma money, lobbying and corporate favors are what shape drug and vaccine policies and this is rampant throughout the system.

Mandatory vaccines fail in Japan

Mandatory influenza vaccination has been tried before across a nation. During the 1980s, Japan had mandatory flu vaccination for school children. Two large scale studies that enrolled children from four cities with vaccination rates between 1 and 90 percent discovered no difference in the incidences of flu infection. As a result, in 1987, Japanese health authorities ruled that flu vaccination was ineffective and was no more than a serious financial and legal liability if it was to continue. The mandatory policy was quickly overturned. By 1989, the number of Japanese taking the flu vaccine dropped to 20 percent. A follow up study at that time found that there was statistically insignificant change in influenza infection rates compared to when the vaccine was mandatory.

Now we are hearing that for the forthcoming 2010-2011 flu season, the H1N1 flu strain will be included in the seasonal flu vaccine. This will be a quadravalent vaccine comprised of four strains including the H1N1. As of this month, the World Health Organization (WHO) continues to evaluate the H1NI virus at a 5 level pandemic and issues warnings to deaf ears now that people realize the WHO's word is disreputable. Nevertheless, we should still brace ourselves for another year of old yarn, fear-mongering, media spin and more voodoo science.

A brief overview of the past H1N1 pandemic boondoggle will help us to understand the addiction of denial permeating the ranks of the CDC's advisory committee. It presents a picture of a delusional bubble, unrelated to medical facts, that the CDC has found comfort to float within. The simple fact remains that **the CDC is disconnected from anything resembling legitimate science** thereby making their recent decision ludicrous and **criminally irresponsible**.

The CDC's predictions of particular strains during past flu seasons has never been especially accurate. In fact, often it has been extraordinarily dismal. The previous swine flu prediction in 1976 resulted in only one swine flu death but hundreds of people suffering permanent disabilities, including death, from the vaccine. For the 1992-1993 flu season, the prediction made for the virus used in the vaccine was off by 84 percent. For the 1994-1995 season, it was off by

43 percent for the primary strain targeted and off 87 percent and 76 percent for the other two strains. The Laboratory Center for Disease Control's study comparing vaccine strains with the strains appearing during the 1997-1998 season found the match off by 84 percent. One would achieve a greater accuracy rate by simply flipping a coin.

The CDC's scare tactics

An article published in the prestigious British Medical Journal in 2005, "Are U.S. Flu Death Figures More PR Than Science" is apropos for addressing the wildly inflated figures by the WHO and CDC to present their case for mass vaccination measures. The article begins, "U.S. data on influenza deaths are a mess." The study reviews the CDC's own statistical data and finds numerous inconsistencies and incompatibilities between "official estimates and national vital statistics data." Although the government's predictions never came close to the "dire outcomes" stated by our health officials, the CDC's own communication strategy was marked by high levels of fear.

The U.S. government's assessment of the past H1N1 scare is another example of flawed science and incompetence. In last August's issue of *USA Today*, the White House's Council of Advisors on Science and Technology, which receives its recommendations from the CDC, warned us that the H1N1 would kill between 30-90,000 American citizens. At the same time, the CDC was predicting 2 million people would be infected and as high as 40 percent of the entire population. The WHO, which sleeps in the same bed with the CDC in their shared complexes in Atlanta, was screaming figures of 7.5 million deaths worldwide. Consequently, the FDA fast-tracked swine flu vaccines manufactured by 5 different drug makers, none which met reliable standards of viable clinical testing and data to determine their efficacy and safety.

And pregnant women, young children and the elderly were primary targets—those also most susceptible to serious vaccine adverse reactions. Over $1.6 billion tax dollars went to Big Pharma on orders of 229 million doses, of which only 90 million were actually administered and the remaining 71 million left to decompose on shelves or dump off on poorer nations out of the graciousness of the American philanthropic spirit.

However, as we witnessed in 2009 and the early months of 2010, people woke up to the false alarm of a swine flu pandemic. Often intuition is better suited to sniff out a hoax and scandal than the pseudo-science our federal health officials give obeisance to behind closed door conference rooms. And in the case of the so-called H1N1 pandemic, intuition proved correct. Our health agencies' warnings and numbers propagandized over mainstream media simply did not add up and have been consistently found to be contrary to more medically reliable and unbiased facts generated by independent sources without ties to the private vaccine manufacturers.

Whenever the CDC, the FDA and the U.S. Department of Health and Human Services post figures, it is a prudent rule of thumb to be suspicious and investigate their accuracy. The fact of the matter is that the CDC is completely clueless about this past season's flu infection rate and the number of deaths due to the H1N1 strain. Let us explain why.

No proper testing was ever conducted

Immediately following the WHO's decision in May 2009 to cease laboratory testing of samples to determine the actual biological cause of infectious cases with influenza-like symptoms, the U.S. followed suit. Therefore, no matter what they tell you, no matter what Dr. Gupta and other tools of the media and establishment have to say, no proper testing was performed. Only PCR technology can determine the actual subset of a Type A flu strain, such as H1N1. But PCR diagnosis was not routinely performed in order to monitor and track rates and the spread of infection. By its own admission, a CDC report found that rapid influenza kits used in hospitals and clinics were wrong as much as nine out of ten times, and on average between 40-69 percent. The CDC determined that the instant tests are "not highly worthwhile for diagnosing H1N1 infections."

So why would any organization responsible for the tracking of an infectious disease believed to be a global health threat, potentially threatening the lives of millions of people, make such a decision to not carefully monitor flu infections is beyond comprehension, unless it knowingly determined, with malice of forethought, that the H1N1 strain was mild and not a national danger. And many independent experts in infectious diseases had been stating this throughout the season but our health agencies preferred to ignore their warnings.

Yet it is the reported death rates due to H1N1 infection that seriously call the CDC's integrity into question. According to the CDC reports, anywhere between 8,870 and 18,300 Americans died from swine flu. For the sake of simplicity, the health feds conveniently circulate the figure of 12,000 deaths.

Projections in the UK were equally off the mark. The British Ministry of Health was expecting 65,000 deaths, but reported only 500 towards the season's end. British citizens, however, were better informed of the scandalous hoax and of the 110 million vaccine doses purchased, under contracts amounting to over $864 million to the drug makers (not including national preparatory measures bringing the total to over $1 billion for a small population), only 6 million Brits, approximately 10 percent, were vaccinated.

What figures does the World Health Organization report for the number of worldwide swine flu deaths? 18,036. That is correct, not millions. That is only 5 percent of the global figure for deaths associated with the regular seasonal flu. I don't need an advanced degree to notice a grave discrepancy here, unless we are to believe that the H1N1 virus was on autopilot to target victims with American birth certificates or citizenship. But the reasons for the CDC's erroneous numbers are quite easy to understand.

The CDC's flawed statistics

First, as mentioned, the CDC did not monitor the swine flu with any precision and accuracy. Our officials don't have, and never had, the data to make any accurate determination.

Second, the CDC does not distinguish between deaths caused by an influenza virus and deaths due to pneumonia. The two are lumped together in their mortality statistics and pneumonia-related deaths are reported as having an initial influenza cause. For example, if we take the combined figure of flu and pneumonia deaths for the flu period of 2001, and spin the figures, we are left believing that 62,034 people died from influenza. The actual figures are **61,777 died from pneumonia and only 257 from flu.**

Even more amazing, in those 257 cases, only 18 were scientifically identified as positive for the flu virus. These are the CDC's own figures. But does the New York Times, Boston Globe, Washington Post and all the others report this? No. Do any of the puppets that mumble on television, with access to official sources and data, actually do their homework? No.

A separate study conducted by the National Center for Health Statistics for the flu periods between 1979 and 2002 reveals that the actual range of annual flu deaths were between 257 and 3006, for an average of 1,348 per year. This is a far cry from the 36,000 annual flu deaths still found on the CDC's website and vomited by the major media.

And here is the catch. If we apply the same criteria to determine the actual number of swine flu related deaths in 2009-2010, serious vaccine adverse effects, besides the hundreds of reported miscarriages, would far outweigh deaths and injury due to the virus.

Third, there are over 150 different viruses during any given flu season that can cause flu-like symptoms, such as adenovirus, parainfluenza, bocavirus, etc. Very few of these are ever tested. For example, in Canada where actual infection rates are more carefully monitored, during the 2004-2005 flu season, the Canada Communicable Disease Report showed that of the 68,849 laboratory tests performed for influenza, only 14.9% tested positive for a flu virus. The remaining 85.1% specimens were a result of other pathogens impervious to flu vaccines. For the following 2005-2006 season, Health Canada received 68,439 tests for influenza like infections. Of these, only 6,580, or 10.4% confirmed positive for influenza. The rest, 89.6%, were other pathogens. So no vaccine would have benefitted or protected those almost 90 percent in Canadians.

In the U.S., however, the CDC relies upon an esoteric witch's brew of figures based upon various mathematical algorithms and speculative projections with no sound basis in reality. On one CDC site we find evidence of their flawed methodology: "Statistical modeling was used to estimate how many flu-related deaths occurred among people whose underlying cause of death on their death certificate was listed as a respiratory and circulatory disease." This is clearly an indication of policy turned dogmatic with utterly disregard for sound scientific evidence. It is all business as usual, negligent disregard for scientific reason, and full speed ahead.

And while the brilliant minds in the CDC decide to expose all Americans to the adverse risks of influenza vaccination—Guillain-Barre Syndrome, schizophrenia, neurological disorders, miscarriages, polyneuritis, encephalitis, multiple sclerosis, intense headaches suggestive or meningeal or brain irritation, aphasia (loss of speech), bronchopneumonia, sexual impotence, angor pectoris, anaphylactic reactions and death—we should not lose sight of what is unfolding across the great pond in the European Union's investigations into the CDC's favorite bed partner—the WHO, an utterly corrupt organization at every level.

Corruption at the WHO

Two reports recently published have indicted the WHO for serious malfeasance and conflict in interests behind the fabrication and propagation of the 2009-2010 H1N1 swine flu pandemic and has been called a "momentous error" in global health oversight. The people at the WHO had as much accuracy in their predictions as the Bush administration did with WMDs in Iraq.

The British Medical Journal printed a research paper by its Features Editor, Deborah Cohen, and Philip Carter from the Bureau of Investigative Journalism in London, charging the largest global health organization with **exaggerating the H1N1 flu and being steered in their decisions and fraudulent fear campaign by the pharmaceutical industrial complex**. According to the authors, "credibility of the WHO and the trust in the global public health system" has been damaged.

A second devastating preliminary report released by the Health Committee of the Parliamentary Assembly of the Council of Europe (CE) found gross negligence and lack of *transparency* in the WHO's handling of the swine flu scare. Throughout the WHO's key advisory committees, particularly a secretive group known as the "emergency committee," which steered the WHO's assessment and predictions of the spread of H1N1 flu virus and advised them to announce a level 6 pandemic, were scientists entrenched in the morass of private vaccine and drug interests, particularly GlaxoSmithKline (H1N1 vaccine and Relenza anti-viral drug maker) and Tamiflu maker Roche AG.

Even worse, **the WHO never publicly disclosed widespread conflict of interests.** Paul Flynn, the rapporteur for the CE's report stated, "the tentacles of drug company influence are in all levels of the decision-making process," and "they vastly over-rated the danger on bad science." Following a lengthy investigation, a preliminary report, which still awaits a final version next month, states the result of the WHO's negligence in proper oversight resulted in the "waste of large sums of public money and unjustified scares and fears about the health risks faced by the European public."

The WHO continues to withhold the names of the 16 members sitting on its secret "emergency committee." However, this week, two of the members resigned, notably Dr. John MacKenzie from Curtin University in Australia, who was the WHO advisor who first urged the organization to call a pandemic and is well known to be entangled in financial interests and investments with the pharmaceutical cartel.

So far the CDC has weathered the WHO controversy in Europe unscathed. A fundamental oversight in the CE's investigation and hearings has been solely targeting the WHO. It ignores the role of government health agencies' complicity in promulgating the H1N1 hoax and the flushing away of billions of dollars into the drug industry, especially during an economic downturn and recession. As we witness the WHO's indifference and denial of wrongdoing crumble, the question remains over whether or not the CDC was complicit in the propagandizing of the astronomically expensive H1N1 hoax.

Of course, the vaccine industry doesn't give a damn about the investigations. Their vaccines, anti-viral drugs, and oligarchic rule over the medical caste system make them immune to independent international scrutiny. And we can be assured none of the lap dogs at the New York Times, MSNBC and other major media would expose their crimes. In the shadow of this medical charade, the drug makers are laughing their way to the banks. No Big Pharma executive is sitting before investigative committees to give an accounting of corporations' role in the pandemic debacle. Instead, after scoring over $6 billion (Associated Press, May 19, 2010) it is again business as usual and another flu season ahead to further increase revenues.

Financial corruption at every level

Similar to the WHO, the CDC's Advisory Committee on Vaccination and Practice, which voted in favor of a flu vaccine-for-all policy, is equally stacked with individuals entrenched in financial ties with the vaccine and drug makers. The Committee's Chair, Dr. Carol Baker from Baylor University, has consistently received research and educational grants and private donations from Big Pharma. She is also on the Board of Directors of the National Foundation of Infectious Diseases, a consulting body of scientists frequently wined and dined and provided perks by the pharmaceutical industrial complex.

Another Baylor University committee member, Dr. Wendy Keitel, received clinical trial support from Novartis, the maker of the H1N1 vaccine most widely distributed in the U.S., Dr. Janet Englund at the Children's University Medical Group in Seattle received financial support for clinical trials favoring vaccines made by Medimmune (the nasal flu vaccine), Novartis, and Sanofi Pasteur. Dr. Cody Meissner received Big Pharma support through Tufts University for his supporting clinical trials for Medimmune's RSV vaccine and for participation in Wyeth's streptococcus vaccine for children, Prevnar.

To put this into greater perspective, since the FDA relies on industry-funded clinical trials and subsequent data to approve vaccines and drugs, there also appeared in the news this month a critical finding from the German Institute for Quality and Efficacy in Health Care, published in the peer-reviewed journal Trials. The study investigated 90 approved drugs in the U.S. (and let us make no mistake, vaccines are drugs! In fact, the flu vaccine is listed as a Category C drug; which means there are no adequate safety studies to determine whether flu vaccination adversely affects pregnant mothers and their fetuses.) and discovered that 60 percent of the 900 papers were unpublished and some were concealed from the federal regulatory agencies. Forty to sixty percent omitted clinical details or changed their final analysis. Among the pharmaceutical industry studies alone, 94 percent were unpublished, and 86 percent of the university studies sponsored by drug makers remained unpublished.

What does this tell us? If they were positive results, the drug companies would without hesitation publish their findings; but if the clinical studies' results contradict their expectations negatively, thereby delaying and preventing regulatory approval and licensure of a product, then there is no incentive for their release. And they are under no regulatory obligation to publish or produce them. Hence **the American public is denied approximately 90 percent of the actual clinical data** performed on any given drug or vaccine."

– Gary Null and Richard Gale *Progressive Radio Network, July 2, 2010*

And now we have the newest scare being rolled out. The dreaded Ebola scare. This comment on a *Natural News* article is telling …

> "In Liberia, where the Ebola outbreak was reported to be the worst, cell phones have 70 percent market penetration and the Internet is a well established reality. Yet not one doctor, not one teenager walking the streets, not one sad mother with a dead child, not one plumber, nurse, police officer, relief worker, soldier, security guard, dog catcher or ANYONE ELSE ever uploaded a SINGLE PHOTO that would confirm the outbreak was real. All we had was the scamming zio press uploading "Ebola photo-scapes" that never showed ONE PICTURE of what they were even talking about. Just a hospital with rows of people in bed, showing no Ebola symptoms on the 6 o'clock news … and a few doctors walking around in white bio-hazard suits. Yet we're all suppose to believe it's all legit? … right."

Figure 2: Ebola virus disease cases reported each week from Liberia and Monrovia

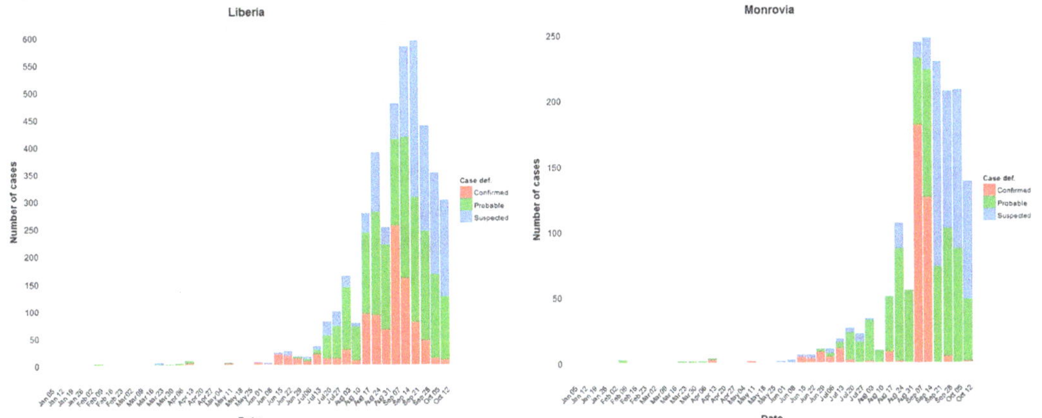

Data are based on official information reported by Ministries of Health up to the end of 12 October for Guinea and Sierra Leone, and 11 October Liberia. These numbers are subject to change due to ongoing reclassification, retrospective investigation and availability of laboratory results.

WHO Data as of October 8, 2014 shows that Ebola has all but disappeared in Liberia, as the western media scares the world with panic. Intentional breaches in protocol and possibly outright murder creates "victims," none of whom display bleeding or hemorrhaging, as of this writing in mid-October, 2014.

The CDC, NIH & Bill Gates Own the Patents On Existing Ebola & Related Vaccines: Mandatory Vaccinations Are Near

– by Dave Hodges 17 September, 2014

"I have previously reported that Monsanto, or Monsatan as many call them, has partnered with the Department of Defense to use a proxy third party company to develop a vaccine against Ebola. The seed money began at $1.5 million. The value of the deal could grow to an estimated $86 million. The company's name is Tekmira Pharmaceuticals Corporation (TKMR) (TKM.TO), a leading developer of RNA interference (RNAi) therapeutics. "TKM-Ebola, an anti-Ebola virus RNAi therapeutic, is being developed under a $140 million contract with the U.S. Department of Defense's Medical Countermeasure Systems BioDefense Therapeutics (MCS-BDTX) Joint Product Management Office." As breaking and shocking of a news story as this has the potential to be, the real story is that this is not the most important part of the Ebola threat which has invaded the United States. The truth of the matter is that these unholy and untrustworthy associations, when it comes to "fighting" the Ebola virus, represent the mere tip of the iceberg.

"The more one digs into who is behind the creation and the development of vaccines for treating Ebola, the more the conspiracy networks widen. The most amazing fact is how incredibly easy it was to locate this information. I want to be clear on this point, Ebola was invented, a vaccine for Ebola has existed for 8-10 years, some government sponsored institutions as well as some of the global elite have positioned themselves to profit enormously from the spread of the virus and the development of and dissemination of mandatory Ebola vaccines and the imposition of total martial law in the process. Here is the proof.

"Amazingly, the CDC owns "the" patent on Ebola and all future strains.

"The "SUMMARY OF THE INVENTION" section of the patent document also clearly claims that the U.S. government is claiming "ownership" over all Ebola viruses that share as little as 70% similarity with the Ebola it "invented:"

"Why would a government organization claim to have "invented" this infectious disease and then claim a monopoly over its exploitation for commercial use? It is clear that the CDC plans to claim royalties on Ebola vaccines. This certainly increases the likelihood that the vaccines will become mandatory, thus increasing the profit potential for the patent holders.

Publication number	CA2741523 A1
Publication type	Application
Application number	CA 2741523
PCT number	PCT/US2009/062079
Publication date	Apr 29, 2010
Filing date	Oct 26, 2009
Priority date	Oct 24, 2008
Also published as	EP2350270A2, 4 More »
Inventors	Jonathan S. Towner, Stuart T. Nichol, James A. Comer, Thomas G. Ksiazek, Pierre E. Rollin
Applicant	Jonathan S. Towner, 5 More »
Export Citation	BiBTeX, EndNote, RefMan

Classifications (21), Legal Events (1)
External Links: CIPO, Espacenet

"Clearly, Ebola is manmade and this patent proves this contention. Why does the CDC need to own the patent on Ebola? Perhaps, we should ask Bill Gates why he is donating $50 million to the UN and the CDC in the name of fighting Ebola. The CDC has partners in the fight against Ebola, namely, Crucell Inc., the National Institute of Health (NIH) and the U.S. Army Medical Research Institute of Infectious Diseases (USAMRIID) and, of course, Bill and Melinda Gates.

"Since when would Gates not expect a return on his investment? Gates and Michael Bloomberg have already contributed large sums of money to numerous vaccination causes such as the Global Polio Eradication Initiative originally launched in 1988 by the World Health Organization (WHO), Rotary International, Centers for Disease Control and Prevention (CDC), and the United Nations Children's Fund (UNICEF). The return on investment has been impressive.

"Gates has announced that he plans to vaccinate every child in the third world with multiple vaccines, which could result in a dramatic population reduction of 10-15%. Do you realize the enormous profits that can be realized by vaccinating every child in the third world? If we apply Gates' penchant for investing in causes which produce a hefty "return on investment" (ROI) then one could reasonably suspect that Gates is positioning himself to profit on the $50 million he has invested in the Ebola cause which conveniently includes the CDC, the holder of the patent for Ebola.

"The NIH presently holds all patents on Ebola vaccines. Crucell is much like Tekimara is to Monsanto in that they are fronting the science for the Ebola vaccine treatment patents.

What You Are Not Being Told: Fast facts From Crucell Inc.'s Website

- Crucell is developing an Ebola vaccine in collaboration with the Vaccine Research Center (VRC) of the NIH National Institute of Allergy and Infectious Diseases (NIAID). It has been shown to completely protect monkeys against the virus with a single dose of the vaccine.

- Under the terms of the agreement with VRC, Crucell has an option for exclusive worldwide commercialization rights to the Ebola vaccine.
- Crucell's Ebola vaccine entered Phase I clinical trials in Q3 2006. Two groups of 16 volunteers were enrolled and vaccinated. The study showed safety and immunogenicity at the doses evaluated.
- In October 2008, Crucell secured a NIAID/NIH award to advance the development of Ebola and Marburg vaccines, with the ultimate aim of developing a multivalent filovirus vaccine.
- The award provides funding of up to $30 million, with additional options, worth a further $40 million.

"Do you understand how much we are being lied to by the media on this topic? The work on an Ebola virus, sanctioned by the holder of the patent for the vaccine, the NIH, has been ongoing since 2004 with clinical trials in 2006. This explains why the CDC and the NIH are bringing Ebola patients into the country to treat. The moment that an Ebola patient crosses the U.S. border, they become the intellectual property of the CDC, NIH and Bill and Melinda Gates! How can we not believe that this is the Hegelian Dialectic run amok in a case of problem creation, solution to the problem and reaction to the problem?

"The involvement of the USAMRIID is noteworthy because the Army has long been rumored to have created Ebola and, for purposes of experimentation, implanted the artificial virus in Zaire in 1977.

"When an unsuspecting public is finally told of the existence of an Ebola vaccine, the Global Fund will be in charge of the distribution of the vaccine. Interestingly, Bill Gates has donated a total of $560 million dollars to the Global Fund. The Global Fund has also positioned themselves to be in charge of the distribution of the "newly developed," and not yet announced, vaccines for TB and HIV. Since the goal is the vaccination of every man, woman and child on the planet with multiple vaccines, Gates' $560 contribution to the Global Fund is chump change compared to the expected ROI. However, on deck is the Ebola virus.

"I mentioned in Part One of this series that my best *military* insider source has told me that the Department of Homeland Security has taken over the plans for mandatory Ebola vaccinations and the imposition of martial law. I also mentioned in Part One how very few soldiers and police officers will actually realize that they are actually enforcing martial law since they are merely reacting to a "health crisis," albeit contrived, which will involve severe travel restrictions and the quarantining of segments of the population of the country. If one really wants to appreciate the depth of this conspiracy and the players involved, I would recommend visiting the Crucell website which is linked above.

"The operational details of the mandatory vaccination program will be forthcoming in a future article."

– by Dave Hodges, September 17, 2014 [62]

Ebola Outbreak and Impossibly Rapid Vaccine Response Clearly Scripted

– by Mike Adams, the Health Ranger, September 19, 2014

"On the very same day that vaccine maker Glaxo Smith Kline is being fined $490 million by Chinese authorities for running an illegal bribery scheme across China, the media is announcing the "astonishing" launch of human trials for an Ebola vaccine.

"Care to guess who will be manufacturing this vaccine once it is whitewashed and rubber-stamped as "approved?" Glaxo Smith Kline, of course. The same company that also admitted to a massive criminal bribery network in the United States, where felony crimes were routinely committed to funnel money to over 40,000 physicians who pushed dangerous prescription drugs onto patients.

"This is the company that is now—today!—injecting 60 "volunteers" with an experimental Ebola vaccine.

Spontaneous vaccine development a scientific impossibility

BBC: "Normally it would take years of human trials before a completely new vaccine was approved for use," reports the BBC. (1) "But such is the urgency of the Ebola outbreak in west Africa that this experimental vaccine is being fast tracked at an astonishing rate."

"Yes, it's astonishing because it's impossible.

"As any vaccine-related virologist already knows, the process of going from an in-the-wild infection of Ebola to a manufactured vaccine ready for human trials *simply cannot be achieved in a matter of a few weeks or months.* Apparently, we are all to believe that a spontaneous scientific miracle has now taken place–a literal act of vaccine magic—which has allowed the criminal vaccine industry to skip the tedious R&D phases and create a vaccine ready for human trials merely by waving a magic wand.

"The first of 60 healthy volunteers will be injected with the vaccine," says the BBC today, and vaccine pushers are of course lining up to proclaim the vaccine miracle which has spontaneously appeared before them like a burning bush:

> "Professor Adrian Hill, director of the Jenner Institute in Oxford, who is leading the trial, said: 'This is a remarkable example of how quickly a new vaccine can be progressed into the clinic, using international co-operation.'"

Near-proof that this was all scripted

"The far more likely explanation, of course, is that *all this was scripted in advance:* the outbreak, the international cry for help, the skyrocketing of the stock price for Tekmira (which has received financial investments from Monsanto), the urgent call for a vaccine and now the spontaneous availability of human vaccine trials. It's all beautifully scripted from start to finish, better than a Shakespearean tragedy played out on the international stage.

"The 'heroes' of this theater have been pre-ordained to be drug companies and vaccines, and it is already written in the script that vaccines will be heralded as lifesaving miracles of modern science *even if they infect people and cause widespread damage* as has now happened to young girls in Colombia who are being hospitalized *en masse* after being injected with HPV vaccines.

"Incredibly, the official response from vaccine-pushing health authorities in Colombia is that all these girls who are suffering from paralysis are merely "imagining" their symptoms and suffering from "mass hysteria." Obviously, if vaccines are created by the gods of modern science—the new cult of our delusional world—then they must be perfect and infallible. Therefore, anyone who suffers side effects of such perfect vaccines must obviously be imagining things. Such is the delusional dogma of modern vaccine pushers.

"This will be the exact same explanation leveled against anyone who suffers harmful effects from an Ebola vaccine, too. After all, the discovery of vaccine side effects simply isn't in the script being played out before us. Therefore, it cannot be allowed, and any person who actually suffers side effects will be immediately deemed to be mentally ill. (Yes, this is how insane and Orwellian the vaccine industry has become. All who now bow down to the voodoo of dangerous vaccines are labeled mental patients and then treated with psychiatric drugs. The vaccine industry has quite literally become the Heaven's Gate Cult of modern medicine …)"

The United States government now owns the patent on Ebola

"This plot gets even more interesting when you realize that a patent on Ebola was awarded to the United States government just four years ago, in 2010. That patent, number CA2741523A1, is available here.

"Astonishingly, the patent claims U.S. government ownership over all variants of Ebola which share 70% or more of the protein sequences described in the patent: "[CLAIMS] … a nucleotide sequence of at least 70%-99% identity to the SEQ ID …"

Furthermore, the patent also claims ownership over any and all Ebola viruses which are "weakened" or "killed," meaning the United States government is literally claiming ownership over all Ebola vaccines. What this means, of course, is that *the U.S. government can demand royalties on all Ebola vaccines.* Even more Orwellian is the fact that the U.S. government can use this patent to halt all other research for treatments or cures for Ebola.

Patent monopoly gives U.S. government legal right to block all non-vaccine Ebola treatments, cures or research

Do you remember the massive medical controversy over the BRCA1 gene tied to breast cancer in women? One corporation claimed patent ownership over the gene and then *they used that patent to shut down all other research, testing or diagnosis of breast cancer* related to that gene. To date, nearly 20% of the human genome has been claimed as "owned" by corporations, universities and even the government.

The controversy went all the way to the U.S. Supreme Court which ultimately ruled that human genes cannot be patented. But the Supreme Court decision actually protected patents on gene sequences for viruses and other pathogens.

The truth of the matter is that anyone who owns the Ebola gene patent can legally use that patent to shut down all research on Ebola, including research for non-vaccine medical treatments and cures. This is how medical monopolies are reinforced—by monopolizing all the research and all the "cures."

Even more frightening, the "ownership" over Ebola extends to Ebola circulating in the bodies of Ebola victims. When Dr. Kent Brantly was relocated from Africa to the CDC's care in Atlanta, that entire scene was carried out under the quasi-legal justification that *the U.S. government "owned" the Ebola circulating in Dr. Brantly's blood.* Thus, one of the very first things that took place was the acquisition of his blood samples for archiving and R&D by the CDC and the U.S. Department of Defense.

(Only the gullible masses think that was about saving the life of a doctor. The real mission was to acquire the Ebola strain circulating in his body and use it for weaponization research, vaccine research and other R&D purposes.)

Anyone infected with Ebola is now deemed to be carrying "government property" in the form of a patented virus

This brings us to the quarantine issue. As the whole world knows by now, the entire nation of Sierra Leone is now under a state of *medical martial law,* where Ebola victims are now being hunted down like fugitives in door-to-door manhunts.

Simultaneously, the United States government is now operating under Obama's executive order #13674, signed on July 31, 2014, which allows the U.S. federal government to arrest and quarantine any person who shows symptoms of infectious disease.

His executive order allows federal agents to forcibly arrest and quarantine anyone showing symptoms of:

> *... Severe acute respiratory syndromes, which are diseases that are associated with fever and signs and symptoms of pneumonia or other respiratory illness, are capable of being transmitted from person to person, and that either are causing, or have the potential to cause, a pandemic, or, upon infection, are highly likely to cause mortality or serious morbidity if not properly controlled.*

Part of the legal argument for justifying such a quarantine in the case of Ebola goes like this: *If you are carrying Ebola in your body, then you are in possession of U.S. government property!*

The fact that the virus is replicating in your body is, legally speaking, a violation of patent law. Because you are providing a host environment for the replication of the virus, you technically are breaking federal laws that restrict the copying and distributed of patented properties, which in this case include the Ebola virus.

Thus, the government has every right to "relocate" you and prevent you from violating patent law by replicating, distributing or spreading THEIR intellectual property (i.e. the Ebola virus).

Lest you think this legal argument sounds insane, just remember that the legal system is full of lawyers who make far more insane arguments on a daily basis, including the argument that human genes could be patented in the first place. And medical officials also make insane, irrational arguments almost constantly, including the argument that all those girls in Colombia who are suffering convulsions and paralysis from the HPV vaccine are merely "imagining" their symptoms. Such explanations flatly defy any attachment to sane thinking.

Ultimately, *the patent on the Ebola virus provides the legal justification for forced government quarantines—and even medical research—on Ebola victims.*

"Ebola is a genetically modified organism"

What I've outlined in this story is just a small taste of the crime against humanity which is taking place right before our eyes. I am now convinced that this Ebola outbreak is very likely not an accident, and many scientists in Africa wholeheartedly agree that the outbreak is actually the deployment of a biological weapon.

"Ebola is a genetically modified organism (GMO)," declared Dr. Cyril Broderick, Professor of Plant Pathology, in a front-page story published in the Liberian Observer. (6)

He goes on to explain:

[Horowitz] confirmed the existence of an American Military-Medical-Industry that conducts biological weapons tests under the guise of administering vaccinations to control diseases and improve the health of "black Africans overseas."

SITES AROUND AFRICA, AND IN WEST AFRICA, HAVE OVER THE YEARS BEEN SET UP FOR TESTING EMERGING DISEASES, ESPECIALLY EBOLA.

The World Health Organization (WHO) and several other UN Agencies have been implicated in selecting and enticing African countries to participate in the testing events, promoting vaccinations, but pursuing various testing regiments.

AFRICAN LEADERS AND AFRICAN COUNTRIES NEED TO TAKE THE LEAD IN DEFENDING BABIES, CHILDREN, AFRICAN WOMEN, AFRICAN MEN, AND THE ELDERLY. THESE CITIZENS DO NOT DESERVE TO BE USED AS GUINEA PIGS!

Africa must not relegate the Continent to become the locality for disposal and the deposition of hazardous chemicals, dangerous drugs, and chemical or biological agents of emerging diseases. There is urgent need for affirmative action in protecting the less affluent of poorer countries, especially African citizens, whose countries are not as scientifically and industrially endowed as the United States and most Western countries, sources of most viral or bacterial GMOs that are strategically designed as biological weapons. It is most disturbing that the U. S. Government has been operating a viral hemorrhagic fever bioterrorism research laboratory in Sierra Leone.

The world must be alarmed. All Africans, Americans, Europeans, Middle Easterners, Asians, and people from every conclave on Earth should be astonished. African people, notably citizens more particularly of Liberia, Guinea and Sierra Leone are victimized and are dying every day.

If you really want to learn the truth about all this, listen to the free *Pandemic Preparedness* audio course available right now at www.BioDefense.com

Nearly one million people have now visited www.BioDefense.com since its launch last week. Find out there what the mainstream media won't dare tell you. Your life may quite literally depend on it.

– Mike Adams, Natural News, September 19, 2014 [63]

U.S. Bioweapons Lab in Sierra Leone at the Epicenter of Ebola Outbreak

– By Jane Burgermeister, birdflu666.wordpress.com

*U.S. bioweapons lab with links to the Bill and Melinda Gates Foundation at core of Ebola epidemic

*CDC admits hospitals and vaccines cause Ebola

*UK and U.S. mainstream media fuel Ebola hysteria

*The Telegraph hypes Ebola as a threat to Britain

*Epidemic and pandemic plans allow for implementation of martial law

A stunning piece of propaganda in establishment newspaper The Telegraph seems to be preparing the British public for a false flag Ebola outbreak at the Commonwealth Games starting in Glasgow on July 23.
http://www.telegraph.co.uk/news/worldnews/africaandindianocean/guinea/10942598/Ebola-out-of-control-in-West-Africa-as-health-workers-rush-to-trace-1500-possible-victims.html

The Telegraph buries a key aspect of the Story – the evidence that a U.S. bioweapons lab in Sierra Leone with links to the Soros and Bill and Melinda Gates Foundation is likely the origin of the current Ebola outbreak.

While The Telegraph buries facts about the existence of this hospital bioweapons research lab and also ignores information in the U.S. Centers for Disease Control's (CDC) Ebola fact sheet which identifies hospitals as the place where an Ebola outbreak is most likely to occur, Washington Post reporter Terence McCoy has entered the realm of fairy tales by blaming the current Ebola outbreak on deforestation
http://www.washingtonpost.com/news/morning-mix/wp/2014/07/08/how-deforestation-and-human-activity-could-be-to-blame-for-the-ebola-pandemic/?tid=hp_mm

"Like most matters involving an Ebola epidemic, chronicling its first horrifying infection is not an easy endeavor," McCoy sighs.

It is easy, Terence. Just read the CDC's Ebola Hemorrhagic Fever Information Packet which says that Ebola comes from hospitals and vaccinations in most cases.
http://www.cdc.gov/ncidod/dvrd/spb/mnpages/dispages/Fact_Sheets/Ebola_Fact_Booklet.pdf

The CDC Ebola fact sheet admits on the very first page that clinics and hospitals are "frequently" the places of Ebola outbreaks.

The CDC fact sheet also states that the first ever Ebola deaths in 1976 were caused by " …(close personal contact and by use of contaminated needles and syringes in) hospitals/clinics" .

In the second ever Ebola outbreak in 1976 in Sudan killing 151 people, the "[]Disease was spread mainly through close personal contact within hospitals," says the CDC in language which could not be plainer.

McCoy prefers, however, to misrepresent the dry facts concerning Ebola originating in hospitals, which everyone can read online, to excite fear in readers with entertaining theories.

"But even in circumstances in which details are hard to come by, certain similarities have emerged," McCoy breathes to create suspense like the best fiction writers. " The first contact often occurs in remote, rural communities where a victim handles an infected animal carcass, and things quickly progress downward from there."

His own report quickly spirals downwards by attributing the current Ebola outbreak to deforestation while providing no evidence.

McCoy also hypes the notion that infected animals cause Ebola, again ignoring the CDC fact sheet, which admits that in cases when humans came into contact with infected monkeys in U.S. quarantine facilities, humans did not get sick or die from Ebola.

Local people in West Africa appear to know without having to read the CDC Ebola fact sheet that hospitals and medical staff are spreading Ebola. The Telegraph reports people wielding knives surrounded a Red Cross vehicle in Guinea.

The involvement of hospitals would also explain why Ebola has appeared in this part of Africa for the first time ever and in so many different locations at almost the same time.

Given that the CDC itself admits that hospitals are, in fact, the likely source of any Ebola outbreak, the question arises which specific hospital could be the origin of the current Ebola outbreak?

At the epicenter of the current Ebola epidemic is the Kenema Government Hospital in Sierra Leone, which houses a U.S. a biosecurity level 2 bioweapons research lab with links to the Bill and Melinda Gates Foundation and Soros Foundation.

U.S. biodefense scientists have been working at the lab on viral fevers such as Ebola since 2011 at least.
http://www.nti.org/gsn/article/biodefense-scientists-fight-lassa-fever/

The partners and people leading the viral fever bioweapons lab inside Kenema Government Hospital read like a roll call of New World Order organizations.

"The Consortium is a collaboration between Tulane, Scripps Research Institute, Broad Institute, Harvard University, University of California at San Diego, University of Texas Medical Branch, Autoimmune Technologies LLC, Corgenix Medical Corporation, Kenema Government Hospital (Sierra Leone), Irrua Specialist Teaching Hospital (Nigeria) and various other partners in West Africa. ... The Consortium intends to expand this program to include other important infectious agents such as Ebola, Marburg and other Arenaviruses that are of great concern to public health and bioterrorism," states the bioweapons lab website.
http://vhfc.org/consortium

The website admits that Professor Robert F. Garry is "currently managing the consortium of scientists who are developing modern diagnostics for several biodefense pathogens."
http://vhfc.org/consortium/people/garry

Dr James E. Robinson " is a collaborating investigator in four large consortia projects funded by the Bill and Melinda Gates Foundation."
http://vhfc.org/consortium/people/robinson

Dr Pardis Sabeti has received fellowships from the Rhodes Scholarship, the Soros Fellowship, L'Oreal For Women in Science Fellowship, according to the website.
http://vhfc.org/consortium/people/sabeti

Scientist Stephen Gire has links to the CDC and U.S. *military*.

He "spent time at the Centers for Disease Control and Prevention researching vector-borne infectious diseases. He then moved on to complete a Masters of Public Health at Columbia University and a three-year fellowship with the United States Army Medical Research Institute of Infectious Diseases (USAMRIID). He has researched viruses such as West Nile, Dengue Fever, Monkeypox and Ebola, and he conducts on-site training in biological techniques to laboratory staff in the developing world."
http://vhfc.org/consortium/people/gire

Connecting the dots, it is reasonable to ask for an investigation into whether this particular U.S. bioweapons lab at the geographical epicenter of the current Ebola outbreak actually caused the Ebola outbreak.

In 2009, Baxter in Austria was caught contaminating 72 kilos of seasonal flu with the deadly bird flu virus in its biosecurity level 3 laboratory. It later emerged from documents posted on Wikileaks that Baxter was a U.S. defense or *military* asset.

Facts and documents as well as current mainstream media hype point to plans for false flag Ebola bioterrorism attacks in hospitals and clinics against U.S. and UK citizens using occasions like the Commonwealth Games in Scotland to spread panic.

The purpose is to implement martial law measures contained in epidemic and pandemic plans and so gain total control of the population at a time when the financial system is close to collapse.

The Bill Gates You Should Really Know

Oct 15, 2014 – Letter to my email list –

In this email are four articles about Bill Gates on food, on geo-engineering (chemtrails), on sterilization and last one on Gates being taken to court in India right now. Their crimes against humanity are catching up with them. Bill and Melinda Gates have killed tens of thousands of people to "keep them safe." They are "philanthropists." According to Bill Gates in conversation with Bill Moyer in 2003, his father was a former head of Rockefeller eugenics Planned Parenthood, and is still co-chairman today of the aggressive Gates Foundation.

In other words, let's line this up properly … Bill Gates was given computer operating system already developed by *military* contractors such as IBM and Honeywell, because he was the son of a trusted Rockefeller racist insider …

There is no way he invented or promoted something without his father's deep New World Order connections. Bill Gates was placed to develop Microsoft with his father always in background and now steering one of the very rich and powerful "foundations" enacting "change" or "*globalization.*" The word "change" is *doublespeak* for New World Order.

Billionaire Bilderbergers, Bill Gates and Warren Buffet, funnel their (our) money into programs run by Rockefeller eugenics globalists, straight up.

It has been postulated that Bill Gates and his wife Melinda, believe a higher standard of living (consumption) leads to less children. Let's ask, where will that higher level of consumption come from, in a resource starved world? If the rich were into higher standard of living for everyone, wealth would not be concentrated, it would be shared. That isn't what they want.

To right, February 2010 TED talk, (Technology, Entertainment, and Design)

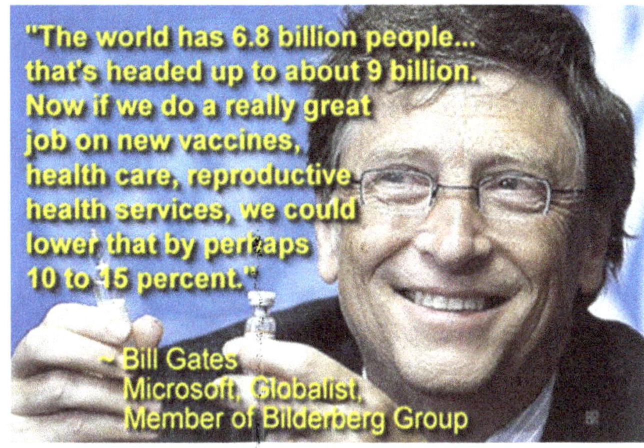

"The world has 6.8 billion people...
that's headed up to about 9 billion.
Now if we do a really great
job on new vaccines,
health care, reproductive
health services, we could
lower that by perhaps
10 to 15 percent."
~ Bill Gates
Microsoft, Globalist,
Member of Bilderberg Group

The New World Order wants population control without empowering the masses because an empowered informed public would see the corruption that maintains disparity in a pyramid society.

We can ask Bill Gates, who told him the population is headed to 9 billion and why did he believe them? Why not some other number? What is he not sharing? "Health care" usually keeps children alive, increasing population. "Reproductive health services" is *doublespeak* term for vaccination or surgical sterilization. (See pages 157-158)

But what about "new vaccines" for lowering the population? There is something undisclosed in the new vaccines that will either sterilize or kill people, and as the evidence below shows, these vaccines are being tested on *indigenous people*, not the relatives of Bill and Melinda Gates.

Gates Foundation support of a polio vaccine in India led to 47,000 cases of paralysis. No surprise, there, as the polio vaccine causes polio. The only surprise is that they are not in jail already for life. Bill and Melinda Gates are mass murderers and should be in jail.

"In 1976, Dr. Jonas Salk, creator of the killed-virus vaccine used in the 1950s, testified that the live-virus vaccine (used almost exclusively in the U.S. from the early 1960s to 2000) was the 'principal if not sole cause' of all reported polio cases in the U.S. since 1961. (The virus remains in the throat for one to two weeks and in the feces for up to two months. Thus, vaccine recipients are at risk, and can potentially spread the disease, as long as fecal excretion of the virus continues .)

"In 1992, the Federal Centers for Disease Control and Prevention (CDC) published an admission that the ***live-virus vaccine*** *had become the dominant cause of polio in the United States. In fact, according to CDC figures, every case of polio in the U.S. since 1979 was caused by the oral polio vaccine. [The flu vaccines every year ensure more flu cases that justify more vaccines.] Authorities claim the vaccine was responsible for about* ***eight cases of polio every year.*** *[Lies, lies, lies.] However, an independent study that analyzed the government's own vaccine database during a recent period of less than five years uncovered 13,641 reports of adverse events following use of the oral polio vaccine. These reports included 6,364 emergency room visits and* ***540 deaths*** *(Figure 3). Public outrage at these tragedies became the impetus for removing the oral polio vaccine from immunization schedules ."* [64]

"... gene-targeting vaccine research technology **purchased by Microsoft** was developed by the company known as Rosetta Biosciences, formerly owned by Merck. Their software is described as a way to "figure out how genes interact with each other, analyze peptides and metabolites, and determine how they relate to gene expression." [65]

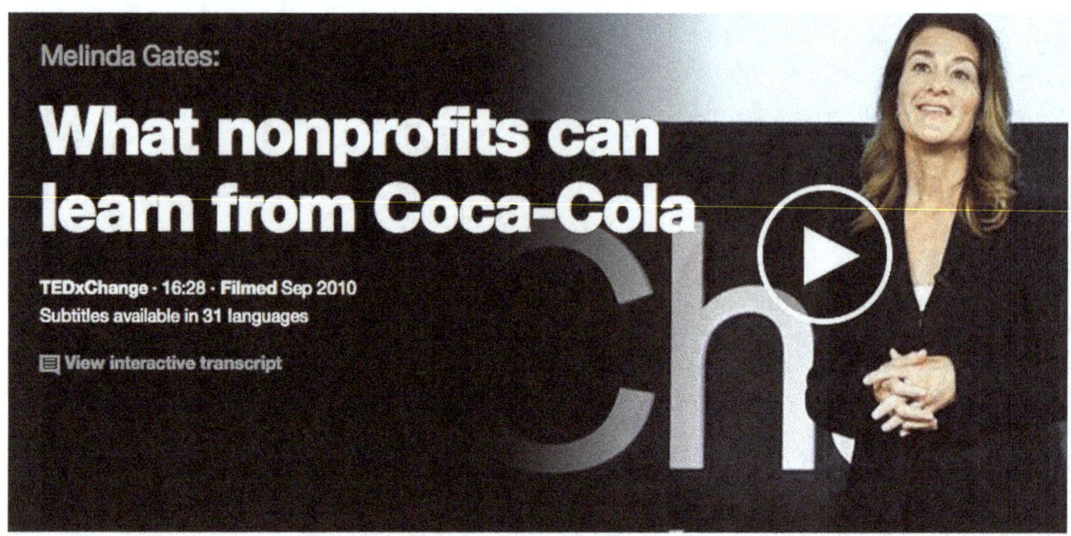

Melinda Gates:
What nonprofits can learn from Coca-Cola
TEDxChange · 16:28 · Filmed Sep 2010
Subtitles available in 31 languages
View interactive transcript

Share this idea      949,657 Total views 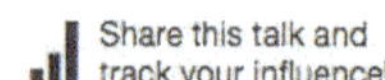

In her talk, Melinda Gates makes a provocative case for nonprofits taking a cue from corporations such as Coca-Cola, whose plugged-in, global network of marketers and distributors ensures that every remote village wants — and can get — a Coke. Why shouldn't this work for condoms, sanitation, vaccinations too? (Filmed at TEDxChange.)

Interactive transcript

Melinda Gates
Philanthropist

Melinda French Gates is co-chair of the Bill & Melinda Gates Foundation, where she puts into practice the idea that every life has equal value. **Full bio**

Above, we see another globalist, Melinda Gates, Bill's wife, co-opting the word CHANGE (behind her), as if the immoral hoarding rich can lead the world in any change that is positive. The rich will decide what is good for those that they keep poor?

"It is likely that the Bill and Melinda Gates Foundation will continue its commitment to global population control, and now, curriculum creation in the nation's schools because they truly believe that they know better than anyone else how we all should live."

– Anne Hendershott [66]

With Melinda Gates, we see the arrogant *monoculture vanity* of the rich control freaks who call themselves philanthropists. Yes, now there is teeth decaying Coca Cola in every village. That isn't progress, it is profit through addictive unhealthy products. Melinda Gates wants to make sure gene specific vaccines containing undisclosed nano-technology gets into every remote village also. Notice what the summary of talk says … Coke "ensures that every remote village wants" a coke. *Social engineering.*

Melinda Gates does not put into practice "every life has equal value." What a total joke. Is her lifestyle shared equally by the 99% she wants to "save" by brain washing them into what they should want?

Why shouldn't all values be marketed just like Coke? Answer … Because Coke spreads addiction and erosion of health and is not at all concerned with anything positive. We need to see through the *doublespeak* of the rich. They don't want independence in this world, they want one dependent world under their vision.

So they can stay rich and powerful.

* * *

Bill Gates, Monsanto, and Eugenics: How one of the world's wealthiest men is actively promoting a corporate takeover of global agriculture

– by Ethan A. Huff, staff writer NaturalNews.com, February 29, 2012

After it was exposed that the Bill & Melinda Gates Foundation, the philanthropic brainchild of Microsoft founder Bill Gates, purchased 500,000 shares in Monsanto back in 2010 valued at more than $23 million, it became abundantly clear that this so-called benevolent charity is up to something other than eradicating disease and feeding the world's poor (http://www.guardian.co.uk). It turns out that the Gates family legacy has long been one of trying to dominate and control the world's systems, including in the areas of technology, medicine, and now agriculture.

The Gates Foundation, aka the tax-exempt Gates Family Trust, is currently in the process of spending billions of dollars in the name of humanitarianism to establish a global food monopoly dominated by genetically-modified (GM) crops and seeds. And based on the Gates family's history of involvement in world affairs, it appears that one of its main goals besides simply establishing corporate control of the world's food supply is to reduce the world's population by a significant amount in the process.

William H. Gates Sr., former head of eugenics group Planned Parenthood

Bill Gates' father, William H. Gates Sr., has long been involved with the eugenics group Planned Parenthood, a rebranded organization birthed out of the American Eugenics Society. In a 2003 interview with PBS' Bill Moyers, Bill Gates admitted that his father used to be the head of Planned Parenthood, which was founded on the concept that most human beings are just "reckless breeders" and "human weeds" in need of culling (http://www.pbs.org/now/transcript/transcript_gates.html). [Gates Sr. also controls food retailer Costco]

Gates also admitted during the interview that his family's involvement in reproductive issues throughout the years has been extensive, referencing his own prior adherence to the beliefs of eugenicist Thomas Robert Malthus, who believed that populations of the world need to be controlled through reproductive restrictions. Though Gates claims he now holds a different view, it appears as though his foundation's initiatives are just a modified Malthusian approach that much more discreetly reduces populations through vaccines and GMOs (http://en.wikipedia.org/wiki/Thomas_Robert_Malthus).

Gates Foundation has invested heavily in converting Asian, African agricultural systems to GMOs

William Gates Sr.'s association with Planned Parenthood and continued influence in the realm of "population and reproductive health" is significant because Gates Sr. is co-chair of the Bill & Melinda Gates Foundation . This long-time eugenicist "guides the vision and strategic direction" of the Gates Foundation, which is currently heavily focused on forcing GMOs on Africa via its financing of the Alliance for a Green Revolution in Africa (AGRA).

The Gates Foundation has admittedly given at least $264.5 million in grant commitments to AGRA (www.gatesfoundation.org/about/Documents/BMGFFactSheet.pdf), and also reportedly hired Dr. Robert Horsch, a former Monsanto executive for 25 years who developed Roundup, to head up AGRA back in 2006. According to a report published in La Via Campesina back in 2010, 70 percent of AGRA's grantees in Kenya work directly with Monsanto, and nearly 80 percent of the Gates Foundation funding is devoted to biotechnology (http://www.organicconsumers.org/articles/article_21606.cfm).

The same report explains that the Gates Foundation pledged $880 million in April 2010 to create the Global Agriculture and Food Security Program (GAFSP), which is a heavy promoter of GMOs. GAFSP, of course, was responsible for providing $35 million in "aid" to earthquake-shattered Haiti to be used for implementing GMO agricultural systems and technologies.

Back in 2003, the Gates Foundation invested $25 million in "GM (genetically modified) research to develop vitamin and protein-enriched seeds for the world's poor," a move that many international charities and farmers groups vehemently opposed (http://healthfreedoms.org). And in 2008, the Gates Foundation awarded $26.8 million to Cornell University to research GM wheat, which is the next major food crop in the crosshairs of Monsanto's GM food crop pipeline.

If you control agriculture, you control the populations of the world

The Gates Foundation's ties with Monsanto and corporate agriculture in general speak volumes about its real agenda, which is to create a monopolistic system of world control in every area of human life. Vaccines, pharmaceuticals, GMOs, reproductive control, weather manipulation, global warming—these and many other points of entry are the means by which the Gates Foundation is making great strides to control the world by pretending to help improve and save it.

Rather than promote real food sovereignty and address the underlying political and economic issues that breed poverty, Gates and Co. has instead embraced the promotion of corporately-owned and controlled agriculture and medicine paradigms that will only further enslave the world's most impoverished. It is abundantly evident that GMOs have ravished already-impoverished people groups by destroying their native agricultural systems, as has been seen in India (http://www.naturalnews.com/030913_Monsanto_suicides.html).

Some may say Gates' endeavors are all about the money, while others may say they are about power and control. Perhaps it is a combination of both, where Gates is still in the business of promoting his own commercial investments, which includes buying shares in Monsanto while simultaneously investing in programs to promote Monsanto.

Whatever the case may be, there is simply no denying that Gates now has a direct interest in seeing Monsanto succeed in spreading GMOs around the world. And since Gates is openly facilitating Monsanto's growth into new markets through his "humanitarian" efforts, it is clear that the Gates family is in bed with Monsanto.

"Although Bill Gates might try to say that the Foundation is not linked to his business, all it proves is the opposite: most of their donations end up favoring the commercial investments of the tycoon, not really "donating" anything, but instead of paying taxes to state coffers, he invests his profits in where it is favorable to him economically, including propaganda from their supposed good intentions," wrote Silvia Ribeiro in the Mexican news source La Jornada back in 2010.

"On the contrary, their 'donations' finance projects as destructive as geoengineering or replacement of natural community medicines for high-tech patented medicines in the poorest areas of the world ... Gates is also engaged in trying to destroy rural farming worldwide, mainly through the 'Alliance for a Green Revolution in Africa' (AGRA). It works as a Trojan horse to deprive poor African farmers of their traditional seeds, replacing them with the seeds of their companies first, finally by genetically modified (GM)."

* * *

Bill Gates Backs Climate Scientists Lobbying for Large-Scale Geo-Engineering

– from *The Guardian,* Sunday, February 5, 2012

A small group of leading climate scientists, financially supported by billionaires including Bill Gates, are lobbying governments and international bodies to back experiments into manipulating the climate on a global scale to avoid catastrophic climate change.

The scientists, who advocate geoengineering methods such as spraying millions of tonnes of reflective particles of sulfur dioxide 30 miles above earth, argue that a "plan B" for climate change will be needed if the UN and politicians cannot agree to making the necessary cuts in greenhouse gases, and say the U.S. government and others should pay for a major programme of international research.

Solar geoengineering techniques are highly controversial: while some climate scientists believe they may prove a quick and relatively cheap way to slow global warming, others fear that when conducted in the upper atmosphere, they could irrevocably alter rainfall patterns and interfere with the earth's climate.

Geoengineering is opposed by many environmentalists, who say the technology could undermine efforts to reduce emissions, and by developing countries who fear it could be used as a weapon or by rich countries to their advantage. In 2010, the UN Convention on Biological Diversity declared a moratorium on experiments in the sea and space, except for small-scale scientific studies.

Concern is now growing that the small but influential group of scientists, and their backers, may have a disproportionate effect on major decisions about geoengineering research and policy.

"We will need to protect ourselves from vested interests [and] be sure that choices are not influenced by parties who might make significant amounts of money through a choice to modify climate, especially using proprietary intellectual property," said Jane Long, director at large for the Lawrence Livermore National Laboratory in the U.S., in a paper delivered to a recent geoengineering conference on ethics.

"The stakes are very high and scientists are not the best people to deal with the social, ethical or political issues that geoengineering raises," said Doug Parr, chief scientist at Greenpeace. "The idea that a self-selected group should have so much influence is bizarre."

Pressure to find a quick technological fix to climate change is growing as politicians fail to reach an agreement to significantly reduce emissions. In 2009-2010, the U.S. government received requests for over $2bn(£1.2bn) of grants for geoengineering research, but spent around $100m.

As well as Gates, other wealthy individuals including Sir Richard Branson, tar sands magnate Murray Edwards and the co-founder of Skype, Niklas Zennström, have funded a series of official reports into future use of the technology. Branson, who has frequently called for geoengineering to combat climate change, helped fund the Royal Society's inquiry into solar radiation management last year through his Carbon War Room charity. It is not known how much he contributed. [Covert geo-engineering using HAARP is not officially mentioned.]

Professors David Keith, of Harvard University, and Ken Caldeira of Stanford, [see footnote] are the world's two leading advocates of major research into geoengineering the upper atmosphere to provide earth with a reflective shield. They have so far received over $4.6m from Gates to run the Fund for Innovative Climate and Energy Research (Ficer). Nearly half Ficer's money, which comes directly from Gates's personal funds, has so far been used for their own research, but the rest is disbursed by them to fund the work of other advocates of large-scale interventions.

According to statements of financial interests, Keith receives an undisclosed sum from Bill Gates each year, and is the president and majority owner of the geoengineering company Carbon Engineering, in which both Gates and Edwards have major stakes – believed to be together worth over $10m.

Another Edwards company, Canadian Natural Resources, has plans to spend $25bn to turn the bitumen-bearing sand found in northern Alberta into barrels of crude oil. Caldeira says he receives $375,000 a year from Gates, holds a carbon capture patent and works for Intellectual Ventures, a private geoegineering research company part-owned by Gates and run by Nathan Myhrvold, former head of technology at Microsoft.

According to the latest Ficer accounts, the two scientists have so far given $300,000 of Gates money to part-fund three prominent reviews and assessments of geoengineering – the UK Royal Society report on Solar Radiation Management, the U.S. Taskforce on Geoengineering and a

2009 report by Novin a science think tank based in Santa Barbara, California. Keith and Caldeira either sat on the panels that produced the reports or contributed evidence. All three reports strongly recommended more research into solar radiation management.

The fund also gave $600,000 to Phil Rasch, chief climate scientist for the Pacific Northwest national laboratory, one of 10 research institutions funded by the U.S. energy department.

Rasch gave evidence at the first Royal Society report on geoengineering 2009 and was a panel member on the 2011 report. He has testified to the U.S. Congress about the need for government funding of large-scale geoengineering. In addition, Caldeira and Keith gave a further $240,000 to geoengineering advocates to travel and attend workshops and meetings and $100,000 to Jay Apt, a prominent advocate of geoengineering as a last resort, and professor of engineering at Carnegie Mellon University. Apt worked with Keith and Aurora Flight Sciences, a U.S. company that develops drone aircraft technology for the U.S. *military*, to study the costs of sending 1m tonnes of sulphate particles into the upper atmosphere a year.

Analysis of the eight major national and international inquiries into geoengineering over the past three years shows that Keith and Caldeira, Rasch and Prof Granger Morgan the head of department of engineering and public policy at Carnegie Mellon University where Keith works, have sat on seven panels, including one set up by the UN. Three other strong advocates of solar radiation geoengineering, including Rasch, have sat on national inquiries part-funded by Ficer.

"There are clear conflicts of interest between many of the people involved in the debate," said Diana Bronson, a researcher with Montreal-based geoengineering watchdog ETC.

"What is really worrying is that the same small group working on high-risk technologies that will geoengineer the planet is also trying to engineer the discussion around international rules and regulations. We cannot put the fox in charge of the chicken coop."

"The eco-clique are lobbying for a huge injection of public funds into geoengineering research. They dominate virtually every inquiry into geoengineering. They are present in almost all of the expert deliberations. They have been the leading advisers to parliamentary and congressional inquiries and their views will, in all likelihood, dominate the deliberations of the UN's Intergovernmental Panel on Climate Change (IPCC) as it grapples for the first time with the scientific and ethical tangle that is climate engineering," said Clive Hamilton, professor of Public Ethics at the Australian National University, in a Guardian blog.

The scientists involved reject this notion. "Even the perception that [a small group of people has] illegitimate influence [is] very unhealthy for a technology which has extreme power over the world. The concerns that a small group [is] dominating the debate are legitimate, but things are not as they were," said Keith. "It's changing as countries like India and China become involved. The era when my voice or that of a few was dominant is over. We need a very broad debate."

"Every scientist has some conflict of interest, because we would all like to see more resources going to study things that we find interesting," said Caldeira. "Do I have too much influence? I feel like I have too little. I have been calling for making CO2 emissions illegal for many years, but no one is listening to me. People who disagree with me might feel I have too much influence. The best way to reduce my influence is to have more public research funds available, so that our funds are in the noise. If the federal government played the role it should in this area, there would be no need for money from Gates.

"Regarding my own patents, I have repeatedly stated that if any patent that I am on is ever used for the purposes of altering climate, then any proceeds that accrue to me for this use will be donated to nonprofit NGOs and charities. I have no expectation or interest in developing a personal revenue stream based upon the use of these patents for climate modification.."

Rasch added: "I don't feel there is any conflict of interest. I don't lobby, work with patents or intellectual property, do classified research or work with for-profit companies. The research I do on geoengineering involves computer simulations and thinking about possible consequences. The Ficer foundation that has funded my research tries to be transparent in their activities, as do I."

This article was amended on 8 February 2012. The original stated that Phil Rasch worked for Intellectual Ventures. This has been corrected. This article was further amended on 13 February 2012. Prof Caldeira has asked us to make clear that the fact that he advocates research into geoengineering does not mean he advocates geoengineering. [What?]

* * *

Bill Gates Talks "Vaccines to Reduce Population" – Excerpt

by F. William Engdahl, author of *Full Spectrum Dominance,* March 4, 2010

… A new form of eugenics?

Gates' interest in inducing population reduction among black and other minority populations is not new unfortunately. As I [William F. Engdahl] document in my book, *Seeds of Destruction,* since the 1920s the Rockefeller Foundation had funded the eugenics research in Germany through the Kaiser-Wilhelm Institutes in Berlin and Munich, including well into the Third Reich. They praised the forced sterilization of people by Hirtler Germany, and the Nazi ideas on race "purity." It was John D. Rockefeller III, a life-long advocate of eugenics, who used his "tax free" foundation money to initiate the population reduction neo-Malthusian movement through his private Population Council in New York beginning in the 1950s.

The idea of using vaccines to covertly reduce births in the Third World is also not new. Bill Gates' good friend, David Rockefeller and his Rockefeller Foundation were involved as early as 1972 in a major project together with WHO and others to perfect another "new vaccine."

The results of the WHO-Rockefeller project were put into mass application on human guinea pigs in the early 1990s. The WHO oversaw massive vaccination campaigns against tetanus in Nicaragua, Mexico and the Philippines. Comite Pro Vida de Mexico, a Roman Catholic lay organization, became suspicious of the motives behind the WHO program and decided to test numerous vials of the vaccine and found them to contain human Chorionic Gonadotrophin, or hCG. That was a curious component for a vaccine designed to protect people against lock-jaw arising from infection with rusty nail wounds or other contact with certain bacteria found in soil. The tetanus disease was indeed, also rather rare. It was also curious because hCG was a natural hormone needed to maintain a pregnancy. However, when combined with a tetanus toxoid carrier, it stimulated formation of antibodies against hCG, rendering a woman incapable of maintaining a pregnancy, a form of concealed abortion. Similar reports of vaccines laced with hCG hormones came from the Philippines and Nicaragua.

Gates' 'Gene Revolution in Africa'

The Bill and Melinda Gates Foundation, along with David Rockefeller's Rockefeller Foundation, the creators of the GMO biotechnology, are also financing a project called The Alliance for a Green Revolution in Africa (AGRA) headed by former UN chief, Kofi Annan. Accepting the role as AGRA head in June 2007 Annan expressed his "gratitude to the Rockefeller Foundation, the Bill & Melinda Gates Foundation, and all others who support our African campaign." The AGRA board is dominated by people from both the Gates' and Rockefeller foundations.

Monsanto, DuPont, Dow, Syngenta and other major GMO agribusiness giants are reported at the heart of AGRA, using it as a back-door to spread their patented GMO seeds across Africa under the deceptive label, 'bio-technology,' a euphemism for genetically engineered patented seeds. The person from the Gates Foundation responsible for its work with AGRA is Dr. Robert Horsch, a 25-year Monsanto GMO veteran who was on the team that developed Monsanto's RoundUp Ready GMO technologies. His job is reportedly to use Gates' money to introduce GMO into Africa.

To date South Africa is the only African country permitting legal planting of GMO crops. In 2003 Burkina Faso authorized GMO trials. In 2005 Kofi Annan's Ghana drafted bio-safety legislation and key officials expressed their intentions to pursue research into GMO crops. AGRA is being used to create networks of "agro-dealers" across Africa, at first with no mention of GMO seeds or herbicides, in order to have the infrastructure in place to massively introduce GMO.

GMO crops have never been proven safe for human or animal consumption. Moreover, they are inherently genetically 'unstable' as they are an unnatural product of introducing a foreign bacteria such as Bacillus Thuringiensis (Bt) or other material into the DNA of a given seed to change its traits. Perhaps equally dangerous are the 'paired' chemical herbicides sold as a mandatory part of a GMO contract, such as Monsanto's Roundup, the most widely used such herbicide in the world. It contains highly toxic glyphosate compounds that have been independently tested and proven to exist in toxic concentrations in GMO applications far above that safe for humans or animals. Tests show that tiny amounts of glyphosate compounds would do damage to a human umbilical, embryonic and placental cells in a pregnant woman drinking the ground water near a GMO field.

One long-standing project of the U.S. Government has been to perfect a genetically-modified variety of corn, the diet staple in Mexico and many other Latin American countries. The corn has been field tested in tests financed by the U.S. Department of Agriculture along with a small California bio-tech company named Epicyte. Announcing his success at a 2001 press conference, the president of Epicyte, Mitch Hein, pointing to his GMO corn plants, announced, "We have a hothouse filled with corn plants that make anti-sperm antibodies."

Hein explained that they had taken antibodies from women with a rare condition known as immune infertility, isolated the genes that regulated the manufacture of those infertility antibodies, and, using genetic engineering techniques, had inserted the genes into ordinary corn seeds used to produce corn plants. In this manner, in reality they produced a concealed contraceptive embedded in corn meant for human consumption. "Essentially, the antibodies are attracted to surface receptors on the sperm," said Hein. "They latch on and make each sperm so heavy it cannot move forward. It just shakes about as if it was doing the lambada." Hein claimed it was a possible solution to world "over-population." The moral and ethical issues of feeding it to humans in Third World poor countries without their knowing it countries he left out of his remarks.

Spermicides hidden in GMO corn provided to starving Third World populations through the generosity of the Gates' foundation, Rockefeller Foundation and Kofi Annan's AGRA or vaccines that contain undisclosed sterilization agents are just two documented cases of using vaccines or GMO seeds to "reduce population." [67]

* * *

The Melinda Gates photo above was at a TED talk, Technology, Entertainment, and Design. These words pretty much summarize the world view of the elite *globalists* who think new technology … meaning control, and Entertainment … meaning dumbing down masses, and Design meaning … funded designers designing society for everyone else who will just have to fit into it. The TED conferences are invitation only, at $7,500 (2012) a seat. (TED talk only, 2015, $135/seat.) This is the rich awarding each other. The *vanity* of the company that owns TED is palpable.

> The Sapling Foundation, "a private nonprofit foundation, a 501(c)3 organization under U.S. tax code. It was established in 1996 by Chris Anderson, who was at that time a magazine publishing entrepreneur. [He was and is just a PR man.] "The goal of the foundation is to foster the spread of great ideas. It aims to provide a platform for the world's smartest thinkers, greatest visionaries and most-inspiring teachers, so that millions of people can gain a better understanding of the biggest issues faced by the world, and a desire to help create a better future.
>
> [By accepting top down ideas and structures.]
>
> "Core to this goal is a belief that there is no greater force for changing the world than a powerful idea …
>
> [Here is the *dominant culture* view of nature, as "chaos" that needs to be ordered (by people lost in their heads) to serve humans to the exclusion of all other species. "Change" means destabilization of ancient ecology and traditions because these are not "modern" and must be re-designed so we can "progress." A "better world" means better for the elite, and everyone else can just get used to what is designed for them.]
>
> "Many factors can amplify the power of ideas: mass media, technology and market forces, to name three. [But not conscience, not spirit, not innate sense of justice, or simply the innocence of simplicity.] In the past Sapling has supported projects that use these tools to leverage every dollar spent and create sustainable change [Liar. "Sustainable change" is an oxymoron. What he means is a prison planet in which all is controlled and everything must change to meet the model.] in areas such as global public health, poverty alleviation, and biodiversity. More than $10m has therefore been granted to en-

> lightened organizations such as the Acumen Fund, Environmental Defense, One World Health, and PATH."

All these organization are globalist tentacles. One World Health is obviously a ONE WORLD, New World Order Globalist mono-culture assault.

This next article is long, but important. This article accurately describes who these people really are. Bill and Melinda Gates are criminals. Especially, this article proves that TED is a *social engineering* organ and nothing more.

In the article below, look out for the name PATH, which Sapling Foundation proudly supports with millions of dollars.

Sapling and TED should be named in lawsuits as complicit in the *social engineering* of popular opinion to commit crime and in the funding of criminal organizations like PATH. Watch for the name PATH below.

Controversial Vaccine Studies: Why is Bill & Melinda Gates Foundation Under Fire from Critics in India?

– KP Narayana Kumar, Economic Times Bureau Aug 31, 2014

In 2009, several schools for tribal children in Khammam district in Telangana — then a part of undivided Andhra Pradesh — became sites for observation studies for a cervical cancer vaccine that was administered to thousands of girls aged between nine and 15. The girls were administered the Human Papilloma Virus (HPV) vaccine in three rounds that year under the supervision of state health department officials. The vaccine used was Gardasil, manufactured by Merck. It was administered to around 16,000 girls in the district, many of whom stayed in state government-run hostels meant for tribal students.

Months later, many girls started falling ill and by 2010 five of them died. Two more deaths were reported from Vadodara, Gujarat, where an estimated 14,000 children studying in schools meant for tribal children were also vaccinated with another brand of HPV vaccine, Cervarix, manufactured by GSK. Earlier in the week, the Associated Press reported that scores of teenaged girls were hospitalized in a small town in northern Colombia with symptoms that parents suspect could be an adverse reaction to Gardasil.

A standing committee on health and family welfare that investigated the irregularities pertaining to the observation studies in India tabled its report a year ago, on August 30.

The committee found that consent for conducting these studies, in many cases, was taken from the hostel wardens, which was a flagrant violation of norms. In many other cases, thumbprint impressions of their poor and illiterate parents were duly affixed onto the consent form. The children also had no idea about the nature of the disease or the vaccine. The authorities concerned could not furnish requisite consent forms for the vaccinated children in a huge number of cases.

The committee said it was "deeply shocked to find that in Andhra Pradesh out of the 9,543 [consent] forms, 1,948 forms have thumb impressions while hostel wardens have signed 2,763 forms. In Gujarat, out of the 6,217 forms 3,944 have thumb impressions and 5,454 either signed or carried thumb impressions of guardians. The data revealed that a very large number of parents or guardians are illiterate and could not even write in their local languages, Telugu or Gujarati."

Earlier this month, taking a serious view of the death of seven tribal girls in the context of the observation studies, the Supreme Court asked the Drug Controller General of India (DCGI) and the Indian Council of Medical Research (ICMR) to explain how permissions were given.

The SC bench of justices Dipak Misra and V Gopala Gowda asked the Centre to produce relevant files that pertained to the grant of license for trial of the HPV vaccine in India. The court also asked the Centre to appraise it of steps taken on the report of the parliamentary committee.

Shoddy Investigations

When a team of health activists from an NGO that specializes in women's health named Sama visited Khammam in March 2010 on a fact-finding mission, they were told that as many as 120 girls experienced adverse reactions such as epileptic seizures, severe stomach ache, headaches and mood swings. [How would reader feel if that happened to your daughter or niece or sister or granddaughter? 145,000 children have died from adverse reactions to vaccinations in the U.S. in the last 20 years.] The Sama report also said there had been cases of early onset of menstruation following the vaccination, heavy bleeding and severe menstrual cramps among many students. The standing committee pulled up the relevant state governments for the shoddy investigation into these deaths. It said it was disturbed to find that "all the seven deaths were summarily dismissed as unrelated to vaccinations without in-depth investigations ... the speculative causes were suicides, accidental drowning in well (why not suicide?), malaria, viral infections, subarachnoid hemorrhage (without autopsy) etc."

The committee said that in the context of deaths of girls classified as suicide, the role of the "HPV vaccine as a possible, if not probable, cause of suicidal ideation cannot be ruled out."

It said that an American NGO — Program for Appropriate Technology in Health (PATH) — had carried out the studies. (PATH which is funded by Sapling that runs the TED talks, where Bill and Melinda Gates lie to the world in 31 languages.)

The committee found that the objective behind the observation studies in India primarily was to collect and record data on the effect of the vaccines on the minor subjects [children]. Another objective was to help the relevant authorities in India make an informed opinion on introducing the vaccine into India's immunization program. Providing a background, the report states that on June 1, 2006, American drug regulator, the U.S. Food and Drug Administration (USFDA) approved the first vaccine — Gardasil — to prevent HPV. According to the World Health Organization (WHO), two HPV types cause 70% of cervical cancers. In the very same month, PATH embarked upon a large-scale, five-year project that involved observation studies, covering Peru, Vietnam and Uganda, apart from India. [But not in United States. It's okay to treat poor illiterate *indigenous people* like guinea pigs according to the elitist *dominant culture.*]

The committee observed that on November 16, 2006, a draft memorandum of understanding (MoU) between PATH and the ICMR was circulated by the latter. The MoU states that the two parties desire "… to explore collaboration to support public sector decision regarding HPV vaccine introduction in India and to generate necessary evidence to allow the possible introduction of HPV vaccine into India's Universal Immunization Program." That idea appears to have hit a roadblock following the deaths of the children during the observation studies. [I wonder why?!]

The standing committee report was a shocker but it became even more significant when it was mentioned that the study was sponsored by the Bill & Melinda Gates Foundation (BMGF).Over the past decade, Bill Gates has transformed from an IT businessman into a global philanthropist. The foundation that he set up along with his wife is involved in hundreds of projects related to healthcare for the poor. Vaccination is a significant area of work and BMGF has projects running in almost every country that's counted as poor. BMGF continues to partner PATH in a number of studies such as the ones for a Rotavirus vaccine and pneumococcal vaccine in several countries, mainly Africa and Asia.

The health ministry also has not stopped PATH, in any manner, from becoming a part of such studies in India. The NGO has been roped in for other vaccine observation studies in India wherein it partners the department of bio-technology and other government departments. Health secretary Lov Verma refused to give an answer when ET Magazine asked why PATH continued to be allowed to carry out observation studies in India even after the studies which allegedly turned fatal.

According to the BMGF, the WHO, the International Federation of Gynaecology and Obstetrics, and the Federation of Obstetric and Gynaecological Societies of India have all recommended vaccination "as a proven and highly effective preventive measure for cervical cancer. "The project used vaccines that are licensed in India and that have been administered safely around the world tens of millions of times, preventing countless cases of cervical cancer illness and death," maintains a BMGF spokesperson in an emailed response (see GAVI & PHFI create incentives …).

Laying the Foundation

The Bill & Melinda Gates Foundation (BMGF) funds several organizations as part of its work on public health. All these organizations partner pharma companies in some form or the other, raising questions of conflict of interest

PATH

Set up in 1977, in Seattle, the US. The not-for-profit organization has carried out several clinical trials, especially in Africa and Asia

Was pulled up by a parliamentary committee in India after the death of seven tribal girls in 2009. *It had conducted observation studies for cervical cancer vaccines using drugs of Merck and GSK. The project was funded by BMGF*

PATH did not reply to e-mailed questions. BMGF says the vaccines were licensed and therefore already established to be ***safe and efficacious***

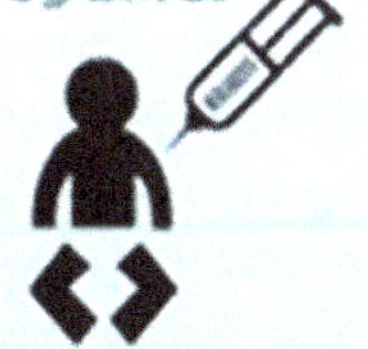

The Wrong PATH

BMGF's role in funding the controversial studies, however, has led to many healthcare activists in India voicing their apprehensions. "BMGF has to take full responsibility because PATH is funded by them. It is also unethical when people championing the cause of vaccines are the same ones who are also investing in vaccine development," said V Rukmini Rao, one of the activists who filed a writ petition before the Supreme Court in connection with the HPV vaccine studies.

BMGF has funded two organizations that over the past five years have played a significant role in the country's immunization program and are both under fire for conflict of interest. The organizations are GAVI (earlier known as Global Alliance for Vaccines and Immunization), a global aid organization that specializes in vaccination, and Public Health Foundation of India (PHFI), a public-private partnership society that BMGF co-founded with the UPA government in 2006.

Activists allege that these two institutions have a working relationship with pharma companies. The main charge against GAVI is that it has representatives from pharmaceutical companies on its board while the PHFI accepts grants from pharma companies. "BMGF and GAVI are pushing the [vaccine] agenda with governments around the world, including India," says Ritu Priya Mehrotra, professor of Social Medicine and Community Health and School of Social Sciences, Jawaharlal Nehru University, Delhi. The community health activist says the biotechnology industry was pushing more and more vaccines into India and that the health ministry was not ensuring that adequate testing was done before recommending their use in government programs.

"We need to follow the precautionary principle when it comes to vaccines. We do need more vaccines … but we should ensure that enough time is given for research to prove the efficacy and safety of new vaccines. The vaccines that are to be brought here should also fit our epidemiological profile," adds Protract. Mehrotra adds that a network of people in aid agencies and the health bureaucracy were pushing this agenda. "They have the advantage of an existing medicalized mindset that believes vaccines are the perfect, safe, effective, low-cost solution for prevention of infectious diseases. There is ample evidence that this is not always the case."

The current trend is to dilute safety testing criteria and cut short on time required to conduct proper observation studies. "The best example is the Pentavalent vaccine against which

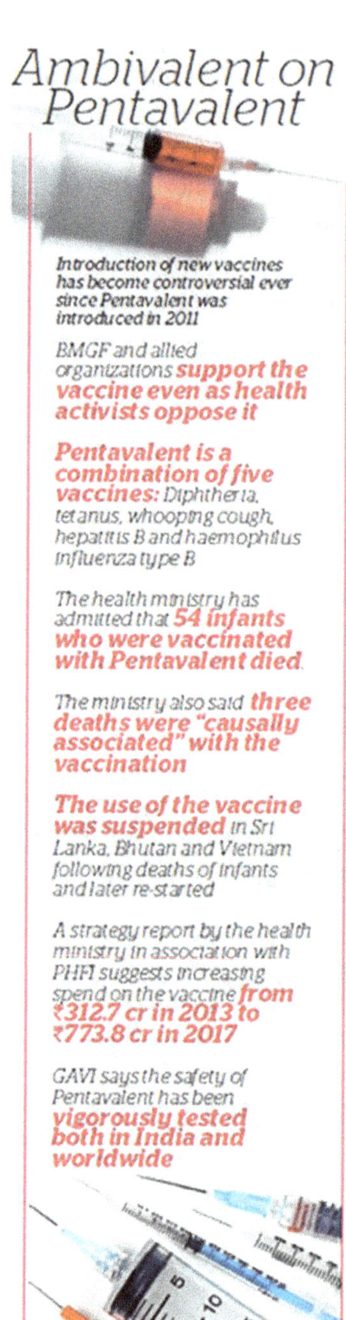
Ambivalent on Pentavalent
Introduction of new vaccines has become controversial ever since Pentavalent was introduced in 2011
BMGF and allied organizations support the vaccine even as health activists oppose it
Pentavalent is a combination of five vaccines: Diphtheria, tetanus, whooping cough, hepatitis B and haemophilus influenza type B
The health ministry has admitted that 54 infants who were vaccinated with Pentavalent died
The ministry also said three deaths were "causally associated" with the vaccination
The use of the vaccine was suspended in Sri Lanka, Bhutan and Vietnam following deaths of infants and later re-started
A strategy report by the health ministry in association with PHFI suggests increasing spend on the vaccine from ₹312.7 cr in 2013 to ₹773.8 cr in 2017
GAVI says the safety of Pentavalent has been vigorously tested both in India and worldwide

there is evidence to be wary of and yet we are going ahead [with its use in the immunization program]," points out Mehrotra.

In recent years, the deaths of many infants allegedly soon after they were immunized with the Pentavalent vaccine, a five-in-one shot, has contributed towards anxiety around vaccines. **The vaccine has been controversial in Sri Lanka, Bhutan and Vietnam, too, where it was temporarily suspended on account of some reported post-vaccination deaths of infants.**

Launched in 2011 in India, Pentavalent is a combination of five vaccines in one: diphtheria, tetanus, whooping cough, hepatitis B and haemophilus influenza type B (the bacteria that causes meningitis and pneumonia). The vaccine created a furore after many infants from across the country were reported to have died after the vaccination. A reply by the health ministry to an RTI application shows that the deaths of three infants in Tamil Nadu have "a consistent causal association to immunization," which means the ministry confirms that there is a connection between the vaccination and the deaths. In all, 54 cases of deaths of infants who were vaccinated with Pentavalent have been classified as 'adverse events following immunization' (AEFI), nomenclature that confirms the deaths have occurred soon after vaccination.

ET Magazine's questionnaires to the health secretary were unanswered. BMGF, GAVI and PHFI are in favour of Pentavalent even as a number of paediatricians and health experts have petitioned the government to take a second look at the vaccine in light of the deaths of infants.

In an opinion piece published recently in Deccan Herald titled "New Vaccines: Gates Foundation's philanthropy or business?," Dr Gopal Dabade of the All India Drug Action Network said that GAVI had committed a $165-million grant for the phased introduction of Pentavalent in India and provides a subsidy of Rs 145 per injection for five years after which the government will have to pay the total cost of the vaccines. "BMGF is a founding partner of GAVI. Its initial grant helped establish GAVI and it continues to support its work. Some of the pharmaceutical companies have affiliation with BMGF to manufacture the vaccine," Dr Dabade said.

The Controversial Report

A recent strategy document on immunization published this year by the health ministry suggests doubling the expenditure on purchase of Pentavalent. The Multi-Year Strategic Plan for the Universal Immunization Programme UIP) makes the case that the ministry needs to double its spend on Pentavalent from Rs 312.7 crore in 2013 to Rs 773.8 crore in 2017. The report also calls for a seven-fold increase in total spend on vaccines—from Rs 510.6 crore to Rs 3,587.1 crore by the same year.

The report was drafted by a team of immunization researchers who work under the PHFI which was co-founded by BMGF and the UPA government as a public private partnership. A few experts from UNICEF and WHO were also part of the team. Interestingly, its on the basis of such multiyear plans that GAVI, also funded by BMGF, disburses grants to countries.

Started in 2000, GAVI is a first-of-its kind funding agency that brings together poor countries, donor nations, global agencies, foundations, individual donors and pharma companies to enhance vaccination in poor countries. The funding is split between governments of the developed world (74%) and corporations, foundations and individuals (26%). BMGF accounts for about a fifth of the total contributions. The HPV vaccine, used as a part of the allegedly fatal observational studies in undivided Andhra Pradesh and Gujarat, as well as Pentavalent are both part of

Reference Report

A health ministry report making projections on vaccine procurement for five years was drafted by a unit under the PHFI, which was co-founded by BMGF and the health ministry

The report ***suggests a massive increase in spend on vaccines***

It indicates ***a spend of ₹1738.8 crore on the pneumococcal vaccine in the first year of its launch in 2017.*** *This vaccine is not a part of the national programme as of now*

It says the total spend on vaccines is to be ***increased seven-fold in five years***

The PHFI said it could not share the methodology used to arrive at the figures *and referred ET Magazine to the health ministry. The ministry refused comment*

a range of vaccines that countries can seek co-financing support for under GAVI's scheme for new and underused vaccines.

The GAVI board comprises of a representative each of the pharma industry from the industrialized and developing countries, a sore point with some experts from the aid world. In an article in the The Guardian three years ago, leaders of international aid agencies such as Oxfam and MSF said the representatives of companies needed to step down from the GAVI board. "Pharmaceutical companies' representation on GAVI's board creates a conflict of interest. The current structure is far too cozy," said the article quoting Mohga Kamal-Yanni, a senior policy adviser with Oxfam.

In a statement to ET Magazine, GAVI defended its model: "As a public-private partnership, GAVI harnesses the capabilities of the public and private sector to maximize its impact on health and development. While we believe this model is critical for our mission, we also recognize that it requires us to manage potential conflicts of interest. Therefore, relationships with the private sector are managed through strict policies. For instance, a board member representing manufacturers will be asked to leave discussions and be excluded from voting on any issue where a potential conflict of interest is identified."

Recently, an additional secretary with the health ministry, Anuradha Gupta, was appointed as the deputy CEO of GAVI. Gupta was earlier in charge of the National Health Mission. Healthcare activists raised a furore as the international agency's board also has representation from pharmaceutical companies. The Alliance Against Conflict of Interest, an organization fighting for a legislation on the subject, highlighted Gupta's move from government to GAVI as an example.

GAVI's defenses is that "Ms Gupta has brought to GAVI her deep passion and commitment to protecting maternal and child health which includes enabling them to access life-saving vaccines. She strongly supports GAVI's vision and mission which is to save children's lives and protect people's health by increasing access to immunization in poor countries."

Conflict of Interest

Similar controversies on proximity with pharma companies and conflict of interest have been raised about PHFI. While PHFI is engaged in public health and is also partnering the government in UIP, it has accepted grants from a number of pharma companies, including vaccine manufacturers. In all, PHFI has accepted grants worth around `57.65 crore from pharma companies, including Merck Sharp and Dohme, Pfizer and Sanofi, which manufacture vaccines. Sanofi is one of the many manufacturers of the controversial Pentavalent vaccine around the world.

PHFI head K Srinath Reddy asserts that the grants "that the PHFI has received from pharmaceutical companies are meant for broader educational activities, and are not intended to benefit PHFI, a pharma company or any other specific organization."

Another point that provides firepower to the critics is PHFI's McKinsey connection. An executive with the consulting company, Gautam Kumra, is present on the governing body of PHFI. Kumra's profile on McKinsey's website declares that his areas of expertise include healthcare. He is also credited with helping "one of India's leading pharmaceutical companies define its 10-year vision, redesign its organization and upgrade its capabilities to execute the vision."

In 2012, McKinsey published a report titled "Transforming India's vaccine market" in association with the Organization of Pharmaceutical Producers of India.

The report suggests that India's vaccine market is much smaller and under-penetrated than its global peers and discusses impediments that have hampered growth of the vaccine market. The report also features a scenario as per which the optimistic case would be that the market would have hit a value of around $3.2 billion in 2020, growing at 30-35% year-on-year from 2012 onwards. "In all likelihood, there will be five "mega" vaccines of over $250 million each in size, constituting 60% of the market, namely the anti-influenza, anti-typhoid, HPV, pneumococcal and Hepatitis A," the report said.

A McKinsey spokesperson said "the consultancy does not have a working relationship with PHFI. Gautam Kumra, a senior partner at McKinsey & Company, is a member of PHFI's governing board but in an entirely personal capacity as a healthcare systems expert and not as a representative of McKinsey." The consultancy also said it had a long history of pro bono and volunteer work for private, public and social sector organizations.

Public health activist and pediatrician Dr Arun Gupta says PHFI's links with pharma companies and McKinsey are unacceptable. "It is a clear conflict of interest. Neither the government nor PHFI has come out clearly and spoken of their relationship with each other ... it seems to be a private club that helps pharma companies make inroads into public policy."

"PHFI is a private society cleverly disguised as a public-private partnership since some of the people in the governing body are or have been senior civil servants or public servants," adds Supreme Court lawyer and activist Prashant Bhushan. Bhushan points out that PHFI appears to have several connections with the big pharma companies and their consultants. "The PHFI appears to have a conflict of interest in advising the government of India and directing the immunization program."

"PHFI's Srinath Reddy stresses that they had received unrestricted educational grants from **pharma companies** towards building the capacity of health professionals for providing appropriate health care of adequate quality in primary health care settings. However, these were not connected with the PHFI's work on the immunization front, he added. "As a not-for-profit organization, PHFI **receives grants from different stakeholders** for funding capacity building programs which address broader public health and health system needs, including quality of healthcare. These grants are in no way tied to any pharmaceutical product and are meant solely for educational activities." But then again the line between transferring medical knowledge and deriving commercial interests is a thin one.

– KP Narayana Kumar, ET Bureau August 31, 2014, *The Economic Times,* India

* * *

... But then again, a rep is not paid to tell the truth or he might get fired. What expectations come with the grants from the "stake holders?" The New World Order wants marketable products and more than that, they want an addicted market. They want a market that is scared into thinking that there is something, for example, called a "flu season".

Corporations, the foundations, and the bought off governments work together. This combo is the matrix of lies we now live in, organized from the top, just as Bill Gates is organized by his dad who has been under Rockefeller influence his whole life. Microsoft is an operation.

The "educational activities" at end of above article could be better called *social engineering* activities to condition the market to the manufactured needs that the "stakeholders" will provide for. A lot like Coca Cola in every village. A lot like the wants and expectations in each of our heads because every remote village includes every one of us. Yes, you the reader, live under the manipulations of the New World Order social engineers, and yes, you and I have been programmed. A big part of the programming is eliminating any resistance to programming as we are about to explore with children's shows and music industry. Full Spectrum Dominance means ALL venues are controlled.

The Gates Foundation and Big Pharma are spending billions of dollars to convince us to take vaccines. The goal is to have habitual world wide vaccinations. As investigative journalism increasingly disappears, it becomes easier to just create fictional crisis as "news." The responsible "educated" citizens with very wrong information, are panicked like a herd as we've seen with Swine Flu or Ebola. Gene specific vaccinations with RFID chips are now being developed to bring the population down to the designed demographic. Gates Foundation is even exploring sterilization through nano-fibers in clothing. [68]

While ocean life disappears, TED talks. Technology, Entertainment, Design. Little food, lots of games.

"Depopulation Vaccine" in Kenya and Beyond

– By Jon Rappoport, November 10, 2014

"You have to understand that every promoted so-called "pandemic" is an extended sales pitch for vaccines ... Depopulation has several objectives. Along one vector, it is an elite strategy designed to get rid of large numbers of people, **in key areas of the world,** where local revolutions would interfere with outside corporations staging a complete takeover of fertile land and rich natural resources. [See rockstar U2 Bono pages in Vol. 3 of this series.]

"We have this current claim:

> "Kenya's Catholic bishops are charging two United Nations organizations with sterilizing millions of girls and women under cover of an anti-tetanus inoculation program sponsored by the Kenyan government.
>
> "According to a statement released Tuesday by the Kenya Catholic Doctors Association, the organization has found an antigen that causes miscarriages in a vaccine being administered to 2.3 million girls and women by the World Health Organization and UNICEF. Priests throughout Kenya reportedly are advising their congregations to refuse the vaccine.
>
> "We sent six samples from around Kenya to laboratories in South Africa. They tested positive for the HCG antigen," Dr. Muhame Ngare of the Mercy Medical Centre in Nairobi told LifeSiteNews. "They were all laced with HCG."
>
> "Dr. Ngare, spokesman for the Kenya Catholic Doctors Association, stated in a bulletin released November 4, "This proved right our worst fears; that this WHO campaign is not about eradicating neonatal tetanus but a well-coordinated forceful population control mass sterilization exercise using a proven fertility regulating vaccine. This evidence was presented to the Ministry of Health before the third round of immunization but was ignored."("Mass Sterilization: Kenyan Doctors Find Anti-Fertility Agent in UN Tetanus Vaccine," November 8, 2014, by Steve Weatherbe, Earth-heal.com)

"An astonishing journal paper: November, 1993. FASEB Journal, volume 7, pp.1381-1385. Authors—Stephan Dirnhofer et al. Dirnhofer was a member of the Institute for Biomedical Aging Research of the Austrian Academy of Sciences.

> "Our study provides insights into possible modes of action of **the birth control vaccine promoted** by the Task Force on Birth Control Vaccines of the WHO (World Health Organization)." [Bill Gates speech page 139.]

"... There is a Task Force on Birth Control Vaccines at WHO. This journal paper focuses on a hormone called human chorionic gonadotropin B (hCG). There is a heading in the FASEB paper (p.1382) called "Ability of antibodies to neutralize the biological activity of hCG." The authors are trying to discover whether a state of non-fertility can be achieved by blocking the normal activity of hCG.

"Another journal paper. The British Medical Bulletin, volume 49, 1993. "Contraceptive Vaccines." The authors—RJ Aitken et al. From the MRC Reproductive Biology Unit, University of Edinburgh, Edinburgh, UK.

> "Three major approaches to contraceptive vaccine development are being pursued at the present time. The most advanced approach, which has already reached the stage of phase 2 clinical trials, involves the induction of immunity against human chorionic gonadotrophin (hCG). Vaccines are being engineered ... incorporating tetanus or diptheria toxoid linked to a variety of hCG-based peptides ... Clinical trials have revealed that such preparations are capable of stimulating the production of anti-hCG antibodies..."
>
> "... In principle, the induction of immunity against hGC should lead to asequence of normal, or slightly extended, menstrual cycles during which any pregnancies would be terminated ..."

"Miscarriage would then be the "normal" state of affairs. These authors leave no doubt about who the target of this vaccine would be:

> "During the next decade the world's population is set to rise by around 500 million. Moreover, because the rates of population growth **in the developing countries of Africa, South America, and Asia will be so much greater than the rest of the world, the distribution of this dramatic population growth will be uneven ...**" [Racist Eugenics – Bill Gates' dad!]

"... The Population Research Institute, in the November/December 1996 issue of its Review, published a report by David Morrison. 'Philippine women may have been unwittingly vaccinated against their own children, a recent study conducted by the Philippine Medical Association (PMA) has indicated.'

" ... as of 1995, there were several large groups researching these [sterilization] vaccines.

- WHO/HRP. HRP is the Special Progamme of Research, Development and Research Training in Human Reproduction, located in Switzerland. It is funded by "the governments of Sweden, United Kingdom, Norway, Denmark, Germany and Canada, as well as the UNFPA and **the World Bank.**"
- The Population Council. It's a US group funded by the **Rockefeller Foundation,** the National Institutes of Health [a US federal agency], and the US Agency for International Development [notorious for its collaborations with the CIA].
- National Institute of Immunology. Located in India, "major funders are the Indian government, the Canadian International Development Research Center and the [ubiquitous] **Rockefeller Foundation.**"

"... West Nile, SARS, bird flu, Swine Flu, Ebola—**the real motive for promoting these "pandemics" is the follow-up: vaccines.** To a highly significant degree, the CDC and the World Health Organization are Public Relations agencies, whose job is to convince the public that stepping up, rolling up their sleeves, and submitting to shots containing germs and toxic chemicals is the most natural and wise action possible ..."

– By Jon Rappoport, Nomorefakenews.com November 10, 2014

http://jonrappoport.wordpress.com/2014/11/10/depopulation-vaccine-in-kenya-and-beyond/

Chapter 7

Just Look In the Mirror

I've been a victim of a selfish kind of love
It's time that I realize
That there are some with no home, not a nickel to loan
Could it be really me, pretending that they're not alone?
I'm starting with the man in the mirror
I'm asking him to change his ways
And no message could have been any clearer
If you want to make the world a better place
Take a look at yourself, and then make a change.

– from song "Man in the Mirror" sung by Michael Jackson
All criminal charges against Jackson were dropped, but the *controlled media* succeeded in smearing his name anyway. The worth-seeing music video [69] for this song contains social commentary disallowed by pop industry today.

Disconnecting vanity (see Glossary) is a neologism (new combination of words) that I am using that points out the *effect of vanity. Vanity* creates disconnection. *Vanity* separates us and thus cuts both ways. *Vanity* cuts nature and it cuts our inner nature. But because our *dominant culture* puts *vanity* on a pedestal, we discount the *effects of vanity* ... the collateral damage, the broken hearts, the maimed children, the broken seas.

The *disconnecting vanity* that hurts both others and ourselves is spreading through the world's various cultures. And it is not an accident. We live in a soup of deception and corruption that is slowly "transforming" us, and all this is painted to be glorious and "brave." We saw the graphs in the previous chapter. There is a disconnect. We aren't keeping our kitchen clean and healthy.

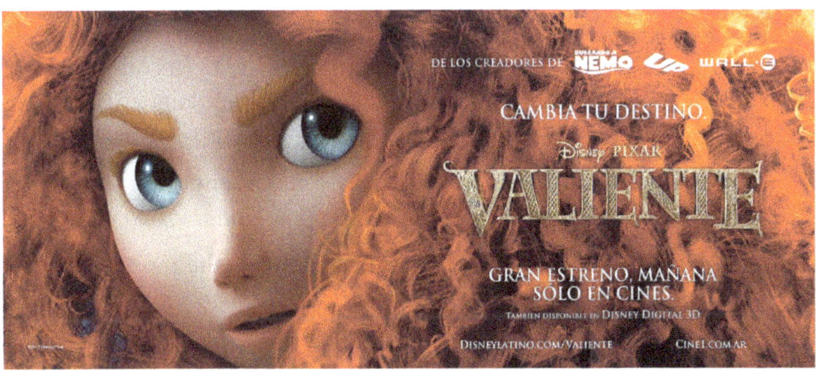

Movie Brave *in Spanish. Globalism is not just an economic model.*

"Cambia tu destino," above, means "change your destiny." In *doublespeak,* "change your destiny" really means, "We elite will change your destiny." We saw how *Globalists* view billions of people as the "BOP." The *Globalists* see all of us as a "cultural bottom of the pyramid" also, and to bring us into the "emerging culture" they have to destabilize our ancient traditions, just as they destabilize economies with trade agreements and destabilize governments with covert ops.

Breaking down traditions cleans the slate and then the *Globalists* can implant values in children worldwide. The character in this movie *Brave* represents "freedom from tradition."

The reader could say, "Well we've always had *vanity* and the abuse that comes from *vanity.* We've always had temptation and sin."

I agree. However, in this book series I will attempt to show that *vanity* has never been as organized and as invasive as what we are experiencing now.

"Progress" has been invasive, not positive. Medical discoveries such as vaccines, for instance, have ended up making peoples' immune systems weaker, not stronger. Invasive fixes just don't work. The values promoted by Disney are invasive and will be negative, because they are not intended to be positive for anyone except the *Globalists.* Disney Inc. is all about cultural destabilization using popular themes like "liberation." At risk are natural societies that sustained us for thousands of years.

The key to not falling for the conditioning you have already absorbed is to look for your triggers. What is it that triggers you? What triggers your motivations? Uncover your triggers and uninstall the button and you will discover your true nature.

When we have *personal sovereignty* we do not react to cultural triggers, which is what Globalist conditioning is all about. We check into something deeper in ourselves that is connected with our longest term goals. Our longest term goals are spiritual, not material.

Now, since our elite want to control us, they wouldn't want us checking into spiritual goals, would they?

This is why ancient traditions that do consider spirit are being eradicated by the control freaks.

* * *

In the most clever way, movies like *Brave* seem to empower the individual. However, this is not what we should want. We should want empowerment of small communities because we are social creatures. We are not islands, we are families. By pushing for "the rights of the individual," all families worldwide become fragmented, and single moms replace male/female bonds and community. Why? Because if individuals come first, everything else comes second.

The "bravery" to be a strong individual is a trojan horse. The real intention of this *social engineering* is fragmentation of community to create the "melting pot" under state collectivism.

I know for sure that there are readers already programmed to defend "the rights of the individual" and you did not like what I wrote, and that is because you are probably already fragmented. You are probably loyal to more fragmentation, not a tradition. You don't have a tradition do you? Thought so. Hopefully you have loving parents, and that is your tradition. If not, the chances are that you are already globalized and programmed primarily by Big Brother.

I am writing to help de-program you. You will discover that community bonds and traditions are the only way any of us will physically survive what we are facing. If that sounds like doom and gloom, please review the broken ocean story again, the graphs, the geo-engineering jet trails, and the injected tracking chips.

I don't think we should be comfortable. Its time to be on edge and get our homes clean and tight and well-stocked. It is time to create alliances with your neighbors.

This book is not an intellectual presentation for your intellectual titillation. This is your life and I'm here to help you wake up.

* * *

The U.S. national anthem has the words, "home of the brave." What does "brave" mean? Bravery is not protecting a fellow soldier who is killing civilians. Bravery is not following orders in an occupation of another country.

Young song writer Christina Perri is speaking about a type of "brave" that is worthwhile below.

> *How to be brave …*
> *How can I love when I'm afraid to fall …*
>
> *I will be brave*
> *I will not let anything take away*
> *What's standing in front of me*
> *Every breath, every hour has come to this*
>
> *I have died everyday waiting for you*
> *Darlin' don't be afraid,*
> *I have loved you for a thousand years*
> *and I'll love you for a thousand more …*
>
> – from song "A Thousand Years" by Christina Perri

What we see in Perri's lyrics is this essence of commitment. "Love you for a thousand more." Bravery has a promise to it, beyond one's self interest. Bravery is not being sassy. Bravery is not being a "strong individual" or being "independent." I feel the key word is devotion. Bravery is *devoted* to something bigger, to someone or something else, not the "individual," and not my tribe. "Blood is thicker than water" is tribal loyalty. But true bravery defends water, pure clear water. Bravery is something very noble that stands up for something virtuous, something beyond what can be held in the hand or what is even visible. For example …

> *"Give me liberty or give me death."*
>
> – Patrick Henry, 1775

The entertainment and music industries encourage us to be "brave" in order to be "different" or "special." It is really a *co-opt* (Glossary) of the word bravery. This is what the *Globalists* do with everything noble, they *co-opt* it. The way they present it, "bravery" is about "taking a chance" to prove one is better than others. In war, globalist "bravery" is protecting your mates in battle, even if the battle is against freedom fighters who are the true heroes. Bravery isn't noble in this *co-opted* version, it is just winning awards for one's own team, not for virtue, not for beauty.

In our world the bravest people of all are the whistleblowers. They are true true heroes.

In the home, the *Globalists* want children to be brave to resist the guidance of parents and this is working quite well for them. We see this in the disrespectful language and attitudes of most children who watch TV or video games. If one watches Disney movies in terms of the attitude toward tradition, the attack on family and males is non-stop. Family is in their way, men are appendages.

The *Globalists* want us fragmented or atomized, because they want to break down communities, so we can all live in a globalized world under one law, one value system, one *monoculture* . The point of this is that the *Globalists* want only one organization in the world, not many, as it should be.

Family traditions are the building blocks of diverse and unique communities, but because they are diverse, the *Globalists* want to "draw them together," which means homogenize them.

To do this, we must be broken down to the simplest most basic unit. It is much like *military* boot camp; break down all loyalties so that what is left is "the individual" without conscience or ethics who will follow orders like a robot. Welcome to the world of "transformation."

Just as boot camp strips a young person of conscience and replaces it with "duty" to be a robot, all citizens are being stripped of virtue and this is being replaced by *consumerism* and obedience to "politically correct thinking," a New World Order term used by the Rothschild Communists one hundred years ago. (My Mom told me this.)

By contrast, a spiritual seeker breaks the layers of tradition in vision quest, but this is not replaced by some concocted new order, it is about breaking old routine consciousness. The true seeker returns to the home tradition with vision. But in the New World Order, returning home is not part of the curriculum. Being globalized means there is no home, and no turf that you are responsible for. (Good to review Education 2000, Page 29)

Cartoons, media, and schools are now pushing a breakdown of tradition, not for vision, but for an opening to place the consumer mentality of me first, my mouth, my taste buds, my genitals, my car, my success. Acquisitiveness. By contrast, traditional people are, for the most part, not acquisitive, they are connected and respectful.

The psychology of test scores creates adults who are competing employees instead of community members. "Team work" in schools is about categorizing interactive behavior which is recorded by the teacher and goes on the student's permanent NSA resume through proprietary software that the school has no control over. [70] Profiling. Although "empowering the individual" appears to respect individuality, globalized students have little ecologic sense of place, thus, stewardship and service to local community never develops. Our children are being "educated" to be indigenously retarded.

A few elderly lifetimes ago, only community rights existed. Now the bankster legal system forced *everywhere* denies *indigenous people* of their ancient community rights. We've been flipped.

* * *

Let me please spell this out, because we all really need to get to the bottom of this. The root of "sin," however you define it, is what? It is selfishness at the expense of others.

The other pole, (see Glossary *Inverse Relationships*) would be "service to benefit others."

> We could say that soul energy (I'm making this up because this can't be put in words) is directed toward helping either "self" or "others." But as we awaken, there is no longer a designation of separateness. I promise this. The more quiet you become, the more you won't be able to find the separation. And you will move toward service. *As we purify, there is no self that is not connected.* Maybe I said it well there. There is no person with a perfectly pure self. There are people who have dropped self and are therefore more pure.

Which pole do the *Globalists* promote in movies and everywhere? This gets tricky. They fragment us to serve and be "heroes," not to serve the circle of life, but *to serve the pyramid of their order.* So we are still "serving," but not serving what is noble and good and true and refined and virtuous.

It is important to understand this trickiness. The *Globalists* can't get rid of altruism, but they can redirect it to their purposes.

We are going to be asked by our *cutouts* to give up everything to serve "world peace" and to sacrifice for "world environmental crisis" by … *obeying their plan.*

The *Globalists* have done this for a long time. One hundred years ago, the original communists like my uncle and my parents, thought they would bring about a fair world for all workers that was free of war. They were tricked, and were bitter when they figured that out. Now there is a new generation and the Zeitgeist Movement is the exact same blueprint of trickery.

> *"This present window of opportunity, during which a truly peaceful and interdependent world order might be built, will not be open for too long …*
>
> – David Rockefeller speaking at the United Nations Ambassadors' dinner, September 23, 1994

Any doubters about who is going to be in control under this "window of opportunity"?

What the *Globalists* need is a crisis to get the sheeple panicked and running. Their plan is to come up with various disasters, so that most people will be quite willing to run to their "safety." Crisis, within a nation, will end local communities, but if international, it will force more cooperation to deal with the international emergency. When cooperation is seamless, sovereign nations no longer exist. Mission accomplished for *Globalists.* And how prescient, the *Globalists* have set up all the structures for just such an emergency in advance, and this new "cooperation" will be the new one world government, or New World Order. Step by step, this is how manufactured crisis is being used.

As an example, think about Hurricane Katrina, and stadiums full of desperate people. Since your community will be crushed, you will have to depend on Big Brother, right? This is the purpose of destabilization/consolidation events and also family fragmentation programs. *The Globalists are desperate now* to crash things so we will fall in line to their "order," because the truth about all their deception is dawning on more and more people. They need a huge disaster as soon as possible! [Katrina was steered. Search Scott Stevens www.Weatherwars.info]

See www.geoengineeringwatch.org … Disaster is already here. It really is "truth versus deception" and the whole Earth is hanging in the balance. That is why your voice, your choice, your heart, your action, your protest is now so important.

The alternative to following the *Globalists* is obvious. Don't. Ditch *globalization*, ditch international trade, ditch the UN, ditch centralization. Rather, you the reader (you!) can start cleaning up your kitchen, stock your pantry, and connect again with your own community and your ecological base. *Your community must survive and you can help that by being a strong member of it.* What is essential is that you start producing something! Cut the dependence. Produce!

We can stop giving energy to an ideological construct like "The World" that has a deceptive script behind it and is really a form of mind control. We can stop being sheeple believers. We can be strong natural men and women with inner quiet and connection who know how to work together again as communities. The teenagers reading this are the most important people in the world. This is the alternative that will turn the tide and also save our spiritual paths. For those who say, "Oh we can't do that," your only other choice is to trust Big Brother.

People are going to tighten their belts and work together. And you will be one of the leaders.

* * *

The western system of law took centuries to build. Our laws protect "personal property" above community. *This means those with the most property have the most protection.*

I'll say that again because it is so important.

Our laws protect private property; therefore, the laws protect the rich who have the most property.

The Queen of England doesn't have to worry about the law.

And *indigenous* peoples who never even conceived of private property are protected the least.

Communities are not recognized in court. If there was such a thing as a legal community, *indigenous* people could have been able to stand up to colonialism legally. But communities don't exist in the *dominant culture* because our culture is based on private property, not community property. Private property is a divide and conquer tactic. The barons of England don't recognize community. They own the land, they own the serfs, and their system is trying to take over the world. In Hawaii, there is a small island off of Kauai called Ni'ihau which has been owned by one Colonial era family and they control the lives of the *indigenous* Hawaiians, who lived there for a thousand years. (Acknowledgement to Keith Robinson, an ardent conservationist.) Our system gives the "property" owners that right, backed up by police and *military*.

In this system, a representative can lie, be replaced by a *cutout* who also lies, and then be replaced by another *cutout* who also lies … so that *indigenous* communities don't even have someone accountable to talk to.

In the U.S., the federal government is taking more power from the states, and the states taking more from the counties. Home rule is on the run. The *dominant culture* overran the *indigenous people* and now is overrunning everyone. This aggressive erosion of natural living can be viewed as fragmented urban life spreading to the countryside.

* * *

Let's pretend the reader has a school assignment. Pretend you are a Globalist with unlimited funds. Your goal is to have a planet that you can completely control. You want it so the inhabitants will have no basis for strength and will depend on your whim for food, energy, entertainment, drugs, transportation, and security. What on the existing planet stands in your way?

The answer is ... any human being with self respect will refuse to go along. Answer two, any parent. Answer three, any grandparent. Hmmm ... so, for a Globalist the family is a problem because it is a source of strength.

Now the reader might recall how the Black slaves in the U.S. from 1619 to 1865 were often divided from their families to make them disoriented, heartbroken, and without a basis for organization. This made them more compliant slaves for the monsters who terrorized them. We recall how children were stolen from *indigenous* families in the U.S. and Canada and Australia to create a lost generation with a fraction of the earth-soul-roots-family connections they had before. It is no coincidence U.S. and Australia had the same policy. They both were controlled by the Rothschilds. We, as *Globalists*, don't even consider how incredibly heartbreaking it was for our *dominant culture* soldiers to come to these peoples' homes and steal their children to get "developed" in our concentration camp schools.

Pupils at the Carlisle Indian School, Pennsylvania (c. 1900)

From the lips of Richard Henry Pratt, who founded the Carlisle Indian School and engineered the forced assimilation policy ...

> *"A great [not!] general has said that the only good Indian [Native American] is a dead one, and that high sanction of his destruction has been an enormous factor in promoting Indian massacres. In a sense, I agree with the sentiment, but only in this: that* ***all the Indian there is in the race should be dead. Kill the Indian in him, and save the man.****"*

[The actual words were, "The only good Indians I ever saw were dead," as spoken to Tosawi of the Comanches, uttered by Union Army General Philip Sheridan, 1868.]

> "The plight of Native American and First Nations children in the United States and Canada as stolen generations cannot simply be brushed off as "ancient" history. Many readers here are aware of the history of Native American boarding schools, like Carlisle, depicted above, and the Canadian Indian residential school system, thanks to the ongoing efforts of editors and writers for *Native American Netroots*, founded by Navajo, both on their site and here at Daily Kos. They have also provided critical coverage of the current [!] South Dakota kidnapping of Indian children—placing them in white foster care, in pieces written by Meteor Blades, and Aji.
>
> "Unfortunately, too many of our fellow citizens remain in complete ignorance. I know this, because I am faced with the censorship of Native American history and invisibility of Native Americans living among us every day. Colleagues and other teachers I'm in touch with across the U.S. concur."
>
> – Denise Oliver Velez, *Daily Kos,* April 14, 2013
> this link includes excellent videos also [71]

Above, stolen aboriginal children in Australia. Believe it or not, every child in the world is now being stolen as you read this, by bringing a new foreign value system into every home through entertainment and global "outcome based" education. Rather than take the children away from the parents, the parenting is being taken from the child right in the home.

So the school assignment of how to create a compliant population is to list ways the family can be undermined to arrive at a population that has no moral coordinates other what the New World Order feeds to people. Here would be my list …

1. Erase respect for parents by creating a sassy generation.
2. Create distrust between men and women. Make fun of men in media and kick them and slap them.
3. Focus on lust, not commitment.
4. Ridicule chastity and promote teen sex by sexualizing children so there will be more teen pregnancies and more kids born without committed fathers.
5. Support single mothers with welfare to backup promiscuity.
6. Confuse sexual identity by *co-opting* the original feminist movement. (Support "equality" rather than respectful complimentary poles and dignity.)
7. Promote mantra of "independent" woman and promote the wimp man. Also support men who are focused on appearance, not their abilities.
8. Remove the head of the family.
9. Promote alcohol and run drugs so more men are less responsible and more abusive and there are more broken homes.
10. Confuse the meaning of marriage to be a "relationship" that any two people of any sex could join in. While real marriage between young men and women is a commitment to service, that is, children, the new marriage is not about duty, but about "my need" to love. "I have the right to love anyone I want." It is selfish. Having children strips this entitlement away. We serve duty itself in a real marriage, not our own rights. By confusing this, the mentality of commitment to service is eroded, and there are more broken homes based on the new selfish ideal.
11. Empower the "strong (selfish) individual" rather than the strong community in cartoons, movies, and laws.

I just listed these off the top of my head. The reader can add more. This is all happening now, and *none* of these things happen in *indigenous cultures.* The Carlisle Indian School program is being administered to all of us everyday. The natural human is being taken out of the person more and more.

The Disney Weapon

Traditional family structures, in whatever culture, are under attack. Movies like *Brave* are a weapon that change what girls think is important and how they view their relationship with parents. Something ancient is being replaced. The girl character in *Brave* is the most unfeminine female ever, but she is hardly alone in the decades of Disney *social engineering.*

In Vol. 1 we met CIA feminist, Gloria Steinem. (The CIA is surely *not* accountable to U.S. citizens or any given administration and here was involved in covert *social engineering.* Therefore the CIA is an arm of *Globalists* and is accurately called "globalist CIA," which funded *Ms. Magazine* in order to take us all away from true human rights issues.)

Women wanted an end to chauvinism and being treated like sex objects, and what they got was "equality" in the pyramid of abuse to abusively treat men as sex objects also. Why did the CIA fund *Ms. Magazine*??? This is the reason I say *globalization* is much more than economic.

This *co-opt* is blatantly stated in below song by Disney manufactured "Diva" Christina Aguilera. This Disney brat is a weapon for the Globalist *social engineering* attack on Latin America, as many of her songs are in Spanish. I cover her in the next chapter.

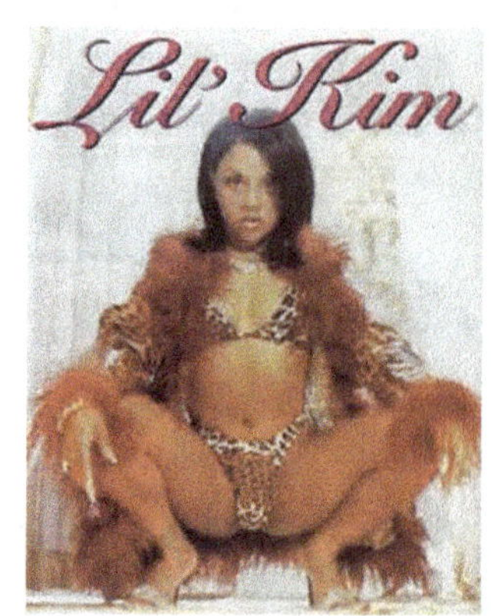

If you look back in history
It's a common double standard of society
[It sounds like a protest against injustice but ...]
The guy gets all the glory the more he can score
[The singer also wants vain glory, not virtue.]
While the girl can do the same and yet you call her a whore

I don't understand why it's okay
The guy can get away with it and the girl gets named
All my ladies come together and make a change
Start ***a new beginning for us,*** *everybody sing*

[So she names an abuse, and original feminism would call for an end to the abuse of vain glory, but *co-opted* feminism calls for "equality" to be just as vainly promiscuous.]

Here's something I just can't understand
If the guy has three girls then he's the man
He can give us some head, sex a roar
If the girl does the same, then she's a whore
But the table's about to turn
I'll bet my fame on it
Cats take my ideas and put their name on it
It's airtight though,
you can't hold me down, I got to keep on movin' *[and f**king anyone]*
To all my girls with a man who be tryin to mack
Do it right back to him *and let that be that*
You need to let him know that his [no longer exclusive] game is whack
And Lil' Kim and Christina Aguilera got your back

– from song "Can't Hold Us Down,"
by Disney creation Christina Aguilera

The explicit message of the Aguilera/Kim song is, "You can act like a whore, but shouldn't be called a whore. Now we sisters should demand equal rights to the glory of promiscuity! You can't hold us down!" This is CIA Gloria Steinem feminism. (Please download Vol. 1 free.) This is how the New World Order *co-opted* the *hero* whistleblower original feminists.

Original feminism wanted a man's and woman's world shared with gentle respect and dignity. Original feminism was a reaction to over dominance by men and called for men to back off and be less pig headed. *Co-opted* feminism wants only a piggish man's world where the women act equally sassy and disrespectful and abusive, just as wrong as the dominant, vain disconnected men. Now, everyone will be a chauvinist pig, including the women, who will be as equally dysfunctional as self-entitled men! "Equality." This is what I mean by attack on the natural feminine, which transfers to how we treat the Earth Mother.

Yin-yang … The compliment of opposites. "Lipstick" is not about being the polar compliment of masculine any more. Our ideal of female is being decoupled from being something unique and special and feminine.

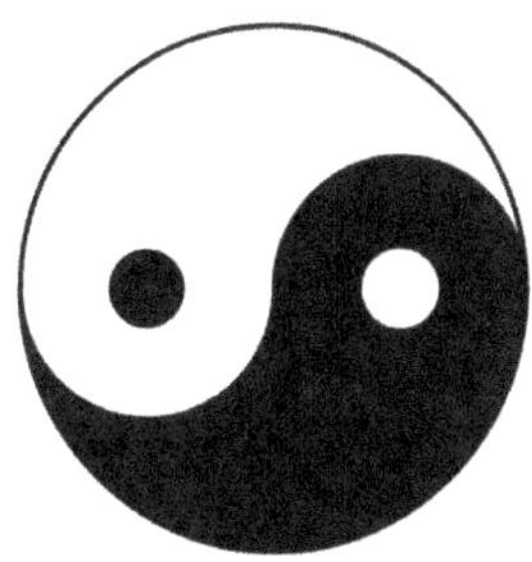

What is a strong woman? What is a weak woman? Is it stronger to stand by someone or to abandon them?

Stand by your man
Give him two arms ***to cling to***
And something warm to come to
When nights are cold and lonely

Stand by your man
And tell the world you love him
Keep giving all the love you can
Stand by your man

– from song "Stand By Your Man"
by Tammy Wynette and Billy Sherrill

This song was attacked as old fashioned submissive weakness, but it is strength. Old fashioned? It sure is. It worked for millions of years.

Now in the *co-opted* feminine, girls are supposed to "come out" and "find their voice" and be sassy and profane, and whor-ible, as in the Disney brat Aguilera song just cited. "Forget yin/yang, let's be profane!"

The Secrets of Isis

From Wikipedia, the free encyclopedia
(Redirected from Isis (TV series))

The Secrets of Isis is the title of the syndicated version of a live-action CBS television series produced by Filmation in the 1970s (originally titled ***Isis***) that appeared during the network's Saturday morning cartoon lineup.[1] The series also aired in various countries other than the United States. As indicated on commentary in the 2007 DVD release of the series, and supported by examining broadcast premiere dates, *The Secrets of Isis* was the first weekly, American, live-action television series with a *female* superhero lead character (debuting September 6, 1975,predating the *weekly* debuts of both *The Bionic Woman* (January 14, 1976), and, *Wonder Woman* (April 21, 1976). In the series, Isis starts out as a seemingly normal, explorer/teacher, who transforms into (a variation on) the Egyptian goddess, when presented with crises that a mere mortal cannot resolve.

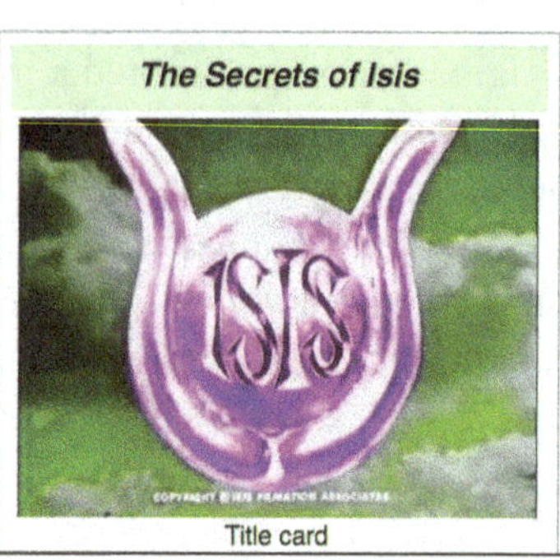

Title card

In the discussion of how women's self-identity has been *socially engineered,* this 70s kids' show character "Isis" reveals some interesting connections.

The name Isis might ring a bell, like those bad guys beheading people over in the Mideast. You know "I.S.I.S.," the name that somehow translates from an alleged Arabic gang (that can outsmart everybody miraculously and steal and know how to use the most sophisticated modern weapons) to come out abbreviated as "ISIS." (ISIS is a NATO operation [72]) This English name was utterly fabricated by whom, the Pentagon? And the name just happens to be an Illuminati deity that is pushed along with other symbolism? We will get more into this ISIS Middle East connection toward the end of series. A thriller has to have some mystery, right?

From watered down Wikipedia …

"She was first worshiped in Ancient Egyptian religion, and later her worship spread throughout the Roman empire and the greater Greco-Roman world. Isis is still widely worshiped by many pagans today in diverse religious contexts …" Hmmm … which pagan religions?

ZURQIEH -ANCIENT EGYPT - LARGE FAIENCE EYE OF HORUS , 1075 - 600 B.C

From United Arab Emirates

$250.00

Buy It Now

Isis was the mother of the Egyptian god Horus (artifacts or replications sold above on Ebay of "Eye of Horus") from where we get the symbol of the all-seeing-eye, which is at the top of pyramid on the U.S. one dollar bill, the logo for intelligence agencies, and will be pushed in children's TV shows, *X-Factor* and *American Idol* talent shows. (See Adam Lambert, Ch. 10)

What pagan religions was Wikipedia referring to? The Illuminati is becoming the dominant anti-spiritual religion of our times, and is doing this with subliminal messages and symbolism which is unquestionably changing our values.

For example, is it just coincidence that Madonna's 2012 half-time Super Bowl costume looks a bit like the symbol from goddess Isis in the carefully chosen logo for kids show, above, and that she is doing an Egyptian move with her hand? No way. One must understand the power of symbols … Symbols create adherence and familiarity without any rational screening. Advertising of logos and brand names is all about creating this adherence. Thus symbols have power.

Not convinced? How do you explain Cher's costume? Coincidence??? This book is an exposé on *globalization* and our place in correcting it. *Globalization* is a very vain and dark project, that in our historical period can be traced back to the *vanity* and disconnection of the Egyptian parasitic elite, and even before that. When we see pop stars like Cher kissing a** to Illuminati symbolism, and its connection to the all-seeing-eye and mass surveillance a la *technocracy*, we need to splash some cold water on our faces. Do you really want to live in *their* culture? (See *cage theme* Glossary)

About the Goddesses

Many people know that the ancient Egyptian goddess Hathor was associated with a cow. She would often be portrayed as having the head of a cow; for example, on the handles of mirrors and on the tops of columns in temples.

Hathor was also often portrayed as a woman wearing a headdress that consisted of a pair of horns surrounding a sun disk, as shown in the drawing to the right. Because of the cow horns, many people assume that this headdress always indicates that the goddess pictured is Hathor.

However, other goddesses could wear the horns and sun disk, including Sekhmet, Tefnut, and Isis.

The drawing to the right could represent either Hathor or Isis. It does not contain enough information to specifically link it to one or the other.

> "Hathor is at times the mother, daughter and wife of Ra and, like Isis is at times described as the mother of Horus ... The cult of Osiris promised eternal life to those deemed morally worthy ... The Ancient Greeks identified Hathor with the goddess Aphrodite while in Roman mythology she corresponds to Venus"
>
> - Wikipedia

> "**Isis** is a DC Comics superhero, as well as a separate Egyptian goddess also living in the DC universe. The recent superhero character is modeled closely after the main character of The Secrets of Isis, a live-action American Saturday morning television program that served as the second half of The Shazam!/Isis Hour. The television character appeared in several late 1970s DC Comics publications. The more recent superhero character was introduced into the in 2006 as a female counterpart ... The Egyptian goddess character has been depicted within the Wonder Woman comic book."
>
> - Wikipedia

From the Internet Movie Database (IMDb): *Isis* with JoAnna Cameron, Brian Cutler, Joanna Pang, Ronalda Douglas. An archaeologist gains an amulet that lets her turn into the superheroine goddess Isis and fight evil.

Isis Movie (Concept)—Isis is not in active development. A young girl finds the bracelet of the ancient god Isis and inherits her powers in addition to awakening a dark force.

In the Disney movie *John Carter* (2012) the characters swear to the god Isis repeatedly. The name was being planted in audience again and again. Why the emphasis? In the script the following narrative was given to audience. *Predictive programming?* The parasitic elite reveal themselves here.

> *"We've been playing these games since before this planet, and we'll continue to do so long after the death of yours. We don't cause the destruction of a world, Captain Carter. We simply manage it. Feed off it, if you like. But on every host planet it always plays out exactly the same way. Populations rise, societies divide, wars spread, and all the while the neglected planet slowly fades."*
>
> - from movie *John Carter* (2012)

Let's focus on the words of Wikipedia screenshot at top of Page 170 (back 3 pages) about the 70s kid's show *Secrets of Isis.*

In the series, an average human female transforms into a super hero. Notice within 3-7 months that similar shows, *The Bionic Woman* (*predictive programming* seeding us with transhumanism,) and *Wonder Woman*, also debuted. The second two shows were being developed before *Secrets of Isis* was really tested by the market. *Secrets of Isis* debuted on Saturday morning, aiming directly at small impressionable children. So we see here that the developers were creating a market, not responding to it. They had a purpose that was more important than making money. Also, please notice that *Secrets of Isis* was released internationally to homogenize all children. *Isis* appeared on the pre-school children's show *Captain Kangaroo*. The theme was simply introduced to all children without any parent's input. This is New World Order to a tee. What exactly did these super women teach little girls, and boys also?

Little girls were given role models of women who are forever young and wear sexy costumes, meaning ready for sex 24/7. They have no kids and fight like men. The natural feminine was replaced. The hook and bait was "equality" and the thrill of power over others, but the standard was not normal life anymore. Injected into the minds of little girls was a "transformed" super woman, who was superior... in male terms! This is what shaped the self-identity of "modern" women who are now in their 50s or younger.

The super women shows were attacks by Illuminati "feminism," which actually hijacked humanist feminism. The attack was aimed at girls internationally and has been very successful. *Very few women so far see that a super woman is an enemy to the feminine and to Earth itself.*

Isis is an Illuminati metaphor and deity. [73] We logically understand the destabilization of families, increase in divorce rates and the growing number of single moms. But why did the Illuminati New World Order introduce the name and symbols of one of their deities? The answer is found in the network of symbolic connections itself, that form the matrix of beliefs which we must awaken from. It is like the Illuminati preoccupation with numerology ... Their deities are simply superstitious crutches that they foist on us all. It is just another limited belief system. Clarity they know not. But it is possible there are actual entities behind the deity worship. Remember Moses, Mohammed and Joseph Smith all channeled outside entities who gave us the Ten Commandments, the Koran, and the Book of Mormon.

What we each call "normal" is like a multi-layered fabric that includes subconscious emotions, archetypal symbolism, connotations, placed nuances, prejudices, loyalties, and the gravity of the repetitive familiar. The "flywheel" of habit. This ubiquitous network or net or fabric isn't just beliefs, it is energy. The symbolism seems superfluous, but symbols contains the intentions of others. People are powerful and power can be routed through any medium of communication, even emails. When two beings are focused on same point, that point can be the bridge and intention can be transferred.

The power of intention is not something we sheeple are taught about, but those at top of pyramid of power use all the tricks. The matrix of lies which we are learning about has a sign language and an intention behind it. The parasitic elite are themselves caught up in bizarre beliefs. Isis, mother of all-seeing-eye Horus is one of their icons. They worship the addiction of grasping for more and more power. They think their symbols are important. It is all a big *vanity* that leaves behind collateral damage and we are pawns in their game.

The self-image of women is perhaps the most important arena of our new consumer choices and, therefore, also of our pollution and our spiritual de-construction. The de-construction of clear sexual polarity is why girls were targeted. Girls were defiled to become aggressive men.

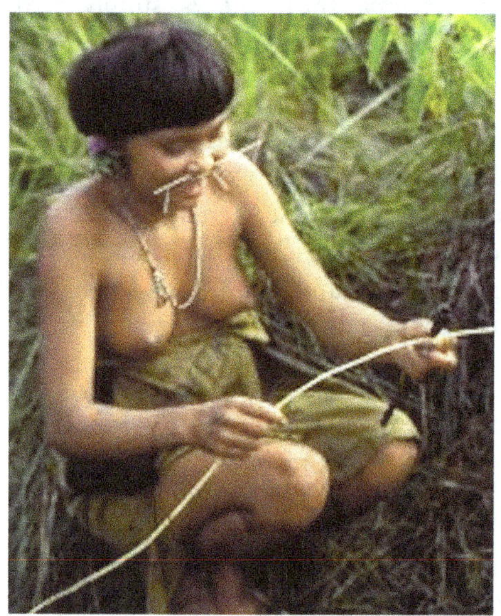

Why does European culture seem so perverted compared to others? You see, these countries were the colonizers, that is, the rapists of the world. Just as Rome was decadent, so the West has been and still is decadent. The Romans were proud of being "penetrators." Sexuality and dominance were melded in Roman Empire and anyone was prey to rape. On the other hand, the top elite Romans were "impenetrable." Sick sh*t. The "Colonial Nations" scraped profit from everyone else, and in their wealth and power, as usual, sickness thrives. Consider who invented brassieres and why. Breasts are for nursing, not to be framed as fetish objects. But now, most of the world is wearing bras, framing the fetish. That is *globalization* for you; the spreading of the unnatural. The center of decadence and perversion now seems to be avant-garde North America.

What triggers are you wasting your life on, and who gave them to you?

The older women in the photo are stronger and more free and can prove it, while the younger women behind them can't because their coordinates of self-identity were marketed into them by the dominant culture. They are weak in comparison. Are traditional people "old fashioned" or still sovereign?

The roots of perverse sexual attitudes are many, but who is it that keeps these perverse attitudes alive generation after generation? If you guessed the elite, that is correct. The top of the pyramid, the richest and most perverse people of all, keep distortion fashionable. The peasants who are having families don't come up with fetish fashion.

I don't think innocent *indigenous* women even considered self image in their own eyes. They were concerned how the community saw them, not how they looked in the mirror to themselves. The women I met in Arnhemland, Australia, had no mirrors.

Khajuraho Temple, Madhya Pradesh, India is a monument to all the ways to have sports sex without concern for family. And some Westerners love this because it affirms their own obsession. But this is not the religion of India! This is one rich man flaunting his false god. This is not example of classical Indian culture, this is an example of classic 1% royal elite decadence. Always follow the money. Who funded this? How did he get so much wealth and power? Who did he take it from at spear point?

Women are now supposed to be aggressive and men are supposed to passively accept this as the new normal. And this is really what we are seeing on the street.

You should be stronger than me
You've been here 7 years longer than me
Don't you know you supposed to be the man,
Not pale in comparison to who you think I am,

You always wanna talk it through - I don't care!
I always have to comfort you when I'm there
But that's what I need you to do ...
Stroke my hair!

You should be stronger than me,
But instead you're longer than frozen turkey,
Why'd you always put me in control?
All I need is for my man to live up to his role,

Always wanna talk it through – I'm ok,
Always have to comfort you every day,
But that's what I need you to do - are you gay?

– from song "Stronger Than Me" by Amy Winehouse

The man now usually defers to a bossy self-entitled female partner. I see it very often. The woman handles the business. But the new boss wearing the pants in the family is more materialistic than ever, because she is not only trained to be materialistic, she also no longer has a *natural feminine* to fall back on. She is now as equally disconnected as disconnected men.

The trick of changing peoples' behavior has been to lead them with the carrot, "I want, I want, I want." The person who wants the most, who has the most *grasping desire*, will be the one who is the most aggressive and "succeeds." This is how a materialistic culture grows like a snowball.

Today, women in very remote places are wearing silly fashion. Unlike one hundred years ago, women of all ages now focus on maintaining an advertised image, created by urban values. Women are now unpaid employees who advertise for commercial interests in a vicious cycle of phoniness. They present a facade. They are posing.

Little girls are imitating their role models, who are lipstick posers. Girls want to be this Diva or that, who, just like the politicians, are controlled *cutouts*. This is important. *The role models for 100 years have been manufactured and placed with a specific psychological goal.* Follow the money. They were placed. Example of placed role model was "feminist" Katherine Hepburn, daughter of a Planned Parenthood founder, funding from aircraft mogul Howard Hughes. [74]

The reader can watch women on TV pose, then spin your head and watch your neighbors pose. Women no longer weave or sew their own clothing. The "look" they wear has no creative inspiration that they could be proud of. No, most urban women are now vainly proud to dress like factory mannequins. *Humans now look like something which mannequins created.* They "strut their stuff" at the end of a factory conveyor belt!

Men don't have to dress like mannequins. They don't have to alter their appearance. They are supposed to just be passive and let a woman manipulate their libidos. My theory is that because lust is more a male characteristic (prostate gland pressure), there is a "market opportunity" for selling lust. The result of this warped emphasis is that men look like people, while women look like painted dolls, to manipulate the men with triggers. Once one adjusts the eyes, the reality of this is rather startling. Half the people you meet in almost any city in the world look like real people, and the other half look like painted mannequins. Half the people are wearing masks!

Every woman who wastes time putting toxic chemicals on her face is saying, "As a woman, I must look like a dolled up mannequin, *otherwise I am not a woman.*" Mission accomplished for the conveyor belt stock holders! The painted face is advertising as a sex object. Or are women doing this for themselves to satiate their *vanity* as defined by the fashion industry?

... All the girls walk by
dressed up for each other.

– from song "Wild Nights" by Van Morrison

Young ladies ... do you know why a prostitute wears a lot of makeup? It is so that she is no longer an individual with a unique personality that a "john" would have to deal with. She is the ultimate retail personality with no real face. She could almost have a paper bag over her head, or no head as "Lady" Gaga proselytizes. She is just a —. That makes her easy to approach if all the man is looking for is pressure relief. So that makes her "sexy" because the man, then, is just a body also, and doesn't have to be an accountable human being. Neither customer nor sex worker has to respect/relate to another human being. He pays and leaves. She re-applies the makeup/mask. Next!

I'm addressing all young women now in regards to above paragraph. What are you?

Women have bought the idea of competing with each other for the most shallow of goals ... appearances. As a reality check, *indigenous* women simply don't do this. We didn't have mirrors for tens of thousands of years!

Toxic cosmetics are a direct attack on the *natural feminine.* Why did I say "toxic?" Ladies, would you let a baby eat your mascara or lipstick or face creams? You would not. But all this gets absorbed into your body through your skin. What chemicals are you putting on your face?

From article "Fox Guarding Hen House" by SmartCosmetics.org

> "The agency charged with oversight of cosmetics, the U.S. Food and Drug Administration (FDA), has no authority to require pre-market safety assessment as it does with drugs, so cosmetics are among the least-regulated products on the market. The FDA does not review—nor does it have the authority to regulate—what goes into cosmetics before they are marketed for salon use and consumer use. In fact, 89 percent of all

ingredients in cosmetics have *not* been evaluated for safety by any publicly accountable institution.

"Ironically, most consumers believe the U.S. government regulates the cosmetics industry the same way it regulates food and drugs sold in this country to make sure they're safe. The truth is, no one's minding the store when it comes to shampoo, skin moisturizers, baby products, lipstick or any other personal care product.

"The FDA's own website explains its limitations: "FDA's legal authority over cosmetics is different from other products regulated by the agency. Cosmetic products and ingredients are not subject to FDA pre-market approval authority, with the exception of color additives."

"The emerging evidence on the body burdens of chemicals in the American people, as well as the new science on *how small exposures to these chemicals* can add up to harm [The key concept missing is cumulative risks.], suggest that there is no health-based rationale for the difference in regulatory powers between the different FDA divisions.

"According to the FDA, '[a] change in the FDA's statutory authority over cosmetics would require Congress to change the law.' To discourage congressional legislation, the cosmetics industry trade group (then the Cosmetic, Toiletry, and Fragrance Association, now the Personal Care Products Council), created a system of voluntary self-regulation in 1976 through the Cosmetic Ingredient Review Panel.

"The Cosmetic Ingredient Review (CIR), the industry's self-policing safety panel, falls far short of compensating for the lack of FDA oversight. According to its website, the CIR "thoroughly reviews and assesses the safety of ingredients used in cosmetics in an open, unbiased, and expert manner, and publishes the results in the peer-reviewed scientific literature."

"Yet in its more than 30 year history, the CIR has reviewed the safety of only 11 percent of the ingredients used to formulate personal care products, and through June of 2008 has found only nine ingredients to be unsafe for use in cosmetics.

"This panel operates in a vacuum of guidance from FDA when it comes to the safety of personal care products. Words on labels like "natural," "safe" and "pure" have no definition in law and no relationship to the hazard inside the packaging. Acceptable levels of risk are entirely at this panel's discretion. [In other words, if your cosmetics say "natural" this means nothing, because there are no standards and no one enforcing. It is just print on a package and any chemical could be in the cosmetics. Anything.]

"To the detriment of public health, the CIR doesn't look at the effects of exposures to multiple chemicals linked to negative health impacts; **the cumulative effect of exposures over a lifetime;** the timing of exposure, which can magnify the **harm for the very young** and other populations; or worker exposures, in both beauty salons and manufacturing plants."

– Safecosmetics.org, *hero* whistleblower website

And what did I mean by the *natural feminine*? The *natural feminine* is what women were for thousands of years before a magazine instructed them on how to present themselves for this year's "look." It doesn't matter if every woman you know wears makeup. That is only the women you know in the bubble of your fabricated culture. It is not the women who have lived naturally on Earth for ages. Is it possible that the reader is lost in a corporate cult of appearances?

Women who play the lipstick doll game are second class citizens who aren't good enough to appear like themselves, but must play a game. Playing a game undermines our inner spiritual nature, which is true and simple, not involved in manipulative tricky games. Wearing a mask is deception.

Gentlemen, aren't you tired of women who are constantly posing? What does she really look like? Don't you want to get to know someone who is real? Are you satisfied lusting for a mannequin? (Yes, the mannequin has no real personality and is great for sex. We covered that, but you are not a "john" all the time are you?) Do you want to court someone who is a poser? In fact you cannot trust a woman who wears makeup, because she hates what she naturally looks like and is terrified you will see her for who she really is. (Deny all you want, ladies. You are spending time each day trying to hide what you really look like, unlike *indigenous* women who always look like what they really look like!)

Guys, your girlfriend or wife's life has become a game of appearances. Not only is her face not real, neither is her personality. After all, she *chooses* to deceive you with how she looks, and presents a painted facade. Do you really want a retail wife? One day you will realize you are with someone who is not the same person you thought you were courting. Her personality, as well as her "look" was an illusion. *Both* were deceptive. You can't judge a book by its cover unless it's a phony cover. What you see is what you get with a phony cover … phoniness.

I have advice for young men. Listen to her voice. Listen to her tone. That tone will last for decades because that is her heart speaking. Listen to the issues in her attitude. Does she have something to prove or is she at peace? The chances are she is from a broken home, and has never had security. You too. So besides being friends, you may need to be someone who offers security. There are a lot of people who are like kittens taken from their mom's teats too soon, and spend their lives unconsciously using their paws to massage anyone, to get the milk they never received. Understand this. Don't get anyone pregnant unless you are ready for real marriage, real long-term commitment. Avoid sex until you find a woman with a voice you want to hear for the rest of your life. She will not be hot for long, (and neither will you), I promise. Fall in love with her voice and you might have found something.

And you may find yourself in another part of the world
And you may find yourself behind the wheel of a large automobile
And you may find yourself in a beautiful house, with a beautiful wife
And you may ask yourself – well … how did I get here?
And you may ask yourself, how do I work this?
And you may ask yourself, where is that large automobile?
And you may tell yourself, this is not my beautiful house!
And you may tell yourself, this is not my beautiful wife!

– from song "Once in a Lifetime" by Talking Heads

PROSTITUTING OURSELVES

Prostitutes wear the same clothing as women going out to clubs. One cannot distinguish a difference. How is it that the young "women" who go out wanting to be seen as "hot" are acceptable, while professional street whores looking exactly the same, are considered dirty? Maybe all the posers in the dance club are lying to themselves. Maybe the prostitutes on the street are more honest.

"But I'm not a prostitute!"

Maybe you are, and maybe your pimps are the *social engineers* who have convinced you to sell yourself to phoniness. Consider this, that most of us, myself included, have a habit of judging everyone's sex appeal based on how they dress. This is not natural. Traditional people all dress the same!

Traditional "undeveloped" *indigenous* women never dress to be "hot."

The main reason for this is that sex equals family in nature.

Indigenous women never try to look "sexy" because a natural man would assume it was a genuine provocation. And actually an *indigenous* man wouldn't trust it. It is unnatural. Young women don't have to try to be anything, they are fresh flowers! So trying to be "hot" just doesn't happen in *indigenous* cultures and the women get to stay innocent and genuine. (I'm not talking about cultures that have been "turned out" by White men for hundreds of years.) Women from the hinterlands are a thousand percent more sincere than our masked, aggressive, phony, "liberated," mannequin women. I'm sorry to say that most "developed" women have no idea what I'm talking about.

"Developed nation" men are supposed to be passive and shut down and ignore the fact they are being sexually provoked/harassed. It is supposed to be impolite to stare.

> "What are YOU looking at!"
>
> "Ummm, your cleavage, which ummm, you are showing off, ummm, to attract attention ... from ummm ... men."
>
> "No, I'm not! I show my breasts because I am AWESOME!"
>
> Right. Like Wonder Woman.

Domesticated men are supposed to clamp down on their life force, wear a tie around their neck (which is definitely a symbol of slavery) and be "civilized," while their attention is below the waist because of constant provocation. After all, men must "be professional" and serve as robot representatives of their industrial culture.

Indigenous men have a hard time relating to institutionalized White men or Han Chinese (China has 56 ethnic groups, with the Han compromising 90%.) *Indigenous* cultures are used to relating face to face and being genuine, not posing and walking on egg shells from a lifetime of "doing their job." In nature, life is the job. There is nothing but life. There isn't a time clock that takes up most of the day. There isn't a boss or surveillance cameras. And there are no uniforms.

If you wear a uniform, any kind of uniform, even the robes of a monk, you are allowing yourself to be domesticated. (I saw this in Arnhemland with Aboriginal men having to wear a uniform to have any job.) You are not being genuine with *the Great Mystery*. You are playing a role for a position, to get "respect" for a reaction, playing a game, being phony. Simply the way we are is the most honest and, therefore, the most truthful and true we can be. To be true is how we grow spiritually. To be true is difficult in a society that judges and grades and ranks us. That is why millions of men in India walk away from society and live as naked seekers. We need to find a balance, but the weight needs to lean toward purity, not phoniness.

To be proud of a uniform is like being proud of a lobotomy.

About the Han in Tibet and other areas, yes, there is more than one *dominant culture* in the world overrunning other cultures. On one side are real people with long deep traditions, on the other are the *dominant culture* robots who were *socially engineered* yesterday.

I'll ask the reader, "Who has more vitality, ethnic minorities or the politically correct?" Don't we see that vitality comes from the frontiers? For example, can we ignore that Americans and Caribbeans with African roots have contributed a disproportionate amount to world music? The center in a *dominant culture* is deadened because we are no longer natural. We've been dehumanized because our *personal sovereignty* was regimented to oblivion. So the "developed" cities are filled with mannequins and robots with ties around their necks.

The *Globalists* want to crush everyone under a New World Order, and we minions help them. We help them even crush our own families by allowing subliminal programs into our homes.

* * *

Commercially, fashion is just cyclic planned obsolescence for profit, and is not about aesthetics as much as the indulgent *vanity* of "edge" and manipulating other peoples' reactions. Pop fashion today makes sure men stay below the waist and women compete with each other as sexual objects.

Say, if someone wants to be slut, that is what they want, but is that what billions of women really want? I'm not judging women here. I am naming the *social engineers* and fashion moguls as disconnected psychos.

Meanwhile, too many older women are trying to look young, even though they are no longer fresh flowers. Ladies, trying to look fresh actually doesn't work. You look like a poser.

Interestingly, *indigenous* tribes in warm climates are basically naked every day and they don't even think about this. These billions of women over the eons were not vain, and the men weren't conditioned to be triggered by nudity either. Each of us have been conditioned by what I've called triggers. A certain look, a certain part of the body, whatever. This is sheeple existence.

Modern culture (*"progress"*) manufactures values in girls from an early age through corporate inputs like Disney movies and music industry "diva" role models. This has replaced community role models. The trouble is that movies and divas are not real people. They are make believe actors. Our steered choices have taken us into phoniness and away from simple integrity.

This makes us more superficial and we aren't paying attention to the direction we are going. Who is at the helm? Who? The continuous input of the superficial is now embedded within our "normal" outlook so that we can barely recognize it. That is, we have been molded into shallow sheeple who don't question or even understand our own values.

I bring this discussion of superficial appearance in early in the book series to show how deep our *disconnection* is, from the real and the natural. Not only are we stripping the planet with *unsustainable* fishing and farming and mining practices, we are stripping ourselves with *unsustainable* self-image choices.

Who am I? Will I look within and find out, or put on a painted mask of game playing?

* * *

Seeking status somewhere above "the boring natural" doesn't improve our character. As we will soon see, "*disconnecting vanity*" is what leads to crime, not just environmentally, and not just militarily, but crime against morality itself. As *Hero* Edward Snowden disclosed, there are government agencies, paid for by citizen tax dollars, that exist to disrespect the rights of the very citizens who fund them.

Perhaps I just defined government corruption.

The criminal mind thinks it is okay *to take advantage of others.* That is what crime is, isn't it? Opposite of the Golden Rule, right?

"Do onto others as you would have them do on to you."

When we think of thugs on the street, let's also think about crimes of *our employees* in the government, who gather data behind our backs or conduct secret wars that we aren't even told about. How many readers understand that the U.S. conducts drone strikes out of Ethiopia or that the U.S. has *military* bases in Columbia on the Venezuelan border? How many people know about the *military* testing of low frequency sonar that is torturing and killing whales?

We are taught that disrespect is necessary. We are told "collateral damage" is necessary. We are told that in the interests of "national security" there is no longer any kind of sin. Certainly, anyone working for the government is taught sin doesn't exist. This is the fruit of *disconnecting vanity.*

The same disrespect of the natural feminine also disrespects human rights or the rights of the Earth. This is a big circle of understanding. I feel that when we harbor respect and appreciation, a more beautiful relationship with the planet is possible. When we harbor disrespect, destruction follows.

Reforming our choices needs to start with how we understand what we are. We are not the face in the mirror. We are something deeper. We could exist quite well if every mirror was thrown away. When we can respect ourselves for what we naturally are, we will not allow ourselves to be manipulated. When we accept the "plain" woman's face without lipstick, we might accept nature without a profit motive.

When we *expect* respect from our governments, we will expect our government to honor all other people also. Then we can end horror wars like Iraq, where 1.5 million civilians have been murdered and are still being killed by American mercenaries (contractors) daily.

When we respect all people, we will respect all animals and plants.

We will not save the planet from *consumerism* until we drop *consumerism. Consumerism* is based on us disrespecting ourselves and thinking we need more stuff to be worthwhile. Unfortunately, we will never find satisfaction with *consumerism. Consumerism* makes us into smelly, pooping, trampling asses chasing a carrot we will never reach.

Selling Disconnection

As noted, to sell this ethic of posing, women are convinced to doubt what they naturally are. Women are supposed to imitate some image. The more they distrust themselves, the more they will buy. Ah, here we see the disease of our times.

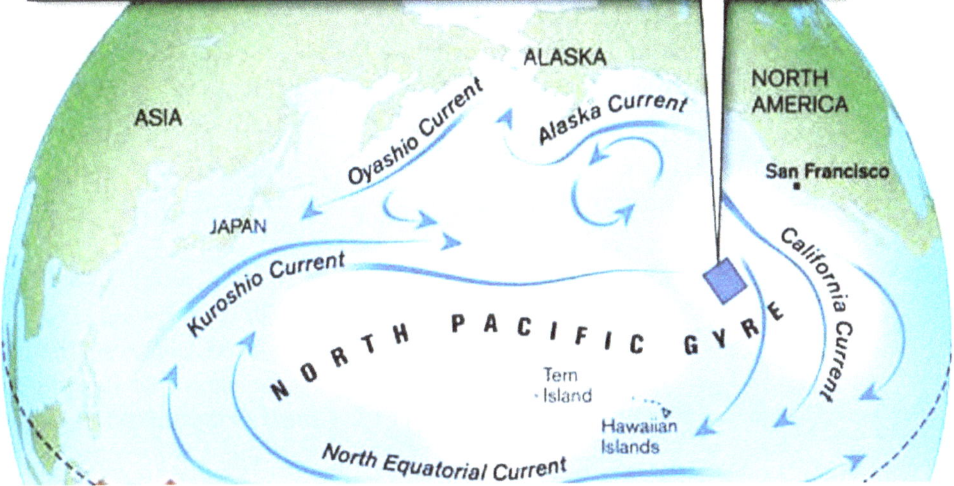
A mammoth garbage pit in the Pacific
The Great Pacific Garbage Patch swirls around an area of the Pacific Ocean about 1,000 miles west of California and the same distance north of the Hawaiian Islands – a week's journey by boat from the nearest port. Scientists disagree about its size, but a marine researcher in Long Beach says it's twice as big as Texas and weighs 3 million tons. Most agree that the mass of garbage is hurting marine life such as fish.
ALASKA
ASIA
NORTH AMERICA
Oyashio Current
Alaska Current
San Francisco
JAPAN
Kuroshio Current
California Current
NORTH PACIFIC GYRE
Tern Island
Hawaiian Islands
North Equatorial Current

Non-sequitur? Not at all. Connect the dots. Our choices … our future. But the solution is not global laws created by control freaks with selfish secret agendas. The solution is personal sovereignty. But you will have to sacrifice for it. The Globalists want you dumb. How does your lipstick look?

Women worldwide try to emulate the look of the European mannequin-models who walk like robots down the fashion runways. Now we see young girls encouraged to walk down imitation "runways" in fashion contests in their home towns scattered across the globe. Unlike airplanes however, these girls are going nowhere except toward *vanity*. The European posers set our standards of so-called beauty. More than that, *ugliness is delineated by contrast*. Ethnic groups who don't follow fashion are seen as losers. Cool is what the posers sell, uncool is what traditional people do.

The *Globalists*, and all those who buy into Globalism, see traditional people as a "backwards" inferior "market," not as people worthy of respect. Respect means hands off. No proselytizing, no covert anything. Respect means we don't covet other peoples' homelands.

Let's run through this again …

> The big race is to "develop" the "emerging" market. The "*developed" countries* have to "save" those "poor" "undeveloped countries." What that really means is that genuine empowered *indigenous people* have to be assimilated as a "market" into phony dis-empowered *consumers* to give the top more cream to skim. More cream means more money, means more bribes and arms and media venues. More influence means more control.

City people (50% of the planet) *never* emulate the look of *indigenous* women because that won't sell products. *Indigenous* women are put down and considered lowly and primitive and not part of the proud march of "modern" civilization. They are considered losers because they don't play the phony game, when, actually, they still have some *personal sovereignty* and offer a better role model for young women than *Vanity* magazine does. They are the winners!

Corporate interests *have created* a society of shoppers, and the *natural feminine* was in the way, so it has been undercut, smeared, ridiculed and ostracized. The *natural feminine* is not only the way we dress or appear. The *natural feminine* is what we were before Wonder Woman sold "attitude" and ambition to climb the corporate ladder so we can buy more stuff, our new religion.

You see, we resist considering the whole circle ... More success in terms of stuff equals that huge garbage pit in the ocean. And that is only the visible garbage. Acidification of the oceans and mercury in fish and other poisons can't be seen.

What is progress? More products? More cosmetics? A new dress? Or spiritual awakening and community health and a wilderness that is still wild?

A young woman who wants to be a homemaker is shunned. A young woman who wants to keep her virginity is shamed. The schools join in on this assault of the *natural feminine.* If a young girl student is asked by her teacher, "What do you want to be when you grow up?," and she answers, "A housewife," the teacher will target that girl for "development."

I do swear that I'll always be there
I'd give anything and everything and I will always care
Through weakness and strength, happiness and sorrow,
for better for worse,
I will love you with every beat of my heart

From this moment life has begun
From this moment you are the one
Right beside you is where I belong
From this moment on

From this moment I have been blessed
I live only for your happiness
And for your love I'd give my last breath
From this moment on …

I give my hand to you ***with all my heart***
Can't wait to live my life with you, can't wait to start
You and I will never be apart
My dreams came true because of you

You're the reason I believe in love
And you're the answer to my prayers from up above
All we need is just the two of us
My dreams came true because of you

From this moment as long as I live
I will love you, I promise you this
There is nothing I wouldn't give
From this moment
I will love you as long as I live
From this moment on …

– song "From This Moment" by Shania Twain

People smile and tell me I'm the lucky one,
And we've just begun
Think I'm gonna have a son
He will be like she and me, as free as a dove,
Conceived in love, sun is gonna shine above.

Seems as though, a month ago, I was Beta-Chi,
Never got high, oh, I was a sorry guy.
And now, a smile, a face, a girl that shares my name
Now I'm through with the game.
This boy will never be the same.

A rainbow in the morning sky is a very good sign,
Strong and kind, and the little boy is mine.
Now I see a family where there once was none.
Now we've just begun, Yeah, we're gonna fly to the sun.

And even though we ain't got money,
I'm so in love with you, honey,
Everything will bring a ***chain*** *of love.*
And in the morning, when I rise,
You bring a tear of joy to my eyes
And tell me everything is gonna be alright.

– from "Danny's Song" by Kenny Loggins

"Oh those songs are so sappy! Oh, she is giving her power away. You cannot devote yourself to nurturing! Caregiving is no career! Marriage is a trap. Love is sex, not devotion. Oh, by the way, here's a condom. Take two!"

The natural traditional essence of a human being, and the meaning and importance of devotion that has been sustainable for millions of years, is now considered a backwards "ignorance" which society must eradicate.

Cosmetics and the irresponsible sexual values taught to youth are mirrors of our planet killing ways. Rather than live naturally within the confines of a quality value system, we live unnaturally as status seeking posers, actually worshipping *grasping desire.* (Glossary) "Free love" and "free pollution" have parallels. Neither respect limits.

* * *

Traditional spiritual teachers have always steered people away from *grasping desire.*

"Painted cakes do not satisfy hunger"

– Zen Saying

But *consumerism* and "the market" and "development" and being "modern" all demand that *grasping desire* be enshrined.

And so we try to fly down the fashion runway towards "progress." And guess what, the result is we don't have quality, we just have more hunger, because we are chasing the carrot of consumption. Quality would be something sustainable, would it not? We would get there, wouldn't we? Instead we chase chase chase. And just like our faces underneath all that makeup, our idealism isn't soft and vibrant anymore either. But we hide that. "More make up! Don't let anyone know! Hey, I'm not one of those people Henry Thoreau wrote about, one of those people living in 'quiet desperation.' I look good in the mirror don't I?"

We are doing the same hide and seek when we describe our economy. There is no economic recovery in sight, no matter how many times the politicians lie to us. The system is broke. No amount of lipstick can cover that fact. Economic growth now means squeezing profit from the middle class, who are drained in order to concentrate wealth in a smaller and smaller investor class. (Interestingly, concentration of wealth by the top 1% of population is now similar to the proportion in 1928 just before the Great Depression. Heads up.)

There is not more growth, there is just more concentration of wealth. So we are not getting younger, no matter how much makeup we put on. We are instead now entering economic and environmental disaster. The more time we spend applying lipstick, the more crime our children will inherit. Lipstick and war crimes.

TAKE A GOOD LOOK AT MY FACE

Consumerism thrives on embracing unspiritual *grasping desire as an ethic.* City life makes this ethic marketable, because city life is so empty of natural connection that being phony seems "fun."

People say I'm the life of the party,
'cause I tell a joke or two,
Although I might be laughing loud and hardy,
deep inside I'm blue
So take a good look at my face,
you'll see my smile looks out of place
If you look close its easy to trace,
the tracks of my tears …

– song "Take a Look at My Face," Smokey Robinson

How can young urban men and women re-connect with the natural?

Disconnection is uncomfortable, so we want to connect. What can young urbanites touch that is real? They don't have nature, after all. So we find in the cities and in the movies that come out of the cities, that having sports sex is one of the few ways people can touch the Earth … that is … each other. Really, in most cities there are few plants and almost no animals. Almost the only thing living and natural is other peoples' bodies.

Sports sex is conquest sex. It is *vanity* sex. It is basically using someone else's body to masturbate with. It is isn't about union, it's about "satisfaction," which only satisfies *vanity*/groin (momentarily), not the heart. In fact, sex without devotion jades the heart. Conquest sex is driven by a need to have ANY kind of connection and is driven by the *vanity* that likes to "come out on top" and "hit a home run." This is the syndrome of *disconnecting vanity.*

Now the reader is probably thinking, what about physical need driving us to …

This is such a deep subject that I can only touch upon it here. I feel this subject could be explored without conclusion forever. For now the reader might do an internet search for "epinephrine sex" and consider what a Vietnam vet once told me, that he got a hard-on in combat. However, also consider the first paragraphs of my Introduction … our Being is deeper than our bodies. Also consider that Europeans have been disconnected for a long time, as evidenced by the Pan/Bacchus cults and words like *libido*, supposedly from Latin, that don't appear in most other languages. Particularly perverse (this is not hate speech, it is discernment) are the French with their words like *ménage à trois, fellatio, douche and burlesque.* But then the French are intoxicated as a culture. *Bon appetit!* (It doesn't mean "good appetite," it means Enjoy!) Does any other culture have an expression that dedicates food to the taste buds? Who else drinks wine rather than water? *Grasping desire* and hedonism and alcohol have been imbedded in French culture for some time. (And all three of these are spreading.) "Paris" is almost synonymous with indulgent partying. "Gay Paree."

> "As early as the 18th century, the word "Gay" was used to describe a person or place of looser-than-the-standard morals. "Gay Paree" and "gay divorcee" were common phrases of the time, which described the uninhibited fun had in the City of Lights, and by recently unentangled folks. By the 1800s, a "gay house" had become a synonym for a brothel."
>
> – article from Mental Floss that is no longer online

Nice to know the prostitution origins of the word "Gay." Homosexuality might seem fun in decadent romanesque bathhouses, but not when someone gets older alone without children or dies young from AIDS. I am not anti-gay, I am pro-sustainability.

> "The French were the first to make an industry out of fashion, not just dress-making, and they have been exporting their style since the 17th century, which is frankly before most of the world had even realized what fashion was. [And didn't bother to know, thank goodness.]
>
> "Today, along with London, New York and Milan, Paris is considered one of the fashion capitals of the world. Fashion has always existed at the crossroads of art and *consumerism and never more so than in today's society* [emphasis mine]. The way we perceive our desires, bodies, and eras shapes fashion every season, *as it shapes us*. Paris fashion is at the center of it all.
>
> "It all kicked off in the 17th century when the association of France with fashion and style was initiated by Louis XIV's court.
>
> "The Sun King made it his business to be at the center of all that was beautiful in the world so the luxury goods industry in France became a royal commodity. The creation of the fashion press in the 1670s catapulted French fashion into the spotlight and the notions of different fashion "seasons" and the changing of styles became available to a bigger audience."
>
> – from www.whatisparis.com, a Tourist Guide website.
> Above is the "official story" accepted as mainstream values.

Louis XIV was a despot, as expressed in the famous quote attributed to him, *"L'etat cc'est moi"* (I am the state). He is alleged, in a recent book, to have been preoccupied with being a good moral role model, while importing the most luxurious items for his sensual lifestyle. Well, that is *disconnecting vanity* for you! Conceit disconnected from what is possible for the masses.

I'm trying to show here that *consumerism* and fashion and decadence are rooted in elite *disconnecting vanity*. Despotic *vanity*! It is this same fashionable *vanity*, or lipstick, that makes it possible for us to abuse. Fashionable *vanity* is what I am calling "lipstick."

European sexual preoccupation may be some kind of psychological complex. Other places, people procreate, but in parts of Europe, sexual experimentation became an obsession. Some think that the Church helped make European sexuality dark. According to this understanding, the Church's dark side (which includes pedophilia) was projected out into mass culture.

Does the reader know why kings have so many concubines? It is because they are vain addicts and can't get enough and are ruled by *grasping desire.* Do they take the time to be good fathers for all the children they create? No. So they are the bastards, not their children. Same with rock stars, same with most politicians. These people are lost in temptation. And these are the leaders of our world.

Virtue is not leading the world, so *we* need to step up and take the lead.

Do *indigenous people* go out on "dates" and "hook up?" They might, but more likely they will get married because they don't have as much *"freedom"* or even desire to be irresponsible, because *they are grounded.* Promiscuity is not the norm in traditional cultures. It is in ours. In nature people want *to live together.* They want teamwork, because teamwork is what survives.

Do *indigenous* people get obsessed like the rich? There are 6,000 languages in the world. We can't use a broad brush with accuracy here. Let me ask, "In general, does living with the soil and seasons and tides and harvests make a community more connected and grounded and responsible?" You answer that one.

(This is why, *in general*, "country music" is less satanic than what we are about to explore in the music industry. I know Christians want some credit here, but I covered that on Page 6, and as country artist Carrie Underwood shows in her video in Chapter 10, being a Christian today doesn't always mean a commitment to wholesomeness.)

When we worship freedom we don't realize that *"freedom"* is *doublespeak* for "irresponsibility," because freedom for us is *more more more.*

Why don't we worship "balance" instead?

The explanation of why we no longer honor balance is that we are members of an irresponsible *dominant culture* run by psychopaths who thrive on warping *what used to be balanced*, to reap profit from the turnover. *Globalists* practice slash and burn agriculture with everything. They practice "slash and burn universe." The "Colonial Era," which was run by elite banksters and royalty, practiced slash and burn with every culture in the world. What we need is a new paradigm called something like *re-localization culture.*

Country people live within the oversight of their small towns, and if someone is lucky enough to still live in their ancient homeland and know the ancient language that describes it, they probably are "undeveloped" enough to still know that sex equals children.

Does the reader feel superior to the young woman in photo, in any way? Are you more or less free than she is? Who lives in a cage? Who is confused about who she is? She has on jewelry and a tattoo on her chin. These are her cultural norms. But is she interested in looking sexy or hot? What does she think sex is for? What do you think sex is for?

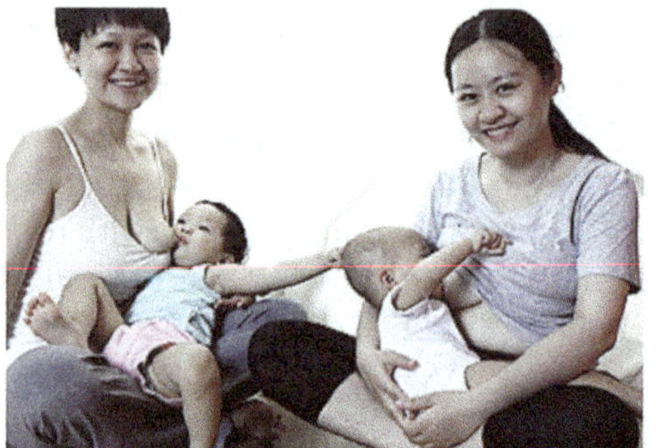

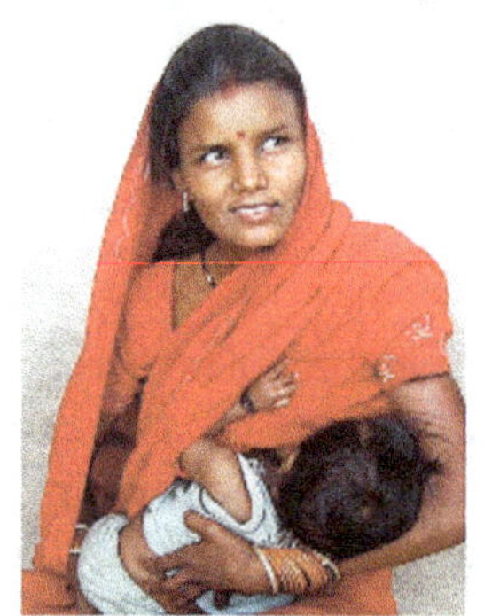
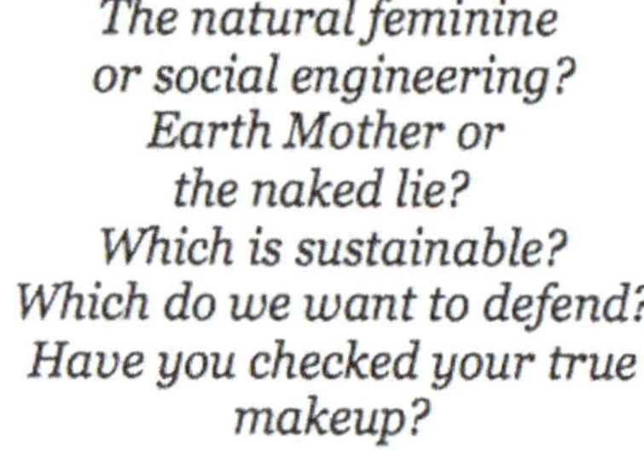

The natural feminine
or social engineering?
Earth Mother or
the naked lie?
Which is sustainable?
Which do we want to defend?
Have you checked your true
makeup?

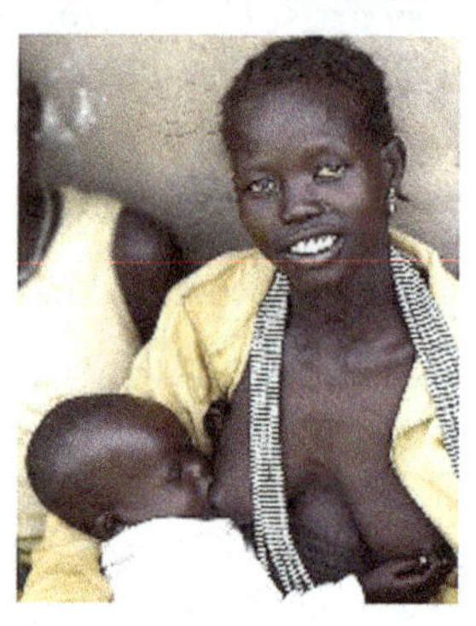

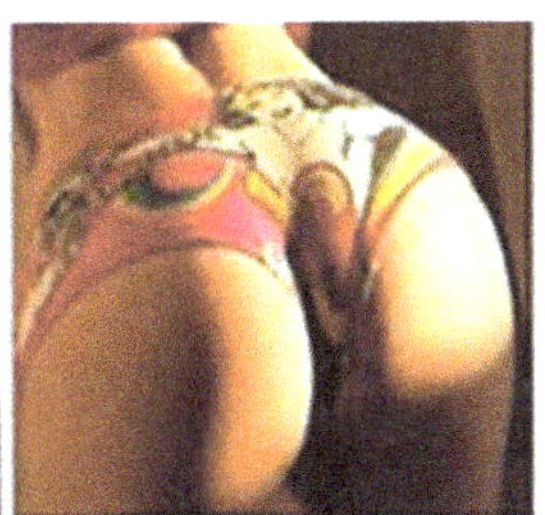

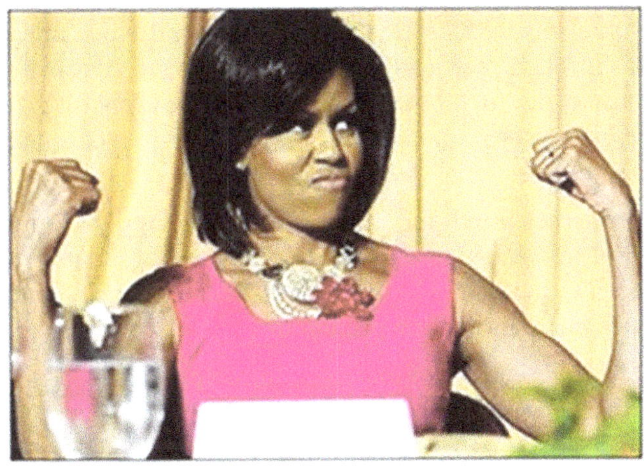

The replacement of natural feminine with lust for dominance leaves no protection for Mother Nature, as the New World Order civilization ravishes life on Earth in an all male paradigm. Lipstick sexual obsession / hate of gentleness replaces feminine heart. Wanna-Be-Men ("Women") are not nurturing our world. Lipstick and War Crimes.

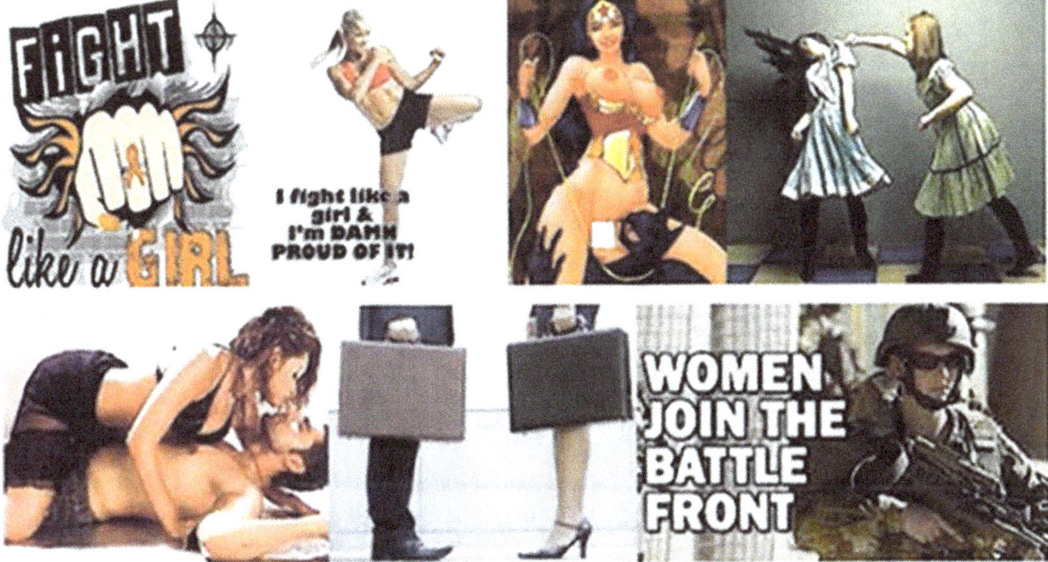

Modern people are disconnected this way, and don't think sex = children = family, which requires marriage. There are readers here thinking, "Why is marriage required?" ... Because marriage means two committed parents. It's called family. Children require family.

Urban people, like the decadent royalty, think that sex is for fun and that pregnancy is a "risk," not the purpose of sex. Most *urban people* don't even realize that breasts are mammary glands for nursing. *Indigenous* men aren't turned on by breasts. They see a baby hanging from one, day in and day out. But some Europeans in some royal courts, as mentioned above, made breasts a fetish. And we inherited the trickle-down perversity.

The purpose of new types of contraception was to compromise our integrity. The *Globalists* control new inventions through sponsorship, buying the patents, or threatening inventors. If a new tech is released, it is not just for money. It has to fit into the Globalist's vision of the future. If something does not fit in, it is not allowed. Altruism is NEVER part of equation with the control freaks.

The reader can do an internet search for "suppressed technology" or "suppressed inventions" or "FDA revolving door" to see how new tech is released or not, and it is not altruistic. If contraception was altruistic, it would only be available to married couples, and that would reduce unwanted pregnancies without promoting promiscuity.

Instead of coming up with new kinds of invasive contraception, children could be taught *personal sovereignty* and that would control population. But that would empower the populace, and the elite would lose their slaves. So this isn't what China or the West are pursuing.

The top of economic pyramid is parasitic upon a dumbed-down dis-empowered base. Memorize this and you will understand our era.

Aggressive Wanna-Be-Men role models have replaced the Natural Feminine. Endless war can be deprogrammed, but only if women call for gentleness and nurturing. The womb of life doesn't need regime change. To rejuvenate the sacred, we need to sing an old song, not a new one.

* * *

In general, country youth cannot dodge consequence as easily because the village is watching, so their actions are more restrained and planned. Also they grow up knowing sex = children, just as they grow up learning that meat comes from a life taken. Country people know the truth of things because they are close to nature. And so, their deeper *personal sovereignty* is engaged and not disconnected from their sexuality and the meaning of procreation.

Disconnected urban life creates obsessions. The "*freedom*" to be anonymous in the cities can be a freedom to be aberrant. The cities are where morality loses traction and perversity gains traction. The cities are where "adult" bookstores and clubs and shops find a market. And this is spreading worldwide.

Notice the very non-traditional girl on the Chinese fashion runway is holding a bird cage. Please remember this image as we explore the subliminal cage theme (See Glossary) *in the next chapter. Remember the cage.*

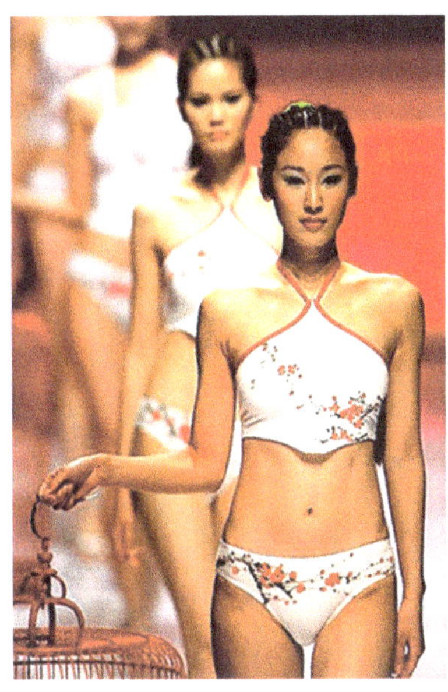

If we are intimate with someone who we don't really know yet, we will probably get burnt. As the reader knows, rarely do two people experience "hooking up" without one feeling dumped afterwards, or worse. That is why so many songs are about broken hearts. Most of us consider fragmentation to be normal, but in traditional places like Bali, where there is no such thing as divorce, people don't live in a culture of heartbreak.

Almost nothing in our present pop culture warns young people. We actually encourage our children to go down the fashion runway of sensualism and reckless temptation.

So let's meet some of the super women role models of indulgent *vanity* or "lipstick," such as Madonna, "Lady" Gaga, Jennifer Lopez and more, who are all ruled by the same Illuminati machine that is connected with the Globalist banksters who funded Illuminati founder Weishaupt from Chapter 2. These artists/agents are funded to the tune of hundreds of millions of dollars each.

Let's meet the change agents of anti-virtue who are inducting us into fragmentation within the "safety" of the *Roth-efeller* New World Order cage.

The biggest problem I have found in giving new information to older people is that they already have a world view built on knowns that they trust. They think the News is true. They think the schools teach true history. They think the Bible has not been warped again and again. To hear new information that runs counter to what they have absorbed all their lives, challenges the ego that thinks it already knows. It is indeed, all they know. But there is an obstinance. There is a one-upsmanship around which one of us is "correct."

So the problem in reaching older people is not their intellect, it is their pride. Thus I have found a complete block by many people who simply are unable to let go of the known, and are often too proud to admit that anything they believe might be based on false data. For this reason I have directed this book toward college students knowing they will be more open to the relevance of the message.

Another problem is "my country right or wrong." I know someone who believes the Bible literally and believes the Ashkenazi people who live in Israel are descendants of the ancient Israelites, which they are not, and since the Bible is the word of the one and only God, whatever Israel does, right or wrong, is right. Even war crimes. Even war crimes are acceptable because these people are committed to a dogma, not to conscience.

A spiritual seeker recognizes the Great Mystery and is surrounded by an endless event horizon in the here and now that cannot be named. There is simply no room for pride here. Pride would block the next revelation.

Open mindedness is not an intellectual stance, it is a reduction of pride. When pride is eliminated, what is left is open mindedness.

Since we are inextricably, in essence, connected with the context of all that surrounds us, open mindedness and reality are one.

Pride and certainty disconnects us from reality.

This series has new information for most people. Don't let pride get in the way of further discovery. And please please please don't let anything get in the way of compassion.

Chapter 8

Shamelessness and the All-Seeing-Eye

Shame is very healthy. Shame means one has a conscience and feels bad about a mistake. That is real shame. False shame is false pride feeling ashamed at being exposed and losing face in front of others. Real shame is humiliating but purifying. Out of real shame comes reformation. Out of false shame comes defensive anger. If the image or ideas you are about to see makes you defensive, I would ask you to go slow. I'm not interested in offending anyone. I am interested in uncovering the *social engineering* of ourselves and our children.

Shamelessness is the idea that one is above making any mistakes, and can break any code of politeness or modesty, and feel above reproach. A shameless person upholds no standards of morality. The are completely "out." They would be an outcast in any traditional society, but in modern urban life, they can be irresponsible. The Rothschild Zionist controlled entertainment industry is just like the Rothschild Zionist controlled governments. That is, Big Brother, including the CIA, now controls Hollywood. Some of this proof is in Vol. 1 where the Feminism Operation was exposed, with one *cutout* after another acting like wrecking balls in their controlled demolition of moral standards. As discussed in the beginning of Vol. 1, this is to create a complacent population that is too confused to take a stand against the designers.

In theatre and music shows now, actors and singers seem to have a split personalty so that the *vanity that disconnects* reigns supreme. Their behavior is shameless, and it seems impossible in their minds to make a mistake because the industry pays them to be shameless and society awards them with popularity *won from placement* on magazine covers and in big Hollywood productions. But theses celebrities paid for that placement with slavery. They are drunk on fame and fortune but are really slaves. Or maybe they aren't? Are they accountable or not?

Unfortunately many of these stars began as mind programmed children (Vol.1). If they want to stay on the ride of fame, they have to stay like unconscious children and abandon any sense of shame, even if they are basically now known for their pornography. These days we don't have men like Elvis shaking their hips. It is almost exclusively women acting like some kind of prostitute, but they really aren't women, like the true older women we saw on page 174. They are actresses and "Divas" staging a performance scripted by the big money that controls their every move. Their personalities are like the emperor with no clothes, but it is literal. Everyone sees they are now porn stars, but they think they are just royal, and indeed are treated royally. Most fans are conditioned by the fame and awards and then accept the subliminal message of the star, their outrageous behavior, which was created expressly to pollute our virtue. The fame prostitutes are artistic *cutouts*, who are used by the royal political *cutouts* in the shameless fame game.

* * *

In early chapters we read about economic destabilization to then construct a new order. But we also studied destabilization in school curriculums. We looked at cartoons. But what about the videos we watch and the big media events like super bowl half time and the popular talent shows? As most older people don't watch music videos, you may be surprised at what teenagers are exposed to. As most teenagers do watch this, you might wonder at the fuss here. MTV has been controlling the values of youth while their parents remained unaware of what was going on. This has the effect that was intended. For young readers, the fuss is that you have been jerked around and you should be angry about this. My generation was given wannabe men. Your generation has been given "women who act like whores" as in first paragraph of Vol.1.

There is simply no model of chastity or even fidelity in our culture now. Most people now would laugh at these words. How did this come about?

This book was fairly safe up till now, because the reader wasn't much in the story, but now we will step into an area so close to home that many readers may be uncomfortable. We will look at how top entertainment personalities shape, not just gender ideals, but sexual behavior.

Because they have already done this to us, it will be predictable for the reader who has been converted to thinking non-traditional behavior is normal, to feel angry at any criticism of gutter morality. Who are you to say anything is gutter!!!

Tradition is a million years old. Very normal. Non-tradition, which the New World Order is pushing, is not normal. I'm going to be asking the reader if there is *anything* that is shameful? And just as I showed consumerism is organized, so is shamelessness organized.

I've added these paragraphs after some friends said I was too harsh with some of the Divas. I listened. They explained that entertainers are locked into contracts, and that they don't have control over costumes, staging, song choices, photo shoots. My question to them was, is anyone accountable? "I was just following orders," is what the Nuremberg Nazis said. Celebrity *cutouts* are the same as political *cutouts*, in that they are paid off to do whatever they are told. Are they not accountable *at all* for the amoral or immoral messages they spread?

I will try to show examples of what is being pushed on young people. It is vulgar. If you find the images repulsive, so did I. That is why I am showing this. For me it is not normal and should never be the new normal, and I am protesting and encouraging you to do so also. I am trying to show that the same powers behind the Bilderberg Group and the UN are behind Hollywood and the Music Industry. One of the common threads, as mentioned, are the Zionist Rothschilds who control both. Another common thread is the common symbolism. All together, they comprise our New World Order which is a *social engineering* master plan (Page 29).

Once we realize we have been jerked with, we each need to de-program. That experience may feel like pulling teeth. All of us who can read this are *dominant culture* non-indigenous people. *Indigenous people* don't need a book like this.

So your sense of what is acceptable is about to be challenged. I'm going to try to show that what we think of as artistic license is really dictated licentiousness.

Entertainment is very important. In the bread and circus formulae for controlling the masses, entertainment is the circus that distracts. Sex is very distracting as everyone has experienced. We have heard, "sex sells," however, as I hope to show, "sex has been sold to us."

My friends explained that entertainers seek edginess and that is just how it is. I disagree. They already told me it is a controlled industry, so the controllers are pushing whatever edge they want to push upon the entertainers. If being wholesome was what the music industry wanted they would select celebrities that would go along with wholesomeness. The message now is …

> "Nothing is shameful. All boundaries and standards should be blurred. Nothing is illicit. Nothing is decadent. Anything goes." Or as Aleister Crowley who wrote the Hollywood bible on satanism said it, "Do what thou wilt."

Now the reader can say, well that is your opinion Ray. Okay, please look at the evidence and come up with your own opinion. The following is a quote from Madonna showing the above message is an agenda. This was spoken by her in an interview to the homosexual magazine, *The Advocate.* She is not just some actress/singer performing what someone else dictated, she is a conscious wrecking ball agent.

> They digest it on a lot of different levels. ["it" means the anti-family agenda"] Some people will see it [lesbian displays] and be disgusted by it, but maybe they'll be unconsciously aroused by it. [And subverted by it.] If people keep seeing it and seeing it and seeing it, eventually it's not going to be such a strange thing.
>
> – CIA Madonna (See Vol. 1), *The Advocate,* May 7, 1991, Page 49

Now right there, some people are insulted because I used the word homosexual. I already explained where the word gay comes from. It comes from the illicit sex of "gay Paree." Gay meant something like carefree and happy, but with a sexual context. "Gay" means irresponsible. Gay men can have as much sex as they want and not worry about pregnancy! Wow, such an achievement!

Licentiousness is supported by the homosexual community, because "freedom" from traditional standards supports what they do, which is untraditional. So they are fundamentally anti-traditional. This is a moral dilemma for gay people who recognize there is such a thing as trash, *but cannot define what is clean.*

Readers who have been programmed by the New World Order (all of us) to want One World Government with One Monoculture which treats everyone "equally" because no one has the right to have a unique culture or unique standards or any standards, are conditioned to be angry with me for even talking about this. We will trace this conditioning in Chapter 10.

The friends I mentioned think that the monoculture should define the age of consent world wide. They also feel that pornography aimed at children is not pedophilia, but I disagree. Media sleaze aimed at children is psychic and emotional pedophilia and almost as deranging as the real thing.

Let's please return to the question I asked at beginning of Vol.1. If a young woman came to you and asked "Why are so many women acting like whores these days?" would you hide your head in sand or say something? Would you encourage her to "let it go" like the song (Vol. 3), or suggest she wait for a quality relationship? What about same sex experimentation? What would you say? Would you agree with "Let It Go" song that there is no right or wrong? CIA Madonna would.

* * *

Almost every society has clear sexual polarity as a bedrock, and I say that because all over the world, men and women wear their hair and clothing differently from each other. *This is to keep the polarity clear.* Why does the reader think this is so? To go against what has worked for untold generations is a bit presumptuous and disrespectful.

Also, traditions that have been tested by time, limit sex to marriage because, as we already explored, in natural life, sex means family. Sex is not free. Sex equals kids!

The New World Order wants to blur all this so that there are no standards. This is called Demoralization (introduced in Vol. 1, the "Trailer"), or the promotion of amorality. Amorality bleeds into immorality rather quickly.

As the reader beholds the evidence that the music industry is organized to use celebrity *cutouts* to blur clear standards, your own New World Order created values might get tweaked. For a lot of people, the word moral is a bad word, for example. Anyone like myself that talks about morals is smeared as a "moralist." Those smearing me were conditioned to feel this. I will ask the question again and again … Is anything decadent? Do we have nothing to say about what media puts on half time sports events that affects our children's peers? How about family television talent shows? Does anything go?

My friends asked why I featured only female *cutouts* in this chapter. I feature male *cutouts* in Volume 3. The famous men are not one tenth as well known as the famous women. They don't sing national anthems or open for the Grammy awards. We don't see Hip Hop artists at the Super Bowl. The reason women are used by the Illuminati is that the natural feminine is the target of their attack. They want to display a "new normal" role model for women that is, to the time tested eye, immoral, meaning without definitions of moral.

The natural feminine is very careful about sex because in nature sex equals kids. Being modest, and careful, and demure are important for not giving the wrong message to men. "I can f--k like any man and I'm proud of it," is the new so-called feminism in which the natural feminine is destroyed. The music industry *cutouts*, like Madonna and Rihanna and Miley Cyrus are the spear points of this *social engineering* to destroy natural sexual caution. Right up there with them is Jennifer Lopez, Shakira (Vol. 3), Katy Perry, Gaga, Christina Aguilera, Britney Spears.

Is sex sacred or profane? Which way does the reader swing?

It is circumspect feminine modesty that keeps crazy male energy behind a fence. Take down that fence, and all is craziness, with single moms providing babies for the State to raise. That is in fact, exactly what is happening. Think about it. Cause and effect. Do you disagree?

The images in this chapter are going to be explicit and yucky. I am trying to point out that cultural shock doctrine using entertainment *cutouts* is organized and has a satanic and Freemasonry origin. The proof is the use of their symbols. Masons reading this may balk, but then, please explain how your symbols are being used by an obviously controlled system which is against clear sexual polarity?

"Satanism" seemed to me to be some urban legend, until I studied it. My friends told me I shouldn't sound opinionated, but you know what, I think satanism and pedophilia are really horrible, sickening, criminal activities by insane perverted criminals. F—k yes I am judgmental about this! But, okay, I rewrote this chapter to be cool.

View of our new Blazing Star set in the checkered pavement of our Lodge by WB Paul Cannon and WB Carl Landwehr.

Model Kate Moss, lesbian photo shoot with singer Rihanna, Freemasonry star with all-seeing-eye symbol.

Neither of these extremely rich women needed this photo shoot. Illuminati arranged it, to pollute all their fans with the "new normal."

Please consider the evidence I am presenting without being turned off. Get through it please because the evidence is all there. This book is about waking up, not about being entertained. It is not important that you like the book. What is important is you want to help solve the mess we are all in. And we must start with uncovering our own *social engineering* and who is feeding it to us. Their purpose has been to distract us from the crimes outlined in Chapter 6 and the wars we will study in this series. Unless we get brave enough to take a **moral** stance, we are done for. Please indulge me and re-read the Yuri Bezmenov quote on fifth page of Vol. 1.

It might help if the reader could now also go to the first entree in the Glossary, about Cage Theme, and read that again. We are about to see the connections between the Illuminati (equals the music industry), Queen Elizabeth, and crimes like the murder of Whitney Houston which is absolutely what happened. The Queen be-knights both celebrities and war criminals. Lipstick and war crimes. This is emotional controversial material and if you don't want to look at explicit mind programming in a very forensic manner, you can stay asleep, but in my opinion, it is very important for you and everyone you love to be awake about the Music Industry.

* * *

November 27, 2013—Seventeen-year-old *X-Factor* USA talent show finalist "Ella" (made up name), seduced by grasping desire for fame, sings as a wide open you-know-what, facing a live audience, on national TV USA. [75]

Believe it or not! This really happened. And this will happen more and more and is not a random occurrence. She did not choreograph this; she was used. She was seen as a vulnerable, malleable, grasping, compromising teenager, and she was used as attack on the moral sensibilities of all youth and particularly the Asian community. A seventeen-year-old girl was told to imitate the indecent antics of the top multi-millionaire stars, and she complied. Is this the future? With its influence on youth, venues such as children's shows, MTV, video games and YouTube music videos are being used and even created by the New World Order as primary *social engineering* projects.

To study this, I spent many hours watching youtubes of past *American Idol*, the *X-Factor USA*, the UK, Australia, Britain and *America's Got Talent*, and *The Voice* episodes. The 2014 *American Idol* contest had over 30 million votes (not voters) per show. We are told 2016 will be last year for *American Idol.* The good news is that the *X-Factor USA* talent show, which set up "Ella" in the photo above, is not popular in the U.S. and was dropped, but this show is just one thread of a many faceted program by the Globalists to destabilize human culture, human morality, human values, and consolidate everyone into a virtue-free zone.

* * *

I feel there are women seeing the above image of seventeen year old "Ella" and are not shocked. Hold on! Is it appropriate for a woman to ever spread her legs in public? Isn't the above photo something one might find in an adult-only strip club? This is national TV viewed by millions. Is there ANY modesty in this display? Is vulgarity no longer defined? We should be shocked. If not, then the "transforming" of our minds by the Illuminati is working, and **we are losing standards that maintain quality over trash.**

International licensing rights for *X-Factor* USA is owned by Sony, Inc., with 29 countries and growing. *X-Factor* coordinator is Simon Cowell, a Freemason. Freemasonry was taken over by Illuminati which we saw George Washington writing about in the Rothschild timeline. (Page 45) The U.S. *X-Factor* talent show is produced by Cowell's company, Syco, and Freemantle Media, which is controlled by Bertelsmann in Germany, which is controlled by some foundations including Bertelsmann Stiftung, that describes itself this way on the Bertelsmann website ...

"The Bertelsmann Stiftung is an independent, non-profit foundation which identifies social problem areas for which it develops and *implements solutions.* Its projects focus on education, economic and social affairs, health and international understanding. The Bertelsmann Stiftung was founded in 1977 by Reinhard Mohn, the former Chief Executive Officer and owner of the majority share of Bertelsmann, in order to continue the socio-political, cultural and social commitment of the founding family, Bertelsmann/Mohn, and to guarantee the continuity of Bertelsmann. Towards this purpose, Reinhard Mohn transferred a large part of the capital share in Bertelsmann AG (now Bertelsmann SE & Co. KGaA) to the Bertelsmann Stiftung in 1993."

According to *The Economist,* October 15, 2009, the late Reinhard Mohn's father's business published "quantities of Nazi novels and propaganda." Reinhard Mohn would go on to monopolize as much as possible and ... "In America, he bought record labels like Arista and RCA Victor, and publishers like Bantam, Doubleday and, eventually, Random House [*controlled media* – Glossary]; in Europe, he acquired 90% of RTL Group, a huge radio and television company."

"As time went by, Mr. Mohn came increasingly to be seen as a benign patriarch who personified the collaborative, we-all-eat-together-in-the-canteen way in which Germans did business. This [don't rock the boat and be a good old boy] helped him to brush off a few embarrassments, notably the publication by *Stern,* one of his magazines, of some bogus diaries supposedly written by Hitler. Potentially more damaging, because it showed that Bertelsmann had not come clean earlier, was the revelation in 2002 by a commission appointed by the company that it had co-operated closely with the Nazis during the war and used Jews as cheap [slave] labour."

"Embarrassing?" We can be sure *The Economist* was very nice here and not exactly digging deep as a whistleblower. Above is the "official story" as released by the company's own "all in it together" commission. Official commissions always seem to whitewash truth. So Mohn's foundation, that has control over *X-Factor*, was lying to the world about who Hitler was. "Its projects focus on education, economic and social affairs, health and international understanding."

X-Factor talent shows in 29 plus countries is one of Bertelsmann Stiftung's projects. Isn't it nice to know that someone "independent" and unaccountable with Nazi roots in Europe is "identifying social problems" and "implementing solutions" in 29 countries?

Above is *globalism* in your face, the lying *social engineering* of your mind and your children's minds by corporations run by tax free "non-profit" foundations.

* * *

"Ella's" song "Mama Knows Best" was changed to *doublespeak* by *Bertelsmann X-Factor* staging and choreography. Simon Cowell told her she might win the 2013 contest based on this spread leg display. The judges refer to this performance as "family television." Five years before this would have been an impossible situation. The corruption of moral values is ramping up very quickly. Without ethical coordinates, youth will have no righteous direction to lean toward. Without ethical coordinates, youth are like raw clay being molded to any shape.

In fact, most people are now conditioned to think morality is being judgmental, rather than being careful or wise.

"Ella's" "mentor" was a 21-year-old industry slave named Demi Lovato, who, like Selena Gomez and Miley Cyrus, was raised, groomed, trained, and scientifically mind programmed by Disney Inc. All three are now placed, promoted, successful singing stars. Their careers are greased and fueled by constant media exposure in magazine after magazine. I wonder if they think they earned any of this? Don't they see they are just *cutouts?* Selena Gomez was recently a poster girl for Kmart, Inc., and will corrupt millions of Latino girls with vain *consumerism*.

These Disney produced stars have sides of themselves that are controlled personalities. I cannot delve deep into mind control in this series, but the reader can study MK-Ultra mind control and multiple personalities online (Please study the mind control links in Vol 1.) In the personalities of these puppets, show business has nothing to do with their "real" selves. They deny in themselves that they are affecting the thinking of pre-teens and teens. Somehow they miss that the purpose of burlesque show business is to titillate and shock, and they somehow don't realize that this side of themselves is not just an act, but *is their manifestation before the world.* They are in denial that they are destroying standards and traditions. They perform something shameful or sing filthy words on stage, then walk around afterwards on the street being gracious and polite as "good role models." They have huge fan bases due to their early work on Disney children's shows. Their songs on YouTube have, combined, many billions of views.

Obviously a 21-year-old Disney puppet like Lovato had very little to say about indecent staging. In fact, like military operations, the music industry compartmentalizes productions so that no one has control and everyone just goes along doing their part. Therefore, Lovato was "just" acting as middle-person pimp for a young Filipina, and helped "transform" "Ella" into a shock object. Lovato watched the process without protecting "Ella" at all. Remember Naomi Kline's book *Shock Doctrine?* Shock applies to destabilizing culture as well as governments or economies. It is called "Pop Shock." "Ella" comes from a modest Filipino family. In fact, in the video, the family is shown reacting negatively to the spread leg display, and this was added to video to thumb nose at people with standards of decency. Even though the family didn't like it, they will bow to "success." "Get used to it," was the message to the Asian community. Producers knew it was shocking and looked for and caught the family reaction. For me this was really rather sick.

Who told her to spread her legs on a chair like that and what was her initial reaction? She knows what shame is, but turns it off on stage for the almighty buck. She is a *willing recruit*. Her "mentor" Demi Lovato supported "Ella" to develop a split personality just like her own, so she can display indecent behavior and then collect herself a moment later as a "decent" person.

Lovato is a nice person with a heart. Nice when person to person—anything her handlers command when "doing her job." She doesn't view herself as a con artist selling depravity with a warm hug. This is the split personality. The more "*disconnecting vanity*" (See Glossary) and selfish ambition a new singer or actor has, the more easily they are manipulated to have this double standard. Swinging before them is the glitter of unimaginable luxury, fame, attention, and most seductive, stoked vanity. These people are led to take their love of music and have it converted to love of attention and money. Vanity and gold. Gold necklaces worn by *cutouts* like Pharrell Williams and Jay-Z are actual symbols of material slavery and these fools don't even realize it or care. They got the material perks. They think they are winners.

Vanity is both the hook and the mask. Having been compromised since a young age, the Disney brat child stars then act as handlers for the next generation, which validates to them that they are responsible, good people. They are in a culture of deception and buy into it. They are always on stage, always acting. They don't know what it is like not to be acting. Conscience and remorse is sublimated so it doesn't get in the way. It is there, but the conscience is *disconnected by the vanity* that pushes it into a corner.

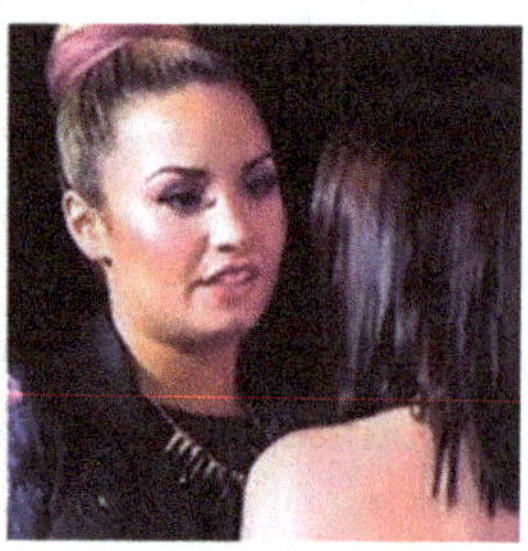

Demi Lovato calming down emotionally distressed contestant. (not "Ella")

Lovato has a heart that will suffer when she realizes (de-programs) someday how she was groomed and used. I see her as a major whistleblower in future, if she doesn't "commit suicide" or have an "accident." She, more than the others, has a likable deep side, in my opinion. She has *compassion*, but she is dangerous because of her conditioning and the industry she supports. She also wants to be a demigod. This is no pun on her name. She tells her fans "I am here for you." It is delusional *disconnected vanity*. She "self-medicates" on drugs, but thinks she can lead others simply because she has a fawning fan base of sheeple. "I've been there," she tells her fans, but no, Demi, you are still there.

In the 2013 *X-Factor* singing contest, "judge" Lovato asked a contestant, Tim Olstad, "Tell me something crazy about you?" This is the value set of *disconnecting vanity* and now youth culture. Since he couldn't come up with anything crazy, because he is sane and comes from a more rural, grounded reality than Disney Lovato, the audience laughed at him, and "compassionate" Lovato made fun of him for not being "wild." The three female judges whispered that he was "boring," but had to eat their words when he got a standing ovation. They want "edge," something that will break tradition, "make them sweat," clean the slate.

The Freemason motto is "Order from chaos." Chaos is needed first. They want wild craziness so they can break down traditional walls, not realizing that time tested walls are what insure cultural sustainability in a multi-verse of entropy. Tradition is solid and reliable. Craziness in random and untrustworthy. Despite being "boring," traditional spouses can be counted upon. Do you remember the professional woman in the Vol. 1 who wanted to sell the idea that professional women are better because they are wild, while the Forbes author was saying they don't make good wives for that exact vain reason?

The encouragement by the entertainment industry to "be wild" is not about empowerment of community, but empowerment of fragmentation through individual egotism. In this way it is anti-community.

These women judges wanted something unpredictable which is understandable in a singing competition, but their real job is to capitalize on someone else's talent. It is like settlers in Canada scraping the land of fur bearing animals to make a profit so some rich snob in some disconnected city can wear a fur coat. The music industry scrapes the population for new talent, not to celebrate talent, but to scrape profit. So the judges are not sincere. They have to bend to the mighty buck. Does a pimp care about the inner beauty of his girls?

They are acting like judges when really they are recruiters. Plainly, these judges are just paid industry scouts and the purpose of *Bertelsmann X-Factor* is to mold new talent *to its designs.* The talent shows are very entertaining and are produced now to include family stories to make them more emotionally touching, but really the music industry is simply using peoples' emotional side.

Let's then add to Albert Einstein's quote from chapter one ...

> *The ruling class has the schools and press [and music and entertainment industries] under its thumb.* ***This enables it to sway the emotions of the masses.***
>
> – Albert Einstein

The young people in these performances are led up the "runway" of *vanity,* and told to look, wear, and act to fit the market. They are selling their souls almost from the beginning, and so are most of us, because we started our apprenticeship as members of the material "outcome based" culture in school. Let's talk a bit about schooling and *social engineering.* Schools are not for education, schools are for producing workers who fit the market. In schools we are told what to think, not how to think. What is important is the right answer for the test score. This is called "outcome based" education. As adults, we "do our job" just as we got good test scores. Without thinking.

Let's remind ourselves once again where school curriculums come from. It appears that the Carnegie Foundation has been replaced by the eugenist directed Gates Foundation. "Common Core" national curriculum was adopted in Hawaii and many other states in 2014. I included the protest letter by 557 New York State principals at the end of Vol. 1, the "Trailer."

"Working collaboratively with the Obama administration, the Gates Foundation subsidized the creation of a national curriculum for English and mathematics that has now been adopted by 46 states and the District of Columbia—despite the fact that the General Education Provisions Act, the Department of Education Organization Act, and the Elementary and Secondary Education Act all protect states against such an intrusion by the United States Department of Education.

"The "Common Core" Standards were developed by an organization called Achieve, and the National Governors Association—*both of which were funded by the Gates Foundation.* The standards have been imposed on the states without any field testing, and little or no input from those involved in implementing the standards. In a post entitled 'Why I Cannot Support the "Common Core" Standards,' educational policy analyst and New York University Research Professor, Diane Ravitch, wrote that the standards 'are being imposed on the children of this nation despite the fact that no one has any idea how they will affect students, teachers or schools ... Their creation was neither grass roots nor did it emanate from the states.'

"Ravitch is especially concerned about the content of the curriculum—what she called the 'flap over fiction vs. informational text. 'Rather than giving English teachers the freedom to teach literature, the "Common Core" mandates that a far greater percentage of classroom time be spent on "fact-based" learning. Ravitch's concerns are shared by others. For example, one teacher claimed that she had to give up having her students read Shakespeare in favor of Malcolm Gladwell's *Tipping Point* because it was 'fact-based' and Shakespeare was not. Of course, *Tipping Point* has a political agenda. [This is *co-opt* of use of 100th monkey idea of tipping point toward awareness. In New World Order *doublespeak* it means tipping point toward *social engineering Monoculture* .] Parents may be concerned if they were to learn that Gladwell [facts] suggest ... that parents should stop worrying about their children's 'experimentation with drugs,' including cocaine because 'it seldom leads to hard core use.'

"'Fact-based' books on climate change [disputed by NASA scientists who say global warming is not good science [76]] are also replacing classic works of literature because they are viewed as offering students an opportunity to learn 'science.' *Freakonomics*—a book that has already been a favorite of public school teachers—is preferable to Poe because students will learn about the positive effects of abortion on reducing crime rates by reducing the population of those more likely to commit crime. [Racist Eugenics]

"While the adoption of the "Common Core" was 'voluntary' by the 46 states that adopted it, it was well understood by these states that **they would not be eligible for Race to the Top funding ($4.35 billion) unless they adopted the "Common Core" standards. [They were bought off.] The Gates Foundation was very much a part of this.** According to Lyndsey Layton of the *Washington Post* (December 2, 2012), 'the Gates Foundation invested tens of millions of dollars in the effort ... The Obama administration kicked the notion into high gear when it required states to adopt the "Common Core"—or an equivalent—in order to [be bought off and] compete for Race to the Top [bottom!] grant funds.'" [77]

The reason kindergarten classes now have homework and first grade curriculum now has little art, is so that *imagination will purposely not be developed in children from now on.* Now we are being "transformed" into robots on a conveyor belt to work for the system. Bucking like a horse and being wild later is the result, and encouraged as a release, while true indigenous inner strength is disallowed.

While *indigenous* children spend their entire childhoods exploring and testing themselves in nature, we "developed people" are trained to be robots on a conveyor belt. On the "runway" we are told how to be a good employee or a model of fashion, with no say in how our industry or fashion impacts nature or culture. "Just sit still and do your homework." In fashion and school curriculum, the novice is herded and molded to someone else's program. We are that novice. Let's recall that the first mandatory public schools were created in Prussia to prepare citizens for martial mentality.

> The state of Prussia began to rise in power and dominance at the beginning of the eighteenth century, led by its first king, Frederick William I. Frederick William believed fervently in paternal despotism and in the virtues of monarchical absolutism. One of his first measures was to effect a huge increase in the Prussian army, founded on an iron discipline [mind control] which became famous throughout Europe. In civil administration, King Frederick William forged the centralizing engine of the Civil Service, which grew into the famous autocratic Prussian bureaucracy. In the commercial world, the King imposed restrictions, regulations, and subsidies on trade and business.
>
> It was King Frederick William I who inaugurated the Prussian compulsory school system, the first national system in Europe. In 1717, he ordered compulsory attendance of all children at the state schools, and, in later acts, he followed with the provision for the construction of more such schools. [78]

This is the opposite of *indigenous* lifestyle. *Power* in nature springs forth from every atom, not from a remote authority. The *indigenous* mind learns from nature, knows nature, and is natural. Nature is the school. Nature is the church. A child's mind is not a raw material to be "transformed." In nature, nature is the mind. The mind is not warped to be something else. As stated, Page 194, the clear mind IS reality.

When we make our own clothes, we know what the style signifies. Our world is understood. If there are symbols on a basket, we know what they mean. There is stewardship. As an *indigenous* child we learned how to work and produce and live by watching. There is no split personality. There is very little sublimation of heart and soul. *Indigenous* people don't appear like they grew up in a psychic refrigerator, the way "civilized" people do. But today, *indigenous* people are known as lazy because they don't readily become retail personalities, soldiers, or any other puppet in the stage production of lipstick and war crimes.

Not only is curriculum being changed to "transform" students psychologically, ***schools are being changed to "transform" us morally.***

THE DISNEY MACHINE

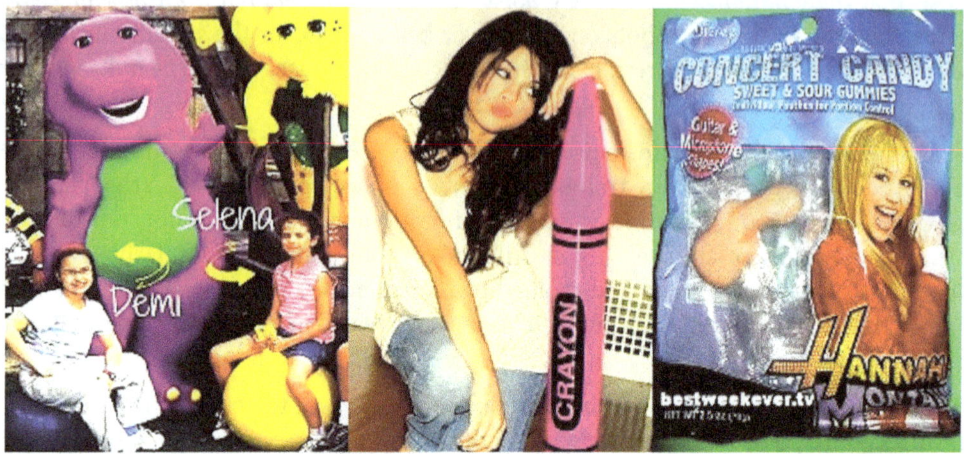

Above we see up and coming *cutouts* Demi Lovato and Selena Gomez as little stooges for industry, being trained to be actors and singers. How many thousands of hours of voice lessons did they receive? In the middle, Gomez is conforming to her handlers' training with phallic crayon photo shoot. She is already sexualized, probably raped as part of her programming, and is sexualizing pre-teens. On the right, selling candy with a flesh colored (Caucasian) penis guitar to subliminally corrupt young girls is Miley Cyrus, then known widely as Hannah Montana. (See Cyrus discussion in *Cage Theme* in Glossary and Vol. 1) The package says the candy has guitar and microphone shapes to suck on at the concert. Subliminal messaging works. "Be fascinated by sex. Experiment with sex. Give it up and score! Chase sex not family. Sex, sex, sex, sex, sex, sex ..."

Despite what Godmother Dolly Parton said in *Time Magazine* in Vol.1, *cutout* Miley Cyrus is not coming up with performances "to make her mark." She is simply obeying the script, as in the above image and as shown in Vol. 1.

Does anyone think celebrities chose which image is selected from a photo shoot to be made public? How about the clothes they wear? They are so controlled that stylists tell them what to wear every day of their lives! They get used to taking orders. Everything is sublimated to the almighty vanity that will do ANYTHING to stay in the lime light. But there are moral stylists also, who make sure someone offers them drugs, someone takes them to a decadent party, someone gives them an Aleister Crowley satanic book to study ...

> **Miley Cyrus Licks Giant Inflatable Penis Onstage at G.A.Y ...**
>
> www.eonline.com/news/540855/miley-cyrus ... penis-onstage ... see-the-pics
>
> May 11, 2014 · That giant phallic object Miley Cyrus is ...

There are people who defend anything "gay" without being at all critical of the *social engineering* agenda coming down from they ask not where. (Chapter 10) Cyrus is being used. By who and for what? My questions are: Is ANYTHING decadent? Do we denounce nothing? I am proud of Mark Dice Youtube channel that roasts celebrities. They don't deserve fame, they deserve shame for being moral wrecking balls. Is Cyrus or any of the *cutouts* accountable for what they do and say? And same goes for Dolly Parton? Is she accountable for what she says? If no one is

accountable, we have the same situation with the Roth-efeller FED and with Roth-efeller entertainment, do we not? No one can be audited. And if we the people have no questions about this, we are the perfect sheeple citizenry that Big Brother wanted and we are not accountable either. So why not kill the oceans? No one did it!
I would like to reverse this so we have some kind of quality control again and some things are worthy of words like trash, decadent, obscene, polluted, criminal, wrong, and slut. In my startling opinion for some, "anything goes" is not a sign of an evolved civilization, but is the sign of decadence. Do indigenous people have the right to opt out of UN definitions of homogenizing "human rights?" Do they or not? Can we opt out of having our children exposed to "anything goes, no taboos" non-morality slutism? I'm willing to take the heat and say that those who defend zero quality control are dangerously mistaken. Societal suicide is not a future in my startling controversial opinion. And morals matter. Perhaps ONLY morals matter.

Importantly, nothing the *cutouts* do is artistic expression. They might have the ego of an "entertainer," but they have the conscience of a robot. Why should *cutouts* get a video award when they didn't create the video? They were just obedient puppets for the social engineers who want to blur all lines of acceptability, as we are about to graphically see. Some people are offended by analogies to prostitution. In being "offended" I feel these people are enabling abuse. Is there anything which "nice" New Age people will denounce as wrong, besides putting down people who can?

So I have replaced the words slut and whore in the rest of this text with the word *cutout* or role model. I was so disgusted with a UK talent show performance that I had put the word slut in front of Jennifer Lopez's name over a dozen times. Though I feel she is an industry slut, I cleaned up the text as my friends suggested. For me, a spade is a spade, but you can decide for yourself.

One friend said I sounded angry. Oh my, angry! Can't be angry! That is not evolved! Again I remind the reader of Jesus physically throwing the money changers out of the temple. Or Paul Revere riding in the night with only a little lantern and shouting, not whispering politely, shouting to wake up his neighbors. But nowadays, oh, you can't be angry! So I changed the text, but I want the reader to feel my anger. If there can be passion behind careful words, I hope you get it because this is serious stuff. Mama Bear needs to growl now.

* * *

Many corporations use titillation, and it is profitable. With Disney, this perverse subliminal rot works to destroy innocence and hurt girls so they lose inner boundaries that protect something sacred within. When youth are sexualized early, they become more easily programmed.

> **Secret Weapons: How Two Sisters Were Brainwashed To …**
>
> www.goodreads.com/book/show/999051 By Cheryl Hersha *Secret Weapons* is about two girls who are trained in an MKULTRA-style behavior modification program to become femme fatales.

The book *Secret Weapons* begins with electrodes attached to the young girls' 5 and 6 year old labia. They were compromised at a level they can never regain and suffer deeply now. Victims of child molestation can feel great guilt because it was pleasurable. Hooked. Manipulated. Exploited.

Chastity is not just innocence, it means maintaining boundaries. This requires *personal sovereignty*, real power. It's hard to hook someone who is chaste, because there's little interest in bait.

Sexualized children are conditioned to look "sexy" and think in terms of bait. They can be seduced by attention to make them feel "special," while a child who maintains boundaries sees flattery as a con game. Guys, if you want to "score," make the girl feel special and take her into so much *disconnecting vanity* that she lets her guard down. That is the technique. Flattery. That won't work with a young woman who is taught about this game by her parents and rests in *personal sovereignty* with boundaries.

(The exact same lesson applies to *indigenous communities,* by the way, who are still being seduced by members of their own tribes who have taken a bite at the apple of "progress." The "chaste" traditional members of the community see through it. The same is happening right now in your community with UN Agenda 21 agents making new laws with bought-off politicians in your region, that affect land use. The meetings take place when you are at work so you have no input. The rascal UN boys are seducing the consumerist *cutout* bureaucrats in your community. On both a romantic date, and in the Board room, the same con game is at work.)

Girls, if you fall prey to *vanity,* you will be used and dumped, because you were an easy conquest. Or you can be used for a year and then dumped. Up to you. I suggest you try something new … something very ancient.

(I warned the reader this would get very close to home. Remember, most of the decisions in your life were not yours. You were programmed. That is why this examination must get personal.)

Sexualized children don't have the chance to develop an independent non-addicted character, based on boundaries. They don't have the chance to develop *personal sovereignty.* The value of chastity is that we are able to save our character and we don't compromise until we are ready to "give it up" to a long term union. I have a friend who sent two girls to college last year and neither had ever kissed a boy. They were too busy developing their unique characters. They weren't on the market. They weren't put on a sexualized runway at an early age.

In nature, young women are not sexualized, they are just married off, often at puberty. This was to avoid illegitimate children and to avoid in-breeding in tribal communities. Is this bad or good? We all lived like this for hundreds of thousand of years. The young mothers of the past grew up exactly like everyone grows up now, except they had kids early and were grandmothers by the time they were 35. What they *did not* experience is becoming sluts. So to this day, in rural areas all over the world, one can find women who are mothers and grandmothers without any fake *vanity* or guile. They are wonderful! There is a big difference between becoming a sexualized game player and becoming a wife and mother! I have friends who can't understand that "love" marriage is known *not* to work in the traditions of most of the world because it is really infatuation marriage or lust marriage, not "love" marriage.

Should girls marry young? Decide that in your community. It is not our business to judge other cultures. Our business is to learn from them. Just as the *Globalists* shouldn't indoctrinate our children with prurient non-values, we shouldn't be *globalists* either and judge or steer other cultures.

Speaking of prurient non-values please check out this globalist assault on the next page. What questions come to your mind?

Hawaii lawmakers: DOE keeping sex education curriculum secret
watchdog.org/121691/hawaii-sex-education

Dec 20, 2013 · Hi Rep. Bob McDermott holds up a copy of notes from an 11-year-old student enrolled in the **sex education** classes in the state's public schools.

Germany – Parents protest bid to teach about sexuality – The Local
www.thelocal.de/20140109/petition

More than 65,000 parents and teachers in southern Germany have signed an online petition against plans to teach children about homosexuality in school.

Washington STATE – Parents Furious After School Teaches Graphic Sex Class …
radio.foxnews.com › Home › Top Stories

By Todd Starnes. Parents in a small Washington State community are infuriated after their 11-year-old children were given graphic descriptions of oral and ***anal sex …***

* * *

Let's get back to the Disney production line and where it leads. Remember, that none of these child stars ever get independence. They are as controlled now as they were when they were children, and following mind programmed scripts now, just as they always did.

Disney brat Miley Cyrus was directed by her "handlers" (her dad's word) to behave like a porn star on live TV for VMA awards October 2013, and then was placed on magazine covers internationally, ad nauseam, because, dear reader, it is all fixed. Left, New World Order *globalization* "twerking" instructor. Right, Cyrus with another Illuminati illicit (can't use the word slut) role model, Katy Perry. They are not doing this for attention, as Dolly Parton claimed, they are obeying their masters' *social polluting* orders. The disgusting part is they actually kissed. Sex without relationship. That is the social engineering model for young people. Sex without love, sex without love, sex without love. "Repeat a lie enough times and people will believe it."

Cyrus' notoriety wasn't earned. Fame is spun and dispensed. Miley Cyrus was "most talked about" because, like the first 1928 Disney cartoon (Page 240), her antics were promoted by the New World Order Media, now a century old. Cyrus was/is a role model for millions of young women her age, who grew up loving her as Hannah Montana, but this is where the Mickey Mouse Club runway has led us all. These images constitute what many young women now consider normal sexuality. (See wrecking ball Cyrus at *cage theme* in Glossary.)

Selena Gomez, Demi Lovato, and Miley Cyrus aren't the only Disney brats that ended up "coincidentally" dominating the pop music industry. The same Disney machine manufactured Britney Spears and Christina Aguilera ten years before. We can be sure another generation of tomorrow's role models are being designed now and they will be rolled out, to become indecent millionaires. Or maybe we will wake up, and say, no thanks.

Mickey Mouse Club roots of Britney Spears and Christina Aguilera, instructed to pose with open legs.

These manufactured people (not fantasy cartoons as shown in the last chapter) are role models for generation after generation of women. They also train men about what men should find attractive, which is basically now just a body to use, and certainly not a lifelong partner. This dumbs us all down, because we see others as objects, not as respectable spiritual beings with boundaries, who also have *personal sovereignty.* This is also the opposite of family values, yet this is what children are exposed to daily.

The goal of our bankster social engineers it to destabilize the human being. We are being *transformed.* The goal is to replace strong relationships with "individual rights" and "attitude." We are now being led like donkeys with a carrot, step by step into adulthood, to accept non-traditional values which have never existed anywhere on Earth before and will never work. They aren't meant to work; they are meant to destabilize.

SOMEONE IS WATCHING

Egyptian Eye-of-Horus (Page 170,284) and YouTube one eye "hieroglyphs." Watch for subliminal images (sigils) in the first moments of videos. MTV has been a big venue for Illuminati subliminal messages, as have video games. I will only discuss visible messages here, as there are invisible ones also below the conscious recognizable level, used widely in advertising. These shape what we value, without us even knowing.

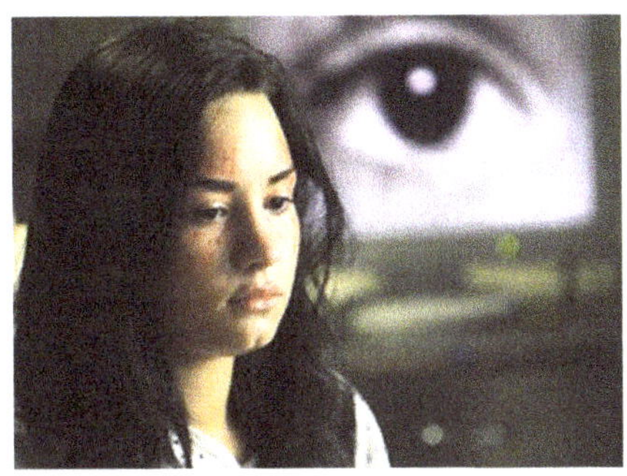

Disney Demi Lovato, "Ella's" mentor from above, is shown here as a placed brat actress, with the old Freemasonry all-seeing-eye, common not only in music Illuminati symbolism, but also on the U.S. dollar bill since 1934.

1798: *"It was not my intention to doubt that the Doctrines of the Illuminati, and principles of Jacobinism, had not spread in the United States. [Demonic Jacob Frank in Vol. 3] On the contrary, no one is more truly satisfied of this fact than I am. [They are here!]. The idea that I meant to convey was, that I did not believe that the Lodges of Freemasons [not yet] in this country had, as Societies, endeavored to propagate the diabolical tenets of the first [the Illuminati], or pernicious principles of the latter [Jacobinism] if they are susceptible of separation. That individuals of them [Illuminati] ... actually had a separation of the People from their Government in view, is too evident to be questioned."*

– George Washington, first President of the United States (1789–1797), from a letter written on October 24, 1798, which can be found in the Library of Congress

Anyone who thinks the Illuminati is a "conspiracy theory" should be shown this quote.

The Illuminati all-seeing-eye on the pyramid appears as the "secret of success" on billionaire Warren Buffet's book cover to right. Secret! Buffet doesn't share, he hoards, and teaches others to hoard and "get ahead." The pyramid always means one thing ... hierarchy with control over the majority by a minority at the top, who keeps everyone beneath them in line with a pecking order of abuse. This is the "normal" of the *dominant culture.*

This is the opposite of the circle of *indigenous culture*, which may have power structures, but the tribe is based on strong members, while a pyramid is based on weak members at the bottom of pyramid (BOP) who make up the masses and are intentionally, institutionally, kept weak. The pyramid is based on subjugation. A *dominate culture* is dependent on victims. The pyramid symbolizes entrenched parasitic economic classes and amoral coordinates. Rather than the Golden Rule, the pyramid teaches that pecking order abuse is normal. It isn't.

Multi-billionaire Warren Buffet gave $2 Billion to the Gates Foundation for globalist centralization projects, hidden as "philanthropy." As revealed in Chapter 6, eugenicist Bill Gates supports sterilization vaccines for targeted populations and is a big investor in Monsanto, the pesticide/GMO company which produces the herbicide Roundup. Glyphosate is now found in everyone's bodies. [79] "Wheat allergy" may be glyphosate allergy. So one of the "secrets" of Buffet's financial success is he is amoral, immoral, and helping to poison the Earth and all of us. (Also review Buffet in Vol. 1)

From Disney all-seeing-eye movies, to Warren Buffet's all-seeing-eye book cover, to Buffet funded Gates Foundation's support of ethnic-specific sterilization vaccines and mono-agriculture, I am trying to show the common organizational all-seeing-eye symbols used by big money, which funds not only politics and industry, but also the engineering of attitudes and values.

This influence has a long and negative history that is willing to kill for profit. The attitude is profit first, and "collateral damage" isn't even second, it simply doesn't matter. Abuse is just a cost of doing business. Killing others is just a business expense for psychopaths, or a job description for special op robots. The entire idea of profit is to make more than one's neighbors and "get ahead" of them. So abuse is built into the "profit motive." This selfish motive is simply not tolerated in *indigenous communities,* where people share or starve. In so-called "civilized" societies, people get fat *by making others starve.*

Consumerism pays off the masses who are chasing the carrot of more stuff, so that a deeper agenda of deconstructing values can occur. In the un-shaping of tradition, one goal is the elimination of any resistance to outside control, because, as we discussed in Vol. 1, a compliant society is desired. This is a number one Globalist goal, and all loyalties or standards need to be compromised so there is no meaning to fall back on. The reader might consider that your sexual standards were manufactured and are not yours. The reader might consider that being sexy or being gay are fads that were fanned to pre-occupy large segments of the population. Many people understand that the news networks are deceptive in order to hide war crimes. They don't understand how lipstick (indulgent *vanity*) is used to trivialize the mind that would judge war crimes.

* * *

> "On December 1, 1963, at the age of 30, Madonna's mother passed away. Madonna was only 5 years old at the time of her mother's death. The loss of her mother significantly affected Madonna's adolescence. Haunted by the memories of her mother's frailty and passive demeanor during her final days, Madonna was determined to make her own voice heard. [Pseudo-feminism. What was message of "her voice?"]
>
> *"I think the biggest reason I was able to express myself and not be intimidated was by not having a mother," she says. "For example, mothers teach you manners. And I absolutely did not learn any of those rules and regulations."*
>
> – biography.com

No, she absolutely did not. (Am I being judgmental? Yes, absolutely, and you should too, unless you lost quality control in your New Age conditioning. Judging means judging behavior, not judging the soul. We have to point fingers at wrong behavior or it won't be corrected.)

Below puppet Madonna passes the mantle of wrecking ball role model to the next generation "diva" puppet Britney Spears. Spears later had a break down, to her credit. I ask the reader, is this behavior a good role model? Why or why not? Would you want any woman or girl in your family to appear like this? Why or why not? Is someone who professes to be beyond manners worthy of fame?

"This is not really shocking. I, your Diva, am doing it. Get used to it, this is normal."

"At the 2003 VMA Awards (MTV), Madonna passionately kissed Britney Spears and Christina Aguilera. The whole incident was actually a mock lesbian wedding. There was a 'wedding chapel' in the set. Madonna was dressed as the butch lesbian, as she was in a tux with a top hat, and Britney and Christina were in the role as the more feminine lesbians. As Madonna stood at the top of a staircase waiting to walk down the aisle to Britney and Christina, the traditional wedding march began. It was after they met at the end of the isle and danced that they kissed one another to bring a climax to the wedding. Together they sang at the end of the song that **they are tired of the "concept of right and wrong."** [80]

Significant is the butch male in the lesbian wedding didn't couple with someone for love, she married two other women, meaning sports sex.

Not only is heterosexuality being trashed, so is monogamy. But please don't blame Madonna or you are missing the plot. She is just a puppet.

I ask the reader, why did the Illuminati controlled music industry which is tied through the symbolism to big money, intelligence agencies, and witch craft, want to create this message for young teenagers watching these awards? None of these *cutouts* produced this performance. Who did and why? There is an agenda to push same-sex experimentation. What more proof do we need?

Disney brats Spears and Aguilera, neither were blond. Here is where Disney led them.

Intimacy without love, without polarity. Did Madonna pass the Illuminati mantle of no manners to next generation Britney Spears or to Christina Aguilera (right with dyed black hair) or to both? Marriage in this attack piece is not between committed mates, but is "transformed" to promiscuity. Is this an assault on traditional values or not? And what was the purpose?

Unnatural behavior is pushed as normal. When it fails to shock, mission is accomplished and on to the next wrecking ball performance. The word decency is not in these people's vocabulary. Thus, neither is the word indecency. This is called "relativism." "Who is to judge?"

People without standards of decency, don't mind violating anyone else's standards with their "relativism." This translates to -"You can't hold anything sacred, because we don't." Sane people with standards also don't have the right to violate their relativism. We are not allowed to say anything derogatory about their behavior or values because "you shouldn't be judgmental!" Then, this is the excuse for an amoral society with no values except what Big Brother says is "fair" for everyone "equally." However, one side that allows anything is protected, while the other which has moral boundaries is destroyed. Mission accomplished.

> *I know that I'm not the best singer and I know that I'm not the best dancer. But, I can fucking push people's buttons and be as provocative as I want. The tour's* ***goal*** *is to break useless taboos. [Useless?]*
>
> – Madonna, on her 1990 Blond Ambition World Tour

Her arrogance is to claim the taboos of other entire cultures are useless. She is then, a Globalist; her values should dominate everyone else. She is more than a *cutout,* she is a conscious agent. She is accountable. She is not only a victim of mind control, she is a co-perpetrator. My question—If the New World Order is going to push this agent on us, why can't we push back and denounce her?

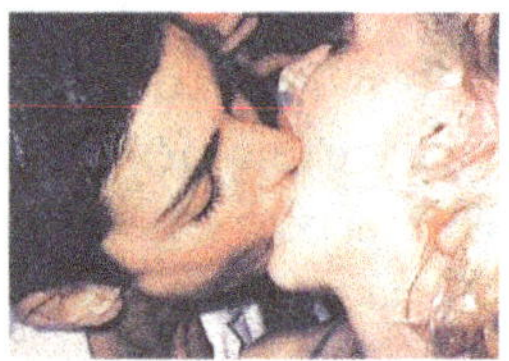

Madonna partying with another woman. For gay people who are getting defensive, is this an example of love or licentiousness? Please think about this because I have gay friends who are always defending love. Did she have a relationship with this woman. She did not.

She is a mature woman here and still into sports sex. She is then, not just a slut role model, she is literally the real thing. If this is her private business, why is it in public? If gay people want to have private lives, why is same sex intimacy now appearing on TV commercials as public displays? Who is pushing this and why? (I explore this more in Chapter 10).

Bi-sexual Madonna was programmed early for her illicit role models. The reader can decide whether Madonna as an allegedly mature adult, respects other women, relationships, family, or a true father for a child. And please remember she was placed and scripted, and still is.

> "The Material Girl once again copped to having a crush on her *Evita* co-star Antonio Banderas, saying she "wished" she had gotten together with him [sports sex] but that his wife Melanie Griffith never left his side.
>
> – Celebrity News March 11, 2015

The implication is she would have tried to have sex with him more than once, if that darn wife wasn't always there. In same article, on "romancing" her CIA trained handler Warren Beatty (Vol. 1) she says, "I have confidence in my skills." The kind a professional would have.

> "Christopher Ciccone's new biography *Life With My Sister Madonna,* accuses her of being a sexual predator – and hints that she's also had lesbian relationships. [Confirmed since.] Christopher – who no longer speaks to Madonna – says before starting a family she drew up a list of men, including basketball star Dennis Rodman and actor John Enos, who could father her child.
>
> "But Madonna's publicist Liz Rosenberg has rubbished the reports, [confirmed by Rodman in his autobiography] saying the singer is deeply hurt by his allegations."
>
> – Celebrity News, July 20, 2008
>
> She got pregnant by Carlos Leon, whom she met in Central Park - even though she was "not sure he fulfills the intelligence requirement." Again, to drive home the point, where is the respect for commitment, family, a real father for a child. Madonna is supported by the fame machine because she has New World Order values that want to replace tradition with fragmentation.
>
> When she romped with JFK Jr., Madonna said, "I feel like I am repeating Marilyn [Monroe] and the president." Please review Presidential Models in Vol. 1.
>
> "It was clear during her childhood in Michigan, Ciccone says, that Madonna wasn't shy about deploying her sexuality to get what she wanted." During her childhood?
>
> "Madonna bedded so many luminaries, it seems, that some notable members of this diverse group … rate no better than a passing mention." – oddphobia.blogspot.com. Again, what word would you use for a person like this? I know it is illegal to mention words like slut. We need to examine our values now.
>
> "Madonna hung a gigantic 8-by-12-foot photo of herself in S&M gear, lying on a bed with dead animals, in full view of her kids." This fits in with her own beta kitten mind programmed past. I do not think she made this decision. Her children are owned by the same handlers that own her. If MK-Ultra trained by CIA, as the Beatty connection indicates, she would not be conscious of her programming. (Please review Vol. 1)

Significant is that magazines that cover Madonna's sexual past do not question her moral compass. But then, tabloids cater to voyeur readers who don't practice *personal sovereignty* and give their power away to following the media puppets. As designed. When we are silent about aberrant behavior, we condone it. In the "anything goes" culture nothing is aberrant.

From New World Order Wikipedia "… Academics noted that with her videos, Madonna was subtly **reversing** the usual role of male as the dominant sex." Meaning, women are to be the dominant sex. The *dominant culture* of abuse now has new recruits through women who also want to be dominating and Madonna was used to plant the seeds of this *social engineering. Penthouse* and *Playboy* magazines published a number of nude photos of Madonna, taken in New York in **1978**: This was an intentional "leak." In other words, Madonna was a placed agent just like Gloria Steinem and Bill Gates. How is it that Madonna became a porn star in her early career? Some suggest she was being programmed for her later role.

1984: "… song, 'Like a Virgin' topped the Billboard Hot 100 chart for six consecutive weeks. It attracted the attention of organizations who [very accurately] complained that the song and its accompanying video, promoted premarital sex and undermined family values. Moralists sought to have the song and video banned. [Moralists?! Here Wikipedia shows it's destabilizing bias. Wikipedia is controlled arm of social engineering just like Madonna.]

"Madonna came under further fire when she performed "Like a Virgin" at the first [this means VMA consciously wanted this performance without any hesitation] 1984 VMA (MTV Music Video Awards, Young people's Grammy Awards) where she appeared on stage atop a giant wedding cake, wearing a wedding dress and white gloves. During the performance, she rolled around on the floor, revealing lacy stockings and a garter. [In other words girls should not save sex for marriage, they should be provocative lust objects. She took marriage and again trashed it.] In later years, Madonna commented *that she was actually terrified of the performance.*"

There it is. CIA Madonna was and is just a puppet going along with the Illuminati who choreographed the performance. If it was her own, she would have relished the whole thing. She was terrified because she was pushed into a performance that she did not create. It is a mistake to attribute creativity to the *cutouts*, be they entertainment or political puppets. Madonna did not create her image nor message, nor did Obama. Are they accountable or not? I think if we don't hold them accountable, we won't find out who their handlers are.

"The next hit was 'Material Girl' promoted by the iconic video, which was a mimicry of Marilyn Monroe's performance of song 'Diamonds Are a Girl's Best Friend.'" –Wikipedia

It might be good to review the Marilyn Monroe material in Vol. 1 to connect the dots between fake-blond Monroe programming and fake-blond Madonna programming.

Rolling Stone Magazine called the 1990 tour an "elaborately choreographed, sexually provocative extravaganza." And who choreographed the extravaganza, and the sexuality in such an elaborate manner? And more importantly, why?

"… The tour was met with strong reaction from religious groups [but they were ignored, their children would continue to be assaulted and "transformed"] for her performance of "Like a Virgin", during which two male dancers caressed her body before she simulated masturbation." [Narcissism and sports sex.]

"Throughout the eighties Madonna broke down sexual boundaries, making eroticism a crucial pop-song element, and challenging [converting] social and religious mores …" – Don Shewey

[Again all these reviewers are continuing the myth that Madonna did these things on her own. We just learned she was terrified. She was *given* the script to break down sexual boundaries. This is a New World Order program. But someone is accountable. She was not just a silly *cutout.* We read her quote. She was a conscious agent, going along with the script and believing in it, just like CIA Gloria Steinem. I would like the reader to consider what the desired outcome of breaking down sexual boundaries was? What was the goal? Keep asking. What was the goal?]

"From the moment Madonna burst onto the nation's radar screen [by being placed, held up and promoted] in the mid-1980s, she did everything in her power to shock the public, and her efforts paid off." – Rodger Streitmatter, author of *Sex Sells!* (2004) [Shock doctrine, but it was certainly not her power at all, not even her script. The promotion and publicity *by her bosses* was effective. They sold their agent, just as they sold us Gloria Steinem or Katherine Hepburn or anyone they want to make famous.]

"Before Madonna, it was possible for women more famous for their voices than their cleavage, to emerge as music superstars. But in the post-Madonna [program] universe, even highly original performers such as Janet Jackson now feel the pressure [from their industry masters] to expose their bodies on national television to sell albums." – Shmuel Boteach, author of *Hating Women* (2005) [Note the title of that book please. All this "transformation" doesn't help women, it trashes women. It trashes the natural feminine.]

"Her [their] influence on pop music is undeniable and far-reaching. New pop icons from Nelly Furtado and Shakira to Gwen Stefani, Christina Aguilera and Britney Spears [Everyone of these names have photo shoots with the all-seeing-eye, Volume 3. None of these women are independent artists.] owe Madonna, a debt of thanks [?] for the template she [not, it wasn't her] forged, combining provocative sexiness and female power [to be a puppet?] in her image, music, and lyrics." – Mary Cross, *Madonna: A Biography.*

"According to Fouz-Hernández, female pop performers [all on his following list are Illuminati puppets] such as Spears, the Spice Girls, Destiny's Child, Jennifer Lopez, Kylie Minogue and Pink were like 'Madonna's daughters in the very direct sense that they grew up listening to and admiring [placed puppet] Madonna, and decided they wanted to be like her.'" They decided nothing. Every move that all these *cutouts* made was also scripted.

The misunderstanding of all these commentators is that CIA Madonna or any of the other industry created super stars, act as independent innovators or plan their own presentation. This is the big mistake. *Cutout* Madonna is part of an Illuminati New World Order program which controls her, she doesn't control it, as quote above about the terrifying performance and the following photos show (also see Freemasonry black and white checkers Volumes 1 and 3).

Above, all-seeing-eye which is drilled into us for subliminal message and also informs other artists that the abusive Illuminati is their slave driver or else.

Notice in fourth photo (above) there is a man's urinal in the background. I call this gutter culture. Oops, I did it again. The all-seeing-eye below, at 2012 Super bowl half-time, subliminally entering the minds of millions of people as a permanent image, was not Madonna's decision. She didn't create the staging. She didn't create the Isis costume she wore, Page 171. Like the Kylie staging coming up, these "divas" are just lost, vain, rich, obscene, disposable *cutouts.*

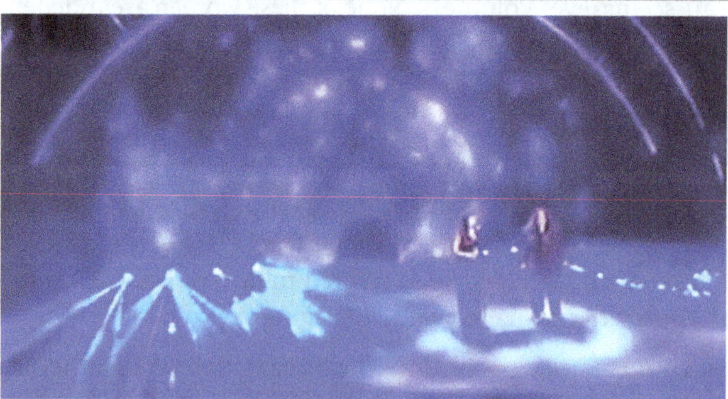

Left-top, 2012 Super bowl half-time. Left-bottom, did 17 year old contestants Jonathan and Charlote, on Britain's Got Talent 2012, create this staging?

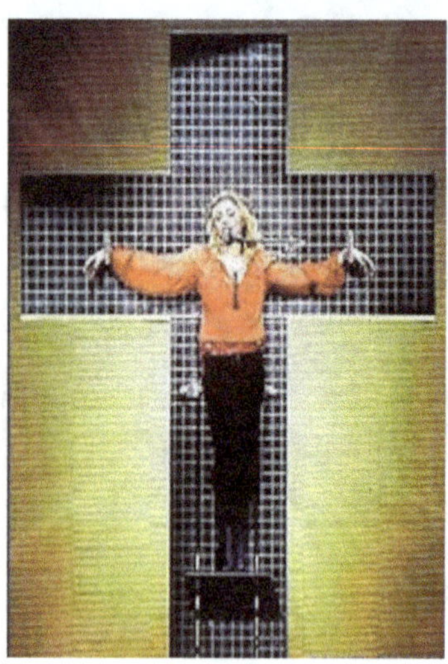

Left, cutout *Madonna at Rome Olympic Stadium concert, trashing the death of Jesus Christ. Profane is the opposite of sacred. The Illuminati hate Jesus.*

Right, cutout *Madonna's jacket with all-seeing-eye on top of pyramid of abuse.*

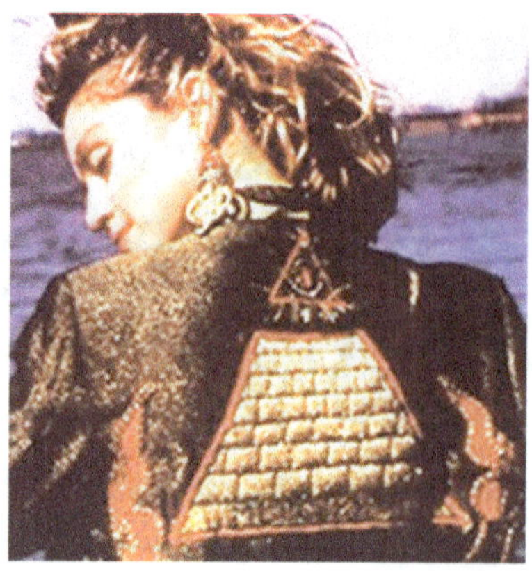

Disney "Hannah Montana" Miley Cyrus, with Madonna. Notice Cyrus holding pistol down below Madonna's waist. "Stay below the waist everyone!" All choreographed, rehearsed, and cutouts *Cyrus and Madonna will walk away and try to be respectable in public. By the way, Madonna is old enough to be Cyrus's grandmother.*

Left, lipstick and war crimes.

By "pushing the envelope" of decency there is the excitement of novelty, always nice for attention or "edge." Remember, our society is into *"progress"* and "edge," *not balance and decency.* However, just like the Romans in the sadistic coliseums of ancient Rome, we have been led into this idea of entertainment.

"In 2012, [Illuminati controlled] Madonna was crowned the "Greatest Woman In Music" by [Illuminati controlled] VH1. As of 2013, some sources report that Madonna's net worth has crossed over one billion dollars. [Illuminati controlled] *Forbes* magazine named Madonna the fifth most powerful and the highest earning celebrity of 2013 with net earnings of $125 million between June 2012 and June 2013." [81] (That is a million dollars every three days.)

After the mantle of Illuminati Queen was rejected by Britney Spears as she had rebelled and shaved her head, Spears went into "rehab," which really means, in her case, forced, probably drugged, into MK-Ultra mind control re-programming to "stabilize" her again as a puppet. According to some analysts, the mantle then went to Christina Aguilera. But Aguilera is now getting old, so Madonna's role is being spread out as Cyrus takes up that *cutout* position.

From Hannah Montana to social engineering wrecking ball would be the "good gone bad" ideal which the *Globalists* would like to push as example to all girls. (Volume 3)

"Throw away wholesomeness girls! Boys, use girls for sex! Have illegitimate children who will not be able to be committed parents when they grow up because they have little example of working female/male relationship in their lives. Maybe you will be like Madonna with no mom to teach you values. Big Brother will take care of you."

Above left, Globalist assault on Latin America. Notice crosses on earrings.

Above right, an ironic title, "not myself." Who is the real Christina Aguilera? When is she herself? Was she herself in the open leg Mickey Mouse Club days? (Page 210) And the devil graphics is not cute, dear reader. Study next image closely, and remember Aguilera did not create this.

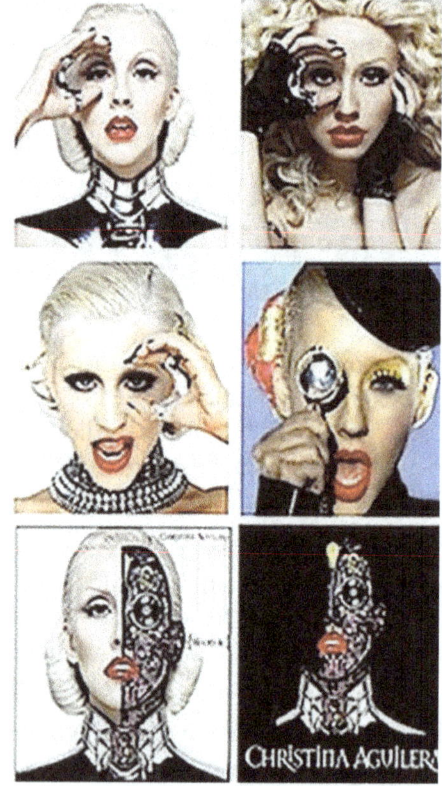

Christina Aguilera, Disney brat, is still a Globalist controlled puppet even as an adult. In the left photo, notice satanist pentagon, black candles, discarded doll on floor, and on right the ubiquitous all-seeing-eye with trans-human agenda. Aguilera graduated from Mickey Mouse Club to become satanist poster girl promoting the all-seeing-eye of the abuse pyramid.

Satanists are not some group of obscure enthusiasts into candles. They are the top leaders in the music industry who are willing to kill people to get what they want. Here Disney Aguilera has been "transformed," to promote satanism. The transformation from human to robot/human has been a repeated Illuminati theme, fed to the public since the movie *Metropolis 1927.* The power of the industrial revolution to convert whole bioregions such as New Zealand from ancient virgin forest into paddocks for sheep was applied to the human mind and society. The future human would be enhanced/compromised by implanted technology, as we are starting to see with the implanted RFID chips, and the cyborg *predictive programming* in films. This human/machine is the planned next step of destabilization/consolidation. (On a positive hopeful note, their transformation will fail, and we won't be damaged goods anymore, we will be good again.)

Dehumanization wasn't lost on the astute, like Charlie Chaplin in his 1936 movie *Modern Times*, in which the human being has to snake through a world of gears. But, *technocracy* goes much further. *Technocracy* and trans-humanism are about bringing the gears inside as seen in the album art of Aguilera, who is used to promote this vision of the new "modern times." Like Chaplin, I utterly oppose this direction. Please refer again to the implanted chips mandated by ObamaCare (Pages 82-83).

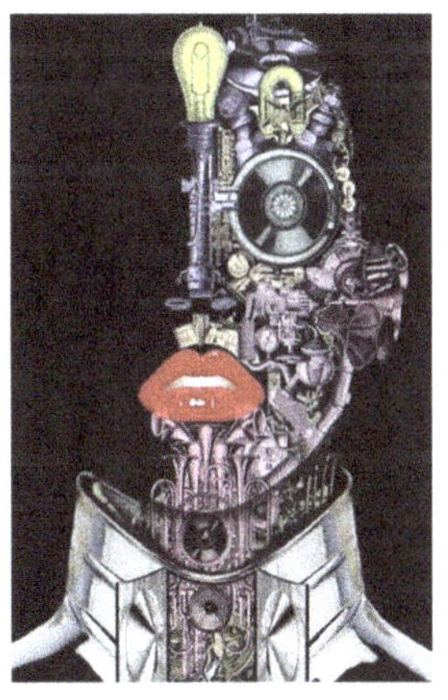

On album cover to right, Aguilera models for the Illuminati program for humanity. She "transforms" from human to human/machine to darkness/machine. Nothing is left of the human. She is now completely transformed, a lipstick mouth with a machine mind. Her soul has been "disappeared." The mouth with lipstick represents the drug of seductive sensuality. This is the only human attribute left on the transformed human ... the part of us that grasps and chases the carrot.

Who made up this art? Let's remember that question when we look at the Beatles' album below.

The popular entertainers keep the Illuminati themes in the public mind as they come into and grow out of popularity. Big Brother's all-seeing-eye message is modeled by almost all celebrities, *or they are not allowed to prosper in industry.* Once they sell out and conform, they are then pushed forward into the mainstream to dilute respectable boundaries with outrageous behavior. Balking would be a "bad career choice."

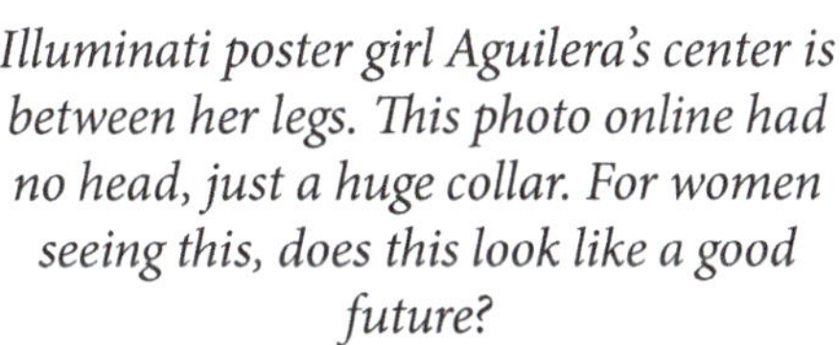

Illuminati poster girl Aguilera's center is between her legs. This photo online had no head, just a huge collar. For women seeing this, does this look like a good future?

What are we pledging allegiance to? Collin Powell lied to us about weapons of mass destruction in Iraq. We never had any business there except maybe to steal their oil, which we have. Should we be proud of our flag? 22 veterans a day are killing themselves. Maybe they know something we don't. Christina Aguilera, the ex-Micky Mouse girl who was taught to spread her legs very early, now grown up and used, to titillate and hypnotize. Then used again to sell the brain washing that we will obey our leaders, right or wrong, and pledge allegiance without any moral discernment whatsoever. Even as she is singing National Anthem she wears sexual triggers, red high heels. We are being *socially engineered* to support war crimes sold to us by keeping us below the waist with lipstick. Lipstick and war crimes.

Indigenous women NEVER pose like the photo, and in fact rarely pose at all. We didn't used to be posers. We didn't have split personalities. Completely manipulated Christina Aguilera was another "judge" on *The Voice USA* talent show 2013-2015. This puts her on TV, makes her more well known, respectable, current, and able to keep influencing your mind. She is now your handler. (Just for the record, she is showing us beta kitten programming. As a cat, she isn't human anymore, and has no natural woman's sexual inhibitions.)

The sex position in image creates a visceral irrational reaction in men. It is an assault. Men are being jerked around. Guys, you have been conditioned and are reacting to your conditioned triggers. Mission accomplished. *Indigenous* men would scrutinize her as some weird creature and in my opinion, so should the reader. That is why I am showing you these displays. Let's re-think how we react to this.

To left the fruit of the Mickey Mouse Club. Who named her perfume "Red Sin?" Answer ... The same people who script her every move. Her "desirability" to trigger sexual response will be used to sell bigger agendas, like who wins a presidential election. (Page 224) Remember, she just follows orders. She doesn't have her own volition. She is just a programmed cutout since childhood, but is she accountable? Is anyone accountable?

In this music video, *cutout* Aguilera promotes the glamour of lesbian sex which works against the feminine/masculine polarity/biological relationships/family. She actually is kissing the other puppet. Was she lucid or not? Notice the checker board looking chair. In photo below, notice dancers in back of her also. This video advertised her brand name perfume *Red Sin* and in the same video she sprays it below her waist, photo below to right. She wears collars as bondage symbols and has prisoners. "Slavery is acceptable."

Know a tree by it's fruit. Disney produces this.

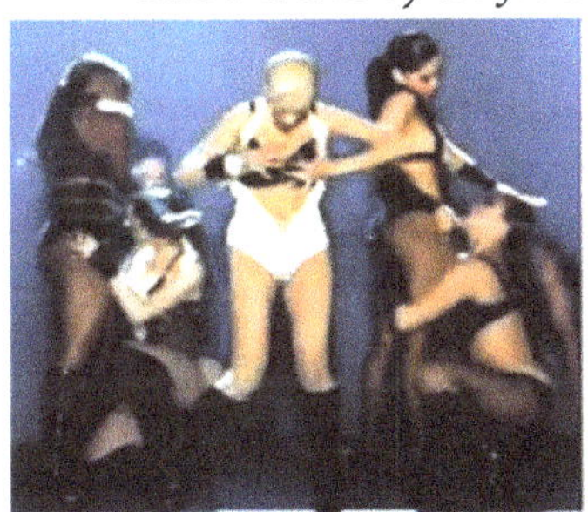

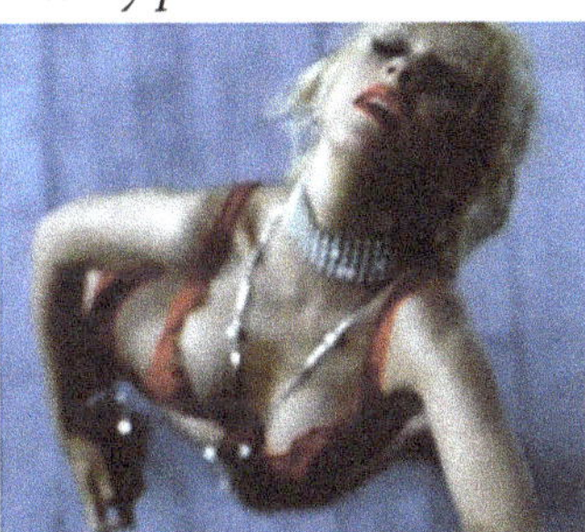

Why did the bosses create this video? What message does the reader get? Gay people can ask, is there any love in this? Or is this something decadent and abusive? It isn't love so what is it? If we are good New Age mature spiritual people, nothing disgusts us and nothing should be condemned. We should love anything and everything, no matter how poisonous, unconditionally. At what point do we shun something as wrong? At what point do we blow the whistle like some of the parents whose children were assaulted with graphic instructions on sex in schools world wide? Or is no one accountable for drawing the line of what is and is not decent? What is the message to her former Disney fans? Is sex disconnected from the heart? Is sex just nerve endings to be stimulated by anyone? What is important in life? What should we give energy to?

We are supposed to accept homosexual red sin as "human rights." The psy-op works like this … "It is wrong to shun anything. It isn't fair. It isn't loving to make someone feel bad. If someone wants to promote red sin, that is okay. It is their right. It is hate speech and against the UN Universal Declaration of Human Rights (One world government crushing ALL cultures to create the "fair and equal" mono-culture) to discriminate according to "gender orientation," which a person can change as often and as many times in their life as they want. If someone seems like a poor role model to have around your kids, and the school district hires that person, too bad. School is mandatory and the school won't discriminate according to "gender orientation" in hiring. If someone has a religion called Red Sin, it is equal to all other religions. It is their human right to not be shunned."

In other words, the Universal (Big Brother) Declaration of Human Rights, tells us we do not have the right to opt out of the UNIVERSAL declaration. Framed as compassion, it is a dictatorship. You don't have any say. But that is because we are fair and not discriminating and believe in peace. After all, if we find something disagreeable, we might say something, and that wouldn't be nice and peaceful. And worse, we might violate someone's else's rights. Just be a good sheeple, and call the police state if anyone steps out of line. Meanwhile keep watching videos.

Since I know Aguilera didn't create this choreography or script, it is obvious to me that this entire staging was designed by her masters to shock/destabilize the natural values of those watching her videos online and condition a new normal into them. The new normal is "anything goes," and hedonism is king.

Who is it hurting? It is hurting everyone, because the only people who win are the *Globalists* at the top of the pyramid of abuse, who pick up the pieces of the confused fragmented people and give them their make-believe "universal aspirations" agenda. (Bush Page 25) How else could their "universal aspirations" be pushed on thousands of different cultures found worldwide, unless those cultures were undermined? The best way to do that is to convince young people it is cool to experiment with sex. The video viewers who gave away their sexual coordinates and experimented, and can no longer bond as husbands and wives to form strong families and raise strong grounded children with boundaries and manners, are the destabilized human beings who will be consolidated under a New World Order. A long sentence, but this is a deprogramming book, and I have to confront the Globalist programming agenda again and again.

Now some bi-sexual women will be up in arms that I question their ability to hold down a stable relationship. People who were raised by a single mom might be up in arms that I doubt their ability to hang in there with a mom/dad relationship. Gay parents who adopted kids might not like that I say they will not be able to give their children an example of female/male polarity, yin-yang energy. These things need to be examined. It makes no sense to argue from a fixed position. The reader can look around. You don't have to go far to see the evidence that I am correct about what confusion yields. Most of us are damaged goods, and these videos make sure more people will experiment, lose their clarity, get addicted to bad medicine and be confused.

Let us ask again and again. Why did the Illuminati create that lesbian sports sex bondage video?

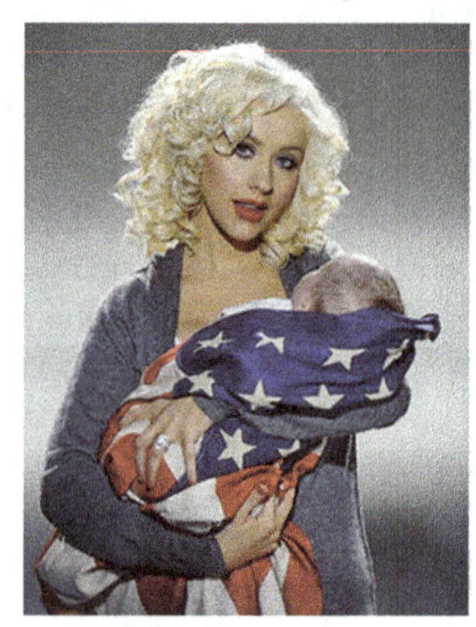

Right, fake blond Aguilera campaigning for Obama in 2008.

I wonder how many people were triggered by the fake photo shoot that invokes patriotism and motherhood. That was the Obama Operation. Did you fall for it?

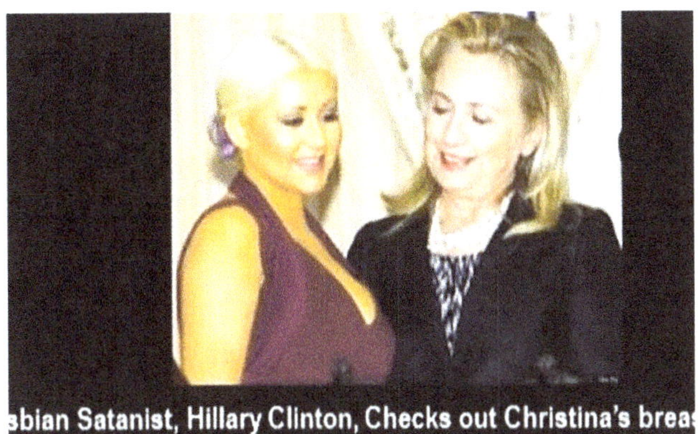

sbian Satanist, Hillary Clinton, Checks out Christina's brea

Hillary Clinton is bi-sexual according to White House sex slave survivor Cathy O'Brien and Bill Clinton conquest, Gennifer Flowers. Hillary also lies regularly. Is she accountable? [82] Hillary is covered in Vol. 1.

When we were *indigenous*, no one posed. There were power structures and warlords, but this was within a tribe, a family. There was not the manufacturing of split personalities. Yes, we were limited by belief systems, but these were unique to our tribe, and thus, there was human diversity. There was no "humanity," there was diversity! Uniqueness has been robbed from us so we could fit into the industrial system and "have a job." Charlie Chaplin was correct … industrialization is inhuman.

Illuminati gave Disney Aguilera songs like this one, "The Voice Within."

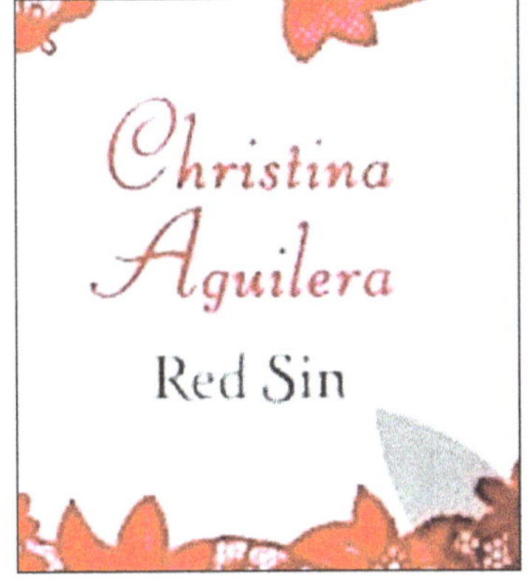

Young girl don't cry
I'll be right here
when your world starts to fall.

Big Brother is waiting for your collapse to teach you there is no such thing as sin, and you will live as an "equal" in a fair world with everything you need in a Smart City.

Being a "Diva" often means being a "tool for dark agendas," but these manufactured stars are not victims. They are people without moral codes to discern what is decent and what is not. If confronted, they would look bewildered and wonder why they were being criticized.

As long as others say it is okay or acceptable and "this is show business," they go along with it, having no moral foundation of their own. At Nuremberg, the Nazis said, "I was just following orders."

Who was following orders? Who is the "I" in the "I was just following orders?" Is the "I" just a robot who follows or is the I a chooser who takes responsibility for her or his choices? By not accepting responsibility we make hell possible.

It's show business, it's war. It's lipstick, it's war crimes. "Do your job!"

POSERS AS TEACHERS

The younger puppets such as Spears, Aguilera, Lovato, Gomez, and Cyrus, produced by Disney Inc., are supported by older manufactured stars, such as Jennifer Lopez, age 46, net worth over $250 million, who began a 2013 concert with this long pose. Here again we have a poser with a dangerous split personality. This is the real Jennifer Lopez, the change agent for an insidious agenda. This is the dark aspect of her energy, her personality, her life, and her concerts. After the day is forgotten, the audience will remember that modesty has no meaning to their idol. Rather, trashing the demure and spreading your legs for anyone is now the inner standard. Before, saving one's sexuality was natural, and being slutty was vulgar. Now being vulgar is cool. Jennifer Lopez is dead serious about "doing her job." What is her job?

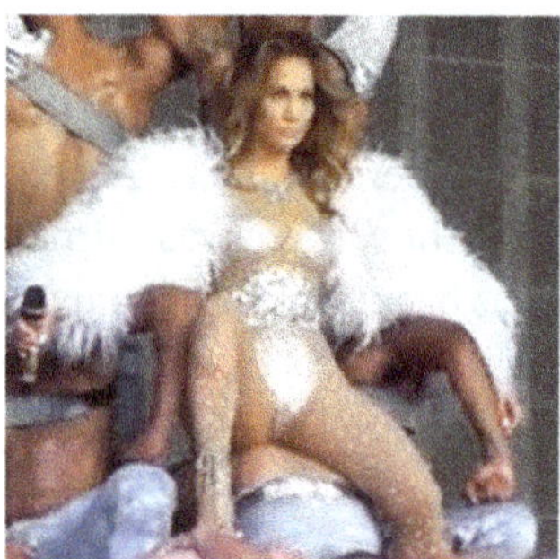

Lopez made sure everyone got a good long look. Jennifer Lopez was making a statement. What was her statement exactly? Was it, "I want you to be shocked by my disgusting pose!" or was it "Look how cool I am disregarding all standards," or was it, "Stay below the waist kids!" Dear reader, is there any difference between these three statements? So we learn here that Lopez doesn't care about anyone. This is the real Jennifer Lopez, make no mistake. Please ask, who does she respect here? Her bosses? This is a woman in her late forties! What is the message? *Cutout* Lopez is obviously ruled by a false sense of self-importance and a thrill of being outrageous and above all laws. In other words, she thrills with "good gone bad."

How would the reader explain why a mother of two kids, who is already rich and famous, would act like this in public? For more fame? For the rush? Is this what she wants to be famous as? Or will she do *anything* for the rush. Or is she just deranged by "*disconnecting vanity*" and no longer lucid? Who would trust such a creature? Well, the talent show curiously called *"American Idol"* made her a "judge," giving her respectability and a place as a role model. And this is her example of how successful women should behave. Believe it or not, there are fans of Lopez that cannot accept ANY questions about her. ANYTHING she does is okay. Well, I am asking, what is the message here?

As mentioned twice already, the super rich have everything money can buy, so their hobby then is to see how much they can control. They need to change *something,* anything, to fuel their need to demonstrate importance. Just as nature must be "conquered to serve mankind," natural morality must be conquered to serve *disconnecting vanity.* The devil is this vain disconnected false pride and false energy.

Breaking all laws for these people is "taking a chance," a recurrent message in youth songs and programs. The erosion of decency seems to be most virulent in the "developed nations," the ones most controlled by the *Globalists. Globalization* is bringing this ethical erosion everywhere.

At this time in the UK, *one thousand children a month are being abducted* while pedophile (U.S. spelling) rings are protected by an advisor of the Bilderberger Queen, Lord Justice Fulford, *founder* of the Paedophile Information Exchange. In other words, perversion is systematic in the great "developed" nation of United Kingdom. [83] Perversion for the elite gives them a kick. "This is fun." Horribly, many of these children are killed. The pyramid of abuse is perverted and lethal, and the entertainer *cutouts* stoke the flame of perversion. Jennifer Lopez was quoted last year as saying the Illuminati doesn't exist. You read the George Washington quote, and in Volume 3, I pile up the celebrities that use the obligatory symbolism. So why did she say that? She knows how much the industry is controlled. So again we need to ask, is she accountable? Or do her deeds speak more than her words?

The Agenda of the *Globalists* is not home making, but home breaking, and every girl on the planet is now targeted to learn to "take a chance."

Below, American Jennifer Lopez appears as guest performer for *Britain's Got Talent* 2013, with young teens as contestants and also teens filling the auditorium. This was aired live before UK national TV. She couldn't do this as blatantly in the U.S. but it is coming soon unless we make noise. In the first photo she is actively jiggling her thighs, stretching them open. I kept this image smaller so the reader wouldn't have to see the crack in her vagina, which was very obvious and she knew it. I personally found this performance revolting, but it was pushed on the good people of UK and the world, to "transform" us, to trash the idea that there are lines that should be respected. "Anything goes, do what thou wilt."

Left, Jennifer Lopez as guest performer on live TV Britain's Got Talent 2013.
Right, "Judge" Lopez performing on 2013 American Idol.

Notice the side dancers also. All our attention and energy is supposed to be below the waist. This is her advice for young people. "Forget the world we are living in and all the environmental problems, human rights problems, surveillance state problems and *live it up!*" This is the name of the song she sang on live UK television, which we will review shortly.

Of course the banksters who don't care about the environment, and who don't care about human rights, and want a technocratic surveillance state with RFID implanted chips in everyone, and no one noticing or protesting, are quite happy with a *cutout* like Jennifer Lopez.

Below is the proof that the top of pyramid that placed CIA Obama, loves *cutouts* like Lopez, since it is not Obama himself that invited Lopez, it was his handlers. This is the New World Order backing up one *cutout* with another to sell us both. This juices their vanity also.

The *Globalists* will push their indecent role model forward, invite her everywhere, give her awards that make no sense, put her in spotlight, give her all the ego candy she wants, because she is helping hide their activities with her "edgy" diversion. Does the reader think that "strong" Michele Obama (photo Page 191), with teenage daughters, will say anything critical about Lopez performances? No she won't, because in this world of *cutouts,* no one is accountable, and since they have the same boss, they are on the same side. The club of the elite hold each other's vanity and disconnection in place at party after party after party and hide each other's crimes.

* * *

Brzezinski, who is quoted in Glossary (*Technocracy*), is consultant of Obama.

Please recall from the "Trailer," Vol. 1, that there is a good chance that Brzezenski was CIA Obama's handler at Columbia. Below, once again, is the statement by Brzezenski, who I believe is another *cutout.* For me there is zero chance that he wrote his books alone. Therefore, we cannot really credit him as writing this. This is the New World Order seeding us with their plans.

> "The Technocratic Age is slowly designing an every day, more controlled society. The society will be dominated by an elite of persons **free from traditional values**, who will have no doubt in fulfilling their objectives by means of purged techniques, with which they will influence the behavior of people and will control and watch the society in all details ... it will become possible to exert a practically permanent watch [all -seeing-eye] on each citizen of the world."

"No doubt" means complete impunity, "influence behavior" means social engineering, "control" means enforce, "watch" means Google, Facebook, Smart Meters, Cell Phones, and soon, implanted RFID chips if we don't all wake up. "The world" means no nations, and also means ZERO indigenous cultures, just a mono-culture, a prison planet of chipped worker sheeple on rations, reduced in numbers, their water, food and time controlled. We are also seeing what "non-traditional" sexuality for women might look like.

Please dear reader connect these dots. The entertainment *cutouts* are being used to "influence" the young to purge them of "traditional values" meaning moral coordinates and the "useless taboos" that agent Madonna spoke of ... Taboos that define decency, modesty, chastity, and fidelity and together constitute the inner strength of a *human being and protect us from straying temptations and dysfunctional aberration.*

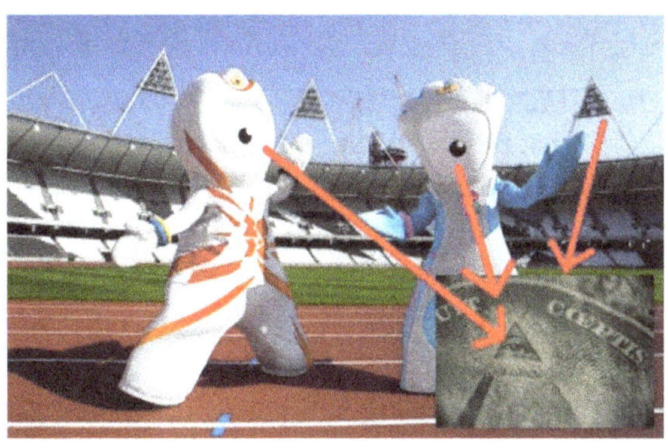

Now back to Lopez's *Britain's Got Talent* performance: even though the UK is filled with people who do know what decency is, their Illuminati Bilderberger Pedophile supporting Queen Elizabeth and Illuminati Stadium builders (London Stadium and Olympic Mascots), and their Illuminati surveillance state technicians, and Illuminati talent show producers like Cowell, will make sure people like Jennifer Lopez are in our face to keep everyone thinking below the waist instead of being responsible, and correcting the direction of our civilization. When we are busy being preoccupied with sex, we won't be demanding accountability from our authorities, because we aren't accountable either.

The online video [84] of this *Britain's Got Talent* episode includes middle-aged Lopez laying on her back and spreading her legs repeatedly, a man laying on her, men playing drum sticks on their crotches, and on and on. Such a performance could only be found in an adult-xxx club where prostitutes might work, until now.

Before *cutout* Lopez starts singing the song "Live It Up," we hear her speaking, along with the lighted words up on the stage …

"*NOTHING LASTS FOREVER … SO LIVE IT UP … DRINK IT DOWN … LAUGH IT OFF … AVOID THE DRAMA …* ***TAKE CHANCES …*** *AND NEVER HAVE REGRETS … BECAUSE AT ONE POINT … EVERYTHING YOU DID WAS EXACTLY … WHAT YOU WANTED.*"

What kind of advice is this? What kind of ethic? "Never have regrets" sounds a lot like have no conscience doesn't it? Exactly. "Do what thou wilt."

Please allow me to de-code this for you. First of all, she was 44 years old and talking to a largely teenage audience, so she is speaking with authority, and imprinting values. A psychological operation must have some truth to be convincing, so she begins with Buddha's first and most important axiom, impermanence. Jesus referred to this reality as "rust." From "*NOTHING LASTS FOREVER*" or "All is change," Buddha derived the second axiom, that our attachment to impermanent things is futile and leads to suffering. Jesus said same thing, that we should invest our hearts in the divine, not the material. The populace, lost in attachment, and the hedonists who are attached to attachment, and the satanists who are attached to power over others, will turn this wisdom to mean, "We might as well get drunk." Her words are "Drink it down." This is the advice of *cutout* Jennifer Lopez and her Globalist owners, the opposite of Buddha and Jesus.

"*AVOID THE DRAMA*" means don't engage. This is why so many young people are hopeless and apathetic, exactly as Ralph Nader described on Page 18. Lopez and her handlers, who go right to the top of the financial pyramid, want to keep you exactly there … Apathetic.

"*TAKE CHANCES*" appears in almost all youth messages. It means don't be careful, don't be wise, don't be measured, or you will miss your chance to stroke your outer *vanity*. You have to "find your voice" like mannerless Madonna or satanist Beyoncé (Trailer and Volume 4) or CIA Gloria Steinem. Take a chance and break out!

"*NEVER HAVE REGRETS*" means have no conscience. This works for *disconnecting vanity* when you are breaking someone's heart or bombing hospitals as a NATO *"hero."*

"*BECAUSE AT ONE POINT EVERYTHING YOU DID WAS EXACTLY WHAT YOU WANTED.*" What point was that? When did anyone do exactly what they wanted? If we were abused as children did we do exactly what we wanted? As adults, didn't we dance with someone else and didn't they influence the dance so they also could make some moves. If we want to dance in any kind of social interaction, we don't do "everything we want," because no one can. We live in a world of compromise if we are sane.

So this last statement is just the statement of "*disconnecting vanity*" that thinks someone is in control of Life. We are not, but we have *some* control of our choices. And no, no one ever, anywhere did exactly what they wanted because they were influenced by the context of their choices (all this around us).

The result of this spoken "advice" is the audience is *now opened up* to the utterly crude below-the-waist f**k fest they are about to witness, which was purposely as shocking as possible. Sorry, but it was unbelievably crude.

So now, as a 44-year-old authority who is "beautiful," "successful," "respected," "rich," and "famous," puppet Jennifer Lopez, mother of 5-year-old twins, with her you-know-what in your face, imprints her cultural standards on millions of young people with this song …

Lyrics to "Live it Up" …

Yeah push me harder, I do the same
Boy I wanna feel you in every way
Don't even wonder, ***it's just a game***
We're rockin' body to body, ***let's go insane***
["Tell us something crazy about yourself"]

I hit the spotlight, all night, ready to go
Give you a hard night, so tight, ready to blow
I'm in the spotlight, all night, ready to go
Give you a hard night, so tight, ready to blow

[Chorus]
Oh, we can do anything we want [anything goes, no moral restraints, who is to judge?]
Live it up, so live it up, live it up, go
Oh, and we ain't stoppin' 'till we're done
Live it up, so live it up, live it up
Go, go, go,

[Spoken]
Make love, don't fight
Let's hook up tonight [sports sex]

Turn up this mother and let it play
I know you like my bumper, [she shows her ass in video, photo above]
don't be ashamed
Don't even wonder, ***it's just a game*** *[life has no meaning]*
We're rockin' body to body, ***let's go insane***

You name it, she's done it
She's the reason that women run it [message to young women to not only drop inhibition but to actually lead in heedless lust, the new "feminism."]
Bet this on a Grammy
Maybe now you understand me [Sex sells and profit trumps everything.]

Clap your hands, go clap your hands, go clap your hands to the beat (x3)
[She encourages audience participation. And the sheeple go along with the programming. They are now totally invested. Mission accomplished.]

The performance ended with white columns of steam bursting through the floor in a big orgasm. It is important to remember that this is not some obscure artist and I am not pointing out some tiny subculture here. This is a world famous name, with one quarter billion dollars in the bank, seen with the President of United States, with a long movie career, doing this on a very popular UK national TV program for all ages, which will be viewed also by millions online. It does not get more high profile. **It was a global assault on decency.** Most of the contestants and people in the audience were young. The camera filming Lopez, laying on her back spreading her legs, was mounted on ceiling above her, looking down, so it was all planned ahead to record her from that angle. Ethically "challenged" Lopez was given "judge" status on the talent show *American Idol* 2012, 2013, 2014. Oh yea, good judgement, that one.

"Your children emulate what you do and I always want to set a good example for them."

– Jennifer Lopez,
December 2, 2013

The only way I can explain Lopez is that she was mind programmed or has some kind of schizophrenia. I call it "the vanity that disconnects" that can give someone selective amnesia. I want to know if she will ever show her girls this performance and say, "I was trying to be a good example for you." Jennifer Lopez, a single mom, was given a parenting award in December 2013 by March of Dimes, which is, not by coincidence, funded by Bank of America, a *Roth-efeller* bank.

THE REAL DEAL (THE TRUTH ABOUT THE MUSIC INDUSTRY)

excerpt by Jeriko One, 2002

"The truth is that big business controls the types of music and artists that get exposure and become popular. The record industry is a $14 billion dollar business [2002]. The five major record labels; Sony, Universal, BMG, EMI and Time Warner dominate 85% of the market when it comes to sales of Compact Discs. Leaving only 15% for the hundreds of independent record labels and thousands of artists out there. And when indies [independents] get too big or an artist starts making noise these major companies usually pick up the artist or label. This way they control the artist/label, get a percentage of the sales and keep competition to a minimum.

"The Big Payoff (radio payola): Ever wonder why you hear the same songs on the radio all the time? It's because major record companies are paying radio stations thousands of dollars to play their records! That's why you rarely, if ever, hear independent music on commercial radio. Most people don't know that virtually all the pop and rock songs they hear on the radio have been paid for by the major record companies. The record labels pay millions of dollars a year to middlemen (independent radio promoters), referred to as "indies," who in turn pass on some of that money to radio stations (they get a portion too), which accordingly play what the promoters ask/tell them to. In exchange for paying the stations an annual promotion budget ($100,000 for a medium-size market), the indie becomes the station's exclusive indie and gets paid by the record companies every time that station adds a new song.

"Launching a single at rock radio can cost between $100,000 and $250,000. If the song's a hit and gets played at hundreds of stations across the country (with added charges for multiple plays a day) the costs can skyrocket enormously. Mercury Nashville president Luke Lewis told attendees at a music conference that his label spent more than $1.5 million on promotion for a Shania Twain single that crossed over to pop radio!

"... Who pays for all of this? The artist. Most record companies recoup their costs for independent promotion from the artist's CD royalties - which of course would not be as high if they did not receive radio airplay. And, ironically enough, the radio stations pay as well, since money that might be used for promotions to build a larger audience is instead diverted into radio programmers' personal bank accounts.

"Big Fish Eat Little Fish (monopoly) There are three companies that own most the radio stations in the US - EMMIS, Radio One and Clear Channel. Over the past two years the Clear Channel company has been on an acquisition binge, spending almost $30 billion [!] on buying radio stations, concert venues and advertising companies. [Centralization for control] The company is building a "monopolistic multimedia empire" that has decreased competition, reduced consumer choice, and driven up ticket prices for concerts.

"Prior to the Telecommunications Act of 1996, a radio company could only own 40 stations nationwide and only four in a particular market. Since that has changed Clear Channel now owns 1,170 radio stations nationwide! One out of every ten radio stations across the United States broadcasts under the Clear Channel's banner and the company's approximate 1,170 stations bill a full 20% of total industry revenue. Clear Channel broadcasts in every top ten market and in 47 of the top 50. These stations take to the airwaves across all 50 states, in almost every major market, reaching nearly every demographic. Clear Channel stations broadcast to over 110 million listeners every week.

"Clear Channel also acquired SFX Entertainment, the world's largest promoter and producer of live entertainment events, including concerts, theater and sporting events. Clear Channel now owns 135 venues, producing 26,000 shows last year (attended by 62 million people) - 70% of the total "live concert" market! Buying entertainment giant SFX cost Clear Channel $4.4 billion, making it instantly the nation's biggest promoter with $2 billion in live-event revenue a year.

"Clear Channel Outdoor owns over half a million outdoor displays (770,000 billboards) around the world. [Globalist monoculture] This gives them and their customers the ability to, as they state on the Clear Channel website "reach over half of the entire U.S. population and over 75% of the entire U.S. Hispanic population". Outdoor is more than just billboards, other products they provide include; bulletins, posters, street furniture, airport displays, convenience store posters, mall displays, mass transit displays and mobile ads.

"Now there's rumors that Clear Channel wants to start their own record label ... hmmm. Think about it. They can play their artists on their radio stations, tour them in their venues and advertise them on their billboards.

"What can you do? Support college and non-profit radio stations in your local area. [Re-localization, de-centralization, don't participate in the pyramid of abuse] These independent radio stations program alternative music as well as specialty shows ...

"... Major record labels sign only what they hope will sell, jumping on the latest trend and flooding the market with sound-alikes. Everything radio and video shows play, sound and look like they *came off an assembly line.* [Including the Divas] Major record companies focus on radio-friendly and videogenic acts and unfortunately exclude new and experimental artists and genres of music.

"Consumers have become lazy and in turn are easily brainwashed by what they hear on the radio, see on TV and read in magazines. People need to be more educated and *take a pro-active approach to music.* Seek out new artists and new types of music, don't let big business *influence* and control what you think is good music or what you purchase. Take what you have just read and inform others of what you have learned - each one teach one. Much respect to all starving artists and independent companies, you are not forgotten and you are appreciated. Keep doing what you're doing and have fun making music.

"A few book suggestions for reading 1. *Hit Men* by Fredric Dannen, 2. *Life and Def* by Russell Simmons with Nelson George, 3. *Off the charts* by Bruce Haring, 4. *Black Vinyl White Powder* by Simon Napier-Bell, 5. *Last Night a DJ Saved My Life* by Bill Brewster and Frank Broughton, 6. *Losing My Virginity* by Richard Branson, 7. *The Rise and Rise of David Geffen* by Stephen Singular, 8. *Bad Boy* by Ronin Ro."

> *The music business is a cruel and shallow money trench, a long plastic hallway where thieves and pimps run free, and good men die like dogs. There's also a negative side.*
> – Hunter S. Thompson

In the Roth-efeller Zionist control of the major music labels and trade organizations that this blog https://thezog.wordpress.com/who-controls-music/ counted in the next image, we see a high percentage of Jewish people predominate. Their sampling was not complete and seemed skewed, so I don't include their percentages, but the Jewish control is simply obvious.

Universal Music Group **35.12% of record sales 2008** Geffen Records, Island Def Jam Music Group, Motown Records, Verve Music Group, Decca Music Group.	**Black Eyed Peas Mariah Carey** **50 Cent** **Elton John** **Jimi Hendrix** **Kanye West** **Shania Twain**	Doug Morris (Jewish) – Chairman - Chief Executive Officer Lucian Grainge (Jewish) – Co-Chief Executive Officer Zach Horowitz (Jewish) – President-Chief Operating Officer
Sony BMG Entertainment **22% record sales 2008** Arista Records, Columbia Records, Jive Records, RCA Records, Epic Records, Victor Records, Legacy Records, Sonic Wave America	**Kelly Clarkson** **Alicia Keys** **Shakira** **Britney Spears** **Usher, Chris Brown** **AC/DC** **Leona Lewis** **Christina Aguilera** **Miley Cyrus**	Rolf Schmidt-Holtz (Jewish) – Chief Executive Officer Kevin Kelleher (Jewish) Executive VP -Chief Financial Officer Clive Davis (Bi - sexual Jewish) – Chief Creative Officer (involved with Whitney Houston murder story, and rise of Usher.)
Warner Music Group **21.12% of record sales 2008** Owner is Jewish Len Blavatnik, named Britain's richest person.	**Madonna** **R.E.M.** **Green Day** **Eric Clapton**	Edgar Bronfman, Jr. (Jewish) - Chairman-Chief Executive Officer, Lyor Cohen(Jewish) Michael Fleisher (Jewish) – Vice Chairman, Strategy and Operations
EMI Music / EMI Group **8.4% of record sales 2008** Capitol Records, Virgin, Blue Note.	**The Beatles** **Coldplay** **Gorillaz** **Rolling Stones** **Robbie Williams** **Katy Perry**	Roger Faxon (White) – Chief Executive Officer Shane Naughton (White) – Chief Financial Officer David Kassler (Jewish) – Chief Executive Officer - Europe
Global Music	**Mark Morrison Lil' Mo, Suga Free**	Arthur Fogel (Jewish) Chairman
Live Nation Entertainment	**Michael Rapino (Jewish) President-Chief Executive Officer** **Irving Azoff (Jewish) – Executive Chairman.**	
Alliance of Artists and Recording Companies (AARC)	**Linda R. Bocchi (White) – Executive Director** **Mike Stern (Jewish) – Director of Royalties** **Bree Dietrich (Jewish) – Deputy Director of Royalties**	
American Association of "Independent" Music (AAIM)	**Jim Cooperman (Jewish) – Member, Board of Directors** **Dan Hoffman (Jewish) – Member, Board of Directors** **Tom Silverman (Jewish) – Member, Board of Directors** **Where are the other board members? The study is a bit skewed.**	
American Federation of Musicians (AFM):	**Ray Hair (White) – International President,** **Bruce Fife (White) – International Vice President** **Bill Skolnik (Jewish) – Vice President from Canada**	
American Society of Composers, Authors, and Publishers (ASCAP)	**Paul Williams (White) – President-Chairman of the Board John LoFrumento (White) – Chief Executive Officer** **Fred Koenigsberg (Jewish) – Counsel to the Board**	
Broadcast Music Incorporated (BMI)	**Del Bryant (Italian) – President and Chief Executive Officer, Richard Conlon (White) – Senior Vice President Corporate Strategy** **Michael O'Neill (White) – Senior Vice President, Repertoire & Licensing**	
Harry Fox Agency (HFA)	**Gary Churgin (Jewish) – President - Chief Executive Officer, Maurice Russell (Negro) – Senior Vice President, Licensing** **Michael Simon (Jewish) – Senior VP, Business Affairs**	
National Academy of Recording Arts and Sciences (NARAS)	**Neil Portnow (Jewish)– President and Chief Executive Officer,** **Kristen Madsen (Jewish) – Senior Vice President** **Scott Goldman (Jewish)– Vice President**	

National Association of Recording Merchandisers (NARM)	Jim Donio (Jewish)– President Holly Rosum (Jewish) Director Membership & Public Affairs Rachelle Friedman (Jewish) Board of Directors
National Music Publishers Association (NMPA):	David Israelite (Jewish)– President-Chief Executive Officer Leeds Levy (Jewish) – Member, Board of Directors David Renzer (Jewish) – Member, Board of Directors There are more than 3 board directors. This shows the sampling was skewed.
Recording Industry Association of America (RIAA)	Mitch Bainwol (Jewish)– Chairman-Chief Executive Officer Cary Sherman (Jewish) – President
Society of European Stage Authors & Composers (SESAC)	Stephen Swid (Jewish) – Chairman-Chief Executive Officer Freddie Gershon (Jewish) – Co-Chairman Ira Smith (Jewish)
SoundExchange	John L. Simson (Jewish) – Executive Director Barrie Kessler (Jewish)– Chief Operating Officer Michael J. Huppe (Jewish) – Executive VP and General Counsel

In the second breakdown of all sectors of the economy seen below, we see that the Roth-efeller/Illuminati/New World Order Cabal controls most of the world in all sectors from a top down pyramid structure of power. The all-seeing-eye is a short cut symbol for the pyramid of abuse.

Please let me remind the reader again that my blood in this incarnation is Ashkenazi Jewish. Don't worry about any of this being anti-semite, as none of these people are dark skinned Semitic people. They, like myself, come from a white race north of the Caucauses, called the Kingdom of Khazar. [85] Anyway, this is not about anti-Semitism or hate, this is about exposure and cleaning the kitchen.

Below, the percentages on the website were skewed because only Jewish Board Members were listed instead of all Board members, so I did not include percentages. However, to deny the disproportionate predominance of the top Jewish officers would be very blind. The big money that really controls these companies makes sure that Zionists rise to the top.

We can be sure if any of these Jewish people exposed Israel war crimes, exposed 9/11, exposed Anti-Defamation League, exposed AIPAC (American Israel Public Affairs Committee) they would be fired.

If a company like Costco rises up, someone like William Gates Sr. becomes a board member and takes over with his money and influence. All venues are controlled. Huffington Post was bought by AOL, etc, etc. This study by thezog.wordpress.com/who-controls-music/ shows that an unusual amount of high level executives are Jewish. This doesn't show us talent, it shows connections and membership.

The Anti-defamation League attacks anyone who exposes the Rothschild network, such as Jewish Hero Henry Makow (Henrymakow.com) and was created by Jacob Schiff who grew up in the House of Rothschild (Page 55-56). The protection of Zionist goals has been a cornerstone of Illuminati control for over 200 years. Israel is above all international laws that are made to control everyone else. Israel can assassinate at will, have uninspected nuclear facilities, and ignore dozens of UN memorandums without any economic embargo, as suffered by any country the Rothschild Central Bankers can't control. Iran and Russia are two recent embargoes.

The Zionist Pyramid, from thezog.wordpress.com/ backed by www.illuminati-news.com/120706a.htm

Sector	Number of top executives	# Jews or have Jewish Spouse
Economy	60	39
Wall Street mutual funds, private equity funds, hedge funds, and brokerages	40	26
Wall Street - banks, trade exchanges, and regulatory agencies	51	37
Goldman Sachs executives	9	7
Goldman Sachs Directors	12	6
Goldman Sachs management committee members	33	20
American International Group directors and trustees	16	12
Treasury Dept.	26	18
Federal Reserve Systems Board governors	7	4
Federal Reserve District Bank Presidents	12	4
Federal Reserve System Chairmen	14	7
Media CBS, NBC, News Corporation (Murdoch), Time Warner, Viacom, Disney	12	9
Major music labels and trade organizations, senior executives	50	39
Hollywood studios, trade unions, and talent agencies	60	50
Television, broadcast, cable, production,	64	57
Radio	46	28
Advertising	46	31
News major television and radio news networks senior executives	67	47
News major newspapers and news magazines senior executives	64	42
Ivy league college and university senior adminstrators	24	20
ADL - Anti-Defamation League, a 100% racist organization	53	53
Southern Poverty Law Center senior program staff members	22	15
American Civil Liberties senior executives	9	4
Group of Thirty has 43 members	43	23
Bilberberg Group - Steering Committee members	35	16
Trilateral Commission Executive Committee	56	23
Council of Foreign Relations (CFR) directors	43	28
Council of Foreign Relations (CFR) think tank members	55	31
Major Think Tank senior executives, American Enterprize, Brookings, Carnegie Endowment for International Peace, Cato, Center for Strategic and International Studies, Council on Foreign Relations, Heritage, Hoover, Rand, Woodrow Wilson International Center for Scholars	30	19
Professional Sports, MLB, MLS(soccer), NBA, NHL (hockey), Athletes First, Boras,Career Sports & Entertainment, Creative Artists Agency, Excel Sports, International Monetary Group, Octogon Worldwide, Premier Sports and Entertainment, Priority Sports, Rosenhaus Sports, Wasserman Media, CBS Sports, ESPN/ABC Sports, Fox sports, HBO Sports, NBC Sports, Showtime Sports, Turner Sports,	60	43

The Illuminati, through Jewish allies also dominate the Porn Industry, though this is now becoming dispersed as teen girls are used in internet porn shoots in an endless parade of reverse vision quest. In vision quest a young person leaves the home to seek vision through purification. Now young girls leave the home to be fast money porn stars and celebrate indulgence, until they realize they were fools, and are now damaged, which takes an average of 3 months. [86] The established old school porn industry is under Jewish control. [87]

The following is from an interview with E. Micheal Jones author of book *Libido Dominandi: Sexual Liberation & Political Control* (2005).

Jones: "The point of pornography, the point of the sexual revolution is to break down morality, because morality is your only defense against the rich and powerful. This is the really insidious nature of the sexual revolution, is that it actually gets inside you, and you actually start to defend your own oppressors! Because you claim it is "freedom," because you want to do what you want to do. [Those who hijack your discernment, and provide stimulating sexual images, control you.]

"And you don't understand that *you only get to do what is right,* not do what you want, no matter what that is. [Anything goes, no taboos]. And if you break away from doing what is right, you will end up being a slave to the people who control the [stimulating] environment."

Interviewer: "The most incredible thing of all, is there is a small group of people that are brain washing us [tempting us] all, absolutely taking the whole society in a direction, as if they wrote it down on a piece of paper and make it reality. And now as you say, you have the oppressed championing the oppressor, thinking it is freedom!"

Jones: "Yea, this is the great thing about sexual liberation, as a form of control. You celebrate your own chains. You have all these people celebrating their bondage by saying they are free."
In another interview—E. Michael Jones www.culturewars.com

"What we are talking about is moral and pre-political. If you can control this aspect [corrupt sexuality], than the politics sort of follows naturally from that. Because first of all, you have established the parameters of control [of media stimulation], that control is something that is acceptable. And it is acceptable because it is not conceived as control! No one perceives this as control. Like the Libertarian argument, "Well, you know, if you don't like it, change the channel." That's not the issue. The issue is who gets to determine what is on the channel in the first place. Once you get that, the other stuff falls into place naturally. And that was the genius of the [top] people who were involved with this. They knew that the morals, let's say, sexual settings, preceded the cultural settings, and the cultural settings proceeded the political settings."
"... The standard liberation is, I am going to liberate you from the ["repressive"] bondage of morality. Well morality [understanding consequence] is another word for practical reason. If you liberate a rational human being from reason, you are turning him into a slave, an animal, and that's what happened. For a lot of people, the only thing that freedom means is the ability to satisfy their passions. And these people [at top] know that, and so the regime becomes the grantor of your ability to satisfy your passions. ... break down the modesty of the young people, for one reason, for control! ... what the controllers realized, is you need a [dumbed down] sexually permissive society." [88]
Also see: Illuminati Use Porn to Wage War on Society, October 11, 2013

www.henrymakow.com/porn_in_the_war_against_you.html

Mass Enslavement through Sex - excerpt by Larsha Darkmoon, May 6, 2014

"It is a tragedy that the Jews should have been allowed to deploy pornography to such good effect that they have succeeded in enslaving entire nations, as [Goddess] Circe with a touch of her magic wand enslaved the Greeks, turning men into swine: an apt metaphor for what lies ahead for the masses under their new masters.

> "A really efficient totalitarian state," Aldous Huxley once noted, "would be one in which the all-powerful executive of political bosses and their army of managers control a population of slaves who do not have to be coerced, because they love their servitude."

"... these porno-centric Jews [don't] have any qualms of conscience in regard to the wholesale corruption of families, whether Jewish or non-Jewish, or show the slightest concern about the tragic descent of children into the hell of compulsive masturbation and porn addiction ... [40% of porn includes violence against women.]

"These sex entrepreneurs, intent on easy profits, have eagerly sought to provide the masses with the cheapest and deadliest of tranquilizers: opportunities for endless orgasms, by way of a ceaseless flow of pornographic images in the mass media they control.

"This is one way to achieve world domination without the need for revolutionary violence or military conquest: to take entire countries and turn them into giant masturbatoria ...

"... Here is what Brother Nathanael Kapner has to say on this subject. It is a neat summation. The fact that Kapner is Jewish makes his words even more compelling:

> "The degradation of Western Christian social life did not merely happen, it was planned, deliberately fostered and spread, as outlined by The Protocols of the Learned Elders of Zion. This systematic undermining of the culture of the West continues today. The instruments of this assault on Christian culture and consciousness are the weapons of propaganda: the press, television, cinema, and education. The chief fount of the propaganda is the cinema.
>
> "From his capital in Hollywood, the Jew spews out an endless series of perverted films to debase and degenerate the youth of America and the Western world. Divorce replaces marriage, abortion replaces birth, and the family becomes the battleground of individual strife. The Jew has attained his goal in destroying Western culture."

"I am afraid I cannot agree with Kapner's sweeping conclusion that the Jews are entirely to blame for the decline and fall of Western culture. If the West has gone to hell in a handbasket, the goyim are as much to blame. Their enthusiastic complicity with their own corrupters has been their undoing ...

"... There is little doubt that the virulent sex epidemic we witness all around us is a deliberately planned sex psy-op. This is what governments want.

"The Puppet Masters who pull the hidden strings of our Western regimes, all masquerading as democracies, have managed to manufacture exactly what we see when we look around us: widespread neurosis, mass misery, the collapse of moral values, Christianity in ruins, and the coarse brutalization of the common man. No need for gulags for those who consent to their own chains."

– Larsha Darkmoon [89]

Gag Order

Let's meet American Lady Gaga, Stefani Joanne Angelina Germanotta, another Disney darling, but adopted as an adult for her ability to be deviant, which obviously Disney is attracted to. Gaga's net worth is estimated between $150 and $190 million.

The one eye is watching. We are all One, right? One world. One Government. One pyramid with the big eye at top. There is only one international financial pyramid that just happens to control NATO and the U.S. Military and the corporate music industry and anyone who wants to "succeed" in the mainstream. This one eye control is a continuation of the control we saw in the historical time line of Chapter Two.

Above, "Lady" Gaga, invokes and empowers the all-seeing-eye. This is not cute playing around. This is membership and the evangelism of something negative called Illuminati Globalism.

Left photo, "Can you tell us anything crazy about you?" This person should be on children's programs, right? She should meet the royalty of the world, right? She should not be banned in any way, right? We should nod our heads and allow this into our living rooms, right? Okay, so we decide to turn it off, but millions of young people watch this kind of stuff daily. What is the message? Who is accountable?

Gaga and famous (famous means placed) homosexual Elton John collaborated on song "Hello, Hello" for another Disney *social engineering* movie, *Gnomeo & Juliet*. Elton John was knighted by Pedophile supporter Queen Elizabeth. Apparently he accepted this gender designation. "Sir" Elton John thinks Jesus was homosexual. [90] He appeared on children's program, the Muppets, in 1978. He is now raising two children who will have no mother. He is dissatisfied with a civil union and wants full marriage so he can have a "husband."

Interestingly, staff at Disney estimate 40% of its employees are homosexual. [91] Homosexuality is the opposite of sustainable *indigenous culture* and is based on a rejection of the circle of life in favor of sex as an end in itself, no pun intended. If this is not true, why don't we hear gay proponents putting down bath houses for what they are, places for sports sex with strangers. My view on homosexuality is it is none of my business until it becomes an agenda to change how my children think, and Disney is all about that.

Again, as in the Lopez song above, the same advice is in this Gaga-Elton John song "Hello Hello" for children. *"Do a dizzy dance, twirl around and* ***take a chance."*** The dizzy part means forget balance, forget traditional wisdom, let go and join us.

It sounds innocent enough except that the same words appear again and again for older listeners. When we see repetition, we are looking at orchestrated mind control conditioning.

With a long history and almost a monopoly on animated films, Disney Inc. is one of the biggest players in Globalist *social engineering*, along with CNN, BBC and institutions like the United Nations. Disney not only raises children to become industry puppets, but invites moral wrecking balls like Gaga and Elton John on to children shows. This is to *socially engineer* children, in order *to condition our values*, which as noted, has been very successful for increasing teen pregnancy, illegitimate children, divorce rates and dependency on government. The "non-traditional" is becoming the norm, and "tradition" is seen as archaic, even though tradition used to prevent the problems listed.

> "Disney, [maker of role models] through the ABC Television Network and its affiliated local stations reaches fully 99% of all U.S. television households. [99%!] The ESPN company held by Disney and, through its agreements with 45 internationally-held sports networks, broadcasts in over 195 countries in 16 languages. Radio Disney (programming marketed for children and "tweens") is carried on 52 stations (41 of which are owned by Disney itself) and covers 60% of the U.S. market, not even including the audiences reached by its broadcast on the internet and satellite sources of radio programming."
>
> – Sourcewatch.org

I've mentioned twice that fame is not won, it is placed. We are told Walt Disney was a cartoonist that made it big. This isn't true. He was placed, just as Bill Gates and Gloria Steinem were placed.

> "On November 18, 1928, [Walt Disney's cartoon] *Steamboat Willie* was shown in a small, independent theater without any advance promotion or advertising. But amazingly(!) the *New York Times, Variety*, and *Exhibitor's Herald* all ran rave reviews of the cartoon the next day. Was this an accident? Did journalists from all these prestigious periodicals just happen to go to this tiny independent theater? No, it was connections."
>
> – From *The 13 Illuminati Bloodlines* by Fritz Springmeier

The word "connections" is an understatement. How did these big Globalist newspapers even know about *Steamboat Willie?* The answer is that this cutting edge media was not Walt Disney's creation. He was given this tech, and also given the notary about the tech, the publicity, the "success." But, in exchange, he was on a leash, and his movies, from the beginning, contained *social engineering* agendas. Walt Disney was a *cutout.* He also happened to be a 33rd degree Freemason.

The six past heads of Disney Inc were …

- 1977–1984: Ron W. Miller (Miller married Walt Disney's daughter and later moved to "Valley of the Kings" Napa Valley, California.)

"Napa Valley, where many members of the Disney family live, has the Illuminati's Opus One temple owned by Rothschilds, as well as two roads lined with meticulously kept wineries owned by Illuminati kingpins and connected via secret underground tunnels. To top off this incredible collection of Illuminati wineries (Rothschild's, Mondavi's, Rutherford's, Christian Brother's, Sattui's etc), on the north end of a series of wineries on highway 29 lays the CIA's medieval-looking Culinary Institute of America Greystone (at 2555 Main St., St. Helena, CA 94574), where numerous people have suffered torture."

– Illuminati Bloodlines by Fritz Springmeier

Napa is close to Bohemian Grove where satanic rituals involving most western political leaders occurs annually. (Just do web search for Bohemian Grove) Ron Miller started Touchstone Pictures so that Disney could create *social engineering* for adults. Miramax and Hollywood pictures were other subsidiaries. Their hundreds of popular movies influence attitudes and behavior towards parents, romance, marriage, consumerism, violence, and war. Lipstick and war crimes.

- 1984–1994: Frank Wells (A Rhodes scholar, globalist grooming. Cecil Rhodes was a racist, a Freemason, a complete imperialist, and some indicate gay. See Vol. 1.)
- 1994–1997: Michael Ovitz (Jewish)
- 1997–2000: Michael Eisner (Jewish)

"A paper trail connecting Michael Eisner and Walt Disney Co. to mind control is their support of the Boys & Girls Club of Napa Valley, which is used for a supply of children for pedophilia and mind-control. The Boy's & Girls Club is used to supply caddies for the Silverado Country Club [now called Silverado Resort and Spa], where these children are also used as mind-controlled slaves [traumatized] for the sexual perversions of the elite. Notice that Napa's Silverado Country Club invites in celebrities (such as CIA asset Pat Boone, Joe DiMaggio ex-husband [handler] of sex slave Marilyn Monroe, Engelbert Humberdinck a slave handler, Digger Phelps Notre Dame's coach who uses slaves, and Jack Valenti CEO of Motion Picture Assoc. & Bohemian Grover) for a golf tournament which is billed as a "benefit for the Boys & Girls Club". The benefit for child slaves is they get to caddie and sexually service elite perverts. Michael Eisner (bn. March 7, '42 in NY) came from old American money of a [Jewish] family that has been rich merchants and lawyers. "

– Fritz Springmeier [A Christian jailed 9 years for writing this book.]

- 2000–2005: Robert Iger (Jewish) … 2005-2015 : Chief Executive Officer
- 2015 Thomas Staggs (Jewish) present : Chief of Operations began career at Morgan Stanley

Please question the odds that one Disney Chief after another is Jewish, when Jews only constitute 2% of population. This is the Zionist Rothschild club that controls and perverts society.

The following comment is mirrored by many other testimonies. Parents should boycott anything that is associated with Disney in my opinion.

Jeannie Cox said ...

"My Mother, two children age 6yrs and 8yrs old, and myself visited Disney World 27 yrs ago. My 8yr old daughter disappeared. The four of us were waiting for the evening parade to begin at 6:30pm. We always would meet at the Ice Cream shop on main street when we separated. Before we entered the park of that July 4th hot day, I put notes in the pockets of my children. The notes had my childrens' name and the meeting place at the Ice Cream shop, just in case we were separated. My daughter saw a popcorn vendor about 30 ft away and decided to get this before the parade started. I watched her walk to the vendor, pay for the popcorn and then suddenly a large group of people gathered around us and I lost site of my daughter. This was less than 10 seconds that I lost site of my daughter. I knew she would be back in a few minutes because our PLAN was to always meet at the ice cream shop. This was at 6:30pm. The parade had started. My mother stayed at the ice cream shop and I went looking for my daughter. Hours passed. I checked in with "CITY HALL" on Main Street at least 15 times and each time my daughters name was not be found on the Lost Child list. My Mom and son did not move from the ice cream shop. For six hours I searched Disney. I rode the ferry, and the train twice, going to my parked car, and eventually started looking under buses and bridges.

"Disney personal were no help at all. I was ignored completely. At the end of the nite after the Park had closed I was still looking for my daughter and I told security that I was not leaving until I found my daughter. Twenty seven yrs ago people did not carry cell phones. I called our Hotel numerous times from a pay phone hoping that for some reason my daughter had gone to the Hotel. No luck. The street was bare at Disney at 2:00 am and my Mother and son had not left their spot at the ice cream shop. I demanded that security call the Orlando police dept and within minutes I saw my daughter running down Main street with another young boy. I did not realize this until I got back to the Hotel, but I had walked so much I had blisters all over the bottom and side of my feet. My daughter told me where she had been and how and why she ended up there. I was furious!

"My daughter said that a policeman came up to her and told her she looked lost. [Remember this happened within seconds of the crowd swarm.] She showed him the note in her pocket and while she was left with another officer, the officer she gave the note to, supposedly came to the ice cream shop and went back and told my daughter no one was there that she described. That was a lie.

"My daughter said that she rode a train underground that took her to the Gerber lost and found children area. Names were supposed to have been called down to City Hall on Main street of the children who had been separated from their parents. My daughters name was not on that list. For 6 hrs my daughter was with these evil people and not once had anyone tried to find us. [All the security had communication.] Hate is a strong word, however I hate Disney. What they put my family through for six hours will never be forgotten. Who knows what my daughter went through, but she claims she was ok. [How could she get on a train to a place that was 20 feet away? They did something to her.]

"What else could I do? I was hoping my daughter could tell me what she had done for the past 6 hours and she said it went fast and *all the lost children* [abducted children] played games at the Gerber shop. [They were accustomed to keeping the kids for hours on end, as if the parents weren't desperate, as if the parent's wouldn't notice within minutes their child was missing. More, if she had not threatened to call police, she probably would never have see child again.] This shop was less than 20 feet from where I last say my daughter. NOT ONCE did the Disney employees or security tell me that lost children were held at the Gerber shop. This shop was not on street level. It was in a basement that you had to walk downstairs to enter.

"My Mother never stopped praying for six hours. I never stopped looking for six hours and no one helped me or seemed concerned. I have since learned of other evil things that have happened on trips at Disney but I have found that you cannot fight someone as big as Disney. I would love to hear from others that had the same or similar experiences." [92]

I included that because I wanted the reader to understand what is at stake. Every child in the world in now targeted for "transformation" and thus far, there is no real resistance. If the reader takes any time to study Disney, there is no good news. Disney has been creating a culture of witchcraft, for example, since its first movies like *Fantasia* and *Snow White and the Seven Dwarves.* We thought it was imaginative, but it was satanic imagination. *Pinochio* features child trafficking. Their ride "Pirates of the Caribbean" at Disneyland also features smiling women sold as slaves. The entire mentality of Disney is manipulative and corrosive, so then, Madame Gaga fits right in.

* * *

Robert Kennedy Jr. has helped write a 2014 book, *Thimerosal: Let the Science Speak* about mercury based thimerosal, which is still in flu vaccines. The connection with Autism is absolute. He exposes the CDC for what it is. A cover up agency. In a speech on April 7, 2015 he states ...

> "All the things that are supposed to stand between rapacious industry and our little children have been dismantled, all those checks and balances, the press, the politicians, the regulatory agencies, the courts, they are all gone. ***And the only thing left is the parents. And now they are trying to get rid of them.***"
>
> - Congressman Robert F Kennedy Jr.

* * *

Strong communities are based on strong families, something that would resist government intrusion. The collusion between business and schools (Page 204) in "guiding" children today means our children are already being raised by the state who is teaching them about value and self-worth. The family is being replaced by *controlled media,* entertainment and curriculums.

Here are lyrics to another Gaga song, "Born this Way" ...

> *It doesn't matter if you love him, or capital H-I-M [It doesn't matter if you are with a man you don't love. Also it doesn't matter if you love anything divine. But whoever you love or don't love ...]*
> *Just put your paws up [legs up like in Muppet photo on Page 267]*
> *'cause you were born this way, baby*
> *My mama told me when I was young*
> *We are all born superstars [the goal is vanity and fame]*
> *She rolled my hair and* ***put my lipstick on***
> *In the glass of her boudoir*
> *"There's nothing wrong with loving who you are" [but you need lipstick]*

She said, "Cause he made you perfect, babe" [so put on lipstick]
"So hold your head up [painted], girl and you'll go far, [vanity]
Listen to me when I say"

I'm beautiful in my way [but need lipstick]
'Cause God makes no mistakes [so accept your condition, don't refine]
I'm on the right track, baby I was born this way
Don't hide yourself in regret [do whatever you want, "do what thou wilt," no remorse, no conscience.]
Just love yourself and you're set [no responsibility to anything else]
I'm on the right track, baby I was born this way

Give yourself prudence [A little truthfulness in the song, which is trashed by everything else she is saying.]
And love your friends, Subway kid, rejoice your truth
In the religion of the insecure [the globalist religion of weakness]
I must be myself, respect my youth
A different lover is not a sin [What is sin in the mind of Gaga?]
Believe capital H-I-M [So she is talking about divine after discounting sin? This is multiple personality conditioning to disconnect conscience.]
I love my life, I love this record [me me me] and
Mi amore vole fe yah

Don't be a drag, just be a queen [if you aren't a queen you are a drag]
Whether you're broke or evergreen
You're black, white, beige, chola descent
You're Lebanese, you're orient [globalist homogenization]
Whether life's disabilities
Left you outcast, bullied, or teased [don't call for justice, accept it]
Rejoice and love yourself today [forget problems in narcissistic hedonism]
'cause baby you were born this way

No matter gay, straight, or bi,
Lesbian, transgendered life, [amoral globalist homogenization]
I'm on the right track baby,
I was born to survive. [material survival]
No matter black, white or beige, Chola or orient made,
I'm on the right track baby,
I was born to be brave. [It rhymes, but brave for what? To accept one's condition? To hide behind lipstick?]

These lyrics are the opposite meaning of the lyrics to Lauryn Hill's song "I Get Out," Page 17. Gaga preaches carnal indulgent unconsciousness, while Hill shares a road to emancipation and *personal sovereignty.* In the examples you have seen so far of Cyrus, Madonna, Lopez and Gaga, do you see purification as a primary value being promoted? Or do you see the opposite? What is the opposite of purification?

* * *

Winner of *Bertelsmann X-Factor* Australia 2013 was Dami Im, a pure hearted, young and married Korean-Australian who taught piano. She was given this song, "Alive" by DNA Songs, as her last performance, which was a successful hit in Australia. We see the same words repeated.

> *Don't keep waiting for an open door*
> *Break the lock and get something more [break down all traditions.]*
> *Make a move 'cause you're alive, alive*
> *We ain't gonna get a second* ***chance*** *[live for today, hedonism]*
> *Life ain't nothing but a* ***crazy*** *dance [common theme in song after song … there is no higher meaning. Nihilism]*
> *Learn the moves [conform to this new crazy dance] 'cause you're alive, alive*
> *I remember all the words you said*
> *That a crazy heart can never rest ["Tell us something crazy about you."]*
> *When your light starts fading out, fading out*
> *[This is prep for collapse, termination, and despair. The same exact themes appear in other X-Factor winner songs and it is not a prep for hope.]*
> *You can always break the rules [Always? The rules are your parents' traditions.]*
> *You can always dare to dance [crazy dance as in song "Hello Hello"]*
> *But you gotta take* ***a chance, a chance*** *[again and again, take a chance to really "live" by breaking from tradition, not by creating anything.]*
> *We're alive, we're alive, we're alive-live.*

These songs celebrate negation, not nourishing or creation. The subliminal themes repeat consistently, from the Lopez song, to the Gaga song, to the Gaga-Elton John song, to the Dami Im song. **"Take a chance, life is a meaningless crazy dance, live for today."**

> "… existential nihilism argues that life is without objective meaning, purpose, or intrinsic value. *Moral nihilists assert that morality does not inherently exist*, and that any established moral values are abstractly contrived. Nihilism can also take epistemological or ontological/metaphysical forms, meaning, respectively, that, in some aspect, knowledge is not possible, or that reality does not actually exist. [Talk about *disconnecting vanity*!]
>
> … The term is sometimes used to explain the general mood of despair at a perceived pointlessness of existence, that one may develop upon realizing [getting stuck in the head and disconnected from the natural world] there are no necessary norms, rules, or laws. Movements such as Futurism have been identified by commentators as "nihilistic …"
>
> – Wikipedia

I maintain that the Golden Rule, "Do onto others as you would have them do onto you," is a universal moral compass found in all dimensions where ever living beings can communicate.

The nihilists are really narcissists who indulge in self-absorbed pleasure because they have lost their compass and connection. The *Globalists* are of this group. This leaves selfishness unchecked, as we are about to see with the "Do what thou wilt" satanists.

QUEENIE

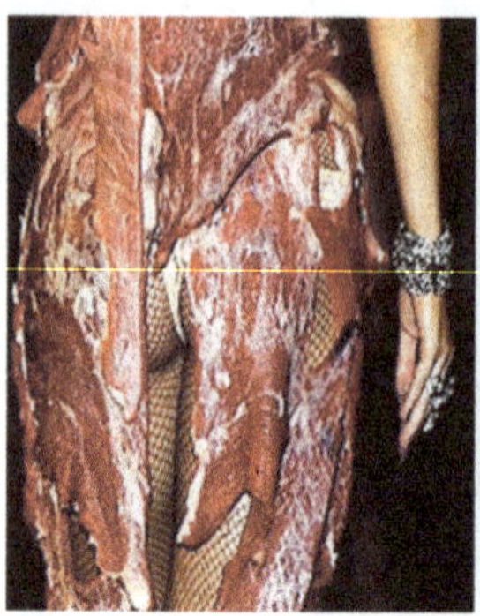

Gaga attire made out of meat with diamonds on wrist and piece of ass showing, letting all women know what it takes to be "successful." This is more than just shock, it's diamonds. Below right, Bilderberger and Freemason Queen Elizabeth honoring cutout *Gaga, who is dressed as Illuminati witch. We will see, next chapter, a similar costume worn by Nicki Minaj at a satanic ritual.*

Whatever the Maltese Cross meant in the last thousand years, it was *co-opted*, as the next few pages show.

The Queen's crowns below include symbols of the Maltese Cross very prominently at top of each crown. This announces who really controls the Crown and England. Certainly Christianity and The Golden Rule do not control the biggest rapists in the world, the British Empire. Certainly the Rothschilds, who are the real rulers of England, are not Christian. And certainly the Rothschilds, who funded the Illuminati co-opted the Knights of Templar and Knights of Malta and the Freemasons. So make no mistake, the Crown of Queen is Illuminati. Please re-read the history of the Rothschilds if this is in doubt, and see youtube *The Zion King*, found online.

> *"Britain is the slave of an international financial bloc."*
>
> – British Prime Minister David Lloyd George,
> June 20, 1934, *New Britain Magazine*

April 15, 2012: "The Sex Pistols, the punk rock band famous for their anti-establishment antics, are to re-release their classic anthem "God Save the Queen" to coincide with the jubilee celebrations this summer.

"... Originally released on May 27, 1977, ahead of the Queen's Silver Jubilee, the single, which featured a defaced image of the Queen on the cover, sparked widespread controversy, [Controversial because there are so many mind programmed British sheeple that they think it uncouth for someone to criticize one of the biggest war criminals in history. The history of the British Empire is an utter shame, as terrible as Henry the VIII.] and was banned by the BBC and the

Independent Broadcasting Authority, which regulated commercial television and radio and independent radio." [So much for "independent" radio!]

– Roya Nikkhah, *London Telegraph*

God save the Queen, a fascist regime
They made you a moron, potential H-bomb
[dumbed you down to be irresponsible]

God save the Queen, she ain't no human being
There is no future, in England's dreaming [unsustainable]

Don't be told about what you want
Don't be told about what you need [don't be programmed]
No future, no future, no future for you
God save the Queen, tourists are money
But our figurehead, is not what she seems
God save history, God save your mad parade [our runway to suicide]
Oh Lord, have mercy! All crimes are paid

When there's no future, how can there be sin?
We're the flowers in the dustbin
We're the poison in the human machine
We're the future, we're the future

No future, no future, no future, no future …

* * *

The organizations in the Emblematic Structure of Freemasonry illustration, next page, are many centuries old and active still. What do they do? This cannot be discussed, because, as with Swiss Bank accounts, something is being hidden. The richest and most powerful people in the world are at the top of these hierarchies, doing something secretive with the support of the organization's masses of lower level Masons who think they are doing something exclusive and therefore important. "Shhhh, its a secret!"

These bottom secret society members have no idea about the agendas at the top. They would deny that there are satanic rituals at the top, because they haven't been initiated into that level of *disconnecting vanity* yet.

On the next illustration, note the Maltese Cross symbols, at top left, of Knights of Malta and Knights of Templar. This is same as cross seen on all the Queen's crowns and curiously, but not coincidently, on a New York license plate, shown in the epilogue of this book. The Knights of Malta are not some extinct club. The private mercenary army Blackwater/Xe in Iraq has links to Knights of Malta, (an easy internet search). Let us put the Queen's association with Knights of Malta in context of Rothschild controlled Europe …

"The Knights of Malta is not merely a "charitable organization." That's just an elaborate front, as should become clear to you later. As the name Sovereign Military Order of Malta (SMOM) confirms, it is a *military* order based on the crusader Knights Hospitaller of Jerusalem and is interwoven with Freemasonry. Most people have never even heard of SMOM, much less that it is a part of Freemasonry. But that is the way the aristocratic elite like it.

EMBLEMATIC STRUCTURE OF FREEMASONRY

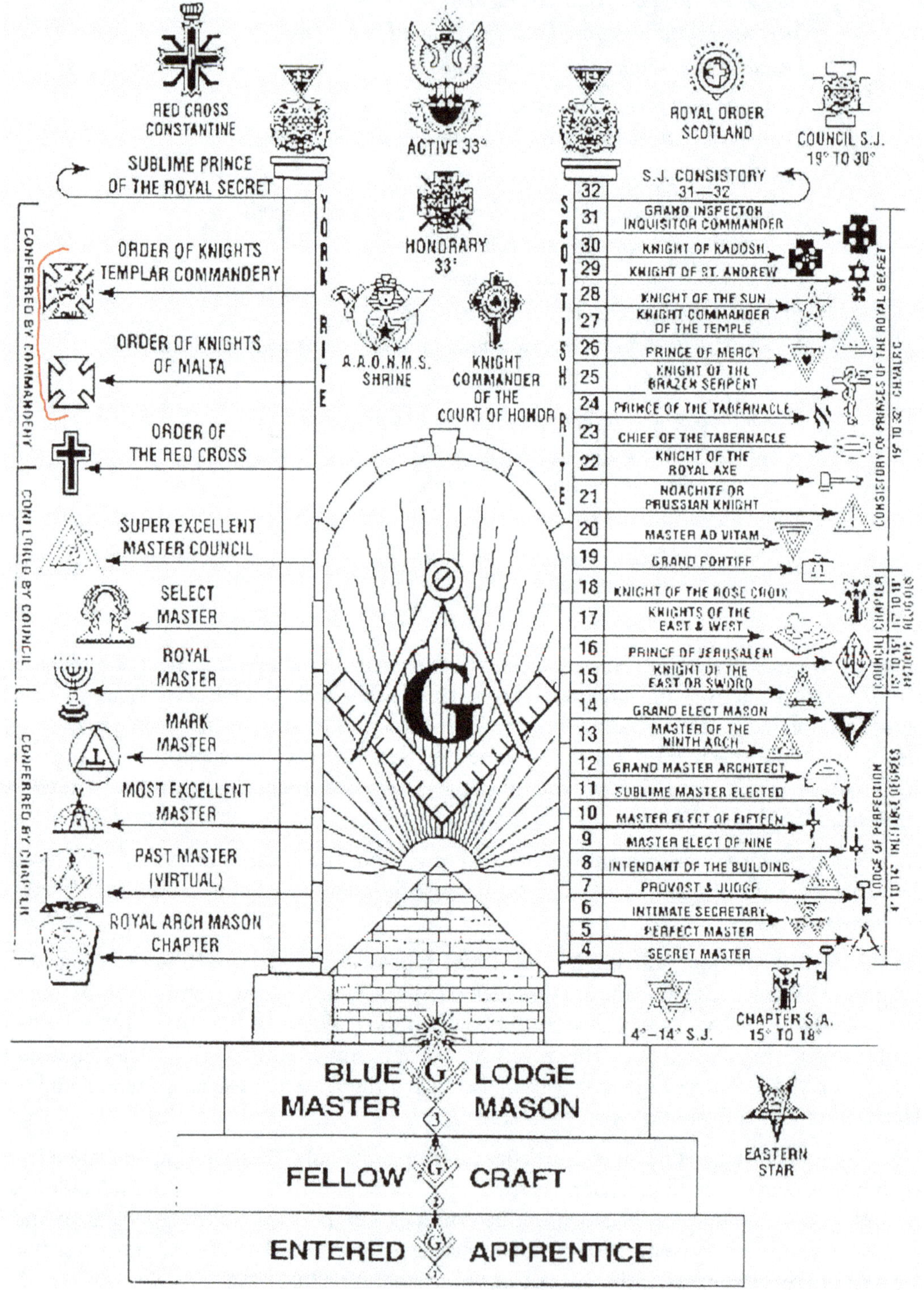

"One of the symbols of the *military* orders of the Vatican, the Masonic double-headed eagle emblazoned with the Maltese cross, signifies omnipotent royal dominion over both East and West. The orb signifies temporal dominion over the globe of Earth, and the scepter signifies control over the spiritual and religious impulses of humanity. This eagle symbol is used in the Masonic rite of Memphis and Misraim, under which it reads, "Order Out of Chaos," the Hegelian method of crisis creation. It is found on the seals of many European and Eurasian nation states including that of Russia, indicating direct Vatican control over those countries. It symbolizes the desire of a predatory elite with virtually unlimited resources to totally dominate the entire world under a New World Order global government system using secrecy, manipulation, coercion and terror, with the ends justifying the means.

"The two-headed eagle emblem of the Byzantine Empire (Roman Empire) on a Red Shield was adopted in 1743 by the infamous goldsmith Amschel Moses Bauer. [Who changed his name to Rothschild and invented modern banking. (Page 41)] He opened a coin shop in Frankfurt, Germany and hung above his door this Roman eagle on a red shield. The shop became known as the "Red Shield firm." The German word for 'red shield/sign' is Rothschild. After this point, the Rothschilds became the bankers to kings and pontiffs alike, among the richest families in the world. Ever since, they have financed both sides of every major war and revolution using the Hegelian Dialectic to engineer society toward their New World Order.

"The Rothschilds and their agents, such as the Rockefellers, have been engineering America and its foreign policy almost since its inception. They and their Skull and Bones Wall Street partners staged and funded both sides in WWII, and out of that hellish nightmare was born their infant global government, the United Nations, and their tool of tyranny, the CIA. The father of the CIA, "Wild Bill" Donovan, was a Knight of Malta. In order to be a director of the CIA you must be a crusading Knight of Malta and it doesn't hurt if you are a member of Skull and Bones either. In order to reach the highest levels in the Pentagon establishment, you must be an illuminated Freemason and/or a Knight of one order or another. Notable U.S. *military* members of SMOM include top crusading generals such as Alexander Haig, William Westmoreland, and Charles A. Willoughby, an admitted Fascist." [93]

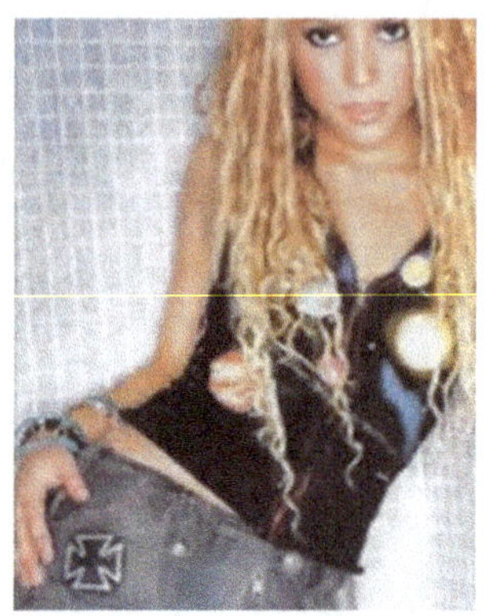

The article above includes a long list of notable politicians and generals as members of Sovereign Military Order of Malta. To right we see Latin singer Shakira with the Knights of Malta patch on her pants. She almost always has Illuminati symbols in her photo shoots. Shakira is another placed *cutout* who we will study in Volume 3.

In the following image, we see how this secret Order was part of the Nazi conspiracy which is covered later in the series. At the top of every organization are people in secret agreements with other players at the top of other organizations in the "Grand Chess Game." Note Maltese cross on breast of Amschel Rothschild (Father of modern banking) in the image below.

"The governments of the present day have to deal not merely with other governments, with emperors, kings and ministers, but also with the secret societies which have, everywhere, their unscrupulous agents, and can at the last moment upset [sabotage] all the governments' plans."

– Benjamin Disraeli, 1876

The Queen of England has honored, by "knighting," many war criminals. Two that stand out recently are "Sir" General Norman Schwarzkopf, under whom in 1991, 400,000 Iraqi men women and children were killed or wounded in 100 hours. Another war criminal, of course, would be anti-virtue "Sir" Henry Kissinger on front cover of this book. Here are just some of the "honorable" people that were given the Grand Cross or Maltese Cross, and again, is anyone accountable? Or, as I am putting forth, are award ceremonies a way to hide accountability and seal actions behind a smokescreen of phony respectability?

Iraq's dead are not worth counting.

– General "Sir" Norman Schwarzkopf

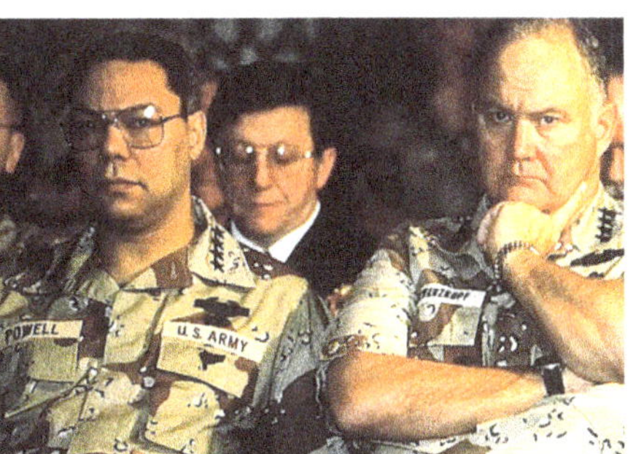

Royal Babylon: The Criminal Record of the British Monarchy

from Margaret Cox

We burned down the thatched huts, starting the blaze with rockets and zippo lighters. Why were we torching houses and destroying crops? Ho Chi Minh had said his people were like the sea, in which guerrillas swam. We tried to solve the problem by making the whole sea uninhabitable. In the hard logic of war, what difference did it make if you shot your enemy or starved him [... her, children, grandparents ...] to death.

(Remember, this was to save the Vietnamese from communism and bring them western "democracy.")

– "Sir" Collin Powell

Powell would go on to lie to UN about weapons of mass destruction in Iraq, and lie about almost everything else as well. It's just the hard logic of war to have no conscience, right? And accept awards for it?

I want every Iraqi soldier bleeding from every orifice.

– "Sir" Norman Schwarzkopf

"Sir" Pedophile Kissinger is on front cover of this book for a reason. He has been commanding the President and Prime Minister *cutouts* since the 70s and, as mentioned, has been called the CEO of the Bilderberg Group. His doctoral thesis was on the Illuminati Congress of Vienna. Please buy and read book *Trance-formation of America* by *Hero* Cathy O'Brien, as well as her follow up book about her daughter, verified with court documents. There you can read about the Queen's pychopathic "Sir" Kissinger, exposed as a pedophile. At hour 1:34 of this interview with Kay Griggs you can hear how Kissinger used grown men. [94]

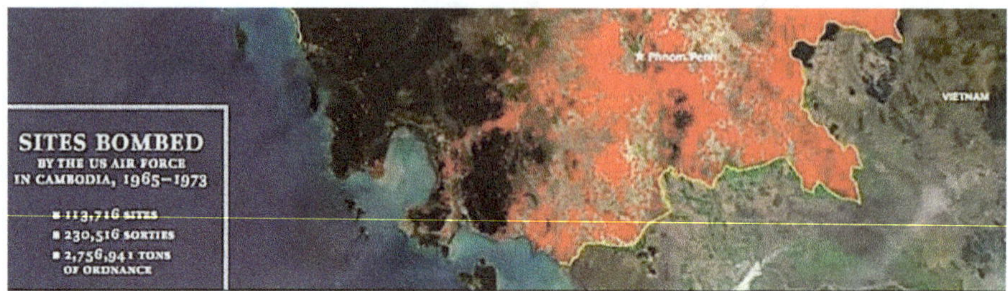

Royal Babylon: The Criminal Record of the British Monarchy

Please search the video above online, youtubes "Royal Babylon" and "The Zion King." Especially Brits might get deprogrammed by these documentaries. 230,516 bombing sorties over 113,716 sites (each hit twice) in rural Cambodia was a gift of "Sir" Henry Kissinger, destroying civil society and creating vacuum of power for the Khmer Rouge, which led to the Cambodian holocaust.

"Why should we flagellate ourselves for what the Cambodians did to each other". [No remorse, no shame, no conscience, live it up! Do what thou wilt.]

"If they put Jews in gas chambers in the Soviet Union, it is not an American concern."

"Today Americans would be outraged if U.N. troops entered Los Angeles to restore order; tomorrow they will be grateful! This is especially true if they were told there was an outside threat from beyond whether real or promulgated, that threatened our very existence. [Ebola? UFO's?] It is then that all peoples of the world will pledge with world leaders to deliver them from this evil. The one thing every man fears is the unknown. When presented with this scenario, individual rights will be willingly relinquished for the guarantee of their well being granted to them by their world government."

– "Sir" Henry Kissinger

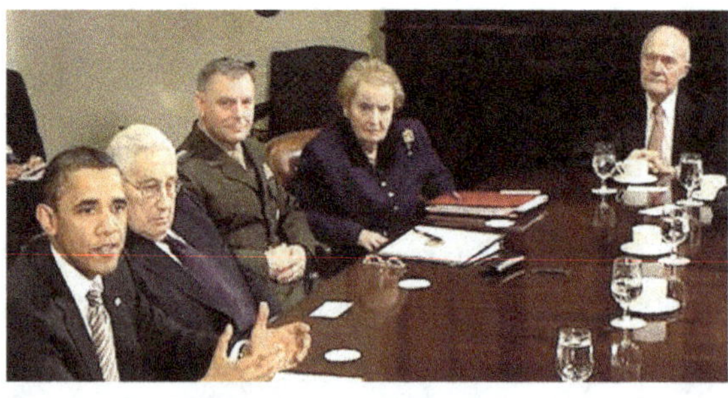

In Obama's White House we see "Sir" Kissinger, Rwanda Holocaust Madeline Albright, and in right top corner Brent Scowcroft. Who is he?

"If we have to use force, it is because we are America. We are the indispensable nation. We stand tall. We see further into the future." [... Because she is illumined! Might makes right! My country right or wrong! But her country is never wrong, so any war crime is excusable. If one nation is indispensable, all others are expendable. This is the non-morality of disconnecting vanity. The Golden Rule does not exist because WE ARE AMERICANS!]

– former Secretary of State Madeleine Albright

60 Minutes – May 12 1996 – Lesley Stahl on U.S. sanctions against Iraq: "We have heard that a half million children have died. [1995 UN Food and Agricultural Organization report—567,000 children starved] I mean, that's more children than died in Hiroshima. And, you know, is the price worth it?"

Secretary of State Madeleine Albright: "I think this is a very hard choice, but the price—we think the price is worth it."

Why is Obama meeting with these monsters? Please review his CIA upbringing in Vol. 1.

Brent Scowcroft Knighted By Queen Elizabeth II

March 18, 1993

Queen Elizabeth II conferred an honorary knighthood Wednesday on Brent Scowcroft, former President Bush's national security adviser.

Scowcroft, 67, received the honorary knighthood, the highest honor that Britain can give a foreigner, for his contribution to Anglo-American relations.

New World Order

According to Keppler Associates, Inc.'s Web Page on Brent Scowcroft:

"With the end of the Cold War and the collapse of the Soviet Union, it was Scowcroft who coined the term New World Order."

Profiles

Scowcroft is also the founder and "president of the Forum for International Policy, a non-profit organization that he founded in 1993 that promotes American leadership and foreign policy." [5]

Scowcroft served as National Security Advisor to both Presidents Gerald R. Ford and George Herbert Walker Bush. He was Vice Chairman of Kissinger Associates, Inc. (1982-1989), an international consulting firm. "In this capacity, he advised and assisted a wide range of U.S. and foreign corporate leaders on global joint venture opportunities, strategic planning and risk assessment." [6]

Scowcroft's prior 29-year "military career began with graduation from West Point and concluded at the rank of Lieutenant General following service as the Deputy National Security Advisor. His Air Force service included Professor of Russian History at West Point; Assistant Air Attache in Belgrade, Yugoslavia; Head of the Political Science Department at the Air Force Academy; Air Force Long Range Plans, Office of the Secretary of Defense International Security Assistance, Special Assistant to the Director of the Joint Chiefs of Staff and Military Assistant to President Richard M. Nixon." [7]

Notice the close association with Kissinger Associates, and "global joint ventures." Globalism. As we already learned, the term "New World Order" is older than Scowcroft and he certainly didn't coin it. But he was quite comfortable using the words, as he is a card-carrying Globalist.

From Wikipedi-lies, "The phrase *Novus ordo seclorum*, Latin for "New order of the ages" appears on the reverse of the Great Seal of the United States, first designed in 1782 and printed on the back of the United States one-dollar bill since 1935. The phrase is sometimes mistranslated as "New World Order" by people who believe in a conspiracy behind the design." [People who have correctly studied the Illuminati, know what a pyramid represents, and aren't willing to be stupid slaves anymore under a pack of secretive conspirators.]

"Sir" Brent Scowcroft at bottom, "Sir" Pedophile Kissinger, and, yep, FED Chairman "Sir" Alan Greenspan who laid the groundwork for the orchestrated 2008 financial collapse.

Below, war criminal, drug runner, sterilizer of Native American women, killer of Guatemalan priests, Education 2000 (Page 29) pedophile "Sir" George Bush Sr. and Iran-Contra scandal "Sir" Ronald Reagan. They were also knighted by Queenie.

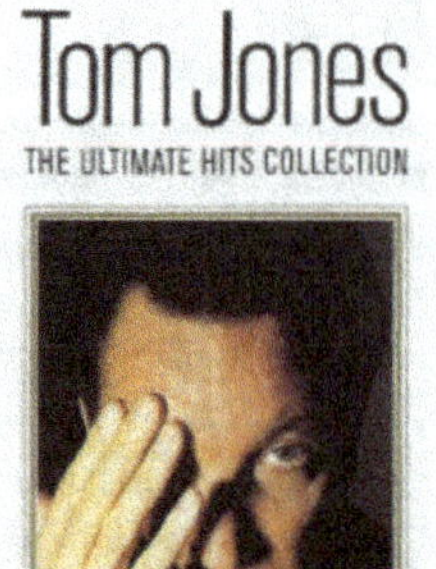

And right with gun "Sir" J. Edgar Hoover, FBI Director from 1935 until 1972, who spied on Martin Luther King for ten years, infiltrated Black Panthers and murdered half of them, and when being just himself, was a sexually confused cross dresser. This is a perfect example where blurred polarity without clear moral lines overlaps into immoral criminal behavior. If one has no right or wrongs with sex, with one's own energy, how does a person have right or wrong anywhere else? Based on what? On being indispensable? Churchill was also bi-sexual as are most celebrities and politicians who use boys. As stated, the top of the pyramid is perverted.

Image of "Sex Bomb" Tom Jones is covering one eye. Of thousands of images of Tom Jones, the industry that controls his album covers chose this one. The Knight is a slave. Is Tom Jones accountable? He did *what* exactly to be knighted? Still, some fawning British sheeple addressed Tom Jones as "Sir" on *The Voice.* And they would address Kissinger or Powell or Hoover or any other serial killer as "Sir" also.

Would you? Would you even shake their hands? Are you waking up? Get off your knees everyone!

Below screen shot of image search for Knight Grand Cross, aka Maltese Cross

Knighted "Sir" Mick Jagger: "… According to Andersen: "Ava Cherry, a backup singer who lived with the Bowies for a time, reportedly told a friend that 'Mick and David were really sexually obsessed with each other. Even though I was in bed with them many times, I ended up just watching them have sex' … Tony Blair, the former Prime Minister, was said to have repeatedly tried to add Mick Jagger's name to the Honours List but was rebuked by the Queen because he was "not suitable", the Daily Mail reported. When *his name was finally added* … she simply arranged to be elsewhere. … asked the Prince of Wales to give him his knighthood instead.

– The Telegraph, July 2012. Who added the name? Keep asking that.

"… A list of Jagger's personal "achievements," in a certain way, epitomize the whole [socially engineered] counter-culture. Having fathered seven children by four different women, he was also rumored to have a fling with fellow rocker David Bowie. Jailed for the use of drugs, and vandalism, he revels in pushing the limits of human excess and degradation in onstage acts too vulgar to mention. The catalog of songs he has authored is famous for demeaning women, and glorifying violence and Satan. [I would disagree, Jagger like all the others is probably just a puppet who authored almost nothing.]

– The Debasement of Knighthood, Marian T. Horvat. Ph.D.

"The inventor of Viagra—a pill designed to enhance sexual performance—has received a knighthood from the Queen in her annual New Year's Honours."

– Davidicke.com January 3, 2015

KYLIE
USA 2009
KYLIE MINOGUE
OFFICIAL
2015
CALENDAR
Royality
= Rothschild
= New World
Order
=Abuse Pyramid
= All-seeing-eye
= Illuminati
=Entertainment
= Indecency
=Dumbing down
= SLAVERY
Kylie has joined The Voice UK
Kylie X2008 - World Tour Opening

In the next photos we see that Simon Cowell, (who runs the Bertelsmann *X-Factor* talent shows for his Sony Inc. boss) and Queen Elizabeth, are both indeed part of secret societies. The Freemasons were resisting infiltration by Illuminati in the days of George Washington, as referenced above, but apparently fell. Queen Elizabeth is probably the richest woman in the world. Not only does she personally own half of Shell Petroleum, but as Sovereign of the British Commonwealth, which includes Canada and Australia and much more, she controls extensive mineral rights. But being a member of the hoarding demonic Bilderberg crowd who like to hold the entire world ransom for their own gain (Page 66), she just keeps working for more power and profit and control. These people are not altruistic. They are trapped in *disconnecting vanity.* They cannot imagine connection. They are quite lost and obviously sick. Who in their right mind would honor the queen?

Masonic symbols on the Queen's nurse's belt, and the same symbols on Simon Cowell's jet ski and on a shrine in Eliat, Israel. Also note pentagon on belt, which appeared in the movie Metropolis, Aguilera photo, and, as we will see, in Hitler's occult rituals.

So now, it is not so surprising that the Illuminati Freemason Queen of England who "knights" serial killers and cross dressers, would "honor" a *cutout* like Gaga. But still, does it stand to reason that a person like Gaga would be promoted by Disney in association with little children? I thought we wanted something wholesome for our kids? But wholesomeness is the illusionary fake image of Disney, Inc. Now we know Walt Disney was placed and everything Disney Inc. ever did was part of a *social engineering* manipulation.

Let's connect the dots. We've seen the production line at Disney that produces entertainers that end up being slut role models, so now we have to rearrange our thinking to understand that Disney actually does not have a wholesome relationship with kids or with society. Disney has a very abusive relationship in a contest against goodness. The goal of Disney is not wholesome entertainment for children. Disney is into sexual deviancy and polluting children. And "The Queen" doesn't honor virtue, she "knights" criminals! Welcome to "where sickness thrives."

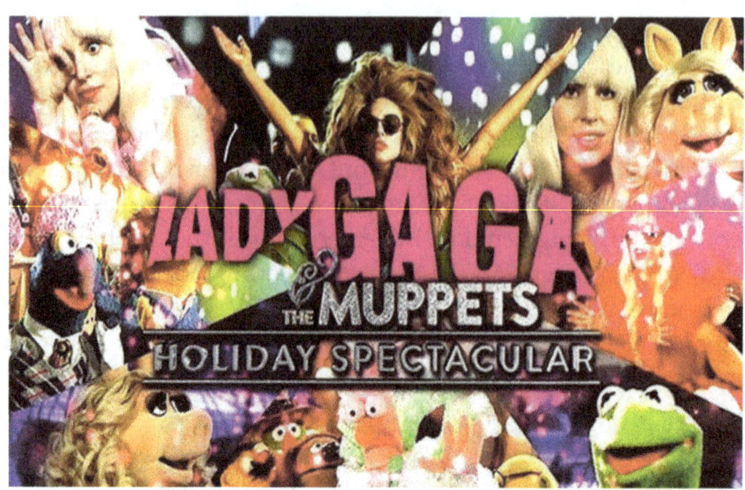

Gaga stumping for all-seeing-eye of pyramid in upper left of poster and on right, open legs (See close-up Page 267). Modesty dissolved for pre-school age kids. Mission accomplished for destabilization/consolidation. Without morals, new "traditions" can be placed.

In the above poster, Disney is not using Gaga to promote itself, but using it's worldwide platform to promote the disrespect for modesty and the filth which Gaga represents. Just as homosexuality is being made normal, being a slut is now supposed to be normal (See next image of singer Rihanna and note the chain of gold around her neck.) It's working. Lots of teenage girls are happy to appear in porn videos. Fifty years ago this would have been impossible. Fifty years ago we had dress standards in school! Those who scoff need to consider what we have now … Shame is "old fashioned." No shame means no blame. No blame means no accountability. Mission accomplished by Illuminati.

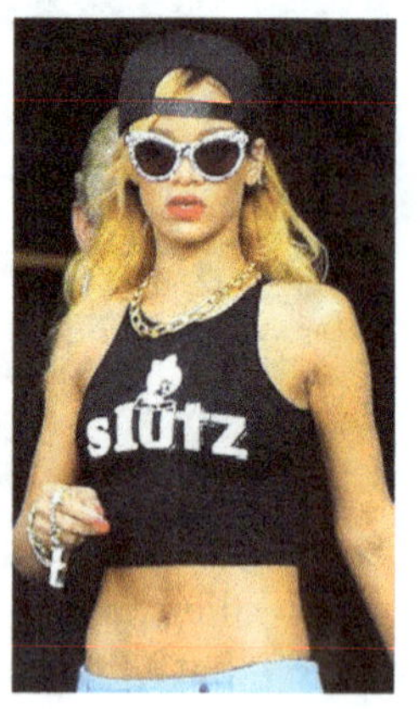

All little kids seeing Gaga with her legs spread (red dress on right of photo above) have this example as a seed in them. Obviously she was told to spread her legs like that, and she went along with it. Or maybe she always does this as a habit? Of hundreds of photos, this one was chosen. Hands open, legs open. No boundaries, no quality control.

Illuminati controlled Celine Dion (next page) is seen in 2014 movie *Muppets Most Wanted,* where the CIA is portrayed as a crime busting organization, which it certainly is not, and the *cage theme* (to be discussed) is pushed with singing characters from a Russian Gulag, which is not portrayed as a death camp, but as place for criminals. *The Muppets* was bought by Illuminati Disney in 2004 and is now a prime venue for *socially engineering* children. By placing Celine Dion on a children's film, older viewers are seduced to think the movie is upstanding, when in fact the movie is filled with subliminal messages. Gaga appears for a few silent seconds in the beginning of the film and singer Rihanna (above), who we will meet in Volume 3, is mentioned. Disney's *Muppets* is pushing Gaga and Rihanna in subliminal mini moments to create the new shameless, no-one-is-accountable normal.

So what can we expect from Disney? We should expect something devious, since Mickey Mouse cartoons and Disney Inc. were sponsored *social engineering* programs, starting in 1928. I ask, "Will you still expose your family to Disney's attack on modesty?"

We can judge a tree by its fruit, and the fruit, such as the celebrity brats Spears, Aguilera, Cyrus, Lovato, Gomez and grafted on gangrenous Gaga, are very bad role models. The fruit of Disney looks rotten. Please go into your heart of *personal sovereignty!* You either enable Disney social corruption and follow like a sheeple … or you boycott and save your family! Support or oppose?

Or if you are *socially engineered* by the New Age movement, you do nothing at all.

Note, in above images, how New Age was *co-opted* with the same *Illuminati* symbols. Original New Age thought was like original feminism, an alternative. It was *co-opted.* The New Age mentality now is that "If I am relaxed and don't judge anyone (not engaging), I am not contributing to conflict and am helping bring peace. Therefore, I should just focus on my own state of mind and feel good. To 'give energy' to social justice issues is to be negative because the only thing that matters is my comfort and relaxation." New Age mentality is both narcissistic and very judgmental of anyone who has a strong stand and points fingers at problems and is passionate. New Age people would judge harshly someone like Jesus, who threw money changers out of the temple.

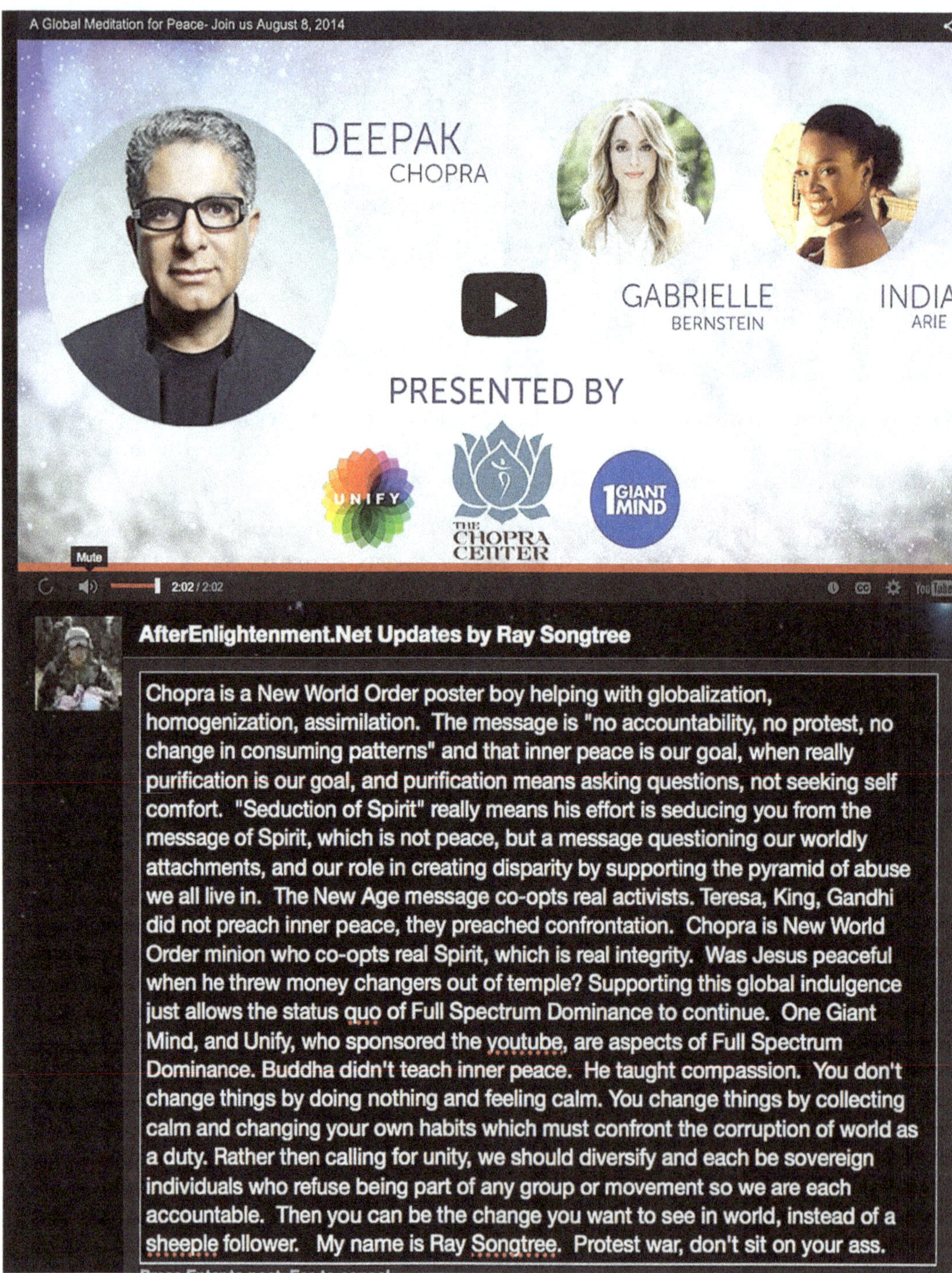

"Global meditation for peace" between shopping for designer clothes and sipping on a latte. One giant mind? No thanks. My comment above to Chopra youtube.

What's wrong with this picture? Answer, the drought in California. See GeoengineeringWatch.org. It is not time to meditate. It is time to protest.

Chapter 9

In Your Own Home

As the series gets deeper into popular culture, control and scripting of musical industry and celebrities, ties with royalty, satanism and methodology of destruction of decency, the reader may ask, what does celebrity idiocy have to do with *globalization*? This seems like gossip!

Please keep remembering this ... *monopolization* is won by homogenization. To reduce all standards to the lowest standards makes resistance very unlikely. Also let's remember to follow the money. Just as the banksters funded Karl Marx and Gloria Steinem, the banksters are funding what we think is popular and shaping popularity itself as a tool of their agenda.

Please let me say it again. It doesn't matter if you like pop music or know something or nothing about it, the youth do know. And even if your kids never listen to pop music or watch TV, their peers do. Even if your son doesn't play with video games all day, most of the boys his age do. Even if your daughter doesn't religiously study fashion magazines, most of her peers do.

Young people's exposure to these split values sets up the disconnecting vanity that can then be mind controlled later in other ways. Once our whole, centered, grounded, connected personal sovereignty is broken, we are like a horse that is broken, and our spirit is never the same.

What do these video games teach? Does a community have the power to restrict what enters their community, or does Globalism have the right to erase any standard? How would you protect your community?

The banner ad below came up when I was researching on YouTube. League of Angels? We know YouTube is Globalist controlled because it bans some whistleblower videos, yet allows ads like this. The shirt on the right says SLUT. These are the images that both boys and girls see in the "developed countries." Did any culture before ever expose their children to this? Will these role models help in a time of crisis? Does this build family and community, or opposite?

I often hear responses to new information such as … "Oh, I don't do that. My kids don't do that …" This is the *disconnecting vanity* that can claim he or she is not part of the problem. In fact, everything that everyone buys is part of the same system that definitely has a problem.

We learned a bit about the New World Order "educational" role of the Carnegie Foundation on Pages 23-24. The following describes the initial funding of the children's series, *Sesame Street.*

> "As a result of Cooney's initial proposal in 1968, the **Carnegie Institute** awarded her an $8 million grant to create a new children's television program and establish the Children's Television Workshop (CTW), renamed in 2000 to the Sesame Workshop (SW). Cooney and Morrisett procured additional multi-million dollar grants from the U.S. federal government, The Arthur Vining Davis Foundations, CPB, and the **Ford Foundation.**"
>
> – Wikipedia

I believe that Cooney was either *co-opted* with conditions as soon as she took money, or more likely, as with CIA Gloria Steinem and *Ms. Magazine,* she was simply a paid agent assigned to the child bending project from the outset. The Carnegie Foundation is a front which produces other fronts to give "charity" to. The foundations are the propaganda/advertising side of corporate control, and those receiving the grants are the foot soldiers. Ford, Gates, Rockefeller, Carnegie foundations are all New World Order cultural destabilization fronts.

Sesame Street features the following partnership illustration on their website. This is real *globalization*, the real thing, which is far beyond economic models …

At home and globally, we build collaborative partnerships with those who share our mission. By matching vital educational needs to our partners' goals, we create real impact together.

"Our continued collaboration provides an opportunity to positively impact early childhood on a global scale with the latest technology."

Kristin Parsley Atkins, Senior Director, Wireless Reach, Qualcomm

USA, Sesame Street

> learn more

"What helps make our Grow Up Great program so effective is the association we established with Sesame Workshop from the beginning. Our collaboration has created an innovative partnership that continues to encourage early learning."

Eva Tansky Blum, Senior Vice President & Director Community Affairs, PNC Bank Chair and President, The PNC Foundation

USA, Sesame Street

We can ask, who at Qualcomm has the right to say what is "positive" for all children world wide? The statement was made by the Qualcomm Director of Wireless. Wireless frequencies have been shown by over 1200 peer reviewed papers at **Bioinitiative.org** to be dangerous, causing cancer and genetic disruption. (Chapter 6)

We can ask how PNC Bank come up with a mission of "early learning" and what they will get by funding and imputting programming intended to condition young children..

The first statement in the screen shot above with green background is *globalization* in your face …

"At home and globally we build collaborative partnerships with those who share our mission [for their own gain, to condition children into corporate values]. By matching vital educational needs to our partners' goals, [of selling more?], we create real impact together."

There you have it. The real *Sesame Street* is a conspiracy of *social engineering* by corporate interests, and worse, to transform children *their way.* We never had a discussion about this kind of *globalization* in school, but this conspiracy of *globalization* is what our schooling was all about.

We can ask, who does *Sesame Street* think it is to determine "vital educational needs" for your children in your home and in the homes of diverse cultures world wide?

"Impact" means warping, seducing, conditioning, controlling your child. Please note that these *dominant culture* conquistadors are egotistically proud of their global impact.

* * *

Above left, the same image as in the right side of the Muppet/Disney/Sesame poster from Page 258, Gaga is imprinting this spread leg non-standard to destroy modesty in kids. The message is very clear … "This is normal. This is how a woman appears in public." This is shown to millions of children. Images imprint the mind and don't go away.

Above right, Elton John on the Muppets, 1978, with an open pink jacket and nothing beneath it, teaching a generation that indulgent queer is "gay." It worked—there is no difference between a vagina and an anus in the politically correct world view pushed by the UN and the many puppet governments. [95]

The line between children's and adult *social engineering* is academic ... there is no line. Let's meet another agent, Nicki Minaj.

To right, we see a similar costume that was worn by Gaga (Page 246 with Queen Elizabeth), also worn by Nicki Minaj (the name in French means a 3-way sexual relationship) at the Los Angeles 2012 Grammy awards. The awards "ceremony" occurred the day after the *murder* of Whitney Houston and was an actual satanic ritual live on TV, planned months or years in advance. [96] At this Grammy awards, Three-Way Minaj sang her song "Roman Holiday." In the dictionary, Roman Holiday means, 1) a time of debauchery or sadistic enjoyment, 2) a destructive or tumultuous disturbance.

The Pope costume is an obvious slap to Catholics, but for those who have studied the Jesuits and the Pope's connections with the Rothschilds, the image of a Pope arm in arm with an Illuminati witch is simply the conspiracy hidden in plain sight. If this seems far fetched, go back to the photo of Pope on Page 250 and Hitchcock's research on Page 49. Remember pedophilia at priest level leads to worse at the top. The face on the dress is who? There is a cult meaning, surely.

Screen shot from youtube. Two large statues of Egyptians were placed on sidewalk before Whitney Houston's body was taken from hotel into ambulance. All planned in advance. They waited 11 hours to take her body from hotel. What ceremonies were they doing?yMost of the celebrities at Grammy Awards knew what it all meant. The lyrics to next song are important. I suggest reading them a few times.

As of this writing, Whitney's daughter is still in coma. The crime is simply horrible and we can't rest until we stop this organization.

"Roman Holiday" by Nicki Three-Way Minaj

Take your medication, Roman [slave]
Take a short vacation, Roman
You'll be okay
You need to know your station, Roman [in the hierarchy]
Some alterations on your clothes and your brain [transhumanism]
Take a little break, little break
From your silencing [dumbing down}
There's so much you can take, you can take
I know how bad you need a Roman holiday
A Roman holiday [debauchery]

You done, you tight? You suck at life?
You don't want a round three, [threat] You'll suffer twice.
Worship the queen and you might could pass [slave]
Keep it real, these bitches couldn't wipe my ass [be a real slave]
Anyway, stylist, go get Bvlgari
I am the ultimate Svengali
You, You bitches can't even spell that
You, you hoes buggin'
Repel that

Let me tell you this, sister
I am, I am colder than a blister
Cause my flow's so sick
And I'm a lunatic
And this can't be cured with no Elixir
*'Cause y'all know who the f*ck, what the f*ck I do*
I done put the pressure to every thug I knew
Quack quack to a duck and a chicken too
Put the hyena in a freaking zoo

Witch, twitch, bitch!
*Motherf*cking right, this is World War 6*
This right here might make a bitch die
And this right here is gonna make a bitch cry
And if you being honest, I am such a great guy
And this what I do ***when a bitch breaks flock***

I'mma put her in a dungeon under, under
No them bitches ain't eating
They dying of hunger

*Motherf*cker I need, who the f*ck is this whore*
And yes maybe just a touch of tourettes
Get my wigs Terrance go and get my beret

Come all ye faithful, Joyful and triumphant [Grammy party goers]
I am Roman Zolanski, Come all ye faithful
Joyful and triumphant, I am Roman Zolanski

Talking about me, you talking about me? ["Me" is the Illuminati controllers.]
I dare a motherf*cker, to be talking about me
Them bitches must be smokin' a couple of OC
They want the outline [the outline, the understanding], I give them a goatee
*God damn, motherf*cker, you talking about me?*
*I dare a motherf*cker, to be talking about me*
Them bitches must be smoking a couple of OC
Ha Ba Ba Ba Ga Gum the goatee

Welcome to the Grammy Awards 2012 …

The reader must understand that Nicki Minaj is a placed *cutout.* She did not write this song alone or sing these words without permission. Though written in the first person tense, it is not she who is speaking. It is not her song, just as it is not her choice to have on the cult dress that she is wearing or to be walking with the Pope. It is her handlers' choice and her handlers' song and it is one message, not many. It is the same people who created the staging, and who made sure Whitney Houston was booked into the hotel where she stayed.

Whitney Houston named her manager, bi-sexual Klive Davis, as abusive in this video interview [97] and became almost distressed when she talked about her relationship with him and it is very apparent she didn't want to say much. She used the word "Svengali" to describe their relationship and the word is used in song. "You bitches can't even spell that." Well, almost no one knows that word, but Minaj is teaching the world about it. Roman Zolanski is not "her gay-boy alter ego." He is the "ultimate" abuser, the controlling force in the entertainment industry. The murder of Houston was planned long in advance, as was the murder of actor Robin Williams, which we have absolute proof of, again in Volume 3 of *Lipstick and War Crimes.* … Not just that he was murdered, but that the plan was years in the making and coordinated. [98] As becomes clear, these are ritual sacrifices, exactly what the Grammy staging portrays (next page).

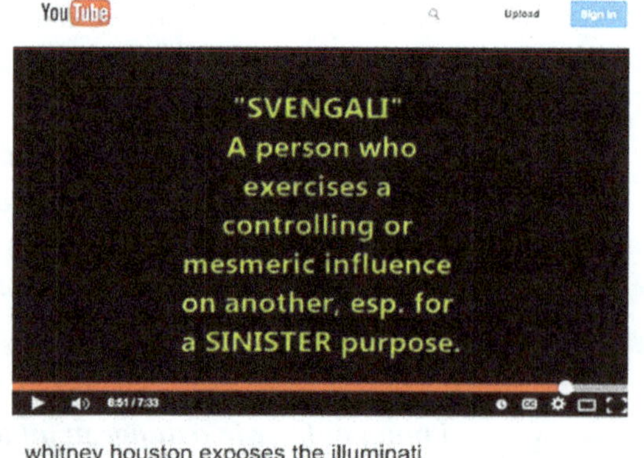

When I first read these lyrics I didn't understand them, but when you imagine that this is the *evil* of Illuminati speaking, then it becomes clear; the handlers are making stellar vocalist Houston an example to terrify the rest of the music industry. Please read it again. The bold lines are talking directly to all the other entertainers about what will happen if they "break flock." And as we will see in Volume 3, they ALL know. The song is a warning backed by murder.

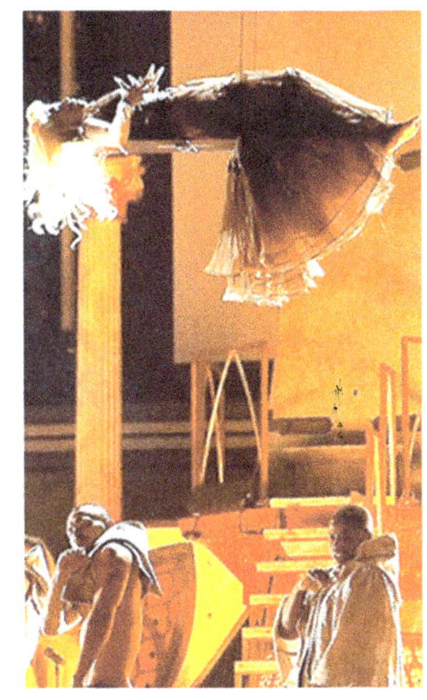

To right, the symbolic sacrifice and "transformation" of Nicki Three-Way Minaj at same 2012 Grammy, which used the real death of Whitney Houston as the actual victim, or does the reader think the elaborate costumes and stage performance, and song "Roman Holiday," and mysterious inconsistent reports about the death of Houston, are all just "coincidences"? [99] The world witnessed an actual satanic ritual, not just some weird crazy random staging. (More on this in Volume 3.)

Just as Three-Way Minaj takes part in mocking the Pope, supposedly the Chinese characters on her arm tatoo means "God is always with me." In what way is God with Nicki Three-Way Minaj, the mistress? (See photo below.) We will see other satanists wearing crosses (Aguilera Page 220), or saying that their religious parents support them, no matter what they do or say. This all undercuts any real meaning to traditions that guide morality. And Kmart Inc. joins in, using someone who trashes standards of decency as their poster girl. Crest Toothpaste will do same with all-seeing-eye singer Shakira. (Volume 3)

Left corner bottom, a (poor quality) screen shot from YouTube of Nicki Minaj slipping into a trance as one of the talent show *American Idol* judges. Upper right, Minaj stumping for *cage theme.* "Get used to it, we are trapped by Big Brother," is the message. And girls, "Your role is for sex without love. Your self-worth depends on being a good slave." Respect for family? Three-Way Minaj is your husband's mistress. That's fine with K-mart.

Puppet satanist Christina Aguilera features puppet satanist Nicki Minaj. Woohoo!

K-Mart promotes Three-Way Minaj with her explicit content. Again we must ask is anyone accountable? Do we excuse these millionaires as victims or denounce them for being horrible destructive role models? Without denunciation, aren't we enabling this? Aren't we accountable?

Sam Bailey sings "Edge of Glory" by Lady Gaga – Live

Youtube screen shot, more *cage theme* (See Glossary) using new talent Sam Bailey (Samantha), winner of 2013 UK *X-Factor* talent show. She is given a Gaga song to boost more fame for the Illuminati super star. This keeps Gaga current so Illuminati doesn't lose a decadence recruiter, not to mention her worth as a revenue stream. Glory (*Vanity* in Glossary) is what Gaga spreads to the masses. More and more *vanity.* Jail bars .... We are all trapped, right?

Above left, Jennifer Lopez promoting human trafficking with a smile, *American Idol* 2013. Respect for women? Above middle, USA *X-Factor* 2013 contestant Rachel Potter is given staging with a *cage theme* fence with a pyramid shape on the cage (her hand is at the peak in the screen shot), but she comes out from behind fence "liberated" and "transformed" as a vixen with black leather boots and leather dress, with red back lighting. The song is converted from talking about love to implying illicit sex. Potter was used. Above right, Disney *cutout* Britney Spears.

The *cage theme* has two messages at least. The first is that the traditional natural feminine is put in a cage and comes out as a sexually liberated, bold, sassy, leopard skin (beta kitten, mind controlled) predator who is all about lust. This is a "transformation" theme. The other is related to imprisonment. The Illuminati bankster *Globalists* apparently are preparing us for martial law. They hope that, just as they have engineered children in how to view relationships and life goals, they can influence us to accept incarceration and riot police to "keep us safe."

One would think the *cage theme* would get old, but instead it is repeated again and again to drill in the conditioning. Thus this choreography is shown, not to be art, but to be *social engineering.*

Staging often has nothing to do with the song. Above left, police soldiers in the song "If I Were a Boy," Grammy 2010. To left, below, young fresh talent, Alex and Sierra, winners of U.S. X-Factor 2013, compromised by riot police staging. "Get used to it. Police state is normal." Again, these repeating themes are not coincidences.

The young couple, Alex and Sierra, were given songs opposite of their actual loving relationship to twist them. The song "Say My Name" featured young sweet Sierra acting "sassy" and the two of them accusing each other of cheating. The sick worded song "Bleeding Love" was given to a former 2007 *X-Factor* UK winner, Leona Lewis, who made the song famous. *Both* the American and British *X-Factor* winners for 2013 (Alex and Sierra, and Sam Bailey) were given "Bleeding Love" to sing. The Illuminati music industry and the *Globalists* don't want purity or love or fidelity because these bring inner strength. They want lust and conflict, which brings competition and lack of unity. They are using same tactic with music as CIA does overseas. Raise hell.

They want nothing wholesome or loyal to oppose their designs. What are their designs? The Pyramid with a top elite controlling and managing the global BOP is their complete plan with no alternatives. NO ALTERNATIVE. That is their plan.

We've drawn a circle of conspiracy around *Sesame Street,* Muppets, Disney, Gaga, Three Way Minaj, K-Mart, murder of Whitney Houston, satanic rituals at Grammy, *cage theme,* perversion of girls, and making riot police "normal." Current popular venues were either created initially to serve as *social engineering* tools, or were *co-opted* and taken over later. Similarly, we saw that Lovato, Gomez, Cyrus, Spears and Aguilera were tools from early childhood, while Madonna, Gaga and Lopez were incorporated/enslaved/paid off. We do not see any popular venue or popular singer spreading a wholesome message. The conspiracy runs on the funding from the *Roth-efeller* foundations. Rothschild Nazi foundations control *X-factor.* (Page 200) Bertelsmann Foundation. Follow the money. Study conspiracy fact. Your mind is on the line.

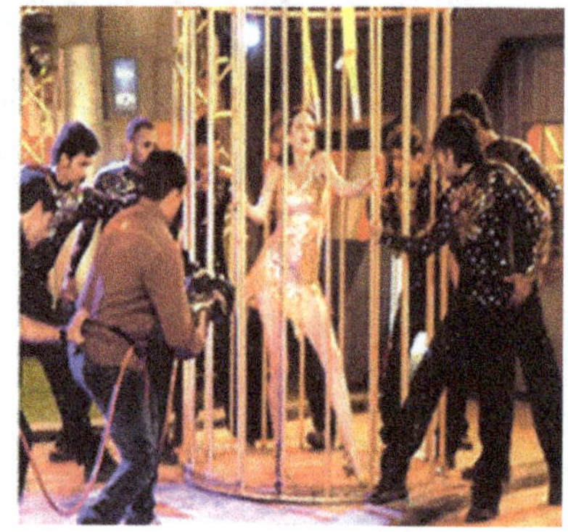

Cage theme *India. On left, "Porn star turned Bollywood actress Sunny Leone did a hot cage dance at the launch of the song 'Babydoll' from her film Ragini MMS 2." The images are clearly of gang rape. There are no baby dolls in traditional cultures. This is the fruit of globalization, in which the most decadent themes are spread like a moral disease. Rothschild-secret-society-controlled-India allows this influence. How will you protect your community? (See Uganda's brave stance Volume 3)*

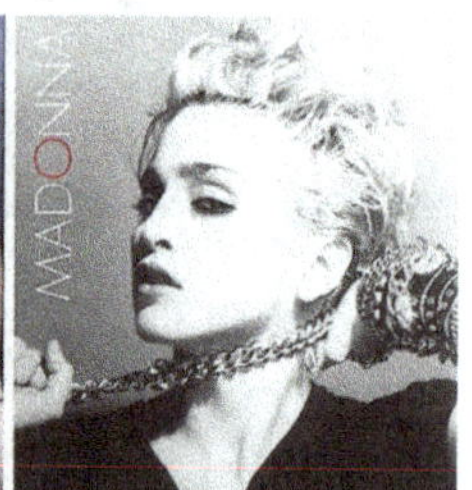

Shakira, Disney Britney Spears, Rihanna, Khloe Kardashian, Disney Miley Cyrus, Madonna Why is there so much violence against women? Use your eyes.

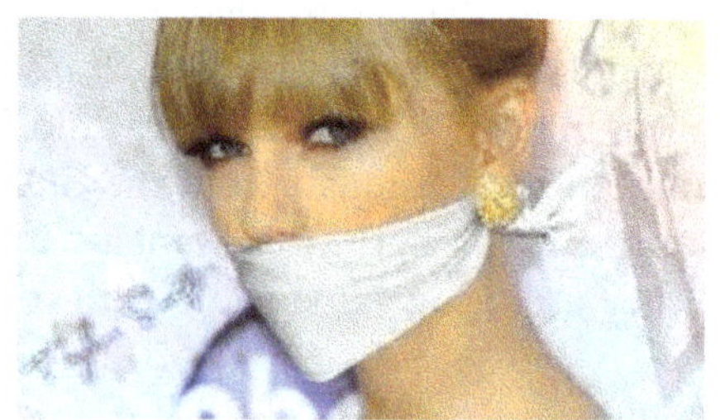

Taylor Swift

Cage theme in real life … U.S. has six times the average of the whole world in prison. U.S. is the opposite of the "land of the free". It is the land of the incarcerated. Is there *"progress"* for Blacks in U.S. society? Whistleblower organizations report higher incarceration numbers than official story, just as the unemployment rate is not reported accurately by government. (Unemployment numbers are based on recent applications for unemployment, not the number of people who are unemployed.)

We will have plenty of jail cells for arresting the elite and their minions when we correct the values in our heads and in our laws. For those who believe in *"progress"* check out the rate of incarceration in last 40 years, next graph.

Notice in these graphs on the next page, how the rate increases when drugs were taken over by the CIA, and Reagan's "War on Drugs" consolidated all the drug running under the New World Order. *If there weren't more drugs available, there could not be more arrests.* Drug use increased, and so did the profits of the prison industry …

"The state of Vermont—Mecca of hemp-wearing, Subaru-driving, Co-op-loving, Frisbee revolutionaries [decadent new age yuppies]—is paradoxically gaining attention for its leading role in supporting the private, for-profit corrections industry … Behind only New Mexico, Hawaii , and Montana, the state of Vermont now houses the largest proportion of its inmates—28 percent—in prisons owned and operated by for-profit corrections firms." [100]

> "In 1984 the Corrections Corporation of America revolutionized the way prisons in the United States operate. The company took over a prison facility in Hamilton County, Tennessee—the first time a private operator was contracted to run a jail. More prison companies were created and contracts continued to flow—between 1990 and 2010 the number of privately operated prisons in the U.S. increased 1600%. This increase has outpaced both the growth of public prison facilities and even the U.S. population.
>
> [Even though the Dept. of Homeland Security was invented after 9/11, drugs continue to pour in. Why is that?]
>
> "Private prisons bring in about $3 billion in revenue annually, and over half of that comes from holding facilities for undocumented immigrants. Private operations run between 50% to 55% of immigrant detainment facilities. The immigration bill battling its way through Washington right now might also mean good things for private prisons. Some estimate that the crackdown on undocumented immigrants will lead to 14,000 more inmates annually with 80% of that business going to private prisons.
>
> "The prison industry has also made money by contracting prison labor to private companies. The companies that have benefited from this cheap labor include Starbucks, Boeing, Victoria's Secret, McDonalds and even the U.S. *military*." [101]

Your latte and Mac Burger and perverted lingerie (Volume 4) were made with slave labor.

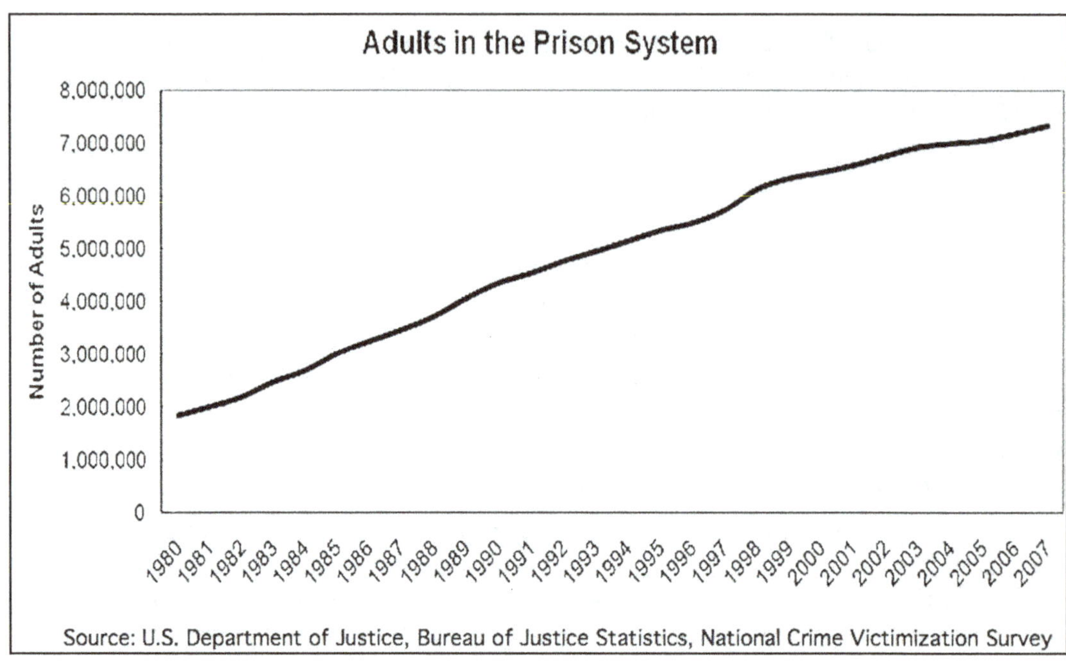

The population didn't quadruple in 27 years, but inmates did.

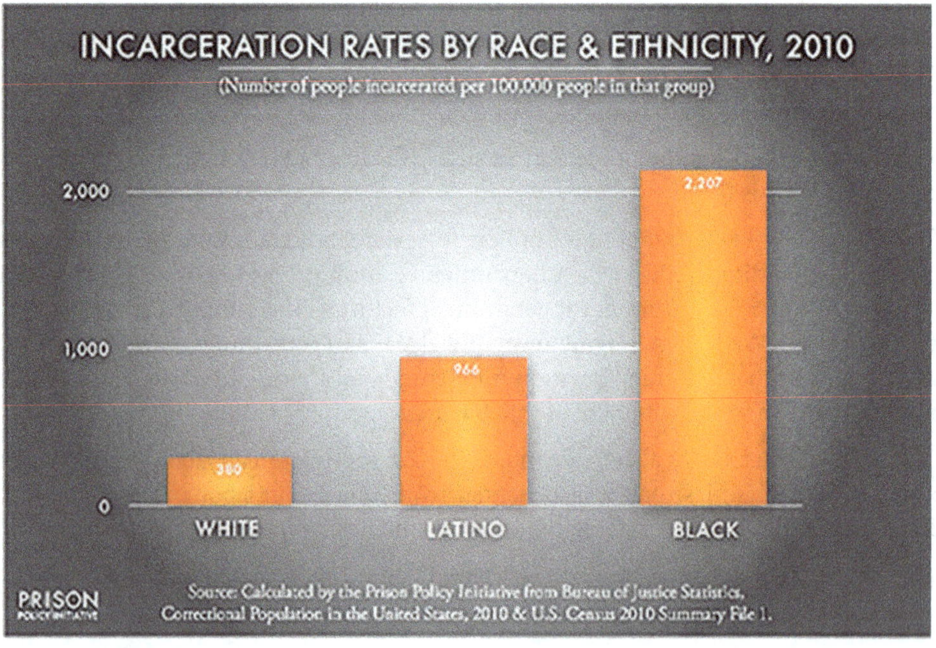

Homeland Security has not decreased drug availability, because their real job is to create a police state which requires ever more arrests. Keep the drugs flowing! And make money doing it! Cage theme! Get used to it!

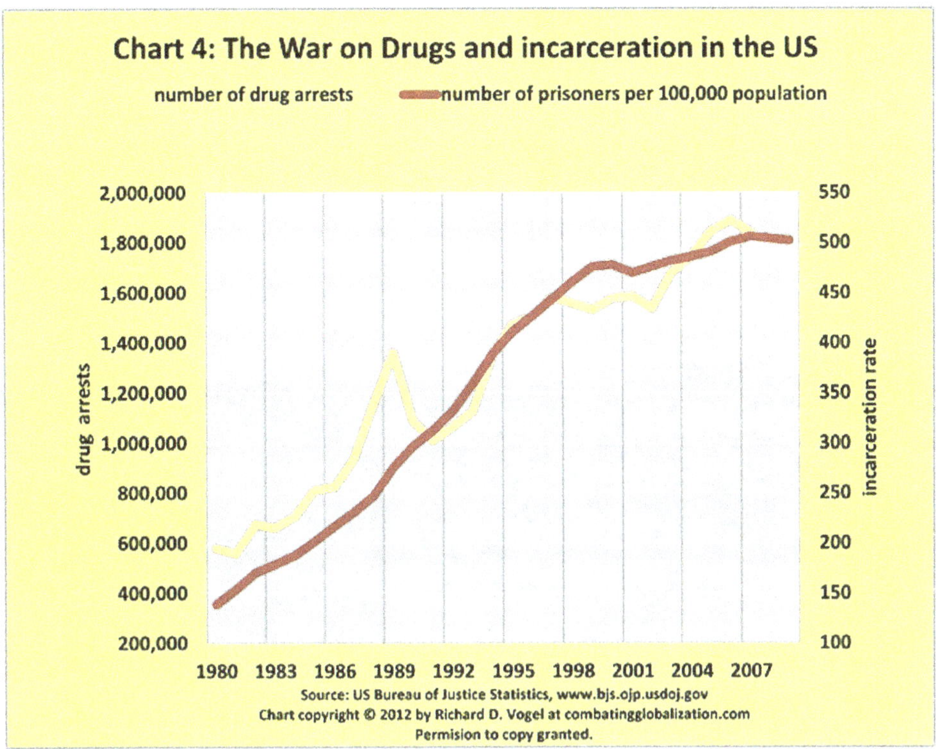

The Cage Theme enters our homes: See next image: The U.S. has twice the jail time for children than any other country, trapping them in our own homes with *social engineering* that creates a culture alien to that of their parents and grandparents. This is New World Order *globalization.*

This generation of couch potatoes will become attention deficit and not be able to focus long on any subject. They will not be as athletic or coordinated as "less modern developed" children. They will probably become obese. TV will teach them *consumerism*, envy, entitlement, sexual identity confusion, sports sex, violence, racial profiling, prejudice against religion, abuse of nature, lies about history, excuses for war, alcoholism, and lust for speed. They will become lazy, sassy and demanding, seeing life from the position of a spectator rather than a participant. In the school of hard knocks they will be weaker, slower, and less adaptable than peers who spent these years interacting with the real world. The TV jailhouse will teach girls that seducing lustful men with spread legs is a woman's place, and that a woman should be equal in obeying any order from the state. That is, "equality." Boys will be taught that if they bomb civilians, they will be called heroes and that freedom fighters are the reason a police state is needed.

Because capitalism demands wealth concentration and ever more "growth"to keep stock prices up, mergers and automatization to make businesses ever more "efficient" will mean fewer and fewer jobs, and more and more people on "benefits." There is no economic recovery. There can't be, because the cheap resources are gone. There will just be more people getting rations (welfare). I suggest that you take no rations from the state whatsoever, and instead earn your own daily bread through hard work that will keep you strong. I suggest you stop going to the doctor except for emergencies. It is vital that you get your kids out of the living room and somewhere that they can learn skills. They need to become good stewards of the land that will keep future generations healthy, and in order to do that, they must know and touch the Earth. Please don't make your child indigenously retarded by keeping her or him in the jail of television and video games. They need to be able to produce something, anything, from scratch. And girls reading this, remember what we learned. The cosmetics industry is flat out deceptive about what chemicals are definitely impacting your health. If it's covered up, it's true. The coverup is the proof of crime.

The youtube below is very important. I urge the reader to see it and share with friends and family, and to start protecting your children. Please examine everything they come in contact with.

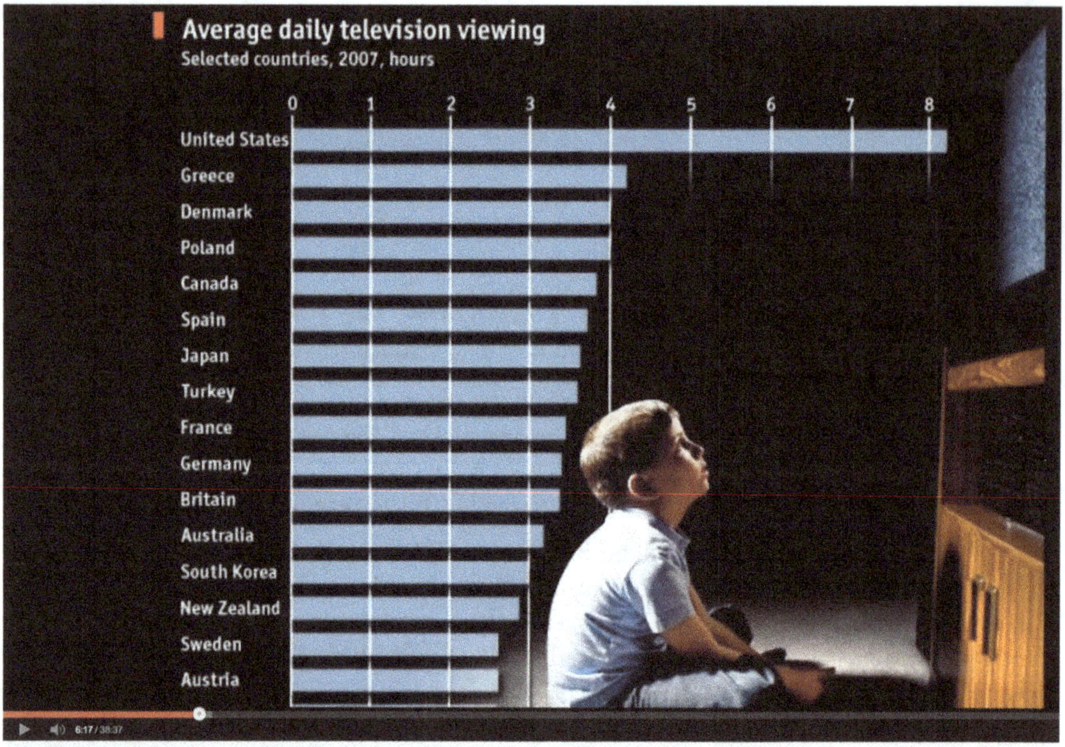

Average daily television viewing
Selected countries, 2007, hours
0 1 2 3 4 5 6 7 8
United States
Greece
Denmark
Poland
Canada
Spain
Japan
Turkey
France
Germany
Britain
Australia
South Korea
New Zealand
Sweden
Austria

Illuminati Hypersexualization of Children Exposed! Disney Pedophilia and Satanic Rolemodels

CHAPTER 10

Is the Gay Movement Another New World Order Social Engineering Project?

The following is a slightly modified article I put together in April 2015, which like Vol. 1 about feminism, is an exposé about the Gay Movement and who is really behind it.

Some of this will be redundant within this book but it acts too as a wrap up summary.

Before any gay people get defensive, your private life is unknown to anyone in the world including me, and is no one's business. But when homosexual behavior becomes a public relations project similar to other *social engineering* projects, to convert everyone else's values, it does become public business. What I will attempt to show is that gay people do not run this public relation's campaign. "Gay" people are being used towards an end that benefits no one except the elite at the top of the pyramid of abuse.

I need to warn anyone who suspects they were molested as a child, that any serious discussion of gay issues is an extremely uncomfortable subject because you probably have buried these childhood memories, which would be a natural thing for anyone to do. This chapter may bring these memories up. It is easier to accept and forget what happened rather than be reminded of an injustice. Here we will be seriously looking at sexual propaganda which will bring up sexual issues, which almost everyone has, whether you were molested or not. If we accept the propaganda that homosexuality is okay, then we can keep our memories buried. If someone like myself points out that lack of taboos is the same thing as immorality, then past actions come under scrutiny and are unburied.

If you were molested in your past, you may not want to read this exposé. If you have experimented with same sex sexuality, and feel ashamed about it, but hide your shame and are "proud," please read this, because you will learn that you were intentionally given a green light about behavior that past traditions outlawed. Traditions exist to avoid confusion.

In other words, the Illuminati banksters erased these taboos to purposely confuse you.

In becoming conscious of this disorienting campaign to confuse you, you will be like military veterans who learned they were tricked into war crimes. Rather than commit suicide, veterans need to become activists for truth to end war crimes. Before getting further confused about your past sexual experiments, *you need to identify who led you into this behavior.* Before the truth sets you free, it may piss you off. You may get angry with me. I have lost friends over this chapter. This is because their loyalty to New World Order gay propaganda is not rational, *by design*, which you will see immediately below. Stick with me. Let's be rational.

* * *

Does the following accurately outline a "gay agenda?" Are the talking points below something the reader has ever spoken? Did you know none of this has anything to do with gay rights? Why did Elton John become famous? Why did Anderson Cooper become famous? Why did Adam Lambert become famous? Is there any connection? Are gay rights activists really patsies for a program they have not examined?

Below are excerpts from a 2007 article by J. Matt Barber, called **"Unmasking the Gay Agenda."** [102]

"... In their manuscript, *After the Ball: How America Will Conquer Its Fear and Hatred of Gays in the 90s* (1989, Doubleday/Bantam), Harvard educated marketing experts Marshall Kirk and Hunter Madsen meticulously laid out the homosexual lobby's blueprint for success in what is widely regarded as the handbook for the "gay" agenda.

[Marshall Kirk was not a marketing expert, his background was neuropsychiatry. Interestingly, gay Dr. William Thetford [103], the co-producer of New Age "A Course in Miracles" which frames Christianity in a way that re-frames the readers values, was a clinical psychologist. Thetford worked for the Manhattan Project, Project Bluebird (MK-Ultra mind control) and the Personality Assessment Program for the CIA during the time "the course" was produced. While Marshall Kirk had a front as a genealogist, Thetford had a front as a rare book expert. Unknown Marshall Kirk was featured in CIA magazines [104] *Newsweek*, *Time* and *The Washington Post* to promote his handbook. The entire *controlled media* and controlled Hollywood manifested the "gay is okay" "transformation" and is doing so today. Marshall Kirk was found dead in his home by two friends. The cause of Kirk's death has never been publicly revealed. All this adds up to likelihood that Marshall Kirk's work was for the CIA, just like Gloria Steinem Feminism and *Ms. Magazine* was a CIA project, [105] (Vol. 1) and just as New Age "A Course in Miracles" was a CIA project.]

"They devised a three-pronged approach that the homosexual lobby [with *controlled media*] has masterfully implemented in subsequent years: Desensitization, Jamming and Conversion. [only first two included here]

"Kirk and Madsen summarized their approach this way:

- Portray gays as victims, not as aggressive challengers.
- Give potential protectors a just cause.
- Make gays look good.
- Make victimizers [The 97% of people's values] look bad.

Desensitization

"Desensitization," wrote Kirk and Madsen, means subjecting the public to a "continuous flood of gay-related advertising, presented in the least offensive fashion possible. If 'straights' can't shut off the shower, they may at least eventually get used to being wet."

If people keep seeing it and seeing it and seeing it, eventually it's not going to be such a strange thing.

– Madonna, The Advocate (gay magazine), May 7, 1991, Page 49

"As previously stated, glamorizing and normalizing homosexual conduct in our public schools [106] is a full time endeavor. But the schools represent only one field of battle in the war over America's body, mind and soul.

"With the aid of a willing [controlled—the author of this article hadn't studied this yet] mainstream media and a like-minded [controlled] Hollywood, societal desensitization has been largely achieved. Blockbusters like Tom Hanks' *Philadelphia*, the late Heath Ledger's *Brokeback Mountain*, and television programs like *Will and Grace* and *Ellen* represent a modern-day fairy tale ...

"The homosexual group, GLAAD, even offers awards to the television networks that most effectively carry the homosexual lobby's water. The more distorted and positive the portrayal of homosexual conduct and the more frequently the networks shows such portrayals; the more likely networks are to win the coveted awards.

"As Kirk and Madsen put it, homosexuals should be portrayed as the "Everyman." ... "In no time," they said, "a skillful and clever media campaign could have the gay community looking like the veritable fairy godmother to Western Civilization." [They were not exaggerating.]

Jamming

"Jamming" refers to the public smearing [hating] of Christians, traditionalists or **anyone else** [emphasis mine] who opposes the "gay" agenda. "Jam homo-hatred (i.e., disagreement with homosexual behaviors) by linking it to Nazi horror," wrote Kirk and Madsen. "Associate **all** who oppose homosexuality with images of 'Klansmen demanding that gays be slaughtered,' 'hysterical backwoods preachers,' 'menacing punks,' and a 'tour of Nazi concentration camps where homosexuals were tortured and gassed.'

"In any campaign to win over the public, gays must be portrayed as victims in need of protection so that straights [97% of population] will be inclined **by reflex** to adopt the role of protector [the "humanitarian intervention" we have seen again and again to justify invasions overseas but used domestically also to trick compassionate people] ... The purpose of victim imagery is to make straights feel very uncomfortable," they suggested.

"But, perhaps Kirk and Madsen's most revealing admission came when they said, "Our effect is achieved *without* reference to facts, logic, or proof." [That is, it is visceral, emotional, irrational programming.]

"And so [hate] words like "homophobe" and "heterosexism" were pulled from thin air, not because they had substance, but because they were effective jamming [irrational] tools. Anyone who holds traditional values relative to human sexuality suddenly became a "homophobe," a "hatemonger," a "bigot."

"Not even churches are safe. [As with the communist take over of Russia and China, the blind irrational dogma replaces anything previously held sacred.]

"Gays can undermine the moral authority of homo-hating [people who understand natural polarity] churches over less fervent adherents by portraying [them] as antiquated backwaters, badly out of step ... with the latest findings [theories] of psychology. Against the atavistic tug of 'Old Time Religion' one must set the mightier pull of science and **public opinion** [emphasis mine] ... Such an 'unholy' alliance has already worked well in America against the churches on such topics as divorce and abortion. ... That alliance can work for gays." [107]

In Kirk and Madsen's writing do we see any respect for 97% of the population, the "straights?" Do we see any respect for religions that are thousands of years old?

The following is from *After the Ball–Why the Homosexual Movement Has Won* [108] June 3, 2004 by Dr. R. Albert Mohler, Jr.

"What about the origin of [the expression] sexual orientation? The success of the homosexual movement can be largely traced to the very idea of "orientation" itself. More precisely, homosexuals advanced their cause by arguing that they were *born* that way. Madsen and Kirk offer this as candid public relations advice ...

'We argue that, for all practical purposes, gays should be considered to have been *born* gay–even though sexual orientation, for most humans, seems to be the product of a complex interaction between innate predispositions and *environmental factors during childhood and early adolescence.*' [Does the reader agree?] Alas, 'To suggest in public that homosexuality might be *chosen* is to open the can of worms labeled 'moral choices and sin' and give the religious intransigents [who believe that some things are wrong] a stick to beat us with. [and warn their children about.] Straights [at least 97% of humanity] must be taught [!] that it is as natural for some persons to be homosexual as it is for others to be heterosexual: wickedness and seduction have nothing to do with it.' " [Therefore no one is choosing, so no one is accountable and there is no such thing as wickedness or wrong or even mistakes.]

"... A quick review of the last 15 years demonstrates the incredible effectiveness of this public relations advice. [carried out by Rothschild Zionist New World order controlled mainstream media] The agenda set out by Kirk and Madsen led to nothing less than social transformation. By portraying themselves as mainstream Americans seeking nothing but liberty and self-fulfillment, homosexuals redefined the moral equation [by ignoring morals]. Issues of right and wrong were isolated [from the realm of choice] as outdated, repressive, and culturally embarrassing. Instead, the assertion of "rights" [to do anything] became the hallmark of the public relations strategy. "

(I cannot cover every thread here in one article but I suggest the reader consider the globalist agenda in the UN Universal Declaration of Human Rights. If there are many cultures, how can there be one code of rights applied to all? In fact the Rothschilds and Rockefellers who created and funded the League of Nations, and the UN, and also funded both sides of World War II, [109] do not want many cultures. They want a One World Government, *their* government, that controls the world under One law, and to get to that goal, taboos have to be consistent, but because taboos define quality by setting perimeters, taboos are better eliminated so that "anything goes." There are then no cultural taboos, only legal taboos, as defined by the state, without conscience or tradition. What better way than to define what the rights are, that every child can expect, despite the culture of the parents? Rights include the right of the child to be exposed to other cultures, that is, globalist propaganda. The state will take away parenting from all parents. This is ongoing now with projects like The Early Childhood Initiative headed by the World Bank which I cover extensively in Volume 3.) [110]

Clinton Fein wrote "The Gay Agenda" [111] in 2005 which the reader can check out. Though she says it is a spoof, this statement was added later, because it is not obviously a spoof. The reader can decide what level of respect she has for people she claims are wrong not to accept her. Interestingly, she writes as if the 1989 well publicized book above never existed.

Does this next woman who is dead serious and not spoofing, represent the "gay agenda?"

> "It's a no-brainer that (homosexuals) should have the right to marry, but I also think equally that it's a no-brainer that the institution of marriage should not exist. ... Fighting for gay marriage generally involves lying about what we are going to do with marriage when we get there — because we lie that the institution of marriage is not going to change, and that is a lie. The institution of marriage is going to change, and it should change. And again, I don't think it should exist. And I don't like taking part in creating fictions about my life. That's sort of not what I had in mind when I came out thirty years ago."
>
> – Masha Gessen [112]

The reader might take stock of how many of the points in this "agenda" have already come about since 1989.

In one sentence I would like to draw a circle that includes the financial banksters (Rothschild, Rockefeller, FED, central banks, IMF, World Bank and World Trade Organization), the political New World Order (UN, NATO, covert ops, Bilderberg Group, Gates Foundation, the Zionists who protect and use Israelis), the Entertainment Industry Mafia-Illuminati, the controlled news media (CIA Project Mockingbird, National Security Agency access to Google, AOL, Skype, Facebook, Apple, Hotmail, Paypal, Yahoo) [113] the international secret society of Freemasons, and ritual sacrifice satanism in which participants are held as blackmail-able puppets. This interconnected, organized and code-of-silence circle has been called "The Cabal." Some also call it the Elite, who work in secret. [114]

How does the gay agenda, as defined above, fit or not fit in with the Cabal? As the reader will see, the real gay agenda is not about gay rights, but is an excuse for a social engineering project by the Cabal for their central goal of total control ... That is, gay rights activists are being used.

EYE OF THE PYRAMID

The person in image to right and below is perhaps the top male gay singer in USA, Adam Lambert. He was runner up in the 2009 *American Idol* talent show. And then what happened? Why didn't he disappear like every other runner up? On the lower part of his shirt is none other than foundational satanist, bi-sexual Aleister Crowley, with pyramid and the all-seeing-eye. Also the checkered shirt is Freemasonry symbolism. Websites that track the entertainment industry, such as Vigilantcitizen.com and youtube.com/user/TheVigilantChristian, [115] have noted the obvious mafia-like control of entertainers and their constant use of freemasonry/satanic symbols. Freemasonry and satanism are two threads combined, as will be explained when we read letter by George Washington. The all-seeing-eye at top of pyramid is a freemasonry symbol that was taken over. It appears on the back of the U.S. dollar bill. The satanist symbols such as 666 and devils horns have their own origin. So on Lambert shirt we see both the Freemasonry all-seeing-eye and checkers, with the satanist Aleister Crowley. As another example, we see Katy Perry, an Illuminati created celebrity, wearing the Freemasonry all-seeing-eye symbol, while her friends wear devil and hell blouses. Pyramid is evil.

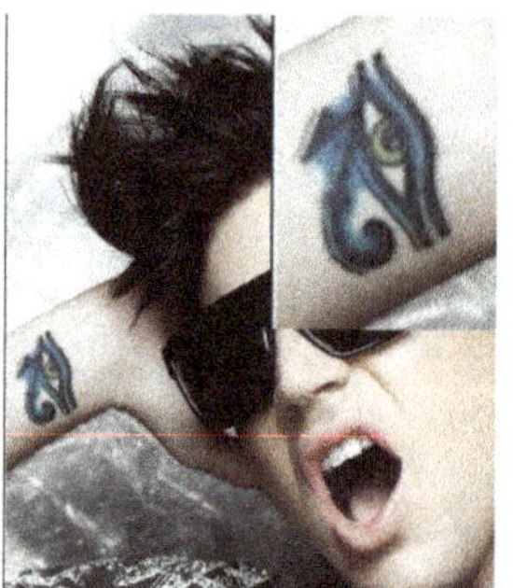

Lambert's shirt has the same symbolism [116] used by other Illuminati puppets in the entertainment industry, and this lets other entertainers know he is controlled/protected. Notice the all-seeing-eye tattoo on his wrist in right image. (Page 170) For agreeing to advertize the branding, he is told he will be rewarded, and he has been. These symbols have nothing to do with a gay agenda in themselves. It only shows that gay entertainers are just as susceptible to control as anyone else. However, the gay community is not protesting this at all. Are they naive? They didn't notice his tattoo or ask what it meant? Are there any gay activists out there who want to endorse satanism?

Perhaps it would be good to back up to see that there really is a hidden conspiracy called the Illuminati. Here is scan of George Washington's letter from 1798 where he discusses the infiltration of the Freema-

once or twice, within the last thirty Years. — I believe notwithstanding that none of the Lodges in this Country are contaminated with the principles ascribed to the Society of the Illuminati. — With respect

I am, Sir,

Your Obt. Hble Servt

G. Washington

sons by Jacobinism/Illuminati. He was not a conspiracy theorist. See youtube on this here. [117] The infiltration became a take over. Now we see Illuminati-Freemasonry symbolism as branding signatures in many many places including the logos for government agencies, corporations, and foundations. Those that understand the symbols understand the membership story they tell.

Placing puppets on stage

Lambert has a satanic orgy music video [118] which tells us something about him and the gay community that doesn't protest his satanism. The screen shot to left of an uncensored video, [119] which was his debut for his first album, included sex slavery and oral sex, which he defends in interviews with lesbian "anything goes" Ellen Degeneres, with puppet Oprah Winfrey, and with David Letterman. This was super promotion. By contrast, Caleb Johnson, 2014 *American Idol* winner got no interviews. Melanie Amaro, 2011 *Bertelsman X-Factor* winner not only got no interviews, but her debut album was shelved. But then, she is a devout Christian, and not someone the satanic music industry can get behind.

In video screen shots above, does Adam Lambert look like a poor gay victim that isn't allowed to love who he wants because of oppressive homophobia? Apparently he is now liberated and can oppress his own slaves. He was brought in as a mentor (tutor) for other *Idol* contestants only one year into his career, a novice, to keep boosting him. No other runner up or winner got this publicity, except perhaps Carrie Underwood, an alleged Christian who nevertheless portrayed herself in a music video as a prostitute in a brothel for her industry masters. The price of fame in today's big label music industry is selling out to perversion or simply being 'out' about it.

Recently Lambert was chosen, out of the blue, to be a judge on *American Idol.* Upping his visibility again brought the "anything goes, no taboos" social engineering to millions of viewers as prescribed in *After the Ball.* The goal is obvious. Young people are being conditioned to feel they can be "free" to experiment with their sexuality, which is almost always just that, an experiment. That is why a person can dress up one night this way, and dress up another way another night, or claim "bi-sexual" orientation, which flies in the face of "being born this way." It is all just an excuse for wanton sex which is considered by the entertainment machine as acceptable "adult," and now family entertainment.

J. Edgar Hoover, the long time FBI director was a cross dresser. Anyone making the assessment these days that such behavior is unstable would be a accused of hate or being "homophobic," as we saw outlined above. Those who use these labels are regurgitating irrational programming, as defined also above.

TV host Ellen Degeneres was also hired to be a judge on *American Idol*, though she knows very little about singing. Her credentials were simply that she was gay. This happened in UK also with a flamboyant gay man being chosen to be a judge on *Bertelsman X-Factor*. This disproportionate representation is example of the *After the Ball* guidance we just read about. Keep remembering please, that gay activists have nothing to do with this.

Lambert was brought on to show as judge, while guitarist Keith Urban, with his Illuminati shirt shown above, was on leave. He was on leave because of the death of the father of his wife, placed actress Nicole Kidman. The father, Antoine Kidman has been named by a survivor as a ritual

"Sir" Tom Jones  | Demi Lovato  | Jennifer Lopez  | Adam Lambert  | Simon Cowell

Will I Am  | Brittany Spears  | Randy Jackson  | Jessie J  | Nicki Minaj

Harry Connick

Pharrell Williams

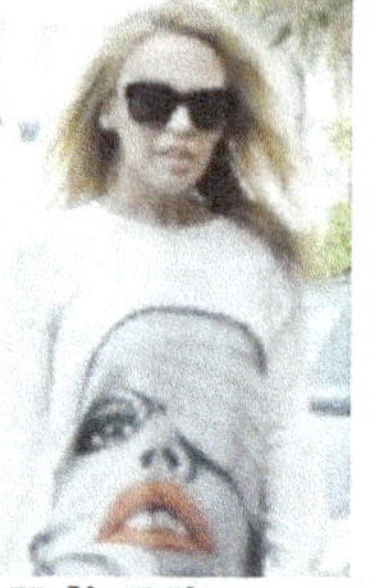

Kylie Minogue

Keith Urban

Usher

pedophile. [120] Keith Urban might protest this, but with his Illuminati slave status, his voice doesn't really carry much of anything. Keith Urban is also shown with the standard all-seeing-eye-at-top-of-pyramid photo shoot in above image of the judges..

American Idol, *The Bertelsman X-Factor* and *The Voice* are Illuminati productions, as shown by the many judges above, who are required to be obedient Illuminati members in order to get "industry love." They are paid well, and receive massive publicity. The Illuminati are using these shows to spread all kinds of messages. Promiscuity, materialism, vanity, patriotism, loyalty to the Queen, zero modesty and "gay is okay" are some of the *social engineering* messages which give the real purpose of why these shows exist. The same is true of the movie industry, which does not exist just to make money, it exists to socially engineer the masses, feed subliminal narratives and memes, and deploy predictive programming [121] which softens us to coming policies or technologies. The talent shows now appear in scores of countries, where on stage standards for contestants are more important than the cultural traditions of their parents. The talent shows are an amazingly powerful way to influence the values of youth and are an important tool in globalization, which basically is the creation of a one world culture under a one world government.

So let's get personal. How does the reader feel about gay people being disproportionately put in the spot light as per the 1989 hand book? If you feel like I do that Lambert is a sick degenerate puppy, how do you feel about him being introduced as an authoritative judge before 20 million viewers? We are supposed to accept anyone's "orientation" or slavery ethics or exhibitionism without blinking, but how do you really feel? How do you feel about Beyoncé Knowles opening the 2014 Grammy awards with her legs spread for millions of children to see as role model? Being a sheeple means we say nothing. We just shut down and go along with the herd. It is considered un-evolved to draw lines in the sand about moral standards against, for example, anal sex. And because we are sheeple we are allowing our children to be taught anal sex in our schools. [122]

Anyone with morals is now labeled as a "moralist." Where did this label come from? This came from the 1989 blueprint outlined above, but the source is much deeper than a couple of authors, who were undoubtedly hired to produce the book. Their ideas were quickly adopted by the controlled media itself without any lobbying by gay activists. The controlled media is hired by the same people who hired the authors. For gay people who are against the New World Order, they need to become suspicious very quickly. You are being used. Interestingly, cabal top players are themselves compromised damaged goods. Henry Kissinger did his PhD thesis on the Illuminati Congress of Vienna. That means he was groomed. That means his rape of women, men, children as reported by survivors [123] with court documents, [124] was probably an out growth of his own abusive programming as a child.

> *The ruling class has the schools and press [and entertainment industry] under its thumb. This enables it to sway the emotions of the masses.*
>
> – Albert Einstein

The purpose of pushing Lambert on *American Idol* was the same purpose as pushing Ellen Degeneres. The purpose is to have young viewers get accustomed to the "gay is okay" idea, but not so that homosexuality will be accepted. Please understand this. The Illuminati could care less about gay people, their rights, women, minorities, the environment, indigenous people or anything altruistic. The gay rights and "gay is okay message" is a trojan horse to bring a wrecking ball into the infrastructure of traditional values. That is the goal, not anything fair for anyone.

Gay people really need to wake up to this fact. Your lack of discretion is being spread to undercut any standard that would resist satanist planning. The Illuminati Cabal want moral breakdown as introduced in Vol.1, and they are using the temptation of sex, as people are encouraged to experiment more by having no boundaries. The zero-taboo role models lead the way.

The Cabal's gay agenda wants "transformation" of the whole. This is the big point to come to grips with. The moral standards, taboos, and guidance of the vast majority are being replaced with lack of moral fiber. This is so everyone can become weak powerless slaves under Big Brother. Does it matter if you are a gay or straight slave?

On the micro level, with our family members and neighborhoods, the fruit of this program certainly is not clear strong young people with noble aspirations. The elite who hold the strings of power want serial relationships that are based on lust, not love. They want broken homes. They want more kids without dads. The agenda of spreading "romance" and "night life" has been going on all our lives. The reader might recall the song "Strangers in the Night" by Frank Sinatra which celebrated sports sex. [125] Sinatra was given this song by those who controlled his material. And what was the message? Was it different than traditional chastity? You haven't heard that word in a while have you?

So I hope the reader now has enough proof that the music industry is indeed controlled by a group that uses satanic symbols, and that you have a suspicion, at least, that unknown gay Adam Lambert and knows-nothing-about-singing Lesbian Ellen Degeneres were put on national TV by the Cabal for *social engineering* reasons. Gay activists had nothing to do with this.

NORMAL OR RARE?

Some say that homosexuality is normal. What they mean really is there is some incidence of it. So what? That incidence in natural indigenous societies of very feminine men who have sex with straight men is so rare that cross-incarnations are not seen as "equal," they are seen as exotic anomalies. Yes, there is a rare incidence of many kinds of behavior, but that doesn't mean all those behaviors are equal. There might be gradations of sexual energy, but world wide, there are men's bathrooms and women's bathrooms, not gradations. Male and female polarity is quite clear for 97% of people. Homosexuality is a very much a minority expression, and not essential to the species. Straight sex creates the next generation while same sex doesn't. So no one should be concerned with homosexuality per se because it is not sustainable. What we need to be worried about is the blurring of all moral standards.

The idea that homosexuality is genetic is ridiculous, when the percentage of people who are "gay" is going up as fast as the *social engineering*. The homosexual phenomenon is a promoted fad, not a genetic orientation. I am saying that if you are "gay," it is most likely due to designed influence that encouraged experimentation. The design was from an evil group. If your surrounding culture had reinforced strictly that sexual experimentation is a mistake and that some things are taboo (WRONG), you wouldn't have tasted the kool aid.

If there are no taboos, what we get is satanic heaven called "anything goes" and then there is no definition of sin or wrong. Evil then has no resistance. That is the goal of the Illuminati, because no resistance means total control.

"The tour's goal is to break useless taboos."

-CIA Madonna, on her 1990 Blond Ambition World Tour

Her statement wasn't hers as she didn't choreograph or arrange the tour, so she is just repeating the value system of the Cabal's agenda. Madonna is a CIA mind controlled puppet who was used in porn films, some say snuff films, when she was a teen. Her words are the opposite of how morals function, as discussed in Vol. 1. Taboos are totally useful! They make a culture unique. Every unique culture has unique taboos. Taboos guide behavior, which is what tradition is all about. The goal of the satanist Illuminati has been to destroy guidance. And now there is a part within many people that is confused. This is what the globalist control freaks wanted. They want confused people. Taboos guide us and actually protect us, and breaking taboos often leads to random confusion and suffering. Are all taboos fair? Hold on, are you a Globalist that is going to judge every other culture with your own rules?

ELTON JOHN AND THE BOY SCOUTS

Elton John has been used to push an Illuminati gay agenda. (Not an agenda by gay activists.) In fact, in my opinion, the only reason we know of Elton John, like every other celebrity, like tattoo Adam Lambert, is that he was placed, framed and given fame. In Elton John's case the reason was to push the "lust, not love" and the "anything is okay" idea upon us all. Madonna was the same kind of agent, as are many of the other role models [126] that the Music Industry rolls out. Elton John was used for this purpose on the children's Muppets Show in 1977, in order to undercut ancient moral guidance for children. His presence on the Muppets would have been a slap in the face for most parents if they had been watching, which they probably hadn't. Again, if you are gay, it is probably because of this kind of social engineering which influenced you. If you had never had any influence like this, and had a tradition with guidance, you probably would have followed the guidance. (Caveat— some feel the rise in gay "orientation" is also due to the amount of estrogen in our drinking water ...) [127]

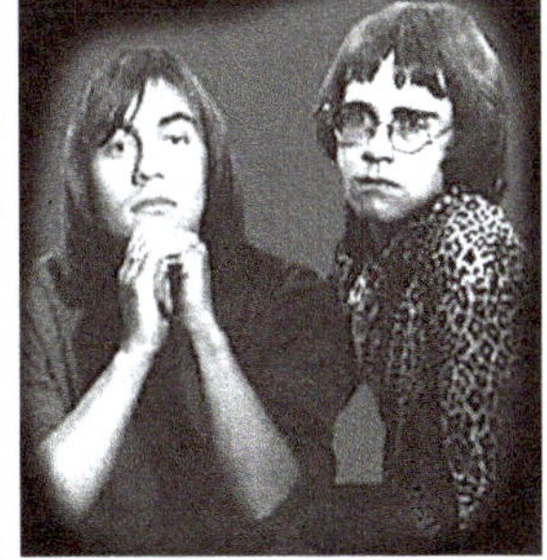

To right, early photo of Elton John wearing Illuminati leopard skin shirt, used for kitten beta programming [128] for women. (Vol. 1 and 3) This indicates Elton John is another mind programmed stooge, like Marilyn Monroe, [129] Madonna, Beyoncé, etc. The programming comes out of Nazi MK-Ultra programming mentioned above with "Course in Miracles" William Thetford. My feeling is that Bernie Taupin, also in image, was and is Elton John's handler.

"Bernie Taupin, [now net worth $300 million] who has lived with Elton John and written most of his lyrics [for over 38 years] stated that Elton John's "home is laden with trinkets *and books* relating to Satanism and witchcraft" (U.S., July 22, 1980, p. 42) ... Taupin admits that he decorates his walls with "satanic art" and has further declared, "the occult fascinates me" (People, June 23, 1980). [In 1991, Bernie Taupin self-published a book of poems called *The Devil at High Noon*]

"Elton John has admitted that he is deceiving his fans, "Its all a big con," and adds, "But as long as the public laps it up, I'm quite happy to go on giving it to them." (Rolling Stone, July 15, 1976, p. 30)

"... Elton John has stated, "In most artists there's a self destructive streak. Drugs, sex and doomed liaisons were my form of destruction."

On his sexual past—"I would walk into a club and see someone I hadn't even met and I would already have them on the conveyor belt," declared John. "They'd come out with a Versace shirt and a Cartier watch at the other end."

"... Elton John has sung about suicide, lesbianism (All the Girls Love Alice), glorified prostitution (Sweet Painted Lady), and sniffing glue (B*tch is Back)." [But he didn't write the lyrics. Who did, and why? I don't believe it was Taupin alone.] [130]

In 1999, Elton John caused outrage by performing at a gay Stonewall charity concert with dancers dressed as boy scouts that then stripped. The song was called "It's a Sin" by the Pet Shop Boys. The song basically blames the church for blaming. Who came up with the boy scout costumes? Stonewall spokeswoman said "the routine was Elton John's contribution" to the event. I ask, who was in charge? Regardless, no one at the rehearsal batted an eyelash about dancers dressed as children stripping to their shorts, getting on their knees and grabbing their groins. This is example of the same old Illuminati theme of "transformation," also called "good gone bad," but extended to society in general, where underage boy scouts are portrayed as players in loveless lust-centered homosexual activity.

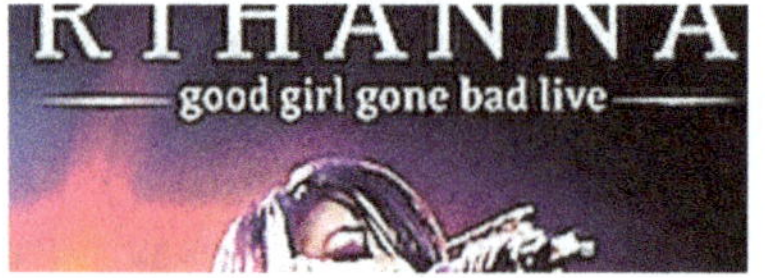

John Fogg, a spokesman for the Scout Association, said at the time:

> "We think it is pretty deplorable and in bad taste in terms of denigrating our uniform and what it stands for. We are disappointed that someone of Sir Elton's standing should involve himself in something of such poor taste. It linked homosexuality with pedophilia. If Stonewall [charity] are completely for the rights of homosexual people, they have not done themselves any favors."

The scout spokesman above said it correctly, "If." Excellent, because in fact Stonewall could care less about gay rights. Stonewall is a front.

Wikipedia—"Stonewall is a lesbian, gay, bisexual and transgender rights charity in the United Kingdom. Now the largest gay equality organization in Europe, it was formed in 1989."

Somebody came up with this performance idea, then Elton John performed it, and an alleged gay rights group didn't question it. Who is accountable here? The "gay is okay" message got mixed in with an abusive satanic "use children" message.

> "It does not surprise me that an unrepentant homosexual [Elton John], who is legally married to another man, would refer to Christians as "Jesus freaks." The underlying power to all occult practices, is Satanism, i.e., the worship of Satan (or Lucifer) in opposition to the worship of God [connection]. It is the worship of Satan [disconnection] which has been the driving force behind the handful of men who have perpetuated the Illuminati conspiracy. Through its various incarnations, the spread of the occult has enabled the Illuminati to create a social climate that has welcomed the advent of the New World Order, and the one-world government that accompanies it."
>
> – David J. Stewart [131]

Religions can argue about the meaning of God, but few religions other than satanism, deny that their is such a thing as sin. What is sin for Elton John? Deceiving his fans? Sports sex? Trading for sex with designer clothes and watches? Attacking boys organizations? Suggesting pedophilia is acceptable? He seems to be confessing occasionally, but where is the reformation? What is sin? Does he use the word? All other religions do, except satanism which is an anti-religion.

Fans of Elton John need to step back for a moment. If Elton John didn't write the songs, why is he so promoted/honored? Why didn't Bernie Taupin, his writer, get knighted? I believe Elton John is a programmed puppet who plays a role for the social engineers. His job is to influence youth.

We see him rolled out for the 2012 Superbowl commercial by Pepsi with naive Christian Melanie Amaro, mentioned above, singing song "Respect" to him. Get it? And notice the Freemasonry checkered floor. (Page 199) This is cutting edge social engineering impacting millions and millions of sports fans, blurring the lines of sexual polarity and moral boundaries. Look how much money was spent, and Pepsi is hardly mentioned in the commercial.

Besides knighting Elton John, the queen has knighted war criminals Colin Powell and Norman Schwarzkopf. She even knighted cross dresser and serial killer J. Edgar Hoover. The queen regularly honors people of questionable character such as Lord Justice Fulford, founder of the Paedophile Information Exchange [132] or singer Kylie Minogue, below.

The Queen and the All-Seeing-Eye Illuminati love "no-taboos anything-goes" Kylie

The queen also knighted Zionist Rudolf Guiliani, the former Mayor of New York City, who was insider on the planned 9/11 attack and helped cover up the real perpetuators, by shipping the steel of the buildings overseas before architects and engineers could investigate why the first steel building in history collapsed the way it did.

Who Told Giuliani the WTC was Going to Collapse on 9/11?

In the following 9/11 ABC News live interview Giuliani states he was warned of the collapses:

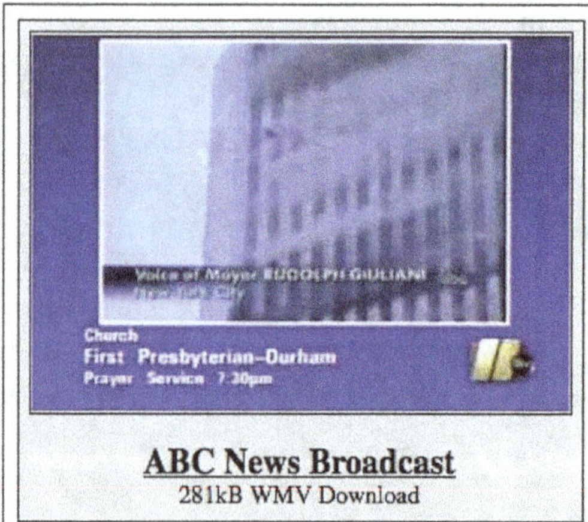

"I went down to the scene and we set up headquarters at 75 Barkley Street, which was right there with the Police Commissioner, the Fire Commissioner, the Head of Emergency Management, and we were operating out of there when we were told that the World Trade Center was going to collapse. And it did collapse before we could actually get out of the building, so we were trapped in the building for 10, 15 minutes, and finally found an exit and got out, walked north, and took a lot of people with us."

Giuliani has subsequently denied making the above comment proving that he has no qualms about lying about an inconvenient truth.

No steel framed building had collapsed through fire prior to 9/11, so how was it known that the World Trade Center was going to collapse? There was no factual or historical basis for this prediction.

When was Giuliani warned?

Below, cross-dressing, 9/11 coverup "Hero," Roth-efeller Zionist, lying "Sir" Rudolf Guiliani.

Guiliani is another *cutout* exactly like Kylie and Elton John. "Obey and we will promote you."

> "Gay rights awareness charity Stonewall will be celebrating today, as their chair, David Issac, has been announced as a recipient of the CBE in the Queen's birthday honors list. Issac becomes a Commander of the Order of the British Empire in recognition of many years of voluntary service."

The Queen is a Bilderberger [133] and has long personal history of pedophilia (see *Zion King* video online), the British have been controlled by the Rothschild banksters for centuries (Chapter 2), and the physical crown itself bears a Maltese Cross used by the Illuminati (Chapter 8), which has nothing to do with Christianity. Being knighted by the queen is not an honor, it is a disgrace if one has taboos against pedophilia and war criminals. This same queen honors Stonewall charity, but it gets worse. Stonewall was always under the Cabal because the Cabal created it.

"Stonewall was established in 1989 by influential Fabians ... what is effectively a branch of the Freemasons ... Fabian members include Jack Straw, Stephen Twigg, Peter Mandleson, the current Prime Minister Gordon Brown [a pedophile, photo to left], and Tony Blair [Pedophile cover up]. [134]

'Stonewall's Ben Summerskill has used his position as Chief Executive of Stonewall to speak at a number of Fabian events [top/down social engineering] all over the world [globalist—one value system for all cultures], and his grandmother, a notable feminist, the late Baroness Summerskill was a notable member of this elite group." [135]

"In 1875 an intriguing organization called the Theosophical Society was founded at New York by Madame Helena Petrovna Blavatsky, editor of a magazine called *Lucifer.* It is currently said by her followers that Madame Blavatsky wanted her Society to be "unconcerned about politics: hostile to the insane dreams of Socialism and Communism, which it abhors...." Nevertheless, upon her death in 1891, the mantle of the Theosophical Society was inherited by Annie Besant, a prolific writer and occultist who was also a member of another cult founded in England in 1884. This powerful organization was called the Fabian Socialist Society. Its avowed goal was the same as that of the Order of the Illuminati: complete control of the world. Madame Besant founded the Fabian Parliamentary League." [136]

Thus we learn that the boy scout performance was not a problem for Stonewall with it's Luciferian Fabian roots. Rather, Stonewall is an arm of the no-taboos agenda. Once again, heads up for gay activists who respect Stonewall. You are being used, and the scout spokesman was spot on.

The pedophilia of Blair and Brown who are New World Order, is connected with Fabians who founded Stonewall, is connected with anti-traditional stance of Theosophy and Satanism. Please re-read page.

Clear lines?

Is there a clear distinction between gay activism and the Cabal? Obviously not. The complete media adoption of *After The Ball* blueprint and the Luciferian Fabian conception of Stonewall prove that. The gay agenda is inextricable connected, initiated, and nurtured by the perverse controllers who truly are involved with satanism.

Here we see the memorial for Princess Diana. She was murdered [137] and the memorial, with Illuminati flame, tells us who did it. Note the satanic pentagon in photo. Elton John helped cover up the murder by singing "Candle in the Wind," which was originally a song to help cover up the fact that natural brunette Marilyn Monroe was a mind controlled sex slave. [138] "Candle in Wind" refers to this Illuminati flame. Now both Monroe and Diana are memorialized as reminders of Illuminati control and terror for those in the club. Please consider how much this memorial cost and what the symbols say. On JFK memorial is an actual flame. That was another signature of who killed him. We will return to Olympic flame, Statue of Liberty, and Columbia pictures logo in Volume 3. For now, speed ahead by seeing this. [139] CIA agent Gloria Steinem did the same with a book about the myth, Marilyn Monroe, mentioned in Vol. 1, "The Trailer."

The same Illuminati that created Stonewall controls the Movie Industry and the actors. As everyone should know by now, when we say the entertainment industry is controlled by the Illuminati, we are also saying it is controlled by sexual perverts.

'The British entertainment industry is crawling with pedophiles, [140] says Ben Fellows, a former child actor who worked in theatre productions and TV. 'I ran a gauntlet of pedophiles—both at the BBC and at other television production companies, and also in theaters, as well as on commercial photo shoots.' During productions, staff would warn him to stay away from certain actors who were known to be pedophiles. He was in danger when he ran into them backstage. He gives an example: 'I was chased around the dressing room by a naked actor who had invited me into his dressing room at the Theatre Royal in Drury Lane—and this actor was *extremely famous*. I was advised by the director of the musical that I was not to complain, or tell anyone of this incident. I was thirteen years old ... so I didn't.' His testimony is full of shocking detail. On one occasion he was seduced by a female BBC producer who regularly had sex with teenage boys. On another he was molested by cabinet minister Ken Clarke MP, who gave him alcohol and groped his penis through his trousers. Ben Fellows says he knows child actors who committed suicide because of the abuse they suffered. However, abuse *by homosexuals* somehow doesn't come under 'bullying.'" [Its legal!] [141]

How many gay activist groups are actively denouncing pedophilia and helping to bring down the Illuminati?

Fans of Elton John or Adam Lambert need to incorporate the information above and re-access your admiration. Gay people need to stop defending anything that is gay just because it is their tribe, because supporting *anything* is very close to the satanic theme "anything goes," or as Aleister Crowley on Adam Lambert's shirt said it, "Do what thou wilt." No taboos.

Aleister Crowley was bisexual, and some say a pedophile. He contracted syphilis. His meglomania [142] produced a treatise in *disconnecting vanity*. The ego, or vanity, loves philosophies that place one's self on high. Dropping self-importance never occurred to Crowley. He wanted to drop inhibition.

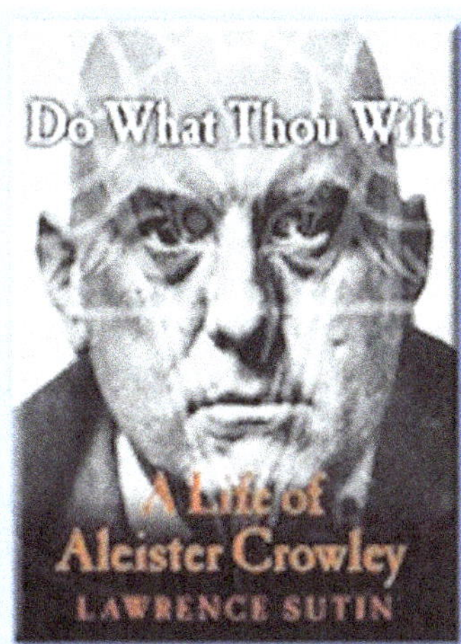

Jay-Z, [143] husband and some say handler [144] of singer Beyoncé [145], is another card carrying satanist.

Like the book *After the Ball* quoted above, Crowley had no respect for Christianity. He wrote "With the cross of Jesus trampled on the floor … Christians' necks our footstool, Heaven itself Our throne." He wanted to replace grace with "will." He hated being restrained by conscience, and wanted a virtue-free zone where he could do anything he wanted. His capacity for sin combined with his intellect won respect of the Jacobinist Freemasons who promoted him quickly to their 33rd degree. Anyway, the present Music industry has various threads and one of them is the immoral thinking of Aleister Crowley, seen on Adam Lambert's shirt above.

There must be moral lines or else virtue gets buried in sleaze and dysfunction and the only winner is Big Brother who will come to save the dysfunctional day with a police state. That dear reader, is definitely planned if you hadn't noticed. Please study "Jade Helm" on internet.

Did Elton John respect the innocence of young people in the boy scout performance shown to right? Where are his lines of morality? Did Stonewall charity respect the innocence of children? Where is their line? What did this performance respect?

I ask Gay Rights proponents, why didn't you also protest this? I believe it is because the "gay movement" has a disrespect for tradition built into it. "Free" experimentation hates moral guidelines. This exactly is why the gay agenda is called immoral. It doesn't respect taboos, guidelines, morals. Not respecting morals is immoral. Period. And this is why gay people are being used by the Illuminati as a wrecking ball, because gay people can be counted upon to have no taboos. Again, the Illuminati gay agenda is to use gay people for the agenda of total control, NOT anyone's rights.

Before the reader comes down on me for daring to say that sex does indeed need moral parameters, please examine the mentality and the satanic background of Elton John.

News anchor Anderson Cooper does not represent gay people. The gay community honored him because he was gay, and forgot he is heir to Vanderbilt 1% wealth, was member of a secret society at Yale, attended CIA training courses for two summers, and now continually brings us watered down news that hides the real culprits behind war and domestic problems. The truly honest people in the Gay community, not the bought off leaders of the gay movement, need to take sides ... to be gay sheeple or to be whistle blowers against controlled media and satanic celebrities.

> "Previous recipients [before Cooper] of the [GLAAD] Vito Russo Award, presented to an openly lesbian, gay, bisexual or transgender media professional who has made a significant difference in promoting equality, include Ricky Martin, Rosie O'Donnell, **Elton John** and Nathan Lane." [146]

Does anyone want to be equal with the someone like Anderson Cooper who works for and represents the indecent policies of the New World Order? How about being equal with "Sir" Elton John, a mind programmed satanist puppet?

Until we see gay activists denouncing Elton John's pedophile messages, Adam Lambert's satanic attire, and the white washing of American crimes by people like gay newscaster Anderson Cooper, the gay community is not doing its job in confronting the New World Order controllers. Rather than denouncing "homophobes," gay activists should denounce poster boy gay people who are part of globalist organized crime.

What does moral parameters mean? It means there must be a clear line beyond which the behavior is deemed WRONG. That is why taboos are useful. Whether we call ourselves gay or straight, we need to have an idea of what is wrong. Sex cannot be free. Sex must be wise. Gay people who don't have the word decadent in their vocabulary need to re-think. Gay people need to have a word for perversity also. Are bondage toys okay in sex shops? Is bathhouse sports sex okay? It doesn't matter how many condoms you use, is it morally safe? Where is the line that defines WRONG besides attacking others as "homophobes?"

When we consider that we are all immersed in intentional *social engineering* campaigns from cartoons, to super bowls half time shows, to the sea of "pushing the envelope" advertising, to most Hollywood movies, to new laws, to song lyrics, can we really say that "consensual sex" between people, straight or gay, is the exercise of free *informed* choice?

The key words in the children's song "Let it Go" from movie *Frozen* (2014) are ... "No right, no wrong, no rules for me. I'm free." (The song "Let it Go" is covered in Volume 3.)

(As a side on that, the DVD *Frozen* was distributed by retailer Costco. Costco, as of this writing, is still distributing the pro serial-killer DVD *American Sniper*, and Zionist Jolie's *Malificient*. For those who aren't aware of it, the true story of Chris Kyle [147] is very different than the movie. Costco is controlled by William H. Gates, who has been on the board of Costco since 2003. He apparently isn't busy enough directing the Bill and Melinda Gates Foundation [148] which is involved with sterilizing young women overseas, geo-engineering, GMO foods, and other despicable globalist projects reviewed in Chapter 6. Costco *is* controlled by the top corrupt elite. The lyrics "No right, no wrong, no rules for me" are why the DVD *Frozen* was carried by William Gates Sr. controlled Costco.)

Children who grow up with this kind of confused amoral programming are *not* later excising free choice with sex. Rather, they, all of us, are just experimenting with implanted images and values coming from the media and internet porn, and getting addicted to sexual habits like sports sex instead of holding to virtue and waiting for a true partner. I fell to this decadent sex-first culture 50 years ago. Isn't it obvious that what we think is normal has been planted in us, and that we are victims of *social engineering*. (See Tavistock Institute [149])

"In the wake of the Supreme Court's historic rulings last week, we were able to blow the lid off Hollywood's Gay Marriage Conspiracy, wherein American writers, producers and television executives spent years manipulating audiences and public officials through mainstream entertainment in pursuit of their marriage equality agenda. And it worked!" [150]

and from India

"Let us not forget that 60% of India's population is under the age of 25. The decriminalization of homosexuality is going to **impact them** as they come of age, develop their increasingly individualistic identities and make **choices** about how they wish to live." [151]

At least this pro-gay India opinion, printed in New World Order *Forbes Magazine* was honest; homosexuality is simply a choice, a whim, a fad for the vast majority of people into same-sex experimentation and it is being steered through programs and laws that "impact."

I ask, why is there more bi-sexual experimentation now than before? What changed?

Can we ignore the Illuminati programs to engineer our values and goals and behavior?

[VIDEO] Forbes: The Illuminati Delusion - YouTube
www.youtube.com/watch?v=uHeVVuNWmlo
By Mark Dice · 5 min · 26,757 views · Added Jul 30, 2013
Forbes magazine says if you believe the **Illuminati** or the Bilderberg Group influences the world, you are "delusional." Subscribe to http://**www.YouTube.com** ...

Homosexuality in The Jewish State - Texe Marrs
TheRapeOfJustice

Tel Aviv, in Rothschild Israel, is now the "gay capitol" of world, meaning the place to go for loveless non-committed sports sex. No taboos, no definition of morals. As we have seen evidence of, the gay agenda comes directly from the satanist Illuminati, who are also the banksters behind UN and the New World Order. 40% of Israeli soldiers say they were raped by other men in uniform according to youtube to left. There is a direct correlation between taboo-less sex and the war crimes of Israel. There is no basis of morality in most of Israel now. Rather, "Me first" tribalism and dominant culture vanity is the creed of that subsidized by American tax payers nation.

"Two years later [1969] there was a riot at Stonewall Tavern by the homosexuals. The Jews found a new avant-garde in the homosexual movement. The man responsible for gay marriage in NYC is [non-orthodox] Rabbi David Saperstein. His wife was formally the head of the NPR newsroom. National Public Radio. This is a powerful force, and he basically claims responsibility and says, if it wasn't for our group of Rabbi's this would have never passed. So what you see is this constant Jewish subversive activity and now the homosexual has succeeded the Negro as the avant-garde revolutionary movement in the United States."

– E. Michael Jones [152] (Saperstein is a Zionist into fake global warming, named in 2014 by Obama as a "Religious Ambassador.")

Not all Jews are lost. Excerpt from "Gay Rights or Gay Wrongs?" By Rabbi David Eidensohn

"...The Gay Lobby is not just about homosexuality; it is about those who want *to tear apart the traditional, biblical, family world.* The billion-dollar entertainment industry sees biblical people as a threat to their profits. It makes money from teaching children *unrestricted sex*, and making music about killing. [Eidensohn was not aware that Zionists run the industry.]

"The college professors who preach in front of young people, believe that only they can open the door to knowledge and wisdom. They have a vested interest in teaching children that tradition is bad, that parents are morons, and that only those who believe that "autoeroticism is spirituality" [satanism] can teach truth as it really is. This attitude permeates the NEA and the teachers' unions at all levels.

"I want my children to grow up wholesome, and to follow my inspiration. The Gay Lobby would tear my children away from me, and indeed, government is now moving inexorably toward substitute parents. A textbook for elementary school has a story about an old fool and a young smart person. The teacher's manual explained that this teaches children that their parents are not wise, only young people with new ideas are.

"I oppose the Gay Lobby because both of us will not be able to thrive in the same society, and I do not intend to get off of the world before my time, nor do I intend to let my children come into a world to suffer, and ask, "Daddy, why didn't you try to stop them?"

If Time magazine pushes it, it is Illuminati. This is the After the Ball blueprint of exposing us endlessly to aberrance to create the "anything goes" new normal. But gay lobbyists didn't create this. Time magazine IS the New World Order that is pushing this.

The orthodox Jew minority in Israel do not approve of same sex relations nor do they approve of war crimes.

Orthodox Jewish Rabbis protest Gay Marriage, NYC

www.youtube.com/watch?v=5wk21I9nCro

On July 24, the first day on which same-sex marriages were legally performed in New York, representatives of Orthodox Jewish communities throughout New …

Riots from ultra-orthodox Jews may halt gay march in Jerusleum …

www.theguardian.com

Ultra-Orthodox Jews Protest Israeli Military Draft Bill

time.com/11492/ultra-orthodox-haredi-jews-protest-military

Hundreds of thousands of ultra-Orthodox Jews protested in Jerusalem Sunday against a law that would require them to serve in the military and end a generations-long …

Orthodox Jews protest 'Zionist Israel' in Brussels …

www.worldbulletin.net/?aType=haber&ArticleID=112269

Thousands of Orthodox Jews coming from different countries of Europe protested 'Zionist Israel' in front of EU institutions in Brussels.

What did the Orthodox Jews mean by "Zionist Israel?" Becoming symbol literate: Above, the Israeli Supreme Court building in Jerusalem with pyramid and all-seeing-eye on roof, built by Dorothy Rothschild. To right, in this 2010, two minute Zionist propaganda video "Israel: Defying the Odds" we can notice it was produced by the Illuminati. Yellow keyhole with eye (Page 211), purple mascot with one eye (Page 229) yellow pyramid, all "coincidentally" at same moment in video. The video is a list of shameful, prideful Zionist lies. [153]

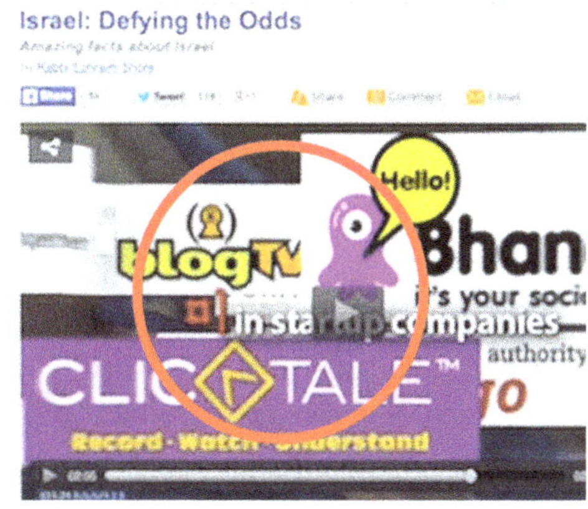

Look at the evidence, don't just believe. You will see these symbols everywhere once you develop a questioning mind and are alert. Remember, asking questions disables how we have been programmed.

The 34th Anniversary of Israel's "independence" was celebrated in 1982 with minted coin on left honoring Baron Edmond de Rothschild's funding of immigrants in 1882.

It says "Centenary of his first settlement activities in Eretz Israel." "Eretz" means much of the Mideast, as shown on another Israeli coin. This is why 7 countries were listed for destruction in 2001 by U.S. and NATO as disclosed by Gen. Wesley Clark. [154]

The connection between Rothschilds and war crimes is immediate. End the Roth-efeller Satanic Illuminati on Earth and an era of peace and restoration is possible.

ISRAELI GEARS

by Jeffrey St. Clair, editor Counterpunch.org, May 22, 2015, excerpt ...

"It started as a rather melancholy Friday afternoon in the west bank. Nothing unusual. Just another funeral for a promising young man who died much too young. Under the implacable shadow of the Wall and in the rifle sights of Israeli soldiers, more than 200 mourners walked down the cobbled street toward the old cemetery in the village of Beit Ummar. Some shouted angrily at the soldiers, condemning Israel for yet another senseless death.

"The funeral was for a college student, Jafaar Awad, who slipped into a coma and died only two months after being released from an Israeli prison, where his serious illness had festered untreated for months. Awad was only 22 when he died, as have so many other Palestinian prisoners, from medical neglect at the hands of Israeli jailers.

"As his family huddled around his grave, the IDF launched a dozen tear gas canisters toward the mourners, scattering the stunned grouping. Then automatic weapons fire strafed the crowd, bullets hitting more than a dozen people, including Jafaar's cousin Ziad Awad. Ziad was struck in the back, the bullet piercing his spine. He was rushed to the Al Ahli Hospital in Hebron, where he died of his wounds. Ziad was only 28.

"A few hours after Ziad's murder at the hands of Israeli snipers, the IDF issued a terse statement saying that Israeli soldiers fired on the crowd of mourners after people where seen throwing stones.

"I'm surprised the IDF even felt compelled to issue a justification for a kind of killing that has become routine: kids were throwing stones, skipping rocks, jumping rope, blowing bubbles, tossing dirt on an open grave. They had no option but to shoot.

"The Palestinians have no redress for these daily acts of butchery: no court to go to judge the legitimacy of shootings, no venue to seek compensation for medical bills, pain and suffering or lost work days, no avenue to find a measure of justice for the slain. How much loss, misery and humiliation are one people expected to endure?

"The Israeli state has never been more violent, the blood toll of Palestinian civilians never so high.

"In 2014, the Israeli military and security forces killed more than 2,300 Palestinians and wounded another 17,000.

"That's the worst carnage since 1967, when the occupation of the West Bank and Gaza intensified in the wake of the Six Day War. [When the *USS Liberty* suffered a false flag attack by Rothefeller controlled President Johnson.] During the height of the last Israeli rampage in Gaza last summer, more than 500,000 Palestinians were displaced from their homes. And, according to a recent UN Report titled Fractured Lives, more than 100,000 of them remain homeless. Detentions of Palestinians inside Israeli prisons are also on the rise. As of the end of February of this year, more than 6,600 Palestinians were being held in Israeli prisons and IDF detention centers, the most in five years. So the gears of the killing machine grind on with impunity, each slaughter only serving to embolden more killing.

"Who will stop them? Certainly not the Israeli state's principle financial investor. For the most vigorous Israeli Defense Force, unblinking in its vigilance, unfaltering in its loyalty, is the [Rothefeller bought off] U.S. Congress. There is a savage synchronicity to an alliance between one nation that drone strikes weddings [U.S. murders in Pakistan] and another that shoots ups funerals.

"Each year U.S. Congress drops a cool $3 billion on Israel. Even in chambers ruled by fiscal tightwads, the only real debate is whether this lavish dispensation, which accounts for more than half of all U.S. military aid worldwide, is enough to satiate Israel's thirst [Rothschild Zionist New World Order experimentation] for new weaponry. Even as Israel repeatedly sabotages U.S. policy across the region, [CIA] Obama has described the U.S. aid package as "sacrosanct."' ...

– Jeffrey St. Clair

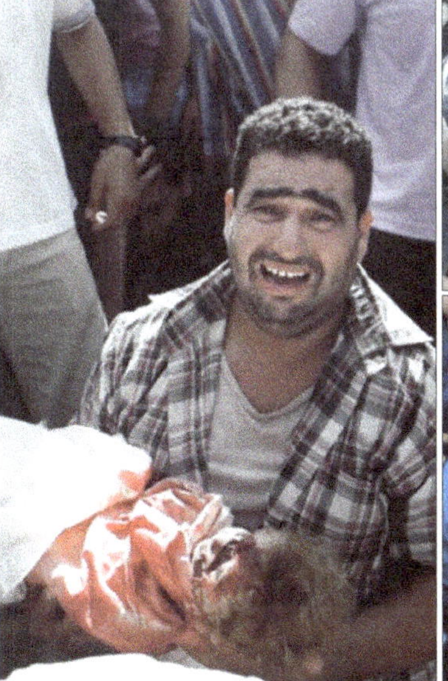

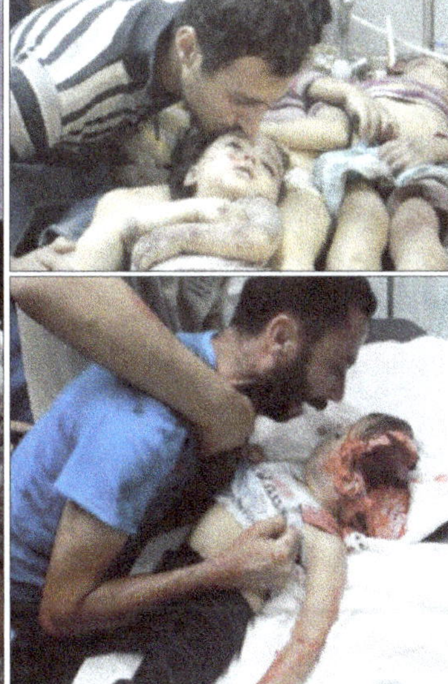

A young bank teller on Maui asked me, "What does War Crimes mean?"

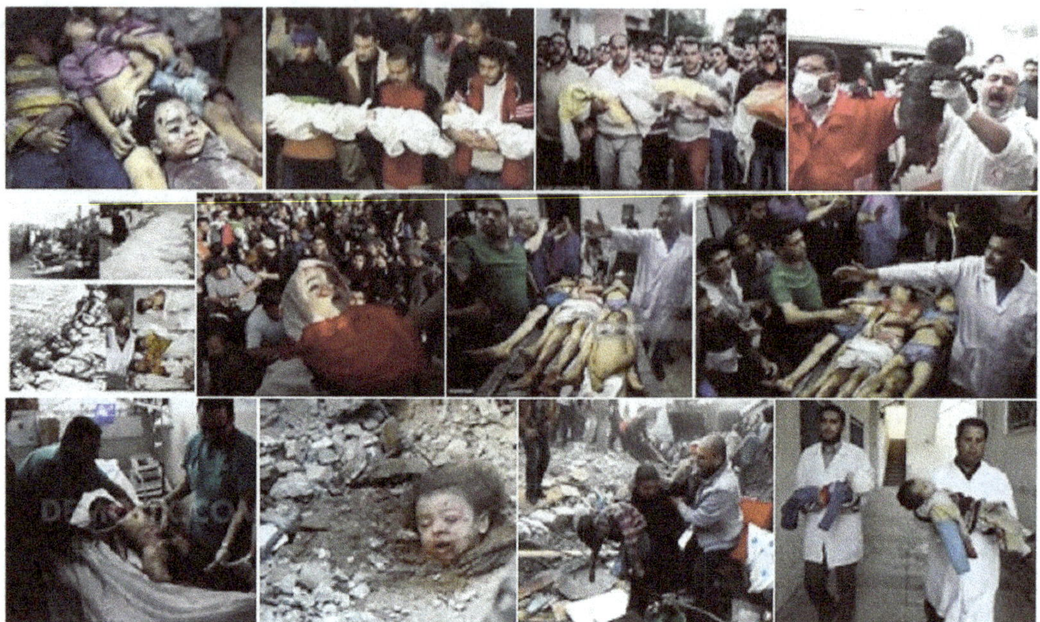

See more images of **palestinian dead children**

News about **Palestinian Dead Children Image**

bing.com/news

Israel Forgives Itself For **Death** of Four **Palestinian Children**

Gawker · 7 days ago

Ahed Atef Bakr and Zakariya Ahed Bakr were ten years old, and Ismail Mahmoud Bakr was nine years old. They were cousins. Photo credit: AP **Images**. ...

Pro-**Palestinians** Host Graphic anti-Israel Demonstration in Amsterdam

Shalom Life · 11 days ago

Local visitors and tourists in Amsterdam's Dam Square were welcomed over the weekend by disturbing **images** of the ...

Israeli military kills **Palestinian** kids, United Nations whitewashes it

Salon · 4 days ago

The report methodically details the devastating impact Israel's prolonged military occupation had on **Palestinian** ...

Hollywood Studios Blacklist Penelope Cruz over Gaza Letter Accusing Israel of 'Genocide'

Excerpt—By Fiona Keating, August 9, 2014, *International Business Times*

"Actress Penelope Cruz and her husband Javier Bardem have roused the fury of Hollywood [Zionist Illuminati] producers (Page 234), with pledges made to snub the Spanish couple. Oscar-winner Bardem and Cruz signed an open letter speaking against "the genocide perpetrated by the Israeli occupation army."

"The letter accused Israel of "advancing on Palestinian territories instead of withdrawing to the 1967 borders.

"'Gaza is living through horror … while the international community does nothing.'

"The Spanish letter was signed by 100 leading figures in the film industry, including director Pedro Almodovar. [Heroes!]

"One top producer who has worked with Cruz says he privately has vowed not to hire her again, according to the *Hollywood Reporter.* [But he didn't have the guts to be named. He is a slave.]

"Another top Hollywood executive also privately expressed his disapproval, saying he's "furious at Javier and Penelope" and wasn't sure about working with the Spanish couple again. [But he didn't want his name published because he is a sniveling slave upholding the Zionist pyramid of abuse.]

Hero Actress Penelope Cruz resisting war crimes

"Relativity Media chief executive Ryan Kavanaugh was the only studio head willing to go public with his views: "As the grandson of Holocaust survivors, I know that anyone calling what's going on in Israel 'genocide' vs. self-defense is either ignorant and shouldn't be commenting or is truly anti-Semitic."

Let's hope Ryan Kavanaugh wakes up. Ryan, please read this book twice and get to know author Henry Makow and everything he has written. You are not someone to call anyone else ignorant on this subject. In fact, you are not even a Semite. You, like my holocaust survivor family, are a descendent of the converted white race from the Kingdom of Khazar. Your relatives have little, if any claim to Palestine. They should return to their homeland in Ukraine, if they are so into homelands. Or if they are urban Jews trying to money-change or socially engineer the rest of the world, they should quit their job and buy some farmland not stolen from someone else, and ground out with nature. A great humiliation and shame is coming for anyone that ever defended Rothschild Israel. And with legitimate rage of being tricked and used, let us demand retribution for Palestinians and an end to any US support of Zionism. No more merceneries for the New World Order!

* * *

Root word "carn" means flesh. Carnal - Carnage. Lipstick and War Crimes. The female and male manifestations of perversion. Both organized by the Roth-efellers who control this era.

Antidote: modesty, chastity, fidelity, honesty, and respect. Boundaries, home rule, no more imperialism, no more globalization, no more outsourcing. Less horror and distraction. Got purification?

* * *

I would like to repeat something, because it is so against the grain of our thinking at this time, that it must be repeated ... Without clear sexual polarity which translates to differentiated sexual roles for men and women, there is no clear right or wrong either. The bottom line is someone is this or that, man or woman. Without that clear foundation, no clear life can be built. A man doesn't ovulate, a woman doesn't have testosterone. A man can have as many surgeries as he wants, he will never ovulate. It is a lie that someone can be a trans-sexual. All they can be is a phony, like Bruce Jenner [155], and why should we respect people who are trying to trick us? Gender is based on biology, not what we desire. We are either male or female, and from that very elemental perception of reality comes the strength to say "This is right," or "This is wrong." Sexual identity confusion blurs our compass, blurs right and wrong and Big Brother can then fill the moral void and dictate society's standards.

Men and women are not equal, that is why there are two such words. We are not equal, we are different, and to deny that uniqueness, sets us up to deny many other things. A homosexual is lying to himself every time he has sex with someone's lower intestines. He knows damn well it is not correct behavior, but *lies to himself that it is not wrong.* This lie makes him unreliable. He has no moral line. He cannot define what is wrong. His idea of being right is that nothing should be labeled wrong, EXCEPT those who draw lines that might limit his lust and hedonism.

Homosexuals have no ideal of purity. They cannot. Inside themselves is a lie that gender doesn't mean gender. So they live in a *doublespeak* world much like the criminals at the top who are all sexual perverts. The *doublespeak* is based on the *vanity that disconnects.* They think in their heads that because they think it, it is true. Rather, why not just observe nature to find out what is true? In birds, mammals and most insects there is gender, not sexual "orientation."

Again, most lesbians were molested, and it has nothing to do with "born this way." Many gay men were molested also as children. The abused person finds familiarity and repeats. The molested "boy" becomes the gay "daddy." The *Archives of Sexual Behavior* reports: "One of the most salient findings of this study is that 46 percent of homosexual men and 22 percent of homosexual women reported having been molested by a person of the same gender. This contrasts to only 7 percent of heterosexual men and 1 percent of heterosexual women reporting having been molested by a person of the same gender." [156] (Link has a wealth of interesting statistics.)

Natural children are naturally boys or girls. Watch boys and girls at play and it is obvious. Girls take pride in becoming women and developing breasts, and they learn about the responsibility of ovulation from their female elders. Boys will never have this experience. Ever! Boys take pride in becoming competent/competitive, strong, skilled men. Their skill is different than womanly skills. No woman will ever experience this, nor will women experience having hundreds or thousands of wet dreams, or know what a blue ball is. You can look that one up, but blue balls come from unescorted dating. Ug.

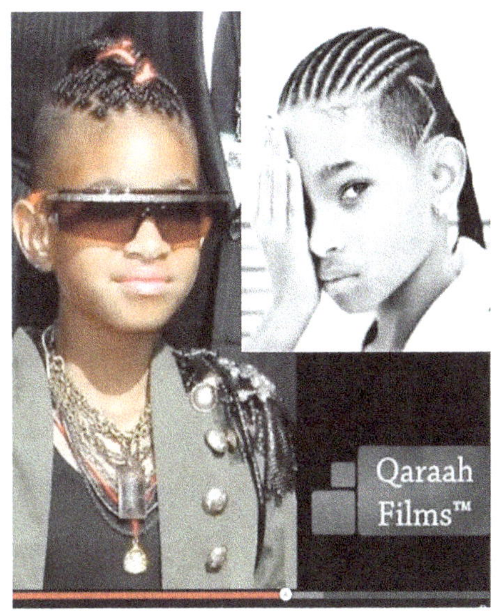

Polarity is real, and confusing polarity, is against nature. Photos to right are actor Will Smith's son being trained to be confused puppy, and daughter, Willow Smith, with all-seeing-eye, a satanic five sided star shaved into her hair, and a satanic star earring, poor slave. The son is also abused, as we will learn in *Lipstick and War Crimes: Vol. 3.* Will Smith is one of the highest paid entertainers. His status is a reward for handing over his own children to the Illuminati. This also happened to Obama's mom, Vol. 1. Once again, please look at the evidence. Pictures don't lie.

A homosexual couple cannot be example to show a boy what a man can be for a woman, nor be a model for a girl, how to be a man's partner. Confusion breeds confusion. Oprah's school for African girls (Vol. 1), for example, will never teach those girls to be good wives who can get along with a strong man, just like Oprah can't. She has not created leaders, she has created dysfunction. Oprah is no leader. If she was, why does she have to promote herself? Her legacy will be miserable, materialistic, vain, entitled wannabe rich women without roots or successful marriages. Teaching a child to be "kind and loving," but not know yin and yang, is not kindness, it is just replicating more confusion. Readers who don't think yin and yang exist, need to get grounded.

Those who think this line of reason is "backwards thinking" might return to the quote at start of this chapter — "Gays can undermine the moral authority of homo-hating churches over less fervent adherents by portraying [them] as antiquated backwaters, badly out of step … with the latest findings [theories] of psychology." (See link on American Psychiatric Society [157])

Again and again, when I have discussed basic right and wrong, or basic sexual polarity with gay proponents, they say I am "backwards." They have been convinced we are progressing, and that all social change is better and progressive. What if it is not? What if it is really worse? What if we are more confused than we were 5000 years ago? What if we no longer touch the Earth and are lost? What if we used to be men and women and now we are just mixed up?

City people don't know the birds and the bees, or the difference between hen and rooster behavior. There are no gay birds, gay bees, or gay chickens! There is nature! For natural people, queer means queer. How can someone who is is clear be equal with someone who is confused? How can someone support gay equality when gay people *are confused* and don't judge sports sex as wrong? Lower intestines are for what? They want license, not wisdom. How can one support that? City people know only *social engineering*, which has made them intentionally carnal and hedonistic, originating as direct mis-guidance from the satanic, pedophile, power freak elite. From *Ms. CIA Magazine* to *Forbes* to *Time* to *the Muppets to CIA Playboy* (Vol.1), with all their actors and divas and politicians, we have seen the elite perversion agenda.

FOR WHAT PURPOSE?

The reader might ask, "If this plot is really true, what would be the ultimate goal of such an elite co-opted Gay Agenda?" The reader can add in Communism, Fascism, the CIA Feminist Operation, the New Age Operation, and the "Galactic Federation" Operation because these all have the same Illuminati/CIA/pyramid origins. Original feminism was co-opted back in the suffragette stage (Suffragettes were offered funds if they would support entrance to World War I, which they did.), and New Age was quickly co-opted after India and Zen were discovered by Western youth in the **60s**. (Ram Dass who wrote *Be Here Now* (1971) was gay. He never was a renunciant in any sense of the term. Alan Watts who wrote about Zen was a drunk.) Those old traditions have clear moral lines drawn in the sand, that is, taboos, but they were replaced by Deepak Chopra and Oprah Winfrey and Ellen Degeneres narcissistic "don't judge anything because anything goes" alleged spirituality without morals. So what would be the purpose of all these operations, introduced in Vol. 1, by Yuri Bezmenov? Well I just gave it away.

The purpose of the Cabal's Gay Agenda is to create another front to destabilize traditional values with divide and conquer antagonism and blurred mixed up people, as delineated by Yuri Bezmenov, and proven by minion New World Order Zbigniew Brzezinski, so that the elite end up finally with a weak, dysfunctional, complacent population of masturbating sheeple to control.

Traditional values are not perfect. They are not sacred. *But most traditional values respect innocence and virtue while the New World Order definitively does not.* The push for "gay is okay" is another front to attack traditional values. I'm not defending any one set of traditional values here, I am defending all old time-tested cultures in general, that all happen to maintain clear forms of sexual polarity. The cultures of entire world are under attack. And the excuse is fairness, "equality," and ultimately peace under the gun of the Globalists. All schools world wide will be teaching anal sex. That is the plan dear reader, unless you start drawing a line in the sand.

Sanity is based on clear codes of right and wrong which is based on clear identity of gender. Confusion on personal identity, leads to confusion. Wrong sexual choices reinforces wrong choices everywhere else. We must be clear on what we are. We are either male or female and we uphold that polarity. We must know this is the right, correct, clear path. With that fundamental sanity about (duh!) knowing what sex we are, we have the strength to resist the New World Order. Without that obvious clarity, we are befuddled and easily enslaved.

In the screen shot to right, we see the women standing together as a pole of clear solid energy. They are not mixing with the men, they are sovereign. In no way are they trying to be sex objects. They are not confused about their gender or the purpose of gender. I recommend this video. It shows the positive future we can strive for, which is not predatory progress, but sane simplicity.

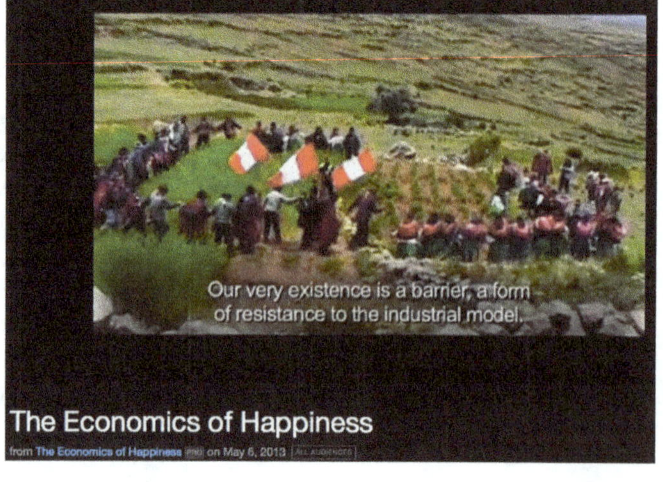

* * *

Zbigniew Brzezinski was the first Director of the Roth-efeller Trilateral Commission, architect of the Afghan holocaust, and is presently a consultant to globalist puppet, CIA "Logo" Obama. He wrote the books *Between Two Ages — America's Role in the Technetronic Era* and *The Grand Chessboard—American Primacy and its Geostrategic Imperatives.*

In his words …

> *"The Technocratic Age is slowly designing an every day, more controlled society.*
>
> ***The society will be dominated by an elite of persons free from traditional values,*** *who will have no doubt in fulfilling their objectives by means of purged techniques, with which they will influence the behavior of people and will control and watch the society in all details … it will become possible to exert a practically permanent watch [all-seeing-eye] on each citizen of the world."*

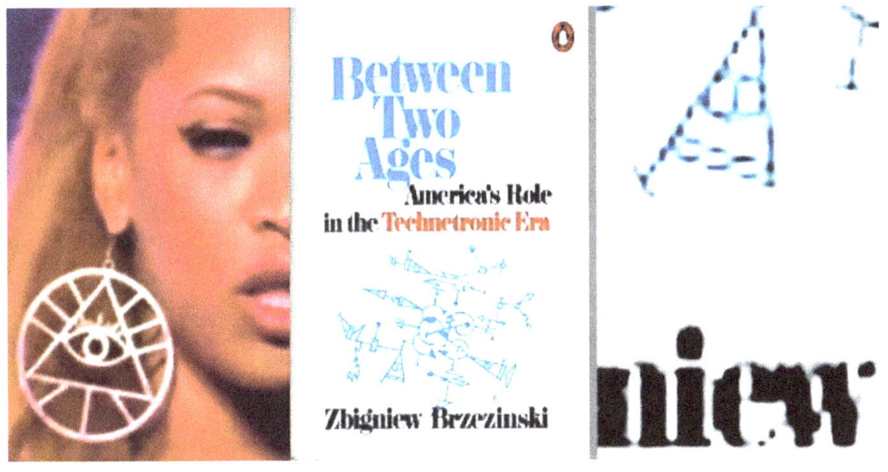

Manipulated sheeple or clear sovereign Human Being? Which way will the reader choose? Lipstick and war crimes or simplicity and compassion? Slavery or Sovereignty?

We go deeper and further in Volume 3.

The New World Order, by Frederick Charles Hicks. (Garden City & New York: Doubleday, Page & Co., 1920, pp. viii, 496.)

This work is in reality a treatise on the new international law of today as it has been affected by the League of Nations and the recent treaties. Most of those who have studied international law up to the present time have felt that numerous changes have taken place during

BROWN AND CAMERON OUTLINE RIVAL GREEN VISIONS

'NEW WORLD ORDER' TO SAVE EARTH

PRIORITIES Brown called for UN action

The logo for the Fabian Society that created gay Stonewall charity is a wolf in sheep's clothing. See www.geoengineeringwatch.org for the real reasons for extreme climate.

"In searching for a new enemy to unite us, **we came up with** *the idea that pollution, the threat of global warming, water shortages, famine and the like would fit the bill."*

– Rockefeller Club of Rome, 1968

FABIAN SOCIETY Fabian Review Members Publications Events

FABIAN WOMEN | YOUNG **FABIANS** | SCOTTISH **FABIANS** | WELSH **FABIANS** | LOCAL **FABIAN**

Bringing it home

In December, politicians, campaigners and diplomats will come together in Paris for the latest in a series of UN negotiations aimed at tackling the world's greatest collective challenge: how to catalyse action on climate change. But whether or not these talks put us on a plausible path to keeping global temperature rises to 2C –...

"Analysis of ice cores shows that the concentration of carbon dioxide in the atmosphere follows the rise in temperatures very closely and lagged warmings by 800±400 years. During the glacial/interglacial cycles the peaks of carbon dioxide concentration have **never preceded the warmings.** Therefore there is no evidence that carbon dioxide is a major factor in the warming of the Earth now."

– Habibullo Abdussamatov

The Intelligent Student's Guide to the New World Order

www.conspiracyarchive.com/NWO/Intelligent_Students_NWO.htm – By Erica Carl

What is the New World Order?

The essence of the New World Order (NWO) or world management system is that it is managemen by social engineers, rather than government based on a written constitution. How you are affected by this management system depends on what the social engineers decide the system should do for you and require of you. The social engineers and system managers think of themselves as scientists applying the scientific method to the control of group behavior. Your behavior and your relationships are regarded as the subject of investigation and control by those who call themselves social scientists. You are among their test animals, and you have no say in, and often no knowledge o experiments that involve you. If the NWO is totally implemented, your independence, individuality, an freedom will be gone.

There is nothing new about the idea of managing others, or even of controlling the whole world. That has been the goal of social philosophers for thousands of years. However, we need not go back over ancient history. We are concerned primarily with what has been going on in our own generations. This we can understand quite well if we confine ourselves to the Nineteenth and Twentieth Centuries.

Goals of the New World Order

To begin to understand the New World Order (NWO) you need to forget what you have been told abou philosophical differences between Republicans and Democrats; left and right; Socialists and Libertarians; business and labor; liberal and conservative; black and white, etc.. The planners of the New World Order know they must use, influence, and cater to all of these groups to accomplish the goals they are seeking, which are:

1. Consolidate everything.
2. Commercialize everything.
3. Classify everything.
4. Claim everything.
5. Control everything.

This concludes Volume 2 of the *Lipstick and War Crimes* series.

Coming up we will learn more about Beyoncé and her card carrying satanist husband Jay-Z. We will meet Shakira, Taylor Swift, Nicole Kidman, Enrique Iglesias, Usher, Justin Beiber, One Direction, Drake, Rihanna, Teddy Roosevelt, Senator Ted Cruz, Nicole Scherzinger, Gary Barlow, William Randolph Hearst, Will Smith, Allen Dulles, Paris Hilton, Kevin Spacey, Robin Williams, and many more pawns in the game. We will also meet heroes like Michael Hastings, Joan Baez, Bradley (Chelsea) Manning, Catherine Austin Fitts, Pete Seeger, Makana, Richard Larry Weaver of the *USS Liberty,* and more.

Then we will explore the meaning of heroism and false heroism, the sick tragedy of *disconnecting vanity* and the life affirming meaning of connection. We will examine where we stand as people (not "a people," but as individuals who are each accountable) living in a civilization which we can no longer believe in.

Remember the fish in the *Nemo* movie image at beginning of first chapter? This book was written as a circle. Please read what the fish are saying in that picture again now, Page 16. I will show in the rest of series that what we are told is NEWS is actually an unending series of lies, so incredible, that you will stand aside from society as you know it and see that image of the fish on Page 16 as a very personal quest. As messed up as the situation seems, remember, the reason we don't like deceit is because *human nature is loving.* We just have to wake up to the responsibility of that truth.

Please now review the Glossary and re-read the book again because so much here is information you never received before. You can use keywords in any sentence I have written to do your own research on the internet, which is enlightening.

Thank you for taking time to educate yourself with *globalization* you didn't get in school. Please visit **Lipstick-and-War-Crimes.org.**

Don't ignore the future, don't look fabulous … be simple, authentic, clear and give a damn! This is your life. Take it seriously. There is an afterlife. You are on an endless spiritual path, and purification is the good road that is worth all your energy and focus. Choose quality. Get to know silence. Visit the wilderness. Gain hand skills. Forget candy, and be strong!

Ray Songtree, August 2015

Epilogue

The reader might be disappointed that this first book of the series actually ended with a question. This is the ego part of us that wants a convenient secure answer. We want to be led. We want to remain sheeple and not stand in our own sovereignty. We want someone to impress us. We want a conclusion. However the answer to corruption is not a statement, the answer is a change of lifestyle and de-colonizing of our minds and hearts. And only the questioning of one's own patterns will get us there. I refuse to enable followship. I expect the reader to live longer than myself and to take responsibility for ending corruption in our times by ending corruption within the self.

Suggestions for de-colonizing your mind and life … (This is somewhat repetitive, written in 2014.)

1. Stop using credit cards, and use cash as much as possible. Open an account with a local credit union. Get a debit card for online purchases. Default on all your credit cards and accept that you will never be eligible for a loan again. Live without debt. Don't feed the beast interest rates. Starve the Roth-efeller banksters. Use the time you will gain not being a debt slave to learn more skills.
2. Stop paying taxes for war crimes and crimes against humanity. Find a way to do this.
3. Support local farmers and craftsmen. Shop for quality in terms of localization, rather than shopping for the cheapest product that allows you to buy more quantity. Buy local. Support everything local, from farm fresh eggs to local power stations. Make something. Produce something.
4. Support "home rule" in your province, your county, your town, your neighborhood. As much as you can, secede from globalization. Convince your municipality to do the same. Pressure your representatives to have a moral stance that money can't corrupt. They draw the line and you hold them to that line as their partner in purification.
5. Turn off your TV. Get rid of it. TV exists to control your values and your choices. Break free. You will gain nothing but a fat ass and lies having a TV.
6. Learn to play a musical instrument. Stop supporting the music industry. Stop being a spectator buying food and games. Grow your own everything, including music. Sing in the shower! Sing!
7. Move out of town. Spend more time outdoors. Be part of the transition back to an agrarian lifestyle because the urban lifestyle is killing the planet, and killing you. Become indigenous. Teach your children about all the plants in your area. Experiment with their uses.

8. Study EMF safety. Hard wire everything and avoid wireless anything. Remove the Smart Meter from your home and join Smart Meter activists in your area. Pressure schools to become wireless free. Ask them for the safety warranty on all wireless products used in school. Show them www.bioinitiative.org. Sue them! Use cell phone only for emergencies. Don't carry it next to your body. Be indigenous, not trans-human. Never allow yourself to be chipped, and remove chips from any card or item you have. Study this. Do search on YouTube "how to remove tracking chip." Protest Obama-care tracking chips and don't listen to those who say this is a myth. Step by step this is where we are heading if we don't wake up. (Page 82)
9. Watch the skies every day and talk about chemtrails and send letters to newspapers, calls to radio shows, and contact elected officials calling for a chemtrail free sky in your area. Demand an Environmental Impact Statement for chemtrails! Sue the EPA for not doing their job. Shasta County in California is one of the leaders on this.
10. Whatever crime in this book invokes your passion the most, become very educated about that crime and become a citizen educator and activist about it. Be a champion on that subject. You really will make a difference. The tipping point of salvation is only a decision away. Make that one issue YOUR issue and go go go!
11. It is not enough to study all this. We must protest. It is not enough to sign online petitions. This will not transform your neighborhood and make your community strong. The education has to be personal, and you must exhibit an alternative to globalized sheeple lifestyle.
12. Stop wearing cosmetics. Remove your tattoos. Remove your piercings. Remove your vanity. Boycott high heels. Never look at a fashion magazine again. Starve the beast!
13. Learn to fast (skip meals for days). You are not entitled to three meals a day for the rest of your life. I promise that. You can change your expectations and come out much much stronger by learning to fast.
14. Consider purification as an alternative value system to consumerism.
15. The wilderness is waiting. Are you preparing for vision quest? You will find your own junk. Prepare by cleaning your mind now.
16. No sex before commitment. Take it from me, sex with someone you don't know well will hurt you very much. Children deserve two stable parents who show them what compromise and care is every day. Just say no to giving away your innocence, trust, sweetness. Just say no to some nerve endings between your legs, and listen instead to something deeper. The waves come and go. Be the sea. Wait for a commitment and don't make a commitment until you have seen your potential partner in a variety of situations over a long period of time. Be modest, be sincere. You want long love, not a short hot ride.
17. Take care of your family. Heal.

18. No more substances. No more alcohol. No more checking out. These times we live in are amazing times. Up your alertness and clarity, don't dumb yourself down. You can't afford one minute of intoxication. We are facing a survival situation. This could be your last day in this life. Your last hour. Live like there is a spiritual path, and you will have a strong spiritual path. Now is your time to choose weakness or strength, indulgence or virtue.
19. Be kind and have faith. This is just one lifetime. We will come back again and again to give our goodness :) We are indomitable. There is no death, just a change of worlds, and you can be the tipping point towards sanity which the Earth begs for. Life is an adventure and we are living in a wondrous Great Mystery. Never forget this for one instant! And all this is connected in the heart, a heart that can see and feel and know. We are alone together. Love to you my friend. Love to you!

– Ray Songtree

Sightings on trip to New York, April 2014

New York has no shame in loser creation. The name "Empire State" demonstrates our culture's marriage to the pyramid of abuse. Spoof license plate below is true. Note Illuminati Maltese Cross on license plate bottom. It says "Veterans of Foreign Wars." This really means wars organized by foreigners in Bilderberg Group, but deceived Americans don't know this. This cross is for real. Symbols are a language, and that is what the language says, wars organized by foreigners in Bilderberg Group. Hidden in plain sight.

em·pire

"The term empire derives from the Latin imperium (power, authority) …

An imperial political structure is established and maintained in two ways: (i) as a territorial empire of direct conquest and control with force (direct, physical action to compel the emperor's goals) or (ii) as a coercive, hegemonic empire of indirect conquest and control with power (the perception that the emperor can physically enforce his desired goals)." [terrorism]

City University New York: CUNY honoring war criminal and state crime cover up artist, Colin Powell in poster. Powell insured his career by covering up the My Lai Massacre in Vietnam. He lied about weapons of mass destruction in Iraq where 1.5 million civilians have been killed to steal their oil. He still helps cover up the truth about 9/11. Shame on CUNY.

A sign in Woodstock, New York, protesting globalization.

At NYC Natural History Museum, Teddy Roosevelt statue dominating Native Americans and Africans. He rides, separated from the Earth, in front of them and above them. The robbed and the enslaved. The *dominate culture* makes a hero out of someone devoted to loser creation, while all along denying the abuse. What an ugly ugly racist, anti-indigenous statue. Regime change needed. Tear it down!

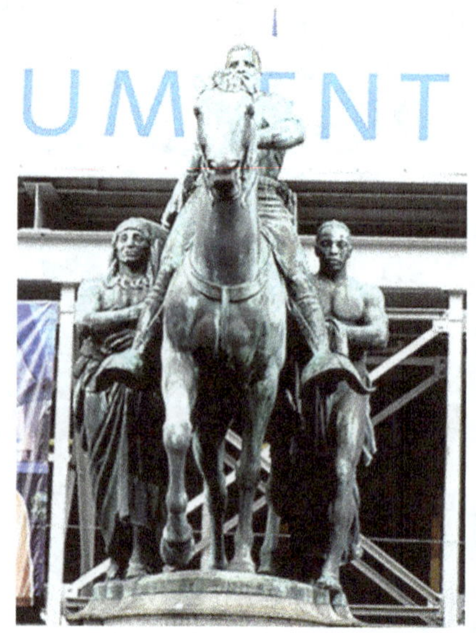

A hero holding informational placard at Times Square, showing current abuses against Falun Gong meditators in China who have been rounded up, and Nazi style, used for profit, their organs harvested. "The Story" on left says … "You don't understand my agony. Those Falun Gong practitioners were alive. It might be easier for me if they were dead, but they were alive." He was surgeon forced to remove corneas from 2000 living people. Photo is of his former wife reading the letter.

A comment from a French traveler in Hawaii … "In France we don't use clothes dryers, we hang our clothes to dry." Wonderful.

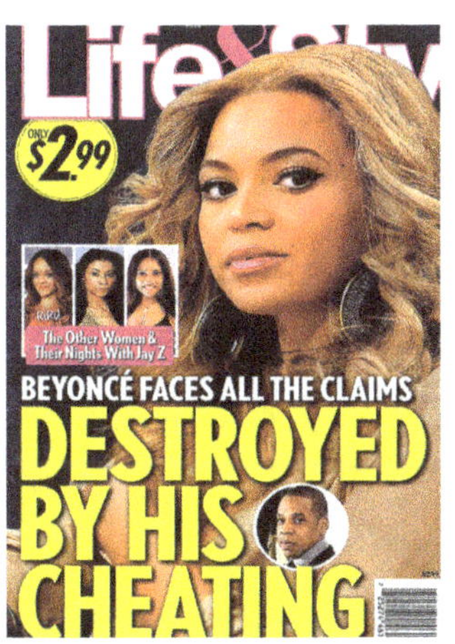

More diva fluff for the masses. Mostly fictional drama. Spread leg Illuminati *cutout* Beyoncé, teaching narcissistic perverted focus for the Grammies, is upset that someone is cheating? Her husband has been using women most of his life. She knew that when they married. Just like Hillary. Can an Illuminati slave leave her handler? Someone could become a discarded broken doll soon. This is interesting, which *Time Magazine* cover spouse will go down? But then "a strong woman" doesn't need a man, and the attack on family is the new normal, as with single moms Madonna and Jennifer Lopez. Perhaps some prayer from everyone can encourage both Beyoncé and Jay-Z to become whistleblowers and support each other in purification. There is a war in the heavens and within each of us, and virtue must win.

Interview April 27, 2014

Catherine Austin Fitts:

"... Let me go back to what we are all part of. How did we get this land? Most of us have ancestors, one way or another, who are part of the process ... We came here, we killed everybody who was here and we stole their land, right? That's how we created the country in the first place. Right? Okay? Then we had a whole financing [through Rothschilds] ... the building out of part of the infrastructure with slavery, right? And then after the slaves went free, what did we do? We went through a process of targeting those [Black] communities with drugs and Lord knows what else, and I'm telling the story in the 90s how we literally rounded up innocent kids, stuffed them into prison, made money on the prison stocks. After you look at who was bringing in the drugs [CIA] it was a genocide policy. There was nothing we were doing, minus the gas chambers, that wasn't the same as the slave labor camps that Hitler was doing. That is our country, that is what we've been doing ...

"This has been going on for a long long time and if we are to change it, then we can't just say let's put some bankers in jail, we have to go deep. *Because, let's face it, one of the ways we have all had a nice middle class life in this country is our military runs around the world and kills people and takes natural resources for cheap, and that's hunky dory with all of us, because it is the basis of our nice life.* [Lipstick and war crimes]

"... For two hundred and fifty plus years, since 1776, we've been talking about respecting each other's rights, but we financed it by running around the world and stealing from everybody else. Not to mention stealing the land we are sitting on. So the time has come where we have to shift the model. We can't stand on the central banking/warfare model. We've been using that for 500 years and it's not going to work because we are so busy killing each other, and the economic warfare is so absurd and so ridiculous, that we are shrinking the total pie, and that means we have to change the model, where we are prepared, globally, to respect each other's human and property rights [sovereignty].

"... The question is, are we as a planet going to institute a totalitarian central government or are we going to find a way out of this kind of economic warfare system we live in?

"That is going to require a deep cultural change, bottom up, not just the United States, but Europe and Japan and the developed world."

– Forbidden Knowledge TV
Alexandra Bruce, April 27, 2014

Catherine Austin Fitts has website Solari.com

Flying home from NYC, I saw chemtrails spreading out to create a continuous white film all the way across the continental United States. The entire sky is manipulated. In foreground the Rocky Mountains of New Mexico.

Glossary of Terms with Central Concepts

Each of us is a series of choices. There is no difference between our choices and their consequences (karma) which, combined, makes up who we are. We are not a mind or a body that makes choices. We are choice.

We exist as choice within context. We think in our heads that we are bodies separated from context, but when we quiet down, we realize we are not separate, we are more or less connected. This is not an intellectual conclusion. It is a quiet and dynamic experience, an actual shift towards what is our true nature. Awakening is not a destination, but a simplification that becomes too quiet to name and grows ever deeper.

In the inescapable context that surrounds us, are other beings. In respecting and appreciating their inalienable right to be here, we choose morality. Thus we live in a moral "universe." ***We can never be free of responsibility.*** *This is an absolute truth that even atheists can embrace. So our choice is to be stuck in our heads and separated and abusive, or to quiet down and connect from the heart and claim our personal sovereignty and do something positive.*

By simplifying and awakening, we help others awaken. By dropping Consumerism, we help others drop Consumerism. By strengthening our own community, we undercut the Globalist plan to centralize and control everything. Re-localization will reverse monoculture and de-throne the parasitic structures of corruption that are threatening to kill the planet.

Since no two of us make the same choices, there is friction within the multi-verse. There is no "universe" or one-verse. There is no universal message or solution. There is no one "humanity." There is no utopia or heaven. Wherever beings choose, there is multi-verse and multi-choice and friction. A spiritual "believer" forgets this and masks this reality with a dogma such as "peace" or "spiritual evolution" or the one and only God, or the one and only Truth. There is no one peace, there is no one direction of evolution, there is no up, there is no Godhead that has infinite sight or keeps tabs on infinite choices, there is no way to express a truth that encompasses infinite choices. Structured belief is a blindness.

Rather than live in dogma, a sovereign individual lives in action that is increasingly informed by connection. That connection includes other dimensions that cannot be explained, but in English we use the words luck, synchronicity, grace, tao, God, spirit, providence (Chapter 16) *to refer to this connection and the beings we connect with. I cannot explain this, nor can anyone.*

We used to live naturally within an ecological community. This is our indigenous roots. Until we return to living naturally within an ecological community, we will kill bioregions with indoor living that blindly rips off the outdoor world. We must both dethrone the Globalist parasites, and touch the Earth again. Thereby we will touch Spirit again and take responsibility for that, each as sovereign individuals. Simplification will survive the disease we call "progress." Overconsumption and monoculture are doomed, but we are not. Young people will adapt!

Index of Glossary and Central Concepts

1. *Cage theme*
2. *Compassion*
3. *Consumerism*
4. *Controlled media*
5. *Co-opt*
6. *Cutout*
7. *"Democracy"*
8. *"Developed" countries*
9. *"Developing" countries*
10. *Disconnecting vanity*
11. *Dominant culture*
12. *Doublespeak*
13. *Entitled*
14. *Evil*
15. *"Freedom"*
16. *Globalists*
17. *Globalization*
18. *Grasping desire*
19. *The Great Mystery*
20. *Hero*
21. *His-story*
22. *Indigenous people*
23. *Informed choice*
24. *Inverse relationships*
25. *Military*
26. *Monoculture or monopolization*
27. *Personal sovereignty*
28. *Predictive programming*
29. *"Progress"*
30. *Purification path*
31. *Recovering from "development" countries*
32. *Re-localization*
33. *Resource depletion*
34. *Roth-efellers*
35. *Rothschild*
36. *Sanctioned disease*
37. *Social engineering*
38. *Technocracy*
39. *Transparency*
40. *Unsustainable*
41. *Urban people*
42. *Vanity*

Glossary

(Throughout the book Glossary Terms will appear in italics.)

1. ***Cage theme*** is a common message in the music industry (Pages 273-275) in which staging for performances and music videos often includes a cage, a bird cage, fencing, walls, prison bars, or riot police (front cover of this book). Usage of *cage theme* in the entertainment industry is intentional and is not some artistic genre. 1) On one hand, we are to accept that we are slaves under a pyramid of abuse and that cages are normal. 2) On the other hand, we are led to believe that liberation from the depressed feeling of this "cage" is the satanist slogan "Do as thou wilt," (Chapter 12) which means do anything you want to, anything goes, no limits, no boundaries, nothing sacred, no traditions, "Live it up, drink it down." (Page 230). As defined in *cage theme*, "breaking out" is liberation to be hedonistic.

   "Its my life, I'll do whatever crazy thing I want, regardless of consequences." The *cage theme* encourages children to be "sassy" and teenagers to abandon responsible creativity and lean toward destructive backlash, which disempowers *personal sovereignty* and sovereign communities. *Cage theme* encourages random experimentation, particularly with sex.

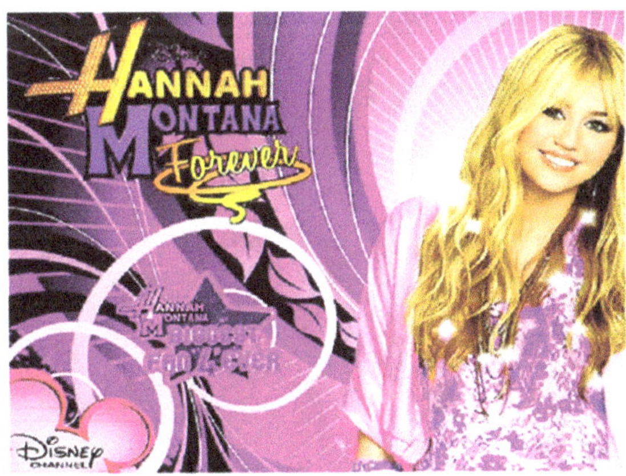

"Hannah Montana Biggest Fan 4 Ever"

Depraved sexuality breaks down traditional walls while creating dependence on a new chain.

The *cage theme* goes along with the broken doll symbol, (Chapter 12) that we are toys to be discarded, that we can be dolls broken into multi-personalities no longer under a sovereign conscience (goodness), and that destroying other people is just collateral damage.

For women, the *cage theme* promotes breaking free of traditional modesty. It also promotes the power tripping vain excitement of bondage and sexual slavery. That is, it promotes the *vanity that disconnects.* For men, the *cage theme* keeps male attention trapped below the waist to see women as seductive enablers of lust. This works hand in glove with role of women as slave sex kittens, another theme which uses leopard skin attire. (Chapters 11-12) In *cage theme*, the "liberated" slave woman exhibits power by being able to seduce. In this *co-opted* feminism, women are "free" to be "equal" and play the materialistic lust game. Such women are "awesome" sluts. (Rihanna photo Chapter 12) They are covered with lipstick, inside and out, and think the new cage is wonderful. (See Gaga, under the word *Vanity* in this Glossary) They got there by being "good girl gone bad," another common theme in entertainment programming. (See Taylor Swift, and Carrie Underwood, Chapter 11.)

Concocted celebrity, Miley Cyrus (photos above and below), for example, is a created personage rolled out by Globalist controlled Disney Inc. (Walt Disney was placed, Page 240) to subliminally use her role model to promote *cage theme*. Her role as Hannah Montana was set up specifically in advance to be trashed later by Cyrus' programmed "liberation," as a wrecking ball smashing down the cage walls of traditional modesty. Other Disney brats, such as Britney Spears, had similar "transformations" but not as promoted. For Cyrus's good gone bad, *cage theme* liberation (none of which was her idea) globalist *Time Magazine* made the 21-year-old a Top 100 Most Influential Person in 2014. We can expect the exact same thing with the next Hannah Montana that Disney tries to roll out. Disney brats do not become settled young mothers.

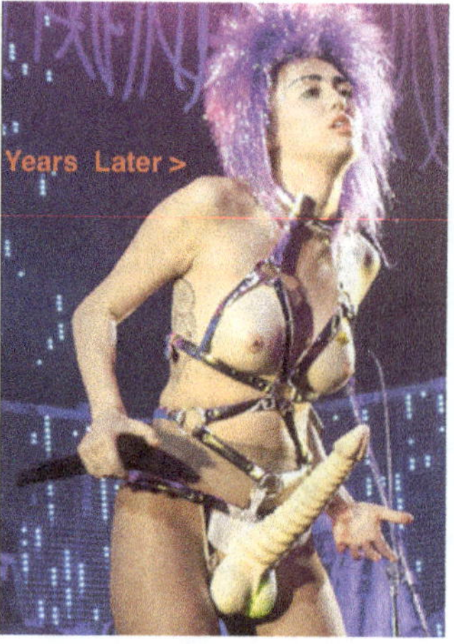

Her vaunted influence co-created by *Time* was the spreading of "good gone bad." (Chapters 10-13) Her message for girls is to escape the cage (Hannah Montana) of goodness and tradition (which the *Globalists* want to destroy in their goal of *monoculture*) to be "free," boundless, and unrestrained. The millions of Hannah Montana fans her age and younger are now set up to no longer believe in anything upstanding. This is cultural "shock doctrine." Her handlers not only trashed her former image, which was not really that wholesome, but trashed wholesomeness for all her fans. Young women are given instead the new alleged mature role model of "twerking" or sports sex in order to "break out." Remember, there are no other role models given this kind of notary. It is a *social engineering* program.

This is not Miley's personal message. She has none. Disney brats have almost no volition of their own. She did not create any of the symbolism she was told to perform or model for. She has been a mind controlled puppet, or *cutout,* since an early age. She chooses almost nothing. The author does not mean to attack Cyrus. She is just a *cutout,* (See Glossary term below), being used.

So, *cage theme* works in tandem with "being free" or "coming out."

In the real world of the expanding surveillance state of SWAT teams and the end of American *Habeus Corpus* (right to trial) when Obama signed the 2013 National Defense Authorization Act (Chapter 29), *cage theme* is not a metaphor. The U.S. has the highest per capita incarceration rate in the world. That is, the U.S. is the least "land of the free" of any nation with the most caged people. But the constant *cage theme* in entertainment industry makes this psychologically acceptable. "Cages are normal. Break out of old cage. Accept new cage." This is classic *social engineering* or what is called "transformation."

Michael Jackson's YouTube prison video of the song "They Don't Care About Us" is a protest against *cage theme* (Chapter 10) as were some of Charlie Chaplin's movies. (Page 221)

2. ***Compassion*** is our true inner nature. *Compassion* is what remains when we drop *vanity* and separation *(disconnecting vanity).* On our *purification paths* (See Glossary term below), it becomes difficult to determine "where" this quality exists, because we lose sense of time and space as we let go of division. This won't make sense now, but it will later on your path. We actually lean on *compassion* to keep us oriented when we drop separation. That is, we become more kind, and kindness gives us a keel. This is perhaps the most important sentence in this book ... kindness gives us a keel to stabilize and direct us on our journeys.

3. ***Consumerism*** does not only mean that we have an addiction of buying unnecessary material things. *Consumerism* is the idea that the purpose of life is to consume sensual experiences. This can also mean consuming movies, consuming music, consuming relationships, consuming sex, or consuming travel experiences. It can mean consuming spectator sports, consuming drugs, consuming status.

   Consumerism is pushed by the *Globalists* as a "food and games" strategy (Roman bread and circus) to keep the masses preoccupied and dumbed down. All spectator sports have this purpose, and are very different than outdoor sports where there is no spectator, just the athlete in nature who is soul surfing. By spectator sports, I mean watching an athlete, rather than doing it! The kids playing with skate boards or basketballs are not spectator consumers, they are engaged. "Food and games" means being a spectator, and being entertained as a distraction.

   My late uncle, Lester Rodney, almost single handedly brought the first African American athlete, Jackie Robinson [158], into Major League Baseball. Without his journalistic agitation, it would not have happened when it did. The sports industry is run by filthy rich investors who buy teams which perform for couch potatoes who drink beer, fart, and are lobotomized by this "food and games" lifestyle. These spectators think that the game is more important than real life or that the game is real life. *Consumerism* is not real life. *Consumerism* is indulgence. Their consumption of commercial sports is a type of mind control. Spectator sports are a direct continuation of the coliseums of the Roman Empire.

   Lester was a city boy who liked spectator sports. To assimilate new races into the elite's controlled *Consumerism* is hardly an accomplishment, but that is how our values are steered. City people need entertainment because they are separated from real life in nature. This makes them consumers of, rather than participants with, nature. My uncle, a good socialist, worked for the *Globalists* and didn't even know it. (Book *Press Box Red.)* In hindsight we can ask, what good is racial equality for African Americans if it makes us into athlete clowns for mass entertainment or into Buffalo Soldiers? (A Regiment of Black U.S. soldiers, 1866-1890s, who helped wipe out Native Americans from their ancient homelands.) Is the goal of racial equality to become bread and circus super star gladiators, that keep people distracted so we ignore killers on the frontier of conquest?

I've now outlined how both the mainstream culture, and the politically correct counter culture, support *Consumerism,* and how consuming entertainment upholds the machine.

Consumerism is the opposite of the spiritual *purification path. Consumerism* makes us weak sleepy addicts of sensual indulgence. The spiritual path makes us sovereign, lean, and awake. The spiritual path promotes simplicity and sensitivity. The path of *Consumerism* promotes complexity, *vanity,* insensitivity, and collateral damage. The main force behind environmental degradation is our *choice* to buy whatever we feel like buying, and not just what we need. The expression from Jesus, "The meek will inherit the Earth" means to me that vain *Consumerism* is *unsustainable.*

4. ***Controlled media*** is the actual covert history of banker-owned media and CIA infiltrated media in the West. In Asia, the same programs are in effect. Free press ended in the U.S. in 1915.

> *"In March, 1915, the J.P. Morgan interests, the steel, shipbuilding, and powder interest, and their subsidiary organizations, got together 12 men high up in the newspaper world and employed them to select the most influential newspapers in the United States and a sufficient number of them to control generally the policy of the daily press ... They found it was only necessary to purchase the control of 25 of the greatest papers. An agreement was reached; the policy of the papers was bought, to be paid for by the month; an editor was furnished for each paper to properly supervise and edit information regarding the questions of preparedness, militarism, financial policies, and other things of national and international nature considered vital to the interests of the purchasers."*
>
> – U.S. Congressman Oscar Callaway, 1917

In the U.S., this control was merged with covert government infiltration by the CIA, called Project Mocking Bird, starting in 1948. Decades later, there are now no information venues that are independent in the U.S., and emerging ones, such as *Huffington Post,* are quickly bought up. The UK *Guardian* was a *Rothschild* project started 80 years ago. The internet still has some freedom, but this is because it is not a "news" corporation, but is a forum for collective research.

Internet freedom is being attacked with the *monopolization* of top venues like YouTube, where important whistleblower revelations are regularly unplugged. Google, Facebook, Yahoo, YouTube, Skype, Paypal, Craigslist and many more are run by the same computers. The reason Craigslist has indexed sexual preferences is to collect personal data to build a profile on you that could be used against you in the future, as Edward Snowden has revealed. So called "independent" venues are produced to catch the unwary. The sites offering encrypted "secure" email are often run by the CIA. *Controlled media* means independent reporting or opinion is being systematically eliminated in order to control what you think. And of course, most people are led to be asleep.

Very soon we can expect a President (*cutout*) to declare a national emergency based on fake cyber attacks so the internet will be shut down because free information that is not controlled by the *controlled media* is a threat to tyranny. Remember, most of our data is controlled by a few companies. The internet may be entirely centralized if we allow it. Our use of Facebook or Google supports centralization.

The only exceptions to controlled internet are websites that ask "Who is in control?" All other news sources are "food and games" for the masses.

"There is no such thing as an independent press. You know it and I know it. There is not one of you who dare to write your honest opinions, and if you did, you know beforehand that it would never appear in print. I am paid weekly for keeping my honest opinion out of the paper I am connected with. Others of you are paid similar salaries for similar things, and any of you who would be so foolish as to write honest opinions would be out on the street looking for another job. If I allowed my honest opinions to appear in one issue of my paper, before twenty-four hours my occupation would be gone. The business of the journalist is to destroy the truth; to lie outright; to pervert; to vilify; to fawn at the feet of mammon, and to sell his country and his race for his daily bread. You know it and I know it and what folly is this toasting an "independent press"? We are the tools and vassals of ***rich men behind the scenes.*** *We are the jumping jacks,* ***they pull the strings*** *and we dance. Our talents, our possibilities, and our lives are all the property of other men. We are intellectual prostitutes."*

– John Swinton, former chief of staff, *The New York Times*,
New York Press Club, 1953

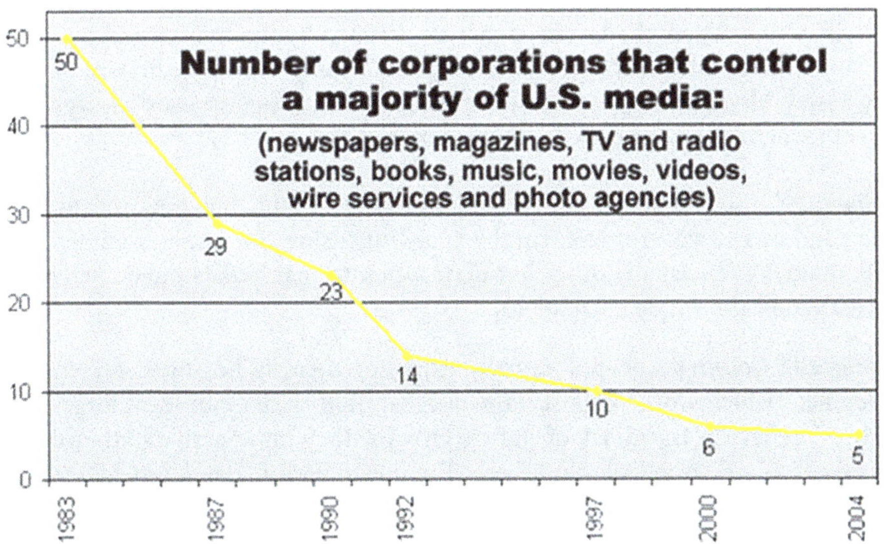

5. ***Co-opt – Definition:*** *To neutralize or win over (an independent minority, for example) through assimilation into an established group or culture: <co-opt rebels by giving them positions of authority>*

   To take into a group (as a faction, movement, or culture): **absorb, assimilate** <the students are co–opted by a system they serve, even in their struggle against it. – A. C. Danto>

   Take over, appropriate <a style co–opted by advertisers>

6. ***Cutout*** is another term for political or economic puppet. Such politicians, CEOs, or divas are like paper *cutouts* of a human being, pinned on to the circus of the political or cultural stage. *Cutouts* have these qualities:

   1) They are either placed or compromised in order to be given a position of influence, or to maintain their position.
   2) They are replaceable and often are thrown away like broken dolls. (Chapter 12). They can also be assassinated if the *Globalists* feel they are acting too independently.
   3) They are well respected and trumped up everywhere. They are well paid and have famous and award decorated careers.
   4) They have split personalities, and are not ruled by conscience.
   5) They will never blow the whistle on anyone unless they are told to throw away another broken *cutout* or to victimize someone. An example of a *cutout* who has no interest in justice is singer Rihanna or Gaga. Another example is Opray Winfrey, who like Walt Disney, like Bill Gates, like Obama, was placed. The governor of Arkansas was invited to a Bilderberg (Page 66) meeting in Europe. A year later this nobody was elected U.S. President. Clinton was a placed puppet *cutout.*
   6) *Cutouts* cannot publicly show any moral backbone. Most celebrities are *cutouts.* They are actor-place-holders for *social engineering* programs which they do not script. *Cutouts* in the music industry are rolled out "divas," who are just like politicians, and follow the behavior models dictated by the music industry, which has Illuminati and Globalist underpinnings. The only difference between a music industry "diva" and a president or prime minister, is one spreads her legs, while the other bends over for the Globalist machine.

7. ***"Democracy"*** used to mean a representative government, but now means a corporate funded and owned government, run by *Globalists* using *cutouts,* and guided by globalist "think tanks." The *Globalists* use *controlled media* to manipulate public perception of the globalist vetted and funded candidates.

8. ***"Developed" Countries*** do not actually exist, for there is no stated target of so called development which would be a *sustainable* goal. Rather than an ideal target, "developed countries" believe in the idiocy of endless growth. They never arrive so they don't actually exist except as a runway going nowhere. The misnomer of "*developed countries*" refers to the rich countries that are ripping off everything else as fast as possible. This is led by the indoor city people who rip off nature but can't see their impact. Because they live indoors, they are disconnected and crave connection which they attempt to purchase as consumer

items. The citizens of the "developed nations," then, have no ideal target either, and are never "developed" enough. These citizens are taught to crave yachts and private jets, and if they could afford it they would have two or three ...

Success in the *"developed" countries* means being able to be lazy and wasteful and vain. The thrill in *"developed" countries* is to go shopping. Women are particularly targeted by advertising and told they are never pretty enough and must buy things to have self-esteem. The goal of women's magazines for at least 40 years is to keep women's self image secure only as female sex objects or as female sexual predators. This keeps everyone "below the waist" and not in their hearts or in their brains. Welcome to "development"!

Citizens of *"developed" countries* are trained to be easily tempted and can easily be bought off. Convenience is never convenient enough, speed is never fast enough, the house is never big enough, there are never enough clothes in the closet. This is the ethic of the *"developed" countries* as their citizens become more and more obese. 35% in the U.S. and Australia are obese with another 30% overweight. The *"developed" countries* are inhabited by pigs. Is this "developed?"

"Development" or *"progress"* is a fake facade that hypnotizes the masses. In reality, 15% of Americans are on food stamps (state subsidies for food) and the U.S. is bankrupt. If the U.S. is the model of *"development,"* why is it printing 30 billion dollars a month to stay afloat? Thus the lie of becoming *"developed"* is a bankrupt fantasy.

The most *"developed country,"* leading the world with culturally invasive programs and policies, is the United States, which spends most of it's money on *military* so it can maintain its predator parasitic position in world.

9. ***"Developing" countries*** are countries targeted for assimilation and conquest by debt. These countries have hundreds of uninvited NGO's (non-government organizations) who come with money dripping off of them to develop *Consumerism and centralization* as fast as possible. This is called "help." An example is an NGO that brings in waste water systems instead of teaching about composting toilets and urban gardening that could use grey water. The waste water systems just waste water and teach careless wastefulness. Carelessness is the Globalist way. NGO's always sweep problems under the rug of "development" and never examine true sources of reform, because that would *not be profitable for those who fund* the Foundations/NGOs.

The pyramid of exploitation has *Globalists* at the top, followed by banks, followed by governments/corporations, followed by "non-profit" foundations, followed by NGOs, followed by assimilation to *dominant culture* values, followed by debt, followed by more regulations. New laws are passed to support insurance companies, multi-national corporations, and a police state. This is what is "developing" in the "developing nations" and all this is called "progress."

The globalist goal of bringing everyone into the "formal economy" is to rip everyone off of local community power and uniqueness.

Regulations are pushed for convenience and safety. We will see a continual call for more "safety" until any independent movement can be seen as illegal. The more "developed" the country, the more police are needed to maintain all the laws. U.S. has 6 times more people in prison than the worldwide average, therefore, if one was to follow the *doublespeak* guidance, developing countries would expect to have more and more people in prison like the "developed" U.S.

"Developing" countries really means someone is developing the resources of a country for extraction to the dominant, foreign, urban countries. To do this the people are "developing" into a market in the global *monoculture* , where one fashion can be sold to everyone in the world and controlled.

"Progress" equals dependence. Thus "developing" is *doublespeak* for enslavement.

10. Disconnecting vanity will be a new concept for some people, and may not exist as words in your native language. It is not just egotism, or narcissism, or false pride, but it could include all these. The energy surrounding *disconnecting vanity* has been called *self-importance,* a central understanding in the writings of Carlos Castaneda who was influenced by *Book of the Hopi* (Page 3).

By putting the word "disconnecting" before the word *"vanity,"* I am trying to point out the fruit of *vanity,* which is destructive disconnection. This makes acting like a whore or a war criminal possible. Lipstick and war crimes. *Vanity* is poison, not some acceptable aspect of human life. In my understanding, there is no "healthy pride." All pride blocks true spiritual awakening. *Vanity Magazine* is an indication that our society is truly sick. And it is no coincidence that the oceans, atmosphere, ground water and soil are also becoming sick.

But to explain it:

Disconnecting vanity disconnects us from our *compassion*ate heart, which is our true quiet nature. *Disconnecting vanity* separates us from each other, from our *compassion* with each other, from our connection with animals and plants and spiritual intuitions. *Disconnecting vanity* allows us to become lost in false pride and egotism. We want to "run the show" and be a hero. We want applause. When we listen to the chattering internal dialogue in our head, and fail to listen to our own heartfelt conscience, we are lost in *disconnecting vanity.* When we obey our boss or sergeant in order to do a "good job" without consulting our conscience, we are bowing to *disconnecting vanity.* When we force romance, we kill romance because we are lost in "me me me." We will suffer and cause suffering when we are tempted by *disconnecting vanity.*

Disconnecting vanity can demonize others (throw stones with our thoughts) to dehumanize them and allow abuse (actually throw stones). When Jesus said, "You who have never sinned, throw the first stone," he successfully exposed *disconnecting vanity* and awoke the crowd to our common connecting *compassion.* When Buddha said "Hatred will not cease by hatred," he pointed out the futile actions of *disconnecting vanity.*

All hierarchies are based on rank, and rank is based on *disconnecting vanity,* for in truth, nothing can be higher or better than anything else. No priest can be closer to Truth than anyone else. No one is more elite than anyone else, unless they buy that false identity and use force to create victims, who they dominate. To think "I am more than you" is egotistic, vain, and actually deranged. Rank and rape are both manifestations of this *disconnecting vanity.* So is greed. The greedy one is the disconnected personality which was created by glorifying "me me me." The deranged elitist is actually addicted to props and awards for his or her self identity. Her personality is thus a house of cards with little real strength. Real strength comes from *personal sovereignty* which needs no status or props and is the opposite of *disconnecting vanity.*

Everyone has an intellect, but the intellect can become isolated and ruthless when *disconnecting vanity* takes control of us. This is what happens to criminals, to priests, to politicians, to scientists, and now to our "*Globalists*," who think they are masters of the multi-verse. Scientists who discover for "science's sake" are lying. Their *disconnecting vanity* is dividing and conquering nature for the sake of "me me me." Being lost in our heads and lost in our pride leads to insane destruction, which is exactly what we are witnessing now. In the pages of this book we examine the crimes of our times. The solution we seek will be in purifying ourselves from "me me me."

Certainly the solution is not more top-down planning by *disconnecting vanity!*

Purification from *disconnecting vanity* is a pole called spiritual love and awakening. The opposite pole is the person who is so isolated from his/her own conscience and *compassion*, that all he/she can hear is his/her own head talking. The extreme of this deluded pole is called satanic or evil.

I made the table under "22. *Inverse Relationships*" in this Glossary to show some examples of our choices. My complete premise is that we live in a moral multi-verse. *To think otherwise is the work of disconnecting vanity.*

We can choose connecting *compassion* or "me me me." The first gives us truth, love, kids who grow up without state terror, and clean rivers. The second leads to lies and *evil* and suffering and destruction.

This whole idea was given to us in a simple petroglyph in Arizona called the Hopi Prophecy (Chapter 22).

Originally I was going to use the words "Separated Ego," however, there is no such "thing" as ego, because ego is not a thing. There is no such "thing" as God because God is not a thing. "I" is not a noun and neither is God. Both are active verbs. So I dodged that whole conundrum and came up with *the vanity that disconnects,* or *disconnecting vanity.*

This places *vanity* as an activity, which it is. It is an activity with consequences.

"*Separated Ego*" was going to signify separated egotism. *Separated ego* or *false pride* is the opposite pole of the *connected* quiet spiritual heart. Scientists use the *separated ego* (or egotism) to come up with divide and conquer designs. (See *technocracy* below) Professors and "scientists" use separated ego to claim authority. The rapist uses separated ego or *disconnecting vanity* to crush his own *compassion* and serve sensual intoxication at someone else's expense.

The *separated ego* wants to "help" other people without considering their *personal sovereignty.* Most "well-meaning" workers employed by Global institutions have this disease. Without being asked, they come to "help" (assimilate) others.

In its far extreme, *disconnecting vanity* manifests intentional pain by trying to be superior. The colonial European powers (Britain, Spain, Portugal, Belgium, France, Germany, Italy, Russia) for 500 years have used *disconnecting vanity* to deny their crimes. Thus egotism or *disconnecting vanity* is rightly called criminal. In the farthest extreme, *separated ego* is insane, and this book proves the lineage of this syndrome among our present leadership.

Examples of *separated ego* is a man so full of pride that he cannot look at his mistakes and is separated from actual reality. *Disconnected vanity* means the same thing. Another example is a king who wants to be remembered and builds monuments in his name, but he uses slave labor. His *disconnected vanity* thinks he will be remembered as "great!," when in fact, he will be remembered as a tyrant who abused his people. Today, every city everywhere has monuments to *vanity* built by people with *disconnecting vanity* who think, for example, war is glorious. In reality, war is hell. But *disconnected vanity* makes up its own reality. This **separation from reality** created by *vanity* or ego is the main reason crime and abuse is supported by our leadership, who are not connected in the heart to nature or other people.

11. ***Dominant culture*** is any group of people who think they are superior and follow their *vanity* to consciously, or unconsciously, destroy and use other cultures. Dominance is based on intolerance. *Disconnecting vanity* rarely wants to learn anything new, and neither does a *dominant culture.* The *dominate culture* wants it's own style of *monoculture* without diversity. *Dominant cultures* believe in class stratification, disparity, and caste entitlement for themselves. They vainly feel glory in domination.

In Cusco, Peru, the Spanish tore down the ancient Inca temple and built upon it's foundations their own temple, and called it "The Triumph." To this day, this *vanity* and hate is not questioned in Peru, and the Church is still chauvinistic and proud. The humility of real spirituality never has been modeled by the West for the entire 500 year Colonial period.

Evidence in literature suggests that in 1193, the Buddhist Nalanda University in Northern India, was sacked by Bakhtiyar Khilji, a Turk. Muslim conquest in India is seen by scholars as one of the reasons of the decline of Buddhism in India. The Persian historian Minhaj-i-Siraj, in his chronicle the Tabaqat-I-Nasiri, reported that thousands of monks were burned alive and thousands beheaded as Khilji tried his best to uproot Buddhism. The burning of the library continued for several months and "smoke from the burning manuscripts hung for days like a dark pall over the low hills."

When the Chinese invaded sovereign Tibet in the 1950s, they murdered thousands of monks and nuns and destroyed monasteries and hermitages with cannon fire.

In Indonesia tens of thousands of Chinese were killed with the excuse they were "communists" because they didn't "believe in God." Many became Catholics just to survive. These are examples of the mentality of a *dominant culture. Disconnecting vanity* runs the *dominant culture* and the *dominant culture* runs the *disconnecting vanity* which is disconnected from sane grounded nature.

Dominant cultures used to be nationalistic but are becoming a world centralizing culture that bundles national cultures. An example is the merging of English and French and Western colonial powers under the NATO (North Atlantic Treaty [War] Organization) who all distribute the same technology, the same news, the same values to their citizens. Most national governments everywhere are *dominant urban cultures* trying to crush local ethnic diversity for more "efficient" control. They do this through laws, "monetary incentives," and national school curriculums to herd diversity.

12. ***Doublespeak*** comes from the book *1984* by George Orwell, which is a method of deliberate deception, using words to trick the thinker. For example *"progress"* sounds so good, that the thinker doesn't see destruction. Another example is the Globalist use of the word "peace," which means homogenization through war. "We will bring *democracy* to Iraq" by killing over a million innocent civilians, is example of the *doublespeak* use of word "democracy." The "Department of Defense," is *doublespeak* for the Department of Aggression. "War Heroes" is an American *doublespeak* term for murderers.

    Our schools do not teach the language *doublespeak*, because this would expose the manipulative deception, such as patriotism, we are now being controlled by. *Doublespeak* is one use of cognitive dissonance to confuse and gain control of other peoples' behavior. It is semantic lying.

13. ***Entitled*** refers to the childish demands and expectations of a spoiled, pampered child. Do you think you are *entitled* to indoor plumbing? Why? A friend of mine, Ted Howard, introduced a new word to me … "entitle-itis," a contagious mental disease now causing the sixth mass extinction event on Planet Earth.

14. ***Evil*** in this series means deliberate cruelty.

15. ***"Freedom"*** used to mean the opportunity which was *not* allowed by former despotism. Now "*freedom*" means escape from personal responsibility and giving power to regulatory agencies, run at the top by *Globalists*. So "*freedom*" now means being a cog in a machine and a "safe" slave who is "free" of responsibility. The last thing most of us want is the trouble of being involved with anything. For almost all urbanites, being anonymous and having no accountability equals "*freedom.*" Above all "freedom" means high consumption. "America is the land of the free," means, now, free to be obese at the expense of wage slaves elsewhere.

    In a *dominant culture,* "*freedom*" means *freedom* for the rich, and "*freedom*" is measured by the impunity to be wasteful. We can be more "free" than someone else and this is measured by our ability to feel *entitled* at the expense of "losers" who we keep at starvation wages with armies of "hero" thugs. Lipstick and war crimes.

16. ***Globalists*** refers to those at top of a world wide (or so they hope) pyramid of power outlined historically in Chapter 2, who want total control through *centralization*. Total control is called "Full Spectrum Dominance." Centralization means local control disappears. In this book series, the noun Globalist refers to actual people and is capitalized, while the adjective globalist, as in globalist agendas, is lower case.

17. ***Globalization*** is *monoculture* under a pyramid of power run by the top *Globalists* who use their primary weapon, secret financial manipulations of interest rates and currency valuations, to manipulate economies, and thereby, governments. The aim of all Globalist programs is to introduce *debt* to local communities, and this is done by buying off gullible leaders. Their citizens become addicted to globally supplied items and speed. These leaders are very foolish, because the supply chain is *unsustainable*. The *Globalists* know this and are planning ahead. There will be no collapse from lack of planning. There will be an organized collapse. The *Globalists* are already "de-populating" the "extra eaters" with *sanctioned*

diseases (See Glossary term below), to create their "efficient" manageable world. They will eventually use the supply chain everywhere, as a chain for slavery and depopulation, or genocide, as they are doing in Iraq, Libya, and Syria today. Codex Alimentarius, the 2009 world food safety law, establishes nutritional standards that are inadequate and will starve any population. The purpose is to set the standards for the rations that will be handed out as the supply chain is tightened. The rations will of course be called "safe."

Those who claim that *globalization* is just organic integration and communication are in denial that the UN, IMF, WTO, World Bank, central banks, most media, and the values in most advertising, were all created and are now controlled by the *Roth-efeller* banksters in a continuous bid for control through debt for over 200 years.

18. ***Grasping desire*** is demonstrated by the monkey that reaches into a narrow mouth jar and grabs a treat, but with his fist clenched, he can't get his hand out of jar. She doesn't want to drop the treat, and so he or she becomes trapped. *Grasping desire* is almost the same as the word "attachment," as used in Buddhism. We think we are the boss and are chasing the carrot, but really the carrot is controlling us because we are letting *grasping desire* control us. And if we are unlucky enough to get a bite of the carrot we will become addicted and want another bite. To be ruled by lust, by want, by craving is to be controlled by *grasping desire.* In Buddhism the seeker cuts this habit and is then free of material bondage. In Christianity, *grasping desire* is the mechanism by which temptation controls us.

The carrot does not control the donkey. The donkey's stomach or taste buds don't control her either. She or he is controlled by the habits of desire. *Grasping desire* might be called unmanaged karma. There are no spiritual traditions that empower *grasping desire*, but there are anti-spiritual traditions that do, and one of them is the Illuminati.

19. ***The Great Mystery*** refers to what really surrounds us and includes us. Unnamable. *The Great Mystery* includes invisible realms of infinite spectrum that interact with our human dimension, but are veiled, often by our own prejudice. *The Great Mystery* includes the workings of our bodies, which we cannot possibly understand. Are you breathing right now? Did you control that? How did it happen? By remembering *the Great Mystery,* we listen, rather than assume. Thus, *the Great Mystery* is the bedrock of honesty, which is the

purification path. The *purification path* leads to *compassion*, which then places us in a moral multi-verse.

20. **Hero** in this series, refers to courageous male and female whistleblowers who have stood up against the threat of being smeared, fired, harassed or killed, to tell the truth.

21. **"His-story"** in this series refers to our lying history, which is the one sided fable of the past, written by the criminal *dominant culture* that enslaved, raped, and colonized the world.

    His-story ignores the crimes of the story teller. "*His-story*" ignores the story of the vanquished. *His-story* is still emerging through false news, such as what is occurring right now in Libya or Syria or Ukraine, or what really happened in El Salvador or Nicaragua.

    Another example is "Noble" prize winners who are really *technocratic* monsters or war criminals. By placing them in the spotlight with praise, and not telling what programs they are part of, "*his-story*" is being written, but not true history that might offer us *informed choice.*

    Wikipedia is perfect example of "*his-story*," never telling the true history of the victims when mentioning "triumphs." Wikipedia sanitizes crimes so no one is blamed. In Wikipedia, Mt. Rushmore is a famous monument, not a desecration of the sacred hills of the Lakota. There are no *evil* Presidents or Prime Ministers in "His-story." Alexander is called "the Great," when true history would name him as a psychopath.

22. **Indigenous people** in this series are defined as people who 1) speak an ancient regional language, 2) produce their own food, and 3) make their own clothing. People who dress like the *monoculture* and eat like the *monoculture* and can't remember their ancestors' local language are no longer *indigenous people* in this series, even if they genetically can claim to be. The fact that these wannabe "rich," so called "*indigenous people,*" expect entitlements and reparations so they can be un-*indigenous* like the *monoculture*, is a confusing point for many apologists.

    For example, an Eskimo community who still speaks Aleut are facing a crisis because they will have to leave their ancient land or all starve and freeze within a year, when the globalist supply chain of machine parts, fuel, and imported food is cut off. Thus their culture is no longer a *living culture.* By the definition above, they are no longer self-sufficient *indigenous people.* They are just *monoculture* globalized "modern" people who speak an old dialect and try to remember their past traditions, but are just waiting for the inevitable cut off. Almost all of us are in this Globalist *unsustainable* boat at this time. This book is meant to help change that so you and your family will survive.

    Most *indigenous people* were free of taxation as they wisely chose not to live in concentrated centers, but chose instead freedom and a direct relationship with the Earth. Unfortunately local gangsters usually had the land divided up into territories, but this was less institutionalized than what Europe and most of Asia had to endure for thousands of years. *Indigenous people* are not serfs! Europeans and most Asians were all serfs or slaves, and did not appreciate *indigenous cultures* when they were encountered. Being on a pecking order of dominance, the colonizers, in turn, made the defenseless *indigenous people* who they "discovered" into serfs, or just slaughtered them.

Today, *indigenous people* are specifically targeted for extinction by the United Nations and the method is to aggressively find them, and expose them to *Globalization* through tourism and "aid." Their leaders are brought to conferences where they experience powerlessness. They are specifically offered astronomical funds to destroy their values and corrupt them, then are offered chances to go into debt. If the regional *dominant culture* can hide the crime, they are simply bulldozed and starved out. The first step to legally taking land is to give *indigenous people,* who never "owned" the land, legal title to private property, (not community property) in the *dominant culture's* system. This has happened all over the world. Common land was made private holdings. Then it can be taxed, (which a non-cash people can't pay), confiscated and sold.

In looking for the proper word for the above I found these synonyms which well describe the activity of the *dominant culture* in relation to *indigenous lands* ... abduct, acquire, amass, annex, appropriate, bag, capture, catch, collect, commandeer, deprive, gather, get, grab, harvest, impound, levy, monopolize, nab, procure, reap, sieze, take, usurp.

Indigenous peoples are also facing intentionally dangerous vaccinations, as described by Mr. Depopulation, Bill Gates, who is not the Bill Gates you thought you knew. (Page 138)

Indigenous people are the opposite of *monoculture,* which is factory culture. As a parallel concept, homemade clothing is the opposite of factory clothing. One is made in the home without chemicals or power grid and the other comes from polluting corporations who hire sweat labor. One has soul, the other makes profit for someone at the top, and cuts as many corners as possible, in order to be "competitive." Those corners include cutting communities and cutting the Earth Mother.

Self sufficient outdoor *indigenous culture* is the opposite pole of indoor artificial city life, which is much more like living in a jail, hospital or zoo. *Indigenous* is ancient, sustainable, and self-propagating, while "modern" non-culture is invented by think tanks and advertising agencies to change us into cogs in a machine to harvest as much as possible, as quickly as possible, for the pyramid of abuse, which is this civilization. We citizens are seen as a market to be molded, not just as servants, security guards and middle men for elite plans, but as happy consumers, so we stay dumbed down and compliant. "The *military* is doing such a good job at all the check points keeping us safe!"

Indigenous is the opposite of this plan, and so is seen as the enemy of Globalist "One World" "modern progress."

The *indigenous* mind sees the hills as sacred. The *dominant culture* mind is the opposite and see the hills as dirt to be sifted for something that can be sold to enrich someone who will "get ahead" of their neighbors and have status and opulence.

The *indigenous* mind is grounded and very simple in the best way. The opposite is the *dominant culture* mind that is lost in *vanity.*

23. ***Informed choice*** implies that each of us, whether we are educated or not, are active choosers. To make good decisions we need accurate information, not lies.

24. ***Inverse Relationships***

    The more urban a civilization is, the more *unsustainable.*

The more *indigenous* a civilization is, the more sustainable.

The more urban, the more complex and vain.

The more *indigenous,* the more simple and innocent.

The more debt, the more slavery.

The less debt, the more freedom.

The more *disconnecting vanity,* the more lust and rape of everything.

The less *disconnecting vanity,* the more *compassion* and care.

The more developed a country is, the faster it will collapse.

The less developed a country is, the less it can collapse.

The Moral Multi-verse of Simplicity and Respect

We live on a continuum of relative purity or relative vanity. There is neither ultimate light nor ultimate darkness. There is no final heaven or enlightenment or moksha, nor a final hell or satan. We are always somewhere in between, learning something, and so is everyone else, including beings in other realms.

Therefore putting anyone or any place on a pedestal or in a pit is ignorant. There are no avatars, there are no devils. There is just all of us. We can make a moral choice in each example below.

Choice of Purification OR "Disconnecting Vanity"

natural		***artificial***
simple		***complex***
inner quietude		***inner scheming***
listening		***talking***
compassionate	*– or –*	***too busy to care***
awakening		***unconscious***
holding to love		***holding to hate***
humble and free		***proud and enslaved***
open minded		***know-it-all***
witnessing		***mapping***
innocent	*– or –*	***compromised***
good		***evil***
communion		***acquisition***
connected		***dominant***
altruistic		***selfish***

forgiving	*– or –*	*judgmental*
empathetic		*efficient*
kind		*cruel*
cooperative		*criminal*
self-sufficient		*insatiable greed*
grace		*sin*
clean		*satanic*
honest information		*deceptive ads*
responsible		*carefree/careless*
respectful steward	*– or –*	*polluting consumer*
sacred		*profane*
sober		*substances*
sincere		*phony*
guileless		*posing*
honoring		*sports sex*
indigenous		*city lights glamour*
allowing diversity		*need more market share*
privacy		*secret data collection*

25. Military now means state-sponsored terrorism to pillage other countries and to force *globalization.* In a globalized world there is less and less need for *military*, yet we see more and more. This is because national security is a lie. The emergency that the *Globalists* are planning for is not attacks from other countries, but the local "insurgent" response to Full Spectrum Dominance. Remember, 99% of terrorist attacks are false flag operations. (Chapter 25) The purpose of *military* is to control all of us. We are the enemy.

In the name of "defense," a police state is being put in place. With the fake "War on Terror" (Chapter 26) this police state became a global goal. The enemy is hiding under your bed. The enemy is everywhere! The main Terrorist organization which is active today is called NATO. In Tibet, the Chinese *military* backs up *dominant culture* oppression of *indigenous people.* Also in China, the *military* persecutes and tortures religious sects such as Falang Gong (Chapter 20). In Iran the Bahai Faith was attacked 30 years ago by the *military* and now the Sufis are under attack. On the island of East Timor, the Australian and American governments ganged up with their puppet, the Indonesian government, to slaughter Christians using the *military.* The *military* is usually an aggressive arm of a *dominant culture.*

The military today would only be needed in a country that refused *globalization* and needed armed troops as a shield, because the only aggressive regime in the world now is that of the *Globalists.*

Now, at this time, the most dangerous *military* comprises 850-1000 U.S. *military* bases worldwide and 55,000 U.S. "special ops," or assassins. This terrorism is also environmental with extremely poisonous substances such as "Depleted" Uranium Ammunition which is not depleted. That name is *doublespeak* lie. The proper name is Radioactive Ammunition.

> "About 55,000 members of the U.S. Special Operations Command are providing humanitarian aid [*doublespeak*] and training soldiers and police in more than 60 countries, according to their commander Navy Adm. Eric Olson.
>
> "*They're building long-term relationships [gangs] in every country,* in every region *in the world, and* we need them there for a long time," Olson said here yesterday, at the 20th Annual Special Operations/Low-Intensity [man to man] Conflict symposium. "Special operations forces—especially Army special operations—do this [killing] better than anyone."
>
> "Olson, and a panel of experts provided insights on special operation activities throughout the world, to more than 300 participants at the February 10-12 symposium. While humanitarian [*doublespeak*] efforts are part of their mission, these deployed special operations forces' main focus is on deterring [killing] America's enemies [freedom fighters in other countries]." [159]

They are "deterring America's enemies" in "every region in the world." This is *doublespeak* for saying that anything anywhere that is not yet controlled is being attacked, and that every region of the world needs to be controlled by force.

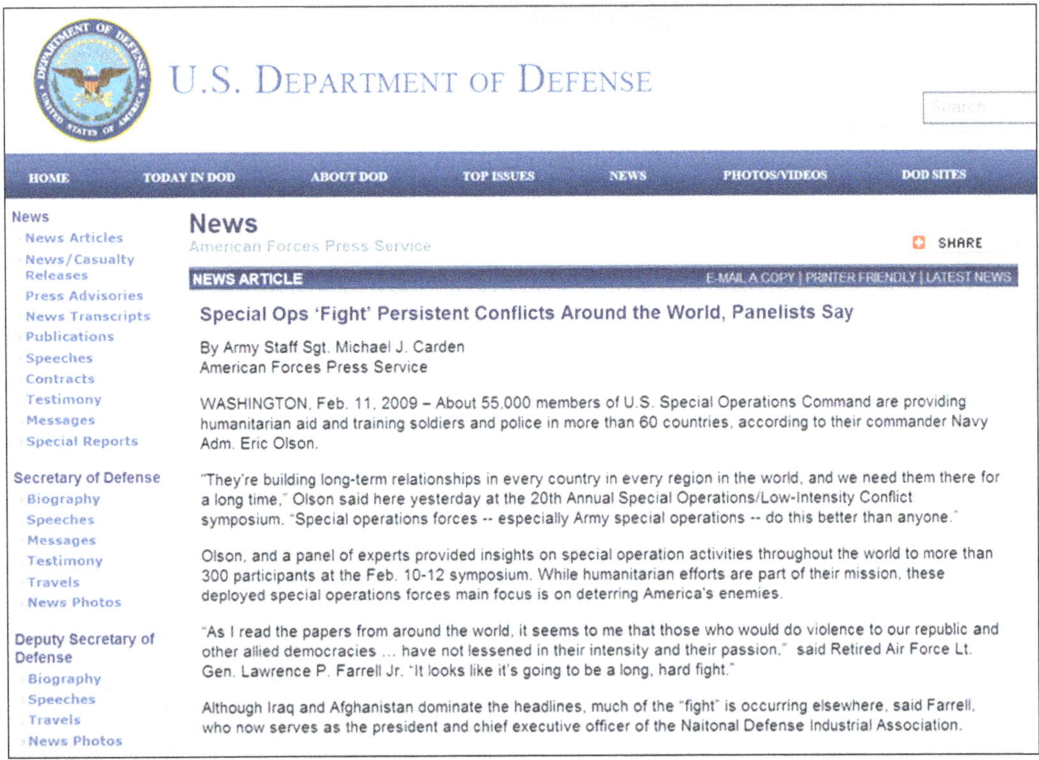

U.S. DEPARTMENT OF DEFENSE

HOME | TODAY IN DOD | ABOUT DOD | TOP ISSUES | NEWS | PHOTOS/VIDEOS | DOD SITES

News
News Articles
News/Casualty Releases
Press Advisories
News Transcripts
Publications
Speeches
Contracts
Testimony
Messages
Special Reports

Secretary of Defense
Biography
Speeches
Messages
Testimony
Travels
News Photos

Deputy Secretary of Defense
Biography
Speeches
Travels
News Photos

News
American Forces Press Service

SHARE

NEWS ARTICLE — E-MAIL A COPY | PRINTER FRIENDLY | LATEST NEWS

Special Ops 'Fight' Persistent Conflicts Around the World, Panelists Say

By Army Staff Sgt. Michael J. Carden
American Forces Press Service

WASHINGTON, Feb. 11, 2009 – About 55,000 members of U.S. Special Operations Command are providing humanitarian aid and training soldiers and police in more than 60 countries, according to their commander Navy Adm. Eric Olson.

"They're building long-term relationships in every country in every region in the world, and we need them there for a long time," Olson said here yesterday at the 20th Annual Special Operations/Low-Intensity Conflict symposium. "Special operations forces -- especially Army special operations -- do this better than anyone."

Olson, and a panel of experts provided insights on special operation activities throughout the world to more than 300 participants at the Feb. 10-12 symposium. While humanitarian efforts are part of their mission, these deployed special operations forces main focus is on deterring America's enemies.

"As I read the papers from around the world, it seems to me that those who would do violence to our republic and other allied democracies ... have not lessened in their intensity and their passion," said Retired Air Force Lt. Gen. Lawrence P. Farrell Jr. "It looks like it's going to be a long, hard fight."

Although Iraq and Afghanistan dominate the headlines, much of the "fight" is occurring elsewhere, said Farrell, who now serves as the president and chief executive officer of the Naitonal Defense Industrial Association.

This 2009 article is not reviewed anywhere that I know of. Note in the last sentence that the speaker, Retired Air Force Lt. Gen. Lawrence P. Farrell Jr., who is giving advise about attitude-policy, was in 2009 employed by the Defense (Aggression) Industry.

Farrel describes the endless war ahead in every country of the world (where U.S. is now murdering people with special ops). He says that there will be a "long hard fight" against those who want to do violence against "the allied democracies," meaning the *Rothschild* owned nations such as NATO. We will see in the later chapters that this "violence" never occurred and was a lie. Remember, the Department of "Defense" is operating *within* the "allied democracies" also, and as of December 2013, can legally kill anyone anywhere, including U.S. citizens, without due process. Habeus corpus is no longer guaranteed. (Chapter 29)

Farrel mentions 60 nations. With U.S. 55,000 covert ops, this means each nation might have hundreds to thousands of very well trained and well supplied covert murderers on their soil, and this count does not include the 850-1000 *military* bases.

The Russians don't have this system. The Chinese don't. The world's enemy is the U.S. according to this statement and no country is safe from U.S. terror in the "long hard fight." Nelson Mandela saw the U.S. in this light also, Page 72. The "War on Terror" is really the War of Terror. In 2011 the U.S. tripled its arms sales to other nations to $66 billion dollars.

26. ***Monopolization*** of control and *homogenization* of market demand is the goal of *centralization*. The goal of the *Globalists* is to create a worldwide *monoculture* that looks, thinks, and acts the same, and which likes it. To do this, any crime is used. *Monoculture* means no diversity or dissidence. *Monopolization* means no competition. *Globalists* want to own the whole planet and every thought on it.

    "Helping local communities" can be very deceptive, when the help offered is the same blueprint of help, no matter what community or tribe or region on the globe is targeted for "aid." So-called "aid" always means bringing local communities, who were independent, into the global *monoculture* of *Consumerism* and debt, known as "the formal economy." Success of "aid" (*doublespeak* for assimilation) is to convince people to become "independent" business people, and take loans. Responding for calls from local communities (who want things that were advertised into their desires for decades) is not helping them, it is just continuing the program of *assimilation*.

27. ***Personal sovereignty*** means we each take responsibility as choosers and also take responsibility for the consequences of our choices. Our choices have impact on others and we care. As sovereign choosers we demand and give respect. *Personal sovereignty* means we respect other peoples' *personal sovereignty*. *Personal sovereignty* is the opposite of what the *Globalists* want. The *Globalists* want unthinking, irresponsible sheep-people (known as sheeple) who they can herd this way and that. We want to be *sovereign choosers*, not sheeple following some subliminal *social engineering*. We are human beings, not sheep or rabbits or grasshoppers.

    "The lord is my shepherd," is a belief of a sheeple that was created by the priests to enslave the masses, while Buddha's dying words, "Be a light onto yourselves," encourages *personal sovereignty* and following no one, including him.

We cannot heal anything until we take *our power of choice* seriously. We can choose to co-operate with injustice or not. We can choose to stay on this planet or not. We each have the ultimate choice right now to go along with something, or not.

28. *Predictive programming* is simply the seeding of the mind of the listener or viewer, with a concept or image, which opens the listener to accept that possibility as an unsurprising probability.

If I showed you a blue fire truck for ten years in movies, you would not be surprised to see one in real life. We do this with children all the time, and this has been called the power of suggestion. *Predictive programming* is used to create fearful despicable unworthy enemies in the minds of masses. Examples are the "Japs," the "Germans," the "Russians," the "Moslems," the "Terrorists," the "Chinese." *Predictive programming* is used to corrupt morals and create promiscuity, or to introduce trans-humanism (Pages 83, 220-221) as a viable future for human beings. Here are some definitions from the web …

> "*Predictive programming* is a subtle form of psychological conditioning provided by the media to acquaint the public with planned societal changes to be implemented by "the powers that be." If and when these changes are put through, the public will already be familiarized with them and will accept them as 'natural progressions,' as Alan Watt calls it; thus lessening any possible public resistance and commotion. *Predictive programming* therefore may be considered as a veiled form of preemptive mass manipulation or mind control, courtesy of our puppet masters."
>
> – bibliotecapleyades.net/sociopolitica/sociopol_mediacontrol66.htm

From MindControlWiki.com—"*Predictive Programming* is the practice of saying something is going to happen (predicting) enough times that people assume it will happen without question. Once they have accepted this future event as a *fait accompli*, their behaviors fall in line accordingly."

And from Wikipedia, the globalist propaganda disinformation website, which would deny that there are any puppet masters or that *social engineering* is constantly in play and influencing much of what Wikipedia claims to cover accurately …

(Wikipedia exists to re-write history and program anyone who uses it … For this reason Wikipedia constantly uses the words "conspiracy theory" instead of conspiracy research, because, for the *Globalists* who control Wikipedia, the public should doubt that anyone official is conspiring anything.)

Wikipedia – "*Predictive programming* is a conspiracy theory [Smear. Thus Wikipedia distorts the obvious, as if the expression *fait accompli* never existed] promulgated by Alternative Media researchers Alex Jones, David Icke, Michael Hoffman, Alan Watt and others. [In other words only official mainstream media is valid, and anyone else is a nut job. This smears the whistleblowers who accurately identify *social engineering* mind control techniques. Thus if David Icke exposes pedophilia, he is to be dismissed as a conspiracy theorist because he is an "alternative media researcher."] The theory [the historical reality] proposes [exposes] that public media (such as films, television, newscasts, etc.) are deliberately seeded with subtle clues to future social, political, or technological changes. According to the theory [reality easily proven throughout this book], when the relevant change is later introduced into the world, the public has become used to the idea through exposure, and therefore passively accepts it rather than offering resistance or opposition. [Precisely as Rockefeller, Kissinger, and others have outlined on Pages 163, 252] *Predictive programming* is therefore thought [strike out the word "thought" because it is not speculation] to be a means of propaganda or mass psychological conditioning that operates on a subliminal or implicit level."

I, the author, include *predictive programming* in this book. I am deprogramming the globalist timeline and seeding the reader with new time lines that might actually help the reader survive and wake up and live a healthy life. To do this I bring in fact after fact to deprogram our sheeple belief in "progress," which is presently suicidal. I replace it with empowering seeds to offset the helpless seeding. Please see youtube on Robin Williams. [160]

29. ***"Progress"*** is the hypnotized religion of the masses under the deceptive *Globalists*, who know that the actual future is quite grim and includes a lot of death or "depopulation," which they themselves are organizing. Thus, the hypnotizing word *"progress"* is actually a lie. However, for most people *"progress"* means "more comfort for me right now, and who cares about the depleted toxic world my children will inherit." "Modern *progress*" is a vain, abusive mistake.

    The religion of *"Progress"* hypnotizes and blinds us to the real future. *"Progress"* is exactly like a drug that deludes our perception. "Modern" is a derivative word of *"progress"* which implies things are getting superior and better, when in fact the opposite is true. We are facing unprecedented crisis because of modern abuse. *"Progress"* means more indulgence for consumers to keep us stupid, which gives more control to the *Globalists*. In this book, *"progress"* will always appear in quotation marks, because it is a *doublespeak* lie. If *"progress"* is not sustainable, then it is an illusion.

30. ***The Purification Path*** is the effort of a spiritual student to drop attachments and desires so that the heart and mind can be clear and able to see clearly. This leads us towards our inner nature which is connected kindness. It also leads to a spiritual experience (not intellectual). This experience is an ongoing and deepening awakening, or it could be called, a dissolving of separation. The *purification path* cannot be accurately described because it leads to union with *the Great Mystery*. The *purification path* exists in all realms with countless traditions. In this book, the Hopi (North Central Arizona) Prophecy succinctly describes the *purification path*. (Chapter 22) In this book Buddha and Jesus are viewed as de-programmers that shared a *purification path* which they themselves had walked.

31. ***Recovering "developed" countries*** are countries that are starting down the road of mass unemployment and *resource depletion* and are beginning to become poor again which is bringing back some sanity after their drunk past. Young people are starting to renounce ever-grasping lifestyle as a mentality and lifestyle. Europe is starting to recover from the glut of colonial global rip-off. U.S. and Australia are still stuck in over-consumption and are lagging in their mental recovery. U.S. stays afloat by using "quantitative easing," or fake dollars, to keep itself propped up, and uses its *military* overseas to capture resources. When this ends, U.S. will start recovering from its obese mentality of thievery.

32. *Re-localization* is the opposite of centralized *Globalization. Re-localization* or "de-colonization" is not only migration out of the cities, (as *resource depletion* makes urban life bankrupt). In this series, *re-localization* also means an empowerment of local community in decision making. *Re-localization* would resist national or provincial regulation for example, because these do not respect *personal sovereignty.* "We won't bow to you. You have to respect us. This is our land and we understand this land. You do not." *Re-localization* would ban aerial surveillance or satellite mapping as an infringement on the sovereign choice of local stewards, for example. *Re-localization* would resist textbooks written somewhere else.

33. *Resource depletion* refers to the fact that easy-to-extract resources have already been stolen from *indigenous people*, and now all resources will be harder to find, and more expensive to bring to market.

(The reader must remember that all of Africa, Americas, Australia and the Pacific are *indigenous* peoples' land, not the land of the occupiers presently abusing these lands and holding it at gunpoint. All these lands were taken illegally by criminals in the last 500 years. The occupiers have no ancient language rooted with the land. They don't know the land and don't intend on ever knowing it. They are just using it up as fast as possible.)

The search for resources is now invading previously barren appearing *indigenous* territory. People using aerial surveys which map underground formations with low frequency technology without permission, see the people living in that area, not as real human beings worthy of respect. So now, underground resources, not apparent before, are being sought after, and anyone in the way will be destroyed.

All resources will become increasingly unavailable every year for the rest of human history. This reality was coined as "Peak Everything" by Richard Heinberg (who presciently endorsed the Transition Towns movement which was a response to Peak Oil research). We have reached the peak on all mineral and resource extraction and are now in a new era of permanent decline.

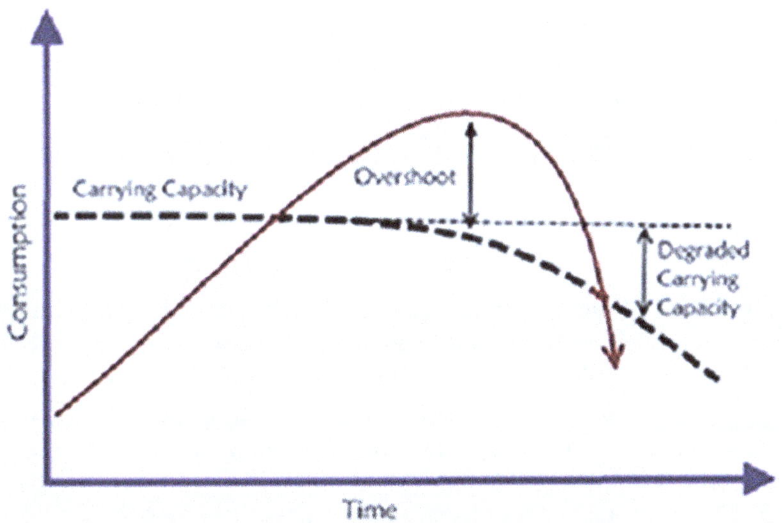

In the graph above, the population peak (red) has not come yet, while the resource extraction peak, which for humans translates as carrying capacity, has. This period of too many animals or people or plants, that over reproduced when times were fat and resources were plentiful, to then in their numbers, face *resource depletion*, is called *overshoot*. In nature, species that face overshoot always face a population crash, as the red line shows. Lots of death.

As demand goes up and supply goes down, prices will increase, and that means more poverty. We are now entering increasing poverty until demand (population) decreases at the same rate as the decline of resources. (The reader can ask whether population will decrease from crisis or *informed choice*? How will the latter be organized without alert, informed sober people?) The only populations who will not have to experience continual downsizing of consumption will be the *indigenous peoples* who know how to be self-sufficient without the industrial supply chain. Their lifestyle represents the stable life that humans had before the past 200 year bubble of cheap energy that led to *overshoot*. Their way is also our future lifestyle, when all the ripoff experiments from cheap energy end.

A point will come when some resources will remain in the ground because they are too expensive to extract. Production must be seen as the key limit, not underground reserves that are 10 miles beneath the surface and might seem endless. So what? We cannot afford to bring them to production. And those who tout "free energy technology" for extracting anything from anywhere do not realize the impact this will have.

There will be no societal or population collapse as many Peak Oil researchers and Deep Ecologists predict. The collapse is already being managed by the Illuminati *Globalists*. A controlled demolition of society as we know it, involving *sanctioned diseases* is already in play.

34. Roth-efellers is a new word combining the Rothschild and Rockefeller family names. The link between these two conspiratorial families is documented and I will offer these examples here. There are mountains of examples.

> *"These International bankers (Rothschilds) and Rockefeller-Standard Oil interests control the majority of newspapers and the columns of these newspapers, to club into submission or drive out of public office, officials who refuse to do the bidding of the powerful corrupt cliques which compose the invisible government."*
>
> – President Teddy Roosevelt in *New York Times*, March 27, 1922

[In fact, Teddy rubber stamped *Roth-efeller* Standard Oil for years, while supposedly carrying out anti-trust campaigns. His father was a *Rothschild* drug runner.]

> "However much of the Rockefeller wealth may be attributed to old John D.'s rapacity and ruthlessness, its origins are indubitably based on his initial financing from the National City Bank of Cleveland, which was identified in Congressional reports as one of the three *Rothschild* banks in the United States, and by his [John D. Rockefeller's] later acceptance of the guidance of Jacob Schiff of Kuhn, Loeb & Company, who had been born in the *Rothschild* house in Frankfort and was now the principal *Rothschild* representative (but unknown as such to the public) in the United States.

"With the seed money from the National City Bank of Cleveland, old John D. Rockefeller soon laid claim to the title of "the most ruthless American." It is more than likely that it was this quality which persuaded the Rothschilds to back him. Rockefeller realized early in the game that the oil refinery business, which could offer great profits in a short time, also was at the mercy of uncontrolled competition. His solution was a simple one—crush all competition. The famous Rockefeller dedication to total monopoly was simply a business decision.

"John D. Rockefeller embarked on a campaign of coercing all competing oil refineries out of business. He attacked on a number of fronts, which is also a lesson to all would be entrepreneurs. First, he would send a minion, not known to be working for Rockefeller, with an offer to buy the competing refinery for a low price, but offering cash. If the offer was refused, the competitor would then come under attack from a competing refinery which greatly undercut his price. He might also suffer a sudden strike at his refinery, which would force him to shut down. Control of labor through unions has always been a basic Rockefeller technique. [Communism was a *Rothschild* creation, Marx was a *Rothschild* employee (Page 52), and unions were never independent, they were tools.] Like the Soviet Union, the Rockefellers seldom have labor trouble. If these techniques failed, Rockefeller would then be saddened [sarcastic] by a reluctant decision to use violence, beating the rival workers as they went to and from their jobs, or burning or blowing up the competing refinery.

"These techniques convinced the Rothschilds that they had found their man. [The *Globalists* always jump on anyone exceptional to incorporate, steer, *co-opt*, in order to use them. All genius, good or horrible, is *co-opted i*mmediately, and if that doesn't work, the exceptional is seen as a threat and crushed.]

"*They sent their personal representative, Jacob Schiff, to Cleveland to help Rockefeller plan further expansion.* At this time, the Rothschilds controlled 95% of all railroad mileage in the U.S., through the J.P. Morgan Company and Kuhn Loeb & Company, according to official Department of Commerce figures for the year 1895. J.P. Morgan mentions in his Who's Who listing that he controlled 50,000 miles of U.S. railways.

"Schiff worked out an elaborate rebate deal for Rockefeller, through a dummy corporation, South Improvement Company. These rebates ensured that no other oil company could survive in competition with the Rockefeller firm. The scheme was later exposed, but by that time Rockefeller had achieved a virtual monopoly of the oil business in the United States. The daughter of one of his victims, Ida Tarbell, whose father was ruined by Rockefeller's criminal operations, wrote the first major exposé of the Standard Oil Trust. She was promptly denounced (whistleblowers are always denounced) as a "muckraker" by the poseur, Theodore Roosevelt, who claimed to be a "trust buster." In fact, he ensured the dominance of the Standard Oil Trust and other giant trusts.

"During the next half century, John D. Rockefeller was routinely caricatured by socialist propagandists as the epitome of the ruthless capitalist. At the same time, he was the principal financier (Rothschild also) of the world communist movement, through a firm called American International Company. Despite the fact that the House of Rothschild had already achieved world control (through international debt), the sound and fury was directed exclusively against its two principal representatives, John D. Rockefeller and J.P. Morgan. One of the few revelations of the actual state of affairs appeared in *Truth* magazine, December 16, 1912, in an article by George R. Conroy which pointed that out.

"Mr. Schiff is head of the great private banking house of Kuhn, Loeb & Company, which represents the Rothschild interests on this side of the Atlantic. He is described as a financial strategist and has been for years the financial minister of the great impersonal power known as Standard Oil. He was hand in glove with the Harrimans, the Goulds, and the Rockefellers in all their railroad enterprises ..."

"Because of these concealed factors, it was a relatively simple matter for the American public to accept the "fact" that the Rockefellers were the preeminent power in this country. This myth was actually clothed in the apparel of power, the Rockefeller Oil Trust becoming the "*military*-industrial complex" which assumed political control of the nation. The Rockefeller Medical Monopoly attained control of the health care of the nation, and the Rockefeller Foundation [that controls Carnegie Foundation], a web of affiliated tax-exempt creations, effectively controlled the religious and educational life of the nation. The myth succeeded in its goal of camouflaging the hidden rulers, the Rothschilds."

– *Rockefellers Secondary to Rothschilds,* By Eustace Mullins, 2008 [161]

The Rockefeller wealth and influence, as of 1975, was organized at "Rockefeller Family and Associates," headed by former Kuhn & Loeb law firm (Rothschild) employee J. Richardson Dilworth, starting in 1958.

Thus, I have introduced the word *"Roth-efellers."* There are more links shown between the two families, including marriage, in Chapter 2. The third book of the series further explores Rockefeller branches and their role in creating CFR, Trialateral Commission, and Bilderberg ties.

35. Rothschild. In this series, I use *Rothschild* as a possessive pronoun, such as *Rothschild* Hitler or *Rothschild* Israel or *Rothschild* U.S.. In fact the *Rothschild bankster* family placed and controlled Hitler, placed and controlled Zionists, created/controls Israel to this day, and owns the FED. In English, "bankster" is a new word combining banker and gangster. The word "bankster" is now being used, as more people study the banking system and realize the crimes of our times. *The History of the House of Rothschild* by Andrew Hitchcock needs to be read a few times in order to re-write true history into your mind. It is extracted from his more complete book *Synagogue of Satan* which I recommend, but without completely agreeing with. No two researchers should completely agree if they have done their own research. Also, Hitchcock seems to feel some races are superior to others, and the *dominant culture* is worthy. I disagree.

Remember, the world is now controlled by those who control debt, and thus, the Rothschilds control our world. It is a false rating that claims that Gates or Buffet are the richest men in the world. These men are just pawns themselves within the hundreds of trillions of dollars wealth controlled by Rothschilds, something a Rothchild rag like *Forbes Magazine* won't reveal.

An example of research that tens of thousands of researchers are producing … http://www.theforbiddenknowledge.com/hardtruth/the_rothschild_bloodline.htm

36. Sanctioned diseases are illnesses that are not discussed by *controlled media,* nor seriously researched by Center of Disease Control (CDC) or World Health Organization (WHO), and are therefore allowed to debilitate and reduce the population. *Sanctioned diseases* are not officially mandated; they are allowed because of silence, censorship of downside information, denial of responsibility, or, sometimes, are simply the result of covert bio-weapons. Examples are autism, Alzheimer's, xenohormone contamination (man made chemicals that act like hormones), effects of fluoride, effects of mercury in fish and dental fillings, effects of aluminum in packaging and vaccines, cancers and genetic disruption caused by wireless frequencies (See www.Bioinitiative.org), cancers and disruptions caused by other electromagnetic frequencies (EMF), radio (RF) and microwave frequencies and radiation, dirty electricity, tobacco (still legal in most countries), alcohol related diseases, etc. The graphs in Chapter 6 are more examples.

Another whole class of sanctioned disease are man made foods that never existed before and which our bodies are not familiar with. As an example …

"You cannot afford to jeopardize your health by consuming [food cooked with] unnatural oils and fats, such as man–made hydrogenated fats (trans-fats) and polyunsaturated fats and oils from vegetable oils (plant sources) except for extra virgin olive oil. These fats and oils are damaging to your entire body because they affect the structure of every single cell in the body.

> "These fats are toxic, increasing the body's need for vitamin E and other antioxidants (substances that guard the body against harmful effects).
>
> "The hydrogenation process used by the oils and fats industry produces trans-fats, which are more damaging than any other oils and fats, because it employs: 1) high heat, 2) a metal catalyst such as nickel, zinc, copper, or other reactive metals, and 3) hydrogen gas.
>
> "This is a volatile combination designed to extract and process oils, but it results in an extremely toxic product that the body reacts to it like it does to other toxins and poisons.
>
> "Also, these fats and oils go rancid (become decomposed) very easily, even when refrigerated, and often they are rancid when purchased at the store." [162]

Another example of dangerous food is modern wheat, which many people experience is "gluten allergy" or "wheat allergy," however they don't have same reaction to organically grown, chemical free wheat. Big Ag wheat is sprayed with massive amounts of Monsanto Roundup—glyphosate—to kill weeds and force more yield in the seed. Gluten allergy could actually be allergy to poison!

Attitudes such as "There are too many people anyway, so who cares?," and "This population is too big and must be reduced somehow," and "How do you know it is *our* company's cancer that is the problem?" unofficially sanction many diseases. *Sanctioned diseases* are made possible by regulatory agencies that have revolving doors of leadership with the industries they are supposed to regulate. Examples are compromised FDA, USDA, FCC, EPA and more. In U.S. these agencies were "cleansed" of integrity during the Reagan administration of the 1980s, which was run by George Bush Sr.

The WHO and CDC are controlled by the UN with its eugenics *Roth-efeller* roots. Intentional death and sterilization through vaccines *a la* Bill Gates, whose father was a *Roth-efeller* eugenics Planned Parenthood co-founder, is another group of *sanctioned diseases.* (Bill Gates was not an innovative entrepreneur; he was a globalist family heir and was given the computer technology and guided every step of the way. He was and is a globalist minion.) The placing of cell phone towers and electric utility Smart Meters in proximity to people are more intentional examples. Vaccine experimentation with *military* recruits is another. Direct attacks on population with geo-engineering jet trails and low frequency antennae clusters (HAARP) is another. The effects of pesticides, herbicides and Genetically Modified Organisms (GMO) are more examples of intentional attacks on our health.

Sanctioned diseases are man made medical problems that are either covert, or hidden in plain sight, but simply glossed over by *controlled media.* There will be an avalanche of cancers in the next few decades, and as of now, this is not an issue for politicians who are neither blowing the whistle, nor prosecuting criminals, because the intentionally dumbed down population is not demanding investigation. When challenged, industry runs whistleblowers out of office by installing their own pro-industry and heavily funded candidates. Political silence sanctions many diseases. This is occurring now on the island of Kauai (in Hawaii State) where the Biotech companies have been asked to be accountable for their use of pesticides in GMO experimentation near schools and public roadways, and their response is lawsuits against the county and the funding of their own pro-industry candidates. In California, $40 million was spent defeating a GMO labeling initiative. The same occurred in state of Washington.

> *"Virtually all of them are diseases of "civilization," i.e. created/enhanced/spread by humans living in an increasingly toxified environment, toxified by the industrial processes we now rely on for this insane way of living!"*
>
> – Ted Howard

37. ***Social engineering*** means secret and undiscussed manipulation of values through planned programs and subliminal messages using movies, TV, advertising, *Controlled media*, textbooks, and now Google, Facebook, YouTube and more, which screen news, censors information, and steer data access.

    An example of *social engineering* of values and identity, is distorted feminism, which now guides most "educated" young women worldwide who are very tolerant of female chauvinism while allowing the degradation of their own feminine nature so they can "get ahead" by adapting dominant male behavior. These millions of women are okay with boys being under represented in educational campaigns because they are bigoted, while they themselves are trying to be kings of the mountain and "be on top." Little do they know that they were targeted by *social engineering* programs that created all these attitudes as agendas to make them workaholic shoppers, dysfunctional mates, and single moms, in order to fragment society at the root, the family.

"Public relations" is no longer discussed out loud, because it has become ever more secretive and invasive.

38. Technocracy is a steered societal direction, but also an ideology. *Technocracy* can be considered a mental disease.

Technocracy, Inc. was co-founded by Marion King Hubbert, the "green guru," in the late 1930s. *Technocracy* is the Globalist use of new technology to control society. An example of use of *technocracy* is ALL data collection. IBM sold "supply machines" to *Rothschild* Hitler to organize and track the murder of six million Jews. The tatoo put on Jews in concentration camps was an IBM code. Rothchild Hitler was a technocrat supported by American technocrats.

> *"A clique of U.S. industrialists is hell-bent to bring a fascist state to supplant our democratic government and is working closely with the fascist regime in Germany and Italy. I have had plenty of opportunity in my post in Berlin to witness how close some of our American ruling families are to the Nazi regime ... Certain American industrialists had a great deal to do with bringing fascist regimes into being in both Germany and Italy. They extended aid [money] to help Fascism occupy the seat of power, and they are helping to keep it there."*
>
> – William E. Dodd, U.S. Ambassador to Germany, 1937

Technocracy wants total control, a *monoculture*, a police state, and an extinction of diversity in the name of "efficient, safe, secure, and peaceful justice for all, under equality." (Equality for a technocrat means rations.) The Trilateral Commission, another Rockefeller funded think tank, believes in *technocracy* as does Microsoft Globalist puppet Bill Gates and Eric Schmidt of Google.

> *"The Trilateral Commission is intended to be the vehicle for multinational consolidation of the commercial and banking interests [Roth-efeller] by seizing control of the political government of the United States. The Trilateral Commission represents a skillful, coordinated effort to seize control and consolidate the four centers of power ... political, monetary, intellectual and ecclesiastical. What the Trilateral Commission intends, is to create a worldwide economic power, superior to the political governments of the nation states involved. As managers and creators of the system, they will rule the future."*
>
> – U.S. Senator Barry Goldwater from his 1964 book, *With No Apologies.*

Zbigniew Brzezinski, first Director of the Trilateral Commission, architect of the Afghan holocaust, and consultant to globalist puppet Obama, wrote the books *Between Two Ages—*

America's Role in the Technetronic Era and *The Grand Chessboard—American Primacy and its Geostrategic Imperatives.*

In his words … *"The Technocratic Age is slowly designing an every day, more controlled society. The society will be dominated by an elite of persons* ***free from traditional values*** *(See Freedom in this Glossary), who will have no doubt in fulfilling their objectives by means of purged techniques, with which they will influence the behavior of people and will control and watch the society* ***in all details*** *… it will become possible to exert a practically permanent watch [all -seeing-eye] on each citizen of the world."*

Every sentence here is horrific (and I don't believe he even wrote this, as it was more likely a collaborative effort by his handlers), but I would like to draw attention to this line … He is saying "the Technocratic Age is designing a society." How can a period of time design something? This would be typical lying of *disconnected vanity,* which denies responsibility, and thus is not even a *sovereign personality.* That is, people ruled by *the vanity that disconnects* are not really human. They are heartless cogs. It is the *choices* of irresponsible heartless cogs like Brzezinski that are *designing* our *technocratic* nightmare, not some glacier called an "Age."

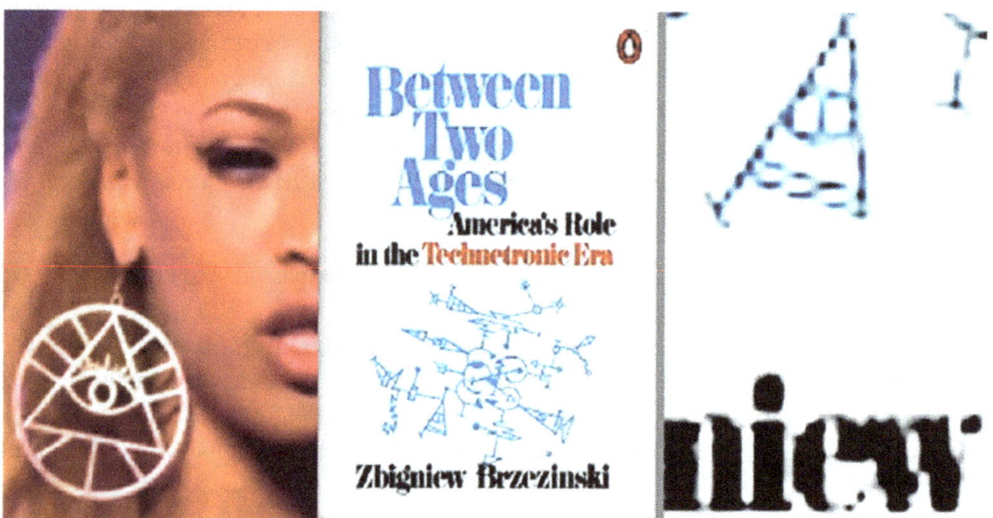

"All seeing eye" on X-Factor talent show earrings and on cover of Brzezinski's book. Lipstick and war crimes, a la Illuminati.

As Brzezinski demonstrates, *technocracy* is run by machine-like, disassociated, disconnected, dominance fixated power freaks, with very little connection to heart or nature. Jacque Fresco of the Zeitgeist movies was also a *technocrat.*

Most urban planners are *technocrats,* as is anyone "designing" someone else's future, or using other people's personal data without permission, such as those using computer tracking cookies or surveillance photos or Facebook. Jacque Fresco actually called himself a "social engineer!" Would you call yourself a "control freak," or a fricking "technocrat!" Controlling the brain activity of whole populations through low-frequency secret technology or fluoride is another example. *Technocracy* is acceptable in academic circles because graduates of 16 or

20 years of "operant conditioning" public school education (programming) have had their hearts separated from their intellects. They actually think it is okay to plan other peoples' lives. They have taken courses in this for many years.

"Ruth" means *compassion*, and *technocrats* are ruthless. *Technocracy* is the arch enemy of anyone who loves nature or their own inner nature or their children. The 2011 global synchronized roll out of spying, dangerous Smart Meters on every home using the same false talking points, is an example of a globalist *technocratic* program. *Technocracy* is explored in more detail in Book 2 of this series, which is about the *co-opt* of environmental concerns.

39. Transparency denotes that public institutions must be public about their business. *Transparency* does not mean that the private sector should give up its privacy.

Transparency then, entails a double standard … Public institutions represent the People, so the people should know everything the public institution is doing. But the institution has no right to delve into the inner workings of the People. Firewalls protect us. In other words, we must be vigilant about maintaining an intentional lack of *transparency* to protect us from tyranny.

The state cannot plead the fifth amendment. Private citizens can and should. This exactly is why the fifth amendment was written.

My home is my castle, means "Don't tread on me." I public institution cannot have this attitude.

An elected official forsakes some of her or his business privacy. However, the public should not have the right to destroy the public servant's private life. That is, paparazzi should not have free reign to harass public figures nor should paparazzi with written words, look for any imperfection in anyone else with vindictive attacks. We do not throw stones.

It is in the private lives of public servants, that we find the uneasy line between public disclosure and privacy. The private sector should be as opaque as possible, the public sector should be as transparent as possible, and in the private lives of public servants is where we find the unclear line. A servant's role is to sublimate the self, to serve. A self's role is to be sovereign.

The choice to be a public servant does mean more scrutiny and is a sacrifice by the servant. Since we don't want to live in a slave state inhabited by servants, government should be small so that there are fewer public servants who give up privacy and their personal sovereignty. That is, we want a society of free people, not slaves who have no privacy. Political freedom means privacy. But the government should have zero privacy and zero freedom, while the People should be as free as possible from monitoring and data collection.

This uneasy relationship is eternal. There is no utopia ever. The definition of Freedom must always re-invent itself. In our temporary digital bubble, *personal sovereignty* cannot be forgotten. We must dominate machines, or be dominated. That is the present conflict that we much watch closely.

40. Unsustainable is a relatively new word in English that can be used in several ways, but in nature it means extinction. *Unsustainable* level of fishing means next year we will have less fish. *Unsustainable* grazing with too much livestock denudes the hills, causing permanent soil erosion and permanent loss of pasture. The *carrying capacity* of the land for sheep or yak or lamas or cows is diminished. (I saw this first hand in Tibet.) Such a land use program is *unsustainable* and the opposite of wise stewardship.

Since the *multi-verse is change* and anything identifiable is impermanent, *no thing is eternally sustainable*, no thing lasts forever, including planets and suns and solar systems. Thus *sustainability* is a relative concept. Obviously, however, some choices are repeatable and sustainable, while others are dead-end experiments (like our present *Consumerism).*

On our planet, with constant climate change and receding or increasing ice ages, no city or city state can be permanently *sustainable* because it is in a fixed location and the climate is going to change. Even seaports will come and go as climate changes. Examples are Venice or New Orleans. Unless a city can be supplied indefinitely by a stable rural area, it is going to use up its available resources. If a city is dependent on transportation that depends on fuels that are in decline, it will have to decrease its population as the transportation decreases. There cannot be endless growth. There must be balance or there is extinction.

On the other hand, none of this is a concern for nomadic or agrarian civilizations that are accustomed to moving on. The Australian Aborigines have lived for 50,000 years on the same land without destroying their very diverse habitat. This is remarkable, and these people were psychically superior to the colonists. Nomadic cultures don't build palaces. There was no rise and fall of civilization in Australia. There was just a *sustainable* civilization. The city of Melbourne will slowly or quickly collapse in the next century because of *resource depletion*, but the Australian bush will still be supporting human civilization (incarnation), for many many thousands of years.

Humans are social creatures. We always live in groups, which is the meaning of civilization. In this series, "civilization" is *also a spiritual configuration*, not a vain, abusive, who-has-the-biggest-monument game. The Romans were a brutal grotesque regime run on slavery and were uncivilized. The Roman arch was built with blood. There is nothing great about the Roman Slave State. It was an experiment in cruelty, and was thus *unsustainable.* It destroyed *indigenous peoples,* slaughtered four-legged incarnations in stadiums, and programmed Europe to accept centralization as normal. We have to reverse this, and see that *re-localization is sustainable*, and that continued slavery is not.

With Agrarian societies, particularly those built on rivers that flood and fertilize the land every year with fresh silt, agriculture has been perfectly sustainable and will continue to be so, indefinitely. Slash and burn agriculture is *sustainable* also when the ratio of farmers to land base is the *sustainable* ratio. Agrarian culture is a better measure of civilization than the excesses of the ancient elite who came and went. The corn eating civilization in the Americas has existed for thousands of years in an unbroken, annual seed collecting and planting cycle. Corn civilization has been very *sustainable.* If this corn planting culture wasn't *sustainable*, corn wouldn't be here, because corn doesn't exist in the wild. The same can be said for the rice or wheat or potato or taro civilizations.

These nomadic and agrarian civilizations are still much greater than the ones that built grand structures with slave labor. Civilizations outside the bounds of tax collectors and slave hunters offer more *personal sovereignty* to the human incarnation. The vain *dominant culture* abusers call them "poor," but they are free. Nomadic and agrarian cultures are more *sustainable* and thus more moral. How odd that some academic researchers can't find an example of a *sustainable* culture. We can just examine the people who were ripped off by the vain rich gangsters throughout history. There we find *sustainability.*

Archeologists who examine the ruins of an ancient Sumerian city, for example, and have theories about the political dramas that caused "collapse," are forgetting that the replanting of wheat by the wheat culture never collapsed. The seed has been replanted in an unbroken cycle every year for at least 6000 years (until the U.S. Invaded Iraq in 2003 and replaced 6000 years of genetic research with GMO wheat at the point of a gun.) The *dominant culture "his-story"* tellers focus on the parasitic cities who lived off of the surrounding farmlands, as their measure of a civilization, probably because they are living in one.

Simple human civilization never collapsed because it was guided by *personal sovereignty* and stewardship and the wisdom to collect and save seed. The present *dominant culture* discounts *sustainable indigenous cultures* as poor, when actually their way of life has persisted and will persist. The vain *dominating culture* cannot see this because it is lost in its own *disconnecting vanity.*

Temporary cities are presented in this book series as the decadent abusers of the rural sustainable civilization surrounding them. These urbanites are not the true humanity which most of us are descended from. The city people died off again and again. Those who touch the Earth never died off. Their lifestyle was and is *sustainable.*

The ancient and *sustainable* food growing cultures that save seed and feed children year after year are now under attack by trans-genic or GMO companies, who are working hand in glove with the United Nations, as proven by the international legalization of Codex Alimentarius (global food "safety" law) in 2009.

For the first time in the history of this planet, the ability to grow food for ones' own children is being regulated, as Globalist companies claim intellectual property rights based on mapping of genetic codes of any plant they can find. These laws are backed up by police. It is becoming illegal to feed one's own children home grown food because it isn't "safe." We already know that parasitic cities are logistically *unsustainable*, but now ancient *sustainability* is being made illegal by the *Globalists.*

Among academic circles there is a *disconnecting vanity* disease called "relativism," which claims that it stands at a far distance and can see things with perspective. This is intellectual snobbery and is deluded, but very vain and authoritative. This consciousness of *disconnecting vanity* is the opposite of spiritual awakening, which sees everything in the now as a union of mind/heart and context. Relativism is detached from reality, while spiritual awakening is a more dynamic caring which participates with reality. Relativism excuses anything. Spiritual awakening excuses nothing because it becomes connected and involved through *compassion.*

Intellectual snobs with adoring students is an old very boring scenario, but another generation of "new science" seems to emerge every other year with a new answer for its own problems. In studying *sustainability*, these relativist "scientists" are lost in space and need to come down to Earth. *Sustainability* is saving seed and planting crops on land where *personal sovereignty* has taken responsibility of stewardship. People who theorize about *sustainability* often have never gotten their finger nails dirty.

University designed *sustainable* "systems" is a joke when sustainable self-sufficient *indigenous* lifestyle has already existed for thousands of years. It is the vain *Consumerism* of the analyst which prevents him or her from seeing this. "They are poor" means "I am superior." In fact the "poor" are stronger, and when the supply chain slows, the poor will carry on their sustainable ways, and the rich will have to catch up and learn how to be poor.

41. Urban people refers to 51% of the world that now live disconnected from soil and plant life and do not know where their food comes from. If you are an urban person, you do not know how your food is grown, where the water comes from to grow it, what habitat existed before the ground was plowed, who the farmers are, what they are paid, what chemicals they are exposed to, how the food is preserved, how it is transported, and whether or not it is even healthy. Everything about urban life is slavery, *vanity,* and *Consumerism.* I found the image Lipstick Alley (Page 88) by accident, but this accurately describes urban culture. *Urban people* survive without knowing how. Thus, compared to *indigenous people, Urban people* are ignorant, irresponsible, personally powerless, drunk, and constitute a cancer on Earth. Their indoor existence threatens the entire outdoors.

The environmental crisis originates from an urban crisis. *Urban people* represent the *dominant culture.* They cannot acknowledge that there are any victims due to their own resource consumption and daily habits. There is not an excess of *indigenous people* on Earth; there are too many city people. If the cities were deconstructed, and young people returned to growing their own food, and making their own clothing, most environmental problems would disappear. This transition back to sanity is called the "long emergency" by the *dominant culture,* the "great unraveling" by impartial observers, "the return to the Good Red Road" by some Native Americans, and "the great opportunity" by spiritual students like the author.

Many so-called environmentalists are urban *entitled* consumers who want to "save nature" in some *indigenous peoples'* homeland while eating food from farms that slash nature. Their daily urban lifestyle of pedicures and videos and Ipads for each member of the family is "free" of consequences. *Urban people* live more for their wants, not their needs. They live for the weekend so they can party. They live to be entertained as much as possible. They live to eat, rather than eat to live, because living in a city is living in a cage, a zoo, a prison, so "entertainment" is a big deal. Most of their "working career," that is, their life, is a "job." They want to be paid their slice of the natural world. That is their reward for working. That makes their cage existence tolerable. So of course, they live to eat, having no life connected with the grand circle of natural existence. They have almost never walked barefoot outdoors in their entire lives, have never held soil in their hands, have never chopped wood, or worked with fibers. The great majority of their life on Earth is actually spent indoors and not on Earth at all. They gravitate to the artificial and dream of a future that is even more artificial. They design a future based on technology, not nature. *Disconnecting vanity* is their culture.

The Pixar film, *Wal-E (2008)*, shows us the disconnected urban future. Note the word FUN in upper left of the technocratic indoor future and the obese convenient look of the citizen.

42. Vanity refers to a head that is separated from the heart and obsessed with appearance. *Indigenous* people had no mirrors. Mirrors came with "progress." *"Progress"* hypnotizes us with mirrors.

Gaga is a multi millionaire Illuminati puppet, deluded by vanity. On the right, she wears Illuminati leopard skin Kitten Programming outfit. (See Cage theme in this Glossary.)

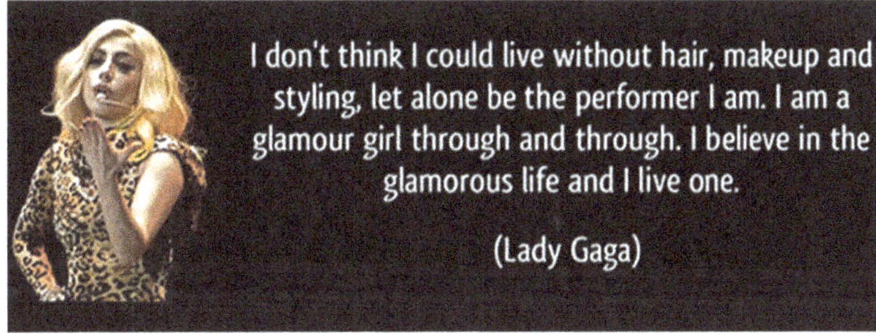

She believes in over consumption. She spreads it. Over consumption is based on taking from others who are left without enough. This is enforced by the military. Vanity leads to violence. Lipstick and War Crimes.

(Do you accept lipstick and war crimes as your new normal?)

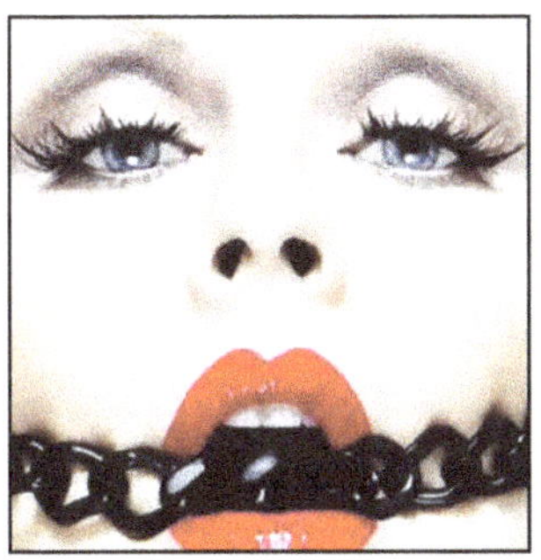

Endnotes

Volume 2

It is my hope that a new department will appear in every college and university called "Unveiled History" in which PhD candidates write exacting uncensored doctoral dissertations which blow open every lie that our destructive, polluting, *social engineering*, top/down, mafia-Illuminati-bankster system is based on. Economics, psychology, and the sciences too will be re-written. These studies will form the new and honest history books for all students. They will learn about the criminal, colonial and globalist culture that almost ended life on Earth, and they will study VALUES like the Golden Rule and the mandate of taking stewardship and personal responsibility seriously. Rather than "think globally, act locally" people will think locally, and remembering the Golden Rule, will not send any pollution downstream. While this honest history is written, millions will be dying from intentional diseases from electronic devices, vaccines, and poisoned food and soil. The lesson of this suffering, directly in everyone's face as we uncover who brought this suffering upon us, will sear deep into human consciousness. Infanticide of deformed babies will become widespread. Sorry, but that is what we are facing. Every place the U.S. has used radioactive ammunition will be scared for a long time and every factory dump that is not cleaned up properly will poison the ground water. The upside might be that the lessons learned will last for thousands of years.

For many, many centuries the lesson will burn. Never again will we trust a pyramid of power and give up our *personal sovereignty.*

– Ray Songtree, November 2014

There is no way all the references below can be accurate. There also is no way they could all be false. Connect the dots! Important information you find on internet should be downloaded to your hard drive before it is scrubbed off the internet. Especially youtubes and Wiki-leaks Documents. If it looks very indicative, save it. Also screen shots are very valuable. But better, start growing food.

Introduction

1 The vow of service extends into future incarnations and into the soul. In Buddhism it is called the Bodhisattva vow. In Native American culture today it is known in English as the Good Red Road. Every ancient culture had an ancient Vow of Service that some people in each culture devoted their life to and were known as seekers or shamans or many other names. Once we enter the road of service, there is no returning to selfish *vanity* as our reason to exist.

2 See World Trade Center 7 video at top of page at
http://www.afterenlightenment.net/hearing_vets.htm\
The full story – https://www.youtube.com/watch?v=O1GCeuSr3Mk

3 "Canned tuna, Americans' favorite fish, is the most common source of mercury in our diet ... Children and women of childbearing age can easily consume more mercury than the Environmental Protection Agency considers advisable, simply by eating one serving of canned white tuna or two servings of light tuna per week."
http://www.consumerreports.org/cro/magazine-archive/2011/january/food/mercury-in-tuna/overview/index.htm
What this article doesn't state is that mercury is cumulative. All top-of-food-chain fish, such as sword fish and Mahi Mahi, are also toxic.

Chapter 1: Organized Consumerism

4 Ralph Nader June 2013
https://www.youtube.com/watch?v=2XoQx9NqZY8&list=FLZ1SmunMl-g89yZg7pkdpkw

5 Controlled Education: William T. Stills, *New World Order: The Ancient Plan of Secret Societies.* pg. 180-181

6 2012 speeches at Harvard Law School
https://www.youtube.com/watch?v=A8kla2T0NQQ&list=FLZ1SmunMl-g89yZg7pkdpkw

7 U.S. helps Iraq use poison gas against Iran
http://theweek.com/article/index/248745/how-the-us-helped-saddam-hussein-use-chemical-weapons-against-iran

8 Chase Manhattan builds Mustard Gas factory in Iraq for Saddam Hussein
http://wearechangetv.us/2013/04/freemasons-chase-manhattan-the-arming-of-saddam-hussein/

9 Alice Bailey links
http://www.conspiracyarchive.com/NewAge/Alice_Bailey.htm
http://www.lucistrust.org/en/books/alice_bailey_books/about_alice_bailey

10 Education 2000
www.ties-edu.org/GATE/Education2000.html

11 Planned 1929 stock crash
http://www.conservativeactionalerts.com/2011/08/short-sellers-destroying-the-market-101/
also
http://21stcenturycicero.wordpress.com/2008/02/11/how-a-group-of-international-bankers-engineered-the-1929-crash-and-the-great-depression/

12 Senator Claremont Pell Earthquake Weapons
www.rense.com/political/weapons/earthqk.htm
www.curezone.com/forums/am.asp?i=18516
https://view.officeapps.live.com/op/view.aspx?src=http%3A%2F%2Fwww.thenewalexandrialibrary.com%2Fsitebuildercontent%2Fsitebuilderfiles%2Fweatherweapon.doc

13 Man made Earthquakes and Tsunamis
HAARP low frequency signals can be directed anywhere and over days can trigger earthquakes ...
http://www.globalresearch.ca/search?q=HAARP+earthquakes

Tectonic weapons http://www.rense.com/political/weapons/earthqk.htm

Santiago Chile Earthquakes
A carpenter from Chile that I know was in Santiago the day of 2010 earthquake, and witnessed the sky turn blood red at 3AM, as the atmosphere was reacting to the HAARP signals that built up to trigger the earthquake the following day. His first hand report is backed by similar accounts from others.
wn.com/Chile_earthquake_and_haarp_colors_in_the_sky
"This morning, the socialist President of Chile, Michelle Bachelet, has accused the American Government, of causing the recent earthquakes … "
worldnewsdailyreport.com/chile-american-haarp … for-recent-earthquake
Do Search Chile Earthquake HAARP

Christ Church 2010
U.S. Homeland Security and FEMA in Christchurch New Zealand day of Earthquake.
http://uncensored.co.nz/2011/03/04/was-the-christchurch-earthquake-a-terrible-natural-disaster-or-was-it-a-terrible-man-made-disaster/
http://beforeitsnews.com/earthquakes/2011/06/christchurch-earthquake-a-fake-haarp-weapon-in-play-713807.html
Military exercise the day before NZ earthquake, like every other disaster. See Haiti Southcom exercise article below, day before also.
http://www.pseudoreality.org/christchurch_earthquake.html
http://www.exohuman.com/wordpress/2011/02/haarp-fema-and-the-christchurch-quake/
Over a hundred pilot whales beached themselves in New Zealand 48 hours before the 6.3 Earthquake hit Christchurch . This is response to the HAARP frequencies torturing whales
www.youtube.com/watch?v=KaWYc9Lq4-M
Do these searches, "Christchurch New Zealand tectonic weapons", "Christchurch earthquake HAARP," "Beached whales HAARP New Zealand Earthquake,"

Hugo Chavez Haiti earthquake
http://www.abc.es/20100119/internacional-/chavez-acusa-provocar-seismo-201001191332.html
Navy exercise same day as Haiti quake http://www.cryptogon.com/?p=13147
Tectonic Weapons Tsunamis
http://whitewraithe.wordpress.com/2011/03/29/tectonic-warfare-aided-by-haarp-specific-cause-of-japans-311-9-1-earthquake-not-due-to-natural-causes/
Collin Powell, Secretary of State, and Jeb Bush reconnaissance 2004 Tsunami
http://www.marketwatch.com/story/sec-state-powell-fla-gov-bush-to-visit-tsunami-areas

14 Tip of iceberg on fukashima conspiracy
www.naturalnews.com/032670_Fukushima_HAARP
www.israel21c.org/news/israeli-surveillance-at-fukushima-plant/

15 Myanmar Cyclone HAARP just search these words: Pakistan Flood HAARP
http://www.pakalertpress.com/2010/08/06/pakistan-flood-photos-haarp-fingerprints-found-allover/

16 Matt Simmons suspicious "heart attack"
http://www.zerohedge.com/article/matt-simmons-has-died-heart-attack
Matt Simmons Exposes BP in an Interview Before His Death
www.youtube.com/watch?v=bcpKSD-Li0A

17 Suspicious vaccines
http://www.abovetopsecret.com/forum/thread916892/pg1
http://www.prisonplanet.com/pandemic-profits-exposed-follow-the-money-on-ebola-fda-and-big-pharma.html
http://www.secretsofthefed.com/whistle-blower-reveals-big-pharma-corps-profit-lifelong-disease/
http://www.sodahead.com/united-states/live-avian-flu-virus-placed-in-baxter-vaccine-materials-sent/blog-68815/?link=ibaf&q=live+virus+pharma+profits

18 History of American Medical Association, Flexner Commission
http://hemphealer.wordpress.com/2012/03/01/the-rockefellers-the-flexnor-report-the-ama-and-their-effect-on-alternative-nutritional-botanical-medicine/

19 Introduction to smart meter dangers
http://www.cellphonetaskforce.org/?page_id=389
also www.bioinitiative.org

20 Problem-Reaction-Solution – David Icke illustrates
http://vimeo.com/29561138
www.youtube.com/watch?v=iEz5fQ_Pm-g

21 *Pawns in the Game:* William Guy Carr
www.gofindpdf.com/pdffiles/pawns-in-the-game-pdf-download.html
Please do Search "Illuminati French Revolution"

22 Ukraine protests engineered by West
http://www.youtube.com/watch?v=SEcZFgSnVP0Do
also search at website Globalresearch.ca for Ukraine

23 Secret recordings at Federal Reserve
http://thinkprogress.org/economy/2014/09/28/3573141/segarra-recordings-elizabeth-warren-hearing/

Chapter 2: All the Man's Kings

24 Many histories, here are two more …
http://greatgameindia.wordpress.com/2013/04/14/the-rothschild-colonization-of-india/
http://www.theforbiddenknowledge.com/hardtruth/the_rothschild_bloodline.htm

25 George Washington letter Library of Congress
http://memory.loc.gov/cgi-bin/query/r?ammem/mgw:@field%28DOCID+@lit%28gw360395%29%29
http://thecounterpunch.hubpages.com/hub/Georges_Washington_did_acknowledge_the_Doctrines_of_the_Illuminati_was_spreading_in_United_States

26 Ben Franklin questions
http://judeo-masonic.blogspot.com/2010/02/3a-american-revolution-addendum.html

27 http://judeo-masonic.blogspot.com/2010/02/4-adam-weishaupt-and-bavarian.html
http://projectavalon.net/forum4/showthread.php?52886-The-Bavarian-Illuminati-Jesuit-Adam-Weishaupt
This dispute is not one I sort out in this book. There are those who argue the Vatican controls Rothschilds, and those who argue the other way.

28 Jack Ruby Speaks
http://www.youtube.com/watch?v=9zd4r4O0o_Y also
http://jfkmurdersolved.com/ruby.htm

29 Buffet, Schwarzenegger, Rothschild Manor
http://www.indybay.org/newsitems/2007/12/02/18464823.php
The source of this article was "by NEW WORLD ORDER Sunday Dec 2nd, 2007 7:08 PM" however I could not find out where or who this was. But most of the information checked out with other sources. Some people think that if they can't find information in their own language on the internet, then it isn't true. There is more information in other languages, than English. Also, it is dangerous to be a whistleblower and source may not want to disclose themselves. I am not happy with this entree, because the writer gave no references, but I feel it is true. This is an entree that is borderline for me. Not as solid as other history, but just barely solid enough.

30 History of Rothschild Anti-defamation League. Definitely *Globalization* you won't get in school. June 27, 1994
http://www.theforbiddenknowledge.com/hardtruth/adl_1.htm

31 The Great American Adventure by Judge Dale
www.scribd.com/doc/95392318

32 The 1999 Shelby Tennessee trial that exonerated James Earl Ray in death of Martin Luther King
http://www.afterenlightenment.net/control_mlk.htm

33 Bill Gates was placed. See more end of Chapter 6.
"In a lengthy interview with Bill Moyers released today, Microsoft billionaire Bill Gates reveals the inspiration for his funding of pro-abortion population control measures. Responding to a question by Moyers on how he came to fund "reproductive issues" Gates answered, "When I was growing up, my parents were always involved in various volunteer things. My dad was head of Planned Parenthood ..." May 9, 2003 – LifeSiteNews.com
Youtube of Gates with Moyer making statement above
https://www.youtube.com/watch?v=EZ6mjx4J7dM
https://www.lifesitenews.com/news/bill-gates-planned-parenthood-president-dad-inspired-pro-abort-funding
Gates Foundation support of *indigenous* destruction
http://www.naturalnews.com/035105_Bill_Gates_Monsanto_eugenics.html#
Bill Gates supports geo-engineering
http://www.theguardian.com/environment/2012/feb/06/bill-gates-climate-scientists-geoengineering
Bill Gates and Sterilization
http://strangerz1989.wordpress.com/2014/03/13/the-hidden-agenda-of-bill-gates-part-b/

34 Apple Inc. hides safety warning, May 12, 2012
http://consumers4safephones.com/apple-warns-customers-to-never-use-or-carry-an-iphone-in-your-pocket/

35 Kissinger the Pedophile
http://waronyou.com/topics/bob-chapman-henry-kissinger-and-the-bushes-are-famous-pedophiles/
http://www.kycbs.net/Kissinger-of-Death.htm

Chapter 3: The Mask Comes Off

36 Rockefellers – Andrew Gavin Marshall
http://www.globalresearch.ca/bilderberg-2011-the-rockefeller-world-order-and-the-high-priests-of-globalization/25302

37 http://colorrevolutionsandgeopolitics.blogspot.com/2011/09/act-one-of-cias-arab-spring-lebanons.html
also Color revolutions
http://ronpaulinstitute.org/archives/featured-articles/2014/february/19/invasions-of-the-mind-snatchers.aspx

38 Do internet search "Kissinger Allende Chile." Many articles.

39 Operation Condor CIA Kissinger, South America
http://www2.gwu.edu/~nsarchiv/NSAEBB/NSAEBB125/index.htm
http://www.latinamericanstudies.org/chile/operation-condor.htm
http://www.globalresearch.ca/operation-condor-campaign-by-us-backed-latin-american-dictators-to-hunt-down-torture-and-murder-tens-of-thousands-of-opponents/5325695

40 Do internet search "Assassination of John Kennedy Jr" on YouTube.
Twenty-two Congressman killed in air crashes
http://www.fromthewilderness.com/free/ww3/110102_wellstone.html

41 www.globalresearch.ca/controlling-the-global-economy-bilderberg
Also Engdahl ... Proof Bilderberg Meeting >Yom Kipper war >oil
shockwww.takeoverworld.info/pdf/Engdahl__Century_of_War_book.pdf Page 130

42 Andrew Gavin Marshall
http://www.globalresearch.ca/controlling-the-global-economy-bilderberg-the-trilateral-commission-and-the-federal-reserve/14614

43 FBI surveillance of Nelson Mandela
http://www.nydailynews.com/news/national/fbi-spied-nelson-mandela-u-s-trip-report-article-1.1809078

44 Gandhi Appendicitis without anesthetics. Gandhi Chapter in *Autobiography of a Yogi*, Paramhansa Yogananda. I also read that President Garfield who was shot, had bullet removed with out anesthetics, but he died anyway.

Chapter 4: Entitlement, the Bad Boy

45 See my essay on the "Australian 2007 Intervention" under Tab "Essays, Letters" at www.Lipstick-stick-and-war-crimes.org

46 Senator Wellstone assassination
http://www.alternet.org/story/14399/was_paul_wellstone_murdered/
The assassination of John Kennedy Jr.
http://www.youtube.com/results?search_type=&search_query=the%20assassination%20of%20jfk%20jr

47 Fake swine flu
http://www.cbsnews.com/news/swine-flu-cases-overestimated/
http://articles.mercola.com/sites/articles/archive/2009/11/24/Superstar-CBS-Reporter-Blows-the-Lid-Off-the-Swine-Flu-Media-Hype-and-Hysteria-.aspx
http://beforeitsnews.com/2012/2014/04/what-really-happened-to-cbs-news-investigative- reporter-sharyl-attkisson-2450498.html
http://www.naturalnews.com/036317_CDC_Swine_Flu_death_estimates.html

48 WHO changes definition of pandemic to now be meaningless. At any time a pandemic requiring martial law can be declared
http://www.spiegel.de/international/world/interview-with-epidemiologist-tom-jefferson-a-whole-industry-is-waiting-for-a-pandemic-a-637119.html

49 Vaccines cause 145,000 child deaths in 20 years
http://www.naturalnews.com/038812_vaccines_childhood_deaths_toxic_chemicals.html##ixzz2vgOnDL2c

50 Experimental vaccines troops
http://www.brasscheck.com/videos/iraq/iraqwar14.html

51 RFID chips Obamacare
www.healthcarevideosite.com/proof-rfid-microchip-is-in-obama-health-care.html

52 Proof of RFID chips in Obamacare. www.fda.gov., www.sodwahead.com,
http://www.youtube.com/watch?v=rsbgqTCS9ZQ#t=79

53 Wyoming children chipped
nationalreport.net/wyoming-school-implant-rfid/

54 RFID with breast implant
www.infowars.com/rfid-microchips-to-be-embedded-in-breast-implants/

55 Billions seen as bottom of economic pyramid BOP
http://www.wri.org/publication/next-4-billion

56 Amnesty international destabilization agent
http://www.youtube.com/watch?v=SEcZFgSnVP0

Chapter 6: The Ocean is Broken

57 Article by Greg Ray
www.theherald.com.au/story/1848433/the-ocean-is-broken/

58 Geoengineering videos
http://www.geoengineeringwatch.org/
What in the World are They Spraying 98 minute
www.youtube.com/watch?v=jf0khstYDLA
Why in the World are They Spraying video
www.whyintheworldaretheyspraying.com
Look up award winning video
http://www.skyderalert.com/

59 Vincent Freeman Chemical Pathogens, April 4, 2014
http://www.redicecreations.com/radio/2014/04/RIR-140404.php

60 A list of *sanctioned diseases*
The original article is no longer online that I wanted to cite. Here are some others.

Cholera brought to Haiti, Lyme Disease, Sars, Crohns disease.
http://forum.prisonplanet.com/index.php?topic=194876.0
http://nstarzone.com/LYME.html
http://rense.com/general69/lyme.htm
http://socioecohistory.wordpress.com/2014/06/30/jim-willie-mers-is-a-bio-weapon-attack-against-the-saudis-sars-was-a-bio-weapon-attack-against-the-chinese/
http://israelect.com/reference/WillieMartin/AIDS.htm
http://exploitationnation.blogspot.com/2007/11/crohns-disease-conspiracy.html

Gum disease, FDA suppression, Radiation
http://articles.mercola.com/sites/articles/archive/2001/07/25/dentist.aspx#!
http://www.robertbarefoot.com/p-17-the-disease-conspiracy-the-fda-suppression-of-cures.aspx
http://agreenroad.blogspot.com/2013/08/hanford-and-multiple-secret-green-runs.html
http://enenews.com/they-lied-to-us-radiation-release-comparable-to-chernobyl-total-core-meltdown-in-all-3-reactors-worst-industrial-catastrophe-in-world-history-cnn-video

61 Fluoride in drinking water
http://canadianawareness.org/2012/03/water-fluoridation-directly-linked-to-eugenics/

62 Ebola article from The Common Sense Show, Dave Hodges
http://www.thecommonsenseshow.com/2014/09/17/the-cdc-nih-bill-gates-own-the-patents-on-existing-ebola-related-vaccines-mandatory-vaccinations-are-near/

63 It's all scripted Ebola article Natural News
http://www.naturalnews.com/046946_ebola_outbreak_vaccines_patents.html

64 Inventor of vaccines, Dr. Salk denounces polio vaccines as causing more polio
http://vaxtruth.org/2012/03/the-polio-vaccine-part-2-2/

65 Microsoft gene targeting software
http://www.naturalnews.com/034848_Microsoft_Merck_eugenics.html#ixzz3Ffyccthd

66 Anne Hendershott quote on Bill and Melinda Gates
http://catholicexchange.com/168244

67 Hidden Agenda of Bill Gates – Part B
http://strangerz1989.wordpress.com/2014/03/13/the-hidden-agenda-of-bill-gates-part-b/
https://www.lifesitenews.com/news/a-mass-sterilization-exercise-kenyan-doctors-find-anti-fertility-agent-in-u

68 Gates Nano fibers deliver contraceptive and HIV drugs
http://preventdisease.com/news/12/120712_Bill-Gates-Awards-Researchers-Development-Electrically-Spun-Cloth-Deliver-Contraceptive-HIV-Drugs.shtml

Chapter 7: Just Look in the Mirror

69 Video worth watching "Man in the Mirror" Michael Jackson. In video Jackson didn't understand that FDR was placed.
http://www.youtube.com/watch?v=lVlY6q6_QfQ

70 Proprietary software tracking school children
http://www.politico.com/story/2014/05/data-mining-your-children-106676.html

71 Excellent article on Native American children
http://www.dailykos.com/story/2013/04/14/1200994/-Native-schools-and-stolen-generations-U-S-and-Canada

72 History of NATO and U.S. created ISIS
http://www.globalresearch.ca/syrian-war-islamic-state-isis-creation-timeline/5472680

ISIS Leader Abu Bakr Al Baghdadi, trained by Israeli Mossad, NSA Documents Reveal. July 16, 2014.
http://www.globalresearch.ca/isis-leader-abu-bakr-al-baghdadi-trained-by-israeli-mossad-nsa-documents-reveal/5391593

More links
http://www.globalresearch.ca/search?q=isis&x=0&y=0

Search "ISIS false" at www.infowars.com

CIA stages atrocities
http://www.infowars.com/flashback-cia-admits-to-staging-fake-jihadist-videos/

73 Occult background of Isis
http://illuminatusobservor.blogspot.com/2008/04/isis-and-osiris-foundation-to-western.html#axzz3Bmr7O7zd

74 Howard Hughes bought the rights to Broadway show *Philadelphia* for Katherine Hepburn, which she sold at a profit and with terms benefitting her career. Once again Wikipedia leaves out the important truth: "Hepburn masterminded her own comeback, buying out her contract with RKO Radio Pictures and acquiring the film rights to *The Philadelphia Story*." She masterminded nothing. The money came from Hughes. So much for an "independent" feminist. See Vol. 1.

Chapter 8: Shamelessness and the All-Seeing Eye

75 See minute 3:45 of this video. You will see also that the words, "I'm not rag doll" in song align with Simon Cowell calling her a puppet the week before, so here she proves she is no phony puppet, she is the real thing, a real rag doll, a real puppet, doing whatever she is told to do. The words go directly against her pornographic gesturing, making the words *doublespeak*. "I am not a rag doll spreading my legs as I am commanded." Hello? This is actual programming before our eyes, where her personality is split.
http://www.youtube.com/watch?v=Yr6w9qJFiJM

76 NASA scientists letter, global warming is bad science
http://climatism.wordpress.com/2014/02/02/former-nasa-scientists-reject-global-warming-crisis/
http://www.inquisitr.com/1234575/nasa-scientist-global-warming-is-nonsense/

77 Education is now *social engineering*, based on screened "facts."
http://www.crisismagazine.com/2013/the-ambitions-of-bill-and-melinda-gates-controlling-population-and-public-education

78 First compulsory elementary schools
http://wiki.mises.org/wiki/Public_education#Prussia

79 Deadly Monsanto Roundup
http://www.naturalnews.com/035050_Roundup_Monsanto_DNA.html#
http://www.scientificamerican.com/article.cfm?id=weed-whacking-herbicide-p
http://www.naturescountrystore.com/roundup/

80 Madonna tired of "right and wrong."
http://truthadvocate.wordpress.com/2011/09/03/the-power-of-music-part-4/

81 Madonna Stats
http://www.celebritiesgirl.com/2013/06/queen-of-pop-madonna.html

82 Hillary Clinton bi-sexual

Cathy O'Brien Testimony

A) Includes Corroborating evidence
www.bibliotecapleyades.net/sociopolitica/sociopol_mindconMKULTRA01.htm

B) Sex: Hilary Clinton and Cathy O'Brien blogspot.com
dutroux.blogspot.com/2008/01/hilary-clinton-and-cathy-obrien.html

C) Cathy's Assault by Hillary
www.scribd.com/doc/63957893

D) Hillary Clinton witness to mutilation of Cathy O'Brien's vagina Page 2
www.godlikeproductions.com/forum1/message1186955/pg2

Gennifer Flowers Testimony
http://www.dailymail.co.uk/news/article-2424555/Bill-Clintons-mistress-Gennifer-Flowers-Wed-today-wasnt-Chelsea.html
http://1984arkansasmotheroftheyear.blogspot.com/2012/02/bill-clinton-confirms-it-hillary-is.html

83 English paedophilia https://www.youtube.com/watch?v=NkudWCm_rGU

84 YouTube of Britain's Got Talent Show 2013 with Jennifer Lopez
http://www.youtube.com/watch?v=Sx0g9BZFZUQ

85 Most Jews are not Semites - origins of the Ashkenazi Jews

Benjamin Freedman
https://lipstick-and-war-crimes.org/the-old-testament-has-nothing-to-do-with-the-zionist-nation-israel/

A note, genetic studies that claim ancient Israelite origins are purely conjecture and not based on science since we have no ancient Israelite DNA. The funding for any study needs to be investigated before the results are considered.

86 Documentary "Hot Girls Wanted"
http://vox-land.com/movie/318256/Hot%2bGirls%2bWanted-2015.php

87 Do web search "porn industry jewish control"
https://www.bing.com/search?q=porn+industry+jewish+control&pc=MOZI&form=MOZSBR

88 E. Michael Jones. This was transcribed from a youtube which I have lost url. Here are podcasts from his excellent site http://www.culturewars.com/Podcasts.html

89 Mass Enslavement Through Sex – Larsha Moon
http://www.thetruthseeker.co.uk/?p=97040

90 Elton John thinks Jesus was homosexual.
http://newsbusters.org/blogs/noel-sheppard/2010/02/21/elton-john-blames-parade-mag-his-jesus-was-gay-comment

91 40% homosexuals at Disney, bottom of page.
http://theconspiracyzone.podcastpeople.com/posts/32979

92 This story has disappeared from net. This is called scrubbing, where Disney had this removed. Investigators like myself are tracked, and information we find is then on a list to be deleted. This also happened with NASA articles about other planets warming, which would of course indicates that Earth warming is a Solar System event. Those articles were scrubbed away. Here is another
http://www.assatashakur.org/forum/florida/12220-keep-your-children-out-disneyland-alone.html

93 Knights of Malta
http://www.zengardner.com/u-s-military-holy-crusade-uncovered/
http://aftermathnews.wordpress.com/?s=malta+blackwater
http://redicecreations.com/article.php?id=23716
http://vaticannewworldorder.blogspot.com/2012/02/knights-of-malta-are-militia-of-pope.html
http://aftermathnews.wordpress.com/2011/02/28/seymour-hersh-targeted-matthew-phelan-writes-on-the-fallout-from-his-exposure-of-the-knights-of-malta-conspiracy/
http://aftermathnews.wordpress.com/2007/10/01/blackwater-knights-of-malta-in-iraq/

94 Interview with Kay Griggs by Jeff Rense. Kissinger discussed at hour 1.34.
https://www.youtube.com/watch?t=5591&v=b4kFYg1A6uo

Chapter 9: In Your Own Home

95 Anal sex taught in schools.
https://www.bing.com/search?q=common+core+curriculum+sex+eduation+protest+anal+sex&qs=n&form=QBRE&pq=common+core+curriculum+sex+eduation+protest+anal+sex&sc=0-0&sp=-1-&sk=&cvid=a6ae0ef59fb14040a7c5ad86ea29e4d6
http://www.infowars.com/chicago-schools-teaching-safe-anal-sex-to-5th-graders/
http://www.infowars.net/articles/january2007/030107UN_Sex.htm

96 2012 Grammy Awards as satanic ritual.
http://vigilantcitizen.com/musicbusiness/whitney-houston-and-the-2012-grammy-awards-mega-ritual/

97 2002 – Whitney Houston Exposes the Illuminati
https://www.youtube.com/watch?v=J9TS7ss7exg

98 Why The Illuminati Killed Robin Williams Conspiracy EXPOSED (Final Cut)
https://www.youtube.com/watch?annotation_id=annotation_299510355&feature=iv&src_vid=lPZCy6G03Tc&v=b-nvpgRk5to#t=6m

99 Ibid 96

100 Privately owned prisons
http://www.nationofchange.org/truth-about-private-prison-contracts-1348147617

101 Slave labor
http://finance.yahoo.com/blogs/daily-ticker/top-5-secrets-private-prison-industry-163005314.html

Chapter 10: Gay Movement

102 *Unmasking the Gay Agenda* by J. Matt Barber
http://www.renewamerica.com/columns/mbarber/080213

103 Gay Dr. William Thetford CIA carreer psychologist writes Course in Miracles
http://www.miracles-course.org/joomla/index.php?option=com_content&view=article&id=171:the-first-acim-teachers&catid=35:tony-articles&Itemid=60
https://inpursuitofhappiness.wordpress.com/2013/12/19/a-course-in-miracles-a-cia-exercise-in-mind-control/
http://www.radiantlunatic.com/wp-content/uploads/2013/10/A-Course-in-Miracles_-a-CIA-exercise-in-mind-control.pdf

104 *Newsweek, Time and Washington Post* are CIA, but with Project Mockingbird, all were infilitrated since the late 1940s.
http://carlbernstein.com/magazine_cia_and_media.php

105 Gloria Steinem *Ms.* Magazine CIA, see extensive documentation Vol. 1
http://theamericanchronicle.blogspot.com/2013/08/meet-gloria-steinem-cia-whore.html

106 Public school homosexual conditioning
https://www.bing.com/search?q=anal++school+curriculums&qs=n&form=QBRE&pq=anal+school+curriculums&sc=0-27&sp=-1&sk=&cvid=011f6d28210049589e530f7c55df84fe

107 'Course in Miracles' CIA project
Ibid 103

108 *After the Ball–Why the Homosexual Movement Has Won* – Dr. R. Albert Mohler, Jr.
http://www.freerepublic.com/focus/religion/1147428/posts

109 Roth-efellers fund both sides of wars
https://www.bing.com/search?q=rothschild+league+of+nations&pc=MOZI&form=MOZSBR

110 World Bank sponsors Early Childhood Initiative to create worldwide monoculture.
https://www.bing.com/search?q=early+child+hood+initiative+world+bank&qs=n&form=QBRE&pq=early+child+hood+initiative+world+bank&sc=0-28&sp=-1&sk=&cvid=74b5c5968861457db-875970611e2c177

111 Clinton Fein's The Gay Agenda
http://annoy.com/features/doc.html?DocumentID=100722

112 Quote without understanding of word "marriage" by lesbian Masha Gessen
http://www.naturalmarriage.org.au/news-posts/abolish-marriage-altogether-says-homosexual-activist/

113 JP Morgan buys up 25 leading newspaper editorial rights
http://www.mindfully.org/Reform/Morgan-Buys-Newspapers9feb17 htm

Examples of controlled media
https://www.bing.com/search?q=bbc+wtc7+20+minutes+early&pc=MOZI&form=MOZSBR
https://lipstick-and-war-crimes.org/hiding-the-verdict-the-1999-martin-luther-king-civil-trial/

114 NSA access to internet
http://www.naturalnews.com/040692_NSA_spying_tech_companies_FISA.html#ixzz3YOvxq1mM

There are many secret think tanks. Oprah Winfrey is part of a billionaire's secret group
https://www.bing.com/search?q=oprah%2C+gates+secret+meeting+jets&pc=MOZI&form=MOZSBR

115 Vigilantcitizen.com is one of top sights for analysing the Illuminati Music Industry
http://www.Vigilantcitizen.com/

Great youtube site for analysis of entertainment industry – good Christian message
https://www.youtube.com/user/TheVigilantChristian

116 There are many good sites on illuminati symbolism. Here are a few.
http://media-conspiracy-manipulation.blogspot.com/
https://www.bing.com/videos/search?q=satanic+symbols+in+music+industry&FORM=HDRSC3

117 A youtube talk on George Washington's Illuminati letter 1789
https://www.youtube.com/watch?v=Pm1995kYjII

118 Adam Lambert's early stage performance with devils and orgy
https://artiewayne.wordpress.com/tag/adam-lambert-uncensored-unedited-video/

119 Adam Lambert's uncensored video portraying oral sex and slavery, which he defended on various TV interviews.
https://www.youtube.com/watch?v=zlZko5PgIT8

120 Ritual pedophile survivor of perpetrator Antoine Kidman
http://childabuserecovery.com/nicole-kidmans-father-dies-amid-pedophile-child-murder-ring-allegations/#.VT37HaZA_Fx

121 Predictive programming
https://www.bing.com/search?q=predictive+programming&pc=MOZI&form=MOZSBR

122 Anal sex being taught in schools
https://www.bing.com/search?q=common+core+curriculum+sex+eduation+protest+anal+sex&qs=n&form=QBRE&pq=common+core+curriculum+sex+eduation+protest+anal+sex&sc=0-0&sp=-1&sk=&cvid=a6ae0ef59fb14040a7c5ad86ea29e4d6

123 Kissinger sex crimes. This is just one of many videos.
https://www.youtube.com/watch?v=03nwLOHt2wQ

124 Hero Survivor Cathy O'Brien's court documented book
https://www.bing.com/search?q=henry+kissinger+access+denied+Cathy+O'brien&pc=MOZI&form=MOZSBR

125 Illuminati Frank Sinatra
http://www.whale.to/b/sp/12 html

126 The industry roles out the satanic role models
http://vigilantcitizen.com/musicbusiness/kanye-west-tidal-is-not-the-illuminati/

127 Estrogen in drinking water
http://chestsculpting.com/the-dangers-of-estrogen-in-your-drinking-water/

128 Kitten Beta Programming, introduced in Vol. 1
https://www.bing.com/images/search?q=kitten+beta+programming&FORM=HDRSC2

129 Marilyn Monroe, mind control slave
https://www.bing.com/search?q=marilyn+monroe+sex+slave+progrmmed&pc=MOZI&form=MOZSBR

130 Bernie Taupin
https://www.bing.com/search?q=bernie+taupin+satanist&pc=MOZI&form=MOZSBR

131 Quote of David J. Stewart on Elton John's smear of Christians
http://whatgetsmehot.blogspot.com/2012/06/elton-john-and-witchcraft.html

132 Lord Justice Fulford, founder Paeophile Information Exchange
https://www.bing.com/search?q=Lord+Justice+Fulford%2C+founder+of+the+Paedophile+Information+Exchange.&pc=MOZI&form=MOZLBR

133 Bilderberg group
https://www.bing.com/search?q=bilderberg+group+conspiracy&pc=MOZI&form=MOZSBR

134 Prime Ministers Gordon Brown and Tony Blair pedophilia
http://www.henrymakow.com/illuminati-pedophiles-run-brit.html

135 Fabian events host Stonewall's Ben Summerskill
http://www.pickledpolitics.com/archives/169

Gay speaker Summerskill's mom a Fabian
https://gaymafiawatch.wordpress.com/2008/10/14/stonewall-and-the-illuminati/#comment-3184

136 Luciferian roots of Theosophical and Fabians
http://www.fourwinds10.net/siterun_data/bellringers_corner/vital_articles/news.php?q=1380385512

137 The murder of Princess Diana
https://www.bing.com/search?q=princess+diane+murder&qs=n&form=QBRE&pq=princess+diane+murder&sc=8-19&sp=-1&sk=&cvid=0319b152d1cd4a4ab67bd074425671b1

138 More on Marilyn Monroe
https://www.bing.com/search?q=marilyn+monroe+sex+slave&pc=MOZI&form=MOZSBR

139 The Olympic Illuminati created flame
https://www.bing.com/search?q=The+olympic+illuminati+flame&pc=MOZI&form=MOZSBR
https://www.bing.com/search?q=statue+of+liberty+illuminati+flame&qs=n&form=QBRE&pq=statue+of+liberty+illuminati+flame&sc=0-28&sp=-1&sk=&cvid=f37e0fc73031458f982027d0e7c14580

140 Entertainment industry crawling with pedophiles
http://21stcenturywire.com/2012/10/11/i-ran-the-gauntlet-of-pedophiles-in-the-entertainment-industry-says-former-child-actor/
http://21stcenturywire.com/2012/10/11/i-ran-the-gauntlet-of-pedophiles-in-the-entertainment-industry-says-former-child-actor/

141 Britain ruled by pedophiles
http://www.henrymakow.com/illuminati-pedophiles-run-brit.html#sthash.3gOVLKb0.dpuf

142 Aleister Crowley, wrote Hollywood bible of satanism "Do what thou wilt."
https://www.bing.com/search?q=aleister+crowley+satanist&pc=MOZI&form=MOZSBR

143 Satanist hip hop JayZ
https://www.bing.com/search?q=jay-z+satanist&pc=MOZI&form=MOZSBR

144 JayZ, handler of Beyonce. Many links on this
https://www.youtube.com/results?search_query=the+satanic+music+industry

145 Beyoncé Knowles, see Vol. 1 and Vol. 4
http://www.rhymeswithsnitch.com/2013/05/beyonces-uncle-exposes-family-secrets.html
https://www.youtube.com/watch?v=Jis4VxmmHRs

146 GLAAD award for CIA trained Anderson Cooper
http://www.usatoday.com/story/life/people/2013/02/20/anderson-cooper-to-be-honored-by-lgbt-community/1934291/

147 The true story of Chris Kyle, American Serial Killer
https://www.youtube.com/watch?v=Jis4VxmmHRs
https://lipstick-and-war-crimes.org/tag/american-sniper/

148 Gates Foundation, well covered in Chapter 6
https://www.bing.com/search?q=the+crimes+of+the+gates+foundation&qs=n&form=QBRE&pq=the+crimes+of+the+gates+foundation&sc=0-21&sp=-1&sk=&cvid=50b8303f03f84f7db3907d820914a7ba

149 Tavistock Institute, should be exposed and shut down
https://www.bing.com/search?q=tavistock+institute+social+engineering&pc=MOZI&form=MOZSBR

150 List of TV shows to push the Gay is normal "transformation" a la CIA Kirk's blueprint
http://www.queerty.com/hollywoods-gay-marriage-conspiracy-it-worked-20130627

151 Indian gay man affirms impact of legislation on choices of youth, supported by *Forbes Magazine.*
http://www.forbes.com/2009/07/06/gay-homosexual-court-decision-opinions-contributors-india.html

152 Quote from E Michael Jones - This was from a youtube I transcribed which I cannot find now. He is brilliant. http://www.culturewars.com/Podcasts.html

153 Israeli lying propaganda video produced by Illuminati
www.aish.com/h/iid/90073102.html

154 Yuri Bezmenov from Vol. 1
https://www.youtube.com/watch?t=10&v=MuQmaupl5Gk

155 Bruce Jenner, placed with massive promotion as part of Illuminati gay trans-humanism agenda
https://lipstick-and-war-crimes.org/heads-up-for-bruce-jenner/

156 Statistics on gay molestation
http://www.frc.org/get.cfm?i=IS02E3

Discussion on blog by survivor.
http://www.timebomb2000.com/vb/printthread.php?t=472730&pp=50

157 The subversion of the American Psychiatric Society
http://thewandererpress.com/featured-today/culture-of-life-101-the-homosexuals-american-psychological-association-coup/

Glossary

158 Jackie Robinson, along with singer Harry Belafonte and actor Sidney Poitier, were supporters of the CIA-linked African American Students Foundation that financially backed Obama Sr.'s (Barack's father) scholarship in Hawaii. Page 14, *The Manufacturing of a President,* must read book by Wayne Madsen.

159 55,000 special ops overseas
http://www.defense.gov/news/newsarticle.aspx?id=53048

160 Obvious *predictive programming* demonstrated as evidence in the planned murder of Robin Williams
"Why The Illuminati Killed Robin Williams Conspiracy EXPOSED (Final Cut)" by Vigilant Christian
https://www.youtube.com/watch?annotation_id=annotation_299510355&feature=iv&src_vid=lPZCy6G03Tc&v=b-nvpgRk5to#t=6m

161 *Rockefeller Secondary to Rothchilds* by Eustace Mullins, 2008
http://www.truedemocracy.net/hj32/21.html

162 Fats in food
http://healthoracle.org/downloads/F/Fats%20that%20damage%20the%20entire%20body.pdf

Some of the Upcoming Images from Vol. 3, Lipstick and War Crimes Series

Cheryl, formally Cheryl Cole, is another illuminati puppet given Judge status on UK *X-Factor*. This hugely escalates the *cutout's* brand name. The all-seeing-eye loves Cheryl Cole.

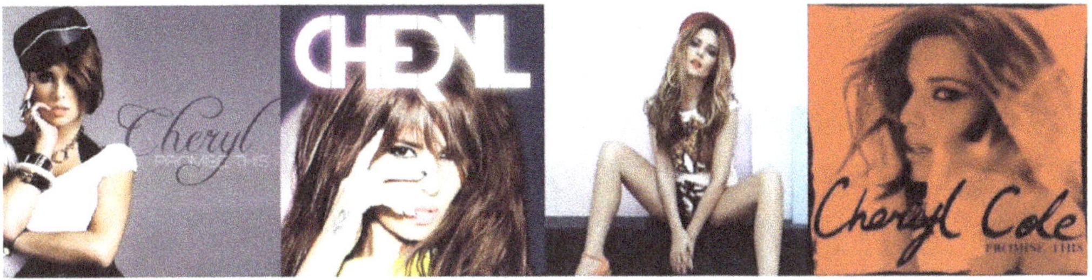

Cheryl is not known because she is a great singer or dancer or because she wears makeup like a good manniquin. She is known because she played the game and by spreading her legs on command, she was promoted. And she is still doing it.

The all-seeing-eye. Lipstick seducing us into accepting war crimes as normal.

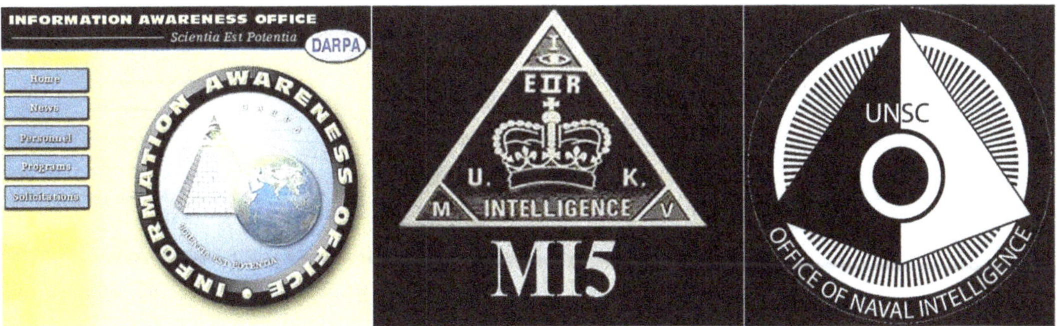

Mickey Mouse Brats - Selena Gomez, Justin Timberlake, Miley Cyrus, Brittany Spears. Let's not forget Aguilera Chapter 8. All these girls became sassy slut models attacking the firewall of natural modesty.

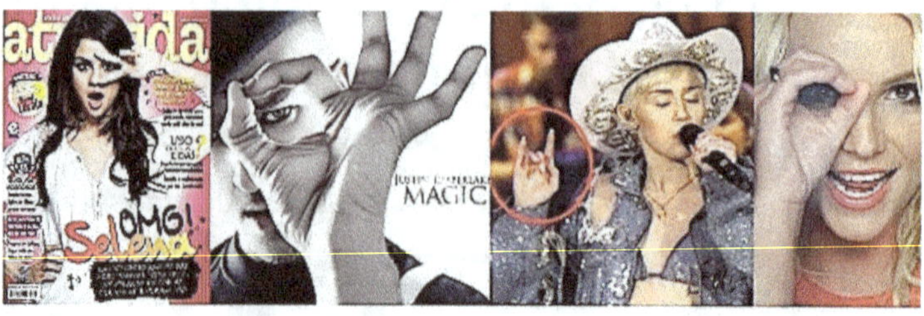

Disney even puts hand signs in their cartoons, (along with their attack on modesty).

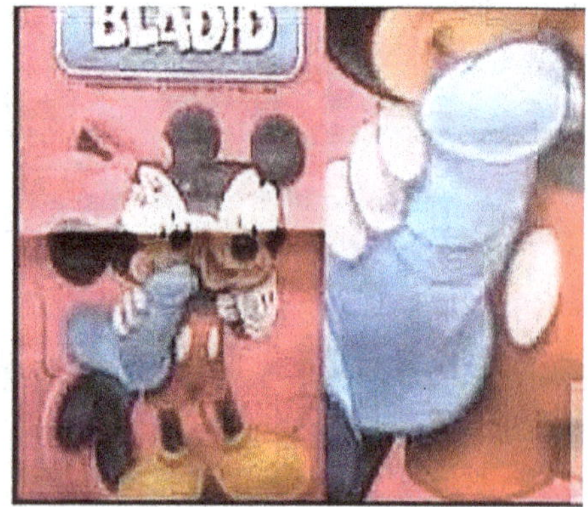

Disney Subliminal Messages: Beauty and the Beast

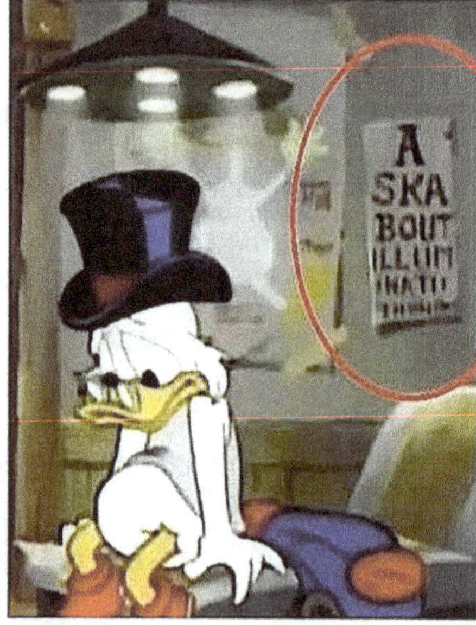

These messages can't be understood in isolation. It is part of a larger campaign. In isolation they seem silly, but as components of a pattern / program, they are an attack.

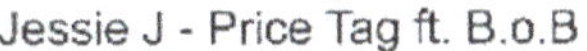
Jessie J - Price Tag ft. B.o.B

Jessie J. "coincidentally" was another judge on UK *The Voice*. Some people will do anything for Illuminati fame. From upper left clockwise... Sassy T-Shirt with Disney Mickey Mouse hat, all seeing eye with three fingers making a 666, pyramid of abuse shirt, devils horns, leopard skin clothing is Kitten Programming, (girls are just sex pussycats), broken doll to be discarded. That would be us to be discarded. Too bad... "Price Tag" is good song. Website left above www.midiilluminati.com Espanol, excelente.

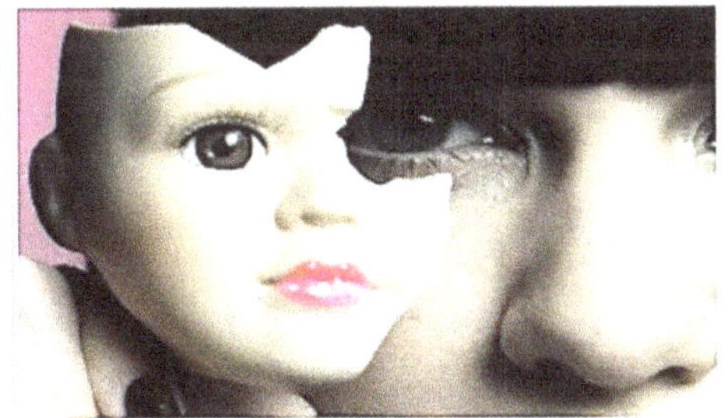

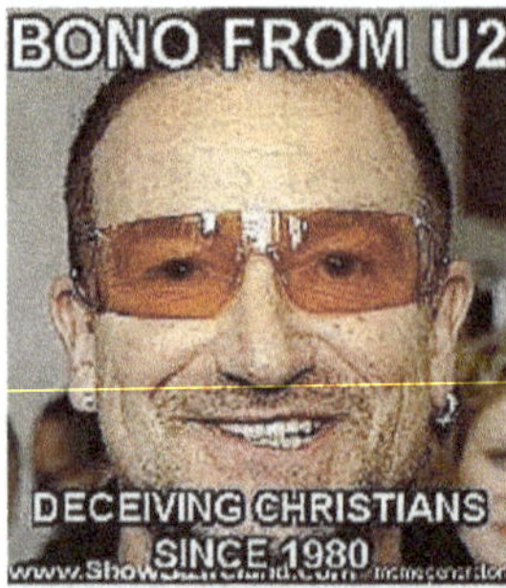

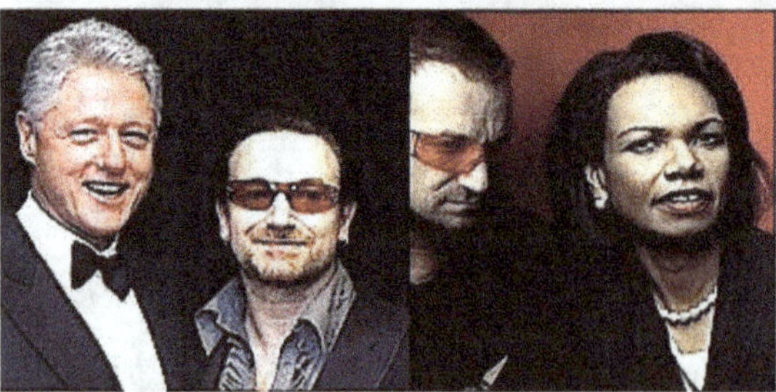

Knighted "Sir" Bono with Cocaine Free Trade Agreement Clinton, cover up of 9/11 and fake WMD in Iraq Condoleezza Rice, Kissinger and Bush Sr – both pedophiles, child killers, and war criminals, third generation CIA Obama, Bill Gates vaccine criminal, and Tony Blair Iraq genocide and cover up of London subway inside-job false flag bombings (Chapter 26). To get this inside with despicable conspiratorial criminals, Bono just had to be a useful con artist who deceives his fans that the parasitic 1% care about us. They don't. "It's all just a con." Notice golden award on neck of "Sir" Bono sitting above with "New World Order" Fuhrer Bush Sr. (Pages 25-27)

"It's all a con - a way of putting people off from the fact that it is a heavy mother. It's probably our most serious record yet, it's the least serious title. It just fooled everyone. They thought we'd lightened up - which is totally untrue. We're miserable bastards."

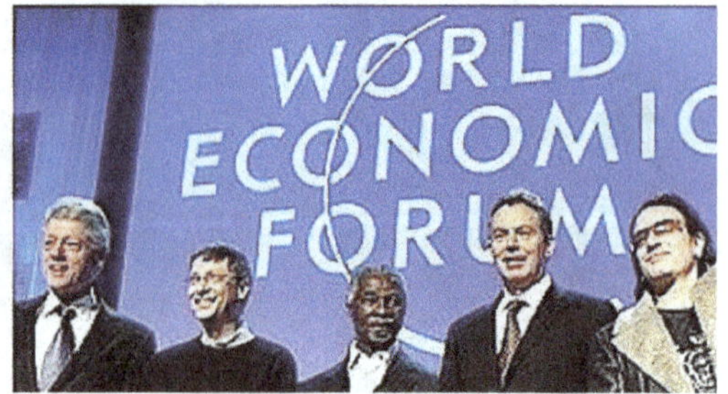

The Entertainment Industry uses Freemasonry symbolism such as all-seeing-eye and checkers. Masons at the lay level think they are part of a philanthropic club. Their higher level leaders are using them for undiscussed programs as evidenced by entertainment industry.

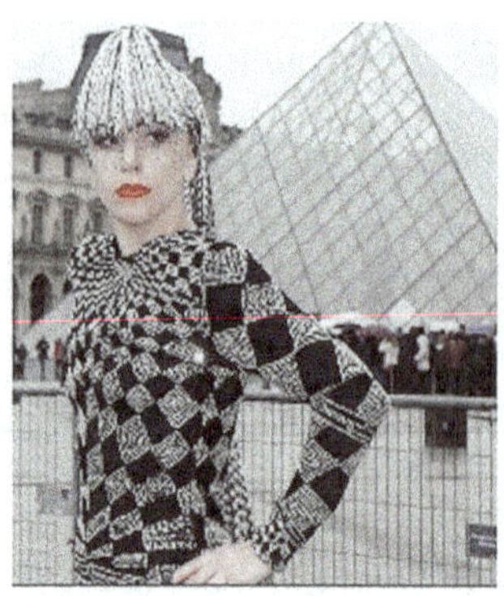

Above Gaga combining four symbols ... pyramid, checkers cage theme, and lipstick.

Left, Madonna with one eye, laying upon slaves in bondage, and spread legs to destroy women, all with checkers.

The New World Order new normal wants no sexual standards ... a virtue-free zone.

Gaga spread legs trigger, shocked looking child to left of her. Shock doctrine. Right, Gaga. (Gaga Page 223, and vanity *in Glossary)*

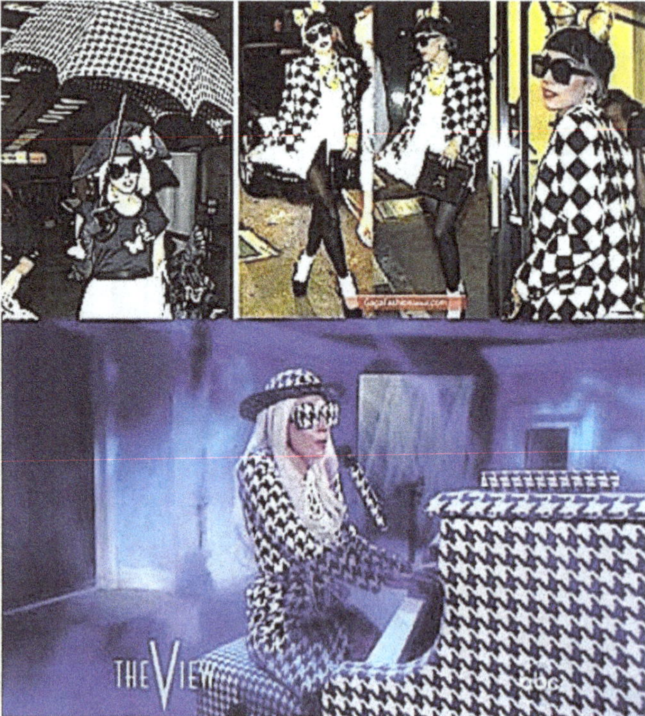

"If people keep seeing it and seeing it and seeing it, [sexual aberration] eventually it's not going to be such a strange thing."

\- Madonna

The World Bank in partnership with the ALAS Foundation presents:

The Early Childhood Initiative

An Investment for Life

Hosted by President Robert B. Zoellick and artist and activist Shakira Mebarak

Monday, February 22, 2010
MC Atrium
Washington, DC
1:00 p.m.

World Bank Group

ALAS

www.worldbank.org/lac

www.fundacionalas.org

Jay-Z, husband of Beyoncé

The event was "hosted" by Bilderberger World Bank President, Robert Zoellick and Illuminati sex object, dyed phoney blond puppet Shakira, who wants to bring "dignity" to all people.

Education for Global Development
A blog about the power of investing in people

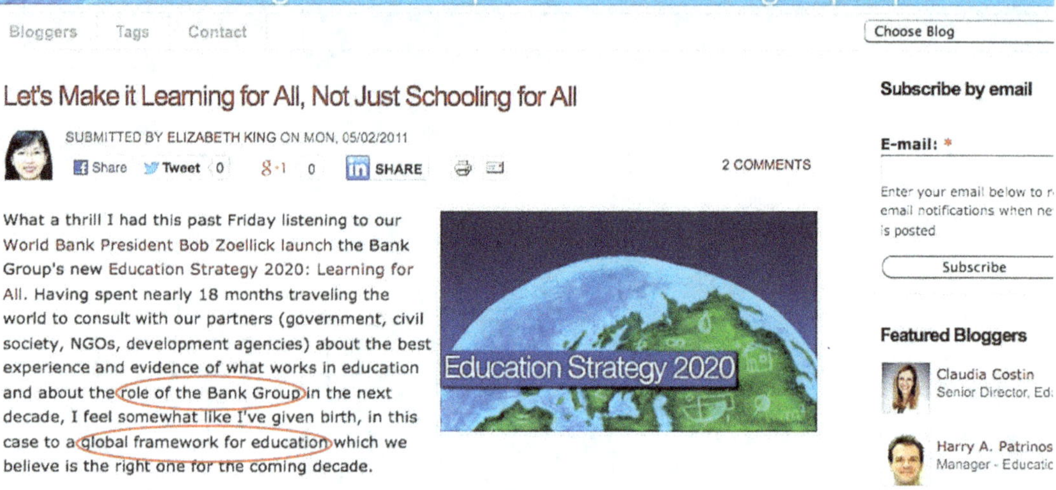

Bloggers
Tags
Contact
Choose Blog
Let's Make it Learning for All, Not Just Schooling for All
SUBMITTED BY ELIZABETH KING ON MON, 05/02/2011
Share
Tweet 0
+1 0
SHARE
2 COMMENTS
What a thrill I had this past Friday listening to our World Bank President Bob Zoellick launch the Bank Group's new Education Strategy 2020: Learning for All. Having spent nearly 18 months traveling the world to consult with our partners (government, civil society, NGOs, development agencies) about the best experience and evidence of what works in education and about the role of the Bank Group in the next decade, I feel somewhat like I've given birth, in this case to a global framework for education which we believe is the right one for the coming decade.
Education Strategy 2020
Subscribe by email
E-mail: *
Enter your email below to r
email notifications when ne
is posted
Subscribe
Featured Bloggers
Claudia Costin
Senior Director, Ed
Harry A. Patrinos
Manager - Educatic

Below image from World Bank, planning "Life Outcomes" and fertility for every child in world. Their plan is to create a global monoculture that is "happy and safe" under one world government, with all diversity and individuality stripped away. To circumvent the paternal instinct, children will be raised by state like stolen indigenous children, as that will be "fair and equal." Parents should consider removing their children from school system now.

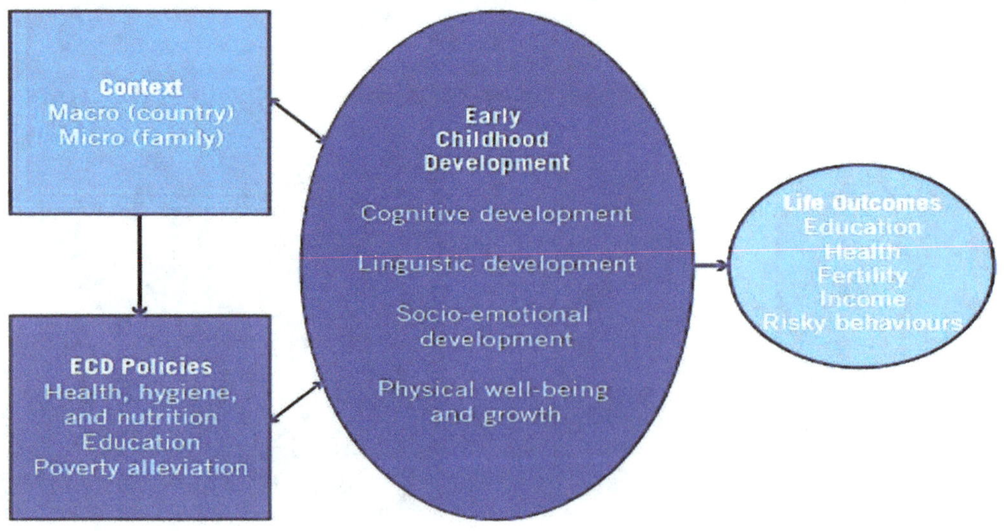

Figure 2 Factors affecting ECD and life outcomes

Source: Adapted from Vegas and Santibañez, 2010

Fame is handed out to those who go along with the perverted sex initiation rituals which are criminal and which maintain the fear and secrecy. This includes CIA Obama and his wife, of course. Either bend over, or you lose your career. Speak out and you can be assassinated like Whitney Houston or Senator Paul Wellstone. Most government officials do not die in plane crashes by accident. The planes are sabotaged or EMF weapons make them fail. Our empire is organized under satanic perversion and terror. The evidence is that the CIA is one and same with the Mafia and uses the same tactics. See youtube online, **"From JFK to 911, Everything is a Rich Man's Trick."** We are being seduced into corruption. Lipstick and War Crimes.

Blurring lines of respect vs. trash, with puppet Obama's blessing. All girls should be sluts?

The subliminal messages and lyrics of pop culture teach the next generation to be ever more crude and irresponsible. Meanwhile, psychological curriculums like Bill Gates Common Core Curriculum and World Bank Early Childhood Initiative destroy diverse cultural expression and prepare humans to be obedient cogs in the designers' machine. The Bankster New World Order took over education and media long ago. Common Core Curriculum is the newest level of invasive control of your child's mind. And the TV will teach your child to "have attitude" in order to, most likely, have a failed marriage. Will Big Brother raise your grandchildren or will you protect and educate your family and push back? Pushing back means practicing personal sovereignty, but you will need a land base, meaning, you must leave city life. See http://transitionus.org/

Good for you.
Good for the environment.
Good for everyone.

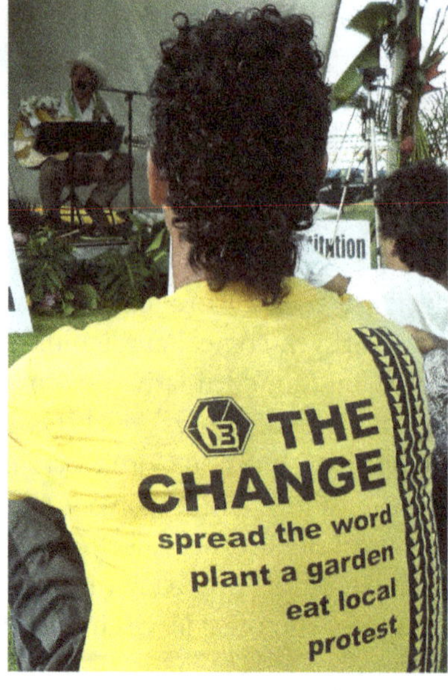
THE CHANGE
spread the word
plant a garden
eat local
protest

Though I went through some nights
Consumed by the shadows
I was crippled emotionally
Somehow I made it through the heartache
Yes I did

I escaped
I found my way out of the darkness
I kept my faith (I know you did), kept my faith

And the river was deep, but I didn't falter
When the climb was high, I still believed
When the valley was low, it didn't stop me, no no
I knew you were waiting. I knew you were waiting for me

With an endless desire I kept on searching
Sure in time our eyes would meet
Like the bridge on fire, the hurt is over,

One touch and you set me free
I don't regret a single moment, no I don't,

Looking back,
When I think of all those disappointments,
I just laugh (I know you do), I just laugh

So we were drawn together

through destiny
I know this love we share is meant to be

I knew you were waiting for me

From song "I Knew You Were Waiting For Me"
by Aretha Franklin and George Michael

Let's save this world folks :)

– Ray Songtree

www.ingramcontent.com/pod-product-compliance
Lightning Source LLC
Chambersburg PA
CBHW081332080526
44588CB00017B/2598
* 9 7 8 1 9 4 1 2 9 3 2 3 2 *